THE NOËL COWARD DIARIES

Noël Coward was one of the most versatile and talented artists of the twentieth century, writing novels, short stories, autobiography, plays, biography, film, poetry, songs and libretti. He was also a celebrated actor, singer, director, producer, and nightclub entertainer. Born in 1899, in England, his first theatre role came in 1909, and he began writing for the stage in 1920. With his play *The Vortex* in 1924 his success was assured. He went on to write many of the most successful plays and lyrics of the century, including 'Mad Dogs and Englishmen', *Private Lives* and *Blithe Spirit*. He died at his home in Jamaica in 1973.

Also by Noël Coward

Present Indicative	Easy Virtue
Oh, Kay	The Queen Was in the Parlour
Lady in the Dark	This Was a Man
I'll Leave It to You	Home Chat
The Vortex	Bitter Sweet
Fallen Angels	Private Lives
On with the Dance!	Design for Living
This Year of Grace!	Blithe Spirit

Graham Payn, who appeared in many of Noël Coward's most successful shows and was his lifelong friend, now lives at Chalet Coward, Noël Coward's last home in Switzerland, from where he runs the Coward estate. With much-appreciated help from Barry Day, Graham Payn wrote *My Life With Noël Coward* in 1994. Sheridan Morley is the drama critic of the *Spectator* and the *International Herald Tribune*. He has presented many radio and television programmes and is the author of the first Coward biography (*A Talent to Amuse*), *Noël and Gertie*, and many other theatre and film books. Sheridan Morley's most recent books include studies of Ginger Rogers, Sir Dirk Bogarde and (with his wife Ruth Leon) Marilyn Monroe, Gene Kelly and the musicals of Sir Cameron Mackintosh.

Graham Payn and Sheridan Morley previously worked together with the late Cole Lesley on *Noël Coward and his Friends*.

THE
NOËL COWARD
DIARIES

Edited by Graham Payn and
Sheridan Morley

PHOENIX
PRESS

5 UPPER SAINT MARTIN'S LANE
LONDON
WC2H 9EA

To the memory of Cole Lesley

A PHOENIX PRESS PAPERBACK

First published in Great Britain
by George Weidenfeld & Nicolson Ltd in 1982
This paperback edition published in 2000
by Phoenix Press,
a division of The Orion Publishing Group Ltd,
Orion House, 5 Upper St Martin's Lane,
London WC2H 9EA

Copyright © Graham Payn, 1982

A CIP catalogue record for this book is available
from the British Library.

Printed in Great Britain by
Clays Ltd, St Ives plc

ISBN 1 84212 066 2

Contents

Introduction

When Noël Coward, playboy of the West End world, jack of all its entertainment trades and master of most, died in 1973, he was as old as the century and its most constant, if often controversial, showbusiness reflection. He left behind him over fifty plays, twenty-five films, hundreds of songs, a ballet, two autobiographies, a novel, several volumes of short stories and countless poems, sketches, recordings and paintings, not to mention the memories of three generations of playgoers on both sides of the Atlantic for whom he had been the most ineffably elegant and ubiquitous of entertainers.

He also left these diaries, chronicling the last thirty years of his life – the years from 1941, when he was starting out on the wartime troop concert tours that were to give him a whole new lease of life as a cabaret entertainer, through the private and professional depressions of the early 1950s, when his beloved England seemed to turn whole-heartedly against him and his work, to the 1960s, when he came home from Las Vegas and Jamaica to the knighthood that had for so long been his due.

These remarkable diaries of war and peace, England and America, work and play, plays and players, at last provide the missing pieces in the Coward jigsaw. Apart from brief extracts which appeared in Cole Lesley's 1976 biography, the diaries have not been published before. Their scope is social, political, historical and theatrical, and their cast of characters ranges from Churchill and Mountbatten through Laurence Olivier and Vivien Leigh to Marilyn Monroe, Harold Pinter and the Beatles. Through the clipped, caustic, often self-mocking tone of the diaries, which were in effect a series of letters from Noël to his own inner self, comes a marvellously funny, touching and revealing account of three decades in the life of the greatest theatrical entertainer of the century, but to understand fully his mood and character at the start of these diaries it is necessary to go back briefly to the beginning of his life.

Noël Coward was born on 16 December 1899, just before the last Christmas of the nineteenth century (hence the name Noël). The second son of an unsuccessful piano-tuner-cum-salesman and a doting, ambitious mother, he grew up in suburban, middle-class South London in genteel poverty. When he was ten, his mother answered a call for child actors in the *Daily Mirror*, and within three months Noël was on stage at the Crystal Palace in a play called *The Goldfish*. A few months later he was Slightly in *Peter Pan* (Kenneth Tynan was to comment years later that he had been Wholly in it ever afterwards) and he then settled, like his beloved friend and partner Gertrude Lawrence, into the life of a fairly successful child actor; in his own view he was 'when washed and smarmed down a bit, passably attractive, but one of the worst boy actors ever inflicted on the paying public'.

Nevertheless Noël survived and by 1917 was already making his first film, *Hearts of the World*, for D. W. Griffith. There followed a brief and unhappy spell in the army, another five years in the theatre and an unsuccessful trip to Broadway, where he hoped to sell some of the comedies and songs he had written. Then, in 1924, at the Everyman Theatre, Hampstead, came the literally overnight success of *The Vortex*, a play about drug addiction written at a time when even alcoholism was scarcely mentioned on the British stage. The roughly equal amounts of interest, indignation, admiration and money generated by the play, which Noël had written, directed and starred in, meant that at the age of twenty-four he went from being a mildly unsuccessful playwright, actor and composer to being the hottest theatrical figure in London – a change so fast that even he took several months and one nervous breakdown to come to terms with it.

There followed, in rapid succession, such hits as *Hay Fever*, *Fallen Angels* and the revue *On with the Dance* (all of which ran in the West End simultaneously with *The Vortex*, a quadruple feat achieved before Noël in this century only by Somerset Maugham and then not again until Alan Ayckbourn), one year of total critical and public reversal when boos greeted *Sirocco* and Noël was spat at by irate theatre-goers, and then in 1929 the start of a period of successful activity remarkable even by Noël's standards.

Within the next two years Noël wrote and staged three of his greatest successes – the operetta *Bitter Sweet*, the comedy *Private Lives* and the epic *Cavalcade* – so that by 1931 the boy wonder of the 1920s had settled into an altogether more stable pattern of theatrical triumph, one which was best characterized by the partnership that he formed with Gertrude Lawrence. For her he had written *Private Lives*, redolent of Riviera balconies, filled with the potency of cheap music and shot through with the sadness of a couple who could live neither together nor apart, a couple who were in many incidental ways Noël and Gertie themselves. Six years later they played together again in his nine short plays, among them *Red Peppers*, *Shadow Play* and *Still Life* that became the film *Brief Encounter*, which made up the three alternating triple bills of *Tonight at 8.30*.

Between these two towering landmarks of their relationship, Noël also found the time to write *Design for Living* for Lynn Fontanne and Alfred Lunt, *Words and Music* for the producer Charles B. Cochran, *Conversation Piece* for Yvonne Printemps and soon afterwards *Operette* for Fritzi Massary. 'Throughout the 1930s, in fact,' wrote Noël later, 'I was a highly publicized and irritatingly successful figure much in demand; the critical laurels that had been so confidently predicted for me in my twenties never graced my brow, and I was forced to console myself with the bitter palliative of box-office success. Which I enjoyed very much indeed.'

If theatrically the 1930s were Noël's best years, politically and socially he cared for them less and less: 'For me', he wrote, 'the pre-war period died on the day Mr Neville Chamberlain returned with such gay *insouciance* from Munich.' He became rapidly and fervently anti-Chamberlain and anti-Munich; having always been bleakly uninterested in any kind of politics he suddenly found himself, on the brink of his forties, increasingly horrified by a world that was rapidly falling apart at the seams. Refuge in the theatre was no longer possible, though ironically the moment when Noël most wanted to leave it was also the moment when most people were telling him he was only useful so long as he stayed there. Churchill told him to go out and sing to the troops, leaving him to reflect uneasily that if the morale of the British Army was at such a low ebb that soldiers could be cheered into battle by his singing 'Mad Dogs and Englishmen' then the country was in even more trouble than he had realized.

Partly therefore to aid his own memory and partly as an acknowledgement of the unusually turbulent and uncertain times through which he was then living, Noël started to write an at first daily note of his activities. The wartime entries, adding up to no more than a logbook of his life, were then used by Noël as the basis for *Future Indefinite*, his second and last volume of memoirs, published in 1954. For this reason, the wartime engagement diary does not form a part of the main body of this book, which opens on VE Day 1945, the day on which Noël ended his own autobiographical publications. However, as a reminder of the kind of war he had, extracts from the wartime entries comprise the Prologue.

It is with the ending of the war that Noël's diaries start in earnest; gradually the brief, pencilled, appointment-book entries give way to longer typewritten essays about the moods and matters, disasters and triumphs, loves and hates of the moment. In a life still often hectic, and with ever-increasing sojourns out of England, Noël did not write every day, sometimes not even every week, occasionally towards the end not even every month, but as the length of time between the entries grows longer, so too do the entries themselves.

As editors, we have not seen a duty to preserve the reputations of those living or dead; nor have we seen it as any part of our duties to censor anything.

We have, however, been subject to the laws of libel, which have demanded certain minor but still regrettable cuts. Other cuts have been made to avoid repetition and on those occasions when the early diaries degenerate into a timetable of lunches, dinners and airline flights. The basic structure of the diaries has, however, been kept intact. Although the very rare errors of spelling and grammar have been corrected, these diaries remain as written or (from the 1950s) as typed. Even the longer, later entries are exactly as typed; Noël did not indulge in any rewriting.

The diaries open in a mood of relief that a long war is at last ending, but also in a mood of uncertainty about the changes that had occurred in the social fabric of a nation which Noël had previously understood and even represented. In his own mind he had neither aged nor changed very much; indeed at forty-five he was hardly a pre-war relic. But much of the world for which he had stood as a showbusiness symbol had been blown to extinction, and suddenly the memories of lost glamour, of 'Noël and Gertie', of balconies in the South of France and country-house weekend parties seemed more of a liability than an asset. Noël had been a figure of the 1920s and 1930s, his own invention and contribution to a period of theatrical and musical history which he had helped to define ('Anyone who cannot see that', as John Osborne once noted, 'should leave the theatre'); but now he had to discover how to become a figure of the 1950s and 1960s, and the learning process was to be long and hard. When Beverley Baxter mischievously asked Noël in 1945 if he could be said to have survived the war, the question was to hang unanswered in the air for a long time. These diaries are the key to that answer; Noël had indeed survived the war – what he now had to survive was the peace.

As editors we are deeply grateful to Ann Wilson, to Martin Tickner, and to Alex MacCormick and John Curtis of Weidenfeld for their help and enthusiasm during a three-year process of editing and research. We would also like here to note that two of the people most closely concerned with Noël's later life and now with the running of his estate, Joan Hirst in London and Geoffrey Johnson in New York, made a vastly greater contribution to his professional well-being than is indicated by their brief appearances in these diaries.

Graham Payn and Sheridan Morley

1941-45
Prologue: The War Years

It was in 1941 that Noël Coward, then just at the start of his own forties, began for the first time in his life to keep a diary. He had already published (in 1937) Present Indicative, *written entirely from memory, detailing his childhood years in south London at the turn of the century and his roller-coaster ride to fame in the early 1920s as 'destiny's tot', an impresario of the self who could alternately shock and delight an audience whether on stage or off. The success of the book – though, as so often with Noël, more popular than critical – meant that there were clearly going to be subsequent volumes.*

The declaration of war in 1939 had found Noël in mid-rehearsal for two new plays, This Happy Breed *and* Present Laughter, *which he had intended (as dramatist, director and star) to tour and then open in London that autumn. Instead he was sent to Paris to set up a British bureau of propaganda in liaison with the French Commissariat d'Information, run by another distinguished dramatist, Jean Giraudoux. This proved a somewhat futile mission and by April 1940 Noël was in Washington, at the behest of the Minister of Information, Duff Cooper, for a brief meeting with President Roosevelt and a more lengthy exploration of official American attitudes to the war in Europe. He failed, however, to get an official posting and resigned himself to Churchill's advice ('Your job in wartime is to sing to them wherever they may be'), spending the rest of 1940 on a prolonged troop concert tour of Australia and New Zealand. He was in fact to discover on such tours that he had a new lease of professional life as a solo singer.*

After this initially confused and frustrating start, Noël's war was highlighted by Blithe Spirit, *written in less than a week during May 1941, and which became one of the longest running comedies in the history of the British theatre, playing hundreds more performances than the more archetypal Coward comedies like* Hay Fever *and* Private Lives. *But the real chance Noël had been waiting for came shortly after he had written* Blithe Spirit: *his friend Lord Mountbatten told him the story of the loss of HMS* Kelly, *and Noël began to see the framework for his major contribution to the war effort, a naval* Cavalcade *and the one that was to become his award-winning film* In Which We Serve.

Saturday 19 April 1941   London

Lunched Dorchester with Bob Menzies[1]. He was absolutely charming. Came away comfortably reassured that I had done a really good job there.

Had a few drinks, then went to Savoy. Pretty bad blitz, but not so bad as Wednesday. A couple of bombs fell very near during dinner. Wall bulged a bit and door blew in. Orchestra went on playing, no one stopped eating or talking. Blitz continued. Carroll Gibbons[2] played the piano, I sang, so did Judy Campbell[3] and a couple of drunken Scots Canadians. On the whole, a strange and very amusing evening. People's behaviour absolutely magnificent. Much better than gallant. Wish the whole of America could really see and understand it. Thankful to God I came back. Would not have missed this experience for anything.

Sunday 25 May 1941

Depressed by loss of HMS *Hood*. Also naturally worried over Crete situation. Hope to God we shall hold on. How horrifying to have to read again and again during this war that we have not enough planes and equipment. Damn those bloody old politicians for all time. 'No recriminations' my foot! They ought to be strung up on lamp-posts for their disastrous mistakes and muddling.

Tuesday 27 May 1941

Very worried on reading in paper that HMS *Kelly* sunk off Crete. Feared Dickie Mountbatten[4] lost. Rang up Ministry of Information. Found that he had been saved. Very relieved.

Sunday 1 June 1941   Coppins

Drove down to the Kents[5]. Found the Duke on the lawn sunning himself.

---

1 Robert Menzies (1894-1978), Australian Prime Minister 1939-41 and again after 1949; knighted 1963. Noël had met him during his Australian concert tour, November 1940 to February 1941.

2 Carroll Gibbons, leader of the Savoy Orpheans band.

3 Judy Campbell (b. 1916), actress; she had been about to play in Noël's *Present Laughter* and *This Happy Breed* when rehearsals were broken off by the outbreak of war.

4 Lord Louis (Dickie) Mountbatten (1900-79), British Sea Lord and administrator, at this time commander of the 5th Destroyer Flotilla; he and his wife Edwina (1901-60) had been close to Noël since his arrival amidst the 'bright young things' early in the 1920s and their friendship had survived his parody of them in *Hands Across the Sea* (1936), one of the plays in Noël's *Tonight at 8.30*.

5 Prince George (1902-42) and Princess Marina (1906-68), Duke and Duchess of Kent, whose country home was Coppins; they had been friends of Noël's since meeting him backstage after a performance of *London Calling* in 1923.

Kents knitting and talking. Air raid and a certain amount of gun-fire.

Monday 2 June 1941

Came down about 12 o'clock having been reading *The Ministry of Wishful Thinking*. Quite an amusing satirical novel.

Long discussion re war and Crete disaster. Astounded at the apathy of the British public, even now. Every station crowded for Whitsun holidays. Even news of clothes rationing failed to damp the holiday spirit. Is this splendid in the face of Crete and the *Hood*, or merely completely unimaginative?

Thursday 3 July 1941   London

Went to private showing of *Down Argentina Way*[1] with Dickie and Edwina. Dined afterwards. Dickie told whole story of the sinking of *Kelly*. Absolutely heart-breaking and so magnificent. He told the whole saga without frills and with a sincerity that was very moving. He is a pretty wonderful man, I think.

Wednesday 9 July 1941

Lunched with Michael Foot[2], whom I liked very much. He hated and hates Chamberlain[3] even more than I. His views, though a trifle too leftist, are sound.

Thursday 10 July 1941   Plymouth

Caught 10.30 train for Plymouth. Drove to Grand Hotel through terrible devastation. A really heart-breaking sight.

Michael Redgrave[4] arrived at 5.30. Extremely healthy and happy. What a magic the Navy does to people. Having left a luxurious film star life to be an ordinary seaman, he is obviously having a wonderful time. We dined and I drove him back to HMS *Raleigh*.

Had drinks at hotel with Dorothy Gilbert, the barmaid. She told me stories of the blitzes here. Quite without conscious drama, therefore infinitely more touching. It certainly is a pretty exciting thing to be English.

Friday 11 July 1941

Spent morning with Lady Astor[5] walking round the devastated town. A strange

---

1 Musical film produced by Darryl Zanuck.
2 Michael Foot (b. 1913), Labour politician and writer; editor of the *Tribune* 1948–52, elected Labour Party leader 1980.
3 Neville Chamberlain (1869–1940), Conservative Prime Minister 1937–40, responsible for the 1938 Munich peace agreement with which Noël had strongly disagreed.
4 Michael Redgrave (b. 1908), actor and director, knighted 1959.
5 Lady (Nancy) Astor, née Langhorne (1879–1964), American-born wife of 2nd Viscount Astor; Unionist MP for Plymouth 1919–45 and the first woman to sit in the House of Commons.

experience. Lady A. very breezy, noisy and *au fond* incredibly kind. Banging people on the back and making jokes. The people themselves stoic, sometimes resentful of her, but generally affectionately tolerant. The whole city a pitiful sight. Houses that have held sailor families since the time of Drake spread across the road in rubble and twisted wood. Lady A. delivered tirade against Winston[1]. Also said (before lunch) apropos of Bruce Lockhart[2] that he could not be really good because he had written a book discussing his travels in Europe with his mistress. This point of view very baffling, and irritating. How sad that a woman of such kindness and courage should be a Christian Science fanatic.

Watched the people of Plymouth dancing on the Hoe. A large dance floor, white-coated band, several hundred girls gaily dressed, dancing very well with sailors, soldiers, marines, etc., in the strong evening sunlight. A sight so infinitely touching, not that it was consciously brave, but because it was so ordinary and unexhibitionist. The English do not always take their pleasures sadly, at least not when they are surrounded by death and destruction.

Saturday 12 July 1941
Arrived London eight o'clock. Spent morning mooching about. Wrote refrain of new 'Duchess' song[3]. Lorn[4] and Joyce[5] lunched, also Larry[6] and Vivien[7]. Larry not very happy. Think it a great mistake for him not to live in Mess.

Saw part of *Blithe Spirit*[8]. Good house. Performance all right except for Margaret Rutherford.

---

1 Winston Churchill (1874–1965), knighted 1953; Conservative leader of the wartime coalition government from May 1940.

2 Robert Hamilton Bruce Lockhart (1887–1970), diplomat and Deputy Under-Secretary of State 1941–45; knighted 1943.

3 'Imagine the Duchess's Feelings', one of four songs (among them 'London Pride') which Noël wrote about this time and used at troop concerts.

4 Lorn Loraine (1894–1967), Noël's secretary, close friend and effectively his manager from 1924 until her death. 'She has been', he once wrote, 'one of the principal mainstays of my life, lovingly and passionately devoted', and it was to her that he would first go for news and welcome on returning from his frequent and lengthy trips abroad.

5 Joyce Carey (b. 1898), actress and close friend of Noël's; she appeared in many of his plays, including *Tonight at 8.30*, *Present Laughter* and *South Sea Bubble*, and also in his films, among them *In Which We Serve*.

6 Laurence Olivier (b. 1907), actor and director, created life peer 1970; at this time he was serving in the Fleet Air Arm. Noël had engaged him in 1930 to play Victor in *Private Lives*; Olivier wrote of his early experience working with Noël that 'he was probably the first man who took hold of me and made me think'.

7 Vivien Leigh (1913–67), stage and film actress, married to Olivier 1940–60.

8 Which had opened on 2 July at the Piccadilly Theatre.

Sunday 13 July 1941

Norman Hackforth[1] lunch. We drove to Hammersmith Palais de Dance to rehearse. Rehearsed with orchestra, drove back, rehearsed a bit more. I performed, shaking with nerves but was pretty good. Songs went well: 'Won't You Please Oblige Us with a Bren Gun' and 'London Pride'. Drove back. Cocktails, Ritz. Joyce and me joined by Fruity Metcalfe[2], who was slightly drunk and very funny. Diatribe against the Windsors and irreverent description of their flight from Paris.

Friday 18 July 1941

Went to Ministry of Information. Had talk with Sir Gerald Campbell. Asked his advice about doing a naval propaganda film myself for Columbia. He said he thought it a magnificent idea and was most helpful.

Tuesday 22 July 1941

Saw Dickie and told him my idea of doing a naval film. He was wildly enthusiastic and said the Admiralty would support me all out. Was awfully pleased that he thought so well of the idea.

Talk afterwards with Thorpe[3] and del Giudice[4]. They will obviously give me complete control. Told them I would give them outline of story within three weeks, then we can discuss shooting dates, terms, etc.

Monday 28 July 1941

Went to Derry & Toms to open roof garden for the Cancer Hospital. Gardens lovely but very few people. Finally received reception committee instead of them receiving me. Made speech. Signed postcards.

Recorded all afternoon. 'Bren Gun', 'There Have Been Songs in England', 'The Duchess' and Carroll's song 'It's Only You'.

Arrived Winchester seven o'clock. Was met by car, which broke down. However, finally arrived at Broadlands[5]. Only Dickie, Edwina and Lady Milford Haven[6]. Later started work with Dickie on rough outline of *White*

1 Norman Hackforth, the pianist who accompanied Noël on many of his wartime concert tours and was to be with him again when he went into cabaret during the 1950s; he later achieved fame as the 'mystery voice' on BBC radio's *Twenty Questions*.
2 Major Edward Dudley (Fruity) Metcalfe, friend of the Duke of Windsor and best man at the wedding of the Duke and Wallis Simpson; in 1940 he had been left stranded in Paris when the Windsors left for Biarritz without telling him.
3 Charles Thorpe, representative of Columbia Pictures.
4 Filippo del Giudice (1892–1961), film producer; according to Noël 'his English was appalling and his enthusiasm boundless', and throughout the making of *In Which We Serve* he 'never allowed his faith in me and the picture to be shaken for a moment'.
5 The Hampshire home of the Mountbattens.
6 Lady Milford Haven (1863–1950), the widowed mother of Lord Mountbatten.

Ensign[1]. He is really profoundly enthusiastic about the whole idea. He told me many touching incidents of the *Kelly*.

Tuesday 29 July 1941

Worked most of the morning with Dickie on naval details. His concentration is really as great as mine. Edwina left after lunch. Dickie went off to meeting. I listed and then typed out what had been done in the morning.

Royal Family discussion at tea with Lady Milford Haven. Very enjoyable. She is a grand old woman with excellent humour. Further work until dinner and on after dinner until 1 a.m. Now have a complete outline clear with a lot of technical stuff too.

Broadlands one of the loveliest houses I have ever seen.

Friday 1 August 1941

Arrived Plymouth just before 8 a.m. Went to Grand Hotel. Called up Commander-in-Chief, who was charming. After lunch told him about *White Ensign* and he was very pleased and called up both the *Raleigh* and the barracks to arrange for me to be shown everything I wanted to see.

Michael [Redgrave] nearly had a fit when I pranced into his hut and everybody had to stand to attention. Had long discussion about RNFC [Royal Naval Film Corporation].

Saturday 9 August 1941 London

Rather depressing financial discussion with Lorn. Obviously, however hard I work, I shall never be able to save any money.

Tuesday 2 September 1941

Telephoned Brooking[2] at Admiralty about *Express* statement regarding me writing and acting Lord Louis Mountbatten. He was very nice and obviously knows this filthy Press stuff is nothing to do with me. He told me that both Brendan Bracken[3] and Walter Monckton[4] had asked him if he did not consider it a mistake for me to play the film. He replied that on the contrary he thought it an excellent idea.

Wednesday 17 September 1941

Filthy article in *Express* about 'Battle of Noël': whether or not I should be

---

1 The working title of *In Which We Serve*.
2 Major Brojah Brooking, Noël's staunch supporter over the film.
3 Brendan Bracken (1901-58), Irish journalist and Conservative politician; Minister of Information 1941-45 and First Lord of the Admiralty 1945; created 1st Viscount Bracken 1952.
4 Walter Monckton (1891-1965), lawyer and Conservative politician, at this time director-general of the Ministry of Information; created Viscount Monckton 1957.

allowed to play Lord Louis Mountbatten. Rang up Admiralty. Brooking furious. Wrote to Dickie.

Thursday 18 September 1941

Spent morning (a) putting off Beatrice and Anthony Eden[1] for weekend, as I must go to Plymouth, and (b) writing long and, I hope, explanatory letter to Jack[2] about our financial tangles. All can be straightened at the end of the war, but at the moment all is very difficult. Took Brooking to lunch at the Jardin des Gourmets. He had what seems to have been a reasonably satisfactory talk with Walter [Monckton] on the telephone last night in which he demanded that pressure should be brought to bear on the *Daily Express*.

Tuesday 7 October 1941

Dined at Ivy. Conversation with Bobbie Helpmann[3] about how difficult it is to keep the Ballet going with people being called up all the time. Thought of Poland, Holland, Czechoslovakia, Norway, Belgium, France, etc., and felt it was indeed terrible not to be able to keep the Ballet going. To do him justice, he was very good about it, but I felt there was something intrinsically wrong with the whole subject.

Thursday 9 October 1941

Arrived in the Strand and found mock tear-gas attack in progress – at least the attack was mock, but the tear-gas wasn't. War news bad. Germans apparently breaking the Russians at last.

Went to the theatre[4]. Received PM and Mrs Churchill[5] in box after first act. He was very amiable and in a good mood. He said the war would last a long time and that he did not think we should have continuous air raids during the winter, just a few rovers.

Monday 20 October 1941

At 11.30 a.m. was served with three summonses by a very amiable police inspector. These deal with currency. It seems that on 26 August 1939 a law

1 Beatrice Eden, née Beckett (d. 1957) and Anthony Eden (1897–1977), married 1923–50 and friends of Noël's since the mid-1930s. He was Conservative MP for Warwick and Leamington 1923–57 and at this time was Foreign Secretary in Churchill's government; Prime Minister 1955–57, created Earl of Avon 1961.
2 John C. Wilson (1899–1961), American theatre manager and Noël's business partner; he had been Noël's closest friend in the pre-war years, but since the outbreak of war Jack had settled permanently in the States and he and Noël were leading increasingly separate lives.
3 Robert Helpmann (b. 1909), Australian-born dancer, actor and director, knighted 1968; he was the leading dancer with the Sadler's Wells Ballet 1933–50.
4 The Piccadilly Theatre, to see *Blithe Spirit*.
5 Clementine Churchill, née Hozier (1885–1977), who had married Winston in 1908.

was passed that all English people with money in America must declare it and not spend it in any circumstances whatsoever. As I had no idea of this at all, obviously all the money I have spent in America – principally on government work – is a criminal offence.

Lunched with Lorn. Went to Bateson[1] at 3.30 p.m. He was most sympathetic and shrewd, but took a gloomy view of the second summons. I gathered from his manner that he suspects that somebody high up is specifically gunning for me. He said, anyhow, that the Treasury were out for well-known blood. Feel ashamed that people should be so vile and getting a bit sick of being persecuted for having done what I thought to be right.

Thursday 23 October 1941

Papers had headlines about 'Noël Coward Summonsed', etc. Determined to rise above it. Obviously I can expect no mercy. My years of success must be paid for.

Tuesday 28 October 1941

Dickie lunched with me with awful cold and terrifically busy, but still had time to be interested in me and my affairs and the film. It's nice to be sure of real friends.

Charming letter from [George] Bernard Shaw advising me at all costs to plead 'not guilty'. I am certain he is right, and deeply touched that he should have taken the trouble to write.

Thursday 30 October 1941

Arrived with Lorn and Bateson at Bow Street at ten o'clock. Case started round about 10.30. Joyce [Carey] and Gladys[2] present. Counsel for the prosecution a snarling little rat. Started by saying I was liable to a £61,000 fine. Magistrate rather grumpy. Gave my evidence quietly and, I think, well. All the truth of my war activities came out except the secret stuff. Adjourned for lunch. Orgy of Press photography. On my return to court, magistrate asked prosecuting counsel what the British Government had expected me to live on upon arriving in the USA with only £10.

Brilliant speech by Roberts[3], then careful summing up by the magistrate (Mr McKenna), who finished by fining me £200 on one summons and nothing on the other two, the minimum fine being £5,000. This was absolute triumph. Left court in a daze of relief and gratitude for the most important fact of all,

1 Sir Dingwall (Dingo) Bateson, an eminent lawyer.
2 Gladys Calthrop (1897–1980), designer, and a close friend of Noël's since they had met on holiday in Italy in 1921; she had begun her design career in 1924 with Noël's *The Vortex* and designed the sets and costumes for all his major stage productions until the early 1950s.
3 Geoffrey Roberts, Noël's defence counsel.

and that is that English justice is worth fighting for. I was treated fairly, courteously and without prejudice. Enormous headlines in evening papers.

Dined with Joyce. Drinks with Winnie[1].

Thursday 27 November 1941

London conference with the whole unit plus Mr Rees (not very nice) who runs the studios[2]. I let fly about general inefficiency and dropped a few dark hints about what might happen if an important propaganda picture like mine should be held up by the mismanagement and indolence of the studios. Spent two hours with Dickie, who told me in detail about his dinner with Brendan. He is certainly a loyal friend all right.

Sunday 30 November 1941

Lunch with Joyce, then drove to Beaconsfield to tea with the James Masons[3]. Discussion ensued during which he talked the most confused rubbish about Hitler not really wanting to conquer England. Wife watching him like a lynx. Fortunately I kept my temper and came quietly away feeling definitely sick.

Friday 12 December 1941

Drove down to Broadlands. Quiet dinner, Edwina, Dickie and Lady Milford Haven. Long discussion with Dickie on general war situation and our naval losses.

More and more convinced that he is a great man. His judgement seems to me to be sound and rational on every major issue. Discussed film script, which he has read. Was highly gratified that there were so few technical mistakes. Brief but hilarious lesson in naval deportment, salutes, etc.

War news not too good.

Saturday 13 December 1941

Quiet morning. Cannot help being delighted about America being so dumbfounded at the Japanese attack [on Pearl Harbor]. This feeling is not malice but a genuine relief that (a) they have at last been forced to realize that this war is theirs as well as ours, and (b) that whatever the future brings they will never be able to say that they came in to pull our chestnuts out of the fire, as they were quite obviously caught with their trousers down.

---

1 Winifred Ashton (1885–1965), better known as the novelist, dramatist, painter and sculptress Clemence Dane; a close friend of Noël's since the mid-1920s.
2 Denham Studios, where *In Which We Serve* was to be filmed.
3 James Mason (b. 1909), the British stage and film actor, and his wife, actress Pamela Kellino.

Sunday 14 December 1941   London

Took Philip of Greece[1] along to see Gladys, who is better but still a bit croaky. Few drinks at the Carlton and Ritz.

Tuesday 16 December 1941

Well, here I am forty-two. Enjoyed my presents. Caviare from Joyce, scent from Lorn and Gladys, books from Winnie, etc. Spent day in bed with cold. Better in the evening. Party which I unexpectedly enjoyed very much. Present – Edwina [Mountbatten], Brooking, Nivens[2], Gwen ffrangçon-Davies[3], John Gielgud[4], Celia Johnson[5], Adrianne Allen[6], Peter Fleming[7], etc.

Wednesday 17 December 1941

War news as far as East is concerned very depressing. It seems that once more we were not ready. Hong Kong being besieged. Singapore in danger.

Jack Beddington[8] rang up from Ministry of Information to say that they considered *In Which We Serve* was bad propaganda for outside England, that the M. of I. could not in any way be associated with it, but that they would grant me certain facilities on condition that I agreed that they should control all advance publicity. When I asked why it was considered bad propaganda, he said it was because a ship was sunk in it.

I controlled myself during this conversation and agreed to meet them to discuss it tomorrow at five. This I have no intention of doing. Absolutely appalled by this utterly infuriating impertinence. Will ask Dickie to take script direct to Winston. Certain that there is a campaign still going on against me. Time will show.

Monday 22 December 1941

Tested people all day from eight-thirty till five. Telephoned Dickie in the morning re M. of I. As usual he was wise and clear, and said that he would handle the whole affair. First of all he wanted a script to take to the King and Queen, with whom he is dining tonight. He will then tackle Brendan.

1 Prince Philip, later the Duke of Edinburgh, at this time a Royal Navy midshipman on leave from active service.
2 David Niven (b. 1909), the film actor, at this time serving in the army, and his wife Primula (Prim).
3 Gwen ffrangçon-Davies (b. 1896), actress.
4 John Gielgud (b. 1904), actor and director, knighted 1953; one of his first jobs had been as Noël's understudy in *The Vortex* (1924).
5 Celia Johnson (1908–82), actress; she was created Dame in 1981.
6 Adrianne Allen (b. 1907), the actress who had played Sybil in the original 1930 *Private Lives* and from then onwards was one of Noël's most constant friends.
7 Peter Fleming (1907–71), writer, married to Celia Johnson.
8 Jack Beddington, director of the Films Division at the Ministry of Information.

Took script to Dickie at War Cabinet. Dickie's militant loyalty, moral courage and infinite capacity for taking pains, however busy he is, is one of the marvels of this most unpleasant age. I would do anything in the world for him.

Tuesday 6 January 1942

Day spent doing scenes over and over again to try and eliminate Noël Coward mannerisms. Saw yesterday's rushes and for the first time was pleased with my performance and my appearance. Ronnie[1] has at last discovered what to do about my face, which is to photograph it from above rather than below.

Tuesday 10 February 1942

Yesterday's rushes excellent. Whole staff working well and efficiently.

War news worse than ever. Singapore obviously not a chance and in a dreadful situation. Our troops retreating in Africa. Winston Churchill read 'production' White Paper before the Commons. I feel that he is losing his touch. He is fine when making stirring speeches but on major issues I doubt his judgement. His prophecies just before the war, when he was a voice in the wilderness, were wonderful but he seems less good in judging strategy and men.

He knows the temper of the people in crisis but I doubt if he really knows the people themselves. It may be heresy to say so, but I feel that if he goes on playing a lone hand, refusing to listen to younger and wiser men, he will fall, and this will be sad because it will damage his legend.

Saturday 28 February 1942

Tiresome morning at the studios. Everyone argued about the colour of the water in the tank. I finally did test shots, submerging myself and shooting to the surface, etc. The water was very thick and highly nauseating, having had in it, in addition to two hundred sailors in full equipment, quite a lot of whiting and endless buckets of black oil.

Wednesday 4 March 1942

The tank in the studio instead of being too cold was very, very hot indeed, so much so that the wretched stand-ins who dived in first scalded themselves. Cold water was pumped in but the whole morning was hell. Really very horrid lying in the hot oil for hours.

Everyone felt faint and got splitting headaches. The afternoon was better, but still far too hot. Finally I was told I was down to fire-watch on Saturday night. This looks like a frame-up on the part of the dear studio workers.

---

1 Ronald Neame (b. 1911), cinematographer and later film director.

They know perfectly well that for me this is the hardest week of the whole picture. Nevertheless, I intend to do it if I die in the attempt. I shall also look to see if the fire-watching organization is efficient and, if it is not, I shall report it.

Wednesday 8 April 1942

A proud and pleasant day. Lunched with Gladys, Joyce and Lorn in dressing-room. At three o'clock the King and Queen arrived with the two Princesses[1], Dickie and Edwina. We took them first to Stage 5, where the King took the salute. Then I did the Dunkirk speech. The ship rolled, the wind machine roared, in fact everything went beautifully. All the time they were perfectly charming, easy and interested and, of course, with the most exquisite manners to everyone. The Queen is clearly the most enchanting woman. The Princesses were thrilled and beautifully behaved. Altogether it was an exhibition of unqualified 'niceness' from all concerned and I hope it impressed the studio as much as it should have – not just because the King and Queen and Princesses of England put themselves out to make everyone they met happy and at ease. There are many who might say, 'So they should, for it's part of their job.' This is perfectly true. It was also part of Pavlova's job to dance perfectly and part of Bernhardt's job to act better than anyone else. I'll settle for anyone who does their job that well, anyhow.

Tuesday 28 July 1942

Slight come-over of war depression in afternoon. Wondering what it will do to all of us. Obviously foolish to expect life to be as it was. I dread the almost inevitable class ructions in this country. The mania for Russia that is going on now will, if it continues, become a grave nuisance. I have a strong feeling that the Russians despise us and dislike us, while we are being worked up by the Press to adulate them and emulate them like a lot of hysterical schoolgirls worshipping a hearty games mistress. I think the Russians are putting up a gallant and brave fight and I am all for supporting and helping them, but I do wish we could all understand that they are not fighting for us nor our beliefs and way of living, but for their own.

Wednesday 26 August 1942

A dreadful morning. Headlines in the papers saying that the Duke of Kent was killed yesterday afternoon in an air crash. I can hardly believe it, but of course that is nonsense because I believe it only too well. It is never difficult to believe that someone young and charming and kind is dead. They are always

---

1 Princesses Elizabeth and Margaret; King George VI was visiting the film set at Denham with his family.

dying. The Duke of Windsor[1] and Hannen Swaffer[2], etc., remain alive but Prince George has to die by accident. Well, there goes a friendship of nineteen years. I shall miss him most horribly. He may have had faults, but he was kind always and I feel absolutely miserable. Years ago I stopped being impressed by him being Prince George, especially in the last years when I have seen him so much. I talked to him on Sunday and made plans about him coming to rehearsals. And now, suddenly, I must know that I shall never see him again. I am taking this resentfully and personally. I am so deeply sorry for the poor Duchess. I wrote to her this morning, of course, a rather inarticulate letter. It is a beastly tragedy. In memoriam I say, 'Thank you for your friendship for me over all these years and I shall never forget you.'

Saturday 29 August 1942

Drove to Windsor and got to the Chapel just before eleven. Was given a seat in the choir very close to everything – almost too close to be borne. The service was impressive and supremely dignified. I tried hard not to cry, but it was useless. When the Duchess came in with the Queen and Queen Mary[3] I broke a bit, and when the coffin passed with flowers from the garden at Coppins and Prince George's cap on it I was finished. I then gave up all pretence and just stood with the tears splashing down my face. I was relieved and heartened to see that both Dickie and the King were doing the same thing. The thought that I shall never see him again is terribly painful.

After it was all over and the King had sprinkled the earth and the Royalties had gone away, we all went up one by one to the vault and bowed and secretly said goodbye to him. Then we went out into very strong sunlight. Margot Oxford[4] came up to me and said, 'Very well done, wasn't it?' as though she had been at a successful first night. I thought this offensive and unforgivable.

Monday 14 September 1942

War news pretty grim. Stalingrad apparently taken. I must admit to a personal

---

1 Noël was not a great admirer of the Duke, who had once cut him dead the day after Noël had spent a long evening playing the piano for him, and he had suggested at the time of the abdication that statues of Wallis Simpson be erected throughout England for the blessing she had bestowed on the country.

2 Hannen Swaffer (1879–1962), journalist and drama critic; his attacks on Noël went back to the 1920s when he had found *The Vortex* among the 'most decadent plays of our time' and, on the disastrous failure of *Sirocco* in 1927, he had written in the *Sunday Express*: 'At last the public seem to appreciate the truth of what I have said – that Noël Coward has nothing whatever to say, that he has no wit, and that his sneers at ordinary, respectable people are irritating to the point of painfulness.'

3 Queen Mary, the Queen Mother; Prince George was her fourth son.

4 Margot, Countess of Oxford and Asquith (1865–1945), socialite and wit of the earlier years of the century, the widow of Prime Minister Herbert Asquith.

apathy now regarding the war. I have tried from the beginning to work constructively for the war effort and now, having been driven back to my own *métier*, the theatre[1], I cannot work myself up about it any more. This may be sheer escapism, but if I can make people laugh, etc., maybe I am not doing so very badly. I only know that to sit at the side of the stage amid the old familiar sights and sounds and smells is really lovely after all this long time. The only things that matter to me at the moment are whether or not I was good in such and such a scene and if the timing was right and my make-up not too pale. This is my job really, and will remain so through all wars and revolutions and carnage.

Friday 25 September 1942

Read the London notices of the film[2], which are absolute superlatives. Nothing but 'great picture' and 'finest film of the war', etc. The most gratifying thing of all is that even the commonest journalistic mind has observed that it really is a dignified tribute to the Navy.

It really is wonderful that the picture should be a success. God knows it has been a long and bloody travail. I cannot help being glad to think of the guns that have been spiked. Max Beaverbrook[3], the *Express*, Jack Beddington, Hannen Swaffer, Graham Greene[4]. How very cross they must be. I have done what I set out to do – a play that was a smash hit, a song ditto[5] and a film ditto. I have also made a definite contribution to the war effort by showing the public what the Navy really is like.

Tuesday 6 October 1942

The war continues to drone along, a horrible background to everything. It appears that the Russians despise us for not starting a second front. I don't think it would matter nearly as much if the Press hadn't been so busy this last year building them up into being the finest race alive and our beloved and staunch allies, etc. Personally, I am convinced that they are no more allies than Hitler and Mussolini. I am also convinced that the world upheaval

---

1 Noël was now in the final rehearsals for a six-month tour of the provinces with *Play Parade*, a repertoire of three of his plays: *Present Laughter*, *This Happy Breed* and *Blithe Spirit*.
2 *In Which We Serve* was about to have its world première.
3 Lord (Max) Beaverbrook (1879-1964), the Canadian-born British newspaper magnate; he had consistently given Noël an unflattering press and hostility began in earnest over *In Which We Serve*, where Noël showed a copy of the *Daily Express* with its celebrated headline 'There Will Be No War' floating alongside destroyers steaming into battle. Beaverbrook reacted to the mockery by trying to have the film suppressed.
4 Graham Greene (b. 1904), English novelist and critic, had been less than kind to Noël in reviews; *Blithe Spirit* he had found 'a weary exhibition of bad taste'.
5 'London Pride'.

would probably have never occurred at all if it hadn't been for their damned Comintern activities since 1917.

This, of course, is merely hypothesis, but what is not hypothesis is that the bastards signed a pact with Nazi Germany in 1939. This fact the English sentimentalists seem to forget and they also fail to realize that the Russian view of life is opposed to ours in every way. They are not fighting for us but to defend their own land, very bravely and effectively, but not for us, and I am sure that if they are not utterly crippled by the war for many years to come, we, with the rest of so-called Western civilization, are going to have a hell of a time with them.

Tuesday 27 October 1942

Lorn telephoned. She told me about a letter from Dickie embodying a suggestion from his cousin[1]. Must think this over very carefully.

Friday 6 November 1942

Began day with two concerts in the Speke [Rootes] aircraft factory[2]. Three thousand seven hundred at each performance. Everything very well organized but the audience, as usual, stupid and dull. There can be no doubt about it, I have no real rapport with the 'workers', in fact I actively detest them *en masse*. They grumble and strike and behave abominably while their very existence is made possible by sailors and merchant seamen who get a quarter or less than a quarter what they do. In addition to this they are obtuse and slow-witted and most outrageously spoilt.

War news still triumphant. Rommel's army still in full retreat. Hope the Press is not overplaying it.

Monday 9 November 1942

Letter from Dickie enlarging on his cousin's idea and my probably favourable reaction. Wonder if Winston Churchill has been obstructive and has had to be overruled.

Monday 7 December 1942

War news a little depressing. The battle for Tunis is raging and, as far as I can see, we are more on the defensive than we should be.

Played *This Happy Breed* to a good house apparently in the last stages of consumption. Supper with Joyce.

1 King George VI; the suggestion was about Noël being awarded a knighthood in the New Year's honours list.
2 Noël had rashly agreed that, on top of eight appearances in three plays every week, he would give four or five concerts to factories and hospitals.

Wednesday 16 December 1942

Well, well, I am now forty-three: one more birthday over. Several nice presents, scent, chocolates and other virile offerings. Highly acceptable, I must say. A very sweet gift from the company and staff, a table-lighter inscribed. Probably the last obtainable in England.

Monday 28 December 1942

In Which We Serve awarded the prize for the best film of the year in America. Rave New York notices quoted in *Telegraph*. Second prize-winner *One of Our Aircraft is Missing*[1]. Dear Ronnie [Neame] and David[2]. Very nice for them. Third *Mrs Miniver*[3].

Thursday 31 December 1942

Dickie had been trying to get me all the afternoon. I finally got him in the course of Beryl Measor's[4] party at the Imperial. He explained that he considered sabotage had been at work, so that's that and I shall not reconsider the matter[5].

Friday 7 May 1943

Anthony and Beatrice [Eden] came to *Happy Breed*[6] and were wildly enthusiastic. I dined with them afterwards at the Perroquet, then went back to the Foreign Office. Anthony is in a black rage with the Russians over the Russo-Polish dispute. Apparently they are behaving abominably. There is also a great controversy going on as to whether or not Anthony goes to India as Viceroy. He seriously asked for my view, which I said would be biased by the fact that if he went I should be able to come and stay. The PM is in favour of him going. Personally think it would be good for Anthony to get away from the House of Commons and be faced with different problems. I don't think he is quite up to being a Prime Minister yet. The question of the peace terms being arranged without him here is troubling him, but he would go on a three-year and not a five-year term.

Monday 17 May 1943

I am writing this with a great deal of noise going on. It really is fantastic this life we lead. Not that there have been any bad raids for ages, but the way everyone has got used to the whole business. I suppose there are still a lot of

1 British film produced and directed by Michael Powell and Emeric Pressburger.
2 David Lean (b. 1908), film director; co-director with Noël of *In Which We Serve*.
3 American film starring Greer Garson and Walter Pidgeon.
4 Beryl Measor, actress, who was touring with Noël in *Play Parade*.
5 Of the knighthood.
6 Now in London at the Theatre Royal, Haymarket.

people who go to shelters the moment an alert goes, but I must say nothing would induce me to.

The Italian situation seems to be getting more and more interesting. It really looks as though Germany were leaving them in the lurch. If so, Germany must be in worse straits than was expected. Italy, I suppose, will sue for a peace. The King [Victor Emanuel III] will abdicate, Prince Umberto will succeed him and Mussolini will either be lightly assassinated or die of a broken everything.

Wednesday 2 June 1943

Was telephoned after the matinée by the BBC asking me to do a broadcast to America immediately, as Leslie Howard[1] had been shot down in a plane coming from Lisbon. This really is a horrid shock. Refused the broadcast as obviously there was not time.

Went down to the cottage[2]. Had supper and went to bed early. Had a long think about death. Imagined all too vividly poor Leslie's last moments. Such a horrible way to die, cooped up with a dozen people in a plane and being brought down into a rough sea. It can't have been so very quick. There must have been lots of time to think and be frightened unless, of course, he had the luck to be hit by one of the bullets. Obviously they were trying to get Winston, who isn't back yet[3]. I must say I have occasional qualms when I think of the amount of flying ahead of me[4].

Sunday 4 July 1943

At twelve o'clock the Prime Ministerial car fetched me and drove me to Chequers. Found Mrs Churchill alone and played a little croquet with her. The PM was very amiable and charming. I played 'Don't Let's Be Beastly to the Germans' over and over again, and he was mad about it.

After tea I had a long talk with him about Willkie[5] and de Gaulle[6] (whom he doesn't like and suspects of being a potential little French Fuehrer). Sarah Churchill[7] appeared on leave. A little more general conversation, then an hour closeted with the PM, during which we played six-pack [bezique] and I took ten shillings off him. At dinner he was very gay and sang old-world Cockney

1 Leslie Howard (1890–1943), British film star, whom Noël had known before the war.
2 Noël had leased a cottage in Kent.
3 Churchill was due to return from an Allied meeting and might have been on the flight.
4 Noël was due to tour the Middle East at the end of the following month.
5 Wendell Willkie (1892–1944), American lawyer and industrialist, the Republican Presidential candidate in 1940, since when he had frequently represented President Roosevelt abroad.
6 General Charles de Gaulle (1890–1970), at this time leader of the Free French Forces in England; French President 1958–69.
7 Sarah Churchill (b. 1914), actress, the Churchills' second daughter.

songs with teddy bear gestures. In the course of the day, he admitted that he had been mistaken over the abdication. Mrs Churchill added later that his mistake had been providential because it had kept him out of office at a moment when it would have been compromising. After dinner we saw a news-reel and I played the piano for hours and then left.

Wednesday 14 July 1943   London

Did two refrains of a new song. Lorn rang up to say that there was a great shindy going on because the M. of I. Censor Department had refused to pass 'Don't Let's Be Beastly to the Germans' for publication or recording or broadcasting because there were lines in it that Goebbels might twist. I rang up Brendan [Bracken] immediately and he said he would look into it. I intend to stand firm over this nonsense and if necessary appeal to the Prime Minister. I am sick of these bureaucratic idiots.

Saturday 23 October 1943

Drove down to Chequers in Prime Ministerial car, arriving at 1.15. The PM was charming to me, but looked rather tired.

Heard at lunch the secret and utterly miserable news that my beloved HMS *Charybdis*[1] was sunk last night. Only a few survivors, among them only three officers. I felt as though I had been kicked in the stomach. I hope the Commander may be a survivor but doubt it. The Captain is gone, definitely. This is the end of the happiest ship I have ever known.

Played croquet with Mrs Churchill all afternoon. Max Beaverbrook arrived for tea and was quite amiable. Tried to have a sleep after tea but lay awake and visualized all my friends in *Charybdis* lying drowned and twisted, and remembered every detail of the ship.

Sunday 24 October 1943

Woke after a practically sleepless night, with a heaviness on my mind. Talked to the PM, who was sitting up in bed. He thanked me really touchingly for all I had been doing for the troops.

Long gossip with Mrs Churchill about Sarah and Vic[2].

Sunday 19 December 1943   Washington[3]

Lunched at the White House. Mrs Roosevelt as nice as ever and the President

1 The ship in which a couple of months earlier Noël had sailed from Plymouth to Gibraltar on the first leg of his Middle East tour.
2 Vic Oliver (1898–1964), musician and comedian, married to Sarah Churchill 1936–45.
3 Noël had arranged to spend a few weeks in the United States prior to a three-month tour of South Africa.

full of vitality[1]. The Morgenthaus[2] were there and young Franklin and his wife and some of their friends. After lunch I sang 'Germans', which the President enjoyed keenly. Morgenthau has asked me to make a recording of it for the Government broadcast, which of course I shall do.

Monday 20 December 1943   New York

Flew back to New York. Dinner party given for me by the Gilbert Millers[3]. After dinner Clare Luce[4] appeared and we had a discussion. She became rather shrill over the Indian question, about which she knows only a little more than I do. I took her later to the Stork Club. I was feeling tired and ill, and I resented being made a sort of show-off target for the Luce shafts at the British Empire. I let Clare and John Gunther[5] talk for ages and remained quiet. Then I upped and said that although they doubtless knew a lot about the Indian question, it was none of their damn business, and if in fifty years they had successfully settled the American Negro question, by which time our Indian problems would have settled themselves, we should be perfectly prepared to let them in on our Dominions solutions on a lease-lend basis. All rather tedious and obvious, and I must say John Gunther was absolutely idiotic.

Thursday 30 December 1943

Gertie[6] came to lunch. Sweet but idiotic.

Elsa's[7] dinner party. Dick Rodgers[8] played and I sang. Garbo[9] was there looking lovely, in fact lovelier than ever. At the end of the evening, I recited – under pressure – '*La Carte de la France*'. Everyone in tears.

Wednesday 23 August 1944   London

Paris has fallen, not to the Americans but, tactfully, to the French. As it is, the

---

1 Noël had first met Franklin and Eleanor Roosevelt in 1940 on his vague mission to the States as a British emissary.

2 Henry Morgenthau Jr (1891–1967) and his wife; he was US Secretary to Treasury 1934–45.

3 Gilbert Miller, Broadway producer, and his wife Kitty.

4 Clare Boothe Luce (b. 1903), American writer and playwright, Republican Member of Congress 1943–47, and later US ambassador to Italy 1953–57; she was married to Henry Luce (1898–1967), founder of *Time* and *Life* magazines.

5 John Gunther (1901–70), American author and journalist.

6 Gertrude Lawrence (1898–1952), English actress, whom Noël had first met in 1913; they had become close friends and famous stage partners, and for her he had written *Private Lives* (1930) and the nine plays that made up *Tonight at 8.30* (1935). She was now living in Massachusetts, married to American impresario Richard Aldrich.

7 Elsa Maxwell (1883–1963), compulsive American party-giver and gossip columnist.

8 Richard Rodgers (1902–79), the American composer.

9 Greta Garbo (b. 1905), the Swedish film star; when Noël had met her in Stockholm in 1935 there had been eccentric Press rumours of their engagement.

French will never forgive us for holding out alone and finally giving them the chance to reconquer their country.

Thursday 31 August 1944

Lunched with Fred Astaire[1] and David Niven. Poor Freddie seemed bewildered by our British flippancy. I hope we weren't beastly, but have a feeling we were.

Went to the first night of *Peer Gynt*[2], a tatty, artsy-craftsy production. Ralph Richardson[3] like a mad bull-terrier. Larry [Olivier] wonderful but only on for five minutes at the end. Dinner at the Savoy and then Mike [Redgrave] came back for a drink. Nice but silly.

Sunday 3 September 1944

Five years ago today Chamberlain declared war, in dismal, defeated tones. Today the news is so fantastically good that it is hardly believable. The Germans are routed in France, the Allies have crossed the Belgian frontier and, in some places, the German lines. Rumour that Maurice Chevalier[4] has been tried and shot, also that Sacha Guitry[5] is in prison awaiting trial. A horrible situation exists in Warsaw. The Russians refuse to help and we can do nothing; have already tried to drop supplies and lost thirty per cent of our aircraft. They obviously rose too soon and are now being massacred by the Germans.

Thursday 21 September 1944

Worked practically all day. Lunch with Rank[6] and discussed the bloody film industry. In the evening went to see Larry in *Richard III*. A tremendous evening. I think the greatest male performance I have ever seen in the theatre. Came out moved and highly exhilarated. He is far and away the greatest actor we have.

1 Fred Astaire (b. 1899), the American dancer and film star, whom Noël had known since the early 1920s when Fred and his sister Adèle starred together in British musical theatre.
2 Ibsen's drama in an Old Vic Company production at the New Theatre.
3 Ralph Richardson (b. 1902), actor and director, knighted 1947; he and Laurence Olivier had this year become joint directors of the Old Vic Company.
4 Maurice Chevalier (1888-1972), the French actor and singer; Noël had done occasional troop concerts with him earlier in the war. At this time he was under suspicion of collaborating with the Germans.
5 Sacha Guitry (1885-1957), French playwright and actor, whom Noël had first met in 1930; their careers were frequently compared; he also was being accused of collaboration.
6 J. Arthur Rank (1888-1972), British film mogul who founded the Rank Organisation and who sponsored Cineguild, the company which had produced *In Which We Serve* and the film of *Blithe Spirit*; created a peer in 1957.

Tuesday 14 November 1944   Paris

Discussed Stage Door Canteen[1] opening here just before Christmas. Rehearsed at theatre 2.30.[2]

Long talk about the collaborationists. Pierre Fresnay[3] is out of prison as he did not denounce anyone, and he now admits miserably that he was wrong. Yvonne Printemps apparently behaved well and will be allowed to play again. Sacha Guitry has been very bad; Gaby Morlay[4] idiotic; and Marcel Achard[5] allowed himself to be flattered by the Germans. Chevalier has been very questionable.

Wednesday 22 November 1944

Lunched at the Directoire. Cost several million pounds, but worth it. Before this had an effusive reunion with Mistinguett[6]. Just before the evening show began, Josephine Baker[7] arrived in a fainting condition, having driven from Paris asphyxiated by the fumes in the car. I sent her off to bed.

My cold is worse and the weather is vile.

Monday 27 November 1944

Maurice [Chevalier] came and sat on my bed and told me that he had appeared once in Germany, the only payment for which was the release of ten prisoners; that he had sung twice over the radio because he couldn't get out of it without getting into trouble with the Gestapo. I believe him and at all events it is not for me to judge.

Sunday 31 December 1944   London

Dawdled about in the morning. Spent the afternoon painting away at the easel. After that dropped in to Loelia Westminster's[8] rout. Everyone was there, from Laura Corrigan to Laura Corrigan[9].

The war news appears to be a bit better. Lloyd George[10] has accepted a peerage. 1945 has *got* to be good.

1 Servicemen's entertainment centre in Piccadilly, London, which was now about to open a Paris branch.
2 For a troop concert at the Marigny Theatre.
3 Pierre Fresnay (1897–1975), French actor, married to French actress and singer Yvonne Printemps (b. 1895); Noël had written *Conversation Piece* for her and Pierre Fresnay. His part was played by Noël later in the run.
4 Gaby Morlay (1897–1964), French actress.
5 Marcel Achard (1899–1974), French playwright.
6 Mistinguett (1874–1956), French actress and dancer.
7 Josephine Baker (1906–75), black American singer and dancer who became a star in France.
8 Loelia, Duchess of Westminster (b. 1902), married to the 2nd Duke 1930–47; Noël later wrote the preface to her autobiography.
9 Laura Corrigan, American socialite.
10 David Lloyd George (1863–1945), Liberal statesman, Prime Minister 1916–22.

Sunday 29 April 1945

The *Sunday Express* announced Germany's unconditional surrender to all three Allies. This headline is mischievous and misleading as it is not true, although it probably will be in the next day or two. Mussolini has been tried and executed. It is hardly believable that after all these dreadful years it is really nearly the end.

It is strange to be back at the Savoy, having been here so much in 1941 when our world was so black. These supremely melodramatic days are somehow anticlimactic and confusing. Report of the deaths of Hitler and Goering. Mussolini shot yesterday and hung upside down in the street and spat at. The Italians are a lovable race.

Tuesday 1 May 1945

Still no complete surrender. Pictures in the paper of Mussolini lying dead with his mistress. The mills of God!

Wednesday 2 May 1945

Went to Wavells'[1] cocktail party, which was fun and very mixed. Dined with Juliet[2]. Just her, the Prime Minister and me. A lovely evening. He was at his most benign and suddenly, at the same moment, we both became emotional about him. He was immensely touched and simple about it. It was a strange but, I suppose, a very natural moment. There he was, gossiping away with us, the man who had carried England through the black years, and he looked so well and cheerful and unstrained, and in addition was so ineffably charming, that I forgave him all his trespasses and melted into hero-worship.

Friday 4 May 1945

Germany surrendering in all directions. VE Day imminent.

1 Field Marshal Earl Wavell (1883-1950) and Countess Wavell; he was Viceroy of India 1943-47.
2 Lady Juliet Duff (1881-1965), society hostess.

1945

The year when the world came back from the war was for Noël, as for many others, a period of drastic readjustment; the society he had left behind in 1939 was no longer a real one, but it was the one of which he had been the most celebrated theatrical chronicler. The playwright of the 1920s and 1930s, the composer of 'Poor Little Rich Girl' and 'Children of the Ritz', the star of Private Lives *and* Tonight at 8.30, *now had to come to terms with an altogether different social and theatrical climate.*

Noël realized, sooner perhaps than many other returning actors and playwrights, that the demands and conditions of his profession had altered drastically. 1939 was already a world away, Gertrude Lawrence was married and settled in America, and what had been successful enough for the theatre in the time of Noël and Gertie might well prove a disaster six cataclysmic years later, when cigarette-holders and clenched smiles were no longer being worn. On the other hand, Noël had both the stage version of Blithe Spirit *and a glossy John Clements-Kay Hammond revival of* Private Lives *running in the West End as the war ground to a halt, both of them nightly proof that a little light escapism never hurt anybody at the box-office.*

Believing, therefore, that in revue also the mixture as before might still prove a tonic, Noël was now writing, composing and casting an only slightly modified version of one of the old pre-war Cochran/Charlot revues. Settings were to be a little less lavish, perhaps, but an evening of light and glamorous escapism was still the plan. It was to be called Sigh No More.

Tuesday 8 May: Victory Europe Day   London

A wonderful day from every point of view. Went wandering through the crowds in the hot sunshine. Everyone was good-humoured and cheerful. In the afternoon the Prime Minister made a magnificent speech, simple and without boastfulness, but full of deep pride.

In the evening I went along to the theatre[1] and had a drink with the company. We all had cold food and drinks at Winnie's[2]: Joyce [Carey], Lilian[3], Alfred and Lynn[4], Lorn [Loraine], Gladys [Calthrop], Dick[5], etc. We listened to the King's broadcast, then to Eisenhower, Monty and Alexander. Then I walked down the Mall and stood outside Buckingham Palace, which was floodlit. The crowd was stupendous. The King and Queen came out on the balcony, looking enchanting. We all roared ourselves hoarse. After that I went to Chips Channon's[6] 'open house' party which wasn't up to much. Walked home with Ivor[7]. I suppose this is the greatest day in our history.

Wednesday 9 May

Second VE Day, slightly anticlimactic but happy by the evening. Piccadilly Circus a marvellous sight.

Lunched at the Savoy with Lorn and we rested our poor feet. My Victory article appeared in the *Daily Mail* together with the King's speech and the

1 The Duchess Theatre, where Noël's *Blithe Spirit* was playing.
2 This VE night gathering at what Noël once called Winifred Ashton's 'rickety little house' in Tavistock Street, Covent Garden, was typical of many and its guest list included most of those within Noël's inner circle of friends. 'If Winifred's walls had ears,' Noël once wrote, 'I only hope she had the sense to plug them with cotton wool years ago.'
3 Dame Lilian Braithwaite (1873-1948), Joyce Carey's mother and *grande dame* of the British stage; her last-minute agreement to take over the role of the mother in *The Vortex* in 1924 helped give Noël his first West End success.
4 Alfred Lunt (1892-1977) and his English-born wife Lynn Fontanne (b. 1882), America's most distinguished and indefatigable stage partnership from the 1920s well into the 1960s, for whom Noël had written *Design for Living* and *Point Valaine*, and would later write *Quadrille*. At this time they were playing in Terence Rattigan's *Love in Idleness* (US title: *O Mistress Mine*) in London.
5 Richard Addinsell (1904-77), composer, probably best known for his *Warsaw Concerto*; he had scored the recently released film version of *Blithe Spirit*.
6 Henry 'Chips' Channon (1897-1958), diarist, party-giver, and at this time Conservative MP for Southend; knighted 1957.
7 Ivor Novello (1893-1951), composer, playwright, actor, and Noël's only rival for the leadership of the British musical theatre between the First and Second World Wars. The two had first met outside the Midland Hotel, Manchester, in 1917 when, Noël later wrote, 'Ivor was wearing an old overcoat with an Astrakhan collar and a degraded brown hat, and if he had suddenly produced a violin and played the "Barcarolle" from *The Tales of Hoffmann* I should have given him threepence from sheer pity.' Both men rapidly moved on to fame and fortune, but ironically their one joint professional venture, *Sirocco* (1927), was the greatest disaster of both their careers.

Prime Minister's. Visited Mum[1]. Went to Juliet [Duff]'s to have a drink and to see Georges Auric[2]. Stayed on to dinner with Juliet and Desmond Mac-Carthy[3] and took them both to the Stage Door Canteen. Made a brief appearance and got a terrific ovation. After I wandered by myself in the crowds and had a lovely time. I sat on a stone balustrade in Trafalgar Square for over an hour and signed a few autographs and watched London rejoicing, and Nelson in his spotlight seemed to be watching too. Friendliness and kindness everywhere.

Friday 11 May

Lunched with Peter Daubeny[4]. Worked all the afternoon with Robb[5]. The Lunts came in and listened enthusiastically.

Dined with Gladys, then we went to Gerald Road[6] for the 'run through' of the revue[7]. Everyone delighted except Madge and Cyril[8], who were depressed with what is probably the best material they have ever had in their lives. On the whole the show seemed good and well-balanced.

Sunday 13 May

A quiet day, interrupted incessantly by the King and Queen. With the Lunts, John [Gielgud], Binkie[9] and the Flemyngs[10], watched them drive to St Paul's.

1 Violet Agnes Coward, née Veitch (1863-1954), with whom Noël, the second and only surviving of three sons, had a close and intense relationship. She had encouraged Noël's theatrical ambitions since childhood and had run a lodging-house to augment the meagre family income – her husband was an unsuccessful piano-tuner. Since his death in 1937 she had been kept in considerable comfort by Noël at Goldenhurst, his house in Kent, and at 10 Eaton Mansions, a Chelsea flat which she shared with her sister Vida Veitch. 'She was the one person who could always tell me outright when something I had written was bad,' Noël once wrote. 'She never lied to me.'

2 Georges Auric, French composer of many film scores.

3 Sir Desmond MacCarthy (1877-1952), critic and author.

4 Peter Daubeny (1921-75), West End impresario and later the founder of the World Theatre Seasons at the Aldwych Theatre; knighted 1973. Noël had first met him at the Liverpool Repertory Company just before the war and they had met again five years later when Daubeny was among the wounded troops Noël was entertaining in a military hospital in Tripoli. Noël was much impressed by Daubeny's courage in facing the loss of an arm; much less so by his 1949 revival of Noël's play *Fallen Angels*.

5 Robb Stewart, pianist, now working with Noël on the music for his revue *Sigh No More*.

6 Noël's studio home in London from the early 1930s to the mid-1950s.

7 *Sigh No More*.

8 Madge Elliott (1898 1955) and Cyril Ritchard (1898-1978), husband and wife theatrical team who had starred in many musical successes in his native Australia as well as in London and on Broadway, and who were heading the cast of *Sigh No More*.

9 Hugh 'Binkie' Beaumont (1908-73), managing director of the theatrical company H.M. Tennent and, as such, the most powerful theatrical producer in London from the 1940s to the mid-1960s.

10 Robert Flemyng (b. 1912), actor, and his wife Carmen.

In the evening I tried unsuccessfully to think of an opening sketch for Madge and Cyril, then had a drink in the bar.

Thursday 17 May

Drove down to Kent. Lovely weather. Visited Goldenhurst[1] which was locked and empty. Found a door open and made a tour of the house. They have left it clean and in reasonably good condition, but never let me know that they had left it at all. Garden wildly overgrown. All a bit heart-breaking, but what is past is past.

Drove home. Interview with Detective Sergeant Hislop, CID, on account of a young man fraudulently selling tickets for a concert in my name.

Saturday 19 May

Made a little progress musically today, but my mind and hands feel heavy. It will pass soon, I hope. I know nothing so dreary as the feeling that you can't make the sounds or write the words that your whole creative being is yearning for.

Monday 21 May

In spite of Churchill's request for a postponement till the war with Japan is over, Labour is insisting on an autumn election. Churchill replies that in that case he will insist on a July one. Personally I think Labour has behaved abominably throughout this war and before it. At least the Conservatives have some sense of leadership and it is idiotic to try and jettison Churchill at this moment. I hope the Labour boys get a trouncing but I am afraid they won't.

Thursday 24 May

Worked all morning, afternoon and evening with an occasional break. During these intervals I read the MS of Gertie Lawrence's book[2]. It is inaccurate, insincere and shy-making.

Churchill has resigned and is putting a caretaker government in until the election in July. The thought of possibly being governed by Attlee, Morrison, Bevin[3] and Co. is too horrible to contemplate. I hope above all things that Winston is returned with a vast majority. He may have faults but he is the only big man we have got. The Labour boys are a shoddy lot of careerists.

1 The farmhouse near Aldington in Kent which had been Noël's country and weekend home since 1926; during the war it had been requisitioned by the army.
2 *A Star Danced*, published in 1945, the autobiography of Gertrude Lawrence, largely ghosted by her American manager Fanny Holtzmann.
3 The Labour Party leaders, all of whom had served in Churchill's war cabinet: Clement Attlee (1883-1967) as Deputy Prime Minister; Herbert Morrison (1888-1965) as Home Secretary; and Ernest Bevin (1881-1951) as Minister of Labour and National Service.

Friday 1 June

Cable from Jack[1] saying he is arriving about the twelfth. Hooray.

Day of storms and stresses owing to Dick being obdurate through his beastly agent over the music of *Blithe Spirit*[2]. Whole thing idiotic. We had a meeting at six o'clock in Binkie's office, where everything was straightened out amicably. We tossed a coin as to whether Dick should get £15 per week for the ballet music instead of £10, or whether he should give it to us for nothing. I won and so we get it for nothing. Honour is satisfied all round.

Saturday 2 June

Saw very rough cut of *Brief Encounter*[3]. Delighted with it. Celia [Johnson] quite wonderful; Trevor Howard fine and obviously a new star. Whole thing beautifully played and directed – and, let's face it, most beautifully written.

Monday 6 June

Dreadful rehearsal in rehearsal rooms. Everyone idiotic. Went with Binkie to the first night of *Jacobowsky and the Colonel*[4]. Turgid and dull. Mike Redgrave put up a gallant fight.

Thursday 7 June

A better day of rehearsal. People showed more signs of intelligence.

Dined with Binkie, Prince Littler[5], Nora Delany[6] and Alec Cruickshank[7] at the Savoy (private room). A really theatrical evening. Old music-hall reminiscences, etc. We discussed future policies. The evening ended with Binkie, Alec and me in Alec's bedroom discussing my suggestion that I should join the Board of H.M. Tennent. Binkie apprehensive. Alec, who is a hard-headed old duck, was highly enthusiastic. Poor Binkie is terrified that I shall be too dominant. How right he is. Argument went on until 4 a.m.

---

1 Jack Wilson was joint producer with Tennent's of Noël's revue *Sigh No More*.
2 One of the numbers in *Sigh No More* was to be a ballet set to the music written by Richard Addinsell for the film version of *Blithe Spirit*, and the problem here was to assess what share of the revue's weekly royalties should go to Addinsell.
3 The film version of a stage play, originally entitled *Still Life*, written by Noël for himself and Gertrude Lawrence as one of the *Tonight at 8.30* sequence of plays. Noël had done the extensive adaptation of it for the screen as well as producing it; David Lean was the director.
4 Comedy by Franz Werfel, adapted by S. N. Behrman.
5 Prince Littler (1901–73), theatrical impresario and theatre owner; at this time he was also a director of Moss Empires, Howard & Wyndham and the Theatre Royal, Drury Lane, and therefore one of the most powerful producers in the business.
6 Nora Delany, actress, married to Prince Littler.
7 Alec Cruickshank (1877–1949), theatre manager and long-time director of H.M. Tennent Ltd.

Thursday 14 June

Rehearsed all day. Lunched with Binkie at Scott's. Went to Bill Astor's[1] wedding reception at Admiralty House. Far too grand. Got home and found that Jack was arriving at Croydon at six o'clock. Arrived just in time to meet him. He looks frightfully well and is sweeter than ever. Series of reunions with Lorn, Gladys, etc. Dinner at the Savoy, Jack, Binkie and me. Further reunions, finishing with the Lunts.

Saturday 16 June

Had a day off from rehearsing. Lunched with Gladys at Boulestin's and painted all afternoon at Winnie's. Took Jack to *Private Lives*[2]. Reasonably good performance and a packed house.

Tuesday 19 June

Rehearsals satisfactory. Lunched with Adrianne [Allen], Joyce Barbour[3] and Dicky Bird[4] at the Ivy. Long talk with Dick Aldrich[5] about Gertie's book. He was very nice and sensible.

Home early. Horribly stiff in the leg from bouncing about too much at rehearsal.

Wednesday 20 June

Stayed in all day after an agonizing night with my leg. Apparently I have strained a muscle. A Swedish masseuse came and treated it and it improved towards the end of the day. Visited Mum and Veitch[6] in the evening. Both well and fairly belligerent.

Edward[7] came to tea. Bed early with a new idea for a song for Graham[8] in my head called 'Matelot'.

1 William Waldorf Astor (1907-66), at this time Conservative MP for East Fulham; became 3rd Viscount Astor 1952. His bride was the Hon. Sarah (Sally) Norton.
2 This revival, the first in London since Noël and Gertrude Lawrence had played it there in 1930, was now in the course of a two-year run at the Apollo, starring John Clements and his wife, Kay Hammond.
3 Joyce Barbour (1901-77), had appeared in Noël's revue *London Calling!* (1923).
4 Richard Bird (1894-1979), actor, married to Joyce Barbour.
5 Richard Aldrich (b. 1902), American impresario, who had married Gertrude Lawrence in 1940.
6 Vida Veitch (1854-1946), Noël's mother's unmarried sister who was always called 'Veitch' by Noël; the two elderly women now lived together in a remarkable love-hate relationship that kept them both on their toes.
7 Edward Molyneux (1891-1974), one of the most fashionable of fashion designers in the 1920s and 1930s.
8 Graham Payn (b. 1918), one of the four stars of *Sigh No More*, now in rehearsal; this was the second of his many appearances in Noël's shows and the beginning of the close friendship that continued for the rest of Noël's life.

Saturday 23 June

Worked with Lorn on the lyric of 'Matelot'. Jack came to lunch and we went to *This Happy Breed*[1], with which he was profoundly impressed. Tea with Mum and Veitch, after which I came home and worked on the verse of 'Matelot'.

Dined at Claridge's with Edward [Molyneux] and Peter Daubeny and we went on to the Lunts' farewell party[2]. The entire company were in uniform.

Sunday 24 June

Finished 'Matelot' and typed it just before lunch. Graham stayed for lunch, after which we rehearsed like mad, then had tea and went to see *National Velvet*[3]. A good picture except for a few Hollywood 'English' mistakes.

Monday 25 June

The election campaign is raging and is almost too squalid to be borne. To read of Mr Churchill's eager repartees after his great phrases during the war is discouraging. How right I was to say to him, 'Don't descend to the arena', and how wrong he was not to smell a little truth in it.

Thursday 28 June

'Wolf on the fold' day. I descended on the theatre like the Assyrian, redid 'Hat' and 'Willy' and 'Bunch of Boys', cut the dance away from 'Matelot' and generally zipped things up. Evening rehearsal much smoother.

Tuesday 3 July

Rehearsed and polished all day. At 5.30 the Duchess of Kent and Princess Nicholas [of Greece] came to Gerald Road. After a drink I took them to the evening rehearsal, which was fairly slick except for 'Bunch of Boys' which stinks. Afterwards we came home for supper. Graham sang 'Matelot' really beautifully.

Sunday 8 July   Manchester

Evening spent in the theatre setting the spot batten and the automatics. We managed to light three scenes by midnight, then we came back to the hotel and, with Ian Dow[4], arranged our plans for the next three days. Everything complicated by the cyclorama arriving the wrong size. It will have to be redone, which buggers up our lighting. In addition to this, we can only

1 The film version, made in 1943, of Noël's 1939 play.
2 They were returning to America, having completed the London run of *Love in Idleness*.
3 The film of Enid Bagnold's celebrated novel, starring Mickey Rooney and a young Elizabeth Taylor.
4 Ian Dow, production manager of H.M. Tennent.

rehearse effectively in the evenings because that is the only time we can get the staff that actually will work the show.

Monday 9 July

A day of frustration, toil, blood and sweat. Disastrous dress rehearsal in the evening. Continued to light 'Never Again'. I am horribly worried about Dick's and Joyce's material[1]. It is all pretty amateurish and gets nowhere. Have suggested to Binkie that we have two weeks at Liverpool or Leeds after Manchester, by which time I shall probably have supplanted them with more vigorous numbers and really pulled the show together.

Tuesday 10 July

Complete run through in the evening. Everybody good. There is still much to be done. The finale is idiotic, so is 'Holiday'. Madge and Cyril have behaved sweetly and it is comforting to work with real dyed-in-the-wool pros. Graham is fine, with style in everything he does. Joyce Grenfell good in all she does on the stage, but she shouldn't write lyrics.

Wednesday 11 July

More rehearsals and polishing and then the opening night. The show went through from beginning to end without one hitch of any kind. Graham's singing of 'Matelot' was the high spot of the evening. Cyril and Madge and Joyce were fine. The whole thing was rapturously received. But oh, what a lot of work there is to be done.

Supper afterwards, then a post-mortem. I have got to be firm from now on and ruthlessly cut anything that doesn't satisfy me.

Thursday 26 July

A highly dramatic day in our 'Turbulent Island Story'. The Labour Government is sweeping in on an overwhelming majority. Winston, I am sure, made a dreadful mistake in descending into the arena. It is appalling to think that our Allies and enemies can see us chuck out the man who has led us so magnificently through these horrible years. The immediate future of the country led by Mr Attlee, Mr Bevin and Mr Morrison[2] looks fairly grim, but I suspect that we shall rise above it.

This certainly gives a salutary lesson to those who set too much store by

1 Joyce Grenfell (1910-79), actress and writer, was one of the stars in *Sigh No More*; in her wartime concert work she had established a partnership with Richard Addinsell as her composer and pianist, and Noël had agreed that she would use in his revue some of the Grenfell-Addinsell songs that had made her name.

2 Prime Minister, Foreign Secretary and Deputy Prime Minister respectively in the new Labour Government.

public acclaim or on the power of the Press. Whatever government rules us for the next few years will have a tough assignment, and it may not be a bad idea for the Labour boys to hold the baby. I always felt that England would be bloody uncomfortable during the immediate post-war period, and it is now almost a certainty that it will be so.

Friday 27 July

Re-rehearsed *Sigh No More* in the morning.

Caught the two o'clock train, arriving London 6.10. Met by Cole[1] and Lorn. Dined with Gladys at the Ivy. She has bought a house just above me at St Margaret's Bay[2].

Wednesday 1 August

Travelled to Manchester with Lorn and Gladys. Saw the show. Joyce G. and Graham first rate but Madge and Cyril really no good. Supper in the suite feeling depressed.

Saturday 4 August

A really bloody day. Woke up feeling awful and coughing my lungs out. Also depressed by Cyril and Madge and the fact that they are spoiling the show. Rehearsed my recording with Robb and Mantovani[3] but without voice. By the afternoon my nerves were beginning to go badly. Finally Binkie arrived and saw the show. Cyril did the 'Indian Army' song with such raucous vulgarity that I nearly stopped him from the stalls. I went round at the end and told the company that, whereas before I had told them I wanted them to be happy and efficient, now I was not remotely interested in their happiness but determined that they were going to be efficient. Back at the hotel I had a real *crise*. Finally Binkie went along and found Cyril and Madge terrified and abject. For nine weeks I have been bored and irritated by their stupidity.

Sunday 5 August

Drove to Liverpool with Joyce, Graham and Bert[4]. The bliss of breathing a

1 Cole Lesley, born Leonard Cole (1911–80), who first worked for Noël as a valet in 1936; he served in the RAF during the war and returned to become Noël's secretary, manager and in 1976 author of *The Life of Noël Coward* (US title: *Remembered Laughter*). It was to 'Coley' and Graham, the two companions of Noël's last thirty years, that his estate was left.
2 Earlier in the year Noël had bought the lease of White Cliffs, a house near Dover overlooking and indeed practically in the sea, which was to be his weekend and country home until Goldenhurst could be made habitable after its wartime army occupation.
3 Mantovani (1905–80), Italian-born British orchestra leader and violinist, who was conducting *Sigh No More*; as usual Noël planned to release his own recording of songs from the show even though he was not appearing in it.
4 Bert Lister, Noël's valet and dresser through most of the war.

little fresh air again and being in a good hotel! At 4.30 I went along to Cyril and Madge with Joyce and Graham to rehearse the new 'Burchells' lyric. Cyril led me into the bathroom and burst into tears and apologized humbly and sweetly. He looked so strained that I felt really sorry for him. Madge was tremulous and on the verge of tears. They have both obviously had an awful time. Now perhaps we shall get some good work done. Binkie's behaviour has been utterly perfect.

Wednesday 8 August

The papers are full of the atomic bomb[1] which is going to revolutionize everything and blow us all to buggery. Not a bad idea.

Friday 10 August

News that Japan has surrendered. If this is so the war is now over. I wonder how many years of *soi-disant* peace lie ahead of us. Here in Liverpool people are preparing for a little gaiety. I wish I had more feeling about it. My mind seems unable to take it in. It has all been too long and too stupid and too cruel. We shall see how sweet the face of peace looks. I cannot help visualizing an inane, vacuous grin.

Wednesday 15 August

Official VJ Day announced last night by Mr Attlee[2]. How smart it would have been if the Labour boys had asked Churchill to announce the victory.

Dined on board the *Sister Ann*. After dinner we let off fireworks and then went below for one for the road. We drank to the King and to the Navy and to those who had died.

Went to the theatre and rehearsed Graham with lights, etc. Everyone screaming in the streets. Felt desolate remembering all the people who have gone.

Sunday 19 August   London

Went to Gladys's flat for a drink. We had watched Mr Attlee making his Victory announcement. Flat, dull and uninspiring. Went to call on Mum. Dined with Graham and his mother at their flat.

Tuesday 21 August

Did the lighting. Everything late on account of Sunday railway strike. Dress rehearsal at 6.30. Chaos. Cyril and Madge awful. Electrical staff exhausted. Went on until 12.30. Home feeling fairly wretched.

1 The Americans had dropped an atomic bomb on Hiroshima two days earlier and on the following day dropped a second bomb on Nagasaki.
2 Hostilities between the Allies and Japan ceased on 14 August 1945.

Wednesday 22 August

Slightly better dress rehearsal, then the first night. A wonderful audience and the show went triumphantly. Joyce and Graham, as predicted, made the outstanding hits. Madge and Cyril got by. We had a party afterwards at Winnie's.

Thursday 23 August

Notices good for box-office but patronizing for me. Joyce and Graham have really got away with it. Evening papers enthusiastic.

Went with Gladys to *Lady Windermere's Fan*[1]. A dull play and over-decorated by Cecil[2]. Isabel[3] very good. Supper at the Savoy and a relaxed discussion of life in general.

Sunday 26 August

Flawless weather. Graham and I drove to St Margaret's Bay and had a picnic lunch on the terrace of the house in lovely sunshine. We bathed and sunbathed. We inspected Gladys's house and then drove to Goldenhurst and went all over it, pushing aside the ghosts. Had a drink with the Freres[4]. Dined at the Mill with Gladys and drove to London, tired, sunburnt and relaxed.

Thursday 30 August

Went to the theatre and received Wavell and Winston Churchill. All went well. Winston, Mrs Churchill and Randolph[5] came up to the ante-room in the interval and had a drink. He was very charming and completely honest over his reaction to the election. He said it had been absolutely bloody and that there was nothing so mortifying as to step forward as a victor and drop through a star trap. After the show the Wavell party came up to have a drink and we all went backstage.

Supper at home and drove down to the country.

1 Oscar Wilde's play in a revival at the Theatre Royal, Haymarket.
2 Cecil Beaton (1904–80), photographer and designer, knighted 1972; he had designed the scenery and costumes for the play and, when it went to America in 1946, took to the boards himself as Cecil Graham in it. Beaton's relations with Noël had been a trifle chilly ever since Noël had told him in the course of a 1930 Atlantic crossing that he was 'flabby, floppy and affected, with an undulating walk, exaggerated clothes and a voice both too high and too precise'.
3 Isabel Jeans (b. 1891), actress playing Mrs Erlynne; she had starred in the film version of Noël's play *Easy Virtue*, produced by Alfred Hitchcock in 1927.
4 A. S. Frere, chairman of Noël's British publisher, William Heinemann, and his wife Pat, daughter of Edgar Wallace; they had a house near Goldenhurst.
5 Randolph Churchill (1911–68), the pugnacious son of Winston and Clementine; 'Dear Randolph,' mused Noël once, 'so unspoiled by his great failure.'

Friday 31 August

Peaceful day. Drove up in the afternoon. Long talk with Lorn about *Future Indefinite*[1]. Went to the Stage Door Canteen. Everything mismanaged, the place was like a furnace, the show too long and the audience restless. I managed to keep them quiet but it was hard work.

Monday 3 September

Six years ago today war was declared. Now we are starting again with officially declared peace and the world in physical and spiritual chaos. History in the making can be most exhausting.

Came up in the train with Beatrice Eden. Graham came to lunch and we went to the National Gallery to see the Tate Exhibition of Moderns. Lovely pictures by Manet, Van Gogh, Degas and others.

Wednesday 5 September

Lorn and I had a ruthless morning and tore up letters and ignored telephone calls. Sibyl Colefax[2] came to lunch and was quite sweet.

Went to the theatre to find that Cyril had lost his voice and was not playing. Watched the matinée and decided the understudy was not good enough. Decided to go on myself for the evening show. Had a terrific reception from the audience. Mantovani was wonderful and the evening a triumphant success. Am playing until Saturday.

Friday 7 September

A horrible day. Woke up voiceless and feeling awful and had to face the fact that to play this evening's show was impossible. Rang up Cyril; he is better and is going back. Postponed Monday's recording until next Friday. Have put off everyone for everything.

Williamson[3] came to talk about St Margaret's Bay and seems optimistic about getting the house ready for me by mid-October.

Tried to read *Forever Amber*[4]; failed. Tried to read *The Bachelor*[5]; failed.

Thursday 13 September

Peaceful day at home. Worked for an hour with Robb. Voice improving.

Am reading through my diaries – 1942 and 1943 – what incredible years.

1 The second and last volume of Noël's autobiography, covering the years 1939-45, which he was now planning to write; it was published in 1954.
2 Lady (Sibyl) Colefax (d. 1950), interior decorator and tireless London society hostess with a penchant for literary and theatrical 'lions'.
3 The architect working on changes to White Cliffs.
4 By Kathleen Winsor.
5 By Stella Gibbons.

The nine o'clock news announced the discovery of the German blacklist. Among the people to be dealt with when England was invaded were Winston, Vic Oliver, Sybil Thorndike[1], Rebecca West[2] and me. What a cast!

Friday 14 September

Recorded most of the day at HMV studios. In the morning did 'Matelot', 'Sigh No More', 'Nina' and 'Never Again' with Mantovani and the orchestra; in the afternoon 'Wait a Bit, Joe' and 'Indian Army Officer' with Robb. I think highly successful, although a bit worried about my voice. Thank God it's over.

Sunday 16 September

Another perfect day at White Cliffs. I don't think I can fail to be happy there. Tea with Gladys and Elizabeth Taylor[3].

Back to London about nine o'clock, full up with sun and sea and fresh air.

Monday 17 September

Lunch with Graham at the Bon Viveur. He gave me a delayed first-night present of a gold cigarette-holder.

Went to the theatre to receive the King and Queen of Yugoslavia.

Friday 21 September

Drove to Dartford with Robb and Bert. Lunched in the MO's Mess. Gave concert to the up patients, who were a very good audience. Tea with about twenty ratings. Visited wards and talked to the bed patients. Watched Dr Cohen performing a tricky operation, removing an abnormal rib from a man's chest. He was skilful and delicate and it was fascinating.

Wednesday 26 September

Mary Borden[4] came to lunch and was enchanting. Went with Adrianne to the first night of *Henry IV*, Part I. Larry was, as usual, magnificent and Ralph was excellent[5]. Had a sharp little set-to in the pub during the entr'acte with a

---

1 Sybil Thorndike (1882–1976), actress, for whom Shaw had written *St Joan* and who played frequently with the Old Vic Company; she had known and admired Noël as a young man, and she and her husband, Sir Lewis Casson, had toured in two of Noël's *Tonight at 8.30* plays in 1937; created Dame in 1931.

2 Rebecca West (b. 1892), author and journalist; on learning that she and Noël had been on the list of prominent English political and literary figures to be arrested and probably executed if the Germans had invaded, she wrote Noël a postcard: 'Just think who we'd have been seen dead with!'; created Dame in 1959.

3 A friend of Gladys Calthrop – neither the film star nor the novelist.

4 Mary Borden (d. 1968), novelist wife of General Sir Edward Spears, with whom Noël had stayed in Beirut in 1944 while doing troop concerts in the Middle East.

5 Olivier was playing Hotspur to Richardson's Falstaff in an Old Vic Company production which they had co-directed.

horrid little German who had written an insulting notice about my appearance at the Stage Door Canteen.

Monday 15 October

Laval[1] was shot at 8.30 this morning. He tried to kill himself with an insufficient dose of cyanide, was stomach-pumped, dragged out, given a volley which did not kill him, and was finished off with a bullet through the ear.

Thursday 18 October

Drove down to White Cliffs in the Ford Brake with Lorn. As usual, the day was wet and bleak until we passed Canterbury, then the sun came out and by the time we reached the Bay it was like summer. Vans and furniture arrived in the afternoon. Later drove Lorn into Dover to catch her train, then Cole and I spent a hectic lamplit evening getting things arranged.

Graham drove down from London and brought a bottle of champagne as a libation to the house. I met him at the top of the hill; there was a full moon making a highway across the sea, the South Foreland was flashing and there were ships far out in the Channel wearing coloured lights. An evening of enchantment. I know this is going to be a happy house.

Saturday 20 October

Went sunbathing for nearly an hour, then worked. Went up to London by the 2.17. Visited Mum and Veitch. Veitch gave me a cheque for £50 as a present for the house.

Wednesday 24 October

A terrific gale and wild seas which would have been lovely if it were not for fresh hordes of beach fleas which come in their thousands. It is only because of the southerly wind.

Worked all day sorting and moving books. Cole and I shopping in the morning and in the evening went to Gladys's for a bath. Graham arrived at midnight with his two test records, which are first rate.

Friday 26 October

A very high sea, at some moments breaking over the house.

A man from the Ministry of Works arrived intent on making trouble. An anonymous letter had been written about the building of a house for Noël

---

1 Pierre Laval, deputy head of the Vichy government in 1940 and Prime Minister, 1942–44; after the liberation of France he had been condemned to death for collaborating with the Germans.

Coward the actor. Got rid of him tactfully and telephoned Lorn to telephone Williamson. I am getting a little sick of being persecuted[1].

Wednesday 31 October   London

Lunched with Binkie. Persuaded him to close the theatre on Christmas Eve, thus giving the company three days' holiday.

I am livid because Mum has been ill for a week without sending for a doctor. It turns out she has had a slight attack of pneumonia. Apparently Dr MacManus was very cross at not having been sent for before. Shall raise hell about this.

Went with Lorn to see *Oedipus* and *The Critic*[2]. Both, in my opinion, boring and too long. Larry very good in *Oedipus*, but as Mr Puff in *The Critic* he was quite perfect. Technically flawless and fine beyond words.

Friday 2 November   White Cliffs

We now have hot water. Gladys came for a drink and brought a kitten which we have christened Atco because it purrs like a lawn-mower.

Saturday 3 November

A warm sunny day, with the sea lying on the shore like a scarf. Drove to Dover with Cole. Did some shopping and had lunch at the Crypt. Read Elizabeth Bowen's new short stories[3]; exquisite writing but a trifle too inconclusive.

Graham arrived on the late train with all the curtain material and, as a wonderful surprise, one of the poodles we saw the other day. It is called Pierre, which will be changed to Matelot. It is very miniature and grey and enchanting. I am mad about it.

Monday 5 November

A wonderful morning. Walked to the other headland. The sea was like misted glass.

Drove to London. Went to the Royal Command Performance at the Coliseum with the Littlers and Binkie. The Queen looked charming. Supper party afterwards at Gow's next door.

Saturday 10 November

Terrible weather and very high seas, which gave me a bad night, aided by a broken shutter banging so much that I thought it would break the window.

1 Questions had been asked in the House of Commons about Noël's wartime activities, and this, together with his prosecution on currency charges in 1941, left him with the impression that English officialdom was out to get him.
2 The Old Vic Season at the New Theatre included a double bill of Sophocles and Sheridan.
3 Published as *The Demon Lover*.

Went out, muffled up in top boots, leather coat, etc., and grappled with the bloody thing in the rain and the spray. I finally broke it from its hinges, hurting my thumb considerably in the process.

Arranged my new painting studio. Shopped with Cole. Spent the afternoon preparing canvases and the evening writing verse.

Monday 12 November

Painted for a bit and then retired to my work room for a number of hours, writing, hemmed in by oil stoves and lamps which smoked and smelt. Read all the Sunday papers. A gloomy proceeding. There is a dreadful feeling of anticlimax in the world.

Jerry Kern is dead[1]. I feel profoundly sorry; no more of those lovely, satisfying melodies. It happened that on Sunday afternoon I spent an hour playing all the old tunes of his that I could remember. This must have been just when he was dying. He is a great loss.

Tuesday 13 November

Painted all the morning. Drove up to London. Long talk with Lorn. Dined with Virginia Cowles[2], Ann Rothermere[3]. Later joined by Esmond[4] and we went to Virginia's flat. Long argument with her husband, Crawley, about the Labour Government, etc. He stood up to the attack fairly well.

Wednesday 14 November

Visited Mum who was very gay, but Veitch is pretty ill. Expected Syrie[5] to lunch but she never turned up. Lorn and I waited, and while waiting suddenly the story that I have been wanting for the operette dropped into my mind whole and complete.

Monday 19 November   White Cliffs

Went for a walk up to the lighthouse. A grey pearly light over everything; very

---

1 Jerome Kern (1885–1945) who, with Cole Porter, was the American songwriter Noël most loved and admired. Noël had recently recorded 'The Last Time I Saw Paris', the song Kern had dedicated to him in memory of the time Noël spent working there for British Intelligence at the outbreak of the war. As early as 1924 the two men had talked of collaborating on a musical; sadly it never happened.

2 Virginia Cowles (b. 1912), American author and journalist, married to Aidan Crawley (b. 1908), then Labour M P for Buckingham.

3 Ann Rothermere, née Charteris (1913–81); her first husband, Baron O'Neill, had been killed in 1944 and she had recently married the 2nd Viscount Rothermere.

4 Esmond Harmsworth, 2nd Viscount Rothermere (1898–1978), chairman of the *Daily Mail* and General Trust Ltd 1932–71.

5 Syrie Maugham, née Barnardo (1879–1955), fashionable interior decorator; married to William Somerset Maugham 1916–27.

lovely. Went shopping with Cole in Deal and bought fourteen old and scarifying paintings with good frames and canvases. Worked on the synopsis from 5 p.m. till 10 p.m. and finished it. Dinner in bed. There is a sea mist and the Goodwins fog-horn is going.

Saturday 24 November

Painted all the morning and part of the afternoon. Was caught by a man called Bindoff from the *Evening News*. Apparently some local people have been complaining and writing to the papers because I have a telephone and they have not, etc. The dear Human Species.

Sunday 25 November

Read Sunday notices of *Brief Encounter*. All enthusiastic except the *Sunday Pictorial*, which decided to take up an attitude.

Spent the evening inventing Samolan history and Samolan language.[1]

Monday 26 November

Drove up to London. Gala première[2] in aid of the Royal Naval War Libraries. The Duchess of Kent came. I made quite a good speech with a few nice cracks at the Government that went down like a dinner. The picture is really very good and Celia is quite wonderful. Party at Gerald Road afterwards; the Duchess, Sybil Cholmondeley[3], Chips Channon, etc.

Thursday 29 November

Went to a vile picture called *Love Letters*. Jennifer Jones and poor Joseph Cotten. In the evening went to *Private Lives*. Hugh and Googie excellent[4]. They played it much straighter than Kay and John and brought the love story out more.

Supper at the Savoy with Joyce, Arthur[5], Lorn and Graham.

Monday 10 December   White Cliffs

A nightmare day. I was having a cocktail before lunch when I heard agonized

---

1 For his new operetta, which he had decided to set on the mythical South Seas island of Samolo; he had already used this island as a setting for one of the plays in *Tonight at 8.30* and later used it in his novel *Pomp and Circumstance* (1960) as well as in the comedy *South Sea Bubble* (1956).

2 Of the film *Brief Encounter*.

3 Sybil, Marchioness of Cholmondeley (b. 1913), Superintendent of the Women's Royal Naval Service 1939-46; married to 5th Marquess of Cholmondeley ('Rock'), Lord Chamberlain 1936-7 and 1952-66.

4 Hugh Sinclair and Googie Withers had replaced John Clements and Kay Hammond in the Apollo Theatre revival.

5 Arthur Macrae (1908-62), comic dramatist, who as an actor had appeared in Noël's *Cavalcade* in 1931.

shrieks and rushed out. Found Patrick and Margaret[1] coming out of Lorn's Bluff screaming. Their baby had been burnt to death. Margaret had dragged it out of the flames and there it lay on the ground. It was poor Patrick who had put the oil stove near the cradle. The doctor who arrived was useless, but the priest who was sent for was very good. Graham was wonderful and took charge of Patrick, and Cole was superb. The whole thing utterly horrible. My heart aches for poor Patrick and Margaret.

Saturday 15 December

Received birthday presents in the morning. A set of Mrs Humphry Ward from Joyce and of Brontë from Mum, a silver egg-cup from Veitch, a Bible from Lorn, etc.

After the show at night drove Graham down to White Cliffs, together with 'Wait a Bit, Joe', a black poodle puppy. Sweet but wicked. Warming reception by Cole, more nice presents and a cake made like a theatre from Madame Floris[2].

Sunday 23 December

Winifred arrived to stay with Gladys, highly enthusiastic about everything. Played some of the *Carousel*[3] records; jolly good. There are mines floating about[4]. Never a dull moment.

Monday 24 December

A charming day ending with a Christmas party at Gladys's. Lovely presents for everyone from everyone in a genial and comfortable atmosphere.

Tuesday 25 December

A thoroughly enjoyable Christmas Day. Walked, slept, played the gramophone, etc. A nice cosy evening.

Wednesday 26 December

Worked at the piano and replayed *Carousel* records. They are so good they make me determined to do better.

Read first volume of Jenny Lind's life[5]. Effusive and turgid and only interesting as a period piece.

1 The couple who looked after White Cliffs and lived in the garden cottage known as Lorn's Bluff.
2 A Soho patisserie.
3 Richard Rodgers' and Oscar Hammerstein's triumphant Broadway musical, which had opened in April of this year.
4 In St Margaret's Bay, a few hundred yards from his garden.
5 *Jenny Lind the Artist* (1891), a two-volume biography of the Swedish soprano by H.E. Holland and W.S. Rockstro.

Saturday 29 December

Had rather a turbulent night with a large black sea-bird which came into my bedroom and got into a panic. I thought it had gone but it had not. It woke at six o'clock and went mad. I finally caught it and put it out. It created rather a scene and gasped and nearly fainted until it saw some of its friends in the morning sky and joined them.

Worked nearly all day. The music is getting richer and more flexible. Graham came down on the late train.

Monday 31 December

Well, 1945 is over; I wonder what 1946 has in store?

1946

Asked at a lunch early in this year whether he could be said to have survived the war, Noël replied, 'Like Mother Goddam, I shall always survive.' It was, however, to be a testing year for him, most of it given over to an ambitious project – the post-war reopening of Drury Lane with a lavish and escapist musical called Pacific 1860, *of which Noël was author, composer, lyricist and director. Permits to repair the bomb damage at the Lane were remarkably hard to come by and much of his year was spent cutting through several hundred yards of red tape before rehearsals could start in the late autumn. Even by then the Lane was far from ready, and ambitious plans for a full week of dress rehearsals (as had been feasible for* Cavalcade *in 1930, Noël's only other production at the Lane) had to be abandoned. The result was, in Noël's own phrase, 'more of a convulsive stagger than a run'. And taken together with the six-month run of* Sigh No More, *it did somewhat tarnish his reputation, which seemed suddenly shaky and irrevocably pre-war. There was, however, rather more to 1946 than backstage bickering at the Lane.*

Saturday 5 January   White Cliffs

An exciting day, because Cole and I started seriously on *Samolo*[1]. We made a map and sketched out various incidents in early Samolan history. We set the longitude and latitude, climate, rainfall, mountains, rivers, etc.

Friday 11 January

Seriously considering Printemps for the operette. She is a superb singer and an excellent actress and I am sure can look young enough. Her great defect is her English pronunciation.

Tuesday 15 January

Wrote rather a good lyric for the verse of 'Bright was the Day'. Tried to set it, but the music wouldn't play. After lunch took the dogs up to the headland. Later the vicar called on me and I felt I must be amiable as his wife had been sweet to Margaret. He talked a great deal of cock and never drew breath. Matelot complicated the interview by attempting to rape him. I removed him saying, 'Matelot, *not* the vicar.'

Worked for four hours at the piano and finally hammered out the beginning of a melody.

Sunday 20 January

The *Sunday Express* came out with a headline that there is to be a question asked in the House on Tuesday about the extensive repairs done to Mr Noël Coward's house. It is too discouraging that our MPs have time, at this critical moment, to ask questions and debate about me.

Monday 21 January

The *Daily Mail* headlined me today. It is all very unpleasant, but although I should write a strong letter protesting against victimization, etc., I have a feeling that I shall remain calm and let all the foolish, mischievous people think and say what they like.

Wednesday 23 January

Apparently the great House of Commons question was dropped. No mention of it anywhere. This Press persecution of me is bound to amount to very little; they invariably go off at half-cock and destroy their own efforts by their own inaccuracy.

Thursday 24 January

The question was asked in the House and the Minister of Works replied

1 Working title for the operetta; Noël always used the French spelling.

stating that I was not the owner but the lessee and that in any case the licences and permits were in order.

Saturday 26 January

Slightly bombshell news that the revue[1] is to close on 16 February. Personally I couldn't care less.

Ivor [Novello], Bobby[2] and Joyce [Carey] arrived at 12.30 bringing with them the *Star* with headlines about Coward writing a new operette for Yvonne Printemps, who is to play opposite Graham Payn. It really is insufferable. However, I am determined not to be stampeded, one way or the other. I am beginning to believe that my news value is higher than that of anyone in the world, with the possible exception of Stalin and James Mason.

Sunday 27 January

Warm sunshine, blue sea and clear sky. Ivor and Bobby were very nice and wildly enthusiastic about the house. We talked theatre *ad nauseam* until supper, when we embarked on Ivor's trial and the injustice[3], etc. I became a little uneasy but he has no qualms whatever. He told me how he evaded fire-watching and flew to the shelter whenever danger threatened.

Tuesday 29 January

A heavy sea, but bright sunshine. After breakfast I started thinking about the operette, but could not concentrate. After a while I began reading Roald Dahl's short stories about flying and war experiences[4]. Then suddenly I found out what was wrong. These stories pierced the layers of my consciousness and stirred up the very deep feelings I had during the war and have since, almost deliberately, been in danger of losing. If I forget these feelings or allow them to be obscured because they are uncomfortable, I shall be lost. Ivor and Bobby and their selfish, pathetic triviality made something click in my mind and brought back the things I knew so clearly during the war; not all the time, but at moments in hospitals and Messes and ships. I must hang on to those moments or I shall not have survived the war.

Saturday 2 February   London

Dressed up in tails for the first time since 1939; they fitted! Dined with Chips [Channon]. A very chic party with the King of Greece, the Duchess of Kent,

---

1 *Sigh No More*, which ran to a total of 213 performances.
2 Robert Andrews (b. 1895), actor, who had appeared in Noël's original production of *Hay Fever* in 1925; he was now living with Ivor Novello and appeared in many of his shows.
3 In 1945 he had been convicted of misusing wartime petrol coupons and had spent a month in prison.
4 *Over to You* (1945).

etc. Very grand and rather agony. Came home feeling a little fried, but not on account of having very much to drink.

Thursday 5 February

Drove Mum down to White Cliffs. A lovely day with a touch of spring in the air. Mum was sweet and gay and cheerful and enthusiastic about the house and everything. She longs to live here and I think it is a fine idea[1]. Of course Veitch is raising hell, but she will have to put up with it. The dogs were charming and welcoming.

Thursday 7 February   London

Went to *Peter Grimes*[2]. Extremely well done and the music, although over-eager to avoid melody, is somehow exciting. It is certainly a considerable contribution to English opera.

Monday 11 February

Worked with Robb [Stewart] for three hours. At 9.30 Mantovani came, also Gladys and Bert [Lister], and Robb and I played through the score. Manty genuinely entranced. Have reluctantly come to the conclusion that Yvonne's English is too bad for the part. I must find someone who can give true value to the lyrics.

Tuesday 12 February

Dinner alone with Binkie, newly returned from America. He told me most unhappy stories of Jack's attitude to him, to Terry [Rattigan] and to this country[3]. True, Binkie exaggerates, but cannot discount his report entirely as, although he came home by sea, neither Jack nor Natasha[4] sent as much as a chocolate. It all makes me feel physically sick.

Wednesday 20 February

Took Sybil Cholmondeley to the reopening of Covent Garden. A gala evening, with the King and Queen, Queen Mary, the Princesses and everyone in

1 Attached to White Cliffs was a row of cottages on which Noël had also taken a lease and he had suggested that his mother and aunt move into one of them.
2 Benjamin Britten's opera.
3 During the war years Jack Wilson had begun to manage many plays in America besides Noël's, including some by Terence Rattigan, and he had thus become Binkie Beaumont's American partner, handling many productions originated by H.M. Tennent in London. However, it was now becoming clear that his interest in the English theatre generally and in Noël in particular was not what it had once been.
4 Princess Natalia (Natasha) Paley (1905-81), daughter of Grand Duke Paul of Russia, whom Jack Wilson had married in 1937 in what Noël described as 'the twenty-first fine careless rapture of youth'.

London. The ballet, *Sleeping Princess*, well done but far too long. Supper at the Savoy.

Thursday 21 February

Visited Mum and Veitch. After lunch visited Winnie as it is her birthday. She was very sweet, but there is a definite change in the atmosphere. She will never forgive me for taking Dick's material out of the revue.[1]

Saturday 23 February

Last night of *Sigh No More*. I watched it and, apart from 'Matelot', said goodbye to it without a pang.

Drove down to White Cliffs with Sybil Payn[2], Graham and Joyce.

Thursday 28 February

Larry [Olivier] arrived with the disappointing news that after all he is not going to do the film of *Present Laughter*.

Made a momentous decision today, and that is to do the operette at Drury Lane and make it a big production. It is a beautiful theatre and it would be exciting to reopen it[3].

Saturday 2 March

Cabled Mary Martin[4] about the operette.

Drove down to Coppins and had a peaceful and pleasant tea with the Duchess and her sister, Countess Törring. Little Princess Alexandra came in, a beguiling child[5].

Monday 4 March

An enthusiastic cable from Mary Martin's husband, Dick Halliday[6], saying she was wildly excited at the idea of doing the operette and that it seemed a practical proposition for the autumn. I am delighted as, although she cannot sing as well as Yvonne, she has youth and charm and a strong personality. At the moment it all seems too good to be true. I do hope that later on in the year I shall not re-read this page amid gales of hollow laughter.

Painted all day, practising doing faces.

1 Richard Addinsell, like Noël, was a close friend of Winifred Ashton.
2 Graham's mother.
3 The Theatre Royal, Drury Lane, had been closed in the war and turned into the operational headquarters of Entertainments National Service Association (ENSA).
4 Mary Martin (b. 1913), Texan singer who had first made her name in such Hollywood musicals as *The Great Victor Herbert* and with the song 'My Heart Belongs to Daddy'.
5 The Duchess of Kent's daughter, Princess Alexandra, was ten years old at this time.
6 Richard Halliday acted as his wife's manager.

Thursday 7 March

Talk with young flying officer in the train; he seemed very disillusioned about his reception in England. Our attitude to our servicemen is deeply shaming.

Went to Sybil [Cholmondeley]'s cocktail party, during which I had a set-to with Mrs Simon, Lord Simon's[1] daughter, who was intelligent but rather rude. She is a roaring Indiaphile and said that while in India she was ashamed of being English. I dealt with her.

Saturday 9 March

Went to the last performance of *Blithe Spirit*[2]. Packed house and gala atmosphere. I made a speech. It was a sad occasion, because it really could have gone on running for another year. However, four and a half years is a nice enough run. Binkie gave a party at the Savoy afterwards. Home much too late.

Tuesday 12 March

I have bought a Vlaminck for £1,000.

Wednesday 13 March

Flew to Paris with Graham and arrived at Le Bourget at 2.45. Diana[3] sweetly sent an Embassy car to meet us. Cole had filled the flat[4] with flowers and it was welcoming and charming.

Friday 15 March

Went to the RAF bar for a drink, then dined with Marlene and Jean[5], who were having a slight row. Tried to smooth things over. We then went to the Boris Kochno-Roland Petit ballet which was, I thought, indifferent. After this

1 Lord Simon, Liberal politician and lawyer; Lord Chancellor in Churchill's wartime government.
2 At the Duchess Theatre, where it was in its 1,997th performance since opening in July 1941.
3 Lady Diana Cooper (b. 1892), beauty and brilliant social figure, married to politician Alfred (Duff) Cooper, who at this time was British Ambassador to France. She had gone on the stage in the 1920s to help finance her husband's career and had been a friend of Noël's since that time despite a somewhat uneasy start to their relationship when, during a dinner party, she remarked that she had not laughed once at his early comedy *The Young Idea*. 'How strange,' mused Noël, 'when I saw you acting in *The Great Adventure*, I laughed all the time.'
4 When Noël was first sent to Paris at the outbreak of war in 1939 to form a bureau of propaganda, he had taken a flat near the Ritz in the Place Vendôme. This had then been occupied by the invading German army, but was now back in the hands of its rightful tenant.
5 Marlene Dietrich (b. 1904), the German-born American film and cabaret star, was at this time in the midst of a well-publicized affair with French film actor Jean Gabin (1904–76). She and Noël had become, and remained, close friends since their first conversation – by transatlantic telephone – in 1935.

we went to a Russian joint where hard-working noblemen play violins and cellos up your nose. Marlene very gay and looked lovely but talked about herself a good deal.

Wednesday 20 March

Lovely weather but I feel beastly because I am overwhelmed with catarrh. A super luxe lunch in a super luxe flat with a curious collection of people: Marguerite Scialtiel[1], Yves Miraude and Colette. At ten to three we started an abortive discussion of *Blithe Spirit* (which was the object of the lunch). I gently intimated that I did not want Yves Miraude to adapt (he was out of the room); Cocteau was suggested, also Colette herself. I find it hard to choose.

Monday 25 March

At the Embassy, just a small dinner for the Windsors. Sat next to Wallis. She was very charming and rather touching. He loves her so much, and at long last I am beginning to believe that she loves him. After dinner I played the piano to help the party out.

Tuesday 26 March

A lovely sunny spring day. Sat outside the Café de la Paix. A brief interview with Madame Champion at the Ministre de la Guerre about petrol coupons in order to get by car to the Riviera.

We dined at the Palais de Porquerolle and then took Marlene and Jean to *Les Parents Terribles*[2], a very good play finely acted, especially by Yvonne de Bray, who has genius. Afterwards we went to hear Edith Piaf[3]. Home late.

Tuesday 2 April   South of France

Went to Maxine's villa[4]. Madame Vandystadt, the housekeeper, let us lie and sunbathe by the pool and showed us over the house. The weather and the Americans have done it grievous harm. I felt the ghosts moving all around me.

1 Marguerite Scialtiel, Noël's French theatrical agent, christened by Joyce Carey 'Grey Daisy' on account of 'a nebulous grey aura which seemed to surround her'; at this time she was in search of a translator for *Blithe Spirit*, among the candidates for which were the French writer Yves Miraude, the celebrated novelist Colette, and playwright and film director Jean Cocteau.
2 By Jean Cocteau.
3 Edith Piaf (1912–63), the celebrated French cabaret singer.
4 Having hired a car and driven to the South of France, Noël and Graham went first to the Château de l'Horizon, pre-war home of Maxine Elliott (1871–1940), the actress whom Noël had first met early in the 1920s and with whom all his memories of the Riviera in the 1930s were inextricably linked. In saying goodbye to her just before the outbreak of war, he had, he once wrote, said goodbye to the world of his youth. The villa had recently been occupied by the American Army.

Maxine, I think, would have liked to know that I was there again. It was not exactly sad. It was more and less than sad, a strange, detached sensation.

We drove to the Château de la Croe[1] and wrote our names in the book as a gesture of politeness, as we are dining there tomorrow night.

Wednesday 3 April

A lovely day spent sunbathing. In the evening we drove to the Windsors. They couldn't have been more charming and are coming over to Monte Carlo on Saturday to dine with me.

Saturday 6 April

In the evening the Windsors arrived. The hotel got itself into a fine frizz and old General Politigor was round my neck like a laurel wreath. I gave them a delicious dinner: consommé, marrow on toast, grilled langouste, tournedos with sauce béarnaise, and chocolate soufflé. Poor starving France. After that we went to the Casino and Wallis and I gambled until 5 a.m. She was very gay and it was most enjoyable. The Duke sat rather dolefully at one of the smaller tables. At the end of the evening I was financially more or less where I started.

Sunday 7 April

Woke with slight hangover. The Duke telephoned me, full of charm, and asked us to drinks and to lunch, both of which I refused.

In the afternoon we joined the Windsors at the ballet, then we had some supper and more gambling. I lost.

Wednesday 17 April   Paris

Marguerite [Scialtiel] came to lunch and we made arrangements about *Blithe Spirit*, etc. Went to Schiaparelli's[2] for cocktails. A gay mix-up, including Mary Pickford[3]. Dined with Edward [Molyneux] and promised to come over on 17 May to do a gala for the RAF.

Tuesday 30 April

Came up to London on the 10.30 and lunched at the Ivy. In the afternoon drove down to Windsor with Neysa[4]. A peerlessly beautiful evening with the castle looking peach-coloured in the late sunlight.

1 Where the Windsors were staying.
2 Elsa Schiaparelli, the Italian fashion designer whose Parisian home had become a centre for American military and ambulance personnel.
3 Mary Pickford (1893-1980), the Canadian film actress who had become the world's sweetheart; Noël had got to know her and her equally famous film actor husband, Douglas Fairbanks, on a transatlantic crossing in 1924.
4 Neysa McMein (d. 1949), American artist much admired by the Algonquin Round Table and a friend of Noël's since he first visited New York in the early 1920s.

Visited Jeff[1] for a drink and a sandwich and then went to the theatre to see *This Happy Breed*[2] and to receive the King and Queen. They arrived in due course. There was a hitch over the lights, which went out just as we were escorting them to their seats, so the whole operation had to be performed in the pitch dark, in the course of which I trod lingeringly on the Queen's train and hacked Princess Margaret Rose on the shin. In the interval we took them to an ante-room and gave them drinks. The Queen was very gay and most charming and the King fairly genial. At the end of the performance I presented Neysa and then, after a little conversation, John Counsell[3] and I saw them off. The Queen thanked me for the play and very charmingly said how sweet it was to see me again. The play was very well played by Mary Kerridge and John Slater and not badly by the rest of the cast. It was excellently put on and lit. Primary fault, inaudibility; primary virtue, reality.

Thursday 9 May

Mr Attlee has announced that perhaps he went too far in stating that the Dominions had been consulted and had agreed to the withdrawal of our troops from Egypt. Faced with such palpable incompetence and dishonesty, I should have thought that the great majority of the people would realize that the present Government, for which they voted with such enthusiasm, was not very good; but I am afraid that the people of this country are too stupid and complacent to grasp what is happening; they will realize later and then, in the face of dire disaster, they will behave with stolid, indestructible courage, by which time it will probably be too late.

Thursday 16 May   Paris

Nobody seems to know about the Gala. It has obviously been mismanaged. Edward is away and will not even be back for the show.

Friday 17 May

A beastly morning spent in that nightmare hell with everything in chaos, Grace Moore[4] being rather tiresome and saying she would not appear because

---

1 Jeffery Holmesdale, Lord Amherst (b. 1896), a friend of Noël's since the early 1920s and the first of his many travelling companions; they were together travelling from Hanoi to Saigon in 1930s when Noël wrote 'Mad Dogs and Englishmen', and it was while waiting for Jeffery to arrive in Tokyo at the start of another voyage that Noël first conceived *Private Lives*.
2 A revival at the Theatre Royal, Windsor, which was the local theatre for the Royal Family when they were staying at Windsor Castle.
3 John Counsell (b. 1905), director and joint manager of the Windsor Repertory Company.
4 Grace Moore (1901–74), American opera singer and film actress, who was also appearing in the concert.

really she was an important singer, etc. She left and came back again, and finally sang 'Rose Marie' too slowly and 'The Merry Widow' much too slowly and the Lord's Prayer a great deal too loudly. After that I rehearsed and so did Graham.

In the evening had a quick meal in the suite, dressed and went to the show. Chaos, with no organization. Finally Diana and Duff [Cooper] appeared, 'The King' was played off key by our RAF band, after which the 'Marseillaise' rang out even more off key. Then I went on and introduced a tough little music-hall girl who, though professional and quite good, went flat; then Graham, who was nervous; he did his numbers well but was not relaxed enough; he went reasonably well, but they were a stinking audience. Then came Marlene [Dietrich], who went marvellously and was very good. Then I did my act and got them completely with 'Marvellous Party', after which all went terrifically; they kept quiet as mice through the French poem and roared and screamed at the end. Then I announced Grace; she came on, apologized for having a bad throat, sang one refrain of 'Rose Marie' and, without warning anybody, walked off. I flew up from my dressing-room, rushed on to the stage and sang 'Mad Dogs' and 'Germans'[1], neither of which I had rehearsed. This really tore the place up, which was jolly gratifying and I felt was deserved, as I had behaved well all day and not lost my temper. Grace again walked off while we were all being thanked and given flowers and magnums of champagne.

Tuesday 21 May   London

Took Neysa to lunch at the Apéritif. She was much occupied with getting some firm of press agents she knows in New York to start a campaign in my favour[2].

Drove Neysa home and said goodbye, as she leaves tomorrow morning. She is a dear darling and I really love her very deeply.

Horrible news that Prim Niven has died suddenly after an accident at a party in Hollywood. It really is tragic and I am dreadfully sorry for David.

Thursday 23 May

Went to dine at Greenwich with Admiral Dickson. Dinner in the painted hall. I suppose it is the most beautiful room in the world. The whole evening was stinking with naval glamour and exquisite naval manners. Even the noisy gun room, where I obliged with a few songs, was beautifully behaved.

---

1 'Don't Let's Be Beastly to the Germans'.
2 Noël's press standing in America was still at a low ebb, following a reference to 'snivelling Brooklyn boys' in his *Middle East Diary*.

Tuesday 28 May

In the morning Lorn had the excellent idea of putting Patience[1] in charge of Goldenhurst, (a) to make the garden profitable, (b) to prevent the house falling down from neglect, and (c) to give her a home and a job in the country which she badly needs. I dealt with letters, cables to Mary Martin, telephone calls to Paris re *Blithe Spirit*, etc.

Long talk with Binkie about the operette. Had some good, reconstructive ideas. Have thought of a title, *Scarlet Lady*. Feel it may be the right one.

Monday 3 June

Lunched at Gerald Road with Gladys and had long discussion about the operette. Went with her to *The Winslow Boy*[2], an excellent play beautifully directed and acted. Drink with Grace Moore at the Savoy. Found Ivor and Bobby in the Grill. They took me back to the flat and Ivor made us an omelette. He was at his most beguiling.

Tuesday 4 June

Satisfactory conference at Drury Lane[3]. The production was finally budgeted at £40,000, but I think we can do it for less. Prince Littler[4] was sensible and calm.

Wednesday 5 June

Went shopping with Lorn and bought an MG eighteen-horse-power drop-head coupé for £1,350.

Thursday 27 June

Drove down to White Cliffs with Gladys. Before leaving discussed Mary Martin's proposed contract with Lorn. It really is a rather arbitrary little document, and I don't think we can let her get away with all that.

A profoundly moving letter from David Niven. He is homesick for England and heart-broken over Prim, but is obviously behaving beautifully.

In the evening I listened to half an hour of my music played rather well on the radio, then to the news which announced that the Government had decided to ration bread. The announced complications of the coupon business sound so idiotic that I imagine housewives and tradesmen will go mad.

Walter Winchell[5] stated the other day apropos of Bevin that he did not approve of a second-rate country having a third-rate Foreign Minister. It is

1 Patience Erskine, a friend of Gladys Calthrop's.
2 By Terence Rattigan.
3 About the production of the operetta.
4 Then managing director of the Theatre Royal, Drury Lane.
5 Walter Winchell, American newspaper columnist and radio pundit.

incredible that this vulgar little man should describe this country as second-rate in 1946, exactly six years after Dunkirk and the Battle of Britain.

Monday 1 July

Well, the atom bomb experiment was made last night[1], with apparently disappointing results. I would like it put on record that I think now, and always have thought, that far too much cock has been talked about atomic energy. I have no more faith in men of science being infallible than I have in men of God being infallible, principally on account of them being men. I have heard it stated that atomic energy might disturb the course of the earth through the universe; that it might cause devastating tidal waves; that it might transform climates from hot to cold or vice versa; make a hole in the bed of the ocean so that the seas would drain away and extinguish the fires of the earth; suddenly deflect our planet into the orbit of the sun, in which case we should all shrivel up, etc., etc., etc. I am convinced that all it will really do is destroy human beings in large numbers. I have a feeling that the universe and the laws of nature are beyond its scope.

I woke early and wrote the first scene of the last act because, atom bomb or no atom bomb, I intend to get the operette finished. In the evening Cole, Joyce, Graham and I went to Deal and saw the film of *Bitter Sweet*[2]. Having only seen it once we had forgotten the full horror of it. It really is frightening that the minds of Hollywood could cheerfully perpetrate such a nauseating hotchpotch of vulgarity, false values, seedy dialogue, stale sentiment, vile performance and abominable direction. I had forgotten the insane coquetting of Miss Jeanette MacDonald allied to a triumphant lack of acting ability. I had forgotten the resolute, stocky, flabby heaviness of Mr Nelson Eddy. I had forgotten the sterling work of the gentleman who saw fit to rewrite my dialogue and lyrics, whose name is Samuels. After this vulgar orgy of tenth-rate endeavour, we sat on the front and watched the hardy English children and a few adults advancing, mauve with cold, into the cheerless waves. The children were touching and sweet. We watched little boys of nine and ten undressing and dressing with such excessive modesty that it took them ages to get their little wet bathing trunks off under their towels. They squirmed and wriggled, contorting themselves into most uncomfortable attitudes for fear that some roving eye might chance momentarily on their poor little privates. What a dreadful and foolish mistake to inculcate that self-consciousness into small children. Oh dear. We really are a most peculiar race.

1 The Americans were carrying out a series of atom bomb tests at Bikini atoll in the Pacific.
2 Not the Anna Neagle-Herbert Wilcox 1933 British film version of Noël's play, but the second one made in lurid Technicolor by MGM in 1940. Noël said that it was 'like watching an affair between a mad rocking-horse and a rawhide suitcase'.

Sunday 7 July

Lovely sunshine again. Worked all morning on Samolan lyrics. Finished the trio and did an extra refrain for 'I Never Knew'. In the afternoon Graham and I decided to change a wheel on the car, just for the practice. We didn't do badly. Fortunately, later on when we were checking up at the garage, I thought to have a look at the wheel we put on; the hub twirled round in my hand like a teetotum. Dicing with death!

Tuesday 9 July   London

Auditions all the morning at the Coliseum. Found three possibles and two less possible.

Came back to change for the Royal Garden Party. Gladys and I went with Sybil Cholmondeley, who was just a tiny bit tiresome. Came home. Tea with Lorn. Thought of the title *Pacific 1860* for the operette. Think this is right.

Wednesday 10 July

Went to the Guildhall to see Dickie [Mountbatten] receive the Freedom of the City of London. A moving occasion, very well done. Dickie was quite magnificent.

Sunday 14 July   White Cliffs

Woke after a fairly sleepless night worrying about Gladys[1]. Went up there at twelve o'clock and, after discussing the show for a bit, went off into a heart-to-heart which was really all right. She was sensible and sweet and at her top best. My heart does ache for her because she is lonely. Nothing can ever change what I really and deeply feel for her.

Am reading more of Oscar Wilde. What a tiresome, affected sod.

Tuesday 16 July   Paris

Went to the Embassy and found nobody about but Winston Churchill. He was very amiable and we talked for about forty minutes and I played him some of the operette tunes. Juliet [Duff] came in later in a frenzy at having missed something. Diana [Cooper] never appeared at all. They urged me to go to the reception tonight for Winston, but I refused.

Delicious dinner with Graham at the Metropole and then went to Edward's. Very enjoyable. Got fried.

Monday 22 July   Biarritz

A truly lovely day. We took the car and a picnic lunch to a remote beach where we lay and sunbathed until five o'clock. The water was velvet and the sun

---

1 Who had been showing signs of nervous strain.

scorching hot. We dined quietly and deliciously at the Café de Paris and gambled unsuccessfully for an hour at the casino. I am glad I am not a real gambler. I can't bear losing more than I set out to lose and, although it seems foolish to lose £20 one night and £10 the next, it is not nearly so foolish as to lose all I've got and have to go borrowing from everyone.

This is being a lovely holiday. There is nothing to do but relax.

Monday 29 July

At last a sunny day. Spent the morning on the beach. Light lunch and then more beach but less tranquil owing to crowds. Came back and wrote letters. Dinner very chic. Felix Youssoupoff[1] sang really quite sweetly with a guitar. He is made-up to the teeth. I looked at him: a face that must, when young, have been very beautiful but now it is cracking with effort and age. I imagined him luring Rasputin to his doom with that guitar and 'dem rollin' eyes'. It was all a little macabre. I sang but not very well. Graham was really wonderful. He was not only socially vital and attractive, but he suddenly proceeded to sing in Russian so much better than Youssoupoff and his friend that the whole party was astonished. It all went on far too long. Home about three o'clock.

Friday 2 August

An agitating but on the whole successful morning procuring *bons d'essence* and extra *bons de l'huile*[2] from various hives of French bureaucracy. From room to room and street to street I went, emerging finally triumphant. It is wonderful what a little determined charm will do, plus American cigarettes.

Friday 9 August   Cannes

A wonderful morning bathing at Eden Roc. The English people are beyond belief; they must all be black-market profiteers. Most of them are Cockney Jews. In the evening we had a drink at the Carlton then went to the Zanzi Bar and had some Pernod. Then to the casino where we saw the Windsors, the Dudleys[3], etc. I gambled, but with some misgiving as money is getting low; I made £80 and, wisely, left the building.

Monday 12 August

Drove over to St Tropez to lunch with Princess George of Greece, Princess Eugenie and a parrot, some children, and old Prince George with a long Blimp moustache and no voice on account of a throat operation.

1 Felix Youssoupoff, Russian prince widely believed to have been responsible for the planning of the murder of Rasputin, though when an MGM-Barrymore film biography of the 1930s suggested this, he was able to sue for several million dollars.
2 Petrol coupons and oil coupons; both were then rationed.
3 Lord and Lady Dudley, friends of the Windsors.

Thursday 15 August

Drove over to Cap Ferrat and lunched with Willie Maugham[1], who is in fine form. We drove over to Monte Carlo in the evening with Robin Maugham[2]. Dined and gambled fairly successfully.

Saturday 17 August

Lunch with Graham and Joyce at the Drap d'Or. Peaceful afternoon resting and bathing. Joyce and Graham went off to dine together and I went to the Windsors. A large party: Loelia Westminster, Odette Massigli[3], etc. I sang and played. The Windsors were charming. I like her and I think that, now, she is genuinely fond of him. They are lovers, so perhaps there is something to be said for the whole set-up. I wonder how their story will end.

Drove back and had a late drink with Joyce in Cannes. Came back to the villa and bathed in the moonlight; beautiful beyond words.

Friday 23 August

Irritating cable from Mary Martin transmitted from Lorn; she wants far too many options and rights and is not going to get them.

Said farewell to Cannes, Jules at the bar, Joyce, etc., with rather heavy hearts and definitely empty pockets. Drove to Hyères and lunched with Simone and Joe Brandel[4]. All very high-spirited. They have offered me the Théâtre Antoine to do a month's season in English next spring which would be enjoyable.

Drove on, loaded with fruit and wine, having evaded all persuasions to stay. A lovely drive to Aix-en-Provence, a good dinner and bed at nine o'clock.

Looking back on the holiday, it is quite one of the happiest, if not the happiest, of my life.

Thursday 29 August   Paris

A dreariness in the air because it is so inescapably the end of the holiday. Went to the Embassy for a drink before lunch: Diana, Duff, John Julius[5]. Lucien Brule came with the design for the *Blithe Spirit* set; very good. Dined with

---

1 William Somerset Maugham (1874-1965), the only playwright apart from Noël to have had four plays running simultaneously in London during the first half of the century; when he turned exclusively to novel-writing it was, he said, because he had been 'placed firmly on the shelf' by the sprightliness of Noël's comedies.

2 Robin Maugham (1916-81), Somerset Maugham's nephew, later his biographer and himself the author of several novels including *The Servant*; his title *Somerset and all the Maughams* was derived from Noël's version of the song 'Let's Do It'.

3 Odette Massigli, wife of the French Ambassador to London 1944-55.

4 Simone and Joe Brandel, French theatre owners.

5 John Julius Norwich (b. 1929), son of Duff and Diana Cooper; succeeded as 2nd Viscount Norwich 1954.

Edward. Valentina[1] arrived with a tin of caviare. Delicious. I am grateful for every minute of this lovely holiday. I hate leaving Paris, but I know that once I am home and the battle is joined I shall enjoy all that in a different way.

Tuesday 3 September   London

An interesting interview with Prince [Littler], in course of which it was decided to get ahead with a lot of the reconstruction work at Drury Lane pending the granting of the licence.

After the interview Lorn, Gladys, Bert and I indulged in an entertainment orgy. We went first to the 12.40 showing of *London Town*, a British attempt at a Hollywood musical. It was dull, common, lacking in tempo and without grace except for the comic genius of Sid Field. A snack lunch and the matinée of *Big Ben*, an operette of such paralysing boredom that we were battered down by it; a series of roguish, pseudo-satirical political meetings very loosely constructed by A. P. Herbert and set to melodic but reminiscent music by Vivian Ellis. In the evening Graham and I went to *No Room at the Inn*[2], a fairly good melodrama so badly acted that we wanted to vomit. Freda Jackson, hailed by everyone for her magnificent performance, overacted throughout and then arrived at her famous drunk scene which she overacted more than ever. I suspect that at the beginning of the run she was much better but now she and the whole cast are a disgrace to the theatre.

Friday 6 September

Orphanage meeting[3]. Caught the 7.15 to White Cliffs. Made particular fuss of Matelot, who has been depressed and sad of late. Poor little dog. Must give him more attention and time.

Saturday 7 September

Worked most of the day on the second act trio. Poor little Veitch fell down this morning. I do hope it isn't serious.

Dined with Gladys, Graham and Peter Stern[4]. Came back and found that Veitch was really pretty bad. The doctor came and thinks she has fractured a bit of her hip. This means that she may never walk again and will have to have day and night nursing. Poor little thing, it really is hard luck. She was so well and bright, but ninety is not a good age to go tumbling about.

1 Valentina, Russian-born fashion designer.
2 By Joan Temple.
3 Noël had succeeded Gerald du Maurier in 1934 as President of the Actors' Orphanage, a charity dedicated to the destitute young of the acting profession. He had declined the offer of a 'figure-head' presidency and had totally reorganized the running of it; during the war he had been instrumental in evacuating many of its children to North America.
4 G.B. Stern, novelist whom Noël had first met in 1918 after writing to her of his admiration for her books.

Friday 13 September

A letter from Admiral Cunningham asking for the first night of the operette for the Royal Naval Benevolent Fund. Of course I agree because (a) it is a wonderful charity and I would like, as always, to do anything for the Navy, and (b) because it will be mighty chic to have a great opening gala shining with naval uniforms and possibly the King and Queen.

Visited poor Sibyl Colefax in hospital. She has broken her hip. Came down to White Cliffs with Gladys, Joyce and Graham. Lovely full moon on the sea.

Saturday 14 September

A restful day. Went to cocktails with Ann Rothermere, Peter Quennell[1], etc. Quiet dinner and played some records.

Friday 20 September

Audition. Out of 115 people selected, only eleven moderates. Later I drove down to White Cliffs through the worst storm I have ever known in England. The gale was infernal and the rain pure Hollywood. Trees were down across the road at several points.

Friday 27 September

Drove down to meet Mary Martin and Dick Halliday at Southampton; drove them to London. They were absolutely sweet and so genuinely thrilled about everything. Dined with Lorn and Graham, then went back to the Savoy to fetch Mary and Dick. We showed them Drury Lane and then played them some of the music. They were madly enthusiastic and we drove them back to the Savoy in a haze of happiness. Personally I think she has authentic magic. She is quite obviously an artist in the true sense. She is easy, generous and humble. Oh dear. In all this excitement there is a dark note. Jack has done everything he knew to dissuade them from coming. They were reluctant to tell me but I made them. He has obviously changed. I don't think he really cares any more for England or for us, which is very sad.

Tuesday 1 October

Prince rang up to say he wanted to see me at five o'clock because he had news. Lunched with Lorn and Graham at the Ivy and went with Graham to *The Big Sleep*[2] (a complicated but fairly enjoyable thriller) with my heart in my boots. Arrived in Prince's office and he told me the application for the Drury Lane licence had been turned down flat. This horrible crisis could have been avoided months ago if I had been allowed to handle it. Came home, telephoned the Prime Minister's secretary and asked if the PM would see me. This was

1 Peter Quennell (b. 1905), poet and biographer.
2 Howard Hawks's film based on Raymond Chandler's novel.

refused, but I was told a letter stating the case would receive urgent attention. I then rang up Bevan[1], who was charming. Went straight round to see him. He was very nice and virtually promised that all would be well; but I won't believe that permit until I see it.

Later, we had our glamorous theatrical party for Mary. All the London Theatre came, dressed to the nines. It was an enormous success, slightly marred by my inner thoughts and by Mike [Redgrave] having had a few too many.

Thursday 3 October

Telephoned Bevan who said it was OK about the licence and that we could go ahead. There is a man whom I have despised and who has behaved to me with the utmost courtesy and kindness. In future I will be more careful in my judgements.

Thursday 10 October

Well, we are off. Opening date set for 19 December. Rehearsals begin 4 November. Scenic conference. Lunch with Gladys. Worked with Robb. Mary, Dick, Joyce, Graham and I dined with Ann and Esmond Rothermere. Others present included Peter Quennell, Ian Fleming[2], etc.

Friday 11 October

Took Mary, Dick and Graham to see *King Lear* and afterwards to dinner at the Ivy with Larry and Vivien. Larry's performance as Lear ranks with his Richard III as being unequivocally great. He is a superb actor and I suspect the greatest I shall ever see. The play, of course, is wonderful, although involved here and there. The production was excellent, but the sets were inadequate.

Wednesday 16 October

Quite a good day, taken all round. To begin with I worked from 7.15 a.m. till 7.15 p.m. and managed to finish everything, even the incidental music cues with Robb, after which I drove up to London, exhausted but triumphant. Spent an hour with Mary at the Savoy. She is in bed with a sore throat.

In addition to the foregoing, Heath[3] is to be executed in London and Ribbentrop, Streicher[4], etc., were executed in Nuremberg. Goering cheated

1 Aneurin Bevan (1897–1960), Minister of Health in Attlee's government.
2 Ian Fleming (1908–64), novelist, at this time a journalist on the *Sunday Times*; he and Noël had instantly struck up a leg-pulling friendship when they had met during the war and in the 1950s they became neighbours in Jamaica when Ian Fleming, much encouraged by Noël, began writing the James Bond novels that made him famous.
3 Neville Heath, English murderer, notorious for his brutal sexual killings.
4 They, with Goering and other Nazi leaders, had been condemned at the Nuremberg War Crimes Trial.

at the last minute and managed to munch up a phial of cyanide of potassium in his cell. The whole business seemed somehow remote and unimportant. If only we could have read about it in 1940, 1941 and 1942. Now, their cruelty and villainy is somehow stale.

Thursday 24 October

Travelled to Paris *en masse*, Cole, Graham, Gladys, Mary, Richard and me. Everything well organized, cabins, coupés, etc. All officials charming and, above all, a sunny day. The flat looked lovely and felt warm and welcoming.

Friday 25 October

Went to a rehearsal of *Blithe Spirit* (*Jeux d'Esprit*) in the afternoon. Thought it flat-footed, obvious and badly directed and the company did not know their words. Finally made a scene and spoke my mind. Pierre Dux, the director, is amiable but lacking in authority. Rested, not feeling too well with a stomach upset.

In the evening, Edward's party. Very spectacular. Everyone in Paris was there.

Wednesday 30 October

Graham and I collected Cole and we went to *La Belle et la Bête*[1], which I rechristened *La Belle et la Bêtise* on account of it being long, dull and badly constructed, but *d'un beauté formidable* every now and then. I wish creative artists like Jean did not consider it necessary to be 'precious', 'amusing' and 'different'.

Sunday 3 November

Drove up to London. Began thinking on the way up about a play on the theme that England was invaded and conquered in 1940, *Might Have Been*, scene a public house somewhere between Knightsbridge and Sloane Square. The whole horrible anticlimax of occupation and demoralization for five years culminating in the invasion of England from France by free English, Americans and French. The family tragedy is conflict arising from Resistance movements, etc. Lovely last scene as the publican, with his wife, daughter and son killed, listens to the secret radio turned on full, announcing the successful invasion from Dover Castle and finishing with 'God Save the King', while the Germans are battering the door down. Think this is really a honey of an idea and it has fallen into place with such remarkable speed that I feel I must do it almost immediately. Oh dear. I do hope it stays as good to me as it seems now.

1 Jean Cocteau film starring Jean Marais.

Monday 4 November

Very good first rehearsal. Went through the whole score with the principals. Voices sounded quite lovely. Sylvia Cecil[1] wonderful. Noticed a few spots which will have to be reconstructed.

Party at the Oliviers which was enjoyable, with Larry beguiling as usual. Maria Montez[2] show-off; Jean-Pierre Aumont sweet.

Tuesday 5 November

Present Laughter New York notices very bad. Obviously a bad performance badly directed. I see clearly that I shall have to have a showdown with Jack. I cannot afford to have my valuable properties bitched up.

Wednesday 6 November

Long letter from Jack explaining the horror of the *Present Laughter* first night in New York. Apparently the audience was social steel and arrived late and put the actors off. I still don't think that they should have been put off, and the whole thing must have been badly directed. However, the business is apparently good.

First reading of *Pacific 1860*. Really very good. Mary very nervous and read mournfully, none of which matters as she is very quick and full of talent. The company is excellent. All the old-timers, Moya, Betty, Maidie[3], etc., were fine. So were some of the newcomers. Took Mary, Dick and Graham to the Ivy. Rehearsed dialogue all the afternoon. Had an egg, and then drove down to White Cliffs. The house welcomed us and wrapped itself round us.

Friday 8 November   White Cliffs

Worked all the morning inventing Samolan words for the chorus of 'Fumfumbolo'. Painted a bit in the afternoon. Did the programme note. Bathed and changed. The Amblers[4] arrived with Joyce and Graham.

At the end of dinner Cole came in and said he wanted to speak to me and explained gently that Auntie Vida had just died peacefully in her sleep. I went over and said goodbye to her. She looked very pathetic and little. Mother was, of course, dreadfully upset but behaved beautifully. The district nurse came and did the laying out and the doctor came, and Mother went upstairs and played patience and recovered herself. I must say poor little Veitch chose the perfect way to die. Just sleep, and the light flicking out.

1 Playing Rosa Cariatanzo in *Pacific 1860*.
2 Maria Montez (1918–51), exotic Hollywood actress, married to the French film star Jean-Pierre Aumont (b. 1909).
3 Moya Nugent, Betty Hare and Maidie Andrews (sister of Bobby) were all actresses who had frequently worked with Noël in the pre-war years.
4 Eric Ambler (b. 1909), novelist, and his wife Louise; they were neighbours at White Cliffs.

Sunday 10 November

Boiler burst so no hot water. Telephone refused to function. Mother upset on account of the coffin arriving and Veitch being put into it.

Drove up to London. Urgent message for Graham that Sybil[1] has had a bad heart attack, so he had to go straight off and be with her and not come to Del[Giudice]'s party. Joyce and I set off in a car sent by Del which we presumed, wrongly, knew the way. We got hopelessly lost and drove for miles and miles about the Thames Valley, so that instead of taking three-quarters of an hour to get there we took two hours and twenty minutes. It was an immense, noisy party with every film star and director in Christendom and Jewry. After dinner, during which we were photographed incessantly, we saw *Hungry Hill*, a dreary, long film with Margaret Lockwood as a suburban-Irish madcap who became a very old and very suburban lady. Oh dear. A new young man called Dermot Walsh was rather good. Cecil Parker and Arthur Sinclair were excellent, Dennis Price not bad, but Eileen Herlie awful. After this, Joyce, Mary, Richard, Winifred and I drove back. Mary and Richard shrieked at the top of their lungs all the way. They are very sweet and I am devoted to them.

Tuesday 12 November   London

Went with Lorn to bury poor little Veitch. Mother was so pleased to see me that I was glad I went. Veitch left a note in her will, after all her little bequests, which said, 'I have nothing good enough to leave my nephew Noël Coward except my love and thanks for all he has done for me and my blessing.' This touched me profoundly. She loved me all my life. Poor little old lady, I am glad she is at rest. I feel awful leaving her in that cold, dark grave. Mother was very upset but recovered wonderfully and came back to the studio for tea and was quite cheerful.

Went to a cocktail party given by Alan Campbell[2], who is leaving for America tomorrow. Then Graham and I went to *Piccadilly Hayride*[3]. Sid Field is a great comedian. I love him. He has the pathos of all great comics and his grandeur is inspired. Talked to him in his dressing-room and then came home.

Thursday 14 November

Rehearsed a little in the morning on 'Fumfumbolo'. Took Beatrice [Eden] to lunch at the Basque. I think she has definitely decided to leave Anthony. She is obviously bored with him.

Rehearsed Mary and Graham in 'Horse Has Cast a Shoe' and 'Bright Was the Day'. Graham is really charming: easy and graceful and unself-conscious.

1 His mother.
2 Alan Campbell (d. 1967), American actor-writer.
3 At the Prince of Wales Theatre.

She is a dream girl, quick and knowledgeable; she has all the mercurial charm of Gertie at her best with a sweet voice and with more taste. Joyce came for a drink and we discussed the Paris theatre and the fairly lamentable performance of *Blithe Spirit*, which is obviously not a great success.

Saturday 23 November

Mary really is remarkable. She suggested, very sweetly, that she wasn't happy with 'Alice' and wouldn't mind if it were taken out. As I have never felt really right about it, we tried it a couple of times and then cut it from the show. I am relieved. She is the only star I have ever worked with who has a real sense of the balance of the show. She is generous about everyone else in the company and never tries to snatch.

Monday 2 December

First rehearsal in the Lane. Set of first act up. Theatre like an icebox and full of hammering workmen and electricians. Perfect hell, but rather exciting. Mary improved since last rehearsal, but I am a bit worried about her diction and general lack of understanding of Elena. However, I think she will get it.

Wednesday 4 December

Did ballroom scene. Mary not really right yet. Polka not good. Graham and I went to dinner with Winifred, also Kit and Guthrie[1]. Darling Kit, it was so lovely to see her. We stayed after they left. I found myself paying Winnie compliments I did not mean. Insincerity quivered in the air. The warm magic that we knew in the war has gone. It is her fault. She has made a change, without reason but with female prejudice. It is a pity.

As I arrived at Gerald Road a girl rang the bell and threatened suicide if I did not talk to her. I did talk to her sharply and firmly and shut the door in her face. Oh dear, how tricky it is to be celebrated.

Thursday 5 December

At 10.30 went to the Stage Door Canteen to help Dotty[2] with the Queen. The Queen, as usual, was enchanting.

Wednesday 11 December

A long and tiring day, Mary with a headache. She is *at last* showing signs of being tiresome, but she has been so good up to now that I suppose she must

1 Katharine Cornell (1898–1974), glamorous American stage star, and her husband, director Guthrie McClintic (1893–1961), who had been friends of Noël since the early 1920s.
2 Dorothy Dickson (b. 1898), American actress long resident in London and now running this servicemen's entertainment centre, which was enjoying a royal visit.

be allowed a little latitude. Even Gladys, her most ardent champion, is beginning to crack a bit. Orchestra rehearsal in evening.

Saturday 14 December

A day of triumph for Gladys. The dresses are the loveliest I have ever seen in any production. The dress rehearsal went all right: flat, of course, and Pat McGrath playing for Graham, who is in bed with his cold. Guthrie fortunately reappeared, his boat having been delayed. He gave one look at Mary's hair (she had stubbornly refused to wear either a hat or a wig) and then he rushed round and ticked her off. At the end of the rehearsal Gladys and I went into the dressing-room to try and persuade her to alter her hair, which is really hideous and completely out of period. Richard, who must have been drinking, suddenly started shrieking abuse at Gladys and calling her a bitch and both of us double-dyed fiends because we wanted Mary to be unhappy in a hat, etc. It was one of the most hideous, hysterical and vulgar exhibitions I have ever known in the theatre. Mary remained quiet but, with one spurt of temper, declared that she would never wear a hat, never, never, never. I have seldom been more angry inside, but I kept my head and told them articulately exactly what I thought. We then left, with Gladys overtired and upset. What a sad pity, just as I was beginning to like Richard in spite of his noise and vulgarity. He has now broken the flimsy edifice into a million pieces.

Sunday 15 December

Went off to a lighting rehearsal at one o'clock. At about five Guthrie appeared, jubilant, having spent two hours with the Hallidays. Mary walked on to the stage with her hair parted in the middle and a lovely bun on the nape of her neck and of course looked ravishing. A few minutes later, after Guthrie had gone, he came flying back even more jubilantly and hissed 'Hat!', whereupon Miss Martin came on in the very hat that all the idiotic fuss had been about. She had told Guthrie that it was for *him* she was doing it and not for Gladys and me. Has there ever been anything more asinine? What has happened is that she will come on looking lovely and correct as I always intended she should. Acids have been upset, rages and violence unleashed by her and Richard, and it has all been a waste of time and energy. I am bitterly disappointed. I had hoped to get through this without rows. Now, although I am still fond of Mary, she is an artist and has charm, I really do not like Richard at all. It is dreadfully awkward and all over nothing. He is a pathological case and is twisted with strange jealousies. I wish the silly ass were at the bottom of the sea.

Went on lighting until 1 a.m.

Thursday 19 December

A hectic, strained day. Worked on lighting until 4.30. Came home, had a bath and changed into tails and went to the theatre. A really triumphant first night. Mary wonderful; Sylvia Cecil stopped the show; Graham magnificent. There was a party afterwards beautifully done by Prince with speeches, etc. Mary's behaviour throughout absolutely impeccable. We all went on to Winnie's. I should have thought this was the natural place to go, but I have been wrong all these years. Winnie never said one word of praise to me and there was in her attitude a deep and genuine hostility. Dick Addinsell never said one word about the music. They were both vile. Everyone else was charming. Winnie has changed so much. She is no longer warm. It is very sad.

Friday 20 December

The blackest and beastliest day of the year. To begin with, a blast of abuse in the Press. Not one good notice, the majority being frankly vile. I don't usually mind but I am overtired.

A gay 'chins up' lunch at the Ivy with Lorn, Gladys and Graham, then a rehearsal for a few cuts. Then I came home to receive the worst blow. Matelot, my little dog, died on Wednesday. Cole is heart-broken and so am I. Coming on top of all the other dreariness, it really knocked me. I loved him so much and now I shall never see him again.

Went to the theatre. A bad audience and the show was flat and went badly. Everyone including the audience was got down by the notices. If only I had had more time for dress rehearsals with audiences I should have got things adjusted before the opening. Elsa Maxwell came and raved with enthusiasm, but I think it may very likely be a flop. The Press was almost too unanimous. It is all very depressing but I shall rise above it whatever happens. Mary behaved superbly. She is a real trouper.

Took Graham home to supper and broke the miserable news about Matelot. He too was horribly upset. Personally I feel sick and drained of all vitality.

Saturday 21 December

Went down after the matinée and pepped up the orchestra a bit. Watched the evening performance. It couldn't have gone worse. Nothing got any applause and the theatre was icy. Oh dear, I do so wonder if it is going to be a rousing flop.

Gladys had a long heart-to-heart with Winnie last night, with Winnie in floods, so tonight I rang her up because I have been fond of her for a long time and hate feuds. She was very touched, and then proceeded to spew, lovingly, all her grievances against me. She told me that for the last three years I had been becoming so unbearably arrogant that it's grotesque; that everyone is laughing at me; that I am surrounded by yes-men; that the reason *Pacific 1860* is so bad is that I have no longer any touch or contact with people and events on account of my overweening conceit; that I have ruined Graham and made him give a preposterous performance; that I have encased Mary Martin in a straitjacket of my own dictatorialness, thereby crushing her personality; that I am disloyal and behaved badly over *Sigh No More* (cutting Dick's music). All this and a great deal more said tearfully, vehemently and from the heart. I said genuinely enough that I would try in future not to be so arrogant, and the conversation ended lovingly.

Now, what is curious is that I am not cross or upset and I really should be one or the other. Perhaps I am too tired. I believe she truly meant what she said and that it has been boiling up in her for ages. I also believe that most of what she said was balls. Her knowledge of my character and Lorn's and Gladys's has never been accurate. As far as her theatrical judgement goes, she loathed Larry as Richard III, loathed *Bitter Sweet*, and loves so many things that are terrible in my sight that I cannot mind her criticism, particularly of anything musical. Anything not composed by Dick or a classical composer is, to her, unethical and lousy. I know they will never forgive me for *Sigh No More*; I know that her mind and emotions are all confused; I also know that she is fond of me and believed all she was saying was true and for my good. I must say I am having a jolly week. I am very tired, but my head is unbowed.

Perhaps I really am arrogant, but I do feel that Dick as a musician is a pleasant amateur and that Winifred as a writer is deteriorating. I also think she is stubborn and conceited to a degree approaching mania. I also think that she is large and warm and generous and somehow dreadfully touching. I think my Christ-like reception of her tirade made her feel happier, but I don't know where we go from here.

Sunday 22 December

Woke early in a royal rage (delayed action) about all the odious things Winnie had said. Had a deep personal look-see and discovered that I was not arrogant or grotesque and surrounded by yes-men, and that the whole thing was a subconscious urge on her part to kick me good and proud when I was down. But I am not down enough for that. Long telephone talk with Gladys, then talked to Nora and Prince, who said that whatever happened to the show they were proud to be associated with it. Prince cheerful and convinced of success. Sunday notices appalling.

Lunched with Graham and Sybil. Went to the theatre and rehearsed 'Uncle Harry'. Later, went to *Lady in the Lake*[1] with Graham; an intelligent thriller. Drinks with Mary and Richard, who were very sweet.

1 Film of the Raymond Chandler story, starring and directed by Robert Montgomery.

Monday 23 December

Spent three hours with Winnie and, after much trial and error, got back to the relationship we used to know. It was a strange and revealing conversation, in which everything, or practically everything, was said. She suddenly, under stress of emotion, became warm again and now all is well. I am glad. I would have hated to lose a friend I valued.

Went back to the theatre. Ivor and party came round and obviously hadn't liked the show but adored Mary. Even Zena[1] was tongue-tied. My deep conviction is that it is a flop, but the big public may like it.

Wednesday 25 December

A peaceful Christmas Day spent in bed talking to people on the telephone. Sybil, Graham, Gladys and I had dinner. Delicious food, including caviare. Later, a party at Binkie's. Very enjoyable.

Friday 27 December

A horrid day. Went to the matinée, which was half-full and dreary. Came back home and discussed reconstructing the first act, then suddenly rebelled and decided that if the critics and the public don't like the show, that's their affair but I won't muck about with it and alter something that I consider charming and accurate and risk pleasing nobody, even myself.

Drove to White Cliffs with Cole. Both of us dreading the arrival on account of Matelot being dead. We were right. We arrived, Joe barked and was quite sweet, but there was no little grey toy to welcome us and I felt unbearably desolate. These are unhappy days. I know they will pass but they haven't passed yet and I am tired and overstrung and the world is heavy.

Saturday 28 December

Slept ten hours. Woke refreshed and no longer morose. Painted a bit and talked to Mum. Gladys came for a drink and we came to the sad conclusion that the fundamental trouble with *Pacific* is that Mary, charming and sweet as she is, knows nothing about Elena, never has and never will, and that although she has a delicious personality, she cannot sing. She is crammed with talent but she is still too 'little' to play sophisticated parts.

Monday 30 December   London

Dined with Gladys at the Ivy. Returned to the theatre and watched the last act. The play went well, with cheers in the end. Five hundred and four pounds in the house. Not bad for Monday. Rehearsed Mary for an hour after the

---

1 Zena Dare (1887–1975), actress with whom Noël had starred in *The Second Man* in 1928 and a long-time friend of both Noël and Ivor Novello.

show. Entirely redid her first scene and finally convinced her that she must play it full out for comedy. She began to do so and the difference was amazing. If only she had done it before. However, we shall see. Home very weary and sick to death of *Pacific 1860* and everything to do with it.

Tuesday 31 December

Went to the Savoy and waited for Mary, Richard and Graham. They finally arrived and we gave them supper and drank the New Year in. I think they were touched and pleased.

Thus 1947 begins. I feel nothing much beyond tiredness. Soon I must snap out of it and get some good work done.

1947

With Pacific 1860 *limping into the New Year at Drury Lane, Noël decided to reach back to the comparative safety of a* Present Laughter *revival for the Theatre Royal, Haymarket; but the year would also see a new play from him about an imaginary Nazi occupation of Britain* (Peace in Our Time) *and the first ever London production of his 1934 West Indies drama* Point Valaine.

   Arctic blizzards, power cuts and fuel crises during the early months did not do wonders for the kind of light escapism in which as a dramatist and songwriter he specialized, and his general temper was not much improved when several thousand tons of chalk crumbled away from the cliff top above his weekend home at St Margaret's Bay and landed on the beach within a few hundred yards of the house. His once beloved England no longer seemed intent on making him feel especially welcome, and his thoughts turned (as so often in the 1920s and 1930s) towards America, where at least the sun shone and Gertrude Lawrence was keen to revive Tonight at 8.30.

Friday 3 January   London

Woke at about five in the morning in a still, dark rage. Had a long think and decided that I am sick of being screamed at and abused. I have had to face a possible flop, vile notices and a great deal of weariness and disappointment. On top of all this I have had Winifred accusing me of every known beastliness, Mary roaring and stamping her foot and, last but by no means least, Gladys losing control and squealing about her integrity as an artist. I have been exceedingly forbearing with the lot of them, but now I have decided to be forbearing no more. Anger is a healthier emotion for me than self-pity. Having made a brisk but firm New Year's resolution to stand no more nonsense, I talked to Lorn on the telephone, who as usual was both sensible and funny.

Gladys appeared soon after eleven, tremulous and proud, and I flew at her violently before she could get a word out. I told her that her arrogance with Mary over the dresses was the root of all the subsequent trouble, and that although her artistic integrity was in the balance it would not weigh against the good of the show. I also told her that the sets looked more like Torquay and Draycott Gardens than Samolo and that her egotism was past bearing. All of which I mean. It was unforgivable to fly at me when I am hanging on by my eyelashes. She went out of the house in a gale of her tears and my words. A little later she telephoned in a calm but distant voice to say she had talked to Richard and was going to design another dress for Mary. She is obviously both hurt and angry, and she can bloody well get on with it.

Lunched with Sybil and Graham. Went to *Great Expectations*[1], a really fine film. In the evening took Joyce to Norman Hackforth's revue *Between Ourselves* at the Playhouse. Awful, with a couple of good ideas bungled and a cast of repellent unattractiveness. Repaired to Drury Lane. Supper party where everyone broke down and agreed that Mary was a disappointment. This surprised me but it did show me that that is the trouble with the play. She is not right for it and never will be, whatever she wears. She is a good trouper and works hard but has no conception of Elena's character and no technical experience as an actress. Her charm and personality are not enough to put her over in a big theatre in a period part. She should be crooning through a microphone. I am sorry because I like her, though at the moment she and Richard are not behaving well.

Saturday 4 January

A day in bed. Worked out more characters for *Might Have Been* with Lorn and Joyce. Watched television with Joyce and Cole. What a hideous and horrid invention. Dinner in bed, feeling more rested.

1   1946 film version of Dickens's novel starring John Mills and directed by David Lean.

Sunday 5 January

Did *The Times* crossword puzzle with Cole. Went with Graham to *Les Enfants du Paradis*, a beautiful film beautifully played[1]. Dined with John Gielgud.

Monday 6 January

Dined with David Lean, who told me all about his marital problems, and his professional problems with Ronnie [Neame] and Tony[2]. Went on to Binkie's and arranged to open *Present Laughter* in Edinburgh on 7 April and at the Haymarket on 15 April. If *Might Have Been* is done, I will alternate them; if not, I will put it on at the end of the three months' season.

Thursday 9 January

Made seven records for HMV, fighting gallantly against thick yellow fog on the vocal chords. Went on recording till five o'clock. Discussed *Noël Coward Vocal Gems*[3] till six o'clock. Came home for a drink.

Sunday 12 January   White Cliffs

Slept badly and woke finally at six o'clock. Lay looking at the ceiling full of dreary thoughts. Then, with an effort, I jerked myself out of gloom, smoked a cigarette and started to read Mr Charles Jackson's novel about a respectable married gentleman who fell in love with a marine. The novel is called *The Fall of Valor* and is by the author of *Lost Weekend*. It is what is known as 'outspoken' and is also fairly silly. The Americans really are adolescent in their approach to the less salient facts of life.

Graham telephoned. Had lunch. Tried to paint; couldn't. Tried to compose at the piano; couldn't. Tried to sleep, could, but without pleasure. Dined with Gladys and we talked and talked and felt better. I presume that eventually we shall smash our way out of the miasma the Hallidays have cast up. I do hate them for it. Binkie told me on the telephone that Richard has a poisoned foot and I said some of his motives must have got into his socks. Binkie also told me that Alfred [Lunt] is having an operation today on his one remaining kidney. I do hope he will be all right. Lynn must be frantic.

Tuesday 14 January

Developed an age-old but, for me, a new ailment; agonizing rheumatism in my right leg. I can see myself at Baden-Baden in a wheelchair being pushed by Cole wheezing with asthma. Stayed in bed all day and took some aspirin with my tea, which soothed the pain very kindly.

1 By Jean-Louis Barrault, Arletty and Pierre Brasseur.
2 Anthony Havelock-Allan (b. 1905), producer, and co-founder with David Lean and Ronald Neame of Cineguild, the film unit that had produced all Noël's wartime films.
3 An anthology recording of his songs.

Thursday 23 January   London

A day spent mostly in bed, girding myself for the Royal Performance. In the morning I sent some flowers to Mary with a pleasant note. Before the show Prince, Nora, Gladys and I went into her room to wish her luck. She never mentioned the flowers and was extremely chilly. The show went well but Mary was not good. The King and Queen received me in the second interval. Graham did his speech at the end very charmingly, after which I presented him, Sylvia [Cecil] and Mary. Mary distinguished herself by saying to Princess Margaret Rose (Princess Elizabeth being absent), 'Give my best to your sister. Bye-bye for now.' I drove away to Dickie's and Edwina's house in Chester Street, where the King and Queen were. I sat next to the Queen at supper. It was all very family: only the King and Queen, Princess Margaret, all the Mountbattens and me. We talked about many things, from the Labour Government to E. Nesbit[1]. The King was gay and relaxed. After dinner I sang a few songs. It was all very lovely and I felt most proud to be there.

Friday 24 January

Morning at the Criterion with Binkie listening to people read for *Present Laughter*. Very interested in a girl called Moira Lister[2] who read Joanna extremely well.

After the show tonight Mary Martin made a speech to the company in which she thanked them for giving such a good performance for the King and Queen. The company received this incredibly naive impertinence in bewildered silence.

Wednesday 29 January

A nightmare morning owing to there being no hot water, everything frozen and the car not arriving in time. Finally it did get to the house and off I went in a frenzy to Waterloo, only to find that owing to the cold the train was two hours late starting[3]. Gladys and Bert were with me. We perished, and finally arrived at Southampton at 2.30. Waited in a queue for ages. Finally got on board and had a fantastic lunch, with white bread and every luxury. Gladys and Bert got off just in time, as the gangway was being pulled up. When they

---

1 Edith Nesbit was always one of Noël's favourite authors; *The Enchanted Castle* was found open on his bedside table the night he died.

2 Moira Lister (b. 1923), South African actress then at the start of her successful stage and film career.

3 Depressed by *Pacific 1860*, tired of the backstage quarrels and frozen by the winter, Noël had decided to head for New York and his first post-war visit to the USA.

had gone I lay on my bed until my bags arrived, then I unpacked, had a turkish bath and a very noisy conversation with Jack Warner[1].

Monday 3 February   New York

Safe and happy arrival. Reporters all most courteous with only casual mention of Brooklyn[2]. Jack came on board, sweet and round-faced. Dinner with Alfred, Lynn and Neysa. It is Alfred's first day out of hospital. Drink later with Clifton[3] and Neysa at '21'.

Tuesday 4 February

Chaotic morning with telephoning, flowers, telegrams, etc. Interview with a horrid girl from the *Brooklyn Eagle* who tried to trap me into indiscretions but did not succeed. Lunch with Jack at the Pavillon. Bought dressing-gown and pyjamas for *Present Laughter* at Sulka's. Leonora[4] came to tea. Dined with Neysa at Voisins and went to *Carousel* which I found enchanting.

Wednesday 5 February

Took Lynn to lunch and to *Annie Get Your Gun*[5], a fast moving, thoroughly enjoyable show. Ethel Merman quite wonderful. Saw Gloria Swanson[6] looking unchanged. Dined with Jack and went to *Years Ago* by Ruth Gordon. Quite charming and beautifully played. Freddie March superb, Florence Eldridge excellent. Supper with Clifton, Valentina and George[7]. Vodka and caviare.

Friday 7 February

Lunched with Charlie Miller and Lew Wasserman[8] at the Colony. They were full of fascinating propositions and want me to make a movie of *Present Laughter* for, obviously, any terms I want. I think they are shrewd boys.

Irene Dunne[9] came to tea. She was so attractive and charming. I do hope

1 Jack Warner (1892–1978), leader and longest surviving of the four Warner brothers who built up one of America's most successful film studios; he called his autobiography *My First Hundred Years in Hollywood*.
2 His reference to the wartime 'Brooklyn boys' was still causing American hostility.
3 Clifton Webb (1893–1966), born Webb Parmelee Hollenbeck, American character actor who had been touring the States in *Blithe Spirit* and *Present Laughter* with immense success; he and Noël had first met on a Davos skiing holiday in 1924.
4 Leonora Corbett (1907–60), British actress who was to have played opposite Noël in *Present Laughter* and *This Happy Breed* in 1939 but rehearsals ended with the outbreak of war.
5 By Irving Berlin and Herbert and Dorothy Fields.
6 Gloria Swanson (b. 1897), American film star, particularly famous on the silent screen, whom Noël had met on a trip to Hollywood in 1930.
7 George Schlee, Valentina's husband and business associate.
8 Charles Miller and Lew Wasserman, American theatrical and movie agents.
9 Irene Dunne (b. 1901), American film star who had recently been much admired by Noël in *Anna and the King of Siam*.

that some day we shall do something, either movie or theatre, together[1]. Adrianne [Allen] came for a drink and a gossip. Dined with Neysa and went to *Present Laughter*. A gruesome evening. Clifton was excellent, lacking in fire and virility but compensating by comedy technique. The production of the play was lamentable. The cast was tatty and fifth rate. Later, at Maggie Case's[2] party, I tackled Jack and told him what I thought. He riposted with wisecracks about *Sigh No More* and *Pacific 1860*. He has let me down by presenting and directing one of my best properties with lack of taste and imagination. The party was gay, but I came home depressed and weary.

Saturday 8 February

Took Leonora to lunch and to *Street Scene*, a musical version of Elmer Rice's play with a score by Kurt Weill. It is beautifully directed and staged. The music is fine and the singing quite superb. A really rich and lovely afternoon in the theatre.

Drove down to Sneden's [Landing][3] with Kit and Guthrie. A lovely evening; pyjamas and dressing-gowns and steak and caviare and that wonderful feeling of long friendliness. To be in this snug, supremely comfortable house again is so very, very good.

Sunday 16 February   Palm Beach

Today should be important because, forsaking all others, I started writing *Might Have Been*. Meant to start in the morning but I woke late, relieved at having killed a cold I started yesterday, and wrote seven pages.

Friday 21 February

Lily Pons[4] and her husband came to lunch. Lily wants to record 'Bright was the Day' and 'Changing World'. I think she most certainly should.

A cable from Lornie; business tottering badly[5].

Sunday 23 February

Lunched with Joe Kennedy and family[6]. Most welcoming and pleasant. I played the piano and, I hope, gave them some pleasure.

1 They never did.
2 Margaret Case, society editor and later special features editor on *Vogue* 1926–71.
3 On the Hudson River outside New York where Katharine Cornell and Guthrie McClintic had a house.
4 Lily Pons (1904–76), French-born opera singer who worked in America, married to conductor, André Kostelanetz.
5 For *Pacific 1860* at what Noël now considered Dreary Lane.
6 Including America's future president, John F. Kennedy.

Saturday 1 March

Caught the train from New York to Fairfield[1]. Lovely peaceful evening with Jack and Natasha. Read the first scene of *Might Have Been* to them and explained the rest. Jack thinks it's good and exciting. Natasha hated the whole idea utterly and completely because she said it was too horrible to put England in such a position particularly now, when everyone is so down. Thought this an interesting point of view. At all events, I am not going to write it yet.

Monday 3 March   New York

Talked to Ken McCormick of Doubleday's about serializing my short stories[2]. Lunched with Neysa. Shopped and bought coats for Gladys, Lorn and Joyce, also bought a lot of theatre make-up. Went with Jack and Natasha to the opening of *The Importance of Being Earnest*[3]. Very well done, in perfect taste and style. I felt proud that English actors could so obviously do what no American actors could ever do so finely.

Wednesday 5 March

Dealt with correspondence, etc., in the morning. Signed the official termination of Jack's and my partnership.

Saturday 8 March   SS *Queen Elizabeth*

Slept for twelve hours. Lunched briefly and back to bed again. Played gin rummy with Edward [Molyneux]. Had turkish bath. Cocktail with Paulette Goddard and Burgess Meredith[4], also Sidney Bernstein[5] and Mr Strachey[6], our splendid Food Minister. Dinner and more gin rummy.

Wednesday 12 March

Well, my holiday is now over and I am extremely glad. Excepting Jack, Natasha, Neysa and the Lunts, there is no one I really love in America. Nevertheless, this trip has done me immense good and opened a lot of windows. I am most grateful to America; it stimulates me and changes my direction. I do not intend another year to go by without going again.

1 Connecticut home of Jack and Natasha Wilson.
2 Doubleday had published his first collection, *To Step Aside*, in 1939; a second, *Star Quality*, was to follow in 1951.
3 An English company headed by John Gielgud was alternating this Wilde play with Congreve's *Love for Love* on Broadway.
4 Paulette Goddard (b. 1911), American actress who started as a Goldwyn girl; she had been married to Charlie Chaplin with whom she had starred in *Modern Times* and was now married to American character actor Burgess Meredith (b. 1902).
5 Sidney Bernstein (b. 1899), became Lord Bernstein 1969; founder and chairman of Granada cinemas, publishing, television, etc.
6 John St Loe Strachey (1901–63), responsible for the Labour Government's unpopular rationing measures.

Thursday 13 March　　　　　　　　　　　　　　　　　　　　London

Disembarked at 7.30. Lorn and Bert met me. Drove up with Lorn. Wonderful welcome at home. Graham looking thin but better than I expected. Gladys arrived and we had a lovely home lunch.

In the evening went to *Pacific 1860*. Company gave excellent performances. Mary awful. Fear that show, seen with fresh eye, really is rather a bore.

Friday 14 March　　　　　　　　　　　　　　　　　　　　White Cliffs

A busy morning with Lorn dealing with piles of letters, etc., and talking on the telephone. Lunched at home with Graham. In the afternoon drove with Gladys and Cole to White Cliffs. Car went badly and finally came to a full stop in the loneliest and most exposed part of the Weald of Kent. It was freezing cold and snowing slightly. Fortunately we got a lorry to tow us into Dover, where we spent a bitter hour in a garage while everyone tinkered at everything. What a performance.

Went to see poor Mum on arrival. She looked pale and weak but not as bad as I feared. Poor old darling, she has had a hellish time and dreadful pain. I do wish the weather would get warmer and give her a chance to recover completely.

Dinner in front of the fire, an acrostic and then bed.

Tuesday 18 March　　　　　　　　　　　　　　　　　　　　London

A good day's rehearsal[1]. Farewell cocktail party to Dickie and Edwina, who are going off to be Viceroy and Vicereine [of India]. I wonder if they will come back alive. I think that if it is possible to make a go of it in the circumstances they will, but I have some forebodings.

Friday 28 March

Letter from Prince saying that all idea of transferring *Pacific 1860* was out and that he is putting the two weeks' notice up tomorrow. Actually I am relieved, but also I cannot help feeling depressed. So much work, energy and time spent and only a dreary four months at the end of it. It is dreadfully hard on Graham whose big chance it should have been. However, that is the theatre.

Lunch with Sybil and Graham. Went to *Notorious*, a first-rate picture beautifully played by Cary Grant, Ingrid Bergman and Claude Rains. Cocktail party at Chips[Channon]'s for the Wavells[2]. Enjoyable. Supper with Graham and a long talk. He is tremendously sane and it is a great comfort.

Monday 7 April

Opening night of *Present Laughter* in Liverpool. For once I wasn't nervous for

1 Of *Present Laughter* at the Haymarket.
2 Returning from India where they had been replaced by the Mountbattens.

one second. The audience was cloddish to start with; the new members of the cast, except Peter Gray, were frightened and slow. I worked like a beaver and the whole thing went off very well.

Monday 14 April   London

A busy day, what with a dress rehearsal, first night arrangements and one thing and another. In the evening went to Winnie's play *Call Home the Heart* with Lorn, Joyce and Graham. It is completely scatty with all values, both psychologically and theatrically, wrong. Oh dear. We were then faced with supper at Winnie's. I managed very well and succeeded in saying what I thought without hurting her.

Wednesday 16 April

Visited Mum, came home for a cup of tea and went to the theatre. Masses of flowers and presents. Wonderful audience, warm and welcoming. Gave a good performance; felt relaxed and in complete control. Tremendous ovation at the end. Felt touched and pleased.

Thursday 17 April

Very good notices. Good audience in the evening. Supper with Gladys and Graham at the Savoy. We popped in to Winnie's farewell party for the Hallidays. Thank God they are leaving tomorrow.

Monday 21 April

Painted in the morning. Drove to London in the afternoon. Still not a puff of nicotine. Agony wearing off a bit, thank God. Evening performance very good; wonderful audience. It really is beguiling being a triumphant success.

Saturday 26 April

Conversation with Teddy Holmes[1]. Apparently the BBC are in a fine flap because I have laid down my terms for a series of broadcasts of my music with Joyce [Grenfell], Graham and Mantovani. They wanted me to do a star broadcast on my own, which I will only do on condition that they do the series. Unless they do what I want they will be out of luck.

Two very good performances. We have apparently broken the Haymarket record on the week.

Drove down to White Cliffs with Graham and Cole. A lovely night. I hope no more of the cliff comes down.

Tuesday 6 May

I am going through one of my periodical worry phases about time and how

1 Teddy Holmes, Noël's music publisher at Chappell's.

little there is of it; there is so much that I want to write and so many people get in the way, to say nothing of eight shows a week. It is difficult to get into the right frame of mind and concentrate in London.

Friday 9 May

Read dear Mr Beverley Baxter[1] in the *Evening Standard*, who has thought up a splendid little gossip article called, in enormous headlines, 'Ivor Versus Noël'. It is all about the great rivalry between us[2]. Really too nauseating.

Tuesday 13 May

Worked all day, mostly planning the last act. Lorn thought of a wonderful title, *Peace in Our Time*. I expect it will get us into trouble but to hell with that.

Played the show to a dreary audience but worked hard and got them going. Straight home and supper in bed.

Wednesday 28 May

Day of momentous decisions. Decided with Binkie to keep *Present Laughter* running at the Haymarket with Hugh Sinclair playing my part and to do *Peace in Our Time* at the Lyric[3]. Think this is a good idea as *Present Laughter* might run on for quite a while.

Sunday 1 June   White Cliffs

A scorching hot day. Lay in the sun for hours. Painted one picture, apart from that did nothing. Feel rested and well. After dinner looked at the films of other years; Jack young and handsome, Gladys ditto, me thinner, Maxine [Elliot], Edward [Molyneux], Gloria Swanson, etc. A little nostalgic sigh.

Monday 9 June   London

Painted in the morning. Came up in the train. Read *The Goldfish*[4], for which I have promised to do a foreword. Oh dear, it really is agonizingly arch.

Tuesday 17 June

First read-through of *Peace in Our Time*. Everyone rather too reverent and a

---

1 Beverley Baxter (1891–1964), Conservative MP and drama critic.
2 Noël once told Ivor, 'If anyone tells you I've been rude behind your back, believe them.' In fact the Press reports of their rivalry were greatly exaggerated and the two men only occasionally moved in overlapping circles.
3 The original plan had been to follow *Present Laughter* with *Peace in Our Time*; the former was to run for another year.
4 The first play (by Lila Field) in which Noël had appeared, at Crystal Palace in 1911.

bit inaudible. I think they will all be good ultimately, but it is going to be a difficult play to do and needs a great deal of cutting.

Wednesday 18 June

Rehearsal. Changed over Ralph Michael and Kenneth More into different parts. Lunch with Duncan Sandys[1]. Very amiable. Winston has suggested that I might be useful in the United Europe movement.

Saturday 21 June

Ronnie Neame came to lunch and we discussed the possibility of doing *Peace in Our Time*[2]. Unfortunately he and David won't work together as of yore, as they both must be directors. This is irritating for me, as together they were more efficient than singly.

Felt awful during the matinée owing to this damned fibrositis. It is a bit hard to have it when I have so much to do. Took three Phensic after the matinée and rested. Gave good evening performance and felt fine. Drove down to White Cliffs with Cole, dictating broadcast announcements all the way[3]. Natasha and Graham were waiting up. Natasha absolutely adorable and sweeter than ever.

Saturday 12 July

A fairly emotional day. My last two performances[4]. Before that we discussed the future of White Cliffs. They will extend my lease for twenty-five years. Visited Gladys's new house. Very impressive. After the matinée the company presented me with a lovely silver cigarette-box signed by all of them. I was very touched. After the evening show champagne flowed in my dressing-room and it was all very sentimental and profoundly sincere and I wouldn't have done without it for the world. It is deeply comforting to know one is loved.

Tuesday 15 July   Brighton

Rehearsed all day, then the opening night[5]. Terribly hot and theatre jammed to the roof with a fairly silly holiday audience. However, the play went terrifically and there was an ovation at the end. Personally I love the play and the cast. From the acting point of view it gives me tremendous pleasure; practically everyone is good and some are superb.

Thursday 17 July

Woke feeling exhausted. Temperature. After the doctor had been and done

1 Duncan Sandys (b. 1908), Lord Duncan-Sandys 1974; Conservative politician married 1935–60 to Winston Churchill's eldest daughter Diana.
2 As a film; it never happened.
3 The continuity links for the songs he had just recorded for BBC radio.
4 He was leaving the Haymarket cast of *Present Laughter*.
5 Of *Peace in Our Time* at Brighton's Theatre Royal.

nothing whatever, it went soaring up and I felt like death. However, by the evening it was only a hundred so I got up and dined at the Criterion and went to the play. The performance was slack and untidy and the effects were muddled, but it went marvellously and again I had a terrific ovation. In spite of all the Press have said about me, I seem to be loved by the public. It is a lovely feeling and I am grateful.

Came back to the hotel and had a cup of tea in bed. Temperature still a hundred but I feel much better.

Saturday 19 July   White Cliffs

Woke feeling much better. Cole came and talked to me and told me he wasn't really happy as he felt there was no future in his work, etc. It was done very sweetly. I talked to him for a long time and he said he felt better. Then something inside me gave an enraged click and I said that however better he might feel, I felt much worse as I was only just recuperating anyway, and to be called upon for such an output of energy was asking too much. The whole thing depressed me immensely all day.

Mum departed in a haze of cats and dogs for her new house[1]. I tried to paint but could not do it well. Finally, went to bed, feeling very low. Graham behaved like fifteen rocks of Gibraltar rolled into one and talked me out of my nervous irritation and self-pity. I now feel much better.

Tuesday 22 July   London

First night *Peace in Our Time*: I haven't heard such an enthusiastic noise in the theatre for many a year. After this cosy little triumph, Binkie gave a party, which was lovely. Got home late but happy. It is a bloody good play.

Wednesday 23 July

Rave notice in the *Telegraph*; insulting one in *The Times*; the rest fairly good, but all a bit grudging and patronizing. The play, however, is a smash hit and no doubt about it.

Lunched at the Ivy with Gladys, Lorn and Graham. Did a bit of shopping and bought myself a beautiful Vlaminck for £300, just to add to the Coward collection.

Thursday 24 July

Morning spent discussing film offers for *Peace in Our Time*.

Went to the Haymarket to say goodbye[2]. Hugh [Sinclair] struggling through the first act with almost total lack of voice. Made quick decision and played

1 In Boscobel Mews, London.
2 Noël was again headed for America.

the last two acts. Rapturous reception from audience and company. Flew along to the Lyric and said my goodbyes.

Wednesday 30 July

Arrived New York. Lovely morning. Ship early, so no sign of Jack and Natasha. Neysa was there and so we drove to the apartment. It has completely changed, the work of the sodding little queen who has rented it. It is full of knick-knacks, the panelling is ruined and there is a general atmosphere of cissy pretentiousness. We shall soon get it cleared of all this artsy-craftsy junk.

Jack and Natasha finally arrived. We lunched at the Colony where we saw everybody. In the afternoon I showed Graham Fifth Avenue, Grand Central, etc.[1] Mint juleps with Ina and Bill[2] at two, then dinner with Jack and Natasha. Then we went to *Brigadoon*[3]. Agnes de Mille's choreography wonderful, music pleasant, production fairly good, book boring. Went out of the air-conditioned Ziegfeld into the oven of Sixth Avenue. Finished up at the Stork Club with Dorothy Parker[4]. Quite a day.

Thursday 31 July

In the evening went with Neysa and Graham to Coney Island. A lovely time had by all; shook ourselves to bits on the roller-coaster, etc. Drove back singing and giggling.

Saturday 2 August

A lovely day flopping in and out of the pool[5]. Both the Clairs[6] gay and charming. In the evening Graham and I drove over to Ferber's[7] with Dick and Dorothy Rodgers. A very good party, including Moss and Kitty Hart[8], Josh Logan[9], etc. Everyone sang and played – not everyone really, mainly Dick and me. Graham sang and Dick played for hours, both old stuff and new stuff. The *Allegro*[10] music sounds lovely.

1 This was Graham Payn's first visit to America.
2 Ina Claire (b. 1895), American actress, and her third husband, lawyer William R. Wallace Jr, whom she had married in 1939 after divorcing actor John Gilbert; Noël had directed her and Laurence Olivier in *Biography* in 1934.
3 Alan Jay Lerner and Frederick Loewe's first success.
4 Dorothy Parker (1893-1967), American writer and wit.
5 At Jack Wilson's Fairfield, Connecticut, home.
6 René Clair (1898-1980), French director of such films as *An Italian Straw Hat*, and his wife.
7 Edna Ferber (1887-1968), American writer and a friend of Noël's since his earliest days in New York.
8 Moss Hart (1904-61), American playwright and director, and his wife Kitty Carlisle (b. 1914), American singer and actress.
9 Joshua Logan (b. 1908), American stage and screen director.
10 The musical Rodgers and Oscar Hammerstein were then working on.

Sunday 3 August

A pleasant day lying in and by the pool. Graham and I drove to Oyster Bay where there was a dinner party: Maggie Case, Christopher Isherwood[1] and a friend, both of whom I liked, and Garbo. A really cosy evening. Finally Graham and I drove back, a two-hour run. Upon arrival we made a bee-line for the kitchen and cooked eggs.

Saturday 9 August   Martha's Vineyard[2]

Peace. Sleep. Lovely food. Swimming. In the afternoon a drive into the town. Delicious dinner of broiled lobsters, etc. Eight-pack bezique. Guthrie gave vivid and exciting description of his plans for his forthcoming production of *Antony and Cleopatra*. When he is really excited he lights up like a carousel.

Thursday 14 August

Telephoned to Gertie. Spent the afternoon finishing a short story, *Stop Me If You've Heard It*. It's good, I think. In the evening we had a clam-bake. Elaborate preparations: chickens, lobsters, corn, clams, etc., etc., were buried in the sand under seaweed and cooked for hours and hours. Net result disappointing. Nothing was cooked enough and everything was full of sand. Kit made a gallant effort to save the situation by building a fire and cooking the underdone dainties until they were black and still full of sand. The white wine was delicious provided you waited until the sand had sunk to the bottom of the mug. Finally we all came indoors and had some milk and angel cake, the lack of sand in which was somehow shocking.

Saturday 16 August

Left Martha's Vineyard. Crossed on the ferry in a biblical storm; most dramatic. Arrived in Boston at 3.30. Rested. Dined and drove out to Marblehead and saw Gertie in *Lily Maria*[3]. She was most enchanting in a bad part and a dull play. Supper afterwards, very reminiscent and gay.

Saturday 23 August

Arrived Chicago[4]. Breakfast with Tallulah who was really very sweet. Delicious lunch and then the matinée of *Carousel*. It is an exquisite show. Dined with Lynn and Alfred and went, with some misgivings, to *Private Lives*. Much

---

1 Christopher Isherwood (b. 1904), English novelist and Hollywood scriptwriter who had become an American citizen in 1946.
2 Where Kit Cornell and Guthrie McClintic had a house.
3 A summer stock production.
4 To see Tallulah Bankhead (1902–68), American film and stage star whom Noël had met on his first trip to America in the 1920s and who had starred in one of his earliest successes, *Fallen Angels*, in 1925; she was now on tour in *Private Lives*.

to my relief, and a certain amount of surprise, Tallulah was extraordinarily good; she is a bit coarse in texture, but her personality is formidable and she played some of it quite beautifully and all of it effectively. The others were unremarkable and the lighting was bad. Drinks with Tallulah, who was touchingly thrilled that I liked her performance and ecstatic when I said she could play it in New York. She insisted on offering me an Augustus John picture that she has in the country. She is a curious character; wildly generous, a very big heart and can be both boring and amusing. Well, well.

Sunday 31 August

Woke late. Breakfast-lunch with Tallulah, then we all went to the Riverview Place Park where we went on everything and thoroughly enjoyed ourselves. We came home, had a bath and changed, then went to dine at Chez Paree in order to see Carmen Miranda[1]. From then on the evening became a nightmare. Carmen Miranda was extremely good and after her show came to sit at our table. Tallulah was nicely thank you and proceeded to be noisy and vulgar from then on. Carmen Miranda wisely disappeared. Tallulah screamed and roared and banged the table, etc., and I wished the floor would open. From Chez Paree we drove all around Chicago to a dive where there is a trombonist, a saxophonist, a drummer and a pianist who play the latest swing and bebop, etc. The audience, mostly callow youths, became hypnotized and began to wriggle and sway and scream exactly like a revival meeting. To me, the whole thing was completely abominable. I loathed it. The heat, the violent noise and Tallulah still shrieking. From there we went on to hear Dixieland music. We were driven back into Chicago and returned to a beastly little club and given a table right under the trumpet, whereupon I walked out and came home. I am forty-seven and sane.

Monday 1 September

Tallulah gay, sweet and apologetic. We went to a private viewing of *Lifeboat*[2]. Very good. After that, we nibbled some caviare and caught the train for New York.

Tuesday 2 September

Rather depressed about the returns for *Peace in Our Time*. I do hope after all the fuss that it is not a flop. Dined with Neysa at the Colony and went to see a revival of *Top Hat* with Fred Astaire. Picture idiotic from every point of view, but he is the greatest dancer in the world, and can sing numbers better than most people. Drink with Neysa and then home.

---

1 Carmen Miranda, celebrated Portuguese singer.
2 Alfred Hitchcock film in which Tallulah starred.

Tuesday 9 September

Overwhelmed with roses from Lillian Gish[1], who wants me to trail out to Bucks County to see her in *The Marquise*[2] and let her present it in New York. I know that no good will come of this, so I intend to evade the issue. Drinks with Valentina, who bared her soul a little over George and Garbo[3]. Poor dear, I am afraid she is having a dreary time.

Dined with Neysa and Graham and went to a movie, *Lured*, which we abandoned after half an hour and went to see Kit and Guthrie. Guthrie full of electric enthusiasm about *Antony and Cleopatra*. I love his capacity for violent enthusiasm. It doesn't really matter if the ultimate production turns out to be good, bad or indifferent. His uninhibited passion for his job is reward enough for him and, incidentally, for me.

Wednesday 10 September

Spent the day indoors doing letters, etc. At six o'clock had a talk with Gertie and Fanny Holtzmann[4] about doing a revival of *Tonight at 8.30*, which I strongly advised her *not* to do.

Saturday 13 September

Constance[5] came to lunch and was perfectly enchanting. In the afternoon drove down to the Nelson Doubledays[6]. A pleasant evening. Both Nelson and Ellen hospitable and sweet. General conversation about the Windsors, modern novelists, etc. I have an idea about turning 'What Mad Pursuit' into a play.

Wednesday 17 September

In the afternoon Jules Stein[7] and Charles Miller came to see me with a fantastic proposition: if I would guarantee Paramount three commitments, either as actor, author or director, they would pay me $500 a week for twenty-three years. I told them it was a wonderful offer but I valued my freedom more. They went on about England being finished, etc., and I suddenly saw the headlines: 'Noël Coward signs up to American Film Company. Another rat leaving the sinking ship.' All my instincts told me violently to refuse. So I did and they were astounded.

1 Lillian Gish (b. 1896), American silent screen star with whom Noël had made his first fleeting screen appearance in *Hearts of the World* (1918).
2 Which Noël had written for Marie Tempest in 1926.
3 Greta Garbo was reported to be living with Valentina's husband, George Schlee.
4 Fanny Holtzmann, indomitable American lawyer who managed Gertrude Lawrence's affairs in New York and also occasionally represented Noël there.
5 Constance Collier (1878-1955), English actress long resident in America.
6 Noël's American publisher and his wife Ellen.
7 Jules Stein, head of the entertainment agency, Music Corporation of America (MCA).

Thursday 18 September

Took Beatrice Eden to lunch at the Colony. Saw Doug Fairbanks[1], who was sweet as usual, but much preoccupied with the affairs of the world. Beatrice was rather touching. I suspect her conscience is troubling her but not enough to make her go back to Anthony.

Discussed with Jack and Graham the possibility of Graham doing *Tonight at 8.30* with Gertie. It might be a good idea. Valentina appeared for a drink in the evening and attacked us for wanting to go back to England. Shut her up effectively.

Tuesday 23 September   Lake Placid

A good day's work. Wrote eighteen pages and finished the act. Telephoned to Graham. He read me a cable from Binkie saying he was not very happy about *Peace in Our Time*. Really, if that play turns out to be a flop I shall be forced to the reluctant and pompous conclusion that England does not deserve my work. That is a good play, written with care and heart and guts and it is beautifully acted and directed. Binkie wants me to write a comedy for the winter. If I do it will get either stinking or patronizing notices and be another flop unless I or a big star play in it. I have a sick at heart feeling about England anyhow. We are so idiotic and apathetic and it is nothing to do with 'after the war' because we were the same at Munich and before that. I want to go back but not for long. I shall have to manage my life carefully in the next few years; I shall have to plan many partings and reunions with not too much time in between.

Sunday 28 September

Today was a big day because I finished the play. I concentrated like mad and wrote 'Curtain' at about 3.30. It really is a wonderful feeling. I think it is pretty good. I didn't think I could have done it in the time. It has been great fun writing in the American idiom. Afterwards I found myself talking about England so very proudly, though I was talking about England in the war years when her gallantry and common sense were married by emergency. It is all very confusing. I think I had better get after *Future Indefinite* and get some of my confusion down on paper.

Wednesday 1 October

Arrived at the New York flat at 8.30. It looks lovely with the new curtains and covers. Lovely letter from Lornie, really the most supremely sensible woman in the world. She obviously feels, without our even discussing it, exactly the

---

1 Douglas Fairbanks Jr (b. 1907), American stage and screen star who had been a friend of Noël's since the 1930s when Fairbanks was living with Gertrude Lawrence.

same as I do about doing another play in London. It is all very well for Binkie to urge me to do one, but counting *Point Valaine* I have had three this year and four would be one too many[1].

In the evening Neysa, Jack and Natasha dined. I read *Long Island Sound*[2]. They didn't seem to be very much impressed. Jack prophesies that the Press will crucify me for it. I shall wait and get a few more opinions. Went to bed feeling a trifle flat. Not seriously, as everyone had had too many martinis and I think they were good and sleepy, or at least heavy. Anyway I didn't enjoy reading it and I had been so looking forward to it.

Monday 6 October

Hot Indian Summer day and the autumn colouring quite fantastically beautiful. Graham and I picked up Gertie at 6.30 and went to dine with the Luces. Gertie looking lovely. After dinner we went to a private showing of *The Fugitive*, one of the most tedious, pretentious, irritating pictures I have ever seen. It is adapted from a book by Graham Greene[3] and has ardent Catholic propaganda. Really Mr Greene has a most unpleasant mind. After this we went to a little party which included Constance [Collier], Helen Hayes[4], etc. Gertie, Graham and I all sang.

Wednesday 8 October

Drink with Fanny Holtzmann. Really she is fantastic. She paints like mad and obviously has considerable uncontrolled talent.

A quiet dinner with Graham at '21' interrupted by the arrival of Jack, who started a bit of show-off about Graham not being able to rehearse without a permit, etc., all of which has already been satisfactorily arranged by Fanny. I pinned him down and made him admit it was nothing serious, but he succeeded in upsetting Graham and our hitherto peaceful evening. I made a joke of it at the time, but when I got home I was sick.

Thursday 9 October

Woke feeling tense with nerves and utterly wretched. Finally calmed myself. I feel this is the end of the friendship between Jack and me. So many things add up over the years, leading up to the reading of *Long Island Sound* the other night. It is a bitter revelation that I can no longer trust him. I am

1 His 1934 drama *Point Valaine*, written for the Lunts, had been given a belated and brief London première at the Embassy Theatre, Swiss Cottage, with a cast headed by Anthony Ireland and Mary Ellis; his other plays this year had been *Peace in Our Time* and the *Present Laughter* revival, which was still at the Haymarket.
2 Title of play based on 'What Mad Pursuit'.
3 *The Power and the Glory*.
4 Helen Hayes (b. 1900), considered to be the 'first lady of the American theatre'.

worried about leaving him to direct *Tonight at 8.30* but I shall take good care to set all six plays[1] before I go.

With all this on my mind we had our first day's rehearsal. The cast is very good. Gertie is enchanting at moments but inclined to be piss-elegant.

Saturday 11 October

I am certainly living through a strange and difficult time. I shall put the events of today down as they happened.

First of all I woke feeling rather worried about Graham's ability to cope with the parts. He had wakened an hour earlier and was studying like mad. We went to rehearsal and started with *Shadow Play*. Graham was virtually word perfect and much better, but still unrelaxed; he was obviously twisted with nerves and trying desperately hard. I noticed Jack scribble a few lines and pass them to Martin Manulis[2], who giggled. After morning rehearsal Graham went out with Gertie to lunch and I invited Howard Young[3] back here as I did not intend to rehearse in the afternoon. During lunch Howard told me he was profoundly worried about a psychological problem, which was that if I left and Jack took over the direction Graham would be crucified. He likes Graham and thinks he is going to be wonderful, but only if he has confidence. He then told me that Jack had shown him what he had written to Martin (under poor Graham's nose) which was, 'I am the biggest baby-sitter in New York', meaning, for the benefit of English ears, that Graham was a passenger. Finally, Howard implored me for Gertie's, Graham's and his sake to stay over and go on directing until the Baltimore opening. I suddenly knew I had to say yes. I went down and told Jack, who was sweet about it but angry underneath. He then made the mistake of going out with Martin to have a drink.

Meanwhile I told Gertie and Graham and the effect was magical; all nervousness disappeared and he played through *Shadow Play* very well indeed. Jack had to leave for Chicago to deal with Tallulah. Graham and I dined with Howard, who was quivering with horror because he had found Jack and Martin hashing everything over in the bar next door. He (Howard) was with the company press agent. Jack insisted that they had a drink too, and proceeded to make a series of witticisms which electrified the press agent and horrified Howard. Howard is an amiable, honest little man obviously ill at ease amidst all this backbiting.

Later in the evening he told me about a thirty-week tour that his company, Lewis and Young, had done of *Blithe Spirit*, in which my royalties had been eight per cent of the gross, Jack's five per cent of the gross for his kindness in

1 There were nine plays in *Tonight at 8.30*, though only six were used in this production.
2 Martin Manulis, Jack Wilson's assistant.
3 Howard Young, producer of this American revival of *Tonight at 8.30*.

letting them do it, together with five per cent of the profits. I certainly did not know about this and I don't think Lorn did either. My mind now is a seething morass of doubts. I only know one thing: I must stay for the opening of these plays. Graham has a terribly tough assignment anyway. Gertie is sweet to him, but with a few nicely phrased witticisms from Jack she might not be. No one could begin to give a performance in that atmosphere. I wish to Christ Lorn was here. I have got to stay but I am tired and sick at heart and I want to go home. However, I shall rise above it as much as I can.

Monday 13 October

Dined with Graham at '21'. Then I went to the Wilson residence and had a heart-to-heart with Natasha until 3.30 a.m. I told her to tell Jack that I was leaving him. We both decided that the only thing to do is to frighten him thoroughly. Unless he shows some change of character I really mean to do it.

Wednesday 15 October

Well, this morning the showdown happened. Jack, having been told by Natasha, came round and I let him have it for two hours. He was abject and gave in all along the line. The net result was that I agreed to give him another chance if he will make a genuine effort to change his character. He swore that he would. In any case it is worth a try. He is coming back to England with me on 12 November.

Thursday 30 October

Talked to Guthrie on the telephone. He was charming about *Long Island Sound* and absolutely honest. He says it does not really stand up to a whole evening and the joke is too attenuated. I feel that he is right and I really felt that Jack was right, but he did not tell me why. He merely evaded the issue by warning me about the critics; a sure way to make me dig my feet in. Guthrie thinks it could be condensed into a short play. I wonder.

Monday 10 November

Caught the train for Baltimore with Fanny [Holtzmann]. Found out some interesting things during the journey. One was that the source of my Bow Street case in 1941 was a lot of the Hollywood and New York British renegades, livid with jealousy about me and resentful that I should ask them to subscribe to the Orphans and not subscribe myself[1]. Learnt lots of other things, among them the fact that my financial affairs in this country have been badly handled for twenty years and that I have been overpaying my tax for years. I have told Fanny to ferret things out and tidy up.

---

1 There had been a fund for transporting Actors' Orphanage evacuees to North America.

Arrived in Baltimore. Went to the opening performance. Graham better than ever. Lighting bad as ever. Electrician being sacked. Supper after the show with Paul Patterson, owner of the *Baltimore Sun*. Quite agreeable.

Tuesday 18 November   London

Arrived at Southampton at two o'clock in drizzling rain and bitter cold. Lorn and Cole met us. Cole and Jack went up in the train and Lorn and I drove up in the car. I told her all the Jack saga, etc. Lovely arriving in the studio[1], which is looking wonderful with pure white paint and the pictures beautifully hung. Gladys arrived. Wonderful welcome. Presents unpacked and all excitement. Popped round to see Mum who is looking fine. Popped back again. Had a drink and dressed, then drove off to Buckingham Palace[2]. A sensational evening. The most lovely sight I have ever seen. Everyone looking shiny and happy; something indestructible. Everybody conceivable was there. Dickie, Edwina, Anthony [Eden], etc. The King and Queen were sweet to me as always. Talked to Philip and Princess Elizabeth, who looked radiant. Also to Princess Margaret Rose and the Duchess of Kent, more lovely looking than ever. The whole thing was pictorially, dramatically and spiritually enchanting. Found many old naval buddies and had a *rapprochement* with Osbert Sitwell[3]. Left at 1 a.m. and went to Binkie's on my way home. Jack was there.

Wednesday 19 November

London *en fête*. Crowds in the streets. Lunched at the Ivy with Lorn, Jack, Joyce and Gladys. Later had a drink with Gladys in her new house which is lovely, then joined Jack at the theatre. *Peace in Our Time* is very moving but, oh dear, the performance has certainly slipped. Bernard Lee is impeccable and so are Beatrice Varley, Elspeth March and Alan Badel. Philip Guard absolutely disgraceful. Gave him hell afterwards and called rehearsal for Friday. Jack obviously deeply impressed. We are going to do it in New York in February with about eight of these principals.

Thursday 20 November

A gala day. Dressed myself up in frock-coat and striped trousers, etc. Drove to Westminster Abbey. Found, to my surprise and pleasure, that I was placed in the fourth row next to Beatrice Lillie[4]. The wedding was most moving and

---

1 His Gerald Road studio flat.
2 To celebrate the wedding (two days later) of Princess Elizabeth and Prince Philip.
3 Osbert Sitwell (1892-1969), author, and brother of the equally famous literary figures, Sacheverell and Edith, with all of whom Noël had fallen out in 1923 after he had parodied them as The Swiss Family Whittlebot in a sketch for *London Calling!*.
4 Beatrice Lillie (b. 1898), Canadian-born actress and comedienne who had starred in Noël's *Set to Music* (1939).

beautifully done. English tradition at its best. Mobbed by crowds while waiting for the car. Lunch at the Rothermeres, where everyone was present. Later, had a sharp argument with Peter Quennell about my attack on the intellectuals in *Peace in Our Time*[1]. Worsted him, aided by Ann Rothermere. Walked home through the crowds and, after a rest, went to a cocktail 'do' at the French Embassy.

Friday 28 November

Blanche Patch[2] came to tea. Enjoyable conversation about GBS. Went with Lorn and Gladys to *Tuppence Coloured*[3], an amateur, mediocre show redeemed by Joyce Grenfell and some witty lyrics.

Dined with Binkie. Just the two of us and Joyce. Read *Long Island Sound*. All enjoyed it but agreed that it wasn't quite a play. This does not depress me as I agree with them and at least they laughed and enjoyed the dialogue. Howard Young rang me up from Hollywood. In spite of rave notices in Boston, the business[4] isn't very good: $17,000 the first week as against $21,000 in Baltimore, which was considered bad. I don't think they should have booked Boston anyhow, as Gertie and I had played it there in the past. I don't much care what happens as long as they play San Francisco and Hollywood.

Wednesday 3 December

Lunched at Claridge's. It was a party for the Queen of Spain and was very agreeable. Dined with Larry and Viv and went to the opening of *St Joan*[5]. Very excited at the prospect of Celia playing that part but was a little disappointed. She was lacking in guts and rather like Peter Pan. Alec Guinness was wonderful; the production artsy-craftsy and fairly bad. Supper with Larry and Viv.

Wednesday 10 December

Invitation from Ward Price on behalf of Rothermere and the *Sunday Dispatch* to write a thousand-word tribute to the King for his birthday on Sunday, in order to offset the bad taste of the *Sunday Express* in publishing the Duke of Windsor's memoirs on that day. Agreed rather reluctantly to do it.

Tuesday 16 December

Very sweet morning, with presents, etc.[6] Mum appeared and was enchanting.

1 In which Noël suggested that after an enemy invasion they would be the first to collaborate.
2 Blanche Patch, George Bernard Shaw's secretary.
3 Revue at the Globe Theatre devised by Laurier Lister.
4 For *Tonight at 8.30*.
5 Old Vic Company production at the New Theatre, with Celia Johnson as Joan and Alec Guinness as the Dauphin.
6 It was his forty-eighth birthday.

She told me stories of her early love affairs. Ronnie [Neame] came to lunch and couldn't have been nicer. After he had gone I retired to bed feeling not very well. Talked to Graham in Philadelphia.

Monday 29 December

It appears that I have some form of rheumatic fever. They are not sure what form of it I have until all the tests are through. This is rather agitating. I am determined to sail on Saturday, whatever happens[1].

Wednesday 31 December

Woke feeling dotty and still in fierce agony. Managed to get myself down to the bathroom on my bottom but nearly killed myself doing it.

Sydney Box[2] and his wife came to discuss the filming of *Tonight at 8.30*, which he owns. They were very amiable and I think I shall be able to keep it under control.

After lunch two specialists arrived, Horace Evans (rheumatics) and Steeler (throat). Was examined all ends up; gout and rheumatic fever brought on by streptococci was the final diagnosis. Pain a bit better. Van Loewen[3] came and we discussed him taking over French theatrical affairs. Temperature rose. More penicillin, more M&B. Peaceful dinner. Pain began to disappear, temperature dropped.

Gladys, Joyce, Jeffrey [Amherst], Ginette and Paul-Emile[4] came in, then the latter three went and Joyce, Gladys, Cole and I drank in the New Year.

1 To join Graham in America.
2 Sydney Box (b. 1907), British film producer.
3 Jan Van Loewen, playwrights' agent specializing in foreign rights.
4 Ginette Spanier, directrice of Balmain, and her doctor husband Paul-Emile Seidmann, closest of Noël's Parisian friends.

= 1948 =

A year spent largely on the American revival of Tonight at 8.30, starring Gertrude Lawrence and Graham Payn under Noël's direction, and the attempt to convert Present Laughter into a boulevard comedy for Paris under the title Joyeux Chagrins, with Noël himself playing Garry Essendine in reasonably fluent French. Money was still tight but a brief Californian visit confirmed Noël's determination not to sell out his professional soul to America in general or Hollywood in particular. The theatre was still where he felt he belonged, and preferably the English theatre, even if at that time it did not seem to be exactly crying out for his services as actor, dramatist or director.

Off-stage, the most important event this year was the discovery of Jamaica as a winter refuge and the purchase of a few acres of land just outside Port Maria on the road from Oracabessa, where he was to build both Blue Harbour and his own small house called Firefly directly above it. But the Rolls-Royce back home at Goldenhurst had to be sold to pay for it, and Lorn Loraine was forever being told to raid his London bank accounts for cash. On one occasion her reward was the following telegram:

DEAR, KINDLY, GENEROUS AND LOVING LORN
SO GRATEFUL AM I THAT I CANNOT SPEAK
THAT YOU SHOULD YIELD SO MUCH FROM PLENTY'S HORN
I SHAN'T NEED ANY MORE TILL TUESDAY WEEK.

Friday 2 January   London

Today I arose from my bed and walked; and lo it was a miracle, although it hurt like buggery; and lo there came unto my house Joyce, the daughter of Dame Lilian, and Edward [Molyneux] and Binkie and Ronnie Neame and Gladys and Arthur [Macrae] and Boxer[1]; and Boxer, the son of a bitch, sprang at my foot and worried it like a rat, but he was so beautiful and newly washed that he was forgiven.

Mum came in the morning to say goodbye[2] and was very, very good. She really is remarkable; not a tear nor a complaint.

Thursday 8 January   New York

Lunched with Natasha. Agonizing two hours with Fanny who talked us to a standstill. Bought two suits and an overcoat at Saks. Dined with Neysa and Lorn at '21', then went to *Brigadoon*, which I enjoyed much more than last time. Long talk with Henry Luce and then with Ann Rothermere.

Saturday 10 January

An enjoyable interview with Wolcott Gibbs[3] for *Life* magazine. I took a great shine to him. Jack and Natasha and Lorn came to lunch. Then Lorn and I went to *A Streetcar Named Desire*[4], a really remarkable play superbly acted and directed. A great afternoon in the theatre. Back home to finish packing.

Arrived at the station[5], fortunately in good time. God's own monumental balls-up over reservations. Finally got on to the train and ultimately, owing to personal determination and charm, we managed to get Lorn her compartment, and now, exhausted, I am back in mine, writing these faltering lines.

Tuesday 13 January   San Francisco

A lovely day and beautiful scenery. We were met by Graham who looks very well. Later at the hotel we had a tumultuous welcome from Gertie. We saw the show and really the standard has been kept up very well and Gertie is remarkable; hardly any overplaying at all; a few things need tightening but nothing serious. After the show we went to the Fairmont and heard Gracie Fields[6]. It was her opening night. She was wonderful, although not all her songs were.

1 A puppy.
2 He was sailing for New York the next day.
3 Wolcott Gibbs, American journalist and dramatic critic.
4 The original New York stage production of Tennessee Williams's play, starring Jessica Tandy and a young Marlon Brando.
5 This being Lorn's first American visit, Noël was taking her to San Francisco where Graham and Gertie were playing in *Tonight at 8.30*.
6 Gracie Fields (1898–1979), popular English singer, who was in cabaret at the hotel; created Dame 1978.

Tuesday 20 January

Rehearsed *Shadow Play* then lunched with Lorn and Graham. Went to the doctor's and had my ears, nose and throat cleaned up. Arrived at the theatre and found the doctor with Graham. Watched performance. *Shadow Play* good; *Fumed Oak* awful, with Gertie overplaying like hell; *Hands Across the Sea* very good. Controlled fury and handled situation tactfully. Graham seems better. Drinks in the upstairs bar.

Saturday 24 January

Went down to see Graham at 12.30[1]. He felt weak and so we decided he had better lay off the matinée and only play tonight. Suddenly decided to play the matinée myself: *Shadow Play* and *Hands Across the Sea*. I flew down to the theatre, started rehearsing at 1.20 and was on at 2.30. I was proud of the fact that I didn't dry up once. The performance was not bad. The company and audience were thrilled but it was all rather exhausting.

Monday 26 January   Los Angeles

A lot of telephoning. Lunch with Gertie and Graham, an orchestra rehearsal, a little shopping and a short rest. Then I went to the theatre, where there was a milling mob. Marlene [Dietrich] arrived on time and we were photographed all ends up. The performance was good and went wonderfully. Then there was George's party[2]. Very glamorous and, like all Hollywood parties, somehow flat. Judy Garland[3], the Colmans[4], Irene Dunne, Joan Crawford[5], the Fairbanks[6], etc., were all there. All very friendly and sweet. Graham made a real success I think, but it is all very agitating and I wish we had opened in New York and the anxieties were over.

Tuesday 27 January

We had a quick breakfast/lunch here and then hired a car and drove to the Fairbanks'. It really is lovely. Mary Lee was sweet and welcoming.

The Chaplins[7] came to dine. Charlie was really brilliant. He told me how he really began his career and how he invented the 'Little Man' character. It was all great fun and I enjoyed it.

1 He had been ill and unable to play the previous evening.
2 George Cukor (b. 1899), Hollywood film director.
3 Judy Garland (1922–69), American singer.
4 Ronald Colman (1891–1958), British actor, and his actress wife, Benita Hume (1906–67).
5 Joan Crawford (1908–77), Hollywood film star.
6 Douglas Jr and Mary Lee Fairbanks, who had married in 1939 following his much-publicized divorce from Joan Crawford.
7 Charles Chaplin (1889–1979) and his wife Oona, daughter of Irish-American playwright Eugene O'Neill, whom he had married in 1943; knighted in 1975.

Thursday 29 January

Went out to Warner's to see Hitchcock[1] directing *Rope*. Lunched with Jimmie Stewart[2]. Then watched Hitch's new camera technique. Really very exciting, a whole reel taken in one go without resetting lights for close-ups and medium shots. The camera silently follows the action, the walls of the set disappear, the furniture is whisked away and the actors play a ten-minute scene without stops. It is a brilliant idea, brilliantly organized. It cannot be applied to all pictures, but from the writer's point of view it is wonderful.

Friday 30 January

Gandhi[3] has been assassinated. In my humble opinion, a bloody good thing but far too late.

Saturday 31 January

Drove out to lunch with Joan Crawford. After lunch we saw the last two reels of *Possessed* and other pictures. The adopted children[4] broke down under the impact of so much emotion and suffering, and bawled their lungs out.

Sunday 1 February

Slept late. Later had a tea party consisting of David Niven and his new wife[5] and Deborah Kerr and her husband[6]. Then had a steam bath and then Clifton [Webb]'s party, which was enchanting. Katie Hepburn[7], Irene Dunne, Ronnie and Benita, Claudette[8], etc. Home rather too late.

Thursday 5 February

Lunched at MGM. Visited various sets. Gene Kelly[9] charming. Saw bits of *Easter Parade* with Fred Astaire and Judy Garland. Really very exciting. Cocktail-cum-buffet party for me given by the Jules Steins. Very enjoyable. Long talk with the MCA boys and Bette Davis re *The Marquise*[10].

1 Alfred Hitchcock (1899-1980), the British film director; knighted in 1980.
2 James Stewart (b. 1908), the American film actor, who was playing the lead in *Rope*.
3 Mahatma Gandhi (1869-1948), the Indian nationalist leader.
4 Of Joan Crawford, one of whom was to write a sensational best-seller about her, *Mommie Dearest*; the films shown all starred Miss Crawford.
5 Hjordis, a Swedish model.
6 Deborah Kerr (b. 1921), the British film star, had married war hero Anthony Bartley in 1945.
7 Katherine Hepburn (b. 1907); the American film star was a much loved friend of Noël's.
8 Claudette Colbert (b. 1905), French-born actress resident in America; she had starred in *Tonight is Ours* (1932), a just recognizable film version of Noël's play *The Queen was in the Parlour*.
9 Gene Kelly (b. 1912), American dancer and Hollywood star.
10 The play written by Noël in 1926 which the American actress Bette Davis (b. 1908) was now thinking of filming; she never did.

Sunday 8 February

Set off with Graham, Fanny and Howard[1] for Tia Juana[2]. Lovely drive and wonderful scenery. Arrived at the border, lots of argument, finally got across.

Monday 9 February

Breakfast at eight downstairs with Fanny, and back over the border. We got through all right, Graham with his quota number and me with my visa renewed for a year. On the way back Fanny, as usual, talked incessantly for four hours and I suddenly revolted in my mind against her and Del[3] and all these people who are trying to promote me and cash in on me.

After a rest at the hotel, dined with Clifton and Mabelle[4] and then went to a private showing of his new picture, *Sitting Pretty*. He is really very good indeed and the picture is quite amusing if a trifle common. Afterwards we returned to the house and had a discussion about *Long Island Sound*[5] with George Cukor. For the second time in one day I suddenly realized something and that was that I would not do a picture in Hollywood. Both Clifton and George talked such balls that I knew I couldn't tolerate much more of it. There is something about the atmosphere here that is utterly defeating. I don't think I could bear it for longer than a brief visit.

Saturday 14 February

Took Gene Kelly to dine and to the theatre; performance fairly good. Then Clifton's for a little farewell drink. This ends my stay in Hollywood. I know I have been over-social and done far too much and have tired myself out. I also know that I could never really be happy here. I have liked it better than before but not enough. There is too much movie mentality about and it is all far too big.

Friday 20 February   New York

The opening[6]: masses of flowers and telegrams. A quite well-behaved audience. Gertie overplayed. Graham was better than he has ever been. I went on and made a speech which later Natasha told me had embarrassed her, why I cannot imagine. There was a terrific ovation at the end. Then Neysa's party which was very enjoyable, then home, dreadfully exhausted.

1 Howard Holtzmann, Fanny's nephew.
2 Mexico, where Graham's American work permit and Noël's visa could be more swiftly organized.
3 Both Fanny Holtzmann and Filippo del Giudice were full of plans at this time for Noël to settle and work in the States.
4 Clifton Webb's mother.
5 Which there was now talk of turning into a film.
6 Of *Tonight at 8.30* on Broadway.

Saturday 21 February

A bitter and horrible day. Filthy notices, all but two of them crucifying Graham. We didn't let him read the notices and I hope he never does. They were beastly about the plays and jolly beastly about him, which is grossly unfair.

I popped down to the theatre and gave a little pep talk to the company and then came back by myself, feeling good and miserable. Talked to Lorn in London. Dined quietly with Neysa and played bezique. Picked up Graham at the theatre and after a couple of drinks in the dressing-room came straight home. Graham's honesty and moral courage are remarkable and I feel a great respect for him.

Monday 23 February

In the theatre all day dress rehearsing. Opening night went extremely well[1]. Gertie was magical and Graham better than he has ever been. *Shadow Play* was really triumphant. Everyone very enthusiastic and sweet. Reunion with Alfred Willmore, now Micheal Mac Liammoir[2].

Tuesday 24 February

Woke with hangover and nerves at 8.45. Collected the morning papers and read the reviews which were abusive all right. Not so bad for Gertie but insulting to Graham and to me. Obviously I mind dreadfully about this. It's a sock in the jaw. Later Jack appeared and couldn't have been nicer, but we were really dreadfully low. Evening notices a bit better but I don't think they are good enough. I fear we are a flop. Now, as far as I am concerned, the sooner we close the better, and then for Jamaica and some sun and some peace.

Tuesday 2 March

Dined with Leonora [Corbett], who took me to see Maurice Chevalier[3]. He was mostly wonderful, but overplayed once or twice. Afterwards we had supper at the El Morocco, which was surprisingly peaceful. Graham arrived and told me that the business tonight was $1,500. That spells disaster. Fanny is frantically trying to pull the wool over everyone's eyes including Lee Shubert's[4] and her own. It is immensely silly not to face the fact that we are a flop. Poor Graham is still behaving magnificently but he is miserable inside.

1 Of the second set of plays that made up the *Tonight at 8.30* sequence.
2 Micheal Mac Liammoir (1901–78), first known as Alfred Willmore, the actor who had been with Noël when they both made their first stage appearances in 1910, and who was now achieving fame as the leading Irish actor-manager of his generation.
3 In cabaret.
4 Lee Shubert (1875–1953), American impresario and theatre owner.

Wednesday 3 March

Lunched with Max Gordon[1], who was his usual, explosively theatrical self. Dropped in to the matinée. Terrible business. Went home and wrote long letters to Binkie and Joyce. Went to Kitty Miller's cocktail party. Talked to Loelia [Westminster] about Ian Fleming's house in Jamaica[2]. It sounds marvellous. He is arriving on Saturday for only twenty-four hours and I must get hold of him at all costs.

Sunday 7 March

The day started peacefully enough and ended, or almost ended, in a sea of horror. Howard and Russell[3] came in looking rather battered. Gertie and the Holtzmanns[4] have been badgering them to keep the show on and take it on tour. Gertie is apparently frantic, poor darling, and offered to play without salary and stand all financial losses. This, of course, is idiotic. Neither of the boys wants to risk the odium of losing her money.

Then I took Graham to hear Maurice Chevalier, who was not as good as he was last time. Then we went on to Leonard Sillman's[5] where there was a frightening party in progress. Harris[6] told me that Louella Parsons[7] had announced over the air that Gertie and I were quarrelling because I had led Graham forward on the opening night and ignored her. This made me feel actively sick. When I told Graham afterwards he flew into a passion; then we both calmed down and decided to rise above it. For sheer baseless malice it takes a lot of beating. We decided dispassionately that this country is really doomed if that sort of muck is encouraged. If there was even a small grain of truth behind it, it would be bad enough, but as Gertie has been behaving like an angel throughout and I am racking my brains trying to think of a new play for her, it is a little hard. It is hardest of all on Graham, but his honesty and horse-sense saved us both.

Saturday 13 March

Went to the theatre to see *Red Peppers* for the last time. Wildly enthusiastic audience. Gertie wonderful in spite of being practically voiceless. The usual 'what a sin to close' dialogue backstage. Then a company supper party in my apartment. Everyone nice.

1 Max Gordon (1892–1978), Broadway impresario.
2 Which Noël was hoping to rent for a few weeks' holiday.
3 Howard Young and Russell Lewis, the producers of *Tonight at 8.30* on Broadway.
4 Fanny and her brother David, who were in business together.
5 Leonard Sillman, American theatre producer.
6 Jed Harris, Broadway producer.
7 Louella Parsons, gossip columnist with Hearst newspapers.

Monday 22 March   Jamaica

Ship arrived five hours late and rammed the pier[1]. Was met by an ADC from King's House[2]. We achieved all our shopping and I got a driving licence and some money from the bank. Then we set off to Oracabessa[3]. We arrived just before dusk. It is quite perfect; a large sitting-room sparsely furnished, comfortable beds and showers, an agreeable staff, a small private coral beach with lint white sand and warm clear water. The beach is unbelievable. We swam, after a delicious dinner, and lay on the sand unchilled under a full moon. So far, it all seems far too good to be true.

Wednesday 24 March

A cloudless and peerless day. More swimming and sunbathing, more searching for coloured fish, this time in a rubber boat.

Afternoon offset for me by having a slight stomach ache; nothing serious, probably a chill from too much immersion. Painted a bit in the early evening and then discussed, over drinks, the possibility of building a shack somewhere isolated on this island and how wonderful it would be to have such an idyllic bolt-hole to return to when life became too frustrating. The climate is so equable and lovely. There are no insects or pests. There is, above all, peace. I am thinking very seriously about all this. Something tells me that the time has come to make a few plans for escape in the future.

Wednesday 31 March

Started definitely on *Future Indefinite*, beginning with my Central European trip in 1939.

Monday 5 April

We caught and murdered an octopus, or rather a small squid. I did three hours' work and have now completed twenty-nine neat pages. Nothing further to say beyond the fact that the stars are enormous and very bright and infinity is going on all round and I don't really mind a bit about the notices of *Tonight at 8.30*.

Sunday 18 April

The day dead calm and very hot. Went over to the property[4] and explored the bathing possibilities which really are much better than I thought. I do feel

1 At Kingston.
2 The Governor's residence.
3 Where Ian Fleming had his house, Goldeneye, rechristened by Noël Golden Eye, Nose and Throat after he had decided that it had all the discomforts of a bad hospital.
4 Some land outside Port Maria which Noël had now decided to buy; it was to be his place in the sun for many years.

that perhaps it is a good buy. It could be made so ravishing. Afternoon spent in making plans and curious house designs.

Monday 19 April

The die is cast. Now I must really admit how excited I am. If we dynamite the cove, it will bring white sand in. Sure it is a good buy. We stayed behind on the point and watched the sunset gilding the mountains and the sea. We also saw a double rainbow and for a few moments the whole land was bathed in a pinky gold light. We drove home through the spectacular sunset and I thought of a name for the house, Blue Harbour. It is a good name because it sounds nice and really describes the view. The house is to be built against the hill on different levels. It will be ready in December. I am very happy.

Tuesday 20 April

Mother's and Hitler's birthday. Worked a bit and lay in the sun.

Sunday 25 April

Graham's birthday, which we celebrated by going down to the lawyer and signing formally the contract for the land. I am now a property owner in Jamaica and it is jolly fine.

Saturday 8 May

Painted in the morning. In the afternoon drove up to Look Out[1] where there is some land at £10 an acre. It is enchanting; an old stone house, roofless but with thick walls and the most fabulous view. I want to buy it, ostensibly as a writing retreat but really with a view to making it lovely for the future, letting or selling Blue Harbour and living in it.

Friday 28 May

Further painting. Finished the first part of *Future Indefinite*. So far so good. Over 35,000 words.

Sunday 30 May

A melancholy day. Went, at sunset, to Blue Harbour and watched the mountains change colour. Gala dinner of soup, black crab, pork curry, sweet potatoes, rice and peas. It was very touching, and very filling. I hate the thought of leaving tomorrow. This has been a wonderful two months and I love this island.

1 A property above Blue Harbour.

Thursday 3 June   New York

Woke feeling nerve-shattered and hating everything to do with New York. Tea-cum-champagne with Gertie, Ray Massey[1], Beattie [Lillie], Mike Redgrave, etc., plus *Life* photographer.

Saturday 12 June

Talk with Nelson [Doubleday]. He insists on giving me a new Buick 8 for Jamaica, having it run in for a thousand miles or so, and shipping it out to me. He also wants me to make a list of any furniture, etc., that I may need. His generosity and kindness really are staggering. I do not know whether or not he will survive the lung cancer operation. I am desperately sorry for Ellen. She really loves him and it is hell for her.

Monday 21 June   London

Arrived at Southampton about 12.30. Greeted by Press with story reported by *Evening Standard* from New York that I was sick of England! Charming! I am getting sick of this Press persecution.

Drove up to London. Lorn waiting at the gate. Lovely to be back. Saw Mum, looking fine. Dinner at the Ivy with Joyce. Went to Binkie's, everyone sweet. Home Sweet Home.

Monday 28 June

Tennessee Williams[2] and Gore Vidal[3] came to dinner. Gore Vidal intelligent and charming, Tennessee less charming but curious. They both gave out a sort of 'end of the world' feeling; they were good company but doomed. I felt sorry for them on account of being happy and emotionally balanced myself.

Tuesday 29 June

Cold and rainy. The Garden Party![4] A heavy shower at midday and another at mid-afternoon. Everyone worked hard and on the whole it was successful and very exhausting.

---

1 Raymond Massey (b. 1896), Canadian-born actor, who had played with Noël in Behrman's *The Second Man* in 1928 and who made his name in America playing Abraham Lincoln on stage and screen. 'He will never really be happy again', said Noël later, 'until somebody shoots him.'

2 Tennessee Williams (b. 1911), the American dramatist; in this year he was awarded the Pulitzer prize for *A Streetcar Named Desire*.

3 Gore Vidal (b. 1925), American novelist and journalist, who had at this time already published *Williwaw* and *The City and the Pillar*.

4 In aid of the Actors' Orphanage of which Noël was still President.

Wednesday 30 June

Discovered that we had taken over £4,000 on the grounds yesterday. A pleasant surprise. If it had not been for the weather we would have made two thousand more.

In the evening dined with the Rothermeres. An enormous party. Sat next to Ian Fleming and had a long gossip about Jamaica. After the dinner we all adjourned to Alex Korda's[1] projection room and were shown *Diable au Corps*[2]. As an audience they were infuriating. None of them really understood it and many tried to be funny about it. It is rather frightening to see something fine and imaginative and true torn lightly to pieces by these sophisticates.

Saturday 3 July

Having read the first act of Roussin's[3] translation of *Present Laughter* [*Joyeux Chagrins*] I am seriously thinking of playing it in Paris in French for a month in November. It would be a terribly exciting adventure.

Thursday 8 July

Lunch with Derek Hill[4] in Hampstead. Saw all his new pictures; very, very good. Went to the Vuillard exhibition; glorious.

Rothermeres' cocktail party. Then went to *Hamlet*[5]. Larry magnificent but the whole thing too drawn out and I am sick of *Hamlet* anyway. Then on to the Mountbattens for a small, select party including Philip of Edinburgh and Sophie Tucker[6]. All highly enjoyable.

Thursday 22 July

Graham and I went to the Savoy to greet Lynn and Alfred, who were wonderful as always. Maggie Teyte[7] came to tea full of *Marquise* plans. Then the Orphanage cocktail party for the helpers. Better than I expected. Came home, changed, picked up Mollie Buccleuch[8] and took her to dine with Sibyl Colefax. A very good party including Dickie, Edwina, the Lunts, and the

---

1 Alexander Korda (1893-1956), the Hungarian film producer, had settled in Britain in 1930 and founded London Film Productions; knighted in 1942.
2 A tragic First World War love story directed by Autant-Lara and starring Gérard Philipe and Micheline Presle; made in 1946 it was the first major success of the post-war French cinema.
3 André Roussin (b. 1911), French comedy writer best known in England for *The Little Hut*.
4 Derek Hill (b. 1916), artist, who later painted an excellent portrait of Noël.
5 The new film version starring, produced and directed by Olivier.
6 Sophie Tucker (1888-1966), the popular American singer.
7 Maggie Teyte (1888-1976), opera singer, created Dame 1958; she wished to revive Noël's *The Marquise* as a musical, but never did.
8 Mollie, Duchess of Buccleuch (b. 1910).

Lewis Douglases[1]. Terrific conversation between Lew and Dickie after dinner about the war situation. Really brilliant, with them both on their toes. Lew, I thought, won because there was a little underlying Russian sympathy in Dickie's arguments.

Wednesday 28 July

London has now become New York in a heat wave. Old ladies dying like flies in all directions and the Government warning us of drought and water shortage. In the morning a meeting of the Festival of Britain Council[2]. Much time wasted but a certain amount achieved. Quick lunch with Lynn and Alfred and then back to the meeting. Home to rest. Took Gladys, Lorn and Graham to the opening of *The Glass Menagerie*[3] at the Haymarket. Helen Hayes's first appearance in England. She was absolutely wonderful, a flawless and touching performance. The rest of the cast first rate, but play directed too slowly by John [Gielgud]. Party afterwards at Sibyl Colefax's.

Friday 30 July

Katie Hepburn came to lunch and was, as usual, enchanting. Actors' Orphanage meeting. Picked up Alfred, Lynn and Graham at the Savoy and drove them down to White Cliffs.

Sunday 1 August

Charles and Ham[4] appeared in the afternoon. They want to start their management with a tour of *Fallen Angels*[5]. I have agreed.

Monday 30 August

Came up to London with Hermione Baddeley[6]. Took Doug, Mary Lee and Graham to dine at the Caprice and on to the Palladium for Dinah Shore's[7] opening night. She had a terrific ovation and was very charming.

Wednesday 8 September

Lorn rang up early in the morning to say that poor Gladys had really broken

1 Lewis Douglas, US Ambassador to Britain 1947–50, and his wife Peggy.
2 Noël was on one of the planning committees until he resigned in protest at the 'shambolic bureaucracy'.
3 Tennessee Williams's play (1945).
4 Charles Russell and Lance Hamilton, who had stage-managed Noël's wartime tours of England with *Present Laughter* and *This Happy Breed*.
5 Noël's play written in 1923 and first produced in 1925.
6 Hermione Baddeley (b. 1906), comedienne, who had appeared in Noël's revue *On with the Dance* in 1925.
7 Dinah Shore, popular American singer.

down badly and been clapped into a nursing home at Swiss Cottage. I went up by the 10.30 and interviewed the doctor. Apparently she is fairly bad. She has been bottling everything up for weeks. It is obviously part of change of life and will pass off in time, but I am desperately sorry for her and very worried.

Friday 10 September

Went to see Gladys. She was infinitely pathetic and lonely, and it upset me inside very much indeed. I talked to her for nearly an hour and I think did some good. It is terrible to see someone you love in any sort of mental state.

Tuesday 14 September   Paris

A morning of great *va et vient* and confusion[1]. Actors and actresses arriving to read scenes and buggering off again. The young man for Roland Maule rehearsing by himself in the dining-room at the top of his lungs. Came home and rested. Gave a cocktail party: Maggie Case, George Schlee, Pam Churchill[2], Charlie MacArthur[3], Doug Fairbanks, Cary Grant[4], etc.

Thursday 16 September

Today in walked Nadia Gray[5]. Extremely attractive, very intelligent and read so well that I decided on her then and there.

Tuesday 21 September   London

Went to see Joyce, who had just come back from Lilian's funeral and really was wonderful[6].

Wednesday 29 September   Paris

Morning of appalling nerves. Really quite idiotic. First rehearsal. Chaos at first. Stage not possible, so we had to make do with the foyer. Got through the first act without the book. Second act more rocky. Nadia Gray very good. Rest of cast OK, I think. Quick drink with [Elsa] Schiaparelli, then dined with Cole[7], Rex and Lilli[8] at Yvonne *et* André Roussin's.

1 Noël was casting *Joyeux Chagrins*, which he was about to direct as well as star in.
2 Pamela Churchill, née Digby (b. 1920), married to Randolph Churchill 1939–46.
3 Charles MacArthur (1895–1956), American playwright and screenwriter.
4 Cary Grant (b. 1904), English-born Hollywood star.
5 Nadia Gray (b. 1923), Russian-Romanian actress who later starred in many European films.
6 Dame Lilian Braithwaite, Joyce Carey's mother, had died on 17 September.
7 Cole Porter (1893–1964), the American songwriter, greatly admired by Noël who had known him since the 1920s.
8 Rex Harrison (b. 1908), the British actor, and Lilli Palmer (b. 1914), the German actress to whom he was then married.

Friday 1 October

Photographed by *Vogue* all the morning. Rehearsed very hard until a quarter to seven. Really exhausted. The concentration required to rehearse in French for four and a half hours without a pause is a great strain.

Friday 15 October

Dined at Versailles. Edward [Molyneux] was there and Barbara Hutton[1], the Bemelmans[2], the Windsors, etc. Long heart-to-heart with the Duchess at dinner. Drove back with Edward.

Wednesday 27 October   Brussels

Well, the adventure has started. Four hours in an unheated train on account of the strike. Very, very cold indeed. Arrived in Bruxelles[3]. Hotel quite nice. Rehearsed after a short rest. Set perfectly frightful, so bad that it is funny. Made scene at the end of rehearsal on discovering that the theatre is not only occupied tonight[4] but tomorrow night as well, and we open on Friday. However, I don't really mind. I need an audience now and if we all look a bit tatty at first it cannot be helped.

Sunday 31 October

Two performances. Matinée rather heavy-going but good practice. Evening much better except that in the second act I was faced with them[5] all choking with laughter. I have seldom been so angry. The French theatre is certainly undisciplined to an alarming degree. If anyone I respected had been in front I would have been for ever shamed. All the management have disappeared, we have no understudies with us and nobody cares.

Saturday 6 November   Paris

Arrived in Paris 6.15. My voice is really awful, virtually non-existent. Went to bed feeling very worried.

Monday 8 November

Mother, Graham and Sybil [Payn] all on the ferry which was held up by fog and rough seas. They all finally arrived at 3.30. Also Joyce, by air. Electrical treatment by Dr Grain, in course of which he assured me that my voice was vastly improved and that I could use it with ease tomorrow night. I had difficulty in thanking him, being virtually speechless.

1 Barbara Hutton, American Woolworth heiress.
2 Madeline and Ludwig Bemelman; he was an Austrian writer living in the United States best known for his 'Madeline' books, named after his wife.
3 Where, prior to Paris, he was trying out *Joyeux Chagrins*.
4 By another production.
5 i.e. the cast.

Arrived at the theatre at 8.30. Chaos. The whole place was alive with jazz musicians who had been giving a radio show. Waited about in mounting fury. Finally started. Got through the first act sweating with the effort and with my voice rapidly going. Finally gave up and knew I could not open tomorrow or the next day or even this week. General consternation.

Got home and decided to go into hospital tomorrow. Gladys, Cole and Graham all wonderful.

Friday 12 November

I am a bit better and suppose I shall be all right by next week. Reading Winston's book *The Gathering Storm*. Superb from every point of view.

Monday 15 November

Princess Elizabeth has had a son[1]. Jolly nice for her and Philip.

Wednesday 17 November

In the evening played the play to the most chic, smart, glamorous and truly awful audience that I have ever known in my life. Apparently it was a great success. I was almost bored. Not nervous but extremely irritated. I gave a good technical comedy performance and my French was good. I got a big reception but the whole thing was an uphill fight. My personal opinion is that I made a success but they did not like or understand the play.

Thursday 18 November

One vile notice. Some others very good. Not sure, however, that the play is a success. Masses of flowers from everyone. Worried about voice, but it felt fine during the evening performance. Public better but they are not very amused with the play.

Friday 26 November

Did letters with Lorn. Lunched alone. Did a six-minute broadcast to America with Mrs Roosevelt[2], whom I love.

Saturday 27 November

Lorn left for London. Lunched with Roussin and Nadia. I love Roussin; he is a genuinely sweet character. Evening performance very good. Play went well but we are not a success really and apparently the weekly Press has been vile. All left-wing and attacking me personally. I certainly seem to be going through a bad patch these years but I don't intend to let it get me down. All the same,

---

1 Prince Charles, later Prince of Wales.
2 Eleanor Roosevelt, now widowed, was in Paris as chairman of the United Nations commission on human rights.

it is disappointing. I expected a warm and loving welcome from Paris and got a sock in the kisser. Heigh-ho.

Monday 29 November

Lunched with Coco Chanel[1]. Not a good word spoken about anyone but very funny.

Wednesday 1 December

Perfectly lovely morning. Diana [Cooper] and I went for a long walk in the Parc de Chantilly. The air was mauve and blue and the trees were hung with frost. It was quite breathlessly beautiful.

Evening perfect agony. Bad audience, theatre half empty. Very hard to bear. Went out with Nadia, Roussin and Orson Welles[2]. The play is a flop and it is no use pretending for one instant that it is not. Personally I want to close as soon as possible and call it a day. Roussin tells me that the day I was taken ill and couldn't be photographed the Press took against me. Personally I am convinced that, although the Press have been cruel, the truth is that the French people didn't care for the play. It is, of course, bitterly disappointing. I suppose this succession of failures is good for my soul but I rather doubt it. I feel depressed tonight. I know it will pass and fade into its right perspective, but the disappointment of having worked so hard, having had the bad luck to be ill and then having a flop is a little heavy on the heart.

Wednesday 15 December

Graham and Nancy Mitford[3] and I drove out to Chantilly to lunch with Diana and Duff, both of whom could not have been sweeter. Evening performance all right but not sensational. Came home and received lovely presents from Graham and Cole. Talked to Binkie and Gertie in London. She has apparently had a wonderful ovation[4]. Well, well. I am now in my fiftieth year.

Thursday 16 December

A happy birthday. Read Gertie's rave notices, which gave me deep pleasure. Audience good. In the first entr'acte the entire company came in *en masse* singing 'Happy Birthday' and bearing three bottles of champagne on ice. I was very touched. Everley Gregg[5] also appeared. Quite an evening.

1 Coco Chanel (1883-1971), French fashion designer.
2 Orson Welles (b. 1915), American actor-writer-producer, who was in Europe for the filming of *The Third Man*.
3 Nancy Mitford (1904-73), English novelist, now resident in France.
4 In Daphne du Maurier's play *September Tide*.
5 Everley Gregg, English actress who had appeared in a number of Noël's plays.

Wednesday 22 December

Evening performance all right but second act bitched by the noise of the night-club opening above. Made a great scene and the orchestra was stopped until the end of the play. After the play went with the Cottens[1] to the club upstairs. A lash-up. Mr Becker, a film director, had pinched my table. Waited in passage until everything straightened out. A young Austrian came up to me, said he admired me very much and wanted to kiss me. I evaded the issue firmly but politely. Finally we went in and spent an hour of supreme discomfort amidst a terrible noise and dreadful heat. As we left, the aforementioned young man rushed at me and kissed me firmly and a Press photographer clicked his camera. It was too obviously a frame-up so I got the photographer to take the film out of his camera. It was all arranged by a charming gentleman from *Samedi Soir*, the dirtiest paper in Paris.

Sunday 26 December

Well, that's that. Two very good performances to very sparse audiences. Gave party afterwards for the company. A great success. Larry and Vivien came and Joe, Lenore and Orson. Everyone drank a lot and the residue left at about 5 a.m. I am sorry to say goodbye to them, but I am immensely relieved not to have to play any more to these dreary audiences. On looking back I know now that I should have played out for a few weeks before opening in Paris. If I had played on the opening night like I have been playing for the last week or two the result might well have been very different.

Wednesday 29 December   London

A loving welcome at Gerald Road. Mum in fine fettle. Joyce, Gladys, Lorn and I lunched at the Ivy. Called on Winnie, who is bright and well. Went with Graham to see *September Tide*. Play dreadful, Michael Gough brilliantly good, Gertie really beyond all praise. I have never seen her play so beautifully or with such heart and truth. She moved me very much. I have quite decided that we must act together again in the autumn.

Thursday 30 December

Long morning with Lorn discussing finance, etc. Lunched with Sydney Box and arranged to do the little extra dialogue required for *The Astonished Heart* for £10,000 on account of ten per cent after the production is paid[2]. Also discussed the film of *Tonight at 8.30* for the summer. *Fumed Oak*, Kathleen Harrison and Jack Warner; *Family Album*, Margaret Leighton and Graham;

1 Joseph Cotten (b. 1905), American actor, and his wife Lenore, who had just returned from Vienna where Joe, with Orson Welles, had been filming *The Third Man*.
2 Sydney Box was then setting up film versions of *The Astonished Heart* and a compilation of three other plays from *Tonight at 8.30*.

and *Red Peppers*, Cis Courtneidge and Jack Hulbert[1]. Graham is to play in two pictures (small parts) starting 21 February, which means he can come to Jamaica.

Friday 31 December

Went to Binkie's party, drank in the New Year, and that is that.

---

1 In the event *Fumed Oak* was played by Betty Ann Davies and Stanley Holloway, *Red Peppers* by Ted Ray and Kay Walsh, and *Family Album* was replaced by *Ways and Means* with Valerie Hobson and Nigel Patrick. The film was called *Meet Me Tonight*.

1949

For an actor-playwright who had once been in absolute charge of his career
and of those whom it embraced, this was a thoroughly chastening year.
Gertrude Lawrence declined to play his Samolan comedy Home and
Colonial *because a London season would not suit her tax situation; John
Clements declined it because the leading male role proved insufficiently
leading; and the impresario Prince Littler informed Coward that if one of
his theatres was to house Noël's new musical (known this year by a variety
of titles but eventually called* Ace of Clubs), *then it would need to be
rewritten, as it was not yet 'up to standard'. For a man of almost fifty to
encounter the kind of refusals and criticism he had last met in his early
twenties cannot have been easy on either self-esteem or morale; yet the diary
reveals Noël's customary resilience, with only an occasional yelp of anguished
pride.*

*Jamaica was proving a considerable consolation, and there was still
enough of the fighting spirit left in Noël for him to oust a miscast Michael
Redgrave from the leading role in the film of his* The Astonished Heart
*and take it over himself. On the typewriter there was now a comedy, a
musical and a collection of short stories. He was not approaching his half-
century in a mood of anything remotely resembling relaxation, despite the
discovery of a place in the sun, but he was well aware that he was at an
all-time professional low and was increasingly inclined to turn towards a
short story or his second volume of autobiography, where at least he could
be sure of publication without protracted negotiation.*

*On stage in London the two Hermiones – Baddeley and Gingold – were
making what he considered a mockery (though a great financial success) of*

Fallen Angels, *while in America Tallulah Bankhead continued to play* Private Lives. *Significantly one song Noël wrote during the year contained the lines 'When the storm clouds are riding/Through a winter sky/Sail Away' and he frequently did just that.*

Monday 3 January   White Cliffs

Got up at eight o'clock and finished *The Astonished Heart*. Did some good work on it. After lunch took Joyce to the station then Graham and I drove over to see Gladys. She really has made her house very sweet but it was perishing cold. She is happy as a bee with it and completely well again.

Wednesday 5 January   London

Dined with Gladys and went to the first night of Sid Field in *Harvey*[1]. He was really magnificent and had a terrific ovation. So did Athene [Seyler], who was extremely good.

Tuesday 11 January

Dingo [Bateson] came to lunch and he and Lorn and I made several momentous decisions: not to buy White Cliffs; to raise a mortgage on Goldenhurst[2] if possible; to keep Fanny [Holtzmann] on provided she does not go too far.

Went to American Consulate, where, as usual, I was treated with the utmost courtesy. Met Graham Greene[3] at long last and belaboured him for being vile about me in the past. Actually he was rather nice.

Saturday 15 January

Worked with Robb [Stewart] and dictated new tunes. Lunched with Gladys. Had long heart-to-heart and told her firmly but lovingly about her tendency to arrogance in the theatre. She was calm and good and took it like a lamb. It had to be done, for her sake.

In the evening she and the Nivens and I dined at Les Ambassadeurs and had a lovely gossipy evening. I talked to Frank Owen[4], who was extremely nice and suggested that I make a gesture to Max Beaverbrook, as he is an old man and desirous of settling old feuds in order, apparently, to join the feathered choir in the odour of sanctity. I shall see how I feel.

Tuesday 18 January

Visited Sibyl Colefax. Talked to Gertie at the Savoy. Lunched at home with Graham and Gladys. Tea with Mum and horribly touching goodbye[5]. I know that in her mind was the thought that she might not see me again. When you are rising eighty-six death is always drawing nearer. She behaved beautifully and I left her with a sad heart.

---

1 Mary Chase's Broadway hit now at the Prince of Wales Theatre.
2 To pay for the necessary repairs to it.
3 Graham Greene (b. 1904), distinguished British novelist and playwright.
4 Frank Owen, one of Max Beaverbrook's editors.
5 He was off to New York and then Jamaica.

Wednesday 19 January   ss *Queen Elizabeth*

Left in good order. Lots of people on board. Loelia Westminster, Evelyn Waugh[1], etc. Max very amiable and asked me to stay with him at Montego[2]. Coco Chanel got on at Cherbourg.

Friday 21 January

No sign of hurricane; sea calmed down. Coco Chanel lunched and we had an entertaining gossip. After dinner further conversation with Max, who was more charming than ever. He is a witty old bastard, and though he has done me much harm I can't help finding him excellent company.

Monday 24 January   New York

Usual last morning agitation. Got through everything smoothly. Met by Natasha, who broke the news that Jack has been and still is very ill. It is purported to be arthritis[3]. He arrived at the hotel looking thinner and papery. He was very sweet. Later we had a drink with Neysa, who I thought looked gallant and weary.

Dined with Jack and Natasha and went to *Kiss Me Kate*[4]. The score is fine, the lyrics brilliant but too dirty, the book vulgar and dull. Alfred Drake superb and Jack's production excellent, fast moving and in good taste. Afterwards drinks with Cole [Porter]. I know now, suddenly, that I hate this town. There is too much bitchiness and cruelty. Before the war it was stimulating and exciting, now I find it merely irritating and noisy and somehow depressing. I don't feel any more that I particularly want to be a success here.

Wednesday 26 January

Long morning telephoning. Marlene came looking lovely and was gay and sweet as ever. Dinner with Arnold Weissberger and Milton Goldman[5]. They took me to *Lend an Ear*[6], a really very good revue. Wonderful dancing and a young cast full of talent. Drink and gossip with Tallulah, who was sweet and talkative as usual.

Saturday 29 January

Lunch party at the Pavillon with Cole [Porter], Marlene, Elsa [Maxwell], Leonora [Corbett] and Graham. Matinée of *Private Lives*. Tallulah overacting violently. House packed and play went really marvellously.

1 Evelyn Waugh (1903–66), English novelist and satirist.
2 Max Beaverbrook had a Jamaican home at Montego Bay.
3 Noël took the view that it was alcoholism.
4 Cole Porter's musical based on *The Taming of the Shrew*.
5 Arnold Weissberger (1907–81), theatrical lawyer and photographer, and Milton Goldman (b. 1914), actors' agent; a celebrated New York partnership.
6 By Charles Gaynor.

Sunday 30 January

To party for Eisenhower[1]. He was charming and talked to me like an old friend. Everyone sang and played and it was a good party, although too crowded at first.

Monday 31 January

Blizzard going on. Lunched with Mike Todd[2], who is very amusing. I like him. Dinner with Marlene, Neysa and Graham and then *La Folle de Chaillot*[3], superbly played by Martita Hunt.

Party at Maggie Case's with Charles Boyer[4], Ruth and Gar[5], Valentina, Cecil [Beaton], Beverley[6], etc. Irene Selznick[7] dropped me home.

Thursday 3 February   Jamaica

Caught the 8.15 plane for Jamaica. Very smooth except for two beastly children who screamed and stamped up and down.

The house is entrancing. I can't believe it is mine, and everyone concerned had taken immense trouble and it really was much more ready than I had anticipated. After various inspecting and interviewing of staff, we went over to call on Ian and Ann[8], who were welcoming and sweet. Back home, we had one more martini and sat on the verandah on rockers, looking out over the fabulous view, and almost burst into tears of sheer pleasure.

Wednesday 9 February

Worked on *Play Parade*[9] preface. Went into Port Maria and ordered some more things[10]. Rest of day spent fussing about and receiving the truck-load of stuff we bought yesterday. Worried about the Surbiton look of the sitting room. It is quite definitely 'Kozy Kot'[11]. Something must be done.

Thursday 17 February

Lunched with Max Beaverbrook who, I must say, couldn't have been nicer.

1 General Dwight Eisenhower (1880-1969), who became US President in 1952.
2 Mike Todd (1907-58), American film and stage producer of considerable flamboyance.
3 Giraudoux's play *The Madwoman of Chaillot* (1945).
4 Charles Boyer (1899-1978), French actor long resident in Hollywood.
5 Ruth Gordon (b. 1896), American actress, married to writer Garson Kanin (b. 1912), with whom she collaborated on several screenplays.
6 Beverley Nichols (b. 1901), English journalist and novelist, who like Noël had been a playboy of the West End world in the 1920s.
7 Irene Selznick (b. 1910), stage producer, daughter of the Hollywood tycoon Louis B. Mayer and once married to producer David Selznick.
8 At Goldeneye, where Ann Rothermere was staying with Ian Fleming.
9 Volume Three of his Collected Plays.
10 For the new house, Blue Harbour.
11 Suburban English, an accusation later levelled by Rebecca West at his final Swiss residence.

He took me to see Ivor's house[1], which is quite, quite horrid. What a fool he is. It is shut in, with not even a decent view of the sea, and is exactly like a suburban villa.

Sunday 20 February

Really lovely day rafting down the Rio Grande[2]. It was great fun. The sun didn't come out much but it was beautifully hot and we splashed about and drank rum and picnicked, then Ian drove Graham and me home and was vastly entertaining all the way.

Saturday 26 February

Made a vow to give up drinking. I don't need it, I don't particularly like it, it makes me feel dull and heavy particularly in this climate, it is fattening and boring, and so no more of it.

The painters have finished the living-room; shrimp-pink and white and I must say it looks charming.

Bill and Barbara Paley[3] and Vincent and Minnie Astor[4] came to lunch and were all absolutely sweet. The lunch was simple and good. I made the iced soup myself.

Tuesday 8 March

Went up to Look Out[5] and decided I must have at least ten acres. It is a lovely place and the view is beyond words. The land is rich in fruit: guavas, avocados, limes, oranges, custard apples, mangoes, etc. I have a feeling that that place will mean much to me in the future.

Thursday 10 March

Finished *A Richer Dust*[6]. Fairly good, I think. Read it to Jack, Natasha and Graham after lunch and they liked it. Now I've got to type and revise it.

Monday 21 March

Rapprochement with Gladys Cooper and John Buckmaster[7] on the beach.

1 Ivor Novello had also bought a Jamaican property.
2 One of Jamaica's tourist highlights.
3 William Paley, Chairman of CBS, and his wife, Barbara Cushing Mortimer.
4 Vincent Astor, head of the Astor family in the US, and his wife, Mary Benedict Cushing.
5 Later called Firefly.
6 His new short story, about an English actor escaping the war by remaining in Hollywood; published in *Star Quality* (1951).
7 Gladys Cooper (1888–1971), English actress, created Dame 1967, and her son John Buckmaster (b. 1915); Noël had first got to know her in the early 1920s and, despite occasional quarrels, they remained friends.

Very glad really because I hate feuds. Lunched with Bill Stephenson[1]. Too many martinis. Slept in the afternoon. More martinis.

Sunday 27 March

Graham left this morning. I shall miss him dreadfully. Ivor, Bobby [Andrews], Olive[2] and Zena [Dare] arrived. After lunch we bounced about on the beach, and at approximately 3.40 Graham's plane went over and we all waved. I took them to Look Out and to see Gladys's house[3], which they loathed. Pleasant gossipy evening.

Monday 28 March

Woke at 6 a.m. Nobody appeared until 8.30. We all went into Port Maria. The day passed pleasantly. None of them was any trouble. Before dinner I read them firmly *A Richer Dust*. It really is a good story. After dinner Ivor played a lot of his new score[4]. Most of it is very good and beautifully professional. One song particularly, 'The Snow Princess', beautifully sung by Olive. I have enjoyed their stay.

Saturday 2 April

Had a long think about what I really want to do. A play for Gertie, or for me or for both, short stories, a book or a musical? Wrote three lyric refrains for 'Josephine'. Worked at the piano. Suddenly a new and lovely tune appeared. Felt the authentic thrill. All right, the musical it shall be.

Wednesday 6 April

Suddenly, while re-reading *Vile Bodies*[5], an idea for a comedy for Gertie fell into my mind. It rang a loud bell, so I constructed it then and there and everything seemed to fall into place. The title is *Home and Colonial*; theme – Lady 'Sandra' Magnus (Diana-Edwina)[6], Government House, Samolo; scandal with local Bustamente. There is more to it than that, but it's a heaven-sent opportunity to get in a lot of Jamaican stuff. Felt really happy. Painted a picture.

---

1 Sir William Stephenson, Canadian millionaire, who in 1941, as head of British Intelligence in the US, had offered Noël a job, which was retracted by Churchill before Noël could take it up.
2 Olive Gilbert (d. 1981), who with Robert Andrews and Zena Dare was a member of Ivor Novello's semi-permanent stage team; all of them were staying with him in Jamaica and were now on a visit to Noël.
3 Gladys Calthrop had also bought a Jamaican property.
4 *King's Rhapsody*.
5 Evelyn Waugh's novel, published in 1930.
6 Diana Cooper and Edwina Mountbatten were models for the central character.

Tuesday 12 April

Interesting morning. Went to the Port Maria Hospital and watched a big abdominal operation (short circuit) with only a local anaesthetic. It was strange and macabre to talk to the patient who, although frightened, was completely conscious and out of pain, while his entire stomach was outside his body and being treated like an unwieldy Christmas parcel. He couldn't see what was going on and, apart from some slight pain during the preliminary injection, he felt nothing at all. His whole organism, however, was affected by shock because I watched his eyes and also the sudden acute trembling of his body. The advantage of the local as opposed to the general is that the after-effects are negligible; no gas pains and gradual, peaceful recovery without vomiting and the danger of bursting stitches. The human body is a most extraordinary mechanism. I watched those pulsating, throbbing organs and tissues being cruelly set upon with steel and catgut, and was once more amazed at the body's capacity for healing itself. When the stitched and operated-upon areas were done with, they seemed to slip back inside with an almost audible sigh of relief, so that they could get on with the business of healing in their own way.

Wednesday 27 April

Started second act and did eight pages. Much better and easier. In spite of good work done I feel livery and not very well. A grey day, too, with rain and wind. Also the news is horrid. The Communists in China firing on our ships and killing our sailors and Mr Attlee doing nothing. The Communist faith is obviously sweeping a great part of the world. What fools people are. Don't they see what a hideous autocracy it is? It is all pretty gloomy and means another war either now or a little later. I think it will be a death-blow to our idiotic civilization, and a bloody good job too if we can't manage life better than we have done.

Sunday 1 May

Ever since I recovered from flu in Paris[1] I have been troubled with heartburn and indigestion. Since I have been here it has been intermittently bad. There are many excellent reasons: I smoke too much, I work too hard and eat too little. I have lost about ten pounds since I arrived, which was intentional. In moments of depression I wonder if anything organic is causing it. I don't really believe it is, because I should feel steadily worse if it were, but I am putting this on record for future reference as it has now been in my mind for months. I will have a thorough check over when I get back to London. I am working hard here and it is an additional effort because of the climate. I am rising fifty

[1] Six months earlier.

and I suppose it is inevitable that I should begin to feel a little of the lethargy of age.

Tuesday 3 May

Worked from 7 a.m. onwards and finished the play at five o'clock. It is very funny I think, but it has been extraordinarily hard work. Whenever Gertie (Sandra) was on, it floated easily but the rest has been tricky. Sandra is a glorious part. My only deep fear is that Gertie may overplay it. It needs everything she has got plus taste. Anyhow, the job is done and I am exhausted but I feel better.

I do like the Jamaicans. Fortunately they like me too and I couldn't be more pleased that they do.

Wednesday 4 May

Telegrams from Gertie and Binkie, enthusiastic but explaining that, owing to Gertie's tax troubles, she cannot appear in London before next April. She wants to open the play in America. This is disaster. It is typically English and topical and now is the time for it. Gertie might get away with it in America but half the point would be lost.

Friday 13 May

Neysa McMein is dead. She died after or during her second operation yesterday. I spent a lonely, wretched day unable to concentrate on anything but the thought that I would never see Neysa again. I so wanted her to come here next year and see the house and play games and laugh as we have done for so many years. New York will be dreadful for me without her. I had just written ordering her to cancel all engagements for the week I was there as she always does. Fortunately she got the letter and it made her laugh. This was just after her first operation. I suspect it was cancer and her poor old heart couldn't stand the shock of two operations one after the other. Perhaps if she had pulled through she would have been an invalid for the rest of her life, which she would have so very much hated. If so, it was better that she died. She has always cancelled every engagement for me; this one she could not cancel. I shall miss her always. She was warm and good and kind and true and, above all, gay. I have a feeling that the last years have been difficult for her but she was far too gallant ever to admit it. I feel a dreadful sense of loss but I must be prepared and armed for the future. I shall be fifty in December, and as one gets older people begin to die and when each one goes a little light goes out. I owe Neysa years of enchanting friendship and so much laughter and so many wonderful jokes. She adored me and would have done anything in the world for me. It is not surprising that I should not love America as much as I used to. So many of my friends have gone: Alec[1], Alice Duer Miller[2], Bob Ben-chley[3], Bee Kaufman[4], all the ones who made it particularly gay for me. Now Neysa, whom I loved more than any of them. I shall never forget her. And now, I intend to rise above it and get on with everything. This has been a dreadful day.

Thursday 26 May

Arrived New York 10.30 and went to the flat. Drink with Jack at '21' and went to *South Pacific*[5]. A very good show, not as miraculous as it is supposed to be, but a great deal to it. Mary was perfectly enchanting. Afterwards Mary and Dick and I had a reunion. It was really touching. Mary was genuinely in tears, and truly happy and relieved that we were making up. I feel as though a weight had been lifted from me. I hate quarrels and feuds, and she had a bloody time in England and I have felt uncomfortable and unhappy about it. Now all that is over and I could not be more pleased.

Wednesday 1 June

Interviewed Gower Champion[6] at the office. He seemed sensible and nice. I do hope he will be able to come to London to do *Over the Garden Wall*[7]. He is a wonderful choreographer.

Went to *Death of a Salesman*[8]. I personally found it boring and embarrass-ing. Lee Cobb overacted and roared and ranted. The mother, Mildred Dun-nock, was good, so was the rest of the cast and the production was occasionally effective. All that symbolic wandering about is considered here to be an innovation. Basil Dean did it in *Hannele*[9] in 1912 and the Germans did nothing else for years. The play is a glorification of mediocrity. The hero, Mr Cobb, is a cracking bore and a liar and a fool and a failure; the sons are idiotic. To me these ingredients do not add up to entertainment in the theatre. At odd

---

1 Alexander Woollcott (1887-1943), irascible American playwright, critic and gossip; a member of the Algonquin Round Table and probably the most powerful literary huckster in America at the time of his death.
2 Alice Duer Miller (1874-1942), American poet best known for 'The White Cliffs', which was made into a celebrated film *The White Cliffs of Dover* (1943).
3 Robert Benchley (1889-1945), American critic, humourist and film actor.
4 Beatrice Kaufman, the first wife of playwright George Kaufman and part of the Algonquin set.
5 Rodgers and Hammerstein's latest hit musical, starring Mary Martin.
6 Gower Champion (1920-80), Broadway choreographer whom Noël wished to choreograph his new musical.
7 The current title of Noël's new musical.
8 Arthur Miller's play.
9 Gerhart Hauptmann's play (1893); Noël had appeared in the 1912 English production, as had Gertrude Lawrence – it was their first meeting.

moments the writing was literate and good and, when it was, it was out of key with the characters. I think this country is deteriorating rapidly.

Friday 10 June   White Cliffs

Visited Mum, who is looking rather frail, but is very well really. Lunched in with Gladys and Lornie. They are all mad about the new songs. Came down to White Cliffs on the 7.15. Oh dear, I think I really love it more than anywhere. Joyce, Graham and I listened to Mary Martin records[1] and then bed in peace.

Monday 13 June   London

Went with Graham, Gladys, Lorn and Joyce to *Daphne Laureola*[2]. Edith Evans magnificent; Felix Aylmer excellent, also Peter Finch. Play untidy but with fine moments. Afterwards we all went on to Binkie's and I read *Home and Colonial* to Gertie. She obviously loved it, as did all present. It is maddening not being able to do it here first, but I fear it is out of the question. However, we must plan it for America (not New York[3]), do it about December until April and then come to London.

Tuesday 14 June

Drove to Pinewood with Gladys. Saw rushes and rough cut[4]. Margaret Leighton[5] and Celia [Johnson] absolutely brilliant, but Mike [Redgrave] definitely not right. Had a talk with him and then, on the way home, decided to play the picture myself. The situation now is tricky.

Wednesday 15 June

Lunched with Tony Darnborough[6], Sydney and Mike. It was mostly a duologue between Mike and me. Eventually he suggested that I play the picture myself. He behaved really and truly superbly, and I will always respect him for it.

Thursday 16 June

Make-up tests. Played a scene for test with Graham. Spectacular scene in the afternoon when I had to send for Rank[7]. His minions suggested that I play

1 Of *South Pacific*.
2 James Bridie's latest play.
3 Until it had been safely tried out elsewhere.
4 Of the film version of *The Astonished Heart*.
5 Margaret Leighton (1922-76), British actress, with whom Noël was now to work for the first time.
6 Anthony Darnborough (b. 1913), film producer; co-director with Sydney Box of *The Astonished Heart*.
7 J. Arthur Rank was in charge of the film's production.

the picture for nothing as a gesture to the British Film Industry! Oi! Oi! There was a great and lovely drama in course of which I beat him down and finished up with a virtual guarantee of £25,000 and a fairly large, as yet unspecified, percentage of the profits. If the picture is a dead flop I only get £5,000. If it is a moderate success and they break even and get their money back, I get another £20,000. If it is a smash success I make on whatever is over the production costs.

Tuesday 28 June

Long day's work[1]. Very hot. Every conceivable mechanical hitch occurred but we managed to act fairly well I think. Celia was wonderful. Talked to Maggie Leighton about possibility of her doing *Home and Colonial* instead of Gertie. Gertie frigging about as usual. Think it essential the play should be done here this autumn.

Sunday 10 July

Talked a bit to Ann [Rothermere], who had a drink with us before we caught the train. I have doubts about their happiness if she and Ian [Fleming] were to be married. I think they would both miss many things they enjoy now.

Thursday 14 July

Recorded broadcast with Gertie[2]: the love scenes from *Private Lives*. After-wards lunched with her and Daphne du Maurier[3] at Larue. Bad food but chic clientèle. She is giving me a miniature poodle called Jollyboy.

Monday 18 July

Drove to Brighton with Joyce and Graham to see *Private Lives*. Peter Graves not bad but too soft. Margaret Lockwood looked charming but cannot act comedy. Tried to persuade her and Sherek not to bring the play into London[4]. The production is inept and the set is hideous. The whole thing has all the chic of a whist drive in Tulse Hill.

Saturday 23 July

A lovely day. Teddie Thompson[5] taught us canasta, a game that will probably waste many hours of my future life.

1 Filming *The Astonished Heart*.
2 She had a BBC radio series at this time.
3 Daphne du Maurier (b. 1907), novelist and playwright, created Dame 1969; Gertie was appearing in her play *September Tide* at the Aldwych.
4 This touring production was managed by the British impresario Henry Sherek (1900–67). It did not reach London.
5 Mrs Teddie Thompson, theatrical socialite and businesswoman; a friend of Noël's from the early 1920s.

Tuesday 26 July

After the day's work at Pinewood I went to Coppins and had a drink with the Duchess of Kent, who was very gay. Her sister Countess Törring was with her.

Thursday 28 July

Dined with Ivor who was really at his best. Went on to Binkie's *Death of a Salesman* party. Apparently it went off all right. Long talk with the author, Arthur Miller[1], who was very nice.

Tuesday 2 August

Worked all day. Saw rough cut up to date. Pretty good, I think, on the whole. Dined with the Vernon Pages (Elsie Randolph[2]) at Larue. Marlene, Hitchcock, Michael Wilding[3], Jane Wyman[4], etc. Quite pleasant. Was nearly bitten by Elsie's poodle which lost its head. Quite an escape, as he might have mauled my right hand.

Wednesday 10 August

Saw yesterday's rushes. Very satisfactory. Lunched with Sydney who told me that the picture has had an offer from America of £100,000, so profit is assured. Did a short silent scene in the afternoon.

Drove home. Preparations going on for a party. I performed very well and everyone seemed genuinely impressed. This was nice as it was rather nerveracking. The percentage of 'looks' and 'celebrity value' was high: Marlene, the Tyrone Powers[5], Ann Todd[6], Zena [Dare], Isabel [Jeans], Celia [Johnson], Maggie Leighton, Michael Wilding, Ivor, Edith Evans[7], John Gielgud, Cyril [Ritchard] and Madge [Elliott], etc. We finally got to bed at 5.30.

Wednesday 17 August

Called at 7.30. Retired to my work room and contemplated my navel. I also contemplated what I have done of *Future Indefinite*, which is good and must be finished. I read through the court records of my two currency trials and really it was a dirty business and obviously a frame-up.

After lunch I painted a bit. In the evening I suddenly got a new tune at the piano, quite a charming one, so the day was not wasted.

1 Arthur Miller (b. 1915), American playwright.
2 Elsie Randolph (b. 1904), British actress, singer and dancer, often Jack Buchanan's stage partner in the 1930s; married to Vernon Page.
3 Michael Wilding (1912–79), British actor; he had been in Noël's *In Which We Serve*.
4 Jane Wyman (b. 1914), American actress; Marlene Dietrich, Michael Wilding and she were in England to film Hitchcock's *Stage Fright*.
5 Tyrone Power (1913–58), American film star, and his wife.
6 Ann Todd (b. 1909), British actress, at this time married to David Lean.
7 Edith Evans (1888–1976), distinguished British actress, created Dame 1946.

Thursday 1 September

Another long, hard day but yesterday's rushes were good and it is obviously going to be a fine picture. Long talk with Lornie when I got home. One of our heart-to-hearts when we discussed the future of this country. We spoke some bitter heresies. We found that we had little to reply to the American criticisms of England. We decided that the present Government[1] is the worst that this country has ever had, and that if the ordinary people do not pull out of their idiotic apathy and learn to want to work again, we shall be taken over amiably by America and serve us bloody well right. A German journalist on the set today told me that Germany was recovering by leaps and bounds, that the Nazis were numerous and that the Germans worked twelve hours a day without cups of tea every hour or so. As he said this, he cast a contemptuous glance round our stage. Everybody in sight was standing about drinking tea. We have a five-day week; two of those days are early days; it is impossible really to put our backs into it and finish the picture. The British Film Industry is on the verge of dissolution. I wonder why?

Monday 5 September

A boring morning on location in Kensington Gardens. Went in the evening with Graham to *The Third Man*, Carol Reed's new picture. Really very fine indeed. Beautifully played by Joe Cotten, Orson Welles and Trevor Howard. Quiet dinner at the Ivy.

Thursday 15 September

Got home from Pinewood in time to go with Graham to Ivor's first night – *King's Rhapsody*[2]. It was a violently glamorous evening. The show was much better than anything he has done before. It had a few embarrassing moments and was, as usual, too long, but Zena Dare was excellent and Vanessa Lee absolutely enchanting; a lovely voice, very good looks and can act. Terrific ovation at the end. We dined at the Ivy and Rebecca West joined us.

Monday 19 September

Woke to the depressing news that the pound has been devalued. This after Sir Stafford[3] had assured the country that it would never, never happen. Atmosphere generally depressed. Film unit depressed anyhow, because we finish the film today and everybody is out of work owing to the British film crisis, brought on largely by executive incompetence and arbitrary union decisions which rob the workers of incentive. Well, well. I thought this country had sunk to its lowest at Munich but I was wrong.

1 Labour, under Clement Attlee, which was pushing through extensive social reforms.
2 At the Palace Theatre.
3 Sir (Richard) Stafford Cripps (1889-1952), Chancellor of the Exchequer 1947-50.

Wednesday 21 September

Went to *Brigadoon*[1] with Gladys in the afternoon. Talked to Charles [Russell] and Ham [Lance Hamilton] from five until seven and dissuaded them from doing *Fallen Angels* with Baddeley and Betty Davies. Said I would only agree if it were Baddeley and Gingold or Googie [Withers] and Kay [Hammond].

Thursday 22 September

Stormy Actors' Orphanage meeting when I flew at everyone, myself included, and I think galvanized them into some sort of awareness of their responsibilities[2].

Friday 30 September

The great decision was consolidated tonight. Kay Hammond and John Clements[3] are going to do the play and are delighted. They will start rehearsal in January, play February out of town and come in in March, which will give Katie time to have a holiday and give me time to finish *Hoi Polloi*[4]. Next spring is going to be a busy time for me.

Monday 3 October

Paris. A beautiful day and a tranquil journey. Arrived to find the flat[5] rather dirty and with lots of things broken, but no serious damage.

Tuesday 4 October

Cocktails with Edward [Molyneux] and then, with Cole and Graham, the first act of the ABC[6] with Mistinguett (hardly able to walk) and the last act of the Folies Bergères with Josephine Baker, who was wonderful as Mary Stuart[7] in a miles long white satin train.

Wednesday 5 October

Lunched with Paul-Emile [Seidmann] and Ginette [Spanier]. Went to *Gigi*[8], a disappointing picture, beautifully played by Danielle Delorme, Gaby Morlay and Yvonne de Bray, but very slow.

1 The London production at His Majesty's Theatre.
2 For fund-raising and general organization of the charity.
3 Kay Hammond (1909–80) and her husband, John Clements (b. 1910), knighted in 1968.
4 The latest title for Noël's new musical.
5 At Place Vendôme; it had been let.
6 Music Hall.
7 In a tableau, singing Gounod's 'Ave Maria'.
8 The film of Colette's novel, later transformed into a more successful Hollywood musical.

Wednesday 19 October   London

Spent the whole morning being X-rayed. I have neither cancer nor an ulcer, which is a great relief, but apparently my stomach has taken to emptying itself far too quickly, which Dr MacManus is giving me some medicine for.

Lunched with Binkie and discussed the play, the musical and many other things. Went with Gladys to *The Beaux' Stratagem*[1], a play of unparalleled boredom and dullness. Katie [Hammond] looked lovely and was just all right; John [Clements] was efficient and noisy. Supper with them afterwards, when we discussed *Home and Colonial*. He wanted his part built up and I refused and it was all very typical and fairly tiresome. It is sad that actors should be so consistently idiotic.

Thursday 20 October

I drove to Silverlands[2]. It has been repainted and is looking not too bad. The Savage-Baileys[3] seem all right. He is obviously a kind man but, I fear, on the weak side. The children were in wild spirits and I was cheered to see that they were not looking downtrodden and dismal. I had a talk with Savage-Bailey about sex and told him not to get too fussed because all children had sex curiosity and too much emphasis on its sinfulness would only make it more attractive, and that as long as he kept it within bounds he could close an eye discreetly every now and then. I am sure this was good advice although perhaps not strictly conventional.

Wednesday 26 October

Dined with the Fairbanks. Sat next to Princess Elizabeth who, I must say, couldn't have been more charming. After dinner we adjourned to Wardour Street where we saw a dreadful picture of Doug's called *The Mighty O'Flynn*. Then we all came back to the house and I sang and gossiped with Princess Margaret Rose. Most of the party were youngsters; it made me feel quite aged.

Saturday 29 October

Went with Joyce to *Streetcar*[4]. Very nice production; Vivien magnificent; audience sordid and theatre beastly. Drove to Notley[5] with Larry and Viv.

Tuesday 8 November

Worked all the morning and came to the conclusion that I love writing fiction.

1 By George Farquhar (1707).
2 The Actors' Orphanage home.
3 The home's administrator and his wife.
4 Vivien Leigh had just opened in the London production of Tennessee Williams's play, *A Streetcar Named Desire*, at the Aldwych.
5 The Oliviers' country home in Buckinghamshire.

It is hard going but it has the lovely satisfaction about it that good, bad or indifferent, there it is and it has not got to be translated through someone else's personality.

Thursday 10 November

Worked with Muir Mathieson[1] on *Astonished Heart* music. Had a showing of the rough cut. There is an essential lack in the picture, and that is that I am never seen being a great psychiatrist and the reasons for my suicide do not seem enough. It is nearly good but not quite.

Friday 11 November   White Cliffs

Read the unexpurgated *De Profundis*[2]. Poor Oscar Wilde, what a silly, conceited, inadequate creature he was and what a dreadful self-deceiver. It is odd that such brilliant wit should be allied to no humour at all. I didn't expect him to enjoy prison life and to be speechless with laughter from morning till night but, after all, there are people even in gaol and he might have had a little warm human joke occasionally, if only with the warder. The trouble with him was that he was a 'beauty-lover'.

Read Maugham's *Writer's Notebook*. So clear and unpretentious and accurate after that poor, podgy pseudo-philosopher.

Monday 14 November   London

Came up on the 10.30. Visited Mum who was fairly awful about the film and informed me that I looked hideous.

Dinner with Frere. Present: Eric Ambler, Priestley[3], Willie Maugham. Very enjoyable and Priestley quite amiable. Willie, of course, enchanting.

Picked up John and Katie at the Ivy and drove down to the country with them. Sat discussing the play until 4.30. Mostly waste of time. Finally coaxed John to play Hali. Firmly refused to rewrite anything.

Thursday 17 November

Letter from Prince saying that the script of *Hoi Polloi* needed extensive changes. Very irritated. I am getting sick of other people's silly unimaginative minds trailing all over my work.

Friday 18 November

Was called at seven o'clock after a bad night during which I had enacted splendid scenes with Prince and told him brilliantly and concisely what I thought of him.

1 Muir Mathieson (1911–75), British conductor and arranger of numerous film scores.
2 Wilde's apologia to his former lover, Lord Alfred Douglas.
3 J.B. Priestley (b. 1894), English novelist, playwright and critic.

Went to Pinewood. Lunched with the Paramount representatives. Discussed next year's *Tonight at 8.30* picture. Thought of really good title for *Hoi Polloi* at last – *Come Out to Play*. Long telephone talk with Binkie, who has read the script twice and given constructive criticism. Have decided to reconstruct and rewrite the second act. Binkie has been a dear and immensely helpful. At least he knows what he is talking about.

Tuesday 22 November

Dined with the Douglases at the American Embassy. Small party. Sat next to the Queen at dinner. She was perfectly enchanting, as always. Afterwards played canasta with Princess Margaret as partner. We won. Then I sang all the new songs for the Queen and she really most obviously loved them. Princess Margaret obliged with songs at the piano. Surprisingly good. She has an impeccable ear, her piano playing is simple but has perfect rhythm, and her method of singing is really very funny. The Queen was sweet on account of being so genuinely proud of her chick. Altogether a most charming evening.

Wednesday 23 November

Caught the twelve o'clock train for Plymouth with Graham. Met by Charles and Ham. Drinks and dinner at the Grand Hotel. They all assured me that I would be pleasantly surprised at the show[1] and that, although Baddeley and Gingold overplayed a little here and there, they were really good. We went to the theatre, and I have never yet in my long experience seen a more vulgar, silly, unfunny, disgraceful performance. *Fumed Oak*[2] was indescribable. *Fallen Angels* almost worse. Gingold at moments showed signs that she could be funny. Baddeley was disgusting. Afterwards I told them exactly what I thought, flew at Peter Daubeny[3] and finally insisted on *Fumed Oak* being cut out entirely. Charles utterly wretched, and serve him right. After this fragrant little evening, I returned to London.

Friday 25 November

Beginning to realize that, after all, Prince was right[4]. The book is not good enough and doesn't only need strengthening. It needs bloody well rewriting.

Monday 28 November

Blissful morning listening to the London Symphony Orchestra recording my *Astonished Heart* music. Afternoon spent cutting the picture. Went to *The*

---

1 *Fallen Angels*, Charles Russell and Lance Hamilton's first venture into management, starring the two Hermiones, Baddeley and Gingold.
2 From *Tonight at 8.30*, done as a curtain-raiser.
3 Also involved, as co-producer.
4 In suggesting that the new musical was 'below Noël's usual musical standard' and was not yet ready for production.

Seagull[1] with Gladys. Very well played. Paul Scofield particularly good. Long talk with Binkie. Everything all right and I feel I am leaving with a light heart[2].

Thursday 1 December   ss *Ile de France*

Read Monica Baldwin's book *I Leap Over the Wall*. Very interesting, I must say. It has strengthened my decision not to become a nun.

Monday 5 December   New York

Went to the Lunts' play, *I Know My Love*[3]. Patchy as a play but they were quite dazzling. Supper afterwards with them. Sweet as ever.

Tuesday 6 December

Forgot to say yesterday that Lorn sent the *Fallen Angels* notices, which were mostly good for the Hermiones but bad for the play. It really is discouraging. How idiotic critics can be.

Thursday 8 December

An hour with [Edna] Ferber, who was in need of comfort owing to her mother having died last week. Long talk to Helen[4] on the telephone about Mary's death. She was wonderful but broke down a little. Dined with Adrianne [Allen]. We all went to Jack's opening night of *Gentlemen Prefer Blondes*[5]. A violently successful opening. Carol Channing had a well-deserved triumph. Music no good at all. Lyrics passable. Décor and dresses good. Dancing untidy.

Monday 12 December

Grande soirée given for me. It was a fairly glamorous party, including Marlene, Danny Kaye[6], Mary [Martin] and Dick [Halliday], Valentina, Natasha and Jack; almost all New York. It was quite enjoyable.

Thursday 15 December   Jamaica

Home again at Blue Harbour and everything unbelievably lovely. The garden has grown so fast that it is quite unrecognizable. The air is warm and soft and so is the sea. I have fallen in love with the place all over again and this time next year I shall install myself for six months instead of seven weeks. I dread the time passing already.

We swam in the velvet sea and tore up to Look Out, which is cleaned

1 Chekhov's play in a revival at the St James's Theatre.
2 For Jamaica, to rewrite the new musical.
3 S.N. Behrman's adaptation of Marcel Achard's play.
4 Helen Hayes, whose young daughter had just died.
5 The musical of Anita Loos' novel.
6 Danny Kaye (b. 1913), American entertainer.

up and looks wonderful. I am alone in the guest house with all my things round me. It is utterly peaceful and tomorrow I shall be fifty and I couldn't care less.

Monday 19 December

Lovely day. Shopping in Port Maria. Letters from home. *Fallen Angels* a terrific success. Livid.

Tuesday 20 December

Did a million Christmas cables. Lay in the sun. Reading Trollope's *Prime Minister* in eight volumes. Absolutely enchanting.

Saturday 24 December

A curious Christmas Eve. We lay in the broiling sun in the morning and floated over the reef on lilos. After that we went over to Port Maria, came home to a lunch of baked parrot-fish, packed and wrapped presents and gave them to the staff.

Dined with Ian [Fleming], more presents, then canasta. All very enjoyable and full of charm. Wonderful letter from Jack who has read the book of *Hoi Polloi* and thought it no good at all. I couldn't agree with him more. I am now preparing to start again from scratch.

Tuesday 27 December

Woke bright and early with a wonderful idea for the show. I am going to do the whole thing virtually in one set – the night-club. There can be a couple of insets and a scrim if I need them, but the story must be the club and what happens in it. Pinkie is the star of it and is being kept by the man who runs it. Harry is the sailor she falls in love with, has an affair with and finally renounces. This set-up will give perfect opportunities for all the numbers because those not in the story can be done in the floor show. One principal built set will minimize the cost of production. In fact it really is a very good idea indeed. The title is *Ace of Clubs*.

= 1950 =

Noël's gangster night-club musical Ace of Clubs *finally made it to the stage under Tom Arnold's banner. It fared better than* The Astonished Heart, *the film of his own* Tonight at 8.30 *play about the psychiatrist, in which he had taken over the screen lead from Michael Redgrave. Ironically, the only real money-maker which did come his way during the year was a project that he turned down: the offer to direct and star in Rodgers and Hammerstein's* The King and I *opposite Gertrude Lawrence, an offer Noël declined on the grounds of his deep loathing of a long Broadway run. He did, however, recommend a then comparatively unknown Yul Brynner.*

Financially all this was to cost him dear; he found he was unable to buy the Paris flat which he had rented since the time he worked there at the beginning of the war, and the improvements to the Jamaica property were rapidly bleeding dry what little remained in his English bank accounts. This was also the year that marked the beginning of the end of his long professional partnership with Gladys Calthrop, whose interest in set designing was waning even more rapidly than Noël's professional fortunes. The year of his half-century was thus not a vintage one; it was, though, to mark the end of this period of post-war failures.

Sunday 1 January   Jamaica

A very stormy day with rough seas and a High Wind in Jamaica.

Worked all the morning, finishing the construction of the first act and am now beginning on the second[1].

We played canasta before and after dinner. A peaceful beginning to 1950.

Monday 9 January

Finished the first act and it is very good. Lost in admiration of my own character. Here I am, being roused from deep sleep every morning at 6.30, before it is light. Not drinking, slaving away and, what is so curious, enjoying myself more than if I were wasting time. The only trouble about not drinking is that other people who are drinking are liable to look a little silly.

Thursday 12 January

Finished *Ace of Clubs* at 11.15. It is really good; tidily constructed and swift moving. I know I have done a good job. The thinking out and preliminary construction was hell but the actual writing of it flowed easily. It is a truly wonderful gift, my natural and trained gift for dialogue. This whole business has taught me a solid lesson and that is that other people far less clever than I am can often be dead right when I am wrong. Prince was right; he could have handled it better perhaps, but if he had it might not have been so effective. I only know that I will never again embark on so much as a revue sketch that is not carefully and meticulously constructed beforehand. I think this will be a success because it seems to me the story and the music will carry it. I feel very relieved and very proud of myself and my self-discipline. I have wasted too much time during these last five years. I have drunk too much, eaten too much and played too much. I have no feelings about this beyond the fact that as I am really happy when I am working well, it is bloody silly to fritter away time not working.

I read the play to Jack and Natasha, who were really impressed. Jack was very sweet and overcame his managerial grandeur, which was good of him and difficult for him.

Ann Rothermere has arrived. She and Ian [Fleming] came to dinner. We gossiped and played canasta.

Saturday 14 January

Rewrote lyrics of 'I'd Never Never Know' and 'Sunday Afternoon'. Read Nancy Mitford's adaptation of *La Petite Hutte*[2] and thought it very well done and extremely funny.

1 Of *Ace of Clubs*.
2 André Roussin's play.

Saturday 21 January

Jack and Natasha left. She is a darling in every way, and Jack is charming, but when he is bitchy he is horrid. His mind is quick but he has a destructive quality. When he is simple, he is so very sweet.

Joyce and I had a peaceful day gossiping. I warned her against being disagreeable and tiresome on occasion, and she took it like a dream. I began a picture. Graham came back after putting Jack and Natasha on the plane. Dined with Ian and Ann. Played canasta and we won for the first time for ages.

Wednesday 25 January

In the afternoon read *Ace of Clubs* to Guthrie [McClintic], Adrianne [Allen], Joyce and Graham. Guthrie was riveted from beginning to end and reacted to every point. Naturally I read it well and sang it well, and it really does feel very good indeed. Jack is wrong about it being overlength. The first act, with numbers and reprises complete, read an hour and five minutes; the second act was a good deal shorter. This means a lot of leeway. He was also wrong about 'I Like America' being out of key. The new lead-up fits it in like a shoehorn.

Letter from Frere saying that, after all, following on much expert opinion, he wants me to do an entirely new book of short stories and not muddle the later ones up with *To Step Aside*[1]. As I have always thought this, I am very pleased. I am getting on well with *Sorrow in Sunlight*, and if I do one more long one and two shorter ones after that, the book will be complete.

Saturday 11 February   New York

Nice suite at the Drake. Went to *The Cocktail Party*[2]. Absolutely lovely until the last act. Beautifully played, particularly by Irene Worth. Party at Cathleen Nesbitt's[3]. Lynn and Alfred, etc.

Sunday 12 February

Peaceful Sunday morning reading the papers. Joyce and Bobby Flemyng for lunch, joined by Natasha. Went to the Danny Kaye film *The Inspector General*, but it was so desperately unfunny that we walked out. Went to *The Fallen Idol*[4] which was very good. In the evening dined at Guthrie's; Margalo[5],

1 Noël's publisher had originally been talking of reprinting some of the stories from the first collection, published in 1939, in the new volume.
2 T.S. Eliot's new play.
3 Cathleen Nesbitt (b. 1889), British actress, who was appearing in *The Cocktail Party*.
4 Graham Greene's screenplay, directed by Carol Reed with Ralph Richardson and Michele Morgan.
5 Margalo Gillmore (b. 1897), English actress long resident in America.

Bob Hope[1], also Alec Guinness[2] and Ruth Chatterton[3]. We sat up till three talking pure theatre and it was lovely.

Monday 13 February

Shopped. Breakfast with Lynn and Alfred. Took them to the Press show of *Astonished Heart*. They were tremendously impressed. Press reception. Everyone seemed to be enthusiastic. In the evening dinner with Kitty Miller, then the première. Great enthusiasm. The picture, in spite of censorship cuts, is pretty good. I think I have made a success. We shall see.

Tuesday 14 February

Jack has had a letter from Gertie being injured about *Home and Colonial*[4]. While at Arnold Weissberger's party I talked to Richard Aldrich about it. Told him the whole story, and suggested that he tell Gertie to mind her manners and that if she wants another play from me she can fish for it. On the whole the party was very enjoyable.

Wednesday 15 February

Read the four morning notices of *The Astonished Heart*. Very grudging. The afternoon ones were apparently worse, but I didn't see them as I was too busy shopping. Oh dear. I really seem quite unable to please. If the picture turns out to be a flop it will doubtless save me a lot of trouble. It's odd, but I really don't mind nearly so much as I should have done a few years ago; in fact, I hardly mind at all. It would, of course, have been nice if they had all come out with blazing headlines saying it was the most marvellous film ever produced. It is only fairly good really, and censorship has certainly done nothing to improve it. I have been paid some really wonderful compliments by Lynn and Alfred and Guthrie, which pleased me very much. At all events, it is dignified and intelligent and my performance is honest and good.

Thursday 16 February

I feel extraordinarily glad to leave America. I used to love it so but now I actively detest it. Apart from my friends and the personal comforts such as trains and shops and drugstores and plumbing, I don't want any part of it. I think as a race the Americans are spiritually impoverished and their vulgarity is much worse than it used to be. The theatre, which before was so vital and competitive and fast-moving, is now sodden with insignificant significances. The dollar as a god is even more enervating than the Holy Trinity.

1 Bob Hope (b. 1903), English-born entertainer.
2 Alec Guinness (b. 1914), distinguished British actor; knighted 1959.
3 Ruth Chatterton (1893–1961), American stage and film actress, later a successful novelist.
4 Which Noël was now offering elsewhere.

Saturday 18 February   London

Cable from Binkie saying that Val Parnell[1] does not consider the book strong enough and so will not do the show either at the Hippodrome or the Prince of Wales. The cable finished by Binkie's apologizing for the 'gloomy news' and sending fondest love. That at any stage of my career Mr Val Parnell's opinion should be of the remotest importance is indeed gloomy news. I cabled back 'Fondest love my foot'. I don't know what's going on but I am bitterly angry. I am more certain of this show than I have been of anything for years. They must be out of their minds. I believe Prince is behind it all. He owns all the theatres and the situation is frustrating and infuriating. I am, I must admit, in a bad state of rage, so I have taken two sleeping-pills and hope my acids will have calmed down tomorrow. The temptation to chuck up the theatre and return to Jamaica and write what I want to write is very strong. Of course I shan't do this because I don't intend to sacrifice anything as good as *Ace of Clubs* on the altar of commercial real estate. Also I cannot let down Pat Kirkwood[2] and Graham and Sylvia [Cecil]. I shall gird my loins and deal with it.

Thursday 23 February

Election day. Voted. Dined with Ian who attacked me about *The Astonished Heart* and said how awful it was. Went to the Camrose[3] party at the Savoy. A howling mob. Sat and listened to the depressing results, mostly no change. Three Conservative gains. Fairly obvious that the Socialists will get in again unless some miracle happens between now and tomorrow.

Friday 24 February

Well, a curious and most typically English miracle has happened. After a day of extraordinary excitement, in course of which the Labour majority was reduced to one and then climbed up again, the Socialists got in with a majority of twenty-five. If the Conservatives had got in with a majority as small as that it would have been really disastrous. As it is, it is virtually a deadlock, with the Labour boys carrying the baby, and I should think that the Budget when it comes will probably send them out on their ear. The Communist vote is non-existent and the Liberals, although they have lost a great number of seats – or, rather, failed to get them – are seven up in the House, which I happen to think is a good thing. Ed Murrow[4] made a wonderful little speech congratulating us as a nation on the decorum, fairness and justice of our parliamentary

1 Val Parnell (1894–1972), London theatre manager who had been sent *Ace of Clubs*.
2 Pat Kirkwood (b. 1921), British actress, who had been offered the role of Pinkie.
3 Viscount Camrose (1879–1954), newspaper proprietor; Chairman of the *Daily Telegraph*.
4 Ed Murrow (1908–65), American journalist and broadcaster who had done much war reporting for CBS from London.

system and the general calm dignity with which the Election has been conducted. It was moving to hear an American praise us so well and it made me feel very proud. As long as we can retain the sense of decency that prevailed all over the country yesterday and today, we shall never go far wrong.

Tuesday 28 February

Val Parnell has got it all round theatrical London that he turned down my book. Pat [Kirkwood]'s agent warned her that my show would be a flop. She replied that she would rather be in a flop by me than in a success with Littler or Parnell. I hope to God she will be all right; I am fairly sure that she will. Her personality is warm and friendly and her vitality tremendous.

Wednesday 1 March

Gladys came to lunch with a not very good design for the set. Rested. Woke up with no voice at all. Rehearsed for an hour and a half. Gargled, sipped port, lemon and honey, and got it back a bit. Binkie came to dinner. At 8.30 they all arrived[1]. I did the whole show. My voice, miraculously, was just all right. They were very impressed and Tom Arnold says he is going to do it and that's that. There is still theatre trouble but we think we shall ultimately get the Phoenix. At all events, we start rehearsing on 3 April and open at the Palace, Manchester, on 1 May, then Birmingham on the twenty-ninth for two weeks and then, we hope, London. Tom Arnold has a wonderful but expensive idea about the cabaret stage sliding out into the audience over the orchestra pit. This might be very effective indeed. Impossible to do on tour but possible for London. I liked Arnold; he was practical and sensible and did not yawn in my face when I was singing[2]. He also thanked me for giving such a wonderful performance. I nearly fainted. I am determined that this show is going to be a smash hit. It is a curious situation now in the London theatre that anyone with my position and reputation and this script and score should have virtually to give an audition to get it on the stage.

Monday 6 March

Telephoned to Clem Butson[3] just to find out how everything was going. His voice sounded strained, with every reason, as he stumblingly explained that he and Tom Arnold were not satisfied with *Ace of Clubs*, although they were impressed with the way I had performed it, and that they didn't think the book was strong enough, etc., and unless it was drastically reconstructed and rewritten they would not do it. This, for a moment, knocked me for six, but

1 Tom Arnold (d. 1969) and his theatre management team, who were now considering *Ace of Clubs*; he put on many of Ivor Novello's musicals.
2 Prince Littler had.
3 Clem Butson, part of Tom Arnold's management team.

I rallied and asked him to lunch tomorrow to discuss it. I was quite cheerful and non-committal. Then I had a bad time. This series of blows in the face is beginning to get me down. My first instinct was to let them all stuff it up and go away and write my book, but this I cannot and will not do. I know this show is good and I also know that I am not going to shelve all those hit numbers or the book just because a few unimaginative, commercial theatre owners lack both vision and faith in me. I talked to Lorn and Gladys and now feel much better. The idea is to do it as simply as humanly possible, with Pat and Graham on percentages, at a small theatre with an intimate atmosphere. It will mean using our imagination and ingenuity like mad. Not only do I think it can be done that way, but I think it is the right way. I would like to prove that talent and material count more than sequins and tits. I will do it with a couple of pianos and a sax and drum if necessary. The more intimate the production is, the more clearly the story and lyrics will be heard. As Lorn so rightly said, let us boss the capital and not let the capital boss us. We shall see.

Thursday 9 March

Binkie is seeing Clem Butson and Tom Arnold next Tuesday and making them my proposition of no royalties until the production is paid back and me guaranteeing two-thirds of the money.

Went to *Venus Observed*[1] with Lorn. A badly constructed, fairly tedious play with patches of fine writing but not enough heart. A very good production and Larry impeccable.

In the evening went with Juliet Duff to the Royal Gala at Covent Garden. A glittering spectacle and the ballets really superb, especially Margot Fonteyn, who was pure magic. Supper afterwards at Warwick House. PS: I was cheered steadily from Long Acre all down Bow Street to the theatre.

Sunday 26 March

The last weeks have been a strain and frustration always exhausts me. Now everything seems set fair. It is one of the pleasanter aspects of getting older that I look forward so much more to quiet than to noise and to comparative solitude than to people. Heigh-ho for the merry fifties!

Thursday 30 March

A gruelling day of auditions[2]. Saw hundreds and picked a few possibles. Really felt worn out by the end of it and oppressed by the thought of those legions of unattractive men and women thinking they were gifted enough to entitle them to appear on the stage.

Caught the nine o'clock ferry for Paris. Went to bed immediately.

1 Christopher Fry's play at the St James's Theatre which Olivier was actor-managing.
2 For *Ace of Clubs*.

Saturday 1 April   Paris

Drove out to Chantilly with Edward to lunch with Duff and Diana. Desmond MacCarthy was there. It was very pleasant and Diana was enchanting. Cocktail party *chez* Ginette *et* Paul-Emile. Very glamorous as regards looks: Nadia Gray, Maria Montez, Pat Kirkwood, Jean-Pierre Aumont, and Binkie and me!

Sunday 2 April

Dined with Ginette and Paul-Emile at Pierre's and went to *Chéri*[1]. Magnificent performance by Valentine Tessier. Jean Marais really very good indeed. The rest of the cast dreadful. Had a drink with Jean Marais[2] afterwards and a rather abortive talk. I like him very much but for discussions of life in the raw I prefer someone a little lighter. Came straight home after toying with the idea of visiting a bar or two. It is most agreeable to be getting old and not feel that one is missing some gallant adventure by going home to bed.

Friday 14 April   London

Long Orphanage meeting. Children behaving very badly, insulting everyone and stealing right and left. Went over their menus and school reports. Interviewed Mr Savage-Bailey, who stubbornly believes that sweet reason, kindliness and long moral explanations is the right way to handle a lot of illiterate young hooligans of very mixed parentage. It is becoming distressingly clear that his theory is not practicable. He is a kind little man but, like so many idealists, he is a cracking fool. The dear children obviously share my opinion and run rings round him.

Monday 17 April   Manchester

First rehearsal[3] went off all right although with a fair amount of chaos. Pat and Graham excellent. Sylvia without a clue so far. The girls[4] pretty bright.

Went with Graham to see *On the Town*[5], a very well done musical. Gene Kelly wonderful; a few good ideas.

Saw Ivor for a few minutes in his dressing-room[6]. He was very sweet and had sent me a welcoming wire today as we were rehearsing at the Palace.

Tuesday 16 May

Atmosphere of tension. Rehearsed bits and pieces and rested. Manchester first night. Quite obviously a smash success. Terrific ovation. Graham nearly

1 Play adapted from Colette's novel.
2 Jean Marais (b. 1913), actor, perhaps best known for his appearances in Cocteau films.
3 Of *Ace of Clubs*.
4 In the chorus.
5 Film by Stanley Donen, co-starring Frank Sinatra.
6 He was playing in his *King's Rhapsody* at the Palace Theatre.

stopped the show twice, with 'Sailor' and 'America'. He became, before the first act was half over, a star. I am fairly bursting with pride and satisfaction.

Wednesday 17 May

All the notices raving with enthusiasm. The evening papers even more ecstatic. Saw matinée and evening performance. Supper party with Tom Arnold. Everything very convivial. Apparently I can have any theatre I want. Am I gloating? Yes, dear diary, I am gloating like hell.

Saturday 27 May

Cole thought of a good title for my theatrical short story: *Star Quality*. Worked on it in the morning. Met Binkie who arrived at 2.15. Gossiped all the afternoon. Discussed *Home and Colonial* and the possibility of Vivien [Leigh] playing it[1]. Took him to the show. He was deeply impressed and most particularly by Graham. All very gratifying.

Wednesday 31 May

Came down to London with Cole. Dined at the French Embassy. Frightfully chic. Loelia [Westminster], Molly [Buccleuch], etc., and the Duchess of Kent. Had a conversation with Mrs J. Astor[2], who was very charming, and Anthony Eden, who was very sweet and old-friendish. The food was good, the wine was good, the whole party was elegant to an alarming degree. I was dreadfully bored. It was suggested that I go on to the Four Hundred Club with the Duchess, but I struck firmly and buggered off home.

Thursday 1 June

Dick Rodgers and Oscar Hammerstein came at five o'clock and asked me to direct *Anna and the King of Siam*[3] next year with Gertie. A very flattering offer but I refused it on account of wanting to write.

Friday 2 June

The great day of the Theatre and Film Carnival[4]. By the afternoon the sun was shining. The Duchess of Kent arrived and was absolutely sweet. The *Daily Mail* had no mention of the affair. All the rest of the Press, realizing that the *Daily Mail* was sponsoring us, left us alone. The result was no advance publicity and the attendance was half what it was last year. We shall have to make £7,000 tomorrow to break even. I am sick at heart and bitterly angry.

1 Kay Hammond and John Clements had changed their minds about the play.
2 Mrs J. Astor, wife of the British newspaper proprietor, John Jacob Astor (1886-1971).
3 Which they were turning into a musical, *The King and I*, at Gertrude Lawrence's request.
4 The annual Theatrical Garden Party to benefit the Actors' Orphanage.

Saturday 3 June

Second day of the Theatre and Film Balls-up. Worked hard from 2 p.m. until 10 p.m. Signed thousands of autographs; sang hundreds of songs, handsomely supported by my dear ones. The public mighty sweet and very well-behaved. Johnny Mills[1], Dickie Attenborough[2], Charles [Russell], Ham [Lance Hamilton], and my own personal bodyguard[3] worked like beavers. We shall have made in two days approximately what we usually make in one. The misorganization has been really remarkable. I hope we have made enough to cover our costs.

Monday 5 June   Liverpool

Lorn rang up to say that the figures of the garden party to date prove that we shall have approximately a thousand-pound loss. I am bitterly angry and the last of it has not yet been heard.

Opening night here. Went wonderfully although the house wasn't quite full. Graham got the biggest ovation at the end that he has ever had.

Wednesday 21 June   Birmingham

Drove to Stratford with Cole. Joined up with Ina[4]. Saw the most exquisite production of *Much Ado About Nothing*. A really enchanting performance. John[5] better than I have ever seen him. I was sad when it was over. Drove back with Ina. Saw the worst performance of *Ace of Clubs* yet given. Even Graham was forcing, everyone else was overacting and the stage management was a lash-up.

Friday 23 June

Read some stories by a new writer called Angus Wilson which are very fine indeed.

Sunday 25 June   London

Great jubilation. Finished *Star Quality*[6]. It is nice and long, about thirty thousand words, and is also, I think, very good.

1 John Mills (b. 1908), British film actor, knighted 1976; Noël had first seen him in 1929 in Singapore and subsequently gave him a London start in *Cavalcade* and *Words and Music*; in 1942 Mills had appeared in Noël's *In Which We Serve*.
2 Richard Attenborough (b. 1923), British actor, producer and director, knighted 1976; his first film appearance was *In Which We Serve* when Noël had met the nervous RADA student with the words, 'You're Richard Attenborough, aren't you? You won't know me, my name's Noël Coward.'
3 Cole, Lorn, Joyce and Gladys.
4 Ina Claire, then visiting England.
5 John Gielgud, playing Benedick.
6 The short story about an actress which would give its title to his new collection.

Went with Joyce to *Odette*[1]. Really very well done and quite thrilling. Anna Neagle extraordinarily good and Trevor Howard quite magnificent. It was all true and honestly done.

Monday 26 June

The Communists have started a war in Korea in direct contravention of the United Nations. It looks like Czechoslovakia all over again. I suppose Mr Truman[2] will soon be flying to Moscow with an umbrella. I think it is serious and may be the beginning of the crack-up. If the human race is that silly, the sooner it destroys itself the better.

Tuesday 27 June

Binkie telephoned to say that Vivien and Larry violently disliked poor *Home and Colonial* and flew at him for encouraging me[3]. They said they loved me far too much to lie to me and that I was not to do the play as it was old-fashioned Noël Coward and would do me great harm. This is a surprising and salutary jolt, and I have a strange feeling that they are right. At all events, I love them for their honesty and moral courage. They may be wrong, but I must admit that the play didn't come easily in the first place and I don't think my heart has ever been deeply in it. I shall think carefully and probably shelve it at least for a year or so. It is all very peculiar but I feel a sense of relief.

Sunday 2 July

Lunched at Warwick Castle. Absolutely lovely and crammed with fabulous Van Dycks and Holbeins and Canalettos. Actually the loveliest living castle that I have ever seen. After lunch Graham and I drove in a leisurely fashion to London, stopping up on the way to have supper with Dirk Bogarde[4].

Friday 7 July   London

Orphanage meeting all the morning. Rather complicated but, I think, constructive. Took Graham to *Treasure Island*[5] to take his mind off the first night. Not very good.

The theatre[6] in the evening tingling with suspense and tension. I got the usual ovation when I went into the box. The show went magnificently and everyone gave a beautiful performance. Sylvia stopped the show with 'Nothing

1 Herbert Wilcox film about World War Two heroine, Odette Churchill.
2 President Harry Truman (1884–1972), elected to a second term of office in 1948.
3 To offer it to Vivien Leigh.
4 Dirk Bogarde (b. 1920), the British film star, whom Noël had met three years earlier and had tried to persuade against signing a film contract instead of acting in his *Peace in Our Time*.
5 Disney film version with Robert Newton as Long John Silver.
6 Cambridge Theatre, London.

Can Ever Last'. The 'Delinquents', too, tore the place up. Graham had a rip-snorting triumph with 'America' and Pat got them roaring with 'Josephine' and 'Charlie'. The whole thing went marvellously all through and when I walked on to the stage at the end there was a lot of booing. I must say I was both surprised and angry. I stood still and waited while a free fight broke out in the gallery. It was very unpleasant and excessively silly. Finally I silenced them and made my speech and that was that. It was a cruel bit of crowd exhibitionism and made me feel bitter because it took the edge off the success and made everyone gossip. I am disgusted with the filthy manners of the galleryites.

Went to Tom Arnold's party afterwards. It was very nice but I longed to be at home with my loved ones.

Saturday 8 July

Notices patronizing, irritating, badly written and silly, as usual, but on the whole very good box-office. The theatre took nearly £1,000 in the two evening shows, which for the second performance was bloody good. The first house was fairly empty but appreciative; the second house was full to capacity and they screamed their heads off. I got in for the end, having been to the last night of the Sadler's Wells Ballet at Covent Garden with Joyce. It was *Ballet Imperial*. It was lovely and Margot Fonteyn was superb. Supper with Natasha and John Sutro[1].

Monday 10 July

Quite a day. Drove with Lornie to Wimbledon to see possible new house for the Orphanage. Not bad. Lunched at the Ace of Spades, then went to see Madge Titheradge[2]; a very moving reunion. She is bedridden with agonizing arthritis and I haven't seen her for fifteen years. Apart from her once lovely hands being swollen and knotted and some lines of pain in her face, she is unchanged. It was so sweet to see her again.

After this we drove to Silverlands. All the children look healthy, happy and well fed. The problem boy is Peter Collinson[3], who has been behaving badly and been threatened with expulsion. I took him out and talked to him. He is twelve and bright and highly strung. He is being torn to pieces between his divorced parents. He is in an emotional turmoil. I talked to him firmly and made him promise me personally that he would behave well in future. In

---

1 John Sutro (b. 1904), actor, journalist and film producer, then in partnership with Alexander Korda.
2 Madge Titheradge (1887–1961), Australian actress who had starred in Noël's 1926 romance, *The Queen Was in the Parlour*.
3 Peter Collinson (1938–80); he was to become a film director and to direct Noël in *The Italian Job* (1969).

return I promised him that I would look after him and be his friend. I honestly don't think he will transgress much again. Actually he practically broke my heart. I may be over-sentimental but a sensitive little boy bereft of all personal affection is to me one of the most pathetic things in the world.

Tuesday 18 July

Understudy rehearsal. Fairly disastrous except for June Whitfield[1]. Went with Joyce to hear Frank Sinatra[2], who was really very fine. Went to the theatre for a bit after dining at the Ivy. Ticked Sylvia off about drinking in the theatre, which was horrid but necessary. Went to Charles and Ham's party for me. As usual a riotous success. Started very glamorously with Tyrone [Power], Cesar Romero[3], Doug and Mary Lee [Fairbanks], Johnny Mills, Dickie Attenborough, etc., and finished with the old guard playing 'the game'[4].

Wednesday 19 July

Well, this is the end of this particular phase. It has been strenuous and fairly exhausting, but the show is going well and Graham has justified everything which makes me deeply happy. This afternoon I went with him to see Eric Portman give a superb performance in *His Excellency*[4]. Really an excellent play. After this, I spent an hour with Dickie and Edwina [Mountbatten], who seemed anxious about Max Beaverbrook and had heard that he and I had had a *rapprochement*. He is still a bitter attacker of Dickie and I sensed in the atmosphere a certain whiff of self-justification. It was all somehow uneasy, as though I were being subtly briefed for any future talks I might have with Max, and equally subtly there was a feeling of appeal. I must say I felt astounded and rather cross. I do so resent having my intelligence underrated.

Friday 21 July   Jamaica

I need hardly say there is a strong norther blowing. I expected more tranquillity in July. The beach is in a muck-up and quite obviously always will be so. I think it will really be the most sensible idea to build a pool so that one can always swim without coming up against rocks or meeting ubiquitous barracudas. A lovely, gentle afternoon and evening wrapped in the luxury of being alone and having nothing specific to do but rest my weary bones.

Tuesday 25 July

A much better day, pressing on with Mr Proust[5]. I have now got four volumes

1 June Whitfield (b. 1925), British actress and comedienne.
2 Frank Sinatra (b. 1915) was singing at the Palladium.
3 Cesar Romero (b. 1907), Latin-American film star and Broadway actor.
4 A form of charades.
5 By Dorothy and Campbell Christie at the Prince's Theatre.
6 He was reading *Swann's Way*.

under my belt. He is an exquisite writer but for pomposity and intricacy of style he makes Henry James and Osbert Sitwell look like Berta Ruck. What a tiresome, affected ass he must have been, but what extraordinary, meticulous perception.

Thursday 3 August

Leonard Cottrell[1] and Wynford Vaughan-Thomas[2] came to lunch. They were very good company, particularly Vaughan-Thomas, to whom I took a great shine. He is a cheerful man with an enjoyable sense of humour and very well-read and intelligent. They both bathed, looking like new bread, laughed a lot, admired everything and talked incessantly. They finally left at about five o'clock. As I had already done my day's work before they arrived, I spent the rest of the evening painting and reading. It looks as though the Americans are about to be shoved out of Korea. Unfortunate, to say the least of it.

Monday 14 August

Cable from Lorn. Last week's business £2,683[3]. Oh Christ! It seems as though it is a flop after all. I really am very, very angry. If the public don't want to see that easy entertainment and listen to those lyrics and that music and if they do want to pack out *King's Rhapsody*, then they can get on with it. I am sad on Graham's account. He is so bloody good and seems so unlucky.

Saturday 2 September   Connecticut

Arrived La Guardia 12.30. Drove straight out to Fairfield. Jack looking very well. Went to the Westport Theatre to see a new play redeemed by one superb performance by a new young actress called Maureen Stapleton; a name to remember. The rest of the cast good.

Sunday 3 September

Very perturbed in my mind about Jack drinking too much, chiefly iced tea which is loaded with whisky. Dick Rodgers wildly keen for me to direct *Anna and the King of Siam*. Very persuasive and flattering. Also wants me to play it[4]. All this very soothing to a bruised ego. Had a long talk to Jack about it and he thinks it would be an excellent thing to do, as I could get two per cent of the gross which would amount to about $1,000 a week for years if it were a hit, also $5,000 down and all expenses. It would entail three months' work. Thought about it very carefully by myself.

1 Leonard Cottrell, British archaeologist; his first book, *The Lost Pharaohs*, had been published the previous year.
2 Wynford Vaughan-Thomas, Welsh broadcaster, who worked with BBC radio and later television from 1937 to 1958.
3 For *Ace of Clubs* at the Cambridge; about fifty per cent capacity.
4 The role of the King, which went eventually to Yul Brynner.

(a) Although probably some arrangement could be made with the Treasury, I should not by any means really get all that money[1].

(b) In three months I could either write a new play for myself or a novel or both or neither. But at least I'd be carrying out my own plan of relaxing for a year.

In fact, tempting and exciting as it sounds, it would actually be a waste of time. I know that this is a moment in my life when I must really be careful. I have earned time to think and I am going to have it.

Monday 4 September   New York

Lectured Jack about drinking. He took it very well. We came into New York in the afternoon and then went to see Helen Hayes in *The Wistaria Trees*[2]. Not really good enough but Helen absolutely superb. She is a wonderful actress. The title ought to be *A Month in the Wrong Country*.

Friday 8 September

Goddard Lieberson came and couldn't have been nicer. He is head of Columbia Records and wants me to do some long-playing records, notably *Conversation Piece* with Lily Pons. Also possibly *Design for Living* with the Lunts. Delighted with this idea as it is not exhausting or nerve-racking and takes at most only a few days. I will get my expenses.

Sunday 10 September

Read *Anna and the King of Siam*. First act only completed. It is very charming. Then went to lunch with the Rodgers. All of us plus Moss and Kitty Hart. Long session with Dick. Fought like a steer. Refused definitely to play it, which they are mad for me to do. It is a lovely part but I know I should go dotty. Then Dick offered to advance the production so that I could get to Jamaica in March. He urged and pleaded. Obviously I could get practically anything I want, within reason. Finally I agreed to think it over further. Jack urging me to do it, also Valentina. We all dined at Ferber's. Talked to Edna about doing *Anna* and she said, 'Nonsense, why should you do a thing like that when there is no "food" in it for you?' I could have kissed her. Later on, music from me and Dick. Went home and found cable saying business up £500[3].

Tuesday 12 September

A peaceful day by myself. In the evening drove to New Haven in the station-wagon. Met Jack, dined and went to the new Irving Berlin musical *Call Me*

---

1 After tax.
2 Play by Joshua Logan based on Chekhov's *The Cherry Orchard* and set in Louisiana.
3 On the previous week's *Ace of Clubs* takings at the box-office.

Madam. Ethel Merman superb, the whole first act tiptop, but the second act not so good. Was implored by George Abbott[1] to give my criticisms and so I did. He didn't seem to mind. Excellent new juvenile called Russell Nype.

Wednesday 13 September   New York

Lunched with Cole [Porter] at the Pavillon. Spent afternoon with Goddard Lieberson. Arranged to record the Ogden Nash verse for *Carnaval des Animaux* on Friday.

Saturday 23 September   Jamaica

Ace of Clubs radio script arrived from the BBC. Incomprehensible and idiotic. Had to spend four hours redoing the whole thing. Would not have done so but that a broadcast will help the show if it is good.

Bathed in the moonlight and I got badly stung by a jellyfish that entwined itself round my right arm and side. Very painful. Treated with ammonia and fresh lime. The arm swelled up with great weals across it. Drove home with damn thing still stinging but lessening in intensity.

Friday 29 September

A lovely empty day to myself. In the afternoon I packed and, when I was done, sat on the verandah watching the sunset, sipping a whisky and soda and reflecting on life in general and my last two months here in particular. I love this place more and more. I have had leisure and peace and time and room to swing a lot of cats. I feel extremely well and I am fairly teeming with ideas. I am enjoying all the planning and scheming about the guest house and the beach, etc. I am looking forward to getting home to my loved ones but, at the same time, jolly sad to be leaving. Actually, the beautiful weather will change soon and it won't be so lovely, but this last week has been exquisite. When I come back the guest house will, I hope, be finished. I am sure that buying this land was one of the wisest things I have ever done. It is here and it is mine and, whatever happens to the silly world, nothing much is likely to happen here. It has been a lovely time and I am truly grateful. Tomorrow I fly home.

Monday 2 October   London

Lovely morning with Lorn. Intensive gossip. Lunch at the Ivy: Lorn, Gladys, Graham and me. Went with Gladys to *Ace of Clubs*. Really very good performances but it all needs tightening. Called rehearsal for Wednesday morning. Dinner at the Caprice.

---

1 George Abbott (b. 1887), American playwright and producer, responsible for the *Call Me Madam* production.

Tuesday 3 October

Supper at the Café de Paris with Gladys, Cole and Graham in order to see Kay Thompson[1], who was brilliant. Took her back to the studio and played Graham's and Cole's new song. Very enjoyable.

Wednesday 4 October   White Cliffs

Woke up with a curious feeling of dreariness about London and England generally. The gas strike is getting out of hand. The whole country seems to be apathetically accepting its obvious regimentation. Nothing but wrong numbers on the telephone and general inertia.

Graham, Pat and Sylvia have all three really held true remarkably well. Lunch with Graham at the Ivy. Lots of Welsh affection from Ivor, etc. Went to the matinée of *The Little Hut*. The lights fused at the beginning of act one and we sat in the dark for forty minutes before the play was resumed. It is really wonderfully directed by Peter Brook. Robert Morley is quite brilliant, David Tomlinson and Joan Tetzel excellent. Set enchanting and adaptation very good.

Visited Binkie briefly but unable to get a word in on account of Gregory Ratoff[2] roaring like a Jewish Russian bull.

Came down to the Bay with Cole. Reunion with Mum, who looks fine but so very frail. Long talk with Cole about the dreadful expense of running this place – not just White Cliffs but all the other houses. Seriously thinking of selling Goldenhurst, retaining several acres of it and retiring there later on. If war should come, we should be thrown out of here immediately. It mightn't be a bad idea to build a compact set-up on my own land. Much as I adore White Cliffs, it is extravagant and I have now got Blue Harbour. Building something new is always enjoyable, anyhow.

Sunday 8 October

Read in the papers a great scare story about flying saucers being visitations from another world. As a matter of fact, everything being so peculiar, it is, I suppose, just possible that they might be. I really don't know how the Catholics would get around that.

Monday 9 October   London

Took Tom Arnold to dine at the Bon Viveur. We went on to a special performance of *Accolade*[3] which Emlyn was giving for the Orphanage. A play of

---

1 Kay Thompson, American actress and cabaret singer.
2 Gregory Ratoff (1897-1960), flamboyant Russian actor-director.
3 By Emlyn Williams at the Aldwych Theatre; about a man whose knighthood is withheld when details of his homosexual past are made public.

considerable expertness and horrifying vulgarity. It was well played particularly by Dora Bryan, Diana Churchill and Noel Willman. I had to make a speech from the box, thanking everybody for everything. Drink with Winnie and Gladys afterwards.

Thursday 12 October   White Cliffs

Came down to the Bay with Cole. Feel I am starting a cold. Supper in bed. While talking to Cole, was suddenly struck with a really wonderful idea for a light comedy. Went on discussing it till after 2 a.m. It fell into place easily which is always a good sign.

Friday 13 October

The idea matured and grew. No title yet but it really could be a wonderful satire on the dear old art lovers; it will have to be kept at a high artificial pitch throughout.

Saturday 14 October

Suddenly thought of a title, *Nude with Violin*, which is really right for the play.

Wednesday 18 October   London

Walter and Helen Lippmann[1] came to lunch and it was very pleasant. Dined with Edward at Kathleen's[2]. I am dreadfully worried about him. He is obviously overstrained, exhausted and unhappy. He is giving up the Paris shop in November and retiring for good. This is breaking his heart, but if he does not stop overworking or even working at all, he is liable to lose the sight of his one remaining eye. I think he will be all right really and he is obviously being sensible. He is coming to Jamaica with me in December.

Thursday 19 October

Made momentous domestic decision after long discussion with Lorn. She now becomes my 'representative' and Cole my secretary. This will make everything much simpler. Lorn really must be relieved of some of the strain and responsibility, and Cole is too intelligent and efficient to go on waiting at table and being a 'servant'. I am sure it will all work out very well. We have changed his name to Cole Lesley[3] and all is cheerful.

Spent two and a half hours with Binkie, who is also suffering from strain

---

1 Walter and Helen Lippmann, American political columnist on the *Herald Tribune* and his wife.
2 Kathleen Molyneux was Edward's sister.
3 From Leonard Cole.

and overwork. Joyce and I worked on him hard and I think had some effect. He too must come to Jamaica.

Friday 27 October

Arrived in Florence at 4.30 p.m. Met by Derek [Hill]. Drove to Fiesole. Beautiful but cold. Went to Derek's dear little house which is a dear little ice-house and very horrid indeed. It was pitch dark.

Saturday 28 October

Cough not improved by the freezing house. Woke feeling lousy. Bathroom *frigorifico* and no hot water. Just my dish. Derek took me over Berenson's villa[1]. It is filled with priceless *objets d'art* and pictures – a great number of immensely famous Madonnas simpering in gold leaf. I know already that I should never have come to Florence. The car broke down so it was hours before we could get away.

On arrival at Derek's house, I made my great decision and told Derek in no uncertain terms that I was leaving his bed and board in favour of the Excelsior Hotel on account of not wanting to catch pneumonia. He was very sweet about it. I packed like lightning and was out of that beastly little icebox for ever. Began to relax at the Excelsior. Retired to my warm bed in a warm room with infinite relief.

Monday 30 October

Marched about Florence. Lovely day. Dinner with Derek. Slight finger-wag from me in course of which I inveighed against the prissy, self-conscious academic beauty of Florence, and said that a young painter trying to paint here would be like sitting down in Rumpelmeyers[2] to make fudge.

Wednesday 1 November

Arrived Paris 10.15. Edward very sweet and behaving wonderfully, although he is really in a dreadful state of unhappiness. He is giving up the shop definitely next week and retiring for good. I worked him up as much as I could about coming to Jamaica. Drove back and went to a cocktail party *chez les jolies* Seidemanns.

Sunday 5 November   London

Morning spent doing letters with Lorn and visiting Mum. In the afternoon did letters with Cole. Took Joyce to the dress rehearsal of tomorrow's Irene Vanbrugh matinée[3]. Really very good. Graham first rate; Diana Wynyard

1 I Tatti, home of the art critic Bernhard Berenson (1865-1959).
2 Famous cake and coffee shop.
3 A memorial tribute to the British actress, who had died the previous November.

wonderful in *Much Ado*; Alicia Markova and Anton Dolin lovely; and Bea [Lillie] supreme, as usual.

Monday 6 November

Matinée a great success. Fortunately, although nervous, I did my speech well and got a wonderful ovation. The Queen and the Princesses came backstage and were charming to everyone, finishing up with Beattie and me.

   Lovely party at Tyrone [Power]'s: Marlene [Dietrich], Michael [Wilding], Monty Clift[1], Gloria Swanson, Clifton [Webb], etc.

Monday 13 November   White Cliffs

Winnie, having dashed off an enchanting 'Conversation Piece'[2] of us playing canasta, departed. Cole and I went to Dover and did a little shopping for canvases and paints and turpentine. Saw Joan Crawford in a dashing melo-drama[3] in which she was jolly ruthless and ruined a lot of gentlemen.

Sunday 19 November

Restful day. Visited Mum. Gladys, Joyce and I dined with Clifton and had a private showing of *All About Eve*[4], a brilliant picture with Bette Davis absolutely superb. Party afterwards *chez moi*: Tyrone, Marlene, Emlyn[5], Binkie, etc., also dear Jack Buchanan[6].

Tuesday 21 November

Went into Dover and watched the arrival of Queen Juliana[7]. Very enjoyable. The Duke of Gloucester saw me and passed out with laughter. Prince Bern-hard waved. Everyone very confused.

Thursday 23 November   London

In the evening went to Buckingham Palace and thoroughly enjoyed it. It was a small party, only about two hundred. The King and Queen were sweet to me. Whirled around breathlessly with Queen Juliana. Joyce Grenfell was there.

Saturday 25 November

In the evening an orgy of theatre-going with Joyce [Carey]. The first house at the Palladium. Frankie Howerd good but the show, including Binnie Hale,

1 Montgomery Clift (1920–66), the American film star.
2 A painting of Joyce, Noël, Ian Fleming and Ann Rothermere.
3 *Flamingo Road*.
4 Written and directed by Joseph Mankiewicz.
5 Emlyn Williams (b. 1905), Welsh actor, playwright and producer.
6 Jack Buchanan (1891–1957), debonair British stage and film actor.
7 Queen Juliana of the Netherlands, on a state visit with her consort Prince Bernhard.

awful. Then the second house of *Touch and Go*[1]: good in parts but everyone overplaying. Called for Graham and the three of us went to hear Dolores Gray at the Empress Club. She was quite enchanting and brilliantly professional. What a relief.

Monday 27 November

Went to *King's Rhapsody* with Hester Chapman[2]. Really enjoyed it very much. It is highly sugary, romantic and extremely well done. Supper at Ivor's flat afterwards.

Thursday 30 November

Worked in the morning. In the afternoon Gladys arrived and we settled down to a curiously profound heart-to-heart and at the moment of writing my heart is high. She was not in the least neurotic or putting up a gallant façade. We discussed her diminishing interest in the theatre, etc. I said firmly that I did not want her to do another big musical with me or indeed anything else unless she was really passionately excited by it. She was completely in agreement over and above good behaviour. Every fermenting doubt was smoothed away and I really feel that she is right back home. We also discussed the possible imminence of war and what was to be done, and arrived at the mutual conclusion that the only place was here.

Thursday 7 December

My last day in England. Visited Mum. Lunched with Ann [Todd] and David Lean. Saw their film of Jamaica, which is lovely. Drove with them down to Silverlands, where a Christmas party was televised; paper caps and crackers and general *bonhomie*. Talk with Tom Arnold. Provisional notice of the show[3] going up next week. Very depressing. Watched the show. Bad audience, but excellent performance. Said goodbye to the company. Party at the studio. Charles, Ham, Cole, Joyce, Lorn, Gladys, Marlene, Arthur [Macrae], Binkie, Bobbie Helpmann and Michael Benthall[4]. Very successful.

Friday 8 December   ss *Liberté*

A day of goodbyes[5]. Mum was the worst because she suddenly became so tiny and touching and defenceless. She cried, unwillingly but dreadfully, and it was bad. Then said goodbye to Lornie and Gladys, Cole and Graham. To

---

1 Revue by Jean and Walter Kerr at the Prince of Wales Theatre.
2 Hester Chapman (1899–1976), historian and novelist much admired by Noël.
3 *Ace of Clubs*.
4 Michael Benthall (1919–74), former actor who was artistic director of the Old Vic through the 1950s when the complete cycle of Shakespeare's plays was produced.
5 He was bound for New York and Jamaica.

love and be loved is the most important thing in the world but it is often painful.

Thursday 14 December   New York

Arrived at crack of dawn. Lunched with Natasha at the Pavillon. Saw Elsa [Maxwell], Linda[1], Maggie [Case], Duchess of Windsor, etc. Did some shopping.

Friday 15 December

Went to Dr Castioviego at 10.15. Immense relief. Nothing wrong with Edward's eye beyond overtiredness[2]. It was dreadfully pathetic to see his face when the doctor told him. He can even paint again in moderation.

Clifton and other loved ones who had decided definitely that he had a brain tumour must feel a big disappointment.

Dined with Jack, Natasha, Peter Brook[3] and Maggie Case. Went to *Guys and Dolls*[4]. Absolutely wonderful and brilliantly staged. Small party at Valentina's afterwards.

Saturday 16 December

Fifty-one today. I've got the key of the parlour door, I've never been fifty-one before.

André Kostelanetz came to lunch with me at the Drake and we went through the *Conversation Piece* score[5]. We then called on Lily at the Met and also called on Cyril Ritchard by request. He wants to sing 'Nina' in a revue. I said no. Drink with Fleur Cowles[6], Irene Selznick and Edward. Later on, drinks with Clifton and, later still, the Blue Angel. Pearl Bailey[7], etc.

Tuesday 19 December   Jamaica

Arrived at Kingston. Pouring rain but fortunately it was warm. Lunch too elaborate, with too many martinis. Saw Edward beginning to disintegrate. Got away as soon as possible, with Edward in a violent, uncontrollable rage. Pouring rain. Charming. Arrived fairly wretchedly at Blue Harbour to find the path to the house a swamp. Oh dear. Rose above everything. New guest house really lovely and beautifully built. Intend to use it exclusively for myself.

1 Linda Porter, wife of Cole Porter.
2 Edward Molyneux had feared blindness.
3 Peter Brook (b. 1925), British stage and occasional film director, later co-director of the Royal Shakespeare Company.
4 The musical by Frank Loesser based on Damon Runyon's stories.
5 Which Noël was to record with Lily Pons under the baton of her husband, André Kostelanetz.
6 Fleur Cowles, American magazine editor, wildlife painter and party-giver in New York and London.
7 Pearl Bailey, the black American entertainer, was in cabaret at the Blue Angel.

Edward went to rest in the little guest house, which had been charmingly arranged for him, and came up almost in tears because the noise of the sea got on his nerves. On the whole, a disastrous day. Beach not a success. The new wall has certainly brought the sand, but it has also taken away the water. Goody, goody.

Saturday 23 December

Spent the morning happily arranging furniture. I am very, very delighted with my new home and my spirits are already soaring at the thought of being able to get away by myself. Edward returned mad about White River and wanting to move in immediately. He really is on the silly side. Horrified at the thought of Edward buying White River (price £25,000) as it is malarial and right on the road, etc. Edward rather pissed. I warned him gently about not being too impulsive about White River, whereupon he flew at me and really was quite insufferable. I kept my temper with a great effort and got him back to reasonable affability, but the strain was considerable. He has so many wonderful qualities but he is curiously petulant and spoilt, and he always was.

Monday 25 December

Although weather abominable, the day was a great success, apart from the fact that instead of Jack arriving at about lunch-time, a telegram came saying his plane had been delayed and would not arrive until 2 a.m. tomorrow. In the evening there was a great giving and receiving of presents. Edward was at his best the whole day and nobody flew at anybody. I managed to get a good bit of work done and all was a good deal merrier than a marriage bell.

Friday 29 December

Long talk and swim with Goddard [Lieberson]. He is a nice creature but, like all sophisticated Americans, neurotic and too sex-conscious. But, unlike many of them, he is exceedingly well-read. Lunched with Max Beaverbrook, who came to pick me up in the car. He was very amiable indeed and I think he has really decided to himself that he is ashamed of having been so vile for so many years.

Sunday 31 December

Expected Ivor and Co. for lunch but a telegram arrived saying they had been held up in Bermuda. Worked. Edward slightly more cheerful. Jack very sweet and very funny. We had a New Year's dinner at Castle Gordon[1]. Returned here to drink at the midnight hour, during which I obliged at the piano, then we went back to Castle Gordon for the festivities and Edward began to get drunk and belligerent, and so we came home.

1 A nearby hotel.

1951

A year of death and quite remarkable rebirth. Before it was half over, news reached Noël in Jamaica of the London demise of Ivor Novello and Charles Cochran, both of whom he had known since the very beginning of his career in the theatre and whose names were synonymous with his own in the annals of 1930s West End success. It was the end not only of a couple of friendships but also of a whole chapter of British show-business.

But then, abruptly, the tide turned. Noël returned to England towards the middle of the year, found that two of the comic numbers he had recently written were at the heart of the success of that year's hit, Lyric Revue, *and then, almost accidentally, discovered a whole new career for himself as well. Faced with the inevitable charity garden party in aid of the Actors' Orphanage, Noël decided to dispense with the usual boring autograph session and instead took a tent, outside which he put up a sign reading simply 'Noël Coward At Home: Admission Three Shillings'. Inside it, he and Norman Hackforth, the pianist who had faithfully accompanied him on years of gruelling wartime troop concert tours, presented a sequence of medleys of all the old Coward songs from 'Parisian Pierrot' across thirty years to 'Sail Away'.*

The triumph Noël had in the tent on that one wet afternoon was to lead within a few weeks to the last major development in his career: his emergence at the Café de Paris – to his own and everyone else's surprise – as one of the most highly paid and highly successful cabaret entertainers of the 1950s. He was already on the road to Las Vegas when Kenneth Tynan, reviewing his début at the Café, wrote, 'To see Coward whole, public and private personalities conjoined, you must see him in cabaret, romping fastidiously, padding down those celebrated stairs on black suede-clad feet and baring his teeth as if unveiling some grotesque monument before giving us "I'll See You Again" and all the other bat's wing melodies of his youth.'

And that was not all. Noël's first successful comedy in almost a decade, Relative Values, *opened at the Savoy Theatre a few nights after his Café première, with a cast headed by Gladys Cooper, Angela Baddeley and Judy Campbell, and reviews nearly good enough to make him forget the insults to which he had been treated by the Press in the long years since* Blithe Spirit. *By Christmas, he was even back at his beloved Goldenhurst; 'On the whole,' he noted with commendable restraint, 'a good year.' In fact, it was one of the best he ever had.*

Monday 1 January   Jamaica

The New Year has begun with a lovely day. We all had a delicious morning on the beach except Edward, who stayed alone in the house on account of not caring for the sea.

Ivor, Bobby, Beattie, Olive, Phyl Monkman, Alan Melville[1] arrived at 12.45 and were all very sweet and admired the house like mad. The buffet lunch was excellent. They were all fairly exhausted but put up a brave show. In the evening we all dined at Castle Gordon.

Tuesday 2 January

Cable from Graham saying that the show[2] is definitely closing on Saturday, and that he will be here on Tuesday.

Friday 5 January

Started to work but was quickly frustrated by a blood row between Evan and Alan[3], one of the beach boys, in course of which they apparently attacked each other with knives. I held a sort of court of enquiry. Everybody denied and refuted and carried on alarmingly. Alan left for good. I delivered an ultimatum that if there was any further quarrelling I would fire the whole lot. Evan, in spite of his efficiency, has a fiendish temper and a *folie de grandeur*.

Max Beaverbrook and his granddaughter, Jean Campbell, came to lunch. The old boy was affable to a degree.

War news appalling. Chinese hurling Americans out of Korea.

Saturday 20 January   New York

Lunched with Linda [Porter] – very sweet. Rehearsed with Lily [Pons] for two hours[4]. Went to *Guys and Dolls* with Graham, having managed to get seats from George Kaufman[5]. It is a great evening in the theatre.

Friday 26 January

Finished the whole record; it sounds very good.

Party given by Doubleday's for me in the evening. Gertie looked lovely and was at her best. Tallulah looked awful and was at her worst.

1 Staying nearby with Ivor Novello were Robert Andrews, Beatrice Lillie, Olive Gilbert, Phyllis Monkman (all but Beatrice Lillie regular performers in Novello shows) and the playwright and lyricist Alan Melville (b. 1910), who was now working with Novello as the lyricist for the last of Novello's musicals, *Gay's the Word*.
2 *Ace of Clubs*.
3 Staff at Blue Harbour.
4 For their double-album recording of *Conversation Piece*, which also starred a young Richard Burton.
5 George Kaufman (1889-1961), American playwright, director and Algonquin wit.

Tuesday 30 January   Jamaica

Still bad weather. I have stinking cold which I caught in the plane. Annie [Rothermere], Ian [Fleming] and Cecil [Beaton] came to lunch – an orgy of photography.

Wednesday 31 January

Cold still heavy. Wrote a lot of letters. Lay in the sun. Quiet lunch and snooze afterwards.

Poor old Cochran died after his horrible accident[1].

Friday 2 February

Until the evening a lovely peaceful day. I worked in the morning and started a new picture.

Then, alas, dinner at Jamaica Inn with Edward, who was pissed and intolerable. He flew at me before dinner and made an ass of himself, and, as far as I am concerned, a beautiful friendship is over. Tomorrow in the cold light of remorseless dawn I intend to tell him so.

Saturday 3 February

A day fraught with drama. At 9.30 I got into the car, drove to Castle Gordon and told Edward exactly what I thought of him. The whole interview was over in about five minutes. Just before he left for Montego, Edward wrote me a heart-broken little note thanking me for all I had done. For the moment I ignored this. I will write to him tomorrow.

Thursday 8 February

Letter from Edward in reply to mine saying he couldn't quite take all I said and would like to have one or two cracks back. I would like to see what happens when he tries.

My first copy of *Star Quality*[2] arrived and very nice it looks.

Monday 12 February

Worked all the morning and all the afternoon – a tough struggle – however I must press on. Rosamond[3] came at 5.30 – a long heart-to-heart. She is dreadfully unhappy about Cecil Day Lewis[4] leaving her after nine years of

---

1 Charles Cochran (1872-1951), the English impresario who had financed and produced many of Noël's great 1930s hits, had been trapped in a bath of scalding hot water.
2 Noël's second collection of short stories.
3 Rosamond Lehmann (b. 1903), novelist, perhaps best known for *Invitation to the Waltz* and *The Echoing Grove*; she was in Jamaica staying with Ian Fleming and Ann Rothermere at Goldeneye.
4 Cecil Day Lewis (1904-72), poet, Professor of Poetry at Oxford 1951-56; in 1968 he succeeded John Masefield as Poet Laureate.

illicit bliss. She is also none too comfortable and will probably be in this house soon.

Saturday 17 February

Dined with Oliver[1] at Jamaica Inn. He is painting beautifully – bought a picture off him for £80 – it is quite lovely.

Wednesday 28 February

First review of *Star Quality* in the *New York Times*. Very bad and keeping on about me being old-fashioned (I don't think it is true).

Tuesday 6 March

A shocking and sad day because Ivor is suddenly dead[2]. He died late last night or early this morning of a heart attack. The first intimation I had was from the *Daily Express* asking me to write an article about him. This I did not understand, as the cable said nothing of his death. Then other cables came.

Graham and Cole were out with Rosamond, so I was all alone and felt awful. I shall miss him very much because, in spite of his plays and his acting, I was very fond of him – also he is another landmark swept away. Poor, poor Bobby [Andrews] – he will be utterly devastated.

Thursday 22 March

An irritating day. Felt dizzy and not well. Tried to concentrate on *Nude with Violin*, but something is holding me back. It really isn't good enough.

Friday 23 March

Good Friday. Very good Friday really. Suddenly evolved a comedy called *Moxie*. It feels the sort of play I want to write – worked it out with Joyce [Carey].

Monday 26 March

Eight pages done of *Moxie* and rather good. The flow is beginning, and oh, the bliss of writing dialogue after prose.

Roald Dahl[3] suddenly appeared and stayed to dinner.

Tuesday 27 March

Left for Port Antonio at 7.30 – arrived 9.30. Rafted down the Rio Grande. Lovely weather.

1 Oliver Messel (1904–78), artist and stage designer.
2 He had died after a performance of his *King's Rhapsody*.
3 Roald Dahl (b. 1916), British novelist and short story writer.

In the evening dined with Errol Flynn and his wife Pat.[1] Drinks on his yacht which is beautiful, then barbecue dinner on his island – palm trees – lit by torches. Both of them extremely nice; a really lovely evening.

Sunday 1 April

Finished the first act. I have decided to change the title from *Moxie* to *Relative Values*.

Wednesday 18 April

Finished the play. Read it through complete to Joyce and Cole – it really sounded very good – it is not too long and I am sure has entertainment value.
  Now I am really going to have a holiday.

Thursday 19 April

Did a lot of letters and telegrams. Nearly finished *Little Dorrit* – what a beastly girl, but what a wonderful novel.
  Meeting about 'Designs for Living'[2]. The money is to be used for training six girls and buying four looms.

Monday 23 April

Got all my notices from New York[3]. All absolutely insulting and nearly all idiotic. I suddenly realized how foolish it is to allow one's mind ever to be irritated by reviews. I write what I wish to write – later on the world can decide if it wishes to. There will always be a few people, anyhow, in every generation who will find my work entertaining and true.

Thursday 10 May

Cable from Joyce saying that Binkie and Jack were genuinely enthusiastic about *Relative Values* – and then a lovely cable from Jack himself.

Wednesday 16 May   Genesee[4]

A very hot day but lovely and peaceful. In the evening read *Relative Values* to Lynn and Alfred, who were genuinely crazy about it – no criticism at all – I was very thrilled and pleased.

1 Errol Flynn (1909–59), the dashing Hollywood star, was at this time married to American actress Patrice Wymore (b. 1926).
2 An American millionaire, Charles Marsh, had given Noël $1,000 to be used for the local community in any way Noël chose; he had decided to set up a local textile weaving business and named it after his 1932 comedy.
3 For *Star Quality*.
4 The Lunts' home in Wisconsin.

Friday 18 May

I want to do a Victorian comedy for Alfred and Lynn if only I can get a good enough idea. We discussed it *ad nauseam*.

A bit troubled with neuritis in my arm.

Monday 21 May   New York

Guthrie [McLintic] and I dined and went to *The King and I*. Gertie absolutely wonderful all through. Yul Brynner fine, production good, direction bad, music and lyrics patchy. Production must have cost $300,000.

Tuesday 22 May

Roald Dahl came to lunch – he is highly intelligent.

Had a bad come-over of dizziness and decided to have a real check-up and went to Dr Wallis. He examined me thoroughly and with almost incredible efficiency. My heart is perfect, my whole condition is fine, and he said that with my constitution I should live to be ninety. What is a little wrong, which I suspected in Jamaica, is my liver, which is a bit congested. My blood pressure is normal when I am recumbent but drops when I stand up. What is wrong is my diet. I must eat more raw foods – fruit and vegetables – and alcohol is definitely bad for me. I shall therefore not drink – I couldn't mind less.

Wednesday 23 May

In the evening went to *The Rose Tattoo*[1]. Maureen Stapleton superb. Eli Wallach was fine. Drove down to Sneden's with Kit and Guthrie.

Thursday 24 May

Saw Kit and Guthrie's new house, which will be lovely. Drove in with Guthrie. Went to New York – *The Moon is Blue*[2] – absolutely charming comedy beautifully played by Barbara Bel Geddes and Barry Nelson. Donald Cook good but too 'mannered'.

Friday 25 May

Had injections. Lunched with Jack. Cables from London. Revue[3] a triumphant success and Graham has made a hit.

Blown out with fruit and vegetable juice and no alcohol.

Wednesday 30 May

Had a drink (no alcohol) with Cole and Linda [Porter]. Dined by myself. Caught the last half hour of *The King and I*. Went with Yul Brynner, Jack,

1 By Tennessee Williams.
2 By F. Hugh Herbert.
3 *The Lyric Revue*, in which Graham Payn (with Ian Carmichael, Dora Bryan and Joan Heal) was performing a couple of new Coward numbers including 'Don't Make Fun of the Fair'.

Natasha and Marlene to see Dean Martin and Jerry Lewis - very funny comedians, but not quite as superb as Jack had said.

Thursday 31 May

Packing, etc. Marlene fetched me - we lunched and drove to the boat. Natasha, Gladys Cooper, John [Buckmaster], the James Donalds[1] and Charles Boyer saw me off. I unpacked, had a turkish bath, dinner and bed.

Tuesday 5 June

Lunched with the Ranks, who really were very sweet. Curious cablegram from Terry Rattigan announcing that there is an extraordinary document awaiting me at Gerald Road, and he hopes I shall still be on speaking terms with him after reading it. What can he mean?

Arrived Southampton. Drove up to London. Terry's astonishing document was a television play he wanted me to do[2].

Wednesday 6 June   London

In the evening went to *The Lyric Revue* with Gladys, Joyce and Cole. Graham excellent throughout and his 'Lucky Day' number was brilliant. The whole revue is a smash success - Dora Bryan[3] superb and Joan Heal[4] excellent.

Thursday 7 June

Three hours with Binkie talking about *Relative Values* - everything he said was sensible and, I think, right. He wants it in three acts instead of two and strengthened here and there. Left him finally to go to a cocktail party at Annie Rothermere's for the Duke of Windsor - did not stay long. Then went to Gladys and told her, as I had discussed with Binkie, the news that I would be having a new set-up for *Relative Values*[5]. She behaved superbly, as always, and I believe in her secret heart she is relieved. At all events she was very fine indeed.

Friday 8 June

Dined with Doug and Mary Lee [Fairbanks] plus Winnie and Gladys. Went to see Danny Kaye[6], who was wonderful. After the show he drove us to Richmond to Johnny Mills's party, which was very gay. Larry, Vivien, Lilli [Palmer], etc.

1 James Donald (b. 1917), British actor, and his wife.
2 Terence Rattigan (1911–77), British playwright; knighted 1971. The play was probably *The Final Test*; Noël declined it.
3 Dora Bryan (b. 1924), British actress and comedienne.
4 Joan Heal (b. 1922), British revue artist.
5 Noël was using a different designer for the first time since *The Vortex* in 1924.
6 Who was appearing at the Palladium.

Tuesday 12 June

Went to the Festival of Britain fun-fair. Really the last word in squalor and completely ungay. The Giant Dipper was disgraceful, like an old-fashioned switchback.

Wednesday 13 June

The best in the theatre in the afternoon – *Waters of the Moon*[1] – and the worst in the theatre in the evening – *Gay's the Word*[2]. The former flawlessly played and directed, the latter stinking with bad taste and the intermixed vulgarity of Ivor and Alan Melville. Cicely Courtneidge a miracle of vitality and hard work, but, oh dear, with that horrible stuff to do. It was rapturously received by a packed house.

Tuesday 19 June

A heavy day but on the whole enjoyable.

The garden party[3] was a success in spite of bad rain in the middle of it. My own show was happily triumphant – I gave twelve or thirteen concerts[4], all of which were rapturously received. After this, feeling bright as a button, I dined with Binkie at 9.45 and sat talking until 4.30.

Wednesday 20 June

Slept until one o'clock. Discussed idea for Victorian play for the Lunts with Lorn. Excellent title – *Quadrille*.

Went with Joyce to *Caesar and Cleopatra*[5] – brilliantly done, and Larry and Vivien wonderful.

Thursday 21 June

Lunch with the Boxes. Discussion about doing picture in October of *Fumed Oak*, *Family Album* and *Red Peppers*.

Went to the Tower Pier at six to go on a yacht party up the river. Very grand and enjoyable, particularly coming back and looking at the South Bank, which looks like a dog's dinner, and the North Bank – floodlit – which, with St Paul's, Somerset House, the Houses of Parliament, etc., was breathtakingly lovely. Felt tears spring to my eyes when one of the ship's crew nudged me and said, 'How's this for "London Pride", eh?' The sordid little party included

1 N.C. Hunter's Chekhovian comedy with Sybil Thorndike and Edith Evans.
2 Ivor Novello's last musical.
3 In aid of the Actors' Orphanage.
4 Twenty-minute song recitals with Norman Hackforth at the piano; out of these came Noël's realization of a whole new career in cabaret.
5 Bernard Shaw's play, which was alternating with Shakespeare's *Antony and Cleopatra* at the St James's Theatre.

the Duchess of Kent, Cecil Beaton, Raymond Mortimer[1] and Bob Boothby[2]. Went back with Bob for a drink at his flat. He told me that we are far more formidably prepared for war than anyone knows, and that the US are ten times more so – and that the Russians are not. Apparently the spy leakages have really frightened the Russians, who have not got enough atomics or the bomb, while the US are fairly plastered with them. Taking into account Bob's slight gift of exaggeration, I suspect there is a certain amount of truth in what he says. I have never yet known him wrong through all the bad old Munich days.

Saturday 23 June

A quiet day. Went with Cole to see *The Lyric Revue* again and thoroughly enjoyed it, after which Graham and I drove down to Notley with Viv and Larry and sat up gossiping over supper until 4.30.

Sunday 24 June

Woke at noon. Visitors arrived. Bette Davis, Gary Merrill[3], Bobbie Helpmann, Peter Finch[4], etc.

Monday 25 June

Drove up in the morning not feeling exactly rested by the weekend. Slept after lunch.

Went with the Duchess of Kent to Covent Garden to hear *Bohème* – Victoria de los Angeles sang well but looked like a musical bun. The whole production was disgraceful and at moments quite hilarious. Took the Duchess to dine at the Ivy, and then on to the Palladium for the Sid Field Benefit[5] – a really star-studded show. Highest spot – Judy Garland. Home about 4 a.m.

Saturday 30 June   White Cliffs

Worked all morning and finished the job[6] – think there is a great improvement. Johnny and Mary[7] arrived in the evening. Ian and Annie came to dinner.

---

1 Raymond Mortimer (1895–1980), writer and for many years literary critic on the *Sunday Times*.
2 Robert Boothby (b. 1900), created Baron 1958, Conservative politician 1924–58 and at this time a member of the Council of United Europe; he later became an outspoken television and radio commentator on public affairs.
3 Gary Merrill (b. 1914), American actor who had become Bette Davis's fourth husband in 1950.
4 Peter Finch (1916–77), British actor whom the Oliviers had met in Australia a few months earlier.
5 The comedian had died the previous year.
6 The rewrite of *Relative Values*, his new comedy.
7 Mary Hayley Bell (b. 1914), playwright, married to John Mills; they were lifelong friends of Noël's, and their eldest daughter, Juliet Mills, was Noël's god-daughter.

They went and we waited up gossiping until Joyce and Graham arrived at 2.15.

Monday 2 July

Graham and Joyce left in the afternoon and I sat in the sunshine with the beach crowded with people and dogs barking and children yelling. I tried to paint, gave it up and went to bed. Then I decided that I am going to give this up and go back to Goldenhurst. It is my own land and so much quieter. I shall miss the sea and the ships, but I shall have the marsh and the trees, the orchard and the croquet lawn. White Cliffs has given me immense pleasure but I have never worked really well here – there is something curiously distracting about it; someone crunches by on the beach or a big ship passes and one's concentration snaps. I am going to Goldenhurst tomorrow to have a look-see – my lease here expires in eight years anyhow.

Monday 9 July   London

Took Joan Fontaine[1] to the Gala Performance at Covent Garden – new Freddie Ashton ballet[2] not good, *Ballet Imperial* lovely. The Queen charming to me as usual. Lost a front stud and sleeve link – emeralds – very cross. Oliver [Messel]'s party very good.

Tuesday 10 July

Buccleuch wedding[3] at the Abbey; absolutely exquisite – wonderful singing and impeccable style. The Queen, Princess Elizabeth, etc. – very, very grand and so typically, indestructibly English. Reception afterwards at Syon House; drove there and back with Doug and Mary Lee.

Thursday 12 July

Orphanage meeting all morning – fairly complicated. Lunch with Peter Brook and John Gielgud. Recorded for three hours at HMV – 'Festival' and 'Sail Away' – very exasperating owing to orchestra being all wrong. Finally got it set.

Friday 20 July

Arrived Cannes after breakfast with René Clair. Second breakfast with Binkie,

1 Joan Fontaine (b. 1917), Hollywood film star, whom Noël had met at a Hollywood party three years earlier: 'It was a nice party,' he wrote to Coley, 'except for Joan Fontaine's titties which kept falling about, and a large rock python which was handed to me as a surprise.'
2 *Tiresias*.
3 Of the daughter of the 8th Duke of Buccleuch.

Arthur [Macrae], J.P.[1], Toby R.[2], Molly Keane[3]. Villa really enchanting – far from luxurious, but with great charm. Gregory Ratoff and André [Roussin]. Later painted a bit.

Saturday 21 July

A lovely day. Painted all morning. Lunched at villa, bathed at Eden Roc, went to Cannes. Drinks at the Carlton with Irene Browne[4], Marie Burke[5], Elsa Maxwell, Dickie Gordon[6].

Monday 23 July

A mistral. Painted in the morning. Lunched with Molly, who is quite bright and doesn't miss a trick. Drinks with Elsa and Dickie plus Freddie Lonsdale[7]. Then the Carlton, where I was presented to Sugar Ray Robinson[8].

Then I gave dinner at the Voile au Vent – perfectly exquisite langouste. Gambled at the Casino, first winning, then losing.

Wednesday 25 July

Not a very nice day. Packed and lunched at home, after which we drove to Eden Roc and bathed, and the sun came out. Drinks at the Carlton with Judy Garland.

Cable from Jack[9] – my play is apparently a success and Claudette is wonderful in it. After a talk with Binkie have decided to fly to America on Tuesday and see it before it closes. I must know whether it is good or not and what Jack has done with it.

Sunday 29 July   White Cliffs

Another long cable from Jack literally beseeching me not to come to America. He has obviously bitched the play by bad direction and doesn't want me to see

1 John Perry (b. 1906), dramatist, director of H.M. Tennent and friend of Binkie Beaumont.
2 Toby Rowland (b. 1916), American-born London impresario, then working for H.M. Tennent.
3 Molly Keane (b. 1905), Irish dramatist and novelist, best known for the play *Spring Meeting* written, under the pseudonym M.J. Farrell, with John Perry.
4 Irene Browne (Brownie) (1891–1965), British actress who had appeared in the film of Noël's *Cavalcade* (1932) and was later to play in his *After the Ball* (1954).
5 Marie Burke (b. 1894), British actress and singer.
6 Dorothy Fellows-Gordon, Elsa Maxwell's lifelong companion; Noël had first met them in 1922, when they had taken him, as a penniless actor, on holiday with them to Venice. He afterwards wrote that 'the life of a gigolo, unimpaired by amatory obligations, could undoubtedly be very delightful indeed'.
7 Frederick Lonsdale (1881–1954), English dramatist, particularly known for his comedies of manners.
8 Sugar Ray Robinson, American boxer, six times world champion.
9 Who was presenting Noël's *Island Fling* (the retitled *Home and Colonial*) in summer stock at Westport, Connecticut, with Claudette Colbert.

for myself. This is a quandary – I don't particularly want to go and yet I would like to see the play played. He is behaving like an abject fool.

Monday 30 July

Came up to London. Long talk with Lornie about the Jack situation. Decided to do nothing about it at all. Saw Norman[1] and we discussed the Café de Paris. I have agreed to open on 29 October for four weeks.

Dined with Joyce and went to the Empire. Michael Wilding excellent in a *Mrs Cheyney*[2] with Miss Greer Garson, who was so piss-elegant that it hurt.

Sunday 19 August

There has been a terrific hurricane in Jamaica which has devastated the airport, killed several people and sunk several ships. Fortunately it came from that direction and I should think Port Maria would have escaped it.

Constance [Collier] and Katy Hepburn came for the day and were absolutely sweet. I love Katy very much.

Sunday 26 August

Wrote a long letter to Jack accepting his suggestion that we finish our theatrical association. This is a relief as I think very little of him as a theatre man.

Thursday 30 August

Letters all morning. Then Leicester Gallery where I bought a Maitland, which is very charming. Lunched at home with Graham. Went to the H.M. Tennent office and looked at Michael Relph's[3] designs for the *Relative Values* set.

Went to the St James's at 10.30 to pick up Larry and Vivien. Drove down to Notley with them and Graham.

Saturday 1 September

Arrival of enchanting Siamese kitten christened first 'Hurricane' and later 'Wordsworth'. Quiet evening. Read *Venus Observed*[4], which Larry wants me to play in New York. It is a lovely part and, at moments, a lovely play, but it is too hard a task and not really my dish.

---

1 Norman Hackforth, who was now encouraging Noël to appear in cabaret at the Café de Paris.
2 Hollywood film version, entitled *The Law and the Lady*, of Frederick Lonsdale's play *The Last of Mrs Cheyney*.
3 Michael Relph (b. 1915), designer and producer-director.
4 By Christopher Fry; Olivier himself had produced and acted in it in London the previous year and still held the rights.

Friday 7 September

Actors' Orphanage meeting – useful but boring. Looked over Mum's new flat[1]. It really will be lovely. Rehearsed with Norman. Caught the 7.15 with Cole and read in the evening papers the appalling news that poor Maria Montez died this afternoon. Apparently she fainted in her bath and was drowned. Poor Jean-Pierre will be demented. I telephoned on arrival and talked to his brother. I am sorry for poor Cole too, having just finished the adaptation of Jean-Pierre's play for her to play in English[2].

Listened to my broadcast appeal for Jamaica[3] – not bad but not particularly good.

Monday 10 September

Meeting at West India House for the Jamaican Hurricane Fund. Lunched at home.

Reading of the play[4] at 2.30 – very satisfactory. Gladys Cooper obviously going to be wonderful, although slow at learning. Judy Campbell read brilliantly – everybody good.

Wednesday 12 September   White Cliffs

Worked as usual. Painted as usual. Ate as usual. Drank vegetable juice as usual. Went to bed early as usual.

Thursday 13 September

Poor Turpin[5] lost his fight with Sugar Ray Robinson. Finished the first act of *Quadrille* and feel it is really good. I do hope the other acts will be as satisfactory and I wish I could stay here until it is finished. However, I must start rehearsing *R.V.* on Monday.

Monday 17 September   London

Rehearsed all day. Everyone going to be good, and Gladys I am sure will make the success of her life. Took her to lunch. Difficult to arrange the moves owing to the shape of the set, but it will come all right I think.

Thursday 20 September

Rehearsed. Home five o'clock and read Lorn first act of *Quadrille* and she genuinely loved it.

1 She was about to move to Eaton Square, Belgravia.
2 Jean-Pierre Aumont had asked Cole Lesley to adapt his comedy *L'Ile Heureuse*, which had been planned as the vehicle for his wife's début on the London stage.
3 After the hurricane.
4 *Relative Values.*
5 Randolph Turpin, English middleweight boxer who in July of this year had beaten Robinson for the world title.

Kenneth Tynan[1] came for a drink and turned out to be charming. A curious young man, very intelligent and with a certain integrity.

Friday 21 September

A good morning rehearsal. Telephone conversation with Alex Korda, who wants me to do a movie with David Lean about the convoys to Russia during the war – oh dear!

Saturday 22 September

Wrote my tribute to Ivor – rather sad and difficult to do.

Annie and Ian produced Cyril Connolly[2] and we all discussed Maclean and Burgess[3].

Tuesday 25 September

Lunch with Tom Arnold who wants me to do a musical for Jack Buchanan and Vanessa Lee[4] – not a bad idea.

Picked up Larry and Viv and went with them to the Jean-Louis Barrault opening of *Les Fausses Confidences*[5] – well done. Party after at Claridge's. Vivien ill with stinking cold, so brought her home.

Thursday 27 September

Disastrous rehearsal owing to Gladys knowing less and less[6]. I am really getting worried. She faffs and stammers and we can never open on Monday fortnight as things are now.

Rehearsed with Norman[7], then went with Cole to *King's Rhapsody* – rather agonizing at moments owing to nostalgia for Ivor. Jack Buchanan really extremely good[8].

Monday 8 October

Disastrous rehearsal with Gladys faffing all over the place. Had restrained showdown with her and in the afternoon she was much better.

Took Joycie to *Tamburlaine*[9] at the Old Vic – Donald Wolfit was good.

---

1 Kenneth Tynan (1927–80), then starting his career as a drama critic on the *Spectator*.
2 Cyril Connolly (1903–74), author and journalist.
3 The British Foreign Office spies, Donald Maclean and Guy Burgess, had fled to Russia.
4 Vanessa Lee (b. 1920), British stage musical star.
5 French star Jean-Louis Barrault (b. 1910), was appearing at the St James's Theatre in Marivaux's classic of 1737.
6 Of her long part in *Relative Values*.
7 For the now imminent cabaret season at the Café de Paris.
8 He had taken over the lead after Novello's death.
9 Christopher Marlowe's sixteenth-century drama.

The play largely idiotic but with some good moments and some funny ones. Dinner at the Ivy.

Tuesday 9 October

Rehearsal good up to the middle of act two, then disaster.

Decided to go to evening word rehearsal – absolute agony but still kept my temper. Gladys really trying hard and I have to admit that, angry as I am with her for not learning the play as I asked her to, she is so good an actress that I have to forgive her. Also I am fond of her. It is the greatest strain to hear her day after day, but at least she is being good about her clothes. She really cannot retain lines. She will be brilliant eventually but, oh, the poor company – and poor me!

Monday 15 October   Newcastle upon Tyne

Did broadcast interview. Another dreadful dress rehearsal. Returned to hotel feeling like death, had a rest and a double whisky and tottered to the theatre. Play a triumphant success but agony for me owing to Gladys's insecurity. Tremendous ovation at the end. Supper afterwards. Binkie wonderful all through. Gladys palpably astounded at all the laughs she got – she gives a remarkable fake performance; charm, heart and authority, but hardly ever the right lines. Quite staggering.

Tuesday 16 October

A quiet day in bed. The notices patronizing and not particularly good. The house sold out for the entire week.

Thursday 25 October   London

Election day. Voted. Rehearsed with Norman. Drinks with Dickie and Edwina. Dinner with Pam Berry[1] – the Salisburys[2], Duff and Diana, the Massiglis[3], Loelia, etc. – very enjoyable. Camrose party at the Savoy. Election results up to the time I left depressing.

Friday 26 October

Conservatives[4] just got in. Lunch with the Rothermeres at the Dorchester – everybody there. In the afternoon rehearsed at the Café de Paris – everything perfect except my voice, which is failing fast. Came straight home feeling

---

1 Lady Pamela Berry (1914–82), society hostess, married to Michael Berry, created Baron Hartwell 1968, editor-in-chief of the *Daily Telegraph* and *Sunday Telegraph*.
2 5th Marquess of Salisbury (Bobbity) (1893–1972), leader of the House of Lords, married to Elizabeth Vere (Betty), daughter of Lord Cavendish.
3 René Massigli, French Ambassador to Britain, 1944–55, and his wife Odette.
4 Under Sir Winston Churchill, now aged seventy-seven.

dreadfully worried. This is the cruellest luck. I feel fine, the microphone is perfect, all London is fighting to get in to see me – and now this happens. I am heart-broken.

Monday 29 October

Agitating day on account of my voice. Rehearsed in the afternoon, visited Mum, came home, rested and woke up practically voiceless. Stayed in bed all evening till eleven o'clock. Musgrove[1] arrived at 11.30 and dealt with my throat.

Went to the Café feeling slightly tremulous. Really triumphant success – tore the place up. Glittering audience headed by Princess Margaret and the Duchess of Kent. All very glamorous – Beattie absolutely wonderful to me[2] – all very enjoyable.

Thursday 1 November

Bed all day, but feeling much better. Went to the opening of *South Pacific*[3]. Show incredibly slow. Audience wildly hysterical. Mary had a great ovation which she richly deserved.

Café de Paris packed. Terrific success. My voice is coming back and I am really beginning to enjoy myself.

Saturday 3 November

Quite a day. Woke almost speechless but rose above that. Went to Oxford[4] with Cole. Saw matinée – capacity house – performance mainly good and play went wonderfully. Caught the 5.50 back.

Hoped voice would improve but it did not. Musgrove came and worked a miracle and I got through my show better than last night. Graham being ill and not able to drive us down to the Bay, we hired a car with an idiotic, slow and over-cautious driver. He got out to piddle just outside Canterbury and could not start the car again. Cole and I got out and pushed, but no use. Fortunately there was a telephone box nearby, so Cole telephoned to Evans[5] to come and fetch us, and we sat in the car till he arrived. Finally got to bed at 5.15.

Friday 9 November

Dined with Binkie, who couldn't have been nicer and is going to deal firmly with Gladys Cooper at Bournemouth. He was really exhausted after a trying

1 John Musgrove, Noël's throat specialist.
2 Beatrice Lillie was already a veteran survivor of Café cabaret.
3 Rodgers and Hammerstein's musical opened at Drury Lane with Mary Martin in her original role.
4 Where *Relative Values* was now playing.
5 Evans, Noël's cook and housekeeper at White Cliffs.

day wrestling with actors, authors and directors. We talked incessantly, drank wine and smoked several cigarettes, after which I went to the Café and sang better than I have ever sung. It was glamour night with Vivien, Larry, Margot Fonteyn[1], Orson [Welles].

Tuesday 13 November

Afternoon spent with Coley. Chose chintzes for Goldenhurst. Binkie came at seven o'clock and was wonderful about *Relative Values* and shrewd as usual. I love him for his personal loyalty to me and for his comforting horse-sense. Delightful dinner with Alex Korda. He is a curious and fascinating man and was highly entertaining and wise, and I enjoyed every moment.

Friday 16 November

Lunch at the Caprice with Michael Joseph[2]. He wants to bring out a *Noël Coward Song Book*. Picture gazing in the afternoon – finally decided on a lovely Boudin for £1,100. Also bought myself a Brianchon.

Went with Coley to see Orson Welles as Othello[3] – he was very fine at moments. The production was a bit fussy, but I enjoyed it. Dined at home and so to work[4].

Tuesday 27 November

Shopping with Cole. Bought Christmas crackers, etc. Very good dress rehearsal of *Relative Values* – Gladys knew all of it at last. Binkie dined with me. Café good – voice better.

Wednesday 28 November

Rested most of the day in preparation for the strenuous evening.

Received the Duchess of Kent and Princess Margaret at the theatre[5]. First act started like ice and warmed up. The royal ladies came up in each entr'acte for drinks and were very sweet. The play went triumphantly. There was a terrific ovation at the end but mercifully no speeches. Then on to Annie [Rothermere]'s party. Then the Café – jammed full and wildly enthusiastic. Dickie and Edwina were there. Then back to the party – sang three songs and left not too late.

Whatever the Press may say, I think the play is a big success.

Thursday 29 November

Well, well, what a surprise! Rave notices. Quite a lot of them irritating and

1 Margot Fonteyn (b. 1919), British prima ballerina; created Dame in 1956.
2 Michael Joseph, book publisher.
3 Orson Welles's first London stage appearance, at the St James's Theatre.
4 At the Café.
5 The Savoy, where *Relative Values* was opening.

ill-written but all, with the exception of the dear little *Daily Mirror*, enthusiastic and wonderful box-office. This should mean a smash hit – very nice too.

Sunday 2 December

All Sunday papers virtually rave notices except Ivor Brown[1], who was a bit pernickety and obviously had not listened to the play very carefully.

Saturday 8 December

Went with Cole to see *Billy Budd* at Covent Garden. Well sung, well put on, but Benjamin Britten's music does not move me. It has the same effect on me as a Braque painting.

Monday 10 December

Went to the Coliseum to appear at the midnight matinée for the Duke of Edinburgh's Playing Fields. Absolute chaos. Was supposed to go on at 1.30 but actually went on at 2.30. Everything far too long. Tommy Trinder[2] saved it for me. I went all right, but I did not enjoy it. Sinatra very good but too slow. The Edinburghs came on to the stage afterwards and were charming to everyone. None of the American women had the manners to curtsey. It was all dull and squalid.

Tuesday 11 December

Stayed in bed feeling fairly exhausted. Rewrote the lyric of 'Old Records' for Mary and me to do at the Café on 13 January[3]. Boy Browning[4] came for a drink.

Dined at Clarence House with the Edinburghs. Sat on Queen Mary's right and she was perfectly enchanting – in more than full possession of all her faculties and did not miss a trick. She is a very great old lady. The rest of the party were Dickie, Edwina and Pamela[5]; Princess Alice and Lord Athlone[6]; Lady Constance Milnes-Gaskell[7], who is a dear; and two gents whose names elude me. After dinner in the private cinema we saw *High Treason*[8]. I did not

---

1 Ivor Brown (b. 1891), drama critic on the *Observer* 1928-54.
2 Tommy Trinder (b. 1909), Cockney comedian.
3 Noël and Mary Martin were doing a charity cabaret there then.
4 Lt.-Gen. Sir Frederick Browning, Comptroller and Treasurer of Princess Elizabeth's household 1948-52, and on her accession to the throne Treasurer to the Duke of Edinburgh 1952-59; married to novelist Daphne du Maurier.
5 Lady Pamela Mountbatten (b. 1929), the Mountbattens' elder daughter.
6 Princess Alice, granddaughter of Queen Victoria, and her husband, the 1st Earl of Athlone, nephew of Queen Mary.
7 Lady Constance Milnes-Gaskell, lady-in-waiting to Queen Mary.
8 British spy drama directed by Roy Boulting.

let on I had seen it before because Princess Elizabeth seemed to think it was a new picture.

The Duchess of Kent was at the Café and has promised to come on the thirteenth. Had a drink with her, then with the Dockers[1] and lastly with Mary Spears[2].

Saturday 15 December

Stayed in all day. Last night at the Café. Sensational. Birthday cake – everyone singing 'For he's a jolly good fellow'. Sang for an hour. Ovation. Champagne with directors, handshakes, autographs, presents, etc. Really very touching. Finished up with Peter Brook and his wife[3], Norman and Pam [Hackforth], Joyce, Arthur and Cole. A very memorable evening.

Sunday 16 December

Probably the nicest birthday I have ever had. It was a shame Graham could not come down because of his cold. We arrived at Goldenhurst at 1.55 – the house and land seemed to envelop me in a warm and lovely welcome.

We spent the afternoon hanging more pictures, etc. Bed at ten o'clock with kidneys and bacon on a tray. Utterly exhausted but deeply and profoundly happy. I am home again.

Wednesday 19 December

Drove up to London. Lunched with Binkie at Scott's. After lunch we went to the Leicester Galleries to choose a painting for my Christmas present from H.M. Tennent Ltd. I chose an enchanting Sickert of *Trelawny of the Wells*. I also found a John Nash going cheap, which I bought for myself. Visited the Savoy Theatre to wish the cast a happy Christmas.

Dined at the Mountbattens: a small dinner party which included the Queen, Princess Margaret, the Edinburghs and Porchester[4]. The Queen and Princess Margaret went off to Buckingham Palace for a servants' ball, but they came back in an hour and, Norman having arrived, I sang my songs. After that everybody sang and it was a gay, uninhibited evening. I really love the Queen.

Thursday 20 December

Rehearsed with Mary Martin for two hours, and drove down to Goldenhurst.

1 Sir Bernard (1896–1978) and Lady (Nora) Docker, millionaire couple whose extravagant life-style attracted enormous publicity.
2 Lady (Mary) Spears; the novelist Mary Borden.
3 Actress Natasha Parry (b. 1930).
4 Lord Porchester (b. 1924).

Tuesday 25 December

One of the happiest Christmases that I have ever known. Pre-lunch present-giving with Gladys. A delicious Christmas dinner. Sleep. Woke feeling awful – then a quick tea and the party began. A triumphant success and a hell of a mix-up. Freres, d'Erlangers[1], Allenbys[2], etc. Christmas tree, presents, crackers, snapdragon. Not *too* late. Really a lovely day.

Monday 31 December

Drank the New Year in in Dora Bryan's dressing-room with most of *The Lyric Revue* company. It has been, on the whole, a good year. There have been the successes of *The Lyric Revue*, the Café de Paris, *Relative Values* and the return to Goldenhurst. Let us hope that 1952 will be as amiably disposed.

---

1 Sir Gerard ('Pops') d'Erlanger, company director and Chairman of BOAC, and his wife 'Smut'.
2 Viscount Allenby (b. 1903) and his wife Daisy Neame.

The successes of 1951 were followed up on all three fronts: more revue songs were written for The Globe Revue, *which repeated the popularity of* The Lyric Revue; Relative Values *was followed by another (though less critically popular) West End comedy called* Quadrille, *which Noël wrote for his beloved Lunts; and there was a second cabaret triumph at the Café de Paris.*

However, this year was sadly overshadowed by the news that reached Noël on Folkestone racecourse via an evening paper's Stop Press headline of 6 September: in New York, suddenly and unexpectedly, at the age of only fifty-four, his beloved Gertrude Lawrence had died of cancer. Earlier in the year he had promised her a new comedy if only she would give up The King and I, *which had been recognized as a risk to her health. Now she was dead, lights were dimmed along Broadway and Shaftesbury Avenue, and Noël was left to collect a few memories of the actress who had been his loving and beloved friend in the theatre and out of it for forty years. 'Her quality was to me unique,' he wrote in* The Times *obituary, 'and her magic imperishable.' 'Noël and Gertie' were no more.*

Tuesday 1 January   London

Michael MacOwan[1] came to lunch and we discussed *The Vortex*.

Wednesday 2 January   Goldenhurst

Woke at 8.30 having hardly slept at all, but feeling fine. Worked on the play[2] in the morning and in the afternoon. Did list of songs for the *Song Book* with Coley.

Finished reading Sir Frederick Ponsonby's *Memoirs of Court Life* – the Royal Family do not emerge as very bright. Winston [Churchill] is crossing the cold Atlantic for a short spell in America. Meanwhile our lives are to be made more miserable than ever by further restrictions, controls, no foreign travel without permits, etc.

Thursday 3 January

Worked from 7 a.m. until 1.15. Slow but, I think, all right. Went into Folkestone with Coley to choose wallpaper for the French room. Bought myself some fleece-lined boots which are paradise. Had hot chocolate and layer cake at Fuller's and a conversation with the waitress, who delivered a tirade against *South Pacific*.

Came home, had supper in bed and a dismal failure over *The Times* crossword. On the whole as nice a day as I could wish for.

Wednesday 9 January

Wordsworth much worse and I think dying. He has caught 'cat flu' and I doubt if there is any hope. I feel dreadfully sad and Cole is miserable. He is such a dear little creature and so full of character.

Took Cole to *Where the Rainbow Ends*. It was poignantly nostalgic going slap-back over forty years and remembering the lines and the music[3]. It was not badly done and the story still holds.

Friday 11 January   London

Meeting of N.C. Limited[4] not too encouraging. More money must be made. Well, I will persevere but *not* at the cost of my talent.

Rehearsed all the afternoon at the Café with Mary and the orchestra. Mary

1 Michael MacOwan (b. 1906), British theatre director, who was planning to revive Noël's *The Vortex*, written in 1923, with Dirk Bogarde and Isabel Jeans.
2 *Quadrille.*
3 Noël had first appeared in this children's classic in 1911, playing William, the spiteful page-boy, and in the 1915-16 revival he had the more showy part of The Slacker. Among 'all we clever little tots', as Noël described himself and the other child actors, was the future star and friend Hermione Gingold.
4 With his accountants.

was really magnificent – she is a marvellous artist. At 5.30 had audition at the Globe and engaged Anthony Forwood for Tom in *The Vortex*. Visited Mum.

Sunday 13 January

Rehearsed with Norman; went through the MS of *Future Indefinite* and corrected it for retyping. Visited Mum. Went to the Café. Received the Duchess of Kent and dealt with everyone. Then the cabaret. Really a triumph – Mary was superb – tore the place up. Financially it will be just all right, but from the point of view of prestige it was very valuable – a highly satisfactory evening.

Thursday 17 January

A happy and productive day because I finished the play. Not only the actual writing but the typing and revising as well. I feel happy because I really think it is good. Hurrah for the holidays!!

Thursday 24 January

Went with Lorn to *Relative Values*: Gladys wonderful, Angela Baddeley and Hugh McDermott overacting, Judy [Campbell] pretty bad. Gave big party – a tremendous success – lasted until 6 a.m.

Wednesday 30 January

Rehearsal of *The Vortex*; extremely good, well directed and played. Dirk Bogarde a little floppy but a fine actor.

Said goodbye to Mum which, as usual, was painful. I know that each time it happens it might be the last time.

Tuesday 5 February   New York

Ship docked 1.45. Jack *incommunicado* and not to be disturbed until four. Natasha appeared and told me the whole story. He is very ill with gout and in great pain, but I think the ulcer business is pretty average silly[1].

Went to the Lunts at four o'clock and read them the play. They are absolutely ecstatic about it, and really could not have been more grateful and sweet. Dined with them and Natasha, and then we went to see Jack. He is obviously fairly ill, although I am not sure how bad really. His hair is white and he looks an old man. He behaved better than I expected, and was cheerful rather than morose. It is all rather puzzling.

Wednesday 6 February

Woke about eight o'clock. Lifted the telephone to call room service and the operator said, 'Have you heard the news that your King [George VI] passed

---

1 Noël was, as always, convinced that Jack's illness was alcoholism.

over?' It was a horrible shock and felt oppressed and miserable all day. I have sent cables to all the Royal Family, and they came from the heart. I am deeply sorry for the poor Queen and Queen Mary. Princess Elizabeth and Prince Philip are flying home from Kenya. She, I am sure, will make a wonderful Queen, but I know how much she loved her father.

Goddard [Lieberson] took me to lunch. Went to Valentina's cocktail party in my honour - everyone from Garbo to Dorothy Stickney[1]. Went to *Pal Joey*[2] with Marlene and thought it very common. Drink at Sardi's with Dick Rodgers and later with Marlene at the Stork.

Saturday 9 February

Dined with Guthrie and went to *Così Fan Tutte* at the Met. Alfred [Lunt]'s production brilliant but I hate Mozart, and I loathed the libretto. Drove down to Sneden's with Kit and Guthrie. Their new house is really lovely.

Thursday 14 February

Dined with Marlene at the Pavillon and went to *Two on the Aisle* - bad revue but Dolores Gray wonderful and Bert Lahr funny as usual. Went to the Stork Club for a bit and then on to Larry and Vivien's - Gertie, Beattie, Rex, Lilli, the Nivens, etc. - a thoroughly theatrical party and very enjoyable.

Saturday 16 February   Jamaica

Evan and the rest of the staff met me eagerly, but no Rygin[3]. I asked immediately where he was and was told he died of distemper two weeks ago. This really shattered me and utterly spoiled my home-coming. I loved him very much and shall miss him every minute. I rose above it as well as I could.

Dined with Ian and Annie at Goldeneye. I sensed that Annie was not entirely happy. Drove home through the lovely warm night.

Monday 18 February

Aggie de Mille[4] suddenly appeared after lunch. Commanded a great orgy of tree lopping.

Megan Lloyd George[5] and Thelma Cazalet[6] dropped in just as I was going

---

1 Dorothy Stickney (b. 1903), actress and dramatist, married to playwright Howard Lindsay.
2 Richard Rodgers and Lorenz Hart's musical, based on stories by John O'Hara.
3 The dog.
4 Agnes de Mille, American dancer and choreographer; she created the dances for *Oklahoma!* and many other award-winning musicals.
5 Megan Lloyd George (1902-66), Welsh politician, daughter of Liberal statesman David Lloyd George.
6 Thelma Cazalet Keir (b. 1899), Conservative MP 1931-45, and later a governor of the BBC 1956-61.

to Look Out. They were very amiable but did not stay long. Look Out was peace and perfection.

Thursday 21 February

A pouring wet day, which cleared towards evening. I wrote a verse to celebrate Annie's and Ian's nuptials[1]. Jack is hobbling about amiably concentrating on his diet sheet. I think he has nothing much wrong with him and is just becoming an egocentric bore.

Saturday 23 February

Drove to Kingston to meet Alfred and Lynn, who arrived on time. They are entranced with Blue Harbour and perfectly sweet. It really is a comfort about old friends.

Tuesday 26 February

Wrote rather a difficult letter to Gladys [Calthrop] explaining why I did not want her to do the dresses for *Quadrille*. I am afraid it will upset her, but it is inevitable. I could not face Lynn and her battling over me.

Wednesday 5 March

Jack and Natasha left – Natasha for New York and Jack for Puerto Rico. Cables from England saying that *The Vortex* had had a triumphant first night with cheers and reasonably good notices.

Monday 24 March

Cable from England saying *The Vortex* is being transferred to the Criterion and that Michael Gough is replacing Dirk Bogarde[2] – he might be very good.

Cole and I were witnesses at Annie and Ian's marriage in Port Maria – a very simple affair, rather nicely done. Later dinner at Goldeneye, which was hilarious. They are leaving tomorrow for Montego, New York and home.

Saturday 5 April

Woke after dreaming vividly of the Queen Mother and there was a registered airmail letter from the Queen herself thanking me for my letter of condolence. A very charming gesture to write it herself when she must have so many thousands to deal with.

Practised drawing all day – it is getting much better. I did a self-portrait staring in the mirror. Evan was quite foxed as to who it was, but there is a

---

1 Ann was now divorced from Lord Rothermere and she and Ian Fleming were about to marry.
2 Who had a film commitment.

faint likeness and it is quite well drawn. Reading *The Caine Mutiny*[1] – very enjoyable.

Monday 7 April

Did two refrains of 'Time and Again'. A wonderful, understanding letter from Gladys and a bitchy, mischief-making letter from Jack saying how dissatisfied the Lunts were[2], and that Alfred would walk out unless Hubert[3] was cut down. As we discussed the whole thing at length when they were here, either someone has gone mad or Jack is lying. I know they go through all sorts of phases before doing a play, and I am prepared for that, but not for mischief-making behind my back.

Tuesday 8 April

Finished reading *The Caine Mutiny* – a very exciting book but nowhere near *The Cruel Sea*[4]. On finishing it I was struck with wonder that the American Navy ever gets anything done at all – the lack of discipline and tradition is appalling.

Sunday 13 April

Drove to Montego Bay. Larry and Vivien arrived at 8.30 – two hours late. Drinks and dinner, after which we drove home stopping for a snifter on the way. Bed about 3 a.m.

Sunday 20 April

Larry is worried about Vivien, who is having a sort of suppressed nervous breakdown. Had a long talk with her and tried to convince her that nervous exhaustion is the result of physical exhaustion, and that she needs a long rest. I love her and can't bear to think of her being unhappy inside.

Gave my annual cocktail party – very successful – all the locals.

Tuesday 22 April

Well, Coley has gone. Larry and Vivien, who have been sweet here, have gone. I am worried about Vivien, who is terribly overtired and obviously suffering from nervous exhaustion. Larry is doing a film[5] – she has nothing for the moment. I love them both and so very much wish them well. It has been a lovely holiday – I feel well and full of ideas and, as usual, I am grateful to dear Jamaica.

1 The best-seller by Herman Wouk.
2 With *Quadrille*.
3 The other male character in the play.
4 Nicholas Monsarrat's best-seller, published the previous year.
5 He was about to play MacHeath in Peter Brook's first film, *The Beggar's Opera*.

Friday 25 April New York

Cables from home. Poor Gertie Millar[1] is dead. Although she has been ill for so long, it gave me a horrible pang. She was my childhood's dream girl, after all. Leslie Banks[2] has also died. Long heart-to-heart with Marlene, who is leaving for Hollywood tonight.

Saturday 26 April

Went to *Gigi*[3] - an orgy of overacting and a vulgar script. Cathleen Nesbitt good and dignified, and the sets lovely. Audrey Hepburn inexperienced and rather too noisy, and the whole thing badly directed.

A drink with Yul in his dressing-room[4]. He is terribly perturbed about Gertie's voice and so, it seems, is everyone else. Went to Ethel Merman's[5] party. Tallulah was there. After she left, everyone performed and it was great fun - real theatrical stuff.

Tuesday 29 April

Lunched with Gertie, who was at her best. Advised her to leave *The King and I* for good. I did not say they were anxious to get rid of her because of her singing, but I think I convinced her that she ought to do a straight play. I also said I would be prepared to rewrite *Island Fling*[6] for her. I am sure that, with some reconstruction, it would be a success with her playing it.

In the evening went to the Copa Cabana with Yul to see Johnnie Ray[7] - quite extraordinary. Talked to Marlene on the telephone. Bed about 5 a.m.

Tuesday 6 May London

Visited Mum - looking a bit frail but very cheerful. The Lunts at six o'clock. Read them the new bits - they were genuinely entranced. I ticked them off gently about being tiresome. Dined at L'Apéritif and went to *The Vortex*. Abominably directed - a good cast - Isabel [Jeans] nearly very good indeed. Michael Gough excellent, but too preoccupied with being young; end of

1 Gertrude Millar, Countess of Dudley (1879-1952), for many years one of the brightest stars in the British musical theatre; as a boy Noël had saved his pocket-money to go and see her once a week in *The Quaker Girl*.
2 Leslie Banks (1890-1952), distinguished British actor.
3 The New York stage production.
4 After a performance of *The King and I*, in which Gertrude Lawrence was starring opposite Yul Brynner.
5 Ethel Merman (b. 1908), American musical star.
6 The comedy Claudette Colbert had tried out in summer stock the previous year.
7 Johnnie Ray, American singer particularly popular in the 1950s.

second act ruined. Last act mistimed, but it held all the same. Supper at Adrianne's – Sherwoods[1], Lunts, Moncktons[2], etc.

Wednesday 7 May

Cecil Beaton arrived at ten o'clock and showed me the set designs[3]. Full of imagination although a bit over-elaborate, but he was as co-operative as could be.

Saw *Relative Values* – packed house – wonderful audience. Gladys perfectly wonderful, rest of cast fine except for Angela in the second act, and Hugh McDermott, who was really appalling. My God, the idiocy of actors! Supper at Binkie's – *Quadrille* casting discussion.

Wednesday 14 May

In the evening went with Gladys [Calthrop] to *The Deep Blue Sea*[4] – a beautiful play superbly played. Peggy Ashcroft perfectly wonderful – Kenneth More, Roland Culver, all impeccable. Went from there to the Bagatelle with Dotty [Dickson], Adrianne, Murray Macdonald[5], Kenneth Carten[6] and Graham to hear Sophie Tucker. Vulgar and noisy but still retaining some star quality.

Tuesday 20 May

Took the Lunts to the Savoy to hear Sylvia Coleridge read Octavia[7] – she did it without the script and was excellent. The Lunts were delighted and she was engaged. David Holtzmann and I discussed the future arrangement of my American finances, and everything is now clear, or at least fairly clear. I am withdrawing from Transatlantic Productions[8] and it all looks much better. Visited Mum.

Tuesday 27 May

Lovely evening. Alfred and Lynn read the first act of *Quadrille* so exquisitely that the tears were in my eyes. They are *great* actors.

1 Robert Sherwood (1896–1955), American dramatist and author, and his wife Madeleine.
2 Bridget Monckton, née Ruthven (b. 1896), and her husband, Walter Monckton, who was now Minister of Labour in Churchill's government.
3 For *Quadrille*. It was the first time the two men had worked together and it proved a happy experience. Beaton had written to Noël, 'I am utterly enchanted by the play… nothing on earth that I know of would prevent me from doing the job.'
4 Terence Rattigan's new play at the Duchess Theatre.
5 Murray Macdonald (1899–1980), Scottish actor turned director.
6 Kenneth Carten, actor turned agent.
7 At a *Quadrille* audition.
8 The Jack Wilson partnership.

Friday 6 June

Stoj[1] reappeared from the past and came to lunch. Fattish with white hair. She was very cheerful and somehow touching because she talked more absolute nonsense than I have ever heard in my life. She is almost jocularly set on saving the world. She is convinced that she, in collaboration with the now defunct J.D. Beresford[2], has been selected by a far greater power than we can contradict to spread the gospel of life eternal, and wage an internal war against dialectical materialism, which is apparently what we are all tainted with. She has been physically celibate since 1928, which accounts for a lot. Her affair with JDB was entirely platonic and on a spiritual plane. (He was a cripple of sixty-five when she met him which, of course, helped.) She is now staunchly persevering with their mutual and entirely self-imposed task. She is quite happy, infinitely superior, capable of sudden quite genuine laughter and an ardent vegetarian. I am writing here at this length because her development from a bouncing, sexy, determined girl into this arid, muddled, moralizing, elderly crank is fascinating. It is her complete compensation for being a failure as an actress, as a writer and as a wife. It is also a supreme compensation to her for my career of nasty, enviable, materialistic success. Yet she is an amiable enough creature, and beneath these soggy layers of confused thought and smugness there is a curious insecurity, as though a deep-down self-conscious instinct in her was regretting the denial of life, but this is far too deeply buried to cause her any doubts or pain – she is supremely self-satisfied and entranced with her mission.

Rehearsed all the afternoon. Had my suit fitted and visited Mum. She is failing a bit, poor old darling.

Wednesday 11 June

Lunched at home. Went to see Gladys Cooper, who fell down last night and hurt her back seriously. Needless to say, she insisted on playing as Judy [Campbell] was off and there was no understudy available. I admire her guts because she was in agony. Came back and worked with Norman[3].

1 Esmé Wynne, a close childhood friend with whom Noël had written his first sketches and songs in 1912–17; their friendship had evaporated in the 1920s, largely because of Esmé's passionate adoption of Christian Science. She had written to him just before this present meeting and asked if he had developed any mental or spiritual philosophy, to which Noël had replied: 'My philosophy is as simple as ever. I love smoking, drinking, moderate sexual intercourse on a diminishing scale, reading and writing (not arithmetic). I have a selfless absorption in the well-being and achievement of Noël Coward. . . . In spite of my unregenerate spiritual attitude I am jolly kind to everybody and still attentive and devoted to my dear old Mother, who is hale and hearty, sharp as a needle and occasionally very cross indeed.'
2 J.D. Beresford (1873–1947), English novelist.
3 For his return to the Café de Paris.

After theatre time an impromptu party – Lena Horne[1], Gene Kelly, etc. Most delightful and enjoyable.

Monday 16 June

First rehearsal of *Quadrille*. Cast excellent. Alfred, Lynn and Joyce [Carey] without books. Band call at Café. Visited Mum. Musgrove came at 10.30; then Norman; then the opening night. Tension very high. Everybody there: the Duchess of Kent, Danny Kaye, Errol Flynn, Claudette, Lunts, Oliviers, Fairbanks. I gave an assured, professional performance but the audience was tough; in spite of a great success I did not enjoy it much. A lot of articulate, generous praise and a mobbing by the crowd outside. I can now look forward to future performances without strain.

Tuesday 17 June

Rave notices about Café opening. Very successful rehearsal all the afternoon. Lynn and Alfred entrancing. Visited Mum. A good long rest. Dinner on a tray. Rehearsed with Norman – then the Café. Better performance than last night – great fun.

Thursday 19 June

Very good rehearsal. Went to the Globe to see rehearsal of 'Bad Times'[2] – quite good. Worked on *Quadrille* music. Café successful and packed to the roof. Took Leonard Lyons[3] and Randolph Churchill on to John Gielgud's party for Arnold Weissberger. I stayed on and talked to John and Emlyn [Williams] after all the others had gone.

Saturday 21 June

Called on Mum for a few minutes on my way to Iver[4]. Drove down in Jaguar. The Queen and I shared a sugar-bowl and she was absolutely charming to me. After dinner I sang three songs, warmly supported by Princess Margaret, who realized it was rather agony and very sweetly came and sat near me to encourage me. After that we played 'the game'. I was in the Queen's team but we were beaten by Princess Margaret. I had to leave at eleven o'clock – got to the Café on time and gave the best performance I have given to date. Mary Martin and Richard [Halliday] were there, also José Ferrer[5], the Fairbanks

1 Lena Horne (b. 1918), black American singing star, then appearing at the Palladium.
2 One of the songs he had written for *The Globe Revue*.
3 Leonard Lyons, Broadway columnist.
4 To a party at the Duchess of Kent's home.
5 José Ferrer (b. 1909), American actor, producer and director.

and Jack Benny[1]. Later drove down to Goldenhurst with Mary, Dick and Cole.

Saturday 5 July

Daniel Massey[2] came to lunch and I gave him a godfatherly, commonsense talk about his career – and Life in General. He is a nice, intelligent boy, but I think inclined to be intense.

Friday 11 July

Globe Revue notices very good. Am feeling much better. Wonderful rehearsal. Dinner with Boy Browning with pleasant Royal gossip.

Throat treatment at 11.15. Café fabulous – packed and violently enthusiastic. Voice a bit better but certainly needs a rest.

Saturday 12 July

Claudette dined with me at 10.30. A glamorous farewell performance that was hell for me as voice virtually non-existent. However, rapturous reception – the place was crammed with stars: Lunts, Claudette, Gene Kelly, Danny Kaye, etc. Said goodbye to all the staff. Late to bed.

Tuesday 15 July   Manchester

Rehearsed [*Quadrille*] during day. Opening night very exciting. Lovely audience. Performance fairly good but a bit staggered by nerves. Tremendous ovation at the end – altogether satisfactory. Party afterwards. Everyone very happy.

Wednesday 16 July

Notices wonderful – one or two even intelligent. All raves. Lunched with Jack and Binkie. Went to an Errol Flynn movie with Cole – very enjoyable. Watched the evening performance. It was a bit fluffy but went marvellously.

Monday 28 July

Jack announced that the Theatre Guild had offered me the dubious task of doing the music, book and lyrics of *Pygmalion* with Mary Martin. It is an interesting proposition, but I must read the play before deciding[3].

---

1 Jack Benny (1894-1974), American comedian, whose hit television show ran from 1950 to 1965.
2 Daniel Massey (b. 1933), British actor; the son of Adrianne Allen by her first husband Raymond Massey, and Noël's godson. Daniel later played Noël in the 1967 film about Gertrude Lawrence, *Star!*
3 He decided against the project, which four years later Lerner and Loewe did as *My Fair Lady.*

The Edinburgh opening night of *Quadrille* was enchanting. Lynn was nervous in the first scene but played the rest like a dream. The audience was deeply appreciative and really warm and sweet. The ovation at the end was terrific.

Sunday 10 August   Cannes

Flew to Nice. Rather hot. Drove to the Carlton. Unpacked, rested and finally descended to the bar. Evaded all invitations. Dined alone at the Symphony. Saw Mistinguett – a truly terrifying sight. Gambled a little and lost.

Monday 11 August

Drove out in my hired Peugeot to Eden Roc and managed to evade being pinned down by a number of people who wanted to talk. Drove back to Cannes and spent a happy afternoon reading *The Traitor* by Alan Moorehead – a truly excellent book.

Met an aged colonel in the bar who could imitate bird noises.

Monday 25 August   Rome

Lunched at the Capriccio. Wandered about Rome – it is an exquisite city but, at the moment, trampled flat by Americans. Called on Tennessee Williams, who has an apartment of desperate squalor. We went out and sat outside Rosati's and watched the world go by. It was pleasant enough, but I longed to be alone, so took a *carrozza* and had a short drive before going home to bed.

Tuesday 26 August

I dined with Tennessee, and we drove out along the Appian Way and looked at all the ruins – lovely except for the horror of Tennessee's driving. I cannot imagine how he got a licence – he admits cheerfully that he cannot see with one eye and cannot drive at all, and yet he has a Jaguar. On the way back we ran out of *essence*, but were able to coast to a petrol station. After this we got lost and drove about wildly in several different directions! It was all very light-hearted, although a trifle dangerous. Not really so, however, because I made him drive slowly. We missed a few trams and buses by inches and finally, at long last, I got to my bed.

Thursday 28 August   London

Did letters with Lorn. Gladys arrived with her drawings for the *N.C. Song Book*. They are quite brilliant. I am so very happy about this from every point of view.

Dinner at the Ivy and then home feeling so happy that my holiday is over.

Friday 29 August

Long, serious discussion about the Orphanage. Decided to make drastic economies – sell Silverlands and get somewhere near London where the Hostel and the Orphanage can be under one roof. If we don't do something soon we shall have exhausted our capital in a few years and have to close down. Much as I would like to resign, I cannot do so until the whole thing is properly solvent. Drove down to Goldenhurst with Coley after lunch. Lovely day. Mum well. The house sweet.

Saturday 6 September   Goldenhurst

A day that started gaily and ended in misery. The happy part was going to the Folkestone races with Cole and Gladys. I backed several winners and it was great fun. Just as I was leaving, Coley told me it was in the Stop Press that Gertie Lawrence was dead. I drove home feeling dreadful. The telephone never stopped ringing – Press all agog.

Fanny called me from New York and was incoherent and in floods. All she could say was that Gertie knew she was dying and had spoken of me. I dined with Gladys, and then came home and wrote an obituary for *The Times*. This was agony and I broke down several times, but pressed on and finished it. Fanny wanted me to fly to New York for the funeral, which I refused to do. Poor, darling old Gertie – a lifelong friend. With all her overactings and silliness I have never known her do a mean or an unkind thing. I am terribly, terribly unhappy to think that I shall never see her again.

Sunday 7 September

A difficult day saved by Graham and Simon Lack[1]. We played croquet in between telephone calls. The newspapers are full of Gertie's death. Talked to David Holtzmann, who said that she actually died of cancer of the liver. I do hope she had little pain, but fear she must have had some. Doug [Fairbanks] rang up and Winifred, and of course Joyce, but no word from the Lunts. It would have been nice if they had rung me up.

Annie, Ian and Cecil [Beaton] came for a drink. After they had all gone, we dined and played canasta. I feel terribly sad inside. I suppose, with time, it will pass.

Monday 8 September   London

Went to the theatre. Alfred and Lynn both gloomy and in a bad mood. Binkie told me confidentially that it was because of my obituary about Gertie[2], but

1 Simon Lack (1917–80), actor, then playing in *Relative Values*; he and Graham Payn were staying with Noël at Goldenhurst.
2 In which Noël had written: 'No one I have ever known, however brilliant and however gifted, has contributed quite what she contributed to my work.'

I feel that such pettiness is too unworthy of them. There is to be a public lying-in-state for Gertie, in which she will wear the pink dress in which she danced the polka in *The King and I*. Vulgarity can go no further.

I shall be glad when this week is over. The weekend has been emotionally exhausting. I am sad about Gertie – particularly about the long ago years, and the Phoenix Theatre[1] is naturally haunted by her.

Thursday 11 September

Photographed for the *Sunday Times* by Douglas Glass. Lunched at home. Did a recorded broadcast about Gertie and broke down after it, feeling utterly miserable.

Went to the third preview of *Quadrille* (in aid of the Orphanage) with Viv, Larry and Michael Benthall – very good. Alfred, after apologizing for muddling a minor laugh of Lynn's, asked me what I was unhappy about. I explained that Gertie had had great pain before she died and that I had been torn up over the whole thing. Alfred told me they are making me a chocolate cake for tomorrow[2].

Friday 12 September

Went with Graham and Joyce to *Meet Me Tonight*[3]. Absolutely awful – vilely directed and, with one or two minor exceptions, abominably acted. Came home and rested.

Opening night of *Quadrille* – took Gladys and Dotty Dickson – very fine performance. Audience respectful and attentive. Obviously a triumphant success. Party at Binkie's afterwards – very pleasant.

Saturday 13 September

Woke up after last night's glamour to find that the Press were unanimous in abusing the play. The Lunts were praised, but the play viciously torn to pieces. Very interesting. We are virtually sold out until Christmas.

Friday 19 September

In the train to Ashford we read the weekly notices for *Quadrille*. The *Spectator* and *Time and Tide* were patronizing and contemptuous. The *New Statesman* was frankly abusive and described it as an absolute and complete failure. I have seldom read such concentrated venom – the notice was written by a Mr Worsley[4].

---

1 He and Gertrude Lawrence had opened the Phoenix Theatre with *Private Lives* in 1930 and played there again together in 1936 in *Tonight at 8.30*; *Quadrille* was about to open there.
2 A traditional gesture of Lunt friendship.
3 Film of *Red Peppers*, *Fumed Oak* and *Ways and Means* (all from *Tonight at 8.30*).
4 Thomas Cuthbert Worsley, drama critic of the *New Statesman* 1948–52.

Saturday 20 September

Read Evelyn Waugh's *Men at Arms* – good in part but a bit soggy with Catholicism. Read also Harold Hobson's *Verdict at Midnight* – a wishy-washy, non-committal book of dramatic criticism, well disposed but silly.

Wednesday 24 September

Went up to London with Cole on the afternoon train. Went to see Doris[1] in the hospital – she was more or less unconscious. Her face looked very peaceful with all lines ironed out – there will be no more worry for her. No fear or conflict, and the sister assured me there was no question of the slightest pain. Approaching death is a curious spectacle – in this instance touching rather than agonizing.

Did some letters with Lorn. Daphne [du Maurier] and Boy Browning came for drinks – long talk to Daphne about Gertie. She loved her very much. Then Larry and Vivien arrived and we all went to Douglas Fairbanks' dinner party for Charlie Chaplin. Charlie was very much aged but very gay. After dinner more people arrived – I obliged at the pianoforte – Mary Martin came to my rescue and we sang together. Charlie did some pastiches – very brilliant but a teeny bit long.

Saturday 27 September

Worked all the morning. Lorn rang up and told me poor Doris was dead, and I had to break the news to Mum, who took it wonderfully. I am so sad for her, because Doris was a great companion for her. However, she rose above her unhappiness with great courage.

Lorn has found a good home for the Orphanage. I shall look it over.

Friday 3 October

Spent the morning reading the scurrilous things the Press wrote about me during 1940[2]. Hannen Swaffer persistently malignant – nearly all of them horrible.

After dinner we watched a political debate on television – Michael Foot disgusting.

Thursday 16 October

Went with Vivien to the opening of *Limelight*. Sat with Charlie and Oona. Charlie wonderful at moments, but picture too long and too trite. His great genius has always been to make us cry with his comedy. In this story he tries to make us cry with his tragedy and doesn't quite succeed. Tremendous

1 Doris Dalton, Noël's cousin, who was dying of cancer.
2 In researching his *Future Indefinite* autobiography, he had come across Press criticism of his mysterious assignment to Paris on behalf of the British Secret Service at the outbreak of war.

hullabaloo – Princess Margaret made spectacular entrance and was quite enchanting.

Wednesday 29 October

Fleming christening[1] and reception. Dinner with Johnny and Mary [Mills] at the Wick – very pleasant – Doug, Mary Lee, Vivien, Larry and me. Drove Viv home as Larry had left early. Long heart-to-heart – she is a darling. We decided to nip over to Paris in the first week of December.

Wednesday 5 November

Went with Vivien and Rachel Redgrave[2] to the laying of the foundation stone of the Vanbrugh Theatre by the Queen Mother. A drizzly day. The cream of the theatrical profession sat in the open air and listened to the QM make a charming speech. Later sherry and a closer glimpse of the Queen Mother. Lunch at home with Vivien and Rachel.

Dined with Hester Chapman to meet Angus Wilson[3], to whom I took a great shine.

Eisenhower is President of the USA.

Thursday 6 November

Derek Hill came to lunch. Then went to Dr Field and decided to have all my top teeth out when I have my gum operation on the nineteenth. Much better get it over and save myself further trouble.

Quadrille – Lynn brilliant – whole performance good. Alfred overplaying a little bit. Supper with them afterwards – very enjoyable.

Saturday 8 November

Saw three of Doug Fairbanks' television films – not bad at all. Went to Mary's last night in *South Pacific*. She gave a superb performance and had a terrific ovation – she is a great artist. Later went with Cole and Graham to hear Pearl Bailey. She was beguiling and curiously witty; she has a streak of madness that is almost surrealist.

Thursday 13 November

Supper with Oliver [Messel] plus Charlie Chaplin and Oona and Graham. Ginette and Balmain[4] came in afterwards.

1 Of Ann and Ian's son, Caspar Fleming (1952–75), to whom Noël was godfather.
2 Rachel Kempson (b. 1910), actress, who had married Michael Redgrave in 1935.
3 Angus Wilson (b. 1913), English writer and academic, whose novel *Hemlock and After* had just been published.
4 Pierre Balmain, French couturier, for whom Ginette Spanier was working.

Friday 14 November

Drove to Notley with Vivien. Peaceful evening playing canasta. Larry very cheerful.

Sunday 16 November

In the afternoon we all drove over to Blenheim. Gay, young house-party headed by Princess Margaret. Larry, Vivien and Graham went back to Notley, leaving me with the *jeunesse dorée*. A lot of piano playing and jolly games. Retired to bed exhausted in the coldest room I have ever encountered.

Monday 17 November

Woke frozen. Shaving sheer agony and glacial bathroom with a skylight that would not shut. Loo like an icebox. Breakfast downstairs. Bert Marlborough[1] none too bright – Mary very sweet. Went round the state apartments; walked in the grounds; took photographs. Saw Princess Margaret off. Pretended I was going to Oxford but actually drove back to Notley, where I had lunch and played canasta. Returned to Blenheim at cocktail time. Small dinner. More piano playing. Back to the Frigidaire. Lit the gas fire like Peggy Ashcroft[2] and burrowed into bed in socks and a sweater.

Sunday 23 November

Great excitement in Press because some Communist on trial for his life in Prague has suddenly confessed that I gave him written instructions to be a British agent, and that I was in a superior position in the British Intelligence Service. His name is André Simon, and I vaguely remember meeting him in Paris in 1940. Wanted to reply to the Press that, owing to recent dental operation, my lips were sealed, but refrained on account of undue flippancy.

Saturday 29 November   Paris

Had to have my plate filed down a bit more by Dr Schachter as it was cutting my lip. Vivien came to lunch. We flew off from Northolt[3] at three o'clock with Larry and the Millses. Met by Ginette and Paul-Emile. Got to the Hôtel France et Choiseul. Suites filled with flowers and Ruth [Gordon] and Gar [Kanin]. Got ourselves organized as far as the Véfour – then *La Dame aux Camélias*[4] with Edwige Feuillère – only fairly good, I thought, and a tatty production. Returned to hotel because Vivien wanted to change her shoes. They all went on to a jolly night-club and I went, gratefully, to my jolly bed.

---

1 10th Duke of Marlborough (1879-1972), who had married Mary Cadogan in 1920.
2 In the suicide scene in Rattigan's play, *The Deep Blue Sea*.
3 For a Parisian weekend.
4 Alexandre Dumas's play (1852).

Sunday 30 November

Enormous cocktail party given by Ginette and Paul-Emile – Maggie Leighton, the Rubinsteins[1], Korda, Ruth, Gar, Irwin Shaw[2], etc. Then dinner party given by Alex Korda at Larue's – delicious food but everyone a trifle too pissed to appreciate it. Went to the Carousel. Graham and I evaded the others and went on to Spivy's by ourselves, which was much more enjoyable.

Monday 1 December

Woke with a hangover. Tottered out into the rain for a walk with Graham and saw him off in a taxi. We all lunched together at Maxim's – wonderful food but my mouth hurting badly. Came back and rested. Went to Ginette's with Vivien. Claudette appeared – the poor darling has been going mad with a skin allergy.

Then Viv and I joined Larry, Johnny and Mary at the Chanticleer, where we had such a good dinner that we decided to miss the first act of *La Dame de Trèfle*[3]. Fortunately we telephoned to say our car had broken down, for when we arrived there was a reception committee with a bouquet for Viv and a row of cameras. A very silly play but Madeleine Robinson is a very fine actress. Went to the Lido with Alex, Alexa[4] and Marcel Achard. Came back with Alex and Alexa, leaving the others to go on.

Thursday 11 December   London

Dined with Binkie, who lectured me on not acting and insisted that I do a play for the Coronation[5] – he suggested *The Apple Cart*[6].

Tuesday 16 December

Fifty-three today. Very nice presents. Lunched with Korda and discussed the film of *Present Laughter* – decided to do it next October. Read *The Apple Cart* – a witty play and a wonderful part for me – will probably do it for a limited run during the Coronation.

Thursday 25 December

A loving, enjoyable Christmas Day. Winnie arrived on a great present delivery expedition. Then a little party at Mum's flat, where she received our presents and had a lovely time. Christmas dinner in the studio – Graham, Sybil [Payn], Joyce and me. Then the Queen's speech, which was most moving and very well done – so much so that I sent her a telegram. Rested.

1 Artur Rubinstein (b. 1887), concert pianist, and his wife.
2 Irwin Shaw (b. 1913), American writer.
3 Play by Gabriel Arout.
4 Lady (Alexandra) Korda.
5 Of Queen Elizabeth II, due to take place on 2 June 1953.
6 George Bernard Shaw's play.

Visited Mum again and went to Binkie's party, which was a sit-down dinner for thirty – Edith [Evans], the Lunts, Mary and Dick, Johnny [Gielgud], Eileen Herlie[1], etc. Left at 1.30. Came home, changed, picked up Cole and drove to Goldenhurst. Home at 3.30.

Saturday 27 December

Woke late after rather a bad night. Slight panic about having to finish the book[2], write song for the Café de Paris, and learn *The Apple Cart*.

Gave buffet dinner party for Annie, Ian, Loelia, the Cyril Connollys, Fione and Peter Quennell. Played 'the game' – great fun.

Sunday 28 December

The die is cast. I am definitely going to do *The Apple Cart*, opening 20 April at Brighton for two weeks and then, I hope, the Haymarket. The Brabournes – Patricia, John and Doreen[3] – came for lunch. Party at the Freres.

Tuesday 30 December

In the evening went to *Richard II* – Paul Scofield wonderful, Eric Porter very good. Supper with Binkie and Michael MacOwan. Long discussion about *The Apple Cart*.

Wednesday 31 December

Got my American visa. The Lunts' party at my studio. They, the hosts, left early and I was left to carry on. Vivien and Larry were sweet – so were Mary and Dick. Drank in the New Year.

---

1 Eileen Herlie (b. 1919), Scottish actress.
2 *Future Indefinite*.
3 Patricia, elder daughter of Earl and Countess Mountbatten, her husband John, Lord Brabourne, and his mother Doreen, Lady Brabourne.

1953

Coronation Year was celebrated by Noël with a further return to the Café de Paris in cabaret and a Theatre Royal, Haymarket, season as King Magnus in Shaw's The Apple Cart, *one of the less than half-dozen occasions throughout his long career as a leading actor when he played in the work of another dramatist. That Noël was now back on top of his popular form can be gathered from the fact that on Coronation Day itself he played the evening performance at the Haymarket, went on to do his regular cabaret appearance at the Café and then, around two o'clock the following morning, did two more shows in cabaret at the Savoy Hotel.*

Tuesday 6 January   Jamaica

Finished the Shaw–Mrs Pat Letters[1]. Arrived Montego Bay in pouring rain at 10.30. Dinner with Sylvia Foot[2], who was dealing with Mrs Churchill[3] – Edward and Kathleen [Molyneux] also present.

Wednesday 7 January

Visited Edward's property. Taken by John and Liz[4] to look over the Roundhill Bluff Hotel site – a complicated project with which they want to involve me – temporized. Saw Mrs Churchill – very amiable.

After lunch drove to Blue Harbour. House and garden looking fine and atmosphere cheerful. Visited Firefly Hill[5] which is coming along fine. It is lovely beyond words to be back.

Thursday 15 January

Wrote all the Bow Street/Mansion House section of *Future Indefinite*. Discovered that even after eleven years the memory of it[6] still enrages me. Polished off the remainder of Act One of *The Apple Cart* – how comforting it is to have a trained memory and the gift of concentration.

In the evening a cocktail party with Sarah Churchill, Mary and Christopher Soames[7] and Mrs Churchill, who was very charming indeed. We had a long heart-to-heart which was fairly illuminating. She was honest about Randolph and, considering that she is his mum, extremely trenchant. She loathes and has always loathed Max Beaverbrook, who she says is malicious and loves giving pain. She very sweetly gave me a £30 order for 'Designs for Living' – the publicity of this will help the shop enormously. She also appeared genuinely impressed by my banana paintings, and carried a large one away with her, frame and all, to show the Prime Minister.

Tuesday 20 January

Started redoing *Middle East Diary*[8] for that section of the book. Mike [Redgrave] and I went to the Churchills' cocktail party. The old man was very amiable. I have taken a great shine to Mary – she is a really charming girl.

1 George Bernard Shaw's love-letters to Mrs Patrick Campbell, published the previous year.
2 Sylvia Foot, wife of the Jamaican Governor, Sir Hugh Foot.
3 Winston and Clementine Churchill were then on a visit to the island.
4 John and Elizabeth Pringle, residents of Jamaica who had become Noël's friends there; they were about to construct a luxury hotel complex at Montego Bay.
5 The renamed Look Out property above Blue Harbour which Noël was planning to rebuild.
6 His conviction in 1942 for evading currency regulations.
7 Mary Soames, the Churchills' youngest daughter, and her husband Christopher Soames, Conservative politician.
8 Noël's book, published in 1944, which covered his wartime tours of the Middle East.

Wednesday 21 January

Worked away like a dog. In the afternoon Mike treated us to a special showing of *The Browning Version*[1] in Port Maria. A very good picture in which he gives a superb performance – Terry Rattigan is certainly a remarkable writer. He has an incisive and almost clinical knowledge of the human heart.

Tuesday 3 February

Drove to Montego. Lunched with Max B. – very mellow and amiable. Drink with Edward who showed me his paintings, which are really first-rate.

Friday 13 February

Finished *Future Indefinite*. Immensely happy and relieved. Too soon yet to know whether it is good or not, but I think it is. Intend to wait a few days before I start to revise.

Wednesday 18 February

A bad day. Woke with a cold. Then came a cable from Lorn saying that Mum was ill – apparently badly ill, but that there was no urgency although she was very frail. This upset me horribly – there was nothing to be done but get through the day.

More reassuring cable when we got home but I have to face the fact that Mum might die at any minute, either now or during the next year or so. I want to be near her when she does, just to hold her hand – she has held mine for fifty-three years.

Tuesday 24 February

Left for Montego after lunch. Met Kate [Hepburn] and Irene [Selznick] outside Jamaica Inn.

Monday 9 March

The news from England is that Mum is much better. The news from Russia is that Stalin is dead.

Yesterday I drove to Tower Isle[2] and collected Graham Greene and his friend, Mrs Katherine Walston – very charming indeed. I brought them back for a drink. He was very agreeable and his beastliness to me in the past I have forgiven but not forgotten. He has a strange, tortured mind but, like most of God's creatures, aches to be loved. Kate and Irene appeared and stayed the night, and it was lovely to have them back again.

---

1 The film of Rattigan's play (1951), which starred Michael Redgrave.
2 Hotel near Ocho Rios.

Sunday 22 March   London

Back in London and starting rehearsals tomorrow. The last part of our time
in Jamaica was fairly social. We gave some jolly drinking parties on Firefly
Hill. Decided to start building on Firefly.

Flew off on Wednesday morning. An hour at Government House, Nassau,
with the Nevilles[1]. Another hour at Bermuda where we heard the first news
of Vivien's breakdown[2]. Direct twelve-hour flight from Bermuda to London.
Mum very much better than I expected but rather frail.

Reunion with loved ones. Supper with Binkie. On Friday, set conference
for *Apple Cart* – sets look excellent. Drove down to Goldenhurst – fog and
cold. Garden lovely. Spent weekend revising and cutting *Future Indefinite*.

Saturday 28 March

Dined with Frere. He was really wise and shrewd about *Future Indefinite* and
said it really would not do in its present form. This I had already suspected.
He said the first part was fine, but the last part too scurried and not objective
enough. All his criticisms were sound and constructive. I intend to serialize it
as it is, with a few essential cuts, because the magazines and newspapers
automatically cut the best bits of writing and concentrate on the narrative
quality. I can get a great deal of money for the serialization, especially in
America, and if I do it right away it will not postpone the publication of the
book, as it would if I waited. I shall not be able to concentrate on rewriting
and constructing until I have finished playing *The Apple Cart*, and then I shall
have time to do it quietly and without rush. Actually I am looking forward to
it. Rehearsals are going well – I think I shall be good. The cast is excellent and
Michael MacOwan so far directing very well and without tiresomeness, except
for a nervously enthusiastic giggle.

Poor Queen Mary died on Tuesday night. She would have loved to see the
Coronation, but I feel it is better for her to die now rather than just before or
just after it.

I took Gladys to Johnnie Ray's opening night at the Palladium. He was
really remarkable and had the whole place in an uproar.

On Thursday I went to *Quadrille*. Alfred was overplaying a bit but Lynn
was superb. Griff Jones and Marian Spencer ineffective and inaudible – the
rest good and the house full except for the boxes. We had a pleasant supper
party afterwards *chez* the Lunts – Lorn and me and Adrianne and Bobby
Andrews.

We are all dreadfully sad about poor Vivien. She is in a mental home and

1 Governor of the Bahamas and his wife.
2 After a tempestuous affair with Peter Finch, she had collapsed on the Hollywood set of
  Elephant Walk and had to be taken home to England under sedation.

has been asleep for a week. She had apparently really gone over the edge, poor darling. Larry, wisely, has gone away to Italy. This is just as well for she has turned against him. It is a tragic story and my heart aches for both of them.

Saturday 4 April   Goldenhurst

Several things have happened this week. Poor Queen Mary was buried. Russia has decided to make peace overtures to the Western powers, and the international atmosphere, although sceptical, is perceptibly brighter.

I went to two comedies: *A Woman of No Importance*[1] - badly directed by Michael Benthall, and intolerably slow; and *The Way of the World*[2] - brilliantly directed by John Gielgud and, although to me largely incomprehensible, the play was so well done that after the first act I enjoyed it.

The Apple Cart rehearsals are going well. I find Michael M. an intelligent director and a great help, and the cast so far is excellent.

On Thursday night I drove down here with Joyce and Graham and Cole. A peaceful day yesterday enlivened in the evening by a hilarious biblical play on television.

Sunday 12 April

The Apple Cart is really getting into its stride. I am improving steadily. Mr Shaw is tricky to play because of his long sentences in which every word counts. The speeches cannot be hurried and yet if they are spoken too slowly they become ponderous - it is essential to find places to pause effectively and *think* effectively. I am very happy with the company - they are all nice personally and all good actors.

Anthony Eden has gone into the London Clinic to have an operation for gall-bladder. I am suspicious that it might be cancer - he had jaundice some time ago as Gertie and Doris had. I do hope it is not. Although he is not a great leader[3], he is an important figure and has integrity.

The television saga of Charles Cochran's life was fairly horrible but redeemed by an excellent performance by Frankie Lawton, and Dennis Price to my relief gave a discreet and not too exaggerated rendering of me.

Russia continues to shower the Western powers with olive branches. We shall soon be having cheap day trips to sunny Moscow!

Rosamond Lehmann's new novel *The Echoing Grove* is beautifully written - at moments brilliant - but on the whole it is introspective and too much on one note. She is, however, a marvellous writer.

---

1 Wilde's play at the Savoy Theatre.
2 Congreve's play at the Lyric, Hammersmith.
3 Anthony Eden had been Foreign Secretary under Churchill since the 1951 election; Noël's fears for him were unfounded.

Emile Littler[1] has given us this whole week for the Orphanage. Every night a gala at the Saville with stars signing autographs and selling programmes. I went on two consecutive nights and was mobbed. The total we shall get will be over £9,000 – I really am very grateful to him.

On Thursday I lunched with the Freres and John Gordon[2], who couldn't have been more anxious to be affable. He has a conscience about attacking me during the War[3] and he also wants the serial rights of *Future Indefinite*.

The *Stars at Midnight* show[4] is still in our hair and driving us mad, but we now have hopes of getting Bing Crosby[5].

On arrival down here on Friday night I had a mysterious telephone message from a Miss Hartley. I called back and it was poor, darling Vivien[6] who has come to after her three weeks' narcosis in the mental home and moved into University College Hospital. It was a heart-breaking conversation. She started in floods of tears and then made a gallant effort to be gay and ordinary, but the strain showed through and she didn't make sense every now and then. I am desperately sorry for her. The whole business is a nightmare and I must help her in any way I can.

Wednesday 22 April   Brighton

The week moved quickly. Rehearsals, of course, all of every day. On Wednesday morning I went to see Vivien in the hospital and was deeply relieved to find her calm and normal and really very sweet. She solemnly promised to be good in future and not carry on like a mad adolescent of the twenties. In the evening Larry came and told me graphically the saga of his married life during the last few years; a curiously depressing saga it was too. Apparently things have been bad and getting worse since 1948 or thereabouts. It is really discouraging to reflect how needlessly unhappy people make themselves and each other. They are now going to start afresh down at Notley, which may work or may not. I shall be surprised if it does. Attractive and enchanting women can certainly wreak havoc when they put their silly minds to it. I am sorry for him and for her. They both have so much and are so lacking in common sense.

On Thursday night I took Maggie Leighton to the opening of Graham Greene's first play, *The Living Room*. It was well directed and played, and finely written in places, but over it all was the familiar Graham Greene smear of despair and sin and squalor. I cannot feel that Catholicism has made him

1 Emile Littler (b. 1907), like his brother Prince, a London impresario; knighted 1974.
2 John Gordon, of the *Sunday Express*.
3 For spending too much time on 'shadowy foreign missions'.
4 The charity midnight matinée for the Actors' Orphanage.
5 Bing Crosby (1904–77), American singer.
6 Vivien Leigh was born Vivien Mary Hartley.

very happy. The conflict between sex and religion is to me fairly unnecessary and extremely irritating, but it has always been a good box-office proposition.

On Friday we had our final rehearsal in London and, in the evening, Cole and I drove down to Brighton[1]. The Sunday evening dress rehearsal, attended by Lynn, Alfred and all of *Quadrille*, went very well. The opening performance was entirely triumphant from everybody's point of view. The production is excellent, the sets lovely, everyone in the cast is good, and I gave a really relaxed and satisfactory performance and got a tremendous ovation at the end. Curiously enough I was not nervous and this made all the difference. I intend never to indulge myself in first-night nerves again. It is a waste of time and unnecessary. This is big talk but I am determined to strain every un-nervous nerve to carry it through.

Monday 18 May
Goldenhurst

During the two weeks in Brighton there were various junketings – a supper party with the Al Parkers[2], another with Maggie L. and Larry Harvey[3], and a party for me and the company. Larry Olivier appeared and was very sweet about my performance.

On returning to London, preparatory to opening at the Haymarket, I was stricken with lumbago again. Really infuriating. During both the previews it was agony, but the opening night, aided by codeine and belladonna plasters, was comparatively painless. Again I was curiously un-nervous and gave a controlled performance. The whole thing was an immediate and triumphant success and has remained so in spite of some silly, patronizing notices. I have done better than usual on the whole, but they[4] will never give me ungrudging praise, or very rarely. We have played to capacity since the opening night and I have cut down on smoking and concentrated on my voice. I gave a party at the studio after the opening night which was great fun.

This weekend there is no one here but Coley and me, and it has been very restful. Last night we played a series of my early records and I retired to bed inadequately lulled by the echo of my thin, feathery voice and the realization that I am getting old! It is a curious sensation to listen to one's younger voice and to become suddenly aware of how swiftly the years march by. The songs I sang were sung twenty years ago, some of them nearly thirty years ago. I tried to remember, listening to them, what was going on in my life at the time they were recorded, but I failed. They are all pitched too high anyway, and although there is a certain charm in my voice here and there, and the phrasing, even then, was excellent, they are not really very satisfactory.

1 Where *The Apple Cart* was to open.
2 Al Parker, theatrical agent, and his wife, Australian actress Margaret Johnston.
3 Margaret Leighton was then living with and soon to marry film actor Laurence Harvey (1928–73).
4 The critics.

Last Wednesday I went to the Comédie Française party on the stage of the St James's[1] to see Larry get the Legion of Honour and be kissed by Monsieur Massigli. Larry made an excellent speech in French and managed, most touchingly, to look like a pompous manager and a wayward small boy at the same time.

On Friday Edith Evans and I were hosts at a luncheon (so-called) to the Comédie Française at the International Arts Club. I spoke in French, Edith in English, and the lunch was quite, quite inedible. The sheer British bloody impertinence in offering a group of French visitors that disgusting meal is beyond belief. I felt bitterly ashamed. The French behaved charmingly and, in spite of the diced beetroot, tastelessly dusty mousse, soggy lettuce and stale cream buns, seemed to enjoy themselves.

Sunday 24 May   Goldenhurst

The week started badly. I felt miserably tired and run down and thoroughly dreary. My throat started hurting and I was racked with dreadful fears because I have so much to do and the prospect of doing it without feeling well was terrifying.

Suddenly, on Wednesday, I began to feel normally well again. My voice is clear and my throat all right except for a slight cough. I have enjoyed every performance and am now looking forward to the Café de Paris without dismay. It is quite wonderful to feel well again. Ever since I opened in *The Apple Cart* I have been operating under strain and difficulty. Now the strain has gone and I am enjoying myself. My performance has improved a great deal and the weather has decided to be perfectly glorious, a sort of romantic English spring in the old tradition. Everything in the garden is, literally, lovely.

London is becoming increasingly hellish, swarms of people and a perpetual misery of traffic congestion. The streets are chaos owing to the Coronation decorations. It will be a comfort when it is all over. I have had much heart-warming, articulate praise at the Haymarket, from Maurice Chevalier and John Gielgud particularly. Jack arrived on Friday and drove down here with Cole and me last night. He has been urging me to play *The Apple Cart* in New York but I don't think I shall. I really don't feel it would be worth the effort. The New York theatre no longer interests me, which is sad because before the war it was swift and stimulating; now it's sodden with pseudo-significance and mighty slow. All the Americans whom I should like to see me play Magnus are over here, so why worry about traipsing across the Atlantic, arguing with the unions, being irritated by a multitude of small tiresomenesses, etc., all for a limited season at ten per cent of the gross?

1 Which Olivier was then managing and where the French company was playing a London season.

Friday 12 June   London

The worst is definitely over. I duly opened at the Café on 26 May. It was a triumphant success and I kept control of my nerves and my material. Roars and cheers and all the trimmings.

The Thursday night, *Stars at Midnight* at the Palladium, was, in spite of all forebodings, a riot. I went on at 3.20 a.m. and found a marvellous audience still alert and enthusiastic. The show made about £19,000 for the two charities, which means about £8,000 for us.

Tuesday, Coronation Day, I spent at home watching the proceedings on television, most excellently done. The English State Ballet at its best. Weather foul and everyone soaked. Our audience at the Haymarket was comatose but we were lucky to have anyone there at all. The Café audience was dull and heavy, after which I faced two more shows at the Savoy[1], getting home at about 4.30 a.m. John Gielgud got a knighthood in the Coronation Honours and high time too. I am really glad because he has deserved it for years.

Since the Coronation, London has been unbearable. Bad weather, teeming crowds, traffic at a standstill, general frustration. Audiences, however, very good and performances both at the Haymarket and the Café excellent.

Dickie and Edwina brought Princess Margaret to the Café last night; very amiable. Benjamin Britten's opera *Gloriana*, for the Royal Gala Performance, apparently a bugger. Dull, without melody as usual with Mr B., and not happily chosen.

London continues to be hell. Anthony Eden has flown to America for a third operation. There is a truce in Korea. Winston Churchill looked both disagreeable and silly at the Coronation. The Nivens came to Goldenhurst last weekend and were enchanting.

Monday 29 June

Finished my four weeks at the Café on the twentieth, still in good voice but determined not to yield to coaxing to stay on, very wisely I think. Life has been much easier since, and I am thankful I got through without cracking up. Have had a bad time over Mum. She was suddenly ill at Goldenhurst and the doctor said it was probably cancer. I told the doctor that if his guess was right I relied on him to see that Mum suffered no pain of any sort and no questions asked. I can't bear to think of her suffering; it is bad enough to see her getting older and older and slowly failing. She cannot now see well enough to read even with a magnifying glass. Old age is cruel, and death much kinder when it is gentle.

The Apple Cart continues to play to capacity. Only five more weeks to go. I am still enjoying it up to a point, but I shall be good and ready to close on 1 August.

1 Hotel, where he was also appearing that night in cabaret.

Anthony Eden has made a remarkable recovery from his third operation and will soon be up and about again. Sir Winston has been ordered a month's rest. The Queen is in Scotland, so we are having wonderful weather.

Thursday 16 July

Busy learning Italian for the holiday. Two weeks more and we shall be off. The Haymarket business continues at steady capacity and the audiences are surprisingly bright and beautiful. I had a nightmare experience last week when I appeared before the Queen and Prince Philip at Hurlingham for the Victoria League. Everything was chaos: a large, overcrowded marquee flapping in a dismal wind, microphones inadequate, lighting non-existent. I cut my medley half-way through because I knew I couldn't get it over. I just managed, by straining every nerve, to get through five numbers. Dear old 'Let's Do It'[1] saved the day. The Queen, poor dear, scowled through most of my perform-ance but perked up at the end. Prince Philip was really sweet and concentrated. Norman [Hackforth] and I, still quivering with inward rage, were presented. Small talk took place, we backed away and went home not even having been offered a drink. We English do love our artists!

During the last week a journalistic orgy has been taking place over poor Princess Margaret and Peter Townsend[2]. He has been posted to Brussels and she is in South Africa with the Queen Mother. She is returning tomorrow, poor child, to face the *Daily Mirror* poll which is to decide, in the readers' opinion, whether she is to marry a divorced man or not! It is all so incredibly vulgar and, to me, it is inconceivable that nothing could be done to stop these tasteless, illiterate minds from smearing our Royal Family with their sancti-monious rubbish. Obviously the wretched Peter Townsend should have been discreetly transferred abroad ages ago. Now it is too late and everyone is clacking about it from John o' Groats to Land's End. One can only assume that the 'advisers' in Buckingham Palace and the Lord Chamberlain's office are a poor lot. A welter of pseudo-religious claptrap is now swirling around the feet of the poor Princess and the unfortunate young man. He was the innocent party in his divorce, but the Church is adamantly squeaking its archaic views. I suspect that she is probably in love with him but, whether she is or not, it should never have been allowed to reach the serious stage. I feel sorry for all concerned but even more contemptuous than usual of the Press.

Larry and Vivien came to *The Apple Cart* last week and supped here afterwards. Vivien looked papery and rather frail but there was no sign of there ever having been a mental breakdown. She was calm and sweet and gay and with no tension. I do hope that she will remain so.

---

1 The Cole Porter song which Noël had now adapted and adopted.
2 Whom she wished to marry. He had been a Palace equerry to King George VI.

For the last five days I have been in real agony with lumbago, so much so that I was seriously worried and had a thorough x-ray. Fortunately it is nothing serious, merely strained muscles from rolling about with Maggie [Leighton] in the second act. I have been living on codeine and veganin and have had a physiotherapist to massage me and at last, at long, long last, it is better. It really is maddening, with only two and a half weeks to play; I still enjoy playing Magnus, but naturally I enjoy it less when I can hardly drag myself onto the stage.

I have decided to turn *Lady Windermere's Fan* into a musical for the Lyric, Hammersmith. Binkie is delighted with the idea and so am I, because it really is up my musical alley.

Sunday 2 August

A slight hangover. Last night was the last night of *The Apple Cart* and I gave a party here[1]. Very successful mix-up; Ina Claire merry as a grig and Ava Gardner[2] most beautiful.

The last week has been fairly hectic and the business at the Haymarket fantastic. It is nice to have had such a thick, warm success and I am duly grateful, but I must never play more than three months; I am just now at the end of my rope. This loathing of routine is curious but very definite; I began to get the trapped feeling two weeks ago. I love acting and I love the theatre but, oh Christ, how people can play heavy parts for long runs I shall never know. I feel now, with the holiday stretching before me, as though a skylight had been opened in my head.

Sunday 16 August   Lake Como

The villa is charming and the garden lovely. We bathe in the lake every morning and spend most of every day painting. In the house, in addition to our host[3], there is a desiccated, voluble gentleman who is a Chilean chargé d'affaires. He is married and has three children but travels with a boy-friend who is pretty, young and fairly idiotic. El Señor speaks French and Italian more quickly and more violently than anyone I have ever met. His English is non-existent. He is a perfect example of the *vieux jeu* European Corps Diplomatique snob, but really quite sweet. We have, during the week, visited one *principessa* and one *duchessa*. The former was born Ella Walker in America and is fabulously rich. She was a friend of Mussolini and had to flee to Switzerland, where she lived for two years in an elaborate clinic, without

1 At the studio in Gerald Road.
2 Ava Gardner (b. 1922), Hollywood film star; she had made her screen début in a 1942 adaptation of Noël's one-act play *We Were Dancing*.
3 Paolo Langheim, a wealthy acquaintance who had invited Noël and Graham to stay at his villa during their motoring holiday in Italy.

enough eggs, and visited constantly by the ex-Queen of Spain. She is eighty-four, very chic, has forty-eight gardeners, twelve menservants, three cooks, one Guardi, one Tiepolo, and two dim grand-nieces in white broderie anglaise who seldom utter and are so *comme il faut* that it is difficult not to call them ma'am.

The Duchessa Sermoneta lives on the top of a mountain in a small square house which she fondly imagines is in '*le style anglais*'. She is only about seventy, has had asthma for two years and is exceedingly grand. She also was in a clinic in Switzerland and was also constantly visited by the Queen of Spain, who appears to be a keen clinic hound. These rich, grand, drained old ladies belong to a world that is dead-o and sigh for the times that are past-o. La Sermoneta had as guests an elderly English queen (grey moustache, Corps Diplomatique, beauty-lover) and his brother, who is a Catholic priest (rather nice), and a startled young man fresh from Oxford with over-eager teeth. I don't know *what* he could have been doing there but I have my ideas.

Mussolini, who of course they all bum-crawled to like mad, was caught and shot just near here on the border. He wasn't, however, hung upside down until they took him to Milan.

Paolo couldn't be kinder, and although the conversation is a trifle monotonous he does everything in his power to make us happy and comfortable. There is to be a ball in Biarritz on 1 September, given by the Marquis de Cuevas. This is of tremendous social importance and is now in jeopardy owing to the general strike in France. Nobody can get in touch with anyone else to find out whether the ball will take place or not, or if so what costume Zuki, Norman, Nada and Nell will or will not wear. It is clearly understood that Titi Something-or-other is going as a red parrot, perched on the shoulder of someone else as Man Friday. Apart from this concrete information we have little definite to go on. The excitement is reaching fever pitch and Chile Pom Pom (the chargé d'affaires) is beginning to show signs of strain. So, as a matter of fact, are we and so we are leaving tomorrow for Lago di Garda.

Wednesday 19 August   Sirmione

This is an enchanting place but, like everywhere else in Italy, there are far too many tourists. There is also Larry Harvey and we went yesterday to Verona to see some of the *Romeo and Juliet* film[1]. From the few reels we saw I suspect that it will be very good. The colour is lovely and the taste excellent. I couldn't judge the sound because the projection room was ill-equipped. It seemed to me that Larry will be very effective; he looks magnificent and spoke the 'Banished' speech well.

On our first day here we drove to San Vigilio and had tea with Diana and

1 In which Laurence Harvey was playing Romeo, with Susan Shentall as Juliet.

Duff [Cooper]. They were very sweet and Diana looked more effortlessly beautiful than ever.

Saturday 22 August   Venice

We have been here for three days and are leaving this morning for Milano, having decided to leave the car there and fly to Rome rather than face the rigours of so long a drive. Venice remains the most fabulously lovely and fantastic city in the world but I doubt if it will much longer. The tourists will stamp it down into the canals. I have never seen so many noisy, horrible people in such terrifying numbers. Launches crammed to the gunwales churn up and down. Germans, Swiss, Americans in vast hordes buying postcards, photographing each other, jostling, shouting, squealing. It is nerve-shattering and very, very depressing. We bathed on the Lido, not the Excelsior beach but the Hotel des Bains', which was quieter. My Italian is improving but my temper is not.

Wednesday 26 August   Palazzo Orsini, Rome

We have been staying here since Sunday with Paolo [Langheim]. The Palazzo is unquestionably beautiful but there is an air of defeat about it. The shutters are closed all day on account of the heat and it feels like an aquarium. Paolo firmly took us to several churches, etc. He also took us to *Aïda* in the open air, which I enjoyed much more. King Farouk[1] came for a drink, stayed far too long, insulted the British and the Romans, but Paolo was thrilled on account of his being a king (ex). Rome is crammed with tourists and hellishly noisy. The Italians seem to thrive on noise – no one drives a car without honking the klaxon incessantly. The Vespa motor-bicycles scutter through the streets in millions, making an ear-shattering din. It is dusty and hot and really very nerve-racking. Paolo has been extremely kind but, oh dear God, how much rather would I be in a hotel. We are flying back to Milano today to pick up the car and drive to Portofino, where we are going to stay with Rex and Lilli.

Saturday 29 August   Portofino

This villa is heavenly. Rex and Lilli have gone to Venice for five days for the Film Festival, leaving us with their house, their jeep and their Chris-Craft. This is the first smell of peace I have had since leaving England. On Thursday morning Rex and Lilli welcomed us and it has been lovely ever since. Portofino is enchanting and, fortunately, the Americans don't care for it much because there is no sandy bathing beach and nothing to do.

---

1 King Farouk, the recently deposed Egyptian monarch.

Saturday 5 September

Today we are leaving with regret. This has been far the nicest part of our holiday. We have swum and sunbathed and painted pictures. We have eaten delicious dinners at Pitsforo's on the Port. We have gossiped with Truman Capote[1] and been entertained on a hideous Edwardian yacht by the Luces and Maggie Case. We have laughed a great deal with Rex and Lilli and revelled in talking our own language again. In fact it has been lovely and I most firmly intend to come again.

Sunday 13 September   Goldenhurst

Home again and for the first time for six weeks a genuine sensation of peace. There is a tang of autumn in the air but the sun is warm and the garden lovely. Joyce is here and Gladys, and our holiday dramas have been told and retold. Cole looks sunburnt and well after a perfect holiday in the west country.

Mum is looking frail; every week, almost every day, perceptibly a little older. It is tragic to watch her efforts to hear and see and be bright. Very old age is no fun, even when cossetted. I hope personally for an earlier exit for myself.

Cole has completed the rough first script of *Lady Windermere's Fan*[2] and done it very well.

Last night, having driven to London in the morning, Lorn, Cole, Graham and I attended the last performance of *Quadrille* at Streatham[3]. It was a fairly gruesome evening. Lynn was wonderful, Joyce excellent and Griffith Jones and Marian Spencer dreadful. The real horror was Alfred, who overplayed badly. He crouched and wriggled and camped about like a massive *antiquaire* on heat. It is so depressing that such a really beautiful actor can go so far wrong. Between the two of them they have pretty well ruined the rest of the cast. If only, if only, they would let well alone. When I think of Alfred's original performance and compare it with what I saw last night, I feel the clammy touch of despair. There is nothing to be done. I shall tell him later on when he is less tired, but the effect of what I say will soon evaporate and he will begin again to rearrange, re-rehearse and change everything about. It is really very tiresome. As far as the American production[4] is concerned, there are only two alternatives: one is for me to be there virtually at every rehearsal and at least twice a week after they have opened. The other is to let them do as they like. I need hardly say I shall choose the latter course because life is short and, as the Genie said in *Where the Rainbow Ends*, we have *far* to travel.

1 Truman Capote (b. 1924), American novelist.
2 Cole Lesley was helping with the new musical, to be known as *After the Ball*.
3 Where it was playing a post-West End week.
4 Planned for the near future.

Thursday 17 September

Just back from London. I went up early yesterday; Cecil Tennant[1] came to lunch and I told him to get MCA cracking over cabaret possibilities in America next year. I propose to go over at the end of November and look at all the rooms[2] and decide which is the best.

Went to *The Confidential Clerk*[3], which was beautifully played by everyone. The play itself is fairly well constructed with some fine writing here and there and some exquisite comments on human relationships. It is *not* in verse although it is supposed to be, neither is it particularly 'significant', which foxed the first-night audience considerably. They were all coming to revere or deplore T.S. Eliot and all they got was a farcical idea which might have been conceived by Ben Travers[4] in a *louche* moment, translated into over-literate English by Mr Eliot.

Today Binkie came to lunch. We discussed *ad nauseam* Alfred and Lynn and the American production. Binkie agrees that the only course is to let them cast it and rehearse it themselves and stay out of range ourselves as much as possible. They really are the most extraordinary couple. They are gay and sweet and warm and friendly; Lynn is mentally slow with flashes of brilliant swiftness; Alfred quick as a knife with flashes of dreadful obtuseness. They are deeply concerned with only three things – themselves, the theatre (in so far as it concerns themselves), and food – good, hot food. Lynn has a strong character and is to be trusted. Alfred is frightened of everybody's shadow except, unfortunately, his own. He is weak, hysterical and not to be trusted on stage. On the other hand he has tremendous charm, great humour and is, or can be, an actor of genius. They are unique and valuable and far too complex to be managed in the same play. They love me very much and will listen to me with respect but after a while, with Alfred anyhow, the words of wisdom dissipate in his mind and are forgotten. It is very confusing and exceedingly irritating, especially because I love and admire them both so much.

Thursday 1 October

Lady Windermere is coming along a fair treat. I have completed the music and lyrics of the opening chorus, fairly long and with complicated rhyming, done a lovely song for Graham as Mr Hopper, called 'I Come from a Faraway Land' all about Australia, some incidental music and a charming song for Lord Darlington in act one: 'Stay on the Side of the Angels'. I wake every morning at seven o'clock and work until 11.30 or twelve. Then I get up, visit

1 Cecil Tennant, Laurence Olivier's agent, who was also doing some work for Noël.
2 Used for cabaret in New York hotels.
3 New play by T.S. Eliot (1888–1965), American-born British poet.
4 Ben Travers (1886–1980), British farce writer.

Mum, lunch, and work a bit more in the afternoon before giving myself up to the pleasures of paint and canvas.

Graham, with great good sense, has joined the Worthing Repertory Company in order to gain experience of playing varied straight parts. He is a very wise character.

Erica Marx has published Robert Greacen's book about my 'Art'[1]. It will be out in a week or so and is beautifully turned out. The book itself is well disposed but neither critical enough nor, I fear, interesting enough. However, it is pleasant and in good taste and will be useful for Christmas presents.

Frere is delighted with the revised *Future Indefinite*, and that comes out in March. I sent Dickie Mountbatten all the excerpts about himself and he wrote back a sweet and detailed letter with a few excellent corrections and suggestions. The *Sunday Express* wanted to serialize it but Max B. objected to the praise of Dickie, whom he hates, so they made me a measly offer for four extracts, which I flatly refused.

Friday 9 October   London

A heavy week culminating in today which has been very unpleasant indeed. On Monday night Alfred, Lynn and I had a farewell dinner at Binkie's. They have decided not to do *Quadrille* in America until next autumn. I think they are genuinely exhausted, in which case it's a sensible decision.

On Tuesday there was the cocktail party at the Café de Paris to sell tickets for our Orphanage Gala on 1 November. Well attended and went well, but was a bore. On Thursday I spent two hours at Philips' Gramophone Company testing microphones for my recording session[2]. The whole set-up struck me as being efficient and very bright. Maybe *at last* I shall make some good records. In the evening Lorn, Joyce, Cole and I went to the opening night of *The King and I*. Valerie Hobson was most charming and made a triumphant success. My heart ached at moments for Gertie but on the whole it was an enjoyable evening.

Today has been hell. A fairly useful Orphanage meeting, then I went to Dr Field to have two teeth out. I took the gas and then apparently went berserk and practically wrecked the joint. I came to after half an hour feeling horrible, to discover that Dr F. had had to leave half my molar in, nerve and all. I insisted on coming back later and having it out. This I did and had Pentothal, which was wonderful. I shall never have gas again if I, or Dr Field, can help it. I am now feeling groggy but relieved. I go to Goldenhurst tomorrow to get on with *Lady W*.

1 *The Art of Noël Coward*, published by the Hand and Flower Press, which was owned by Noël's Kentish neighbour Erica Marx and which was known for high-quality productions of the work of young poets, of whom Robert Greacen was one.

2 He was to do the first of his 'compilation' LPs of previous song hits, from 'Mad Dogs' to 'Mrs Worthington'.

Friday 23 October   Goldenhurst

A week of fairly intensive work in which a great deal has been achieved. The music is pouring out and I can scarcely go to the piano without a melody creeping from my fingers, usually in keys that I am not used to and can't play in; it is most extraordinary and never ceases to surprise me. The *Song Book* is out and has had extremely good reviews, except for an embittered essay in patronage by Spike Hughes[1]. He will never forgive me for what I said about 'reserved musicians' in 'Lie in the Dark and Listen'[2] and for being continually successful.

Monday 16 November

Bobby Helpmann[3] is here. We have been through the score and lyrics and he is genuinely enthusiastic. He has suggested Doris Zinkeisen[4] for the décor and dresses, and has shown both sense and sensibility over the whole project.

Yesterday evening the Freres came with Willie Maugham and the Nivens as well. We had a stand-about buffet supper and everyone had a fine time.

Saturday 21 November

It has been quite a week and I am now tired but cheerful. On Tuesday I traipsed up for *Antony and Cleopatra*[5]. Mike magnificent, Peggy[6] fine but ruined by appalling clothes. Before, I popped along to see King Umberto[7], who was very, very sweet and, not unnaturally, rather *triste*. It can't be very cosy being exiled.

Yesterday afternoon I went up to London again, having been invited by the Queen Mother to Clarence House for a small farewell party for the Queen and Prince Philip[8]. It really was enchanting. I wisely took Norman, and sang well. Peter Ustinov[9] did his 'impressions', brilliant but too long. There were only about thirty people present. Everyone looked lovely and I had long conversations with the Queen Mother whom, as usual, I adored. The Queen and Prince Philip didn't leave till after three and so I didn't get to bed until four.

---

1 Spike Hughes, music critic, who had accused Noël of 'appalling taste and mischievous disregard for public feeling' after he had broadcast his 'Don't Let's Be Beastly to the Germans' in 1943, and who had remained a consistent non-admirer.
2 A wartime poem in which Noël had commented harshly on professions unavailable for military service.
3 Robert Helpmann was to direct the new musical.
4 Doris Zinkeisen, Scottish-born designer.
5 The Redgrave–Ashcroft production from Stratford.
6 Peggy Ashcroft (b. 1907), distinguished British stage actress; created Dame 1956.
7 King Umberto, ex-King of Italy who had been banned from his country since 1947.
8 Off on the first prolonged Royal tour of the new reign.
9 Peter Ustinov (b. 1921), actor, dramatist and raconteur.

Monday 23 November

The weekend has been charming and peaceful. Winnie has started a painting of me sitting at the piano. This was my idea because I could relieve the tedium of sitting still by getting on with the score of *Lady Windermere*. Actually I hammered out two good melodies while Winnie bashed away. The picture is already remarkably good. Tonight I watched on television the departure of the Queen and Prince Philip from London Airport. It was immensely moving. The Queen looked so young and vulnerable and valiant, and Prince Philip so handsome and cheerful. A truly romantic couple, star quality *in excelsis*. True glamour without any of the Windsors' vulgarity. We felt truly sad that they were leaving us for such a long time.

Tuesday 1 December   London

On Wednesday I lunched with Willie Maugham at the Dorchester. I only hope that when I am eighty I shall be as bright and charming.

I worked from Thursday to Saturday at Goldenhurst, worked very well too, music flying from my fingers in keys to which I am hideously unaccustomed.

On Monday night (last night) I went to the opening of the French Ballet with Odette Massigli and the Duchess of Kent. Very enjoyable, supper at the French Embassy afterwards.

1954

Following the now traditional Jamaican winter, the year was spent largely at work on After the Ball, *the adaptation of Oscar Wilde's* Lady Windermere's Fan, *which was to be the last Coward musical launched in London rather than on Broadway. And March saw the publication of his second and last volume of autobiography,* Future Indefinite, *covering the war years 1939–45.*

Privately, though, this was a year of considerable sorrow. On 1 July Noël's mother, who was ninety-one and had been ailing for many months, died peacefully at her flat in Eaton Square. She had been his one close relative, his greatest friend and ally, and her death – though long feared – set him back for many months. But professionally the year ended happily, thanks to the arrival at the Café de Paris (where Noël was again in cabaret) of a New York agent called Joe Glaser, who blithely announced that a season could be arranged in Las Vegas for which Noël, in return for two concerts a night, could pick up $35,000 a week playing to what Coward was later to call Nescafé Society. The offer proved irresistible.

Friday 1 January   Jamaica

The year begins greyly rather, because there is, I think, the beginnings of a norther and there is no sun as yet, but it is still early, 7.30, and the horizon is light.

Last night Cole, Graham and I drank the New Year in without undue solemnity, after looking at some rather scurried colour films of a huge, washed-up, dead dolphin being devoured by sharks right in the enclosed part of my beach. This was startling, because I have, until now, subscribed to the blind but comforting faith that *no* big fish could get through the reef. Actually there were about a dozen sharks and the dolphin itself which, dead or alive, must have got in without difficulty. The beach was crowded with onlookers and, on the flat sandy bit where we always bathe, in about four foot of water, a twelve-foot shark was lassoed and dragged in shore, thrashing its angry blue-black tail and champing its dreadful jaws. It is comforting to reflect that I have built a pool. I shall never feel quite secure again, floating out to the reef on a Lilo. The natives had hacked the dolphin to bits and its blood was obviously what lured the sharks into such shallow water, but even so the fact remains that there they were. In these waters sharks are actually not so terribly to be feared because they are supposed to scurry off if you make a great splashing, but barracudas are a different proposition entirely and much more dangerous. And if twelve-foot sharks can get in, so can they, with the utmost *insouciance*. I must try to veil this information from my guests.

We all three left London for New York on the evening of my birthday, after a *Lady Windermere*[1] gathering at the studio – Mary Ellis[2], Binkie, John [Perry], Bobbie [Helpmann], Doris [Zinkeisen], Larry and Vivien. The latter just popped in to say goodbye. My parting from Mum had been conducted with perfect behaviour a short while before. She really is a wonderful woman. My heart ached of course at having to leave her, but her own extraordinary integrity and common sense made it comparatively easy.

After we had unpacked a bit, we went round to Jack and Natasha. From then on it was fairly horrid. They were both fried and not making sense. We were given some dusty smoked salmon and some cold mutton, and everyone talked balls at once. I was really worried about darling Natasha, who looked puffy and jittery. Jack was as he usually is when he has had too much, petulant and silly. We retired home to the Drake [Hotel] considerably deflated.

Our two days in New York passed in a whirl. Personally I hated every minute of it with the exception of an hour with Mary [Martin] and Richard [Halliday] who were sweet. We did, however, see *Picnic*[3], a sex-sodden piece

1 Noël's musical version of which was now virtually completed.
2 Mary Ellis (b. 1901), American actress and singer, who was to star in the show.
3 Play by William Inge.

about small town adolescence; *Wonderful Town*[1] with Roz Russell who was excellent, and *Me and Juliet*, the new Rodgers and Hammerstein, which was quite enjoyable but not good enough.

The flight to Jamaica was perfect. Smooth, delicious food and an atmosphere of holiday gala. Adèle Astaire was on board with her new husband[2]. We touched down at Montego exactly six hours after taking off, and although the weather was cloudy the blessed heat seeped through our city clothes and, in spite of the fact that we were kept standing about in the airport for an hour and a half, it didn't really matter because we were warm again.

John[3] took us over Roundhill, which I think will probably be a great success. It was arranged that I should give a beach bonfire barbecue party on the night of the seventh, two nights before the official opening. The management will pay for the party and half the island is to be invited. Norman [Hackforth] arrives on the fifth and so I said that I would oblige at midnight with a few classy selections from my repertoire. After lunch at Sunset Lodge with poor old Carmen[4], who has been dreadfully ill and is on a diet of rice and garlic sauce for a year, we piled ourselves and our luggage into a hired car and drove home.

Our Christmas social activities have been fairly hectic but not too much so. There was a mammoth cocktail party on Christmas Eve, in the course of which fireworks were let off by the casual Jamaicans, and rockets and Roman candles, having been insecurely set in the ground, shot on to the verandah with violent explosions and scattered the guests like chaff. A number of dresses were ruined by drinks being nervously emptied over them.

In between, among and around these activities, I have contrived, under considerable pressure, to write a lyric and counter-melody lyric for Mrs Erlynne in act one, a 'Letter' song for Lord Darlington in act two, and a really good Cowardesque trio called 'Why is it the Woman who Pays?'. This is a great relief to me because a comedy number was badly needed and I was becoming panic-stricken and barren of ideas. I was reading *Blessed Girl*, the fascinating letters of Lady Emily Lutyens, and came across the phrase 'Why should men be allowed to sin as much as they like without incurring more than the slightest criticism, whereas if a woman makes one slip she is socially damned for ever?' This was not the exact phrase but it gave me the idea, and yesterday I worked like a beaver and completed the number, music and words, all except a brief coda which I shall finish today.

The animals are in fine form. Serena has had four puppies, one of which

1 Musical by Leonard Bernstein.
2 Adèle Astaire (1898–1981), musical comedy star, now Mrs Kingman Douglass.
3 John Pringle, now about to open his new Jamaican hotel and luxury cottage complex at Roundhill, in which Noël had invested.
4 Carmen Pringle, John's mother.

died. The remaining three are named respectively Lady Agatha, Lord Darlington and Mr Hopper. Emily is due for another family in a few days. The
cats are temporarily unpregnant but the place is becoming very like Whipsnade
Zoo.

On Monday we go to Montego to move into my Roundhill bungalow, meet
Natasha and Norman and prepare for the great Beach Bonfire Barbecue.

Sunday 17 January

Last night, just before dinner, I finished the last note and the last word of
After the Ball. This was the vocal exit of the men from Lord Darlington's
rooms. Now all is done and the relief is immense, particularly as I know that
it is very good indeed. I have been very much *en veine* and have turned out
some of the best lyrics I have ever written.

Norman is here and has been slaving away every day. We got to Montego
the evening before to find the whole of the Roundhill arrangements altered.
No cottages ready and not even the hotel open. Finally on the evening of the
seventh I gave the party[1] and it was a triumphant success. There were two
bonfires on the sea on zinc rafts, rows of flaming bamboo torches and
hurricane-lamps, and wonderful food. At 11.30 I sang and, thank God for a
perfect mike, sang well. Sylvia Foot was charming and so as a matter of fact
was everyone else, even the Press.

I was also forced, bitterly against my will, to read Esther Chapman's[2] *Too
Much Summer*. She presented it to me with an inscription. It was all about a
tiresome English woman called Lloyd who has an affair with a coloured
gentleman called Van. She also has an English girl-friend called Laurence who
has lots of affairs with lots of coloured gentlemen who, I feel, should be called
Muriel, Cynthia and Babe. There is a great deal of lurid sexual description –
'His soft wet tongue explored her mouth while she felt his muscular brown
hand unbuttoning her blouse and caressing her nipples', etc. All highly
distasteful and, emerging as it does from the curious recesses of Esther's mind,
almost terrifying. Rosamond Lehmann once described her as looking like a
corsetière, which is wickedly accurate but one does not expect corsetières of fifty
years of age to embark on such unpleasantly lurid sexual reveries. Or perhaps
after all one does! It was a shock to read such frustrated pornography after the
letters of Lady Emily Lutyens.

Sunday 31 January

I am reading at the moment a fascinating book, *Sex in History*, by a psycho-
analyst. It is well-informed, clearly written and horrifying in its descriptions
of religious persecutions through the ages. The arguments I think are fairly

1 To mark the official opening of the hotel, despite parts being still unfinished.
2 Esther Chapman, novelist, and editor of the Jamaican journal, the *West Indian Review*.

sound and there is a dreadful ring of accuracy about the whole book. Human nature, when analysed over the centuries, emerges very poorly. That such ignorance, hypocrisy, cruelty, bigotry and stupidity should exist and function under the name of Christianity, today almost as much as it did in the Dark Ages, is jolly unfair to poor Jesus who really can't be blamed for any of it.

The days whisk by. I have my lovely long mornings to myself. I read and paint pictures, very enjoyable, painting in a new style in gouache with a Flomaster pen to make the outlines. It is effective and quite unlike anything else I have seen. Edward [Molyneux], whose opinion on painting I value, was impressed and said I had found a new technique and must give an exhibition in London! Oh dear. At all events my drawing is improving a great deal. I am working on the preface for the fourth volume of *Play Parade*.

Poor little Moya Nugent died suddenly at a rehearsal the other day. This was sad news. She has worked with me so loyally and well through all our years in the theatre. Too many people have been dying lately. Since I have been here people I know have popped off on an average of two a week. Lee Shubert, Dorothy di Frasso[1], Duff Cooper, Chester Wilmot[2], Pat Kirkwood's husband 'Sparky'[3], and now Moya. It is obviously one of the sadnesses that people in the fifties must be prepared to face.

I drove Graham to Montego and we spent the night at Roundhill. I hated him going as I always do. He is good company, except when he is fussing about his bloody singing, when he is quite unbearable. However, both Cole and I lectured him severely about this and he snapped out of it completely. He arrived back safely, thank God. I am never really relaxed when he is between the sea and sky.

Jack stayed four days and has gone back to Montego to cope with furnishing his cottage at Roundhill. It is a dismal sight to see him now and remember how handsome and amusing he once was. He has changed in every way so shatteringly that it is only occasionally that I can catch a glimpse of what he used to be. Nowadays I have no contact with him at all. His views and values are diametrically opposed to mine, in addition to which years of overdrinking have sozzled his brain and made him frankly idiotic for most of the time. Natasha knows all this and we have discussed it. We can neither of us think of any solution. Wagging my finger in his face is of no use any more. He is too old to be reformed and too set in his lazy self-indulgence to welcome, or even listen to, any intelligent counsel. Whether or not he is happy I cannot tell. I don't think he can be, but he has always lacked loyalty and moral courage, although when he was younger and gayer these deficiencies were not so

1 Dorothy di Frasso, Hollywood socialite, much in the gossip columns.
2 Chester Wilmot (1911–54), BBC war correspondent and writer on military affairs for the *Observer*.
3 Spiro de Spero Gabriele, her second husband.

apparent. Now that he is fifty-four, four months older than I, he is petulant, repetitive and unbelievably boring. He looks about sixty. I am deeply sad about this. It is difficult to believe that the snows of yester-year should vanish so utterly. He meant so much to me for so many years and now I find even a discussion of the weather is a strain. He has no real friends left because over the years his wicked tongue has alienated them. In addition to all this, poor dear, he has had three flops in a row this year[1]. I am afraid he has let himself go too far to be reclaimable and, as far as I can see, his future is black. Natasha is as worried as I am, if not more so. I have made her promise to come to Europe this year at all costs, to get away from the dreariness of their life in New York. I suppose this general *dégringolade* started during the war. If only, if only, Jack had had the courage and the sense to come to England and be with us all again, it might never have happened.

The sun is shining, the sea is blue, Emily has had three puppies concealed in a hollowed-out coco-palm. They are called Knight, Frank and Rutley. Life goes on like mad.

Sunday 14 February

Jack departed for Montego after four days, leaving, I fear, sighs of relief behind him. Natasha refused flatly to go with him as she prefers the peace of Blue Harbour to the martinis of Montego Bay. We had a gay and charming week. She is no trouble in the house and makes no demands whatever and I am deeply fond of her.

Roald Dahl and Pat[2] came to dine the other night. His new book of short stories[3] has just gone into four editions and got rave reviews. The stories are brilliant and his imagination is fabulous. Unfortunately there is, in all of them, an underlying streak of cruelty and macabre unpleasantness, and a curiously adolescent emphasis on sex. This is strange because he is a sensitive and gentle creature. Perhaps he has lived in America too long and caught some of the prevalent sex hysteria.

Sunday 21 February

I started writing *Nude with Violin* on Wednesday morning and finished the first act yesterday. I think it is going to be good. The story is strong and so far the dialogue has flowed easily. Whether or not it will be too esoteric a satire for the general public remains to be seen. I shall try to evade this danger by making it as light as possible. I have been carefully reading Wilenski's *Lives of the Impressionists* and really no burlesque however extravagant could equal the phrases he uses to describe the 'Abstract' boys. Quite a lot of it is

1 On Broadway, where Wilson was still in management.
2 Patricia Neal (b. 1926), American actress, married to Roald Dahl.
3 *Someone Like You.*

completely unintelligible. He talks a great deal of 'emotive force' and 'lyrical colour' and 'constant functional forms', etc., and after he has described a picture in approximately these terms you turn to a coloured plate and look at a square lady with three breasts and a guitar up her crotch. At any rate I am grateful to him for giving me a lot of hilarious material.

Sunday 14 March

My last day in Jamaica. The morning was lovely so I just consolidated my sunburn and lay on a Lilo in the pool for two hours. Last night we had our 'free for all' cocktail party. Over fifty came and it was a howling success.

I finished *Nude with Violin* on Friday morning. It is very funny, I think, but whether I shall tie myself down to playing it myself remains to be seen.

Tomorrow I leave for Miami and then New York and fly home to England on the twenty-ninth. I have enjoyed these three months. I think it is possible that I may come out in July for a few weeks entirely alone and get my brain nice and clear. *After the Ball*[1] is playing to capacity business and going very well, but there is obviously something not quite right.

Monday 29 March

Marlene drove me out to the airport and saw me off as usual. Her presence at Idlewild[2] caused a slight stir and there was some autograph signing and photography.

I have enjoyed New York this time more than I have since the days before the war, perhaps because I devoted myself almost entirely to theatre-going and stayed on Broadway rather than the East Side. Joe and Lenore Cotten gave a really enchanting party for me on Saturday night which went on until 5 a.m. Harold Arlen[3] played the score of *House of Flowers*, a musical that he is writing with Truman Capote. Ina [Claire] was there, Constance [Collier], Deborah Kerr, Cathleen [Nesbitt], Audrey Hepburn[4] and a mass of my friends, and it was warm and cosy and properly theatrical.

I spent Sunday afternoon watching a rehearsal for television of a Rodgers and Hammerstein show[5]. The cast glittered with stars, headed by Mary Martin, who was wonderful. The show itself was spoiled for me by the fact that it was untidily constructed and over-eulogistic. I love and revere Oscar and Dick's contributions to the musical stage but the air of reverence was a trifle excessive, almost as though it were a memorial service.

I have seen seventeen shows since I arrived. The most impressive was *The*

1 It had opened in Liverpool on 1 March and was to play a twelve-week provincial tour before reaching London in June.
2 Renamed John F. Kennedy Airport in 1963.
3 Harold Arlen (b. 1905), American composer.
4 Audrey Hepburn (b. 1929), Belgian-born British actress.
5 A concert anthology of their hit songs.

Caine Mutiny[1], superbly directed and acted to perfection by Hank Fonda, Lloyd Nolan, etc. Ina Claire, in *The Confidential Clerk*[2], was exquisite and quite beyond praise, but the rest of the cast, notably Joan Greenwood and Claude Rains, were not.

Tea and Sympathy[3] was well played by Deborah [Kerr] and the rest of the cast, but the play itself was a mixture of naivety and dishonesty. Homosexuality is *à la mode* this season and in this particular instance it is treated untruly and lasciviously.

Sabrina Fair[4] is a workmanlike, well-played comedy. *Ondine*[5], directed by Alfred [Lunt], ineffably dull but then it always was. It was ineffably dull to me when I saw it in Paris years ago with Louis Jouvet; I fear my mind is ill-attuned to Gallic whimsy.

Apart from these theatrical forays, I saw a film of Helen Keller's life, shown privately for me by Nancy Hamilton[6] who wrote and constructed it. Aside from two or three moments when its nobility spilled over and became unintentionally funny, it was immensely moving. Helen Keller herself, whom I met and loved instantly, emerges as a great character, which obviously she is.

I felt at home again in New York, a feeling that I thought the idiocies of the war had killed for ever. In theatres strangers were suddenly sweet to me and convinced me that I really must play on Broadway again before I am too old to drag myself onto the stage.

I lunched with Max Gordon, but Marlene I saw most of; she is sweet company and such a permanent pleasure to the eye.

Thursday 1 April   Bristol

Last night was my first view of *After the Ball*. Joyce and Cole came with me. It was a long-awaited occasion and, like so many long-awaited occasions, disappointing. Admittedly the theatre was so enormous that it entirely dwarfed the production, but that I was prepared for. What I was not prepared for was the absence of style in the direction. It was restless and untidy and, owing to everybody moving about so much during the dialogue scenes and the numbers, a great deal of the performance was inaudible. The dance in the last scene is enchanting and so is the direction of 'The Woman Who Pays'. There are also a few other moments of imagination and charm, but not enough, not nearly

---

1 Play by Herman Wouk adapted from his novel.
2 The American production of T. S. Eliot's play.
3 By Robert Anderson.
4 Romantic comedy by Samuel Taylor.
5 By Jean Giraudoux.
6 Nancy Hamilton (b. 1908), American actress, playwright and lyricist: this film was a documentary of how Helen Keller (1880-1968) overcame her disabilities.

enough. Graham, thank God, was really very good indeed. Vanessa [Lee] sang divinely but acted poorly. Irene [Browne] gave a fine, exterior comedy performance. Mary Ellis acted well but sang so badly that I could hardly bear it.

The orchestra was appalling, the orchestrations beneath contempt, and poor Norman[1] conducted like a stick of wet asparagus. If the show opened in London as it is, it wouldn't run a week. Bobbie [Helpmann] has made a few transpositions and cuts which will have to be put back. He is not yet, I fear, a good enough director; being a dancer and choreographer he has an instinctive dread of repose. When he gets over this – if he gets over it – he may be very good indeed. I foresee a lot of hard, hard work. Thank God we have another eight weeks. In fairness to poor Bobbie, he was utterly dumbfounded by the horror of the first orchestra rehearsal, so much so indeed that he wanted to open in Liverpool with only a piano.

The whole score will have to be re-orchestrated from overture to finale and Norman will have to be fired. I have rehearsed all day today and reduced unnecessary movements wherever possible. I have also insisted on follow spots[2] in all the numbers because, believe it or not, last night there were none at all. It was impossible to judge the décor and dresses fairly; however, I am very sure that there must be several changes. I will have to start dealing with everything immediately. I expected that I would have to do some polishing and re-rehearsing, but I did not expect to be faced with a series of major operations. However, away with melancholy, I feel well and there is time enough, my dear love, time and to spare! Or is there? In any event, God help Manchester, Leeds, Newcastle, etc.

My arrival home on Tuesday morning was lovely. The flight had been perfect and I was met by Lornie, Coley and a first copy of *Future Indefinite*, which looks very impressive. I visited darling Mum, who was gay and sweet but looked very frail. In the evening we had a small party at the studio afterwards to celebrate Gladys's and Joycie's joint birthdays and my home-coming. Winnie came and Vivien, Larry, Binkie, John [Perry], and Bobbie Helpmann, and it was all most warming and cheerful.

Wednesday 21 April   Newcastle

The week at Leeds was productive and a great deal happened. We rehearsed all day and every day, and Cole and I rewrote and reconstructed the ballroom scene, giving Irene Browne a lot more comedy and generally pepping up the whole enterprise. We rehearsed the new scene on Thursday and popped it in that same evening. Brownie was really wonderful and carried it through triumphantly. It went so very, very much better that I am forced to admit that

1 Norman Hackforth, Noël's faithful pianist, had now been promoted to conductor.
2 Movable spotlights trained on individual players.

the more Coward we can get into the script and the more Wilde we can eliminate, the happier we shall all be.

On Saturday night, the Princess Royal and the Harewoods[1] came and expressed muted approval. He looked more than ever as though he ought to have a lemon in his mouth but was very amiable. I am sure the appalling discords and wrong notes in the orchestra must have filled him with pleasant nostalgia for his own dear Benjamin Britten[2].

Sunday 9 May   Goldenhurst

Two weeks have gone by, two prevalently Scottish weeks. *After the Ball* was very well received by the audiences in Edinburgh but, curiously enough, the business was disappointing. Usually Edinburgh is a sell-out for anything of mine.

The opening night in Glasgow was a tremendous charity 'première' to which all the Scottish nobility came in full regalia. I sat teed up in tails in a box with Ian and Margaret Argyll[3], and there was a party afterwards. The show went very well and the audience really did look lovely in their kilts and cairngorms and tiaras.

I am terribly disappointed about *After the Ball*. The whole project has been sabotaged by Mary not being able to sing it. Unfortunately she is a strong personality and *plays* it well, otherwise I would of course have had her out of the cast weeks ago.

Sunday 30 May

A great deal has happened during the last few days. Coley and I worked feverishly against time and contrived to get the reconstructed version ready for the second week in Brighton. It is much, much better and a gleam of light is appearing on the horizon at last.

Bobbie has been witty and great fun to work with and it is a tribute to us both that there has been no conflict between us at all.

I am worried about Mum; she is failing rapidly. The poor old darling can hardly see any more and of course her deafness is worse than ever. It is agony to visit her really because she makes such gallant efforts to hear and understand, and I know that the moment I leave she relapses into exhausted melancholy. Old age is a protracted, cruel business. It would really have been so much better if she had died a year, or even a few months, ago before this dreadful process of decay really started. It is heart-breaking to see her waiting for me so eagerly at the window and then barely recognizing me when I walk

1 The 7th Earl of Harewood (b. 1923) and his first wife, pianist Marion Stein; he is the elder son of the Princess Royal, daughter of King George V and Queen Mary.
2 Benjamin Britten (1930–76), British composer; made a peer in 1976.
3 The 11th Duke and Duchess of Argyll.

into the room. I don't think she can last much longer. I dread her dying but I also long for it. I have always hoped that I would be able to hold her hand at the end, but my heart sinks at the thought of it.

Sunday 6 June

I have been here since Thursday. The beginning of the week in London was enlivened by an amateur performance of *The Frog*[1] presented and performed by high society at the Scala Theatre and co-directed by Judy Montagu[2] and Princess Margaret. I went with Vivien, or rather I went by myself and was joined by Vivien later, after she had finished her performance in *The Sleeping Prince*[3]. The whole evening was one of the most fascinating exhibitions of incompetence, conceit and bloody impertinence that I have ever seen in my life. With the exception of young Porchester[4], who at least tried to sustain a character, the entire cast displayed no talent whatsoever. Billy Wallace[5], the leading man, ambled on and off the stage with his chin stampeding into his neck; nobody made the faintest effort to project their voices; Elsa Maxwell appeared in a cabaret scene and made a cracking ass of herself. Douglas Fairbanks played a small part in order, I presume, to prove that he was more one of 'them' than one of 'us'. As a matter of fact, by now, he almost is.

It was a hilarious evening on the whole, if only it hadn't been so irritating. It was certainly a strong moral lesson for all of us never to be nervous again on opening nights. Those high-born characters we watched mumbling and stumbling about the stage are the ones who come to our productions and criticize us! They at least betrayed no signs of nervousness; they were unequivocally delighted with themselves from the first scene to the last which, I may add, was a very long time indeed. In the dressing-room afterwards, where we went civilly to congratulate Porchy, we found Princess Margaret eating foie gras sandwiches, sipping champagne and complaining that the audience laughed in the wrong places. We commiserated politely and left.

The next evening, Wednesday, was the other side of the medal. Joyce, Cole and I went to John G's production of *The Cherry Orchard* at the Lyric, Hammersmith. A magical evening in the theatre; every part subtly and perfectly played, and a beautiful production so integrated and timed that the heart melted. We came away prancing on the tips of our toes and very proud that we belonged to the theatre. I do hope that Princess Margaret, Judy Montagu, Billy Wallace and the Fairbankses manage to get to see it, but I

---

1 A thriller by Ian Hay based on an Edgar Wallace novel.
2 Judith Montagu (1923-72), an active society figure.
3 Terence Rattigan comedy in which she was playing the showgirl opposite Olivier's Grand Duke.
4 Lord (Henry) Porchester.
5 Billy Wallace, then a frequent escort of Princess Margaret's.

doubt if they will; after all, the season is only just beginning and they really won't have a minute.

Here all is calm and peaceful as usual. Jack arrives this evening. *After the Ball* takes the high jump on Thursday but before that we shall have to endure the usual chaos and torment including a dress rehearsal and a social charity première.

Sunday 13 June

The week, as I suspected, was fairly nerve-racking. The scenery, contrary to expectations, has *not* been refurbished to fit the Globe; it has not even been adequately repainted where it needed it. The dress rehearsal and première were dreary but the opening night a good deal better. It was an obvious success. Irene Browne and Graham were the best. Mary was bloody good and at least sang quietly. Vanessa charming, Peter [Graves][1] all right. The quartets and trios all excellent and every word clearly audible. Afterwards there was a party at John Perry's at which Irene got pissed and insulted Joyce and a good time was enjoyed by nearly all.

The daily Press was idiotic as usual but well-disposed and good box-office. Today's papers are, on the whole, very good, particularly Harold Hobson in the *Sunday Times*, who is quite lyrical. I think it will do big business for quite a while, but I feel in my heart that the fact that almost a third of the score has had to be cut will mitigate against its success with the general public. It is now, subtly, a bit lopsided. Personally I would give it about six to eight months, which is definitely better than nothing.

Sunday 20 June

Jack has gone home again. He has been entirely sweet during this visit and at his very best. We went together to see Joyce Grenfell[2] and she was quite brilliant. Marlene arrived on Wednesday and there was a tremendous to-do. She looked ravishing and was mobbed and fussed over and photographed. I took her to *After the Ball* which she didn't care for much. She opens tomorrow night[3] and I am writing a little verse with which to introduce her[4]. She is worried, rightly, about the band at the Café de Paris; she is also worried,

1 Peter Graves (b. 1911), British actor; became 8th Baron Graves 1963.
2 In *Joyce Grenfell Requests the Pleasure* at the Fortune Theatre.
3 In cabaret at the Café de Paris.
4 It ended:

> Though we all might enjoy
> Seeing Helen of Troy
> As a gay cabaret entertainer,
> I doubt that she could
> Be one quarter as good
> As our lovely, legendary Marlene.

rightly, about the lighting. However, I have sent an SOS to Joe Davis[1] and he is on the job. I watched her rehearse and my personal guess is that she will have a triumph.

Sunday 27 June

It's been a busy week, a hectic week and a worrying week; worrying because of Mum and hectic because of all that had to be got through. On Monday I went to a cocktail party at Lavinia Annaly's[2] to meet the Queen Mother. Then there was Marlene's opening at the Café de Paris. Vivien, Larry, Ina, Graham, etc., were at my table. At a given moment the spotlight discovered me and I spoke my introductory verse, which went very well. Then My Lady came down the stairs looking ravishing and assured and the epitome of glamour. She sang her songs beautifully and had a triumphant success.

From then on until Thursday we had all the last-minute preparations and rehearsals for *Night of a Hundred Stars*[3] at the Palladium. Considering the magnitude of the operation it ran astonishingly smoothly. On the night itself I took the Duchess of Kent, Princess Alexandra and party to *After the Ball*, then to supper at the studio and on to the Palladium, where we all filed into the royal box amid general acclamation. The show went wonderfully and was really very good with the exception of a few dull spots, notably Errol Flynn and Pat Wymore, who stayed on for twenty-five minutes instead of ten and by sheer tactlessness and vulgarity nearly wrecked the whole enterprise. I followed them and got the biggest ovation of my life; much of it, I suspect, was relief. Then Marlene came on and we finished up by singing a duet which neither of us knew. It was all good clean fun, however, and we made a clear profit of £10,000 for the Orphanage. The efficiency of the Palladium and everyone connected with it is really beyond praise. If we can do this once a year, and there is really no reason why we shouldn't, the Orphanage can survive. Charles and Ham[4] did a miracle of organization and altogether the whole business was gratifying in the extreme. News of my cosy personal triumph spread round theatrical London like *feu sauvage*.

Underneath it all, of course, was the deep personal sadness about Mum. I know that she can't last much longer and it is such agony to see her disintegrating. She can hardly see at all and hears nothing, so there is nothing to do but sit and hold her hand. I tried to tell her about all the excitements. It would have meant so much to her if only she had been able to take it in, but she couldn't.

1 Joe Davis became her resident lighting director.
2 Lavinia Annaly, wife of 4th Baron Annaly, formerly Lady Lavinia Spencer.
3 The midnight matinée in aid of the Actors' Orphanage.
4 Charles Russell and Lance Hamilton organized this and subsequent Palladium charity shows for the Orphanage.

Thursday 1 July   London

Mother died yesterday at a quarter to two. I went round at eleven o'clock and she recognized me for a fleeting moment and said 'dear old darling'. Then she went into a coma. I sat by the bed and held her hand until she gave a pathetic little final gasp and died. I have no complaints and no regrets. It was as I always hoped it would be. She was ninety-one years old and I was with her close, close, close until her last breath. Over and above this sensible, wise philosophy I know it to be the saddest moment of my life. Owing to my inability to accept any of the comforting religious fantasies about the hereafter, I have no spurious hopes that we shall meet again on some distant Elysian shore. I know that it is over. Fifty-four years of love and tenderness and crossness and devotion and unswerving loyalty. Without her I could only have achieved a quarter of what I have achieved, not only in terms of success and career, but in terms of personal happiness. We have quarrelled, often violently, over the years, but she has never stood between me and my life, never tried to hold me too tightly, always let me go free. For a woman with her strength of character this was truly remarkable. She was gay, even to the last I believe, gallant certainly. There was no fear in her except for me. She was a great woman to whom I owe the whole of my life. I shall never be without her in my deep mind, but I shall never see her again. Goodbye, my darling.

Sunday 11 July   Paris

I have been here since last Saturday. The funeral was in the early afternoon and I caught the 4.30 plane. The funeral, except for one awful moment when I saw the little coffin trundling into the chapel, was virtually without pain and drearily unimpressive. The bloody old clergyman gabbled the service gracelessly and without heart. The relatives looked like morose dummies. Auntie Ida bellowed and had herself a field-day. She was visiting several other graves too and was really enjoying herself. Gladys, Lornie, Graham, Coley and I stood around the grave and listened to the nonsense, but it had nothing to do with Mum. We drove away through the damp suburban streets and made a few jokes.

One thing has impressed me deeply and that is the kindness of people, apart from intimates. Never let it be said that letters of condolence are useless or a bore; they are curiously warming. I had so very many, some of them from most unexpected and unlikely people. Lots of them were silly and filled with godliness and flowery, vicarious grief, but all of them were kindly meant. A few were true and deeply touching and came from the heart.

On the evening of the day she died I had arranged to dine with Rebecca West. I didn't put her off because I felt that her clear, astringent mind would be a comfort. I was quite right. We dined quietly and talked of all sorts of things. She knew, of course, that I was miserable and made no effort to cheer me; she merely talked away and we laughed a lot and she cheered me a great deal.

This week has been fairly idiotic. I have drunk a lot, not excessively, seen heaps of people, gone through each day and night, not tragically, but dully. I haven't thought a great deal or made many plans. Mum, with her usual tact, has been content to sit quietly in my subconscious and not bother me. The only bad pang I have had was having to turn aside from the impulse to send her a postcard.

Sunday 18 July   Villa Mauresque, Cap Ferrat

I flew here yesterday after a busy week which included some high-powered recording for my LP record and a financial conference; perhaps my affairs will be less convulsively conducted in the future.

This house is exquisitely comfortable as always. Willie Maugham[1] merry as a grig and very mellow and sweet. The sun is shining and there is nothing to do but read and relax and talk and eat and swim in the pool. A very good beginning to an escapist holiday.

Sunday 12 September   Goldenhurst

There is a big jump since I last addressed myself to these pages, a jump of nearly two months. To have reported these two months day by day, week by week, or even fortnight by fortnight would have been dull, merely a catalogue of recorded pleasures (?). The query after 'pleasures' is significant because there really haven't been very many. Physical pleasures certainly, sunshine and heat and suntan and beautiful sights, but all spoiled by an inside dreariness. Reaction after Mum's death and a sort of minor nervous breakdown. Nothing serious really but a feeling of nullity and an inability to sleep peacefully. Also a very tiresome head cold which turned to a bloody awful cough and generally depleted me. The week with Willie was enchanting, no complaints; I would like to be certain that I shall be as entertaining and cheerful when I am rising eighty-one.

The four days in Paris were quite fun. Ginette and Paul-Emile dear as ever, Marlene in fine fettle. Then five days in Venice. I will never go to Venice in August again. It was like being shut up in a hot wet box and noisier than all hell. Kate H.[2] was there and Constance [Collier] and darling Natasha. I coughed my lungs out every night and might well have expired like Camille if Kate hadn't given me some codeine. It was all quite gay, but my quiet little nervous breakdown was going on inside and I enjoyed very little of it. From

---

1 With whom Noël was staying.
2 Katharine Hepburn was then filming *Summer Madness* (US title *Summertime*) in Venice for David Lean.

Venice I took the night train to Rome, a hideous experience, where Paolo Langheim met me and whisked me off to Naples on the afternoon train to his island villa at Posillipo. It looks out over the Bay of Naples to Vesuvius, Sorrento, Capri and Ischia.

Capri was beautiful as always but there were far, far too many people. I was having nervous 'come-overs' and not feeling very happy, but on the whole I enjoyed myself. Beattie [Lillie] was there, with entourage, and we bathed together every day. Gracie Fields too. We sat every evening on the piazza and drank cinzanos and bought sweaters and trousers and various other holiday adornments. Sam Spiegel[1] arrived on a little yacht with some hangers-on. I was supposed to join them but, after one look, hurriedly invented urgent calls from England. There was a farewell party given for me by Beattie. On the next morning at dawn I was on the steamer, chugging across to Naples where I caught a BEA direct flight to London.

That was the end of my escapist holiday and here I am, with the sabbatical year I planned blown to hell by my own volition. I don't want *not* to work for a year. I can't bear *not* working. Memories of the visual aspects of the holiday I can recapture by looking at my stereoscopic photographs. Very good they are too. There is the shining sea and the lovely island and the gay, friendly people. How enviable it all looks, squinting into the 'viewer'. I wouldn't, however, live a moment of it again. I was trying to be too bright, too soon. I should have been better advised really to have stayed at Goldenhurst, weather or no weather, and relaxed and read and got myself together. I'm older than I look, but not nearly so old as I feel. This feeling of depletion will, I know, soon fade away but I must go to work again.

I gave a party for Sam Spiegel on Thursday night; it was a great success but I didn't enjoy it very much. *Waterfront* is a good picture. Rex Harrison has fallen in love with Kay Kendall[2] and is breaking Lilli's heart. *After the Ball* is dropping and will not run beyond November. Charles and Ham are planning, with my permission and financial encouragement, a tour of *Blithe Spirit* with Dennis Price, Margot Grahame, Irene Handl and Kay Kendall. Larry and Vivien are fine. All my loved ones are cheerful. Val Parnell wants me to go to the Palladium next year. I intend to do four weeks at the Café de Paris this year, as I was brightly informed that I was £19,000 overdrawn! This has infuriated me. It is not as terrible as it sounds, because by December there will be some big cheques coming in, but I am livid at not having been warned. A big economy drive is now about to begin.

1 Sam Spiegel (b. 1904), Hollywood producer whose films include *On the Waterfront*, released this year.
2 Kay Kendall (1926–59), British actress, who became Rex Harrison's third wife in 1957, following his divorce from Lilli Palmer.

Sunday 3 October   Dublin

It is an undisputed fact that the Irish have charm and it is being brought home to me most strongly. Coley and I arrived here yesterday[1] and found the Irish spell genuine enough. It does really seem absurd to think that I have never been here before. I shall certainly come again and I long for time to explore and see the peat-thatched cabins and the west coast and the colleens. In the meantime I suppose I must content myself with Irene Handl and Kay Kendall who are, at this moment, twittering with nerves and preparing for the dress rehearsal. The city is really charming: lovely reddish Georgian houses with porticos and wide, sashed windows, a feeling of romantic nostalgia in the air and a lot of feathery, gentle Irish rain.

Thursday 7 October

We are flying back to England today, really regretfully. I would love to stay longer. Everyone has been charming to us. The play is playing to capacity and the audiences are extraordinary. They really come to the theatre to enjoy themselves. The first night on Monday was jam-packed and filled with the flower of the city. They gave me a terrific ovation and it felt genuine and warm.

Kay Kendall is a good girl, I think, in spite of having an affair with Rex and upsetting Lilli. Her wig was no good so she dyed her hair grey, which showed enthusiasm and horse-sense. She gives a performance of great charm; all she needs is experience and a bit more technical assurance. Dennis [Price] gives an excellent performance and it is he who really holds the play together. Irene Handl, who *could* be brilliant as Madame Arcati, is still floundering and mistiming and poor Margot is ghastly. She is just a large, breasty, good-hearted hunk of tangerine meat.

Sunday 24 October   Goldenhurst

I opened triumphantly at the Café de Paris last Monday. I wasn't particularly nervous; there was nothing wrong with my voice and I really did tear the place up. The new songs all went wonderfully and 'Piccolo Marina'[2] is obviously a rouser. Everybody was there and it was a highly satisfactory evening. Towards the end of this last week, however, the weather has changed and my voice has begun to get furry. It is always dangerous for me to sing at this beastly time of the year. However, I am less nervous about it than I used to be because I have proved that the audiences don't give a hoot whether I am in good voice or not so long as I can get the comedy numbers over.

1 To oversee the start of the *Blithe Spirit* tour.
2 Written while staying on Capri watching 'hordes of middle-aged matrons pouring off every boat, all set to have themselves a ball'.

Sunday 7 November   London

Two more weeks gone by; routine stuff mostly. Crowds of people at the Café every night. I am fighting for my voice. This time I am finding the waiting a strain; the evenings are long, before I go on at 12.15. The best way out is to dine with people and talk a lot; this eases the chords. If I go to a play it finishes too early, and if I stay at home and cosset myself I can hardly speak when I get to the Café. I have taken to sleeping until 1.30 or 2 which helps, but I don't really like turning the day inside out. I have definitely decided not to do the six weeks but to finish after four, on the thirteenth.

On Monday I appeared at the Royal Command Performance at the Palladium. It was a glittering occasion, crammed with stars, all shaking like aspens. The moment I arrived in the dressing-room and found Bob Hope tight-lipped, Jack Buchanan quivering and Norman Wisdom[1] sweating, I realized that the audience was vile, as it usually is on such regal nights. In the entr'acte Cole and Charles [Russell] came round from the front and said it was the worst they had ever encountered and that I was to be prepared for a fate worse than death. This was exactly what I needed and so I bounded on to the stage like a bullet from a gun, sang 'Uncle Harry', 'Mad Dogs' and 'Bad Times' very, very fast indeed and got the whole house cheering! I was on and off in nine and a half minutes. The next day the papers announced, with unexpected generosity, that I was the hit of the show. This was actually true but it wouldn't have been if I had stayed on two minutes longer. Bob Hope had them where he wanted them, and then went on and on and lost them entirely. I have quite definitely decided *not* to do a season at the Palladium. Much as I love the theatre and the efficiency and niceness of all concerned, it's not really my ambience. I could hold them all right for a quarter of an hour or even twenty minutes but not forty-five minutes. Oh no. Me for the more intimate lark to my own type of audience. After the show we lined up and were presented to the Queen, Prince Philip and Princess Margaret. The Queen looked luminously lovely and was wearing the largest sapphires I have ever seen. She was very charming, everyone was very charming, and that was that.

Sunday 14 November   Goldenhurst

Arrived here at 4.30 this morning after a riotous last night at the Café. I had to sing for over an hour and the audience was wonderful. I was sad to say goodbye to the staff because they are all so very friendly and nice. This is my last weekend here and the weather is suitably doleful. Steady autumnal rain and the garden sodden. It was a busy week; I did a broadcast[2] (recorded) on Friday and I think it was very good. It lasted an hour; Vanessa [Lee] sang two songs – 'Sweet Day' and 'Changing World' – and I did the rest. On Tuesday I dined

1 Norman Wisdom (b. 1925), British actor and comedian.
2 To drum up trade for the closing weeks of *After the Ball*.

with Annie and Ian [Fleming] and it was somehow tiresome. Annie is such a darling when she is alone with Ian but when surrounded by her own set – Judy [Montagu], Alastair F[1], etc. – she changes completely and becomes shrill and strident, like one of those doomed Michael Arlen characters of the twenties. I am really surprised that Ian doesn't sock her in the chops and tell her to shut up.

A jolly dinner with Alex Korda on Thursday, when I had a long talk with Georges Simenon[2], whom I took a great shine to. He told me that he works for three hours a day, 6.30 to 9.30 a.m., and always finishes a book in eleven days. This, of course, delighted me and struck sparks from my own writing impulse which is raring to go. On Thursday I lunched with the Maugham brothers. I felt very sorry for poor old Lord Maugham[3]. His book has not been a success on account of being dull and, I fear, wrong-headed. Willie was full of beans, almost gloatingly so. After all, he is eight years younger than his brother who is eighty-eight!

A character called Joe Glaser[4] flew in from New York to sign me up for Las Vegas. A typical shrewd, decent, sharp agent type. The discussion was satisfactory financially, everything being contingent on whether or not I like Las Vegas, so he is escorting me there for a couple of days so that I can case the joint and decide which room I prefer to appear in, if any. If I can salt away £20,000 free of tax by appearing there for three weeks in the spring, I have a strong feeling that I should do it whether I like it or not. I need the money and that amount, tax-free, is certainly not to be sneezed at. Joe Glaser watched my performance at the Café and was obviously bewildered as to why the audience liked it so much. We are getting together in New York.

Wednesday 17 November

Dined with Binkie last night; I have a curious feeling of sadness about him. There is no concrete reason for this but an inner instinct tells me that he is due for unhappiness. I may be entirely wrong, I hope I am.

On Wednesday Fanny Holtzmann appeared and tried to force me to write a foreword to Richard Aldrich's book about Gertie[5]. I said I would read it. Later on I did read it and it threw me into a frenzy of irritation. It is not outrageously bad in the obvious illiterate sense but subtly it is very bad indeed, false right through and also dull. I have refused firmly to have any part of it.

1 Alastair Forbes (b. 1918), essayist and critic.
2 Georges Simenon (b. 1903), Belgian novelist particularly famous for his Inspector Maigret books.
3 Lord Maugham (1866–1958), Lord Chancellor 1938–39; he had just published his memoirs which contained one sole, last-page reference to his brother Somerset Maugham – 'a writer of novels'.
4 Joe Glaser, New York theatrical agent.
5 *Gertrude Lawrence as Mrs A.*, a biography dealing only with the ten years of their marriage.

I lunched with Maurice Winnick who has television plans for the future.[1] I told him I had already formed my own television company so as to keep control of all my material. I am very glad I have, too. I went to say goodbye to the *After the Ball* company, a dreary little enterprise. They close on Saturday and go off on a six-week tour. The whole thing felt flat and depressing. I dined with Larry and Viv and Johnny G. Graham came later, after the play, and we drove home through thick smog, hugging the pavements. I am so very glad to be leaving, except for leaving him. But I think he is fairly happy. There are one or two offers coming along and he has certainly consolidated his position by his performance of Mr Hopper, which is as fresh and charming as it was at first. He is a remarkable character and I love him dearly and for ever.

Wednesday 1 December   New York

Tonight I leave for Las Vegas on the 1 a.m. plane with Joe Glaser. The week has been crowded and hectic but, taken all in all, not too bad. First of all *Quadrille*, which I saw the first night I arrived. It is very well done, mostly better than in London. Lynn and Alfred are superb, Edna [Best][2] brilliant and Brian Aherne[3] passable. He looks fine and has authority. On Thursday evening I went, by myself, to *The Pajama Game*[4] and loved it. Slick, gay and well done all the way round. After that, a party at Nancy Hamilton's, very cosy: Lynn, Alfred, Mary, Richard, etc. Thanksgiving turkey. On Friday I saw Mary play *Peter Pan*[5]. Except for moments in the first act it had little to do with the original. She was wonderful and whenever she had Barrie's lines to speak there was a 'true' quality. Her flying was miraculous. Cyril Ritchard was not good as Hook. The Lost Boys (real boys) were sweet. The original music has all been banished and some honky-tonk Broadway numbers substituted. Jerome Robbins[6], who directed and *rewrote* it, is apparently opposed to sentiment; in this case Barrie was not the author to choose.

My great worry is Jack. He was amiable and determined to be sweet, but he has been drinking so much and for so long that he is now virtually sodden and frequently doesn't make sense. The Lunts are on to this and talk of leaving his management, for which I do not entirely blame them. However, I told them firmly that they mustn't do any such thing. I lectured him firmly but without vehemence and made him promise to stop drinking entirely. Of course he

1 Maurice Winnick, television impresario, was concerned with the imminent creation of ITV.
2 Edna Best (1900–74), British actress who had starred in Noël's *Fallen Angels* (1925).
3 Brian Aherne (b. 1902), British actor.
4 Musical by George Abbott and Richard Bissel, with songs by Richard Adler and Jerry Ross.
5 An American musical version.
6 Jerome Robbins (b. 1918), American dancer and choreographer.

won't keep his promise because I fear he is too far gone. I dread doing the play with him next autumn[1] and yet if I leave him it will be the last straw and he'll be utterly done for. He still bolsters himself up with the delusion that he is a good director but I *know*, not only from personal experience but from Cole Porter and others he has worked for, that he can't direct at all. Natasha is feeling all this terribly. Few people invite him out any more, he sleeps interminably and potters through every dreary day. He is about to direct two musicals, both of which sound fairly dreadful to me. Whether or not there is the remotest hope of his pulling himself together I just don't know. I don't even know why I should mind so much. I suppose there is a core of deep sentimental pride in me that refuses to let him rot: pride or conscience or whatever it is, I am so very responsible for his career, such as it has been, and I feel profoundly sad that I can't do anything really constructive beyond nagging and bullying and hoping for a change in the weather.

Friday 3 December   Las Vegas

This is a fabulous, extraordinary madhouse. All around is desert sand with pink and purple mountains on the horizon. All the big hotels are luxe to the last degree. Even now, in the pre-Christmas slump, there are myriads of people tearing away at the fruit machines and gambling, gambling, gambling for twenty-four hours a day. The lighting at night is fantastic; downtown where 'The Golden Nugget' is and the lesser dives, it is ablaze with variegated neon signs. In the hotels, where the casinos are more classy, beams of light shoot down from baroque ceilings on the masses of earnest morons flinging their money down the drain. The sound is fascinating, a steady hum of conversation against a background of rhumba music and the noise of the fruit machines, the clink of silver dollars, quarters and nickels, and the subdued shouts of the croupiers. There are lots of pretty women about but I think, on the whole, sex takes a comparatively back seat. Every instinct and desire is concentrated on money.

I expected that this would exasperate me, but oddly enough it didn't. The whole fantasia is on such a colossal scale that it is almost stimulating. I went from hotel to hotel and looked at the rooms. They are all fairly large and much of a muchness. Expert lighting and sound and cheerful and appreciative audiences who are obviously there to have a good time. I noticed little drunkenness and much better manners than in the New York night-clubs. The gangsters who run the places are all urbane and charming. I had a feeling that if I opened a rival casino I would be battered to death with the utmost efficiency and despatch, but if I remained on my own ground as a most highly paid entertainer that I could trust them all the way. They are curious products of a most curious adolescent country. Their morals are bizarre in the extreme.

1 Noël was planning a Broadway run of *Nude with Violin*.

They are generous, mother-worshippers, sentimental and capable of much kindness. They are also ruthless, cruel, violent and devoid of scruples. Joe Glaser, whom I have taken a great shine to, never drinks, never smokes and adores his mother. He is now fifty-eight and, rather naturally, over the moon with delight at having got me under his wing. My name is big prestige stuff for a brisk little Jewish go-getter who hitherto has mainly booked coloured acts and promoted prize-fights. My heart, and reason, go out to him because he at least took the trouble to fly over to London to see me at the Café and give me a concrete offer. If it all ends in smoke I don't think it will be his fault. I believe him to be honest according to his neon lights. He is shrewd, sentimental, noisy and generous. The situation is that I will appear here for the first three weeks in May providing all the money part of it is satisfactorily arranged.

Friday 10 December

Here I am rattling along[1] across the flat hinterland. There are odd shaped mountains, some of them sawn off at the top and some craggy and bulbous. I needed a couple of nights' rest after my five days in Hollywood. Clifton [Webb] was sweet and I was really pleased to see him again. He is, however, not very happy I fear, in spite of his successes and his wonderful contract with Twentieth Century-Fox and his luxurious dressing-room on the lot and his equally luxurious home. I think, in fact I know, that he feels trapped. Poor old Mabelle[2] is getting gaga and is turning more and more to the past. He, too, is suffering from a bad case of '*nostalgie du temps perdu*'. So many of his old friends have died, nothing today seems to him as glamorous and gay as the twenties and thirties. It is a natural enough malaise, this idealized remembering, but should not be encouraged too much. There is no future in the past. I see his point though. New York will never be the same to him as it was when I was younger and Neysa [McMein] was living and Alec [Woollcott] and Gertie and Alice Duer Miller and so many others. Some of them are still alive but the great American Neurosis seems to have dimmed them.

However, Clifton cheered up no end in my honour and we had a great party and all the stars came and twinkled. Judy Garland sang, Van Johnson[3] sang, I sang, Clifton sang; the years rolled back for a little and it was great fun. Apart from this, I dined with the Goldwyns[4], charming; lunched and dined with Darryl Zanuck[5] who, David Niven wickedly said, is the only man alive who can eat an apple through a tennis racquet! He, Darryl, has a comfortingly awe-stricken reverence for me and offered me anything I wanted if I would

1 On a train from Los Angeles to New York.
2 Clifton Webb's mother was now in her eighties.
3 Van Johnson (b. 1916), American film star.
4 Samuel Goldwyn (1882–1974), Hollywood film studio mogul, and his wife.
5 Darryl Zanuck (1902–79), American film producer and director.

only do a picture for Twentieth Century-Fox. I shall consider this proposition seriously. These, so far, are good years for me and I had better use every trick I know to put something aside for that grim old age which is advancing on me in leaps and bounds.

One of my nicest encounters, apart from a sweet dinner with the Nivens at the Beachcomber, was a quiet lunch with Fritzi Massary[1]. There she is, retired, in her seventies and chic as ever in her bandbox of a house. Wise and shrewd and sensible. '*Nostalgie du temps perdu*' to a certain extent, but lightly done and without pain. Her life is over, her memories are mostly pleasant and she makes no demands on the present or the future. She has a few acquaintances who come in and play canasta and samba. She has, I think, few regrets. She also has, owing to her own shrewdness, enough money to keep her in reasonable comfort until she dies. It was lovely seeing her again and astringent, no lachrymose introspection. A valuable encounter.

Thursday 16 December   Jamaica

Fifty-five years ago today my darling Mum ejected me into the suburban world of Teddington, Middlesex. I believe she had a bad time with me for I was truculent apparently about being born and made, with my usual theatrical acumen, a delayed entrance. Up until the actual moment when I was deposited, scarlet and squalling, in her arms, she hadn't really wanted me. The tragedy of Russell's death[2] at the age of six and a half had broken her heart and she dreaded further maternal anxieties and possible miseries; however, it seems that our first meeting went off very well and we were together ever since until last June when she gave that heart-breaking little sigh and went away. Fifty-five years is a long time; in fifteen more years I shall be seventy, which is longer still. It is a curious, incredible thought, not dismaying particularly, just unlikely.

On Saturday I spent the afternoon and evening in Chicago. I shopped a bit but the Christmas rush was beginning and it was not very enjoyable. Yul Brynner took me to dine in the Pump Room; he was in full make-up as the King of Siam[3] and our meal was made convulsive by autograph hunters. Later I went to *A Star is Born*[4]. What has happened to the famous, once famous, American timing sense? In spite of fine acting performances by Judy Garland and James Mason and a lavish, highly-coloured production, it dragged interminably. Every song was attenuated to such a length that I thought I was going mad. One in particular, 'Born in a Trunk', started brilliantly but by the

---

1 Fritzi Massary (1882–1969), Viennese singer who had starred in Noël's *Operette* (1938).
2 Russell Coward, Noël's older brother, had died of spinal meningitis in 1892, seven years before Noël's birth.
3 He was touring in *The King and I*.
4 George Cukor's film musical.

time it was over and we had endured montage after montage and repetition after repetition, I found myself wishing that dear enchanting Judy was at the bottom of the sea. The picture ran for three hours; if it had been cut down to two it would have been really exciting.

In the KLM plane to Kingston I had a long talk with the Dutch captain, a charmer if ever I saw one. He had crashed during the Battle of Britain and been horribly burnt; however, he had been provided with a new and very attractive face by plastic surgery. He was in doubt for some years whether or not he would fly again, but finally back he went and is now caught up in the routine. He has a wife and several children in Curacao which he hates: I could detect, in his sad eyes, a nostalgia for the war, a longing for a bit more adventure and derring-do. He was in the heroic mould but cast up on the beach high and dry with his heroism behind him in the diminishing past. I found myself almost wishing for his sake that the undercarriage would fall off or the wings buckle, just to give him the satisfaction of making a sensational forced landing.

The drive across the Junction Road in our new station-wagon was lovely as ever. Blue Harbour welcomed me appropriately with sun rather than shadow. I swam in the pool, looked approvingly at my new bedroom, over which Coley had been slaving, and began to give myself up to the warmth and peace. Later Cole and I popped up to Firefly and had some gin and watched the stars come out. It was as magical as it always is but I was terribly exhausted and felt papery, as though my nerves were sticking through my skin. Bed early and that was that.

Friday 24 December

Oh how nice it would be, just for today and tomorrow, to be a little boy of five instead of an ageing playwright of fifty-five and look forward to all the high jinks with passionate excitement and be given a clockwork train with a full set of rails and a tunnel. However, it is no use repining. As things are, drink will take the place of parlour games and we shall all pull crackers and probably enjoy ourselves enough to warrant at least some of the god-damned fuss.

The news from home is mainly concerned with disaster, floods and gales and houses collapsing. I am very lucky to be here in the warmth and so I will crush down the embittered nausea which the festive season arouses in me and plunge into gaiety with an adolescent whoop.

Tuesday 28 December

Johnny [Gielgud] is a charming house guest, amusing, talkative and most considerate. He leaves on Saturday.

I have been rereading all the mass of notes and ideas I wrote down some years back on 'Samolo'. It really is imaginative and full of possibilities. I had no idea I had been so thorough. I wonder if I shall really get on with it. I am at the moment in a 'suspended' period. Lots of ideas but nowhere to begin. My writing impulse is itching to be up and at it but as yet I have fended off the moment. There is so much, so much that I would like to write about, so many different people and things and, of course, so little time to do it. Now, however, there is more time than usual. I have at least a few months in hand before I resume singing and acting and showing off and being a fascinating public legend.

1955

This was the annus mirabilis *for which Noël had been waiting ever since the end of the war. A profitable Jamaican winter included the rewriting of* South Sea Bubble *and the start of a novel (*Pomp *and* Circumstance*). These, together with* Nude *with* Violin, *gave him two new plays and a book to bank. Las Vegas in midsummer proved a riot; at the age of fifty-five, armed with little more than that increasingly oriental face, some ageing songs and an irrepressible talent to amuse, Noël sang to capacity Desert Inn audiences twice nightly for the most profitable month of his life. A headline in* Variety *said it all: 'Las Vegas, Flipping, Shouts for More as Noël Coward Wows 'em in Cabaret Turn.'*

And success, once she had taken Noël back to her bosom like a maternal boa constrictor, kept him there. Mike Todd gave him a Bonnard street scene for one day's work on Around the World in Eighty Days, *and in New York CBS television came up with a lavish offer if Noël would promise them three 'specials' – two were to be productions of his comedies in which he would star, and the third was to be a special cabaret concert lasting ninety minutes in which he would appear with Mary Martin but nobody else.*

Via Las Vegas cabaret and then New York television, America had rediscovered Coward at a time when in his own country he was still without profit or honour. Unsurprisingly, therefore, his thoughts began to turn towards emigration; England still meant overdrafts and bad reviews and rain. What he now wanted was success and sunshine, and that seemed to mean, if not America, then perhaps a nearby tax haven such as Bermuda. His thoughts were firmly set on leaving England for ever, and that was a decision which was to cause him the worst Press of his life.

Saturday 1 January   Jamaica

The first day of the New Year. We drank it in last night at a curious party consisting of most of the locals, ghastly and fun at the same time. Our hostess was not only pissed but raving mad, but there was something about her that I liked. Our host, younger than she, was podgy, good-looking and, I thought, a pig but I may be misjudging him.

I have started writing and am feeling consequently a great deal happier. The sentences seemed to construct themselves, the right adjectives appeared discreetly at the right moment, there were no repetitions and tiresome brain-rackings; out it came easily and clearly. I don't know who it was who said, 'The only time I believe in God is when I write', but whoever it was said a mouthful.

Thursday 6 January

Jack is here, on the wagon since I talked to him in New York. He looks a bit better but something is wrong. I have a feeling that he is either (a) sozzling in secret, (b) doping, or (c) has something serious the matter with him. He, who used to be so alert, is slow, slow, slow, paws the air with a sort of arch petulance and exaggerates his American accent. Last night we dined with Claudette [Colbert] at Jamaica Inn and I found myself being irritated all the evening; this was entirely on account of Jack, who embarrasses me acutely. Cole is being driven mad too. Oh dear, oh dear.

Tuesday 11 January

I have already done 19,000 words of my story, which is on the long side anyway, and I am nowhere near the end. I think so far it is well written except for the usual splurge of qualifying adjectives and adverbs. I have now made a great decision which is to start the whole thing from the beginning again, this time directly on to the typewriter, and turn it into a full-length novel. Not a long novel, about 70,000 to 80,000 words. I'm feeling rather excited about this and pray to God I shan't get bogged down.

Claudette is still here (at Jamaica Inn) and she and the Seidmanns[1] and I are flying over to Haiti on Saturday for four days just to have a look at it.

Jack left yesterday to our intense relief. He has become an embarrassment and a bore and I'm not going to try any more life-saving. He's been going on a great deal about being on the wagon, but I could tell by his manner and his breath that he was lying. I went and poked about in his room the other morning when he was in Port Maria and discovered a bottle of vodka 100° proof nearly empty in the bottom bureau drawer. He is a god-damned fool and obviously bent on self-destruction, and as far as I am concerned he had better get on with it.

1 Paul-Emile and Ginette (Spanier) were staying with Noël in Jamaica.

Thursday 13 January

I have started the short story as a novel and at the moment I am convinced that it was the right thing to do. It has, even at this early stage, begun to flow and in the first little bit, about three thousand words, that I have already done, there is a lot of authentic Samolan atmosphere and, I think and hope, quality.

The Parachini funeral[1] was almost comical. It was also strident with local colour. The hearse and the funeral cortège were late and were unable to turn into the church gates and had to go straight on into Port Maria and then come back on the other side of the road. When the hearse finally drew up we observed that a common little Palmolive soap van had wormed its way into a position just behind it and directly in front of the relatives' car. On the side of the van in large letters was a slogan which read, 'A Lovelier Skin in Fourteen Days'.

Saturday 15 January   King's House, Kingston

I have enjoyed my two days here. Sylvia Foot is a dear, kindly and with much humour. HE[2] is less immediately approachable but I like him. We had a long talk about the 'Jamaica 300' celebrations and also about Princess Margaret's impending visit. He told me in detail the programme planned for her: fairly onerous but not too much so and with a certain amount of time to herself. Apparently it has been laid down that on no account is she to dance with any coloured person. This is, I think, a foolish edict. Jamaica is a coloured island and if members of our Royal Family visit it they should be told to overcome prejudice. I should think that any presentable young Jamaican would be a great deal more interesting to dance with than the shambling Billy Wallace. The famous retrogressiveness of pompous English officialdom, like the 'old soldier', never dies; unfortunately it doesn't fade away either.

The JLP [Jamaican Labour Party] lost the election and the PNP [People's National Party] got in with a small majority. The handsome and astute Mr Manley[3] is now Chief Minister. His party was apparently purged of its more obvious Communist elements some while ago but only, I think, apparently. HE, being a Foot and a rabid socialist, is delighted with the election results. Whether or not the PNP being in power will affect our island life much remains to be seen. At all events, after ten years of Bustamante's[4] demagoguery, a change won't be a bad thing.

1 John Parachini, a neighbour of Noël's in Jamaica, had died the previous week.
2 His Excellency, Sir Hugh Foot, created Lord Caradon 1964; Governor of Jamaica 1951-57.
3 Norman Manley (1893-1969), founder of the PNP, Jamaica's Chief Minister 1955-59 and Prime Minister 1959-62.
4 Sir Alexander Bustamante (1884-1977), leader of the JLP and outgoing Chief Minister; Prime Minister 1962-67.

Wednesday 19 January   Haiti

We are leaving today. Claudette takes off this afternoon for Hollywood, and
Ginette, Paul-Emile and I catch the ten o'clock plane for Kingston. We have
had an enjoyable time on the whole. Claudette I adore. She has been a darling
and very gay and funny. Irving and Ellen Berlin[1] are in the hotel and it's
been quite fun. Our car driver is a dream. His name is Jean-Paul and he is a
stalwart buck nigger, coal black with a real Gold Coast face. He speaks
soft, ancient French and the contrast between his voice and his appearance
is fascinating.

Haiti is less exotic than I thought it would be, but of course we only saw
Port au Prince and the mountains behind it. I expect it changes, like Jamaica,
when you get to the further coasts. We saw some genuine voodoo, *not* arranged
for the tourists. It was a family party which took place in a small, stifling hut
in the mountains. We had to leave the car in the road and clamber up a steep
and difficult path. The party apparently was planned to last three days and
nights. The hut was lit by a few stubs of candles and inside it were about 150
Negroes and Negresses. The drums played incessantly and everyone jigged
about and did some circumscribed contortions. Every now and then one of
them started to shriek and thresh his arms whereupon everyone near leapt on
him and held him until, babbling and moaning, he subsided on the floor. This
was only the first day of the orgy so it was comparatively restrained and there
were no animals disembowelled and no marked sexual manifestations. It was
weird and interesting, particularly before they realized that we were there;
when they did, and brought chairs politely, the atmosphere changed and they
became self-conscious. We didn't stay long because it was very hot and smelly.
We staggered down the path and got into the car and drove home. When we
passed the place the next afternoon, after lunching in a mountain restaurant,
we could hear it still going on, the drums and moans and occasional shrieks.

Sunday 23 January   Jamaica

I have read Ian's new thriller in proof[2]. It is the best he has done yet, very
exciting and, although as usual too far-fetched, not quite so much so as the
last two and there are fewer purple sex passages. His observation is extraordinary and his talent for description vivid. I wish he would try a non-thriller for
a change; I would so love him to triumph over the sneers of Annie's intellectual
friends.

I love this island dearly and I shall have to search far to find anywhere else
as sweet, but alas I think I shall have to begin searching. Each year more and
more people appear and I cannot be flat rude and say I won't see them, so

1 Irving Berlin (b. 1888), American songwriter, and his wife.
2 The third of Ian Fleming's James Bond books, *Moonraker*.

many of them are old friends, but it *isn't* peaceful enough any more. I have my long mornings, of course, which I insist upon but that is all.

Saturday 19 February

Well, I have been away and have now come back again, having learnt several lessons. The first of these is that it is no use imagining that I can escape the consequences of my own fame and that I am bound to be set on and exploited by people wherever I go. The second is that it is extremely unlikely that I shall find anywhere on any other island a view and an atmosphere like this one.

On Tuesday last, the eighth, I decided, after consultation with Cole, to duck and run. The weather was dreary. I was feeling really bored and tired and obsessed with the idea of finding some other more inaccessible island, so I flew off to Trinidad where I spent the night, and on to Tobago the next day.

It is a very, very sweet little island but there is a down-at-heel feeling; the natives are friendly but I knew I could never live on so small an island where everybody knows everybody else's business. The whole place was wallowing in the aftermath of Princess Margaret's visit, feuds were flourishing, some people had been presented and some hadn't, and umbrage was all over the place.

The next morning I took off for Grenada, an hour's flight. There was no water, hot or cold, and the electricity only worked for certain hours. I proceeded to hire a drive-yourself car which had no windows, and so I drove a little way and returned soaked to the skin. The next day I drove right round the island. It is staggeringly beautiful and the lushness of the vegetation is incredible.

I cannot say that the reconnaissance trip was a success but it was a good thing to make a break and get away for a little. I know now, or at least I am pretty sure, that I shall never find anywhere as lovely as this. It is largely my own fault that I have allowed people to spoil it for me and I am bloody well not going to let it happen again. The basic trouble has been having the house full since Christmas. If I am alone here with Coley, it is a pleasure sometimes for people to come to dinner, but when there are five of us here already it becomes distracting and nerve-racking.

I arrived back to several dramas. Cole had had a car accident in Oracabessa and had been run into by a truck. *Quadrille* has suddenly stopped being a smash hit and become a dead flop and is closing! The negotiations about Las Vegas are being held up in London and by general incompetence all round, *and* I have a hacking cough which I presume will ultimately disappear. I now intend to relax and let life take a gentler course. God's in his heaven and Princess Margaret arrives today and the garden looks terrible, but the sun is shining and I have just finished Peter Quennell's book on Byron which is very good though a little convulsive in style as becomes a literary critic. At least I can count my blessings. I have not got a club-foot or Caroline Lamb.

Sunday 27 February

Princess Margaret's visit has been a very great success and everybody says she has done it exceedingly well. On her last evening I drove over to Port Antonio for her private 'beach' party. The only other outsiders beyond her staff, the Manleys and the Foots, were Adlai Stevenson[1] and myself. We sat on each side of her at dinner, which did *not* take place on the beach on account of rain and wind. However, we went down afterwards and all the ADCs gambolled in the sand like puppies. It was an extremely pleasant evening. She was sweet and gay and looked radiant. Manley I find impressive, a great deal more so than Bustamante ever was, brilliantly well read and most charming. Adlai Stevenson I was a little disappointed in. He was very affable but commoner and less polished than I had expected. I'm sure he must be a good man and a potentially fine President but I found his appearance rather off-putting.

Thursday 10 March

Quadrille is closing on 12 March. This is a sad blow and a very nasty little surprise. The Lunts, deaf to all pleading by Jack and the company, resolutely refuse to play out the season in Philadelphia and Chicago where they could recoup losses. Whether this is because they are old or cross or tired or just stubborn I don't know, probably all four. I think, for the sake of the company, the management and me, they should make the effort but I don't know what is really going on in their minds. They have, after all, played it a long time and I don't think either of them is very well. I have said nothing one way or the other. It is sad about *Quadrille*, I am so fond of it and had such faith in it. Perhaps all the critics were right[2] and I was wrong. I find this *dreadfully* difficult to believe. It has also been a flop in Paris, with Alice Cocea and Pierre Dux. This does not surprise me because Paul Géraldy's adaptation seemed to me to have robbed the play of all meaning. I had an enraged letter from Ginette who went to the opening night and said it was vile.

Meanwhile I have been pressing on with *Home and Colonial*[3] and have rewritten the whole play except for the hut scene and a few good bits here and there. It has been a salutary experience. It really *wasn't* good enough and was curiously overwritten. I seem, in later years, to have lost my gift for economy. This has been, and in the future must continue to be, remedied. It is now very good, I think, light and undated. I have reverted to one of the other

1 Adlai Stevenson (1900–65), the Democratic Presidential candidate against Eisenhower in 1952 and again in 1956.
2 Reviews on Broadway had not been much better than in London.
3 The original title for *Island Fling*.

original titles, *South Sea Bubble*. I am reading it to Claudette tomorrow (she came back to Jamaica Inn yesterday). I think she will probably play it. This has all been hard work but worthwhile and I feel relieved to have salvaged a property which was really too intrinsically good to be allowed to moulder away.

Charles and Ham have been extremely efficient in New York and have procured a concrete offer for me to do three television shows: (1) an hour's singing with Mary Martin; (2) *Present Laughter*; and (3) *Peace in Our Time*. For these three programmes I get $500,000, out of which expenses and cast have to be paid. Roughly approximated, I should realize $250,000 at the end of it. This, of course, is enormous money and I shall certainly do it. Even if my remainder is taxed in America I can still get enough to make the whole enterprise more than worthwhile. I intend, within the next two years, to have at least £100,000 in the bank *tax-free*. Then I can feel secure, or at least calm, about the inroads of old age. I'm sick of being choosy and prestige-conscious. At the moment my stock is high in America, largely because I have said no so often. Now I intend to cash in and the English theatre can do without me for a little.

In addition to all this there is the offer to do *The Sleeping Prince*[1] in Hollywood with Judy Holliday, and a curious project to have *After the Ball* done in a tent in the round in summer stock. These shows are apparently extremely successful and all the principal musicals have been done and triumphed. Let them have it is all I can say.

Now my intention is to relax for a little, rewrite the small bits that have to be rewritten in *Nude with Violin*, have a desultory jab at my neglected novel, polish up some lyrics for Las Vegas, paint some pictures and read a book.

Monday 14 March

Things are certainly popping but fortunately my liver is *not* among them. I haven't had a drop of alcohol for over a week and the difference in my well-being is quite fantastic. I am feeling smoother and better in every way than I have felt for a very long time.

I finished *South Sea Bubble* and read it to Claudette. The first act is, although much improved, still too weak. Nothing happens and I have fallen back on my dialogue facility, which is not enough. I realized this while reading it aloud. Afterwards there was a discussion. Claudette is scared of it anyway because it is too English for her, and in this she is right. She would be (and was, I believe) charming in it, but actually her personality is not right for a rather flighty English governor's lady. She is too down-to-earth and practical, and although she would play it well technically and be a big draw from the

---

1 Rattigan's play as a film; it was eventually made in England by Olivier and Marilyn Monroe as *The Prince and the Showgirl*.

public point of view, she really isn't ideal for the part and knows it. So that's that. I have an idea for redoing the first act and bringing in more political satire and strengthening the plot. This is not an enormous task and shouldn't take long. Having taken so much trouble I might just as well get the bloody thing really right.

Charles and Ham arrived quivering with excitement with a concrete proposition from CBS[1]. Also two others from General Motors and Chrysler (the latter for $600,000). I think, however, I shall settle with CBS ($450,000) because their organization is the most efficient. Mary Martin is delighted with the idea of appearing with me, and Claudette wants to play Liz in *Present Laughter*, so all that is highly satisfactory.

Saturday 19 March

The Nivens arrived on Tuesday. David was feeling rather ill and the next morning he burst out into a flaming attack of chicken-pox. This, combined with a sun rash he got the first days he was here, has laid him very low indeed. His temperature has fluctuated between 100° and 104° and he has hardly slept at all owing to violent itching. Everything has been tried but so far nothing has relieved it. This means that they will have to be here for three weeks instead of one. Oh dear! It also means that any one of us may have caught it, particularly poor Cole who hasn't had it before. Meanwhile life presses on peacefully enough. My LP record has arrived from England at last and it is really very good. A cable from Mary Martin has also arrived, ecstatic about our project, so *that's* all right. I have tidied up *Nude with Violin* and written a short extra scene which I think has made a great difference. *Quadrille* has closed in New York but picked up in Paris. I am beginning to paint rather better and my strength is as the strength of ten because my liver is pure.

I am reading Arthur Koestler's *The Invisible Writing*. It is a fascinating and finely written account of his early adventures in Russia as a Communist. I cannot honestly say that it entirely lacks humour, but he himself must lack humour otherwise he could never have been so dismally taken in in the first place. It is almost inconceivable to me that an intelligent adult could be deceived by such obvious propaganda tactics – almost, but not quite, because there are still millions of presumably intelligent adults who are besotted by Communism at this very moment. It is so obviously the negation of all one really minds about – creative instinct, freedom of thought and expression, individualism, etc., in fact everything that makes life worth living. It is also, palpably, a more rigid and violent dictatorship over human beings than Mussolini or Hitler ever dreamed of.

I notice, particularly in *Time and Tide*[2], an increasing bias towards religion.

1 For the American television specials.
2 A weekly magazine sent out to him from London.

Each week there are long articles emphasizing the importance of turning to God. These articles are well-written and intelligent, and they confuse me almost as much as the belief in Communism. What possible hope is there for mankind if it persistently reverts to superstition and legend at the expense of precious Time (and Tide)? How can we ever succeed in tidying up this life if half our minds are concentrated upon an unproven and most problematical afterlife? Personally I wish only for ultimate oblivion, which is fortunate because I think it is all I shall get. It sickens me that a world so potentially exciting and enjoyable should be so beset by dark fears and superstitious mysticism. There is so much that is, and will always be, unexplained. Why not get on with the material and experience at hand and try to make the best of it? Whatever may or may not happen to us afterwards must be dealt with when the time comes. I am neither impressed by, nor frightened of, death. I admit that I am scared about the manner of my dying. I hope *not* to have to endure agonizing pain or violent panic, but even if I do have to face these things, there is nothing I can do about it, and I can only hope that my life will be interesting and fully lived until the moment I have to say goodbye to it.

I have discovered on the whole that most very religious people are far more obsessed with death-fear than I am. The other day when I was in the throes of my gastric indigestion I wouldn't have minded dying a bit. I remember distinctly lying on the bed, racked with pain and nausea, thinking of death and almost wishing for it. I thought, 'All right, if I never saw Goldenhurst again, or my loved ones, or the sun rising over the sea, or Piccadilly Circus, so what?' I know when I was watching darling Mum die that she was neither scared nor unhappy. Death seems to me as natural a process as birth; inevitable, absolute and final. If, when it happens to me, I find myself in a sort of Odeon ante-room queueing up for an interview with Our Lord, I shall be very surprised indeed.

Another book I am reading is Richard Aldington's blistering, debunking attack on Lawrence of Arabia. I do not care for Richard Aldington's mind, and his malice is a little too apparent; nevertheless quite a lot of it – as far as I have read – sounds suspiciously like the truth. Lawrence *was* an inverted show-off and I have myself heard him talk the most inconceivable balls. Even at the time I was inwardly aware of this, but his legend was too strong to be gainsaid and I, being a celebrity snob, crushed down my wicked suspicions. He was charming to me anyhow, with a charm that could only be repaid by affection and a certain arid loyalty. We had, of course, nothing in common. To revert for a moment to my death theme, the only thing that really saddens me over my demise is that I shall not be here to read the nonsense that will be written about me and my works and my motives. There will be books proving conclusively that I was homosexual and books proving equally conclusively that I was not. There will be detailed and inaccurate analyses of my motives for writing this or that and of my character. There will be lists of apocryphal jokes I never made and gleeful misquotations of words I never said. *What* a pity I shan't be here to enjoy them! All the same, Lawrence is well out of it, poor dear. He would certainly not have enjoyed Richard Aldington's book. But then a sense of humour was never his strong suit.

Sunday 27 March

Another week has gone in a flash. David is really better at last, most of the spots have gone. Hjordis has gone too because we all decided that if she caught chicken-pox and had it here the whole process would be interminable. She went beetling back to Hollywood last Tuesday, leaving poor David very low. He is now, however, bright as a bee and leaves on Tuesday.

I have worked not at all but painted a lot. I am drawing much better and, I think, evolving a style of my own, primitive and highly coloured but quite professional looking.

Sunday 10 April

I've finally finished *South Sea Bubble*, written in a new scene and made the whole of act one much stronger. It now has a shape and a plot, which it didn't have before.

I have read this week, among other things, *The Nightmare* by Forester, a book of short stories about the Nazi atrocities, well written and absolutely horrifying. I hope a great many people read them. The fact that such bestial, inhuman cruelty could happen in the *soi-disant* enlightened twentieth century should be marked, learned and very inwardly digested by all woolly-minded idealists, Christians, appeasers and pacifists. Of course, it won't be. Most of the horrors are already forgotten and 'Don't Let's Be Beastly to the Germans' has become the pivot of European political strategy. The fact that this is only dictated by fear of the Russians makes it no less shameful in my opinion. The Germans have been aggressive, cruel and humourless all through their dismal history, and I find it quite impossible to forgive them, however politic it may be considered to do so. They are a horrid, neurotic race and always have been and always will be and, to my mind, none of their contributions to science, literature and music compensates for their turgid emotionalism and unparalleled capacity for torturing their fellow creatures.

The life of George Eliot by Lawrence and Elizabeth Hanson is riveting. The Hansons are really brilliant biographers. I have now read all their five books – *Gordon*, *The Brontës*, *Carlyle*, *Gauguin* and this one – and been held and interested and, at moments, enthralled by all of them. George Eliot was a dull, morose, humourless lady with more than a touch of genius. What makes the book so fascinating is the evocation of the period and the people. The Victorian writers certainly made life as difficult for themselves as possible;

what with their flaming temperaments and religious misgivings and moralizings and soul-searchings combined with permanent ill-health from lack of air and exercise and overeating, they really had a lot to bear. The fact that most of it was unnecessary obviously couldn't have made the bearing of it any easier. Everything I have read lately has confirmed my long-held suspicion that Christianity has caused a great deal more suffering, both mentally and physically, than any other religion in the history of mankind. The jolly human sacrifices of other earlier faiths were nothing compared to the implacable cruelties and struggles between various Christian sects. A wretched virgin being sliced up occasionally on a tribal altar seems small beer compared with the endless succession of tortured, oppressed, Puritan-ridden generations that have resulted from that unfortunately over-publicized episode at Jerusalem 1,955 years ago. I must say it is a little hard on Jesus Christ to be for ever associated with such a monumental balls-up.

Friday 15 April

Today I fly back again. Back to all the people and the excitements and the febrile carry-on and the theatres and the different hours. I have been here over four months and they have, as usual, gone in a flash. Next year, however, I am going to take more care and *not* have my valuable peace spoiled for me by my loving friends. Next year, anyhow, the great new project will be a *fait accompli*. I have told Pat Marr-Johnson[1] to start building my house up on Firefly Hill. He has done a charming design and it is to have three verandahs, each looking out at a different view, also a studio. The whole thing will cost between four and five thousand pounds. I intend, next year, to live in it most of the time. It will be a real get-away from my god-damned friends. They can disport themselves at Blue Harbour and keep out of my hair. It will be more peaceful up above anyway and further from the noise of the sea. Last night Coley and I went up and sat on the verandah and it was more magical than ever. The stars were enormous and so were the fireflies, and we had a peaceful, enchanting time.

Now it seems that everything is satisfactory and when I have finished Las Vegas and the three television appearances I should have, tax-free and tucked away, at least £100,000. It is all very exciting. I know that there will be dramas and irritations and frustrations and nerves and worries about my voice and far, far too much publicity, but at least, apart from the four weeks at Las Vegas, there will be no steady, deadening routine. There will also, I hope, be a great deal of exhilaration and fun and some good jokes. I intend to watch myself carefully and not get over-strained.

I cannot, happily, say that my time here has been wasted. *South Sea Bubble*

---

1 Pat Marr-Johnson, an architect friend and neighbour in Jamaica.

and *Nude with Violin* are both strong new comedies, and although I got led astray over the novel, there are at least 40,000 words of good writing to be turned to account when I have time to devote myself to it. In addition to this I have read a lot, absorbed a lot and learned a lot. I now drink hardly at all and feel much the better for it. I even smoke a little less. My mind is clear and my personal dynamo is chugging away very satisfactorily. My philosophical out-look is set fair. I have envisaged, fairly lucidly I think, the possibilities ahead. If I die today, or tomorrow, next week or next year, I have no complaints. If I live until I am ninety-six there will, of course, be complaints but I trust they will walk hand in hand with humour and pleasure.

I am tremendously excited about Firefly Hill. It deeply enchants me and is the loveliest place I have ever known. If I can really make the money I hope to make during the next few years, there it will be, to offer me peace and time. I shall live most of next winter in the new little house and, if it is as lovely as I think it will be and if all continues to go well financially, I shall build the main house up there, install a swimming-pool and pump the water up from the sea, and eventually sell Blue Harbour. There are endless possibilities. All indications point to the fact that this coast is going to develop more and more. The more it does, the more valuable Blue Harbour will become. I believe, with the pool and everything, I should get somewhere between twenty and twenty-five thousand pounds for it. This means that even with all the new building and planning at Firefly I shall not be out of pocket at all.

I regret, dear journal, this unworthy, sordid preoccupation with money, but I have worked hard all my life, I am £15,000 overdrawn in London, I am fifty-five years old and I fully intend to end my curious days in as much comfort, peace and luxury as I can get. If the Great Reaper elects to forestall me I shall at least have had the fun of making the plans, and doubtless somebody will benefit from them. If a great big hydrogen bomb war starts I shall retire here with as many loved ones as I can persuade to join me and hope for the best, eat yams and pray that the sea doesn't become radioactive enough to bugger up the fish! There will be no more heroism and secret missions and pulling my weight in the boat. I've *had* all that. I intend to survive, if possible, and lay in a lot of Worcester sauce and lethal drugs (in case of nasty, slow and painful dying) and books and paints and writing paper. I shall also lay in toilet paper, the *Encyclopedia Britannica*, a donkey and cart, and a lot of tinned soup. If the Russians drop an H-bomb here on purpose, or the Americans by accident, it will be just too bad.

I am going out into the great big world again and shall start a new entry in this diary on Sunday week. I have always believed in keeping the Sabbath Day holy.

Sunday 24 April   Goldenhurst

Blossom by blossom the spring begins, but rather slowly on account of the wicked and heavy winter. However, the wood is full of primroses and windflowers and the daffodils are out in the garden. Oddly enough, the sun is shining and there is hope in the air, in spite of a sharp east wind.

My sojourn in New York was successful. I contrived to remain fairly peaceful and get a good deal done. Bill Paley wants the first TV play I do to be *Blithe Spirit* instead of *Present Laughter* because he is frightened of the sex angle of the latter and fears angry letters rattling in the mail-box, written by outraged Methodists in Omaha complaining about illicit love being brought into their very homes by me and my sponsors, whoever they may be. This is irritating but I don't really mind because my object in the whole operation is to make money.

Las Vegas is virtually fixed. I shall get $15,000 a week, out of which I pay my expenses, Norman's salary and expenses, Cole's board and lodging, and Joe Glaser's commission. An extra $60,000 will be paid by The Desert Inn[1] for an option on some shares in my TV company[2]. This apparently will be tax-free as it is capital gain. It is quite legal although perhaps a trifle transparent. It is a good idea, but obviously cannot be worked too often.

Jack sounded clear enough on the telephone but there are disturbing rumours about him hitting the bottle. Natasha was sweet but, I fear, rather silly. I suspect that she is taking something because one evening when she arrived to go to the theatre with me she was jerking and jumping and stabbing the air with her hands and generally not making sense. There is no doubt that the Wilsons are a serious problem and I see little hope of the problem lessening with the years.

We went to Tennessce's new play *Cat on a Hot Tin Roof* - full of adolescent sex, dirty words and frustrations, but at moments very fine. It was beautifully played, but over-directed by Elia Kazan, half symbolic and half realistic and curiously old-fashioned, like the Piscator productions in Berlin in the twenties. *The Desperate Hours*[3] was good hokum but a bit too noisy. *Bus Stop*[4], a not particularly striking little play but, surprisingly, a smash hit. *Plain and Fancy*[5], a musical which I went to with Marlene, was dullish but not unpleasant, a sort of poor man's *Oklahoma!* I saw an act and a half of *The Dark is Light Enough*[6], Kit Cornell very lovely and charming but not up to Edith really. Tyrone

1 Where he was to appear in cabaret.
2 Formed to benefit from the new CBS deal.
3 By Joseph Hayes.
4 By William Inge.
5 By Joseph Stein and Will Glickman.
6 Christopher Fry's play in which Katharine Cornell was playing the role created by Edith Evans in London.

Power I thought very good and, of course, wonderful to look at. The best thing I saw was Eugenie Leontovich in *Anastasia*[1]. The play was common but she was superb, a really great performance. The girl, Viveca Lindfors, was excellent but inclined to overplay; the rest of the cast tatty. But Leontovich lives in my memory for some really glorious moments.

I went to a Russian Easter party at Valentina's, fairly dull but enlivened by Garbo who was in an unusually merry mood, and by Madeleine Sherwood whom I love.

I flew away, seen off as usual by Marlene. A lovely homecoming. That evening I went to the Café de Paris to see Graham[2]. He really was most charming and, although nervous because I was there, betrayed no signs of it and appeared to be completely relaxed and in command of himself and his medium. He sang five numbers gently and without forcing, then did three dances. Altogether a fresh and agreeable act. I think and hope that he has at last learned to enjoy singing and loosen up.

Sunday 1 May

May Day in the morning. A biting east wind, watery sunshine and a last-minute cancellation of the railway strike. Yesterday I had tea with Lady [Nancy] Astor, still full of vitality but sad at heart, obsessed with the idea that her life is over. In spite of her tiresome Christian Science and temperance tirades, I have a great affection for her. She is a remarkable character, frequently wrong-headed but I don't think wrong-hearted, and undoubtedly a tremendous personality.

After this I dined with Annie and Ian. They are, as I thought they would, tiring of White Cliffs[3]. On Easter Sunday the son of their next-door neighbours, a boy of fifteen, hanged himself in the garage. This horrid business has haunted the place for them and small wonder. I refrained from telling them about Pat Howe's baby being burned to death in 1945. Perhaps the place has a tiny curse on it. Owing to the young man's suicide the Press have been busy and there is a rumour rife all over London that a young man of seventeen had shot himself in my studio and that the story had been hushed up on account of the newspaper strike. Charming. I am feeling, *malgré moi*, a certain depression about England. It feels smug and dull and I love it less. This is a sad admission and possibly only temporary. We must hope so.

Rebecca West lunched with me on Wednesday. We had a lovely heart-to-heart which could have gone on much longer if only we had had the time. I am very fond of her and full of admiration too. It is pleasant to think we are such old friends.

1 Marcelle Maurette's play, adapted by Guy Bolton.
2 In cabaret there.
3 The Flemings had taken over the lease after Noël.

My theatre-going has been fairly intensive. On Monday, Johnnie Ray's first night[1]. Squealing teenagers and mass hysteria, quite nauseating, but he gave a remarkable performance both on the stage and later at supper at the Embassy, where he fondled Terry Moore[2] for the cameras. Poor boy. On Tuesday I went to *Time Remembered*, well acted, pseudo-intellectual drivel. No form, no construction, just Mr Anouilh[3] carrying on his stylized, intricate patterns. Not for me. After this I dined with Binkie, who was at his best, and read him *Nude with Violin* which he seemed to like. On Friday I came down here alone and read about the homosexual problems of poor Ludwig II of Bavaria. A silly young man and no mistake.

On Monday night the sad news that darling Constance [Collier] had died suddenly of a heart attack. This upset me very much. I am glad she died swiftly and apparently easily, but I shall always miss her. It's wretched to think that that rich, gallant humour is extinguished for ever.

Sunday 8 May   London

Last Monday Joyce and I went to Stratford to see *Twelfth Night*[4] and enjoyed it immensely. Vivien was adorable and looked glorious, of course. Alan Webb as Sir Toby impeccable, nearly all the cast good and the production charming. Larry was absolutely superb. He's a great actor and that's all there is to it. His accent was hilarious, never overdone and beautifully sustained. The fact that he and Vivien and the whole thing got appalling notices enrages me when I trouble to think about it. We stayed the night with them and chattered away happily until four in the morning.

On Wednesday I lunched with Dickie and Edwina. They were as easy and cosy as they used to be and altogether it was heart-warming; we laughed a lot and some of the years rolled away.

In the afternoon Graham and I flew to Paris where Ginette and Paul-Emile met us and dined us at the Véfour, which was ambrosial, so ambrosial indeed that I wisely rammed my fingers down my throat before going to bed and brought the whole lot up. There was a vast Seidmann cocktail party on Thursday. Very star-spangled: Edwige Feuillère[5], Micheline Presle[6], Pierre [Fresnay] and Yvonne [Printemps], etc. A magic took place towards the end when Yvonne began to sing. Fortunately I remembered the 'Mozart' and 'Mariette' songs and a lot of 'Trois Valses'[7]. She sang as beautifully as ever and tears were shed, tears of genuine pleasure and of nostalgia.

1   At the Palladium.
2   Terry Moore (b. 1929), Hollywood starlet.
3   Jean Anouilh (b. 1907), French playwright.
4   Gielgud production, with Olivier as Malvolio and Vivien Leigh as Viola.
5   Edwige Feuillère (b. 1907), distinguished French actress.
6   Micheline Presle (b. 1922), French film and stage actress.
7   From Noël's 1934 *Conversation Piece* in which the Fresnays and Noël had all played.

It was a good plan to come back for this little jaunt but, apart from seeing Graham and Lornie and Joyce and enjoying a few good moments, I haven't *really* cared for being back. I hope this remote feeling of dissatisfaction is only temporary. I know I love Goldenhurst dearly and London too, but I keep finding myself longing for Firefly Hill and the soft warm air and also, strange to say, the stimulus of America. I really don't suppose this will last long because I have known it and wearied of it before, but I cannot evade the fact that I find my darling homeland a bit dull and complacent. Perhaps Mum not being here any more has loosened my 'roots' grip. Such uninvited disloyalty is confusing. It may not even be genuine. Time of course will tell. I expect after the synthetic carry-on of New York, Hollywood and Las Vegas I shall be only too glad to fall back on this gentle English smugness. I hope so, indeed I hope so, but it doesn't really matter much. There is a lot to do and settling down anywhere for long is not for me.

Sunday 15 May   New York

Here I am installed in a luxurious suite on the thirty-second floor looking out over the Park, a perfectly glorious view. It seems incredible that only a week has passed since last Sunday.

On Monday I took the Duchess of Kent to see Bea Lillie[1], who was wonderful, and on to supper at the White Tower, a cosy, pleasant evening. On Tuesday the mammoth party for Clifton [Webb], very successful and mixed; everyone had a good time, I think, from the Mountbattens to Hermione Gingold, who looked as though she hadn't washed for seven years.

At lunch with Binkie he had a wonderful idea; we were going mad trying to cast Sebastian in *Nude with Violin*. I can't play it, Rex [Harrison], Alec [Guinness], Larry and Robert Morley[2] are all unavailable. Suddenly Binkie suggested a brisk change of sex and having Yvonne Arnaud[3]! I immediately knew it was a brilliant bit of miscasting and so we telephoned her, sent her the script and she is going to do it. It will mean only a little rewriting and in no way interferes with the theme of the play. Yvonne is a superb comedienne and I have always wanted to work with her. We start rehearsals about 15 July.

Sunday 22 May

It has been a heavy week and much has happened. First of all, on Mary Martin's advice I went to see a man called Alfred Dixon who has a special method of breathing which, once you have mastered it, can banish fear of losing your voice. I am usually sceptical about these miracle men but I trust Mary's common sense and so I have now worked with him for five days and

1 In *An Evening with Beatrice Lillie*.
2 Robert Morley (b. 1908), British actor.
3 Yvonne Arnaud (1892–1958), French actress and pianist.

the effect is extraordinary. It is a trick really, but a trick of using breath correctly and the results are virtually immediate. I do a series of exercises, no more than five minutes a day, during which I make noises like a bull moose and, suddenly, there is the voice, clear as a bell with no fluff on it.

On Friday I dined with Marlene who was in fine fettle, and later drove to Sneden's, where I spent the weekend peacefully with Kit and Guthrie. Unfortunately Kit inveigled me into having Daiquiri cocktails with mint on Saturday before lunch, and I had another of my god-damned gastric liver attacks and had to take to my bed. I still feel fairly beastly and should have my head examined for being such a fool. Alcohol again! Will I *never* learn?

Sunday 29 May   Beverly Hills

Another hectic week but very pleasant. I am happily lodged in Clifton's house and I drive Clifton's Mercury dashingly along the endless boulevards. The weather is disappointingly chill but everything else is fine. Cole arrived at three on Thursday morning having had a much delayed flight. There have been several parties. The Nivens, Claudette, Charlie Feldman[1] (a real Hollywood rout), and a jolly, small dinner at the Cottens with Judy Garland and Rita Hayworth, etc. Peter Matz[2] has arrived and we have been rehearsing. He is quick, intelligent and a fine pianist.

Today Frank Sennes (the booking agent for The Desert Inn) gave a stupendous cocktail party for me in his gracious home. It was actually very well done but of course hilariously funny. It started at four and went on till seven, during which time I was photographed 390 times. This is accurate and not an exaggeration. The swimming-pool was filled with roses which swirled round and round, and there were four cadaverous violinists who also swirled round and round. Over three hundred people came, including Zsa Zsa Gabor[3], Greer Garson[4], Jean Simmons[5], the Nivens, the Bennys, Louella Parsons, Monty Woolley[6], all the Press, and a great many of Frank Sennes's buddies. It was still going quite strong when I left at seven and had a quiet dinner at Chasens with Cole, the Nivens and Michael Wilding.

Sunday 5 June   The Desert Inn, Las Vegas

Coley and I arrived here on Wednesday. The daily temperature is generally over 100°, which I love. My voice is in fine form and I have cut down smoking

1 Charles Feldman (1904–68), American agent and film producer.
2 Peter Matz, American pianist who had just been engaged by Noël as his accompanist, after Norman Hackforth had been refused a work permit for the USA.
3 Zsa Zsa Gabor (b. 1919), Hungarian-born Hollywood actress.
4 Greer Garson (b. 1908), Irish-born Hollywood star.
5 Jean Simmons (b. 1929), British film star.
6 Monty Woolley (1888–1963), American actor.

to the minimum. We have been to see dinner and supper shows at the other hotels. Rosemary Clooney really charming. Jane Powell a very pretty little thing with a fine soprano with a slight gear-shift. Sammy Davis Jr, a rich talent and a brilliant performer but he goes on too long. All the hotels are on the same pattern. A gambling casino with angular shafts of light falling on to the gamblers; the perpetual noise of the slot-machines and the cries of the crap shooters; a bar lounge with a separate four- or five-piece band playing continually. The din is considerable but you get used to it. The men's shops here are wonderful, and as everything I buy can be charged to my hotel bill and is therefore deductible, I am being, most enjoyably, very extravagant indeed. I have hired a car for $50 a week. It is a yellow and black Ford convertible with automatic drive and every known gadget. It also shuts and opens itself when one presses a button.

Sunday 12 June

Well, it is all over bar the shouting which is still going on. I have made one of the most sensational successes of my career and to pretend that I am not absolutely delighted would be idiotic. I have had screaming rave notices and the news has flashed round the world. I am told continually, verbally and in print, that I am the greatest attraction that Las Vegas has ever had and that I am the greatest performer in the world, etc., etc. It is all very, very exciting and generous, and when I look back at the grudging dreariness of the English newspaper gentlemen announcing, when I first opened at the Café de Paris, that I massacred my own songs, I really feel that I don't want to appear at home much more. I have just had a batch of notices from London of Larry and Vivien's *Macbeth* at Stratford, and their ignorance and meanness and cruel, common personal abusiveness have made me sick. I *know* they can't be right, but even if Larry and Viv were not perfect (which I doubt), the tone of the notices is beneath contempt. Much the same as I usually get from the mean, envious little sods.

At any rate – pull the ladder up, Joe, for I'm all right! The place is packed every night at both shows; the audiences, even at the dinner show which is notoriously dull, are quiet as mice and beautifully attentive and they always pull the place down at the end.

Perhaps by the end of my time here I shall be longing for the softer, gentler ways of home, but at the moment I am so fascinated – and helped – by the professional 'expertise' in all departments. I am also touched and warmed by the generosity of their reception of me. Here, a rave notice is *not* considered bad news as it is at home. Here also there is a genuine respect for, and understanding of, light music. I am not gibed at for not being a 'singer', because they recognize immediately here that not being a 'singer' is one of my greatest assets. They know I know how to sing, and they are used to, and largely prefer, performers who perform songs rather than 'sing' them. Light music has been despised and rejected in England for years. Modern music, including variations of jazz, is not considered important by the savants. Benjamin Britten, yes, with all his arid, self-conscious dissonances, but then that is 'serious' and 'significant'. Here, light music has its own genuine values, which are recognized not only by the public but by the Press. The orchestral arrangements and variations are incredible – vital and imaginative. Sometimes they go too far for my own personal taste, but I cannot fail to be impressed by the expert knowledge of instrumentation. Pete Matz, at the age of twenty-six, knows more about the range of various instruments and the potentialities of different combinations than anyone of any age I have *ever* met in England. I suppose music is in the air more here and the mixture of Jewish and Negro rhythms has become part of the national consciousness because it is a goulash of all races. Very exciting and stimulating.

The first night, from the social-theatrical point of view, was fairly sensational. Frank Sinatra[1] chartered a special plane and brought Judy Garland, the Bogarts[2], the Nivens, etc.; then there were Joan Fontaine, Zsa Zsa Gabor, the Joe Cottens, Peter Glenville[3], Larry Harvey, etc. The noise was terrific. The next day there was a quarter of an hour's radio talk devoted to me in course of which they all lavished paeans of praise on me with the most uninhibited and heart-warming generosity. The Press have been courteous and the photographers insistent but considerate. On Friday I was driven out into the Nevada desert, where I was photographed for *Life* magazine in my dinner-jacket sipping a cup of tea.[2] The temperature was 118°.

Sunday 19 June

The mood lasted but God in his infinite wisdom struck me down with a violent fever on Monday. I staggered through two performances with a temperature of 103°, and on Tuesday the doctor absolutely refused to let me play, so I lay here in bed, sweating and writhing and feeling terrible. Meanwhile the news was flashed round the world and there were cables and telephone calls and great fuss. On Wednesday I tottered back and have not missed a performance since. The weather changed suddenly and a hailstorm happened which flooded the whole place and caused three million dollars' worth of damage. Two days after I got better, Cole went down with the same virus. I am now virtually all right again and he, after thirty-six hours in bed, is up and about.

The triumph continues and is even greater than at first. I receive a screaming

1 Frank Sinatra (b. 1915), American actor and singer.
2 Humphrey Bogart (1899-1957), American film actor, and his actress wife, Lauren Bacall (b. 1924).
3 Peter Glenville (b. 1913), English stage and film director.

ovation at every performance. Last night the Goetzes[1], Burns and Allen[2], and the Jack Bennys came. Also darling Kay Thompson. Tonight Joe Cotten again and Jeanette MacDonald.[3] The business is fantastic and hundreds are turned away at every performance. I must say it is very, very gratifying and I am enjoying myself like crazy.

News from London that Yvonne won't do *Nude with Violin* after all and is going to do the Alan Melville play[4]. Secretly this is a relief because I didn't really, in my heart, want to rewrite Sebastian into a lady! Michael Wilding now wants to do it but cannot stay in England more than six months and not even that until after January. I have cabled Binkie to ask whether he wishes to wait, and am expecting a reply tomorrow.

In the meantime I am pressing on; sleeping a lot, eating very little, drinking no alcohol at all, and really giving the best performance I have ever given.

Sunday 26 June

One more week to go. The time has certainly passed incredibly swiftly. I don't think I should like any longer playing two shows a night. It is fairly tiring but on the whole I am enjoying myself.

Lots of people come from Hollywood. The Goldwyns came the other night and were wildly enthusiastic. The audiences continue to be wonderful with the occasional exception of a dull dinner show, but even when they are dull they are at least attentive.

Sunday 3 July

On Monday and Tuesday Goddard Lieberson was here with his myrmidons, and four performances were recorded for a long-player of me at Las Vegas. Happily all four audiences were wonderful and applauded and laughed like crazy. The experts are delighted with the recorded results and so at last I shall have a good American LP on the market. I added 'Matelot' and 'A Room with a View' to the repertoire, also 'Alice'.

The Wednesday night supper show was thrilling. Cole Porter came and Tallulah and the Van Johnsons, and it really was sensational. I was so glad because I so wanted Cole to see me at my best and he certainly did. Last night was the let-down of all time, both audiences stuffed cod's heads, but the supper show really vile. I pressed on and got them in the end, but it was gruelling hard work.

---

1 William Goetz (1903–69), American film producer, and his wife Edie.
2 George Burns (b. 1896) and Gracie Allen (1902–64), American comedy duo whose hit television series ran from 1950 to 1959.
3 Jeanette MacDonald (1902–65), American singing star.
4 *Mrs Willie.*

I went to a sweet party given by one of our dancing-girls, Jeanne Gregory. Her husband is a handsome young Pole who came to Gerald Road twice during the war when I was giving the GI parties. We sat in the garden under oleander trees and had barbecued hotdogs and potato pancakes with chives and sour cream, and it was delicious and peaceful and I stayed cheerfully until dawn.

Tuesday 5 July

Well, it's all over. The bags are packed, the farewell presents given, and the paper streamers drooping in the hot desert wind. Last night was exciting and strangely moving. The management presented me with a beautiful silver cigarette-box and I made a speech and everyone became very sentimental. Ethel Merman[1] was in the front row and in floods. Then I gave a party in the Sky Room to all the boys and girls plus Merman, Tallulah, etc. At long last, when all goodbyes were said, I lost $15 very quickly at blackjack and went to bed. It has been an extraordinary experience and one of the most reverberant successes I have ever had. I am really proud and pleased that I succeeded in doing what no one suspected I could, and that is please the *ordinary* audiences. Obviously on certain nights crammed with movie stars and chums I had no difficulties and every number went wonderfully, but the dinner shows, filled with people from Kansas, Nebraska, Utah, Illinois, etc., were what really counted and their response was usually splendid. Occasionally they would start dull and remain so, but as a general rule I got them in the end. How much I owe to those hellish troop audiences in the war. After them, anything is gravy. This afternoon we fly to Hollywood. It has all been a triumphant adventure and I feel very happy.

Monday 11 July

At this moment we are flying over the flat brown plains of Kansas, both Cole and I fairly exhausted from far too much entertaining. I am certainly the belle of the ball again and there have been red carpets everywhere. All the studios are vying with each other for my services and all the agents are tying themselves in knots. Mike Todd showed me the new Todd A-O process which is really tremendously exciting, the sound is wonderful and the colour also. Paramount want me to do a picture with Danny Kaye and *The Sleeping Prince* and/or anything I bloody well like on my own terms. MGM want me to play the Prince in *The Swan*[2]. Twentieth Century-Fox are sitting with their fingers crossed.

The entertaining has been incessant. On Tuesday night Cole Porter gave a small dinner – Claudette, Fred Astaire, etc. After it Cole and I had a lovely,

---

1 Ethel Merman (b. 1909), star of American musicals.
2 Film of Ferenc Molnar's play.

rather pissed-up heart-to-hearter. On Wednesday Merle Oberon[1] gave a glamorous dinner for me, really everyone *and* the dinner looked most nice. The Kirk Douglases[2], the Jimmy Stewarts, the Joe Cottens, the Van Johnsons and Marlon Brando[3], who was gentler and nicer than I expected. He is a handsome creature. On Thursday a vast stag, or rather gazelle, party was given for me. It was miles away and Rex Evans[4] drove me out. The party was tremendously grand and extremely respectable. It was also fairly silly. Special mauve 'leis' had been flown in from Honolulu and dinner was in the garden with braziers – thank God – between each table. Afterwards we adjourned indoors and there was some wonderful piano playing by Bobby Short, a young Negro. A pleasant evening but a trifle foolish.

Friday was the Bogarts' turn. A barbecue party by the pool. Really great fun although it got a bit nippy and I was delighted to get indoors. The same familiar glamorous faces.

On Saturday Frankie Sinatra gave a tremendous rout for me at Romanoff's in the private room upstairs. He is such a charmer and I love him. He was a wonderful host and a lovely time was had by all. He sang like a dream, I sang less alluringly, circumstances were not propitious, no mike and bad acoustics; however, everyone expressed great enthusiasm. Charlie Vidor[5] tore off his amethyst and gold buttons and links and gave them to me; I protested mildly and pocketed them.

Last night I gave 'le cocktail d'adieu' at the house and everyone came, after which I dined quietly with Tom Tryon[6].

A violent week and now I am going into hospital for three days to get a real proper check-up. Lots of it may be beastly and uncomfortable, but I know it's a good and sensible thing to do.

Tuesday 12 July   Chicago

Here I am, in the Passevant Hospital, for a three-day check-up. I arrived last night under the assumed name of Nicholas Cole. Coley unpacked for me and then he and Alfred departed for Genesee Depot, leaving me weary but cheerful enough in a small green room with a functional bed. The curtains refuse to draw completely, the waste plug in the lavatory basin doesn't work, and outside in the warm humid Chicago air the Shriners are holding their Annual Convention. This consists of many thousand old men and young men dressed in fancy clothes marching about to a series of excruciating brass bands. A

1 Merle Oberon (1911–79), Australian-born film star who had settled in Hollywood in the 1930s.
2 Kirk Douglas (b. 1918), American film star, and his wife.
3 Marlon Brando (b. 1924), celebrated American actor.
4 Rex Evans (1903–69), British character actor.
5 Charles Vidor (1900–59), Hungarian-born film director.
6 Tom Tryon (b. 1919), American film actor and author.

pleasant doctor (Walters) came to see me and extracted my life's history, after which he examined me with the utmost thoroughness even to tickling my balls and, after giving me a sleeping-pill, left.

This morning I woke at seven owing to the light striking my eyes like a sword through the non-drawing curtains. A series of different ladies appeared from time to time, some on errands, some apparently vaguely as though they had nowhere else to go. One of these latter said 'How ya comin?' I replied that in my present mood I saw little hope of such a contingency arising, whereupon she looked at me blankly, said 'Okay' and went away.

Another lady arrived and, having stuck a large syringe into one of my arm veins, extracted a lot of my blood and also went away. She was followed by a big, moist William Bendix[1] character who, with almost maternal sympathy, rammed an enema up my bottom and that was that. Presently some cereal was brought to me, and a cup of coffee. While I was enjoying this, a very ramshackle man arrived with a ladder to fix the curtains while the Shriners struck up 'God Bless America'. Presently Dr Bigg himself arrived looking very like Michel St Denis[2], and we had a purposeful little chat. Following on his visit, two men came in to fix the wash-basin, which they failed to do, then a few other ladies bounced in and out for no apparent reason. At about 10.30 I was taken down in the elevator by a personable young Jew called Tony. Here I was led into a small lavatory and told to take off my dressing-gown and pyjamas and put on a strange garment which tied at the side and made me look like a rather skittish Roman matron. In this I was led into a large, depressing room and laid on a slab. Over me and all round me were vast machines. Two men appeared and proceeded to administer a barium enema, a very unpleasant procedure indeed. One of them inserted a tube into my arse while the Shriners, slightly muffled by distance, struck up 'The Darktown Strutters Ball'. Then, in the pitch dark, accompanied by whirrings and whizzings, I was blown up with barium until I thought I should burst. Meanwhile the whizzings and whirrings were photographing what was going on. One of the men massaged my stomach and genitals rather hard, which was painful. At long last it was over and I was allowed to retire to the loo and sit on it until most of my inside had dropped out. Dr Walters appeared and gave me a cigarette. After half an hour or so I was taken to another room and my chest was x-rayed.

Then I was led back to my room and allowed to relax for a few minutes until yet another very brisk lady came in with an electric apparatus. She proceeded to sandpaper different parts of my skin until it glowed like an ember and clamped electric things on to me and switched on the current. It was quite painless and apparently took a movie of my heart. When she had gone a grey woman arrived with a menu. I chose and marked devilled-egg salad, cheese,

1 William Bendix was a rough-looking film actor frequently cast as an amiable simpleton.
2 Michel St Denis, distinguished French theatre director in Paris and London.

rye bread, French dressing and iced tea. An hour or so later a tray was brought me on which was a cup of vegetable soup, a pear in a bed of lettuce with mayonnaise, a hunk of hamburger covered in ketchup accompanied by two moist boiled potatoes, a corn on the cob which I didn't attempt on account of my teeth, and a pistachio ice-cream which tasted like brilliantine. I ate very little of all this ambrosia, but enjoyed the coffee which came instead of the iced tea. So far that is all that has happened to me today, and thank God the Shriners have at last moved off in ragged formation to lacerate the nerves of the rest of Chicago.

Wednesday 13 July

This has not been a good day. Whatever I write of it will be prejudiced by nervous exhaustion, physical exhaustion and quivering exasperation. First of all, let me state unequivocally that I do not think American women make good nurses. With one or two exceptions those I have encountered in this hospital are smart, bossy and overwhelmingly pleased with themselves. They represent the dominant sex all right in this country and they bloody well know it. The male orderlies are kind, gentle and cowed. Last night, after a meal of fruit only and a pleasant conversation with Dr Bigg, who is obviously a wise man and a first-rate doctor, I retired to sleep at 11.30 with a sleeping pill. I have been moved into a much nicer room which overlooks the lake (it also overlooks a parking lot in process of construction, a fact that was withheld from me until this morning when the hydraulic drills began at 7.30). At 3.30 a.m. I was torn from a deep sleep by a light being flashed in my eyes and a brisk nurse saying, 'I'm only checking up; go to sleep again.'

From that moment I was done for and never closed an eye until 5.30, when I gave up trying and read Tolstoy's *War and Peace* which has saved my reason. From 5.30 until 9.30 I waited without breakfast because I was to have barium for further x-rays. During this time the drills went on outside, while inside different nurses bounced in and out for no apparent reason. After I had returned from the second x-ray jaunt at 2.30 I was allowed breakfast. I ordered poached eggs, bacon and coffee, but when the tray finally arrived the eggs were lying sullenly in the water they'd been poached in, which was not very appetizing. By mid-afternoon I began to feel really beastly and the slight infection in my urinary tract started to give me trouble. Dr Bigg appeared and, to my intense relief, all my organs are healthy: liver, prostate and heart particularly so. He was wise and comforting and of course the main cause for jubilation is that I am neither festooned with ulcers nor riddled with cancer. Finally, after he had given me a belladonna and opium suppository to ease my discomfort, he went.

Friday 15 July   Wisconsin

Yesterday was fairly restful except for the hydraulic drills which happily stopped at 4.30 p.m., having been going since 7.30 a.m. At about five o'clock I had a long talk to Dr Bigg. He lectured me firmly about my future health, with emphasis on my 'nervous' stomach. He said nothing organic was wrong with me, except a slight curving of the spine which can be remedied or at least prevented from curving more by watching my posture and walking and sitting with more care, but that I must remember that I am fifty-five and not twenty-five, and live sensibly and moderately and *not* give myself so much to other people and their problems. He also said that I should create more and perform less and, for the rest of my life, drink as little alcohol as socially possible. He also told me not to be fussy about my diet, but to eat little and well. He specified that roughage was bad for my colon, which apparently is over-sensitive, like so many of my friends. He said that all the old wives' tales about cooked green vegetables being good for me was nonsense and that meat and fish, eggs, potatoes, bread and sugar were much better! He advised the latter in moderation on account of my figure. In fact he advised moderation in everything. We then got into a long discussion of morals and sex taboos and homosexuality, which convinced me that he is one of the wisest and most thoroughly sensible men I have ever met. I shall go to him once a year.

I arrived at Milwaukee at 3.15 and was met by Lynnie and Cole. We had a peaceful evening, played my Las Vegas record, which is excellent, and I went to bed early and finished *War and Peace*. Yes, yes, yes, it *is* a great book but it is far too long and although all the characters are brilliantly drawn they are, most of them, bloody bores, particularly the hero and heroine, Pierre and Natasha, whom I personally find absolutely idiotic. Prince Andrei is, to me, the only sympathetic creature in the whole book and even he gets a bit fuzzy and mystic before he kicks the bucket.

Well, I have finished it and I am very, very proud.

Saturday 23 July   New York

It is very, very, very hot indeed, the sidewalks are sticky, the humidity is terrific and the atmosphere so solid with heat that it is as if we were wrapped in a perpetually hot blanket. Personally I do not find it unbearable because I never find heat unbearable, but it is certainly fairly fierce.

On Wednesday night Jack and Natasha came to dine. Both Cole and I were dreading it. Jack was sober and consciously aware of virtue; Natasha, on the other hand, was high as a kite and perfectly idiotic. I sympathize with her being distraught over Jack, but I am getting very, very tired of people getting drunk. What the hell am I to do when either or both of them want to come to Blue Harbour next year? My heart sinks with boredom at the thought of it.

Chuck Bowden[1] came to see me. He and his partner Richard Barr want to do a revival of *Fallen Angels* with Maureen Stapleton and Nancy Walker. They are both good actresses so I have said yes. It's an old play and if it's a flop it doesn't matter much and if it's a success, which it might be, so much the better.[2]

Last night I dined with Mike Todd. Highly entertaining. I have agreed to do one small scene (two days' work) in *Around the World in Eighty Days*[3]. For this I will not be billed or paid but he will give me a nice Corot or Bonnard or Vuillard, to be chosen when I get back. Apparently Gregory Peck[4], Gary Cooper[5] and Bogart are also being offered small bits on the same profitable and equitable basis.

Sunday 31 July   Goldenhurst

Coley and I had a perfect flight home. All the covers of the studio[6] are new and it looks most shiny and pleased with itself.

Went to the Café de Paris to see Marlene. She was very good indeed, better than last year, but afterwards, when we repaired to her suite at the Dorchester, she was fairly tiresome. She was grumbling about some bad Press notices and being lonely; she also gave an account of singing privately for the Queen, which was obviously meant to be highly amusing but merely turned out to be silly and bad-mannered. Poor darling Marlene. Poor darling glamorous stars everywhere, their lives are so lonely and wretched and frustrated. Nothing but applause, flowers, Rolls-Royces, expensive hotel suites, constant adulation. It's too pathetic and wrings the heart.

Last night (Saturday) we went through it all again. We dined at the Ivy, went to *The Reluctant Debutante*[7], which was charming, and then to the Café with Clifton. I introduced Marlene as it was her last night. She was really in wonderful form but afterwards at the Dorchester again, this time before a room full of people, she started off on her royal saga in spite of my efforts to stop her, and it really was embarrassing and I so wish she wouldn't. She is such a darling in so many ways and she *should* know better. However, we made a get-away and drove down here, Coley, Graham and me, through the dawn. The road was clear all the way and it was lovely, arriving in full light with the birds chirping their heads off.

1 Chuck Bowden, American theatre manager.
2 It ran respectably and became an excellent touring vehicle in summer stock for Nancy Walker during the years ahead.
3 An all-star screen version of the Jules Verne novel.
4 Gregory Peck (b. 1916), American film star.
5 Gary Cooper (1901–61) had appeared in the 1934 Hollywood film of Noël's *Design for Living*.
6 In Gerald Road.
7 Comedy by William Douglas Home.

Sunday 7 August   London

Last night at Stratford-on-Avon I saw Larry Olivier play Macbeth, and it was one of those rare magical evenings in the theatre when the throat contracts, the eyes fill with sudden tears, and there is nothing to say afterwards but abandoned, superlative praise. It was a truly great performance. It had terror and compassion, brutality and tenderness, and it had at moments, particularly in the murderers' scene, a dreadful false geniality. It had also, and this I have never seen before, a curious quality of philosophy, an acceptance of too strong coincidence. Above all, the wonderful poetry of the play was given full value. Vivien was, in my opinion, quite remarkable as Lady Macbeth. She had a sort of viperish determination and a physical seductiveness which clearly explained her hold over Macbeth. In the banqueting scene she was brilliant, and her efforts to calm Macbeth and keep her guests at their ease were utterly convincing. In the sleep-walking scene she was really fine. The production was not up to standard. Some of the performances were all right but the sets were very bad indeed. None of this mattered, of course, because Larry rose and shone and dominated and swept the whole evening into another realm.

After this glorious treat I went back to the house with them and observed, to my true horror, that Vivien is on the verge of another breakdown. She talked at supper wildly. She is obsessed, poor darling, by the persecutions of the Press[1]; her voice became high and shrill and her eyes strange. This morning when she had gone to a fitting, Larry came and talked to me. He is distraught and deeply unhappy. Apparently this relapse has been on the way for some time. She has begun to lose sleep again and make scenes and invite more and more people to Notley until there is no longer any possibility of peace. Their life together is really hideous and here they are trapped by public acclaim, scrabbling about in the cold ashes of a physical passion that burnt itself out years ago. I am desperately sorry because I love them both and I am truly fearful of what may happen. The cruelty of fifth-rate journalists has contributed a lot to the situation but the core of the trouble lies deeper, where, in fact, it always lies, in sex. She, exacerbated by incipient TB, needs more and more sexual satisfaction. They are eminent, successful, envied and adored, and most wretchedly unhappy.

Lilli Palmer arrived with her new lover, Carlos Thompson[2], and they drove me back to London. Lilli is now over her miseries about Rex and is madly in love with Carlos, who seems charming and so *she*'s all right for the time being. She is a close friend of Viv's and we discussed the situation *ad nauseam*. If only the Oliviers could continue to be together as far as the public is concerned,

---

1 *Macbeth* reviews had been especially bad for her; Kenneth Tynan had suggested that Olivier was doing himself professional damage by continuing to work with her.
2 Carlos Thompson (b. 1916), Argentinian actor who later became her husband.

and yet live separately and sleep separately. If only Vivien could hold out until this season finishes in November and then set her career in a different channel from Larry's. However good she is, she will *never* be accepted in the big tragic roles. She should develop along her own lines and become a witty, light comedienne, which she could do better than anyone I can think of because she has wit and humour and could achieve a position in which she was unassailable. I must try all I can to help her, but I sadly fear that the trouble has gone too deep.

On the credit side this week, *After the Ball* has been a success at Lambert-ville[1] and the notices are excellent. Mike Todd bought me a lovely Bonnard for £4,500.[2] I myself bought a Maufra, which is enchanting, for £450. My life insurance money is returned to me and I have now £20,000 in my deposit account and another £20,000 (Las Vegas loot) has been sent to Jamaica. So my financial concentration, dating from last November, has certainly borne luscious fruit. Now for the television lolly and Bob is definitely my uncle.

Annie Fleming came over to Goldenhurst last Sunday for dinner bringing with her Evelyn Waugh, Diana Cooper, Freddie Ashton[3], and Raymond [Mortimer]. The evening was a great success. Diana, whom I haven't seen since Duff died, was extraordinary. Her appearance is unchanged and she was gay and enchanting. Evelyn's new book, *Officers and Gentlemen*, is not, I fear, very good. It has obviously good moments but it is untidy and lacks construction.

Graham, Cole and I are doing a great deal of painting, mostly vast nudes for *Nude with Violin*.[4] It is astonishing how easy modern painting is, I mean modern in the semi-abstract sense. I should think Braque could do a picture a day without turning a camel-hair.

Friday 19 August

The Olivier situation is worsening by the hour. Graham and I drove down to Stratford with Cecil Tennant on Tuesday. He is deeply perturbed and wanted to discuss the whole business. On arrival we dined and went to the opening night of *Titus Andronicus*. Peter Brook had done a stupendously good production, really most impressive and extremely clever in avoiding pitfalls. Larry[5] was wonderful although, at moments, a little funny. Vivien[6] was frankly not

1 Its American première in New Jersey.
2 For doing *Around the World in Eighty Days*.
3 Frederick Ashton (b. 1906), British dancer and choreographer, knighted 1963; director of the Royal Ballet 1963–70.
4 Graham's was chosen by the management but destroyed when the play opened for being too obscene.
5 In the title role.
6 As Lavinia.

very good. She looked lovely throughout regardless of ravishment and her tongue being cut out and her hands cut off. Her clothes and hair-do were impeccable and her face remained untouched by tragedy. It is a very, very silly play with some good moments. Vivien was in a vile temper and perfectly idiotic. Larry was bowed down with grief and despair and altogether it was a gloomy little visit.

Personally I think that if Larry had turned sharply on Vivien years ago and given her a clip in the chops, he would have been spared a mint of trouble. The seat of all this misery is our old friend, feminine ego. She is, and has been, thoroughly spoiled. She also has a sharp tongue and a bad temper. This, coupled with incipient TB and an inner certainty that she can never be as good an artist as Larry, however much she tries, has bubbled up in her and driven her onto the borderline. Fond as I am of her and sorry as I feel for her, I would like to give her a good belting, although now I fear it might push her over the edge and be far, far too late.

Last night I dined with Tarquin[1] 'on guard' at St James's Palace. It was a perfectly sweet evening. Three very young officers and one slightly older one. Lovely manners and good old shabby, traditional glamour. Tarquin is bright and attractive although too small. He obviously is worried about Vivien and Larry. He's been at Notley a good deal and seen it coming. I do so hope, if only for his sake, that another rip-snorting scandal can be avoided.

I am popping over to Paris this afternoon just for the devil of it. I always miss Paris more than anywhere else when I am away in America and this is my only chance of seeing it again for a long while. Ginette will meet me and I shall eat delicious food and probably get thoroughly livery, but to hell with it.

Sunday 28 August   Goldenhurst

A peaceful week, painting and reading and, occasionally, staring grimly at television.

There has been a great fuss and fume because Mike Todd asked me to ask Larry to play the scene with me in *Around the World in Eighty Days*. Larry, as usual, havered and said he might, then finally said he wouldn't. Today Mike called me to say that Johnny Gielgud was going to do it.

I am about to say goodbye to Goldenhurst for a considerable time. I thought of wandering from room to room, touching the beloved furniture like Madame Ranevska[2], but discarded the idea as there really isn't time. I said a mute goodbye to the garden, and now we're off.

---

1 Olivier's son by his first wife Jill Esmond; he was one of Noël's many godsons.
2 In Chekhov's *The Cherry Orchard*.

Friday 2 September   London

Tonight I fly away again with Coley and Graham. Yesterday there was a farewell cocktail party: a mixed bag, Beattie, Mike Todd, a Spanish bullfighter and his wife, Clifton, Binkie, John [Gielgud], June Whitfield, Juliet Duff, etc. Later, I took Clifton (pissed) to dine at the Matelot.

On Tuesday I got up at crack of dawn and went to Elstree. It was a very successful day and Johnny and I managed to do the whole scene. Johnny was charming to work with. He was, as usual, a little false in his performance but very effective. If Larry had played it in a dreadful, refined Cockney accent it would have been hilarious; as it was, it was perfectly all right. All the people at the studio were extremely nice and I thoroughly enjoyed the day. Before leaving, Mike presented me with a cheque for £100 which, together with the Bonnard, brought my day's salary up to £4,600. Mustn't grumble.

Friday 9 September   Jamaica

Here I am safely installed again and feeling as if I had never been away. We had a comfortable flight, enlivened by the company of Ninette de Valois[1] and Sol Hurok[2]. In New York our plane to Montego was delayed from noon to three o'clock. Early the next morning we dashed up to Firefly to see how the house was progressing, knowing in our hearts that it was hardly progressing at all.

The weather is perfect. Lovely sunshine every morning and a nice biblical thunderstorm every afternoon at 2.45. The house looks spotless and the garden is a-growing and a-blowing. I have written two excellent opening numbers for Mary and me – 'Ninety Minutes is a Long, Long Time' and 'Together with Music'[3]. I have also written a brief opening scene.

I am happy every minute of the day, and the long mornings are heavenly. On Monday we drove into Kingston for some intensive shopping in course of which, apart from meat and groceries, I bought a new Austin in which I drove home, and a beautiful Bechstein grand, which was put on a truck with my other piano and was waiting for me when I got back. I also bought a small radiogram to have here in my sitting-room so that I can have music while I paint or play patience. A richly extravagant day and thank God for Las Vegas and, later on, for American television.

A cable arrived yesterday from Vivien, madly enthusiastic about *South Sea Bubble* and wishing to go into rehearsal in January. This is very good news

---

1 Ninette de Valois (b. 1898), British dancer and choreographer; director of the Royal Ballet; created Dame in 1951.
2 Sol Hurok (1888–1974), Russian-American impresario.
3 Which became the title of Noël and Mary Martin's CBS television spectacular, the first special ever to go out live in colour on American television.

because she will be ideal in it and it might quite conceivably set her on her emotional base again. Altogether everything is rosy rapture and it is lovely beyond words to be back here again. Pete [Matz] arrives on Sunday and Mary and Dick on Tuesday; peace will evaporate a little but I shall still, with the utmost determination, keep my mornings sacrosanct.

Wednesday 14 September

Mary and Richard arrived yesterday. They rested in the afternoon and in the evening Pete and I played them 'Ninety Minutes' and 'Together with Music'. To my horror Mary took against 'Together with Music' very firmly indeed. I admired her honesty but it was dreadfully irritating and disappointing. Actually I am afraid she's right, and so I am now in the throes of rewriting the entire number and making it more romantic.

Thursday 15 September

'Together with Music', second version, is finished. It is better than the first really but it was bloody hell to do. However, now it is done, and Mary's delighted and everyone's delighted.

I was right about peace departing with the arrival of the Hallidays. They are both quite incredibly noisy. Richard never stops emitting shrill, whining screams for no reason at all. Mary has a naturally piercing voice, and between them both mealtimes are deafening. Otherwise they are no trouble at all and retire firmly to bed immediately after dinner, which is wonderful. Pete is working like a slave, orchestrating all day long while I grind out lyrics.

Thursday 22 September

Trouble has come inevitably because Richard, we must face it, is not only neurotic, hysterical, noisy and a bad drinker, but a bad character as well. All this was clearly apparent years ago in 1946 when we had the uproar over Mary's dresses for *Pacific 1860*. Now, on looking back, all is explained. Fortunately Mary, over the years, has discarded her rose-coloured spectacles and is no longer deluded. I am deeply sorry for her. She is a great artist within her limited scope and this scope is only limited by her lack of education and by her general naivety. She still remains at forty-two a tough, honest girl from Texas with a rich talent for singing songs and a rich, natural warmth. She is a curious mixture of wisdom and innocence. For years – fifteen years – she has allowed Richard to order her life, run the house, deal with all business and social matters, oversee her dresses, do her hair and generally protect her from any extraneous slings and arrows. This has left her, not entirely willingly, free to develop her talent and build the triumphant career she so very much deserves. But lately she has begun to realize that she has been too assiduously sheltered. She has watched Richard over and over again in every production she has been concerned with, making sudden unpredictable scenes, losing his head and insulting people right and left, thereby not only undermining her own popularity but leaving acres of debris to be shovelled away, and a dreary trail of acrimony and misunderstandings. She has admitted to me that while our idiotic feud lasted she cried for two years. She loves and respects me, and I love and respect her. I have had few opportunities to talk to her alone. Actually, during the whole time they were in London for *Pacific 1860*, I only once talked to her without Richard being present and that was driving home one day from a rehearsal at Chiswick Empire.

The other evening at dinner, after we had been up to Firefly for drinks, Richard suddenly turned on me with snarling, whining hatred, accusing me of cheese-paring and not being willing to spend enough money on the production, etc. All this without the slightest lead up. I turned on him in no uncertain manner and ultimately silenced him. Mary also turned on him without any compromise and altogether it was a horrid little episode. Later he wept and apologized and wrote me a long, humble letter suggesting that he withdraw from any further participation in 'Together with Music'. Over-touched by his remorse and feeling awfully sorry for him, I foolishly calmed him down and, to comfort him, told him how important his judgement was to us, etc. Two nights later he started up another drunken tirade, which Mary and I managed to calm before it got out of hand. The next morning, after a long talk alone with Mary in which we both agreed that he must withdraw from the production, I told him firmly that I couldn't guarantee my own self-control during the ardours of later rehearsals and that it would be better for all of us if he bowed out as he himself had suggested. He took this very well and that is now how the matter stands. However, it wasted a lot of time and energy. Personally I think he is heading for a nervous crack-up. He isn't a confirmed alcoholic like Jack, but two drinks set him off and I really can't risk having to order him out of the television studios in front of everyone and engender a first-class scandal in all the news columns.

Since this has been decided, all has gone well. Mary and Pete and I have worked very, very hard, going over harmonies again and again. I feel sure the show will be good. She is wonderful to work with and the programme has much variety. Pete is being really marvellous. He is not only a fine musician but an enthusiast, so professionally all is rosy.

Sunday 25 September

Mary and Richard have left this morning, escorted loyally to Montego by Cole and Graham. Pete and I are left with a lot of work to do and the threat of a hurricane which is rapidly approaching the island. We have to have the radio on all day in the main house so that we can get hourly governmental instructions. We have filled all the baths with water and taken every possible precaution.

Last evening we gave a cocktail party. Mary and I firmly performed so that we could get some sort of audience reaction. Of course everybody adored everything. Actually I wasn't very good; I became suddenly aware that in deference to Mary I had agreed to do all our double numbers in her key rather than mine. As she has a much stronger voice than I have anyhow, this placed me at a disadvantage and I found myself forcing instead of relaxing. It doesn't really matter as there are several places where I can change melody and hop up to my cs and ds. The heat was really appalling and we and our entranced public dripped with sweat. Mary was really magical. She gave out as if she were doing a command performance. Now they have gone and I have ten days of comparative peace until I go to New York and really take the plunge.

Wednesday 5 October

Well, here I go again, flying off through the 'inclement skies'. They look fairly clement at the moment but *'quien sabe'*, as the Spanish say. We have had a series of gargantuan thunderstorms and the house has quivered and shaken and the dogs have quivered and shaken. Apart from this the last few days have been peaceful. I have painted two pictures, a slight change of style which I think is an improvement. Dimmer colours, not quite so much fantasy and more solidity. I have also written the required second verse for 'What's Going to Happen to the Tots', and so the last of my lyric-writing is done for the moment.

A long letter arrived from Binkie who had seen Larry and Vivien and who is palpably worried about Vivien's health. It would be so wonderful for her and for all of us if she could do *South Sea Bubble* and make a success in it, but she is apparently in a bad state mentally and I personally doubt if she will be able to last out the Stratford season without cracking up again. This is cruel bad luck for she is madly enthusiastic about the play. Perhaps 'madly' is too much the operative word! At all events I have written to Binkie telling him to press on on the assumption that everything will be all right. It is all very worrying.

Sunday 9 October   New York

This is a pleasant suite: sitting-room, bedroom and bath and a small kitchenette, comfortable and unpretentious, with a lovely view over the Park. The sitting-room is bottle-green and Steinway's have sent me a baby grand. There is also a television set over which I crouch occasionally to learn a little of this curious medium. What I have learned so far is that, apart from a few special personalities and talents, the standard of entertainment is poor, the lighting unpredictable, and the commercial emphasis very overstressed. I have seen to date few evidences of imagination in production and no sense of experimentation.

I arrived on Wednesday evening after an agreeable flight and was met at Idlewild by Charles and Ham and some Press photographers. The publicity so far is being well handled. I am well aware that this is a fairly dangerous undertaking but my nerves are still and my attitude one of stately calm. Having got away so triumphantly with Las Vegas I can hope, but certainly not be sure, that I can get away with this. However, I intend to leave as little to chance as possible. Mary seems nervy and depressed about Richard, who fortunately is in hospital. Less fortunately he comes out on Monday, but I doubt if there will be much trouble because the scenes in Jamaica were salutary. The CBS personnel are amiable and appear to be completely co-operative, and the course is set and so there is nothing to do but pray for fair winds and trust to the stars, at least to two of them.

I lunched with Jack and Natasha on Thursday and a small miracle has undoubtedly taken place. He is clear-eyed and clear-witted again. How he has contrived this metamorphosis nobody seems to know. Anyhow at the moment all is well and I only hope it will remain so. I am still wary and suspicious, but I think much will be proved when he goes into rehearsal with his new musical at the end of November.

I have given out that I am terribly, terribly busy and unable to be social at all, so I have had a very pleasant time wandering about on my own and going to movies and going to bed early. I have read an excellent novel, *The Man in the Gray Flannel Suit*[1], and a vulgar pornographic essay in exhibitionism called *The Deer Park* by Norman Mailer who wrote *The Naked and the Dead* and should have known better. I have also had lunch today with Bobby Flemyng, in the course of which we talked and giggled about everyone and everything, also a long heart-to-heart talk with Ann Todd about Ann Todd, which only goes to prove that there is time for everything if only one plays one's cards right.

Sunday 16 October

Rehearsals are going very well. Richard, wreathed in amiability, has only been to one. When he is absent, a purplish ex-drunk stands in for him, presumably to guard Mary's interests. She also has several other transient hangers-on which I find rather a bore, but I am rising above it. She is frightened of doing the 'Madame Butterfly' burlesque, rightly at the moment because she isn't doing it very well. If she suddenly decides she won't do it we are in bad trouble because all the dialogue I have written to bind the show together depends on it!

Our camera director, Jerry Shaw, is extremely nice and very biddable, so I

1 By Sloan Wilson.

think all will be well. I have always found the whims and fancies of leading ladies fairly irritating, but whereas in the old days I was prepared to fight them, now I really feel I cannot be bothered. Mary is a great performer and a very good character. She is painfully naive and has no clue about playing comedy and never will have. She also has a strongly developed 'Rebecca of Sunnybrook Farm' quality and a desire to be perpetually sweet before the public, which is death to sharp comedy lines. She infuses our 'comedy' bickering with saccharin and shies away from any riposte which sounds as though she were being 'mean' to me. This is *not* a help in scenes which have been written on the assumption that we are having a light professional quarrel. The result will be that I shall play rings round her. None of this much matters but it is certainly aggravating.

We had a Press reception on Monday and charm was laid on with a trowel. It was apparently a great success and my face now stares up at me from many magazine covers.

Wednesday 19 October

Cole and Graham arrived on Monday. We have our first preview tomorrow evening. Pete as usual has been a rock of Gibraltar throughout.

It's a little startling to discover that the television boys are not as bright as they should be. For instance, there is a hard and fast rule that they take a 'kinescope' of the actual performance, that is, a film and sound recording. This they look at on the following day when it is obviously too late to profit from it. I have insisted that they take a kinescope of the Friday preview so that there will still be a little time to correct mistakes. They consider this a splendid idea and are most impressed. Personally it looks to me perilously like ordinary common sense.

I have won my battle over the blue floor and the footlights and another battle when I was informed that the Ford Motor Company (our sponsor) was prepared to go to any lengths to prevent me from singing certain lines, *offensive* lines, that would upset the puritan viewers. Among these lines (all the best ones, of course) was 'Sycophantic sluts wriggling their guts' in 'Nina'. The message conveyed to me was that it was a question of taste! I remained commendably calm and replied that I too was prepared to go to any lengths, and that although the contract had been signed it had not yet been posted and would not be until after the performance. I added that for thirty-five years I had been concerned with productions of impeccable taste, that I considered their interference impertinent and that, as the object of the whole enterprise was for me to entertain the majority, I had no intention of being dictated to by a minority. This caused some agitated clucking among the executives, but beyond that no more has been heard.

Monday 24 October

Well, it is all over bar the shouting, and the shouting is louder than it ever has been in my whole career. The Press notices are unqualified raves and it appears that, apart from being clever and pretty and wittier than anyone in this whole big wonderful world, I have also revolutionized television by proving that two people, without support of an elaborate production, can hold for an hour and a half. I have had really marvellous acclaim for my own performance and I feel immensely relieved and happy and pleased.

The preview on Friday night was flat and 'second-nightish' and I knew it. I saw the kinescope on Saturday morning, having been warned that it was a rush job and that we should look fairly dreadful. They were right to warn me. I looked like an emaciated bull moose.

It was not this, however, that concerned me. I knew that kinescopes were always pictorially discouraging; what *did* concern me was that a great many of the camera shots were muddled and diffuse and taken from too far off, and that the sound balance was appalling. I therefore spent the rest of the day re-rehearsing the whole show and insisting that practically all of it should be done in close-ups. It is no use me trying to sing witty lyrics if you can't see my eyes. This was a considerable job. Mary, who had refused to look at the kinescope, fully agreed with me and we worked away until 5.45, when I went home feeling suddenly nervous. This infuriated me so I had a sharp talk with myself and slept firmly for an hour, then I had a minute steak, some ice cream and coffee, and went off to the studio.

The atmosphere was sizzling. Masses of flowers and presents and high nervous laughter, all the usual opening night carry-on. When the moment came to start I noticed that Mary was quivering, so I gave her a sharp, loving lecture and on we went. I discovered to my relief that whatever nerves I had had in the afternoon were stilled and that I was in complete control and determined to enjoy myself. Lynn and Alfred, Margot Fonteyn, Clifton, etc., were in the audience, but I remembered my kinescope lesson and ignored them with my eyes, though not with my ears, and sang everything slap into the cameras. I knew from the outset that I was giving a good performance, and thank God I kept it up.

Mary, after the first scene in which she dried up and became rather baby-talky, was absolutely superb. She infused magic into 'Kick out of You', 'I've Only Got Eyes for You' and 'Daddy'. We *just* got away with 'Butterfly' and our final medley was fine and tore the place up. My biggest successes were my own medley, 'Mad Dogs', 'Texas' and 'Tots' which, considering it was a new number, I did very well.

At the end of the performance chaos set in. Everybody was in a fine state of ecstatic appreciation. Clifton was in tears. Marlene called me immediately from Vegas and her voice had gone up four tones. Telegrams arrived like confetti from all over the country. A couple of strangers rang me up from a small town in Michigan and said they had never seen anything so wonderful in their lives. Finally, when Mary and I left to go to the party at '21', there was a howling mob in the street. There was a genuine 'triumph' feeling about the whole thing. The party was one long paean of praise, an agreeable party, I need hardly say.

Yesterday, Sunday, was one long telephone session. I have never had such varied praise in my life. Apart from the genuine sweetness of my friends, I was terribly touched by the messages from strangers all over the continent. What an extraordinary medium. It is hard to imagine all those millions and millions of people all looking at me at the same moment. Then, of course, today the reviews came out. Well, well. When I think of the grudging patronage of the English Press compared with this whole-hearted, *pleased* generosity, my heart does sink a little.

Apart from *Together with Music* I have noticed in the Press certain references to Princess Margaret wishing to marry someone or other. I really must try to control this yawning.

Sunday 30 October   Jamaica

Everything looked lovely when we arrived home. Graham and Coley had been busy with cement after I left and now the outside of the kitchen looks like an Athenian pleasance and there is a fountain which, as yet, doesn't work. Cole and I have two new names for the property; his is 'Concrete Proposition', mine is 'You Were Cement for Me'. A cloud, considerably larger than a man's hand, descended on us when, hot and stinking and tired, we discovered the swimming-pool empty and the pump not working. Lots of dark gentlemen are crushed into the pump house fiddling with it, but so far to no avail. We have been up to Firefly and it has progressed enormously. It really is going to be an enchanting house. It is irregular, built on different levels and altogether charming. The dogs are well and rampageous and the cats are well and pregnant. How Evelyn can carry on with her flaming sex life at her great age is truly remarkable. In cat language she must be rising eighty. It must be lack of religious scruples that has kept her so rorty.

I feel immensely, overwhelmingly tired, but a pleasant tiredness, neither nervy nor strained. It has been a terrific week, a heroic, white-headed-boy week, a thoroughly wallowing week. Wherever I have walked or driven or lunched or dined, ecstatic strangers have loaded me with praise and gratitude; one lady who meant well but had an unhappy turn of phrase said, 'I never liked you until Saturday night but now I love you!' Another, with wild blue hair, rushed up to me on Madison Avenue and cried shrilly, 'You are out of this world and I'm from East Orange!' Two fascinating statements in one.

On Monday I attended a gargantuan cocktail party given by the publishers in honour of my new paper-bound book.[1] I shook hands with hundreds of people, was tirelessly charming, and made cheerful, modest little jokes. Fortunately none of my loved ones was there to witness such a fawning, saccharin display. Afterwards, at '21' where Edna Ferber and I had gone to have a quiet, undisturbed, chatty supper, I was serenaded by the entire Yale Glee Club. They stood in a semicircle, dressed in tails and looking painfully young and pink and cherubic, and sang the 'Whiffenpoof Song' and 'Anchors Aweigh', the latter presumably as a gesture to my well-known predilection for the Navy. What they were doing at '21' I shall never know. At any rate it was very touching and gratifying, although supper was less tranquil than we had hoped.

On Wednesday, after a long day of Press interviews (more modest little jokes), I went with Maggie Case and Jack and Natasha to the opening of Enid Bagnold's *The Chalk Garden*. Over-literate but beautifully written and exquisitely acted by Gladys Cooper and Siobhan McKenna. All the characters speak in the same idiom, rather Ivy Compton-Burnett-ish[2], but the words are charming. It should be a success.

On Thursday evening I went to Valentina's, a small cocktail party, very gay. Garbo was there for a little, looking lovely but grubby. On Saturday I had a day of peace and went to *Rebel Without a Cause*, a horrifying film about juvenile delinquency. Poor James Dean gave a wonderful performance. It is a great loss to the screen that he should have been killed.

Thursday 3 November

Poor Princess Margaret has made a sorrowful, touching statement that she will *not* marry Peter Townsend. This is a fine slap in the chops for the bloody Press which has been persecuting her for so long. I am really glad that she has at last made the decision, but I do wish there hadn't been such a hideous hullabaloo about it. Apart from church and royal considerations, it would have been an unsuitable marriage anyway. She cannot know, poor girl, being young and in love, that love dies soon and that a future with two strapping stepsons and a man eighteen years older than herself would not really be very rosy. I am terribly sorry for her. Private sorrow is bad enough but public sorrow is almost unbearable. I am sure she is right to stick by the job. It has all been a silly, mismanaged lash-up and I cannot imagine how the Queen and the Queen Mother and Prince Philip allowed it to get into such a tangle. At least she hasn't betrayed her position and her responsibilities, but that is arid comfort for her with half the world religiously exulting and the other half pouring out a spate of treacly sentimentality. I hope she will not take to religion in a big

---

1 A reprint of some short stories.
2 Ivy Compton-Burnett (1892-1969), British novelist.

way and become a frustrated maiden princess. I also hope that they had the sense to hop into bed a couple of times at least, but this I doubt.

Thursday 10 November

Another week has gone by, a week of peace and comparative idleness. I say comparative because I have painted several small pictures, one or two for Christmas presents and the rest for my exhibition.[1] I am slightly agitated about this because although there is certainly a flair for decorative design in my painting, and although I am learning more and more as I go along, I am not *really* good enough yet for an exhibition. Of course, compared with some of the pretentious muck that is shown month after month in the London galleries, my amateur efforts appear brilliant. They have a sense of colour and design and do at least convey a fantasized impression of Jamaica, but as yet I am still at the stage where I break rules without having learned them. There will inevitably be jeers and patronizing sneers from the critics, but this would happen anyway whether the pictures were good, bad or indifferent. At all events, to back out of the exhibition now would be cowardly, and as I go on painting such a lot something *must* be done to dispose of the results and some of them are bound to be bought, if not from genuine artistic appraisal, at least for celebrity snobbism.

Last night the Bennet Korns[2] came to dinner. Mrs B.K. is Moura Lympany the concert pianist, very attractive and pretty. She started off nervously on the Bechstein, which is already hideously out of tune, and then warmed up and played some Ravel, Debussy, a Chopin prelude and the Brahms variations, this last very well indeed. She is not a great musician but she is an excellent pianist, and we sat in my sitting-room sipping whisky and soda while the electric fan whirred and moths barged in and out and a sort of magic was infused; the notes glittered and shimmered evoking a dusty, European concert-hall nostalgia while the tree frogs shrilled outside and Bennet Korn, a grey, sympathetic little man, glowed adoringly at his wife while she picked away at the notes like a determined and dedicated bird.

Relative Values opened in Paris and is apparently absolutely appalling. A vile cast, a bad theatre and a vulgar and shameful production. I read the *Figaro* notice, which is not only vile for the play but goes on to say that it is the shoddiest production ever seen!

The London *Times* came out with the news that the magistrate's court in London had voted down the proposed plan for altering the barbarous laws about homosexuality with an overwhelming majority. This, apart from being shameful and idiotic and bad for England, will obviously have an effect on all British colonial possessions. It is hard to believe, in this scientific, psychiatric

1 A London gallery had offered to stage this.
2 Bennet Korn, an American television executive, was married to Moura Lympany 1951-61.

age when so many mysteries have been made clear, even for the layman, that a group of bigoted old gentlemen should have the power to make the administration of British justice a laughing-stock in the civilized world. But there it is, the lethal remnants of canon law are still malevolently influential. Emotional, uninformed prejudice can still send men to prison and ruin their lives for a crime that in the eyes of any intelligent human being is not a crime at all. The seduction of minors, either male or female, should obviously be punishable, but the fact that two men well over the age of consent should be penalized for going to bed together in private is a devastating revelation that we have learned nothing from history, literature, biology, science or psychology. To regard homosexuality either as a disease or a vice is, we know, archaic and ignorant. It has always existed and always will exist. It has always been a minority in every country of the world and always will be. To attempt by law and punishment to eliminate it is as foolish as to try to eliminate hair colouring and skin pigmentation by the same methods. This malignant, cretinous decision by the English magistrates will cause irremediable suffering and, like the ill-starred Prohibition era in America, encourage and force people to break the law and provide an open field for blackmail and unending persecution.

This farcical-tragic gaffe of the respected high-ups in England will be found to have hideous repercussions, one of which is obviously happening here. The police are empowered to frame private individuals, to extort terrified and probably inaccurate confessions and betrayals from scared young men. There can be no redress. What is to prevent a stranger to whom I have given a lift in my car from going to the police and asserting that I have made indecent overtures to him? What is to prevent these quivering little coloured *tapettes* in Kingston from giving any celebrated names that come into their minds? As usual in such cases, the local homos have behaved foolishly. There always comes a stage when they become over-confident and arrogant and impossible, and I cannot think that a cautionary lesson will be bad for them. Any sexual activities when over-advertised are tasteless, and for as long as these barbarous laws exist it should be remembered that homosexuality *is* a penal offence and should be considered as such socially, although not morally. This places on the natural homo a burden of responsibility to himself, his friends and society which he is too prone to forget; this, although it may appear self-righteous, is merely common sense. The human urge to persecute is always at the ready. When there isn't a major war in progress to satisfy man's inherent sadism, the Jews must be hounded, or the Negroes, or any nonconforming minority anywhere.

Success also must be resolutely attacked. In America today there has emerged a squalid rash of weekly periodicals, *Confidential, Rave, Hush, Private Lives* (this to my personal chagrin). Anyone successful and in the public eye is fair game and, libel laws in the USA being curious to say the least of it, these magazines are permitted to assert freely that so-and-so is a dope addict, so-and-so likes little girls, and so-and-so's private life is one long homosexual orgy, etc. The so-and-sos in question are public figures and usually very popular ones. The circulation of these magazines is apparently enormous and rising steadily. It seems nothing can be done to stop them. Marlene, the Windsors, Elsa Maxwell, Van Johnson, Valentina, Garbo, Tab Hunter[1], Bob Mitchum[2], etc., already have been vulgarly pilloried.

Before I went to Las Vegas I said to Cole, 'Wait and see how soon it is before *I* get it.' Apparently I was quite right because yesterday Cole confessed to me that a month ago, just before I went to New York to do the television, there was an article in *Rave* which, complete with photographs, stated that I was the highest-paid British 'tulip' (better than 'pansy', I think) who had ever been imported into America; that during the war I sang 'Mad About the Boy' to an RAF officer at Biggin Hill and was ducked in a pond by his incensed comrades; that I had set up a young man in Jamaica in a travel agency. All this was printed clearly and with a refreshing lack of innuendo. Graham and Cole decided not to tell me about it for fear of upsetting me, which was sweet of them, but they really should know by now that I am tougher than that.

It doesn't upset me but it does give me to think. I wonder, for instance, how the little man who wrote it dreamed up the Biggin Hill episode? How had he ever *heard* of Biggin Hill? I couldn't expect him to know that I *never* sing 'Mad About the Boy' (a) because it is a woman's song, and (b) because it is too high for me. How also did he manufacture the story of my setting up a boy-friend in a travel agency? There must have been some hint, something said by somebody to start the thing off in his mind. Generally in these periodicals there is some shadow of truth on which their scurrility is based, but in my case there is absolutely none. All of which forces me to the wryly satisfactory conclusion that if I had been seen naked in an opium den with several Negroes stripped for action and the story appeared the following week in *Rave*, I should be in exactly the same position I am now. Those who wished to would believe it, those who didn't would either laugh or become angry on my behalf. But to what avail? I would, of course, never dream of suing them and turning the whole thing into a headline scandal. This, of course, they well know and the same applies to all their celebrated victims. None of it, I think, really matters beyond its intrinsic proof of the nastiness of human nature.

Now, today, having made this sensational success on television, I am in an even more vulnerable position. I must gird my slandered loins and be prepared for fresh onslaughts.

1 Tab Hunter (b. 1931), American film actor.
2 Robert Mitchum (b. 1917), tough American film star.

Sunday 20 November

I suddenly decided, last Sunday, to begin an entirely new novel. The idea of it came swiftly and clearly and I am very happy about it. I started right away and have already done twenty-nine pages, an average of two thousand words a day. It is gay and irreverent and with little sentiment and *no* significance; about the Queen and the Duke of Edinburgh visiting Samolo and the effect the visit has on the community before, during and after. I am calling it *Pomp and Circumstance*, writing it freely in the first person as a cheerful married woman with two children and a nice husband. So far it is, I think, very funny and has flowed easily. I know that my greatest gift is comedy and this gives me wonderful opportunities for all sorts of irrelevancies because my heroine has a light mind and through her I can have a lot of fun with all the colonial types. At all events, *I* am thoroughly enjoying it which is a good thing. I have worked steadily for five hours every morning, painted in the afternoons and practised at the piano for an hour each evening before dinner. An ideal existence.

Sunday 27 November

Binkie is very keen for Johnny Gielgud to play *Nude with Violin* and so, although I do not think him ideal, I have consented. He is a star and a box-office draw, and although his comedy is a bit heavy-handed his quality will be valuable. Fortunately there is no love element and no emotion in the part, and if he plays it down, as I have implored him to do, he will probably, with a strong cast round him, make a success of it. This will mean that I shall have two new comedies opening at about the same time, because *South Sea Bubble* with Vivien goes into rehearsal in February. I expect both plays will get bad notices because in England they always do; however, they are both light and entertaining and both played by stars and so I suspect that the public will be interested.

Sunday 4 December

Last Sunday evening at King's House was agreeable as usual. HE had an upset stomach so couldn't appear at dinner which was sad; however, Theo Seely, the editor of the *Gleaner*, came and was humorous and intelligent, although he betrayed occasional indications of the dreadful trade of journalism. There really is something sinister about journalism, it has an insidious effect on character and distorts viewpoint. I am convinced that the reason I distrust and dislike journalists as a general rule is that after a while, like politicians, they become subtly corrupted by their job. They develop a facile cynicism based on superficial observation, and the real truths below the surface of people and events evade them. Max Beaverbrook is their god – dynamic, saturated with power, autocratic, charming when he pleases, in mortal fear of death, and spiritually one of the greatest vulgarians that have ever lived; he is the object of their true allegiance.

Max when young, devoured by ambition and full of guts and drive, must have been fascinating. Now, rising eighty and bloated with the power he longed for, he is no longer fascinating but rather repellent. The charm is still there but all his years of cynical exploitation of morons, of playing down to the lower aspects of human character in order to sell his newspapers, of misrepresenting facts and shamefully bellowing a patriotism he is far from feeling, this has all diminished him while at the same time placing him at the top. How can young men, dark or light, embarking on this sinister profession, fail to be impressed by such palpable success? And how can they be expected to see through it to the muddled thinking and corroded values behind? Nowadays an efficient journalist (excepting war correspondents) can only succeed in the so-called popular Press by encouraging false values, vulgarizing the English language, substituting sentimentality for true sentiment, exploiting prurience and synthetic indignation, and parodying the human heart.

The degrading 'commonness' of the recent 'royal romance' is a case in point. None of the impassioned clichés about 'A young girl's right to marry the man of her choice' and 'Margaret must choose between love and duty', etc., was even remotely sincere. They were marshmallow phrases for unthinking minds, headlined by cheap, cynical sub-editors.

Enough about journalism now. It is my 'black beast' and it upsets my acids even to discuss it.

I have decided, after some months of thought, that it is fairly ridiculous for me to spend eight weeks in England out of one year and to pay, for that privilege, roughly £20,000 in income tax! It is here, on this island, that I accomplish my creative work and it is in America that I earn the money to make my living here possible, therefore I am going to give up my English domicile, turn over Goldenhurst and Gerald Road to separate companies, establish residence in Bermuda where there is no income tax at all, and contrive to extract from these next few years enough capital to insure my old age. This has nothing to do with lack of patriotism, it is merely a perfectly legal method of defeating the monstrously unjust tax situation in England. It will mean that I cannot spend more than a few months in England each year, which will not inconvenience me as I don't wish to anyhow. I shall still be British and domiciled in two British colonies, nominally in Bermuda and actually here. If at some future date I want to act again in London, I can perfectly easily do so for a limited period, which is all I have done for the last twenty-odd years. If necessary I could rehearse and open in Dublin, thereby giving myself a full three months in London.

It is a sad reflection that owing to these muddled and disagreeable circumstances one should be forced to such devious methods to hold on to what one earns. But there it is. I am fifty-six years old, or shall be in twelve days' time. I have, after a lifetime of hard work, no investments, no capital, nothing but a little property and my talents and health. Neither of the latter can be guaranteed indefinitely. There must come a time when I shall be forced to slow down and look at the view, and when this time comes I do not intend to look at it through eyes misted with tears of regret because I have allowed the British Government to rob me of the material fruits of my labours.

Away with melancholy and on with the dance.

Monday 12 December

Well, I think the die is cast all right. Lornie, whose common sense and integrity I trust to the last ditch, is whole-heartedly in favour of the project, in fact she is almost violent about it. She says, rightly, that however much I earn during these next few years I shall never be able to get straight in England, and not only be unable to put anything by, but be living from overdraft to overdraft. This of course is silly. Unlike poor Larry and Viv and the Redgraves and the Mills, I can work away from England or America. I don't care for living in England anyhow and never have, and during the last few years I have spent very little time there.

It is almost inconceivable what this decision will save me. As things are I am liable to pay the Inland Revenue anything from £25,000 to £50,000 a year. As things will be, all that money will be sitting tax-free in my bank in Bermuda. In five years' time, when I am sixty-one, I should, if all goes well, have amassed a capital of several hundred thousand pounds on which I can live in ease and luxury until the end of my life. I might even be able to afford to live in England again if I tire of sunshine and equable weather and wish to lay my old bones, creaking with rheumatism, in my own dear land, which for years has robbed me of most of my earnings, withheld all official honours from me, sneered at me and abused me whenever possible and, frequently, made me very unhappy. The ordinary English people are fond of me, I know, and quite a lot of them are proud of me, and I sincerely hope that, through my work, they will continue to be, but the knowledge of this abstract affection and pride will not sustain me when I am old and tired if I haven't enough money to live on after all my triumphant years.

So that is that and when I have finished with *Blithe Spirit* in Hollywood[1] I shall spend a few days in New York and then fly to Bermuda and buy a house. Actually the idea of spending a month or so a year in Bermuda rather appeals to me. I'm not mad about the place but the air is wonderful and I can write in peace. Lornie is going back to England on the twenty-first and will immediately put my principal pictures up for sale at Christie's. She will also put Goldenhurst up for sale and sell the Jaguar. She and Cole will form a

1 The television production for CBS.

company, Corolen Ltd, to take over Gerald Road, and when I return in May I shall stay at the Savoy.

All this is very drastic and I suppose I should feel more sentimental pangs than I actually do. If Goldenhurst is sold I shall mind dreadfully, but perhaps it won't be. If it isn't, Corolen will have to take that over too. The programme of the next few years seems as ideal as I could wish. I *love* moving about. I *love* having houses in different places. I can spend a few months a year here at Firefly, a month or so coming and going in Bermuda, three months a year if I wish to in England, and as much time as I have to in America. On capital transactions such as films and television rights, I can go out for large sums to be paid directly into my Bermuda company. There will be no need to spread the payments over years to avoid tax because there just won't be any tax at all. It is almost unbelievable.

For a creative artist, someone who carries his factory about with him, to have domicile in England is no longer sensible. It is impossible to live there and keep your head above financial water. I have paid God knows how many hundreds of thousands of pounds to the British Government during my life and the privileges I have received in return are actually negligible. I love England with my roots and I would never become an alien citizen and renounce my allegiance to it, but I'll be god-damned if I'm going to allow myself to be rooked any more. Bermuda is a British crown colony and I am and shall remain a Britisher and, I hope, a bloody sight richer one.

I have done fifty pages of *Pomp and Circumstance* and will return to it when I get back. In the meantime Firefly is practically finished and in my absence Coley is going to furnish it and get it boat-shaped for me to move into – pronto.

I leave tomorrow for Havana where I stay one night, then to Mexico where I have two nights and a day, then Hollywood on my fifty-sixth birthday. The joke will certainly be on me if one of the planes I take elects to plunge me into eternity, but if it does my first gesture in the afterlife will be to form a limited company, establish residence and set about avoiding (not evading) any celestial income tax that may be demanded of me.

I have just read a book called *How Not to Write a Play* by Walter Kerr[1]. Quite a lot of it is intelligent and well-written but the net result is sterile. He is an excellent dramatic critic, the best, I think, in America at the moment, but like all critics, poor beasts, he devotes too much time to analyses of motives, largely imagined, and, although he begins by being objective, little by little his own ego obtrudes itself and he makes you aware of how much *he* has read and how clever *he* is, none of which is offensive but merely vitiates his arguments.

It's no use, I must face the fact that I find literary and dramatic criticism

1 Walter Kerr, drama critic of the *New York Times*.

tedious, and always have. Even Shaw and Max Beerbohm are only, to me, readable in very small doses when they are criticizing their fellow artists. I am unable to work up any real interest in what so-and-so has to say about Shakespeare's object in writing such-and-such. I would rather read such-and-such and draw my own conclusions or, better still, draw no conclusions at all; just enjoy it and marvel at the poetry, the choice of words, the dexterity, the depths of emotional understanding and so on. I don't want to peep behind the scenes and scuffle about backstage while the ideas and lyrical phrases are waiting for their entrances. I don't really care if Shakespeare wrote the Sonnets to Willy Herbert or to Mary Fitton; 'Shall I compare thee to a summer's day?' is enough.

I would certainly be interested enough in any proven facts about the causes of a writer's inspiration. I would be fascinated to read personal letters from which I could form my own opinions, but I am *not* interested in the inevitably prejudiced theories of professional critics. Shaw, with all his brilliance and dynamic talent, was shrill and foolish when he discussed Shakespeare. And, I suspect, equally invalid when he discussed Wagner. Max Beerbohm, with all his wit and satirical humour, becomes strangely watery when he scratches at the giants. Dear Alec Woollcott's views, when spoken, were amusing and provocative; on paper they are neither, but become rigid and somehow trite.

Willie Maugham, on the other hand, I find enchanting when he embarks on literary criticism, perhaps because it isn't so much literary criticism as an entirely objective assessment of what he likes or dislikes and why. He is too sure an artist himself to lay down the law and *his* ego never obtrudes suddenly when you are not expecting it. It doesn't need to obtrude because it is there all the time, benevolently or apparently benevolently, in charge of the whole proceedings and in complete control from the first line to the last. Unlike Mr Kerr or the industrious Mr Tynan, he never overwrites. He has never, since his very early youth, become besotted with words, drunk on the Oxford Dictionary.

Verbal diarrhoea is a major defect in many American writers. They have learnt assiduously *too many words* and they wish you to know that they know *far more words* than other people and, what is more, long and complicated words. This adolescent crowing becomes quite deafening sometimes and gets between them and what they are trying to say. Every now and then, after a tortuous sentence fairly shimmering with emotion, they suddenly introduce a vulgarism, a slang phrase, such as 'phoney' or 'That's okay by me'. This, I am sure, is a subconscious desire to prove that in spite of their impressive learning they are in fact 'regular guys' like you or me. On a higher level Mr T. S. Eliot is an enthusiastic employer of this trick. He will give you a lyric passage filled with moonshine and romantic symbolism and then suddenly say 'garbage' or 'manure'. A tiresome habit to my mind, because it is coy and pretentious, almost arch. It also betrays insecurity.

Christmas Day   Beverly Hills

In the middle of it all again[1]. This house is really very nice and I have a dusky Jamaican lady to look after me who is lackadaisical and hums constantly. There have been a series of parties as usual, each one indistinguishable from the other, culminating last night in the Bogarts' Christmas Eve revel which was great fun and highly glamorous to the eye. The Christmas shopping has been frantic as usual. Clifton is sweet but inclined to bouts of slightly bibulous self-pity on account of being lonely. Mabelle is indestructible and gets on his nerves, also he has no picture settled, so he is idle. We had a successful reading of the play at the Bogarts' last Sunday and everyone read well. Betty Bacall[2] will be good, I think, and anyhow she is word perfect which is wonderful considering she was shooting a picture until yesterday.

I have acquired some nice Christmas loot. Exquisite gold and ebony monogrammed links from Frank Sinatra, and a lovely black dressing-gown and pyjamas to match from Marlene, and hand-worked bedroom slippers from Merle which are charming. A lot of other nice gifts too, but oh I *do* wish Christmas hadn't coincided with *Blithe Spirit*. There is so much to be done and, it seems, so little time to do it.

1 To start rehearsing the television production in Hollywood of *Blithe Spirit*.
2 Lauren (Betty) Bacall was playing Elvira opposite Noël's Charles.

= 1956 =

*A year of quite remarkable turbulence and activity; it brought two long-
lasting London stage successes,* South Sea Bubble *and* Nude with Violin,
*both of which light comedies overcame grudging Press reaction and settled
in to long popular runs, proving yet again that nobody in the post-war world
liked Noël except the public. He himself spent much of the year in America,
appearing on television there to considerable acclaim in his own adaptations
of his* Blithe Spirit *(broadcast live from California) and* This Happy
Breed *(broadcast live from New York). He also found the time to record
another long-playing album of his own songs, give a lengthy person-to-
person television interview to Ed Murrow, and narrate Ogden Nash's verse
for* Carnival of the Animals *at Carnegie Hall.*

*But this was also the year when his resolution to settle abroad for tax
reasons made every front page in Britain, and brought down upon his absent
but still caring head a torrent of journalistic abuse. The fact that he was
leaving England to avoid future taxation rather than money already owed
to the Inland Revenue, and the fact that it was still every Englishman's
inalienable right to live where he chose, escaped largely unnoticed. Noël was
the first publicized figure to leave Britain for tax reasons in the 1950s, and
he paid a price unknown to the hundreds of actors, singers and footballers
who were later to follow in his footsteps.*

Sunday 1 January   Palm Springs

Graham and I drove here this morning to stay with Frankie [Sinatra] and the Bogarts. It is enjoyable but not the acme of peace on account of people of all shapes and sizes swirling through this very small house like the relentless waves of the sea. Their swirling is accompanied by a bongo drum band in the living-room. Tonight we are dining *en masse* at the Beachcomber. Frankie is enchanting as usual and, as usual, he has a 'broad' installed with whom he, as well as everyone else, is bored stiff. She is blonde, cute and determined, but I fear her determination will avail her very little with Betty Bacall on the warpath. The Danny Kayes, the Vidors, the Romanoffs[1], the Goldwyns, Lucille Ball[2], Mike Todd, etc., are all in and out and the noise is considerable. Bogey pushed Irving Lazar[3] into the pool and Irving Lazar pushed Bogey into the pool and there is a great deal of 'fucking' and 'shitting' and other indications that the new year will be no less bawdy than the old one. The prevailing chaos is curiously dominated by Frankie, who contrives, apparently without effort, to be cheerful and unflagging and, at the same time, sees that everyone has drinks and is looked after. He is a remarkable personality – tough, vulnerable and somehow touching. He is also immeasurably kind.

I was right when I prophesied at Blue Harbour that Claudette [Colbert] was likely to be tiresome. She has been. *Extremely* tiresome. To begin with she arrived at the first rehearsal[4] not yet knowing the words, after I had particularly asked her to be word perfect, with the first act anyway. She explained that this was not her method and that she had been a star for twenty-five years. In the second place, she is exceedingly bossy. In the third place, she can only be photographed on one side of her face, so all grouping of scenes has to be arranged accordingly. In the fourth place, she has changed her mind right and left over her dresses and now nothing is likely to be ready in time. In the fifth place, she is determined to play Ruth as a mixture of Mary Rose and Rebecca of Sunnybrook Farm, and very, very slowly. I have already had two stand-up fights with her, not very edifying and a hideous waste of time.

All this is a sad pity because, if she troubled to play the part for what it is worth, she would be very good. She is, within her limits, an excellent actress and these limits she imposes on herself. I have for years had a definite affection for her as a person, but these rehearsals are wilting it considerably. Betty is charming and no trouble; also, unfortunately, no comedienne, but she moves

1 Mike Romanoff (1890–1972) was a penniless European immigrant who assumed and later renounced the title of Prince, and became a successful Hollywood restaurateur.
2 Lucille Ball (b. 1910), American actress and comedienne.
3 Irving Lazar, Hollywood literary agent known as 'Swifty' for his business acumen.
4 Of *Blithe Spirit* in which she was playing Ruth.

beautifully, looks ravishing and is trying like mad. Mildred Natwick[1] is wonderful: true, subtle and hilariously funny without ever being in the least grotesque. She will make a fabulous success.

I visited Ethel Barrymore[2], who was entrancing, sitting up in bed and exuding magnetism and charm, but I fear she is pretty ill. It was lovely talking to her. Fritzi [Massary] too I have visited. She is as bright as a button and brimming with vitality. She went back to Europe in the summer and this made her realize that Hollywood was not really a suitable place for her to end her days. I don't think she will stay much longer. These two encounters with these two great old stars renewed much of my theatrical enthusiasm. I am sure that they also were fiends in their heyday but, my God, they *did* deliver the goods and now with most, if not all, passion spent they seem so wise and assured compared with the lesser fry.

Wednesday 11 January   Beverly Hills

Three days of agony and despair and the first preview[3] before a picked audience tomorrow evening! On Monday, our first day of camera blocking, I woke in great pain and was barely able to move my right leg. I went to Clifton [Webb]'s doctor and asked him to inject the painful part of my thigh with Novocaine so that I could at least get through rehearsal. He obligingly inserted a large needle, upon which a lot of pus shot out. Cultures and x-rays were taken and he decided that I had an abscess on my sciatic nerve. By this time I was so sick with pain that I couldn't stand. Clifton and Graham got me home to bed where I have been, heavily doped, until today.

This afternoon I insisted on going to rehearsal. My stand-in had been carrying on for me, and Claudette hadn't been any too helpful and anyhow I *had* to go through the play with cameras and establish my positions. I hobbled down to the studio on a stick and watched the first run-through from the booth. My understudy was word perfect and dull, but quite adequate.

When I got up to play the second run-through, my leg, from being in one position for an hour and a half, had seized up and was agony. The doctor was sent for and injected the damn thing eight times with the thickest needle I have ever seen. This was, I think, the most agonizing pain I have ever endured and I lay, bright green and trembling, for a quarter of an hour after it. Charles [Russell], who had been standing outside the door, nearly fainted. I only wish that I could have *quite* fainted. However, the Novocaine apparently did the trick and numbed the pain and I managed to struggle through. I am now in bed feeling completely drained and slightly panic-stricken. However, the pain is definitely better.

1 Mildred Natwick (b. 1908), American actress.
2 Ethel Barrymore (1879-1959), distinguished American actress of stage and screen.
3 Before the live telecast of *Blithe Spirit*.

Sunday 15 January

It is all over and a triumphant success. How it managed to be I shall never know. On Thursday I woke completely free of pain – an absolute miracle – I can only conclude that the Novocaine frightened the bloody abscess to death. We went through the play twice during the day and gave a performance to most of Hollywood in the evening, not a very slick performance. Claudette uncertain and far, far too slow. After everyone had come backstage and said how gorgeous it all was and buggered off, I asked Claudette to play a bit faster, whereupon she flew at me and refused point blank. I kept my temper with difficulty and allowed myself only one riposte, which was when she said bitterly, 'Don't worry dear, you'll never have to see me again after Saturday', to which I replied that it was not *after* Saturday that was worrying me but until and *during* Saturday.

The next morning I woke feeling dreadful. Someone had said that I was too 'grim' in my scenes with Claudette, and I realized that if I or she allowed our personal feelings to show the play would be ruined. So, crushing down my pride manfully, I called her up, apologized abjectly for everything including being born and coaxed her round to amiability. *Then* we went to the studio to see the kinescope of last night's performance. Oh, dear. It really wasn't very good. There were terrific arguments, in the course of which I roared for more close-ups and better lighting. Claudette and I remained Paolo and Francesca throughout the day. This *rapprochement* with me released her completely to boss everyone else about. She spent a happy few hours telling everyone what to do, how to do it and where to stand while doing it. Then we gave our second preview; not much better than the first, but a little. More people came round and said how absolutely wonderful we all were, and then Harry Ackerman[1] informed me that we were two and a half minutes over time. So I sat down then and there and we cut judiciously some more good lines.

The next morning at 9.30 we saw the second kinescope. Owing to a genuine, but most unfortunate, oversight Claudette had not been told and had to be sent for. She arrived just at the end, fuming and with her hair in curlers. She insisted on seeing the whole thing through, so we left her to it, but not before I had delivered a calculated tirade to the 'experts' about close-ups. I fairly let fly and when I had finished there was no comeback from anyone except the wretched Harry Ackerman, who said he had some other notes, to which I replied that no other notes were necessary and all I wanted was close-ups and more close-ups. Then down we went to rehearse and re-set most of the shots.

Meanwhile Claudette sat alone in the projection room facing the unpalatable truth that owing to her muddling and insistence on only being photographed from one side, during the breakfast scene particularly, all that was to be seen

1 Harold Ackerman, the show's director.

of her was her famous left jaw line, whereas I was in full face close-up throughout. We re-set a few shots but there wasn't, of course, much time.

We went on the air at 6.30, having worked up to 5.45. During this fascinating period I had about seventeen cups of black coffee, one hot-dog and a Dexamyl. When the play started I bounced on and, thank God, the curious miracle that happened to me last time happened again. I played without nerves and *on* nerves, and felt oddly detached as though I were watching myself from outside. The result was that the performance went like a bomb. Claudette played her hysterical scene well, her first scene too slowly and too sweetly, and managed to bitch up two of her best speeches by fluffing and gasping and panting. She wore tangerine lace in the first act, black and pearls in the second and a grey ghost dress that would have startled Gypsy Rose Lee. Her appearance throughout was charming and entirely inappropriate to the part and the play. We parted lovingly at the end and that was that.

Clifton gave a *gentil* 'company' party to which we all went except Claudette, who lost the way because, she explained to Clifton later, she had mislaid his address. To mislay both Clifton's address and a perfectly good friendship in one evening is quite an achievement. God preserve me in future from female stars. I don't suppose he will, but I might conceivably do something about this myself. I really am too old to go through all these tired old hoops.

Sunday 22 January   Bermuda

The wind is blowing, the rain is crashing down, it is very cold and I have no heater in my bedroom. The flat shapes of Bermuda are vaguely discernible through the wild weather and the outlook is disconsolate. I have had two letters, one from Gladys and one from Joyce, sadly attempting to dissuade me from my project[1]. They have obviously had a get-together and Gladys has been doing a bit of propaganda. They have, I think, got hold of the wrong end of the stick. Joyce, judging by the very discreet tone of her letter, has written against her will. At all events the letters have depressed me and I am tired anyhow. Whatever happens I do not intend to make any final decision until we have discussed the whole project exhaustively from every angle. From what I can gather it will not be possible to play any tricks. Goldenhurst must genuinely be put up for sale and stripped bare of furniture. So also must Gerald Road. This is a bad wrench and, of course, sentimentally I feel miserable. Yes, it is a wrench all right, but I *know* I cannot maintain Goldenhurst *and* Jamaica, and it will be better to say goodbye now, when I can at least profit by it, than wait for a few years and be forced to part with it at a loss of thousands. In the meantime I intend to start house-hunting here with Graham tomorrow.

We left Hollywood last Tuesday and flew to New York, arriving on Wednes-

1 To take up residence in Bermuda.

day morning. We lunched with Jack, who looked puffy and ill and was obviously straining every nerve to give a good performance of being perfectly all right. It is horrid and tragic and I hate all of it.

In the evening Marlene, Graham and I dined at Sardi's and went to see *Fallen Angels* which, strange to say, is a hit. Nancy Walker, who has had rave notices, is, I must admit, hilariously funny. She is frequently outrageous but never vulgar as Hermione Baddeley was. The play got considerably lost in the process but I recognized a few of my lines here and there. The audience rolled in the aisles, and everyone was delighted.

Last night we went to *A Hatful of Rain*[1]. Shelley Winters, Ben Gazzara and Antonio Franciosa, the latter marvellous, the other two excellent. The play squalid, exciting, melodramatic, theatrically effective. A lot of dope-ridden, neurotic twitchings and groanings and some very, very plain speaking. No particular message but a great deal of social significance.

Sunday 29 January

The die is cast all right[2] and from now on no repining. There have been two good days this week, the rest depressing in the extreme. We have traipsed back and forth over the island roads with a pleasant house-agent in a tiny Morris. He has bad teeth but is quite efficient. Prices in Bermuda are astronomical and none of the houses we have seen, except one, is the faintest good. The one, however, is charming and is called Spithead Lodge. The price at the moment is £23,000 furnished, but it may be possible to get it for £17,000 or £18,000 unfurnished, half on mortgage. This is a terrific price, of course, but considering what I shall eventually gain by having it, it will surely be worth it.

Dingo [Bateson] insists that there be no chicanery and that both Gerald Road and Goldenhurst must be put up for sale before 5 April, which is the beginning of the financial year. I must not set foot in England on any pretext between now and April 1957, and then only by special dispensation and for a very brief visit. After 1957, however, I can return every year for not more than three months. Apart from the first year, this in no way dismays me. I don't wish or intend to stay in England for more than three months in any year. Graham and Coley will return in March and help Lornie with the packing up and disposal of furniture, etc. Patience [Erskine] will stay on at Goldenhurst as gardener and the Evanses as caretakers. If and when the house is sold I will build her a cottage somewhere nearby. Graham will take a flat in London, which he and Cole will share when they are in England. Lorn will set up the office in her own house. I have immediately to resign my presidency of the Actors' Orphanage, which frankly is a great relief; it has cost me a lot of time,

1 By Michael V. Gazzo.
2 He had definitely decided to settle in Bermuda.

energy and money for twenty years and is now established on a more solid basis than it has ever been.

The great snag is *South Sea Bubble*, which opens in Manchester on 19 March with Vivien [Leigh], Alan [Webb], Arthur [Macrae], Joyce, Ian Hunter and Peter Finch, a wonderful cast. It is supposed to open in London at the end of April, but I have written to Binkie imploring him to play two extra weeks out of London and let the last week be in Dublin, where I can fly to see it after my television on 5 May. I do so much hope he will be able to, otherwise I may never see it at all unless Vivien and the public are prepared to endure it for over a year which, to say the least, is doubtful.

John Gielgud has postponed *Nude with Violin* until the summer because, owing to surtax troubles, he has to do a film of *The Barretts of Wimpole Street* with Jennifer Jones.

My heart is lighter than it was. There's no sense in shilly-shallying about. I *must* save something for my declining years and this is the only possible way to do it, so to hell with *nostalgie du temps perdu* and away with regrets. Life is so full of a number of things.

Sunday 12 February   Jamaica

I have been putting myself through a rigorous course of play reading in order to get myself into the right mood for work. During the last few days I have read the following: *Strife, Mid Channel, The Wild Duck, The Liars, Six Characters in Search of an Author, Riders to the Sea, The Red Robe, Post Mortem*[1], *Hay Fever* and *Hotel Universe*. I enjoyed most of them, especially *Post Mortem*, which is much better than I thought it was even when I wrote it. On looking back I think that it was foolish of me not to have had it produced at the time. It is wise to listen to other people's opinions but not always wise to be guided by them. Alec [Woollcott] adored the witty side of me but distrusted my sentiment. He had a perfect right to say what he thought, but I had no right to allow myself to be so easily swayed by anyone so peculiarly prejudiced as Alec and a critic into the bargain! *Post Mortem* is passionately sincere and just as important a facet of my talent as *Private Lives*. They are in no way comparable, any more than *Bitter Sweet* is comparable with *Design for Living* or *Cavalcade* with *Blithe Spirit*. I should have realized more strongly then that with my prolific output it is impossible to please all discerning people. Winifred [Ashton], for instance, loves me and my work but detests *Bitter Sweet*, whereas most people consider it one of my best works. *I* love *Quadrille*, although all the English and most of the American critics tore it to shreds. There are even people extant who rave about poor *Operette*, whereas I think it was a very weak sister indeed. I think on the whole I am a

1   An anti-war, anti-Beaverbrook play, which was written (in 1930) by Noël, as was *Hay Fever*.

better writer than I am given credit for being. It is fairly natural that my writing should be casually appreciated because my personality, performances, music and legend get in the way. Some day, I suspect, when Jesus has definitely got me for a sunbeam, my works may be adequately assessed.

Reading those old plays was interesting. *Strife* is first rate all through. *The Red Robe* excellent until the implausibility of the last act. *The Wild Duck* bitter and fine. *Six Characters* pretentious and confused. *Riders to the Sea* so over-Irish as to be burlesque. *Mid Channel* well constructed but badly written. *The Liars* extremely well done and, although limited by its period, a rattling good comedy. Dear *Hay Fever* still funny and comparatively undated, and *Hotel Universe* a fine idea with some good moments.

Sunday 19 February

The swift result of my intensive bout of play reading was that I sprang at *Present Laughter* like a surgeon and carved an hour and ten minutes out of it[1] without, I think, impairing its essential quality. There was a moment, I admit, when I strode up and down the room quivering with panic and despair crying, 'I can't! I can't! It's no good going on, the play is too tightly constructed to whittle down to an hour and twenty minutes, and by eliminating the majority of its sex implications so that millions of Bible-thumping, puritanical, asinine televiewers should not have their half-baked sensibilities outraged, I shall emasculate the whole thing and have nothing left but a febrile shambles of mangled witticisms.'

However, I wriggled my way out of this Slough of Despond and pressed on valiantly, and now it is done. It will play, as far as I can judge, just under the prescribed time and, strange to say, it is still funny, still entertaining and still a magnificent star part for me. This cutting of my plays down for television is certainly a salutary experience, and I believe that the next time I embark on a full-length play for the theatre, I shall find that I have profited by it. I shall have learned, for instance, to dispense with amusing irrelevancies that have no direct bearing on the story and to get back to my original method of saying what I have to say in as few lines as possible with a minimum of atmospheric padding and linguistic flourishes.

This time I intend to take no chances over the technical side. I am going to plan for camera angles and close-ups from the very beginning. I am also, I devoutly hope, not going to allow myself to be irritated and thrown out of gear by the tantrums of ageing leading ladies. These are brave words, I know, and may turn out to be whistling in the dark. No one can accurately foresee or circumvent the diverse and exasperating exigencies of female stars, but in *Present Laughter* at least mine is the dominant role and whoever plays Liz or Joanna can be handled more effectively than Ruth in *Blithe Spirit*,

1 For American television.

which was a key part upon the playing of which I largely depended for my effects.

I have had a cable from Binkie saying that the reading of *South Sea Bubble* was a great success and that the cast is excellent. I also had another cable from him saying that it was very unlikely that he could do the play in Dublin for a week before the London opening. Apparently there are complications about availability of theatre, etc. This is a great disappointment to me. I have cabled back imploring him to strain every nerve. If he fails I shall have to face it with fortitude and reflect that, even without seeing *South Sea Bubble*, I shall be gaining a great deal more than I am losing. I have written officially to the Actors' Orphanage resigning my presidency and privately to the committee and the subscribers, explaining my reasons. My cottage at Roundhill has been sold for $35,000, which gives me a profit of £3,000. I think this is the first time I have ever sold anything at a profit in my life. It seems that money begets money, and perhaps at long last I may be on the way to real solvency and get enough money in the bank and invested to guarantee a reasonably affluent old age. It seems too good to be true.

There is a 'great freeze' in dear green England and the Government has imposed still more restrictions on gracious living. Anthony Eden's[1] popularity has spluttered away like a blob of fat in a frying-pan. The Queen and the Duke of Edinburgh have returned from their triumphant tour of Nigeria, in the course of which they attended countless religious services and encountered a great many quaint native children who danced for them, sang at them, and presented them with humble bouquets and various specimens of native crafts. There is a rumour that Princess Margaret is about to become a Roman Catholic. This was started by the American *Daily News* which, as we all know, is in constant contact with the Vatican.

A.A. Milne[2] has died. Lord Beaverbrook has not. Mr Attlee – Lord Attlee – has been involved in a minor motor accident. Larry and Vivien have decided to present a united front to a deeply concerned world, and so Peter Finch is *not* going to be her leading man in my play or out of it. Larry is going to make a movie of *The Sleeping Prince* with Marilyn Monroe, which might conceivably drive him round the bend but, as I always say, *il faut vivre* and, after his ill-paid season at Stratford, during which he gave the greatest performances of his career and was miserable throughout owing to poor darling Vivien's carry-ons, a good, solid, commercial enterprise will be very comforting and to hell with eminence.

I have taken to cooking and listening to Wagner, both of which frighten me to death.

1 Anthony Eden had succeeded Winston Churchill as Prime Minister in 1955.
2 A.A. Milne (1882–1956), British author, famous as the creator of Winnie-the-Pooh.

Sunday 26 February

On account of my 'great decision' and the plans and discussions between Graham and Cole and me, and the letters and cables flying to and fro across the Atlantic, and the uncertainty as to whether Binkie will be able to arrange to play *South Sea Bubble* in Dublin or not, the air is altogether too full of wild surmise to permit me to settle down to my novel. There is also the pressure of time, because in five weeks from now I shall be in New York beginning rehearsals for *Present Laughter*. Therefore I have decided to utilize my peaceful mornings by writing a tentative film script.

It is as light as the sensational omelette Cole and I made the night before last: a brittle, stylized, sophisticated, insignificant comedy with music and it is called *Later than Spring*. It is about a fascinating *femme du monde* (Marlene) and an equally fascinating but prettier *homme du monde* (me), a fairly fascinating American young man and young woman (possibly Van Johnson and Betsy Drake), and an articulate pair of companion secretaries (Graham and Marti Stevens). The intricate course of the story will be plainly obvious to the audience from the very beginning, and from the suspense point of view it will be as unexpected as *Così Fan Tutte*, but I hope the dialogue and lyrics and general treatment will redeem its apparent banality and make it a successful entertainment. At the moment I am enjoying it enormously. I feel the urge to make another movie and also to appear on the silver screen in a lighter mood than I have hitherto. In *The Scoundrel* I was drowned and spent a lot of time in the water; in *In Which We Serve* I was submerged in a tank for a large part of the picture, and in *The Astonished Heart* I was utterly miserable, soaked with rain and finally committed suicide. I would like to play a part in which I was cheerful throughout and bone dry. I feel also that from the vulgar financial point of view this ought to be a profitable idea and, what to me is most important, it would be fun to do. However, we shall see how it progresses.

The *Daily Express* has come out with a stirring 'more in sorrow than in anger' article explaining that I am giving up English residence and selling Goldenhurst and Gerald Road, etc. On the whole the article is mild and quite amiable, but it has apparently caused quite a stir and I cannot feel that it can do anything but good. Apart from a myriad journalistic inaccuracies, it is basically true. I *am* giving up English residence and selling properties there and I *am* becoming a resident of Bermuda, and my reasons are as clear as my conscience, but I suspect that there will be a certain amount of head-shaking and disapproval from those of my friends who have not taken the trouble to assess the situation realistically. Among these is Gladys, who is apparently outraged by the whole project. This is silly of her but typical. Her judgement has always been faulty ever since Munich[1].

1 Unlike Noël, she had approved of Neville Chamberlain's 1938 peace agreement.

I had a loving letter from Patience [Erskine], whom the whole business obviously affects more than anyone else. It's a very good letter indeed and I salute her for it. She makes no bones about being upset and sad but she also sees my reasons clearly. What she doesn't know, however, is that I will see to it that she always lives there, where she is happy. Of course, I still have certain tugs at the heart-strings, but they are lessening because although goodbyes are sad I have found from experience that once they are said and the tears have dried, the sun comes out again and the future takes on new and exciting possibilities. The immediate years ahead seem to me to be fraught with interest and adventure.

I had an enchanting cable from Vivien last night. Rehearsals are apparently going well and she is straining every nerve to try to arrange the Dublin week. So there is still perhaps a little hope, because she is a determined girl and usually manages to get her own way. It is miraculous that she is now, it appears, completely herself again and the second crack-up, which I thought was inevitable, has been averted. I am deeply fond of her and of Larryboy, and it really does look as though they have arrived at a sensible working arrangement. I have a feeling that *South Sea Bubble* had a good deal to do with it, and if this is true then I am gladder than ever.

Cole and I have cooked dinner every night this week. I am inclined to put in far too much flavouring, as in painting I put in far too much colour, but I am learning restraint. I am also learning to be fearless with eggs and undismayed by deep fat and flour and breadcrumbs. It all comes under the heading of living dangerously and maybe the day will come when I can cook a joint, stuff a chicken's arse with butter, and make pastry so light that it flies away at a touch. My solo triumphs to date have been a chocolate mousse (plus cinnamon, Nescafé and Crème de Cacao), some rather curiously shaped croquettes, Kitchener eggs, sensational salad dressing with bacon rinds, various experimental soups originating from tins but rising to ambrosial heights after my pudgy fingers have been busy with herbs and garlic, and last but by no means least a *coquille* of shrimps and smoked oysters.

The house and the paving outside is, or are, now virtually finished. Graham dashes about planting bananas, Spathodea, flowering shrubs and grass. Sylvia Foot brought us some orchids, which we have clamped to the trees on the patio where they appear to be flourishing.

Capital punishment in England has almost, but not quite, been abolished. Apparently Anthony [Eden], with an unexpected display of obstinacy, has dug his trotters in and is fighting the repeal tooth and claw. I entirely agree with him. I realize that it is horrible that human beings should be arbitrarily despatched from this vale of tears but, by and large, I have little sympathy with murderers. I don't think that arrogant young delinquents who batter old ladies to death, roving ex-corporals who rape ladies in woods and then strangle them with nylons, and husbands who gleefully poison their wives with arsenic are likely to become reputable citizens after twenty years' confinement, and I don't think that the British taxpayer should have to support them until some future date when they are liable to emerge and very possibly kill someone else. I am sure that the fear of the gallows is a strong deterrent and I feel that the humanitarians who are so eager to abolish it are guilty of woolly thinking. *Crimes passionnels* and murder under extreme provocation are a different matter entirely, and I think, when adequately tried and proved, should be treated with mercy. But cold-blooded, premeditated murderers who kill for money or insurance policies or because, for their own convenience, they want someone out of the way, should be despatched from this world as swiftly and efficiently as possible.

Sunday 4 March

All hopes of seeing *South Sea Bubble* in Dublin are now dead. I had a long letter from Binkie explaining that, apart from the date difficulties, which might have been overcome, Ronald Lewis[1], who is playing Hali in place of Peter Finch, has a contract with London Films which stipulates no more than five weeks' try-out. So that is that, and the play will open in Manchester on 19 March and in London at the Lyric on 25 April. This is, of course, a disappointment but I am rising above it.

A cable arrived yesterday from Lornie saying that Gerald Road had been definitely sold for £11,000. This, although obviously good news, depressed Graham, Cole and me very much. It is worse for them than for me really because they will have to go back and pack it up and wander about the memory-sodden rooms, touching the walls and furniture like Madame Ranevska and saying their adieux, whereas I am at least making a clean cut. It is nonetheless horrid to feel that I shall never live there again, never 'have relish in the magic power' of walking briskly up the alleyway, bounding up the stairs, leaving a 'To be called' note on the round table and retiring to my cosy little bedroom where, let's face it, *a great deal* has occurred during the last twenty-six years. The myriad 'somethings on a tray', the mornings after opening nights, the interminable telephone conversations, the morning seances with Lorn, the ideas conceived, the plans made and, above all, the jokes – the rich, wonderful jokes – with Lorn and Cole and Graham roaring with laughter and me hopping out of bed in the middle of all the hilarity and rushing down to the loo. As Sylvia Cecil sang with such lyric gusto in *Ace of Clubs*, 'Nothing can last for ever', and, as many a prima donna has sung with equal gusto and superior orchestration, '*Adieu notre petite table*'. I hope that whoever occupies that lovely place will have as happy a time in it as I have had.

I have had a long letter from Gladys, who is in Italy, a very good letter and

1 Ronald Lewis (1928–82), British actor.

a comfort. She has apparently got over her dismay and now sees the point of the whole business.

The opening of the new 'Designs for Living' premises[1] was a great success. The local Canon, with a bang, opened the proceedings and blessed the enterprise, imploring the Almighty, without whose personal supervision the designs of man are but as nought, to look kindly on our endeavours. I do hope that if the Almighty is really going to take an interest he will find some means of dissuading Mrs Phillips from sewing sequin flowers on to raffia baskets, but I fear that this is too much to ask[2]. After the canon had mildly thundered, I sprang on to a table and made a speech declaring the whole thing open. It was all very sweet really and lots of local friends rallied round.

Charles [Russell] is arriving on Tuesday and Ham [Lance Hamilton] at about the same time, to discuss the casting of *Present Laughter*. Bill Paley and CBS are most anxious for me *not* to do it but they haven't yet read my expurgated script and perhaps will feel differently when they do. In any event I intend to do it whether they like it or not. It is a wonderful part for me and I shall not be too dependent on fractious leading ladies. I am *not* looking forward to it; whether I do it in Hollywood or New York, it is bound to be irritating, frustrating and exhausting but I shall murmur to myself in moments of crisis, as I did during *Blithe Spirit*, 'Thirty thousand pounds, thirty thousand pounds, thirty thousand pounds!' and, with this artistic ideal constantly shimmering before my mind's eye, I shall press on and do my utmost to make it as, if not more, successful than the other two have been. In my innermost heart I doubt if I can really pull it off a third time. However, even if the worst happens and it is a flop, it is the last one and after it I shall be free for a little while.

The film script is coming along, but slowly, as with so much on my mind I find it impossible to concentrate for long. There is so much in the air, so many plans and arrangements to be made, so much necessary switching of the mind from one thing to another. Also there is the time pressure. In under a month from now I shall be in Bermuda again and then New York for my appearance at the Carnegie Hall with Kostelanetz and the New York Philharmonic[3]. This, of course, won't be much trouble but will take a certain amount of time. Then *Present Laughter* and then Paris. I shall probably go by sea because by that time I shall need a little opportunity to put myself down and unwind a bit.

---

1 The local craft business sponsored by Noël had moved to a larger building.
2 Mrs Phillips was one of the most stalwart workers of 'Designs for Living' who, unlike Noël, had realized that a successful local souvenir did not need to be tasteful.
3 Noël had agreed to narrate Ogden Nash's verse to Saint-Saëns's *Carnival of the Animals*.

Sunday 18 March

I feel relaxed, happy and bursting with endeavour, and all because the Ford Motor Company, with a waspish malevolence which is apparently inseparable from really big business, announced in the Press, without warning me, that my next television appearance was cancelled because the ratings on *Together with Music* and *Blithe Spirit* had not been high enough! The first intimation I had of this was an agitated cable from David Holtzmann quoting the Press. The next morning a cable arrived from Charles and Ham explaining a bit more, but not enough. This was naturally a shock and for the moment I felt humiliated and enraged. I decided, then and there, Tuesday morning at 11.30, to fly to New York and investigate. Cole and Graham dashed off to get me on the plane which leaves Montego at 4 p.m. Twenty minutes after they'd left I remembered that my passport was in Kingston. I started off after them in the Austin and met them on the way back, they having realized the same thing. They had, however, made me a reservation. It was by this time 12.30. We telephoned to Elsa Aarons[1] and told her to get hold of Gardiner and his private plane; get him to pick up my passport at Palisades Airport and pick *me* up on the Boscobel airstrip at three o'clock. All of this took an hour of agonized waiting for the telephone to ring. However, it was miraculously accomplished. Graham drove me to the airstrip, where we waited with some goats and horses for the plane to appear. When it did, I clambered in, got to Montego, with passport, five minutes before the plane left.

I got to New York at 9.45 with a light suit, no overcoat, and snow. Charles and Ham were not there to meet me as they had not received Cole's cable. I got their telephone number from Information and told them to make me a reservation at the Essex House and meet me there. They were, naturally enough, in a fine frizz. We ordered chicken sandwiches and I called up Bill Paley, who was harassed in the extreme. I fixed an interview for eleven o'clock the next morning, and then we gave ourselves over to triple rage and planned Press campaigns and this and that, and I finally got to sleep at about four.

The next morning I talked to David Holtzmann, who was quite sensible. The boys arrived and we decided that my only policy was stately reticence and outraged dignity. Poor Bill Paley received us twitching with apprehension, but I soothed him and he was extremely nice and helpful. We drafted a Press statement announcing that my next television appearance had been postponed until October, when I would launch the new CBS *Playhouse 90* series with *This Happy Breed*. Ford and J. Walter Thompson, their advertising agency, had made their announcement to the Press without consulting CBS, obviously to humiliate me as publicly as possible. Unfortunately for them they haven't

1 Elsa Aarons, a local friend.

quite taken into account the fact that my two appearances have been triumphant successes, ratings or no ratings.

Apparently the reason for Ford's rage is that I ridiculed them in my
Hollywood Press interviews[1]. This is quite true and I don't regret it for an
instant, as they were discourteous and idiotic from the very first and tried to
dictate to me about my taste and material. I do not share the almost universal
American reverence for money and sponsors. I like to get the money but not
at the cost of cutting my material. Incidentally, their announcement that my
ratings were inadequate is, according to Bill Paley, untrue.

At all events I decided not to speak to any of the Press at all. The hullabaloo
will soon die down and, oh dear, dear Ford Motor Company, I shall not have
to do another television until October. I shall have time to come back here
alone on 8 April after my Carnegie Hall appearance and concentrate on *Later
than Spring* and my novel. It's a wonderful feeling of release and if only they
knew the favour they'd done me they would be even crosser than they already
are. I was dreading having to do another appearance so soon after the other
two. As things are now, I shall do *Happy Breed* in October with a much better
chance of success because enough time will have elapsed and, after all this
palpably malicious publicity, I shall have the Press well on my side. Above all,
I have 'time stretching before me' and I am as happy as a bee.

All this shindig has had a curiously salutary effect on me. The moment I
was in the plane to New York a metamorphosis began to take place. Like
darling Mum, I fairly blossom in a crisis. I realized I was in for a fight and it
stimulated me. Since I came back here from Bermuda, in spite of the loveliness
of the new house and everything, I have not been really at ease. The 'great
decision' and all its complications were harrying my mind and I felt incapable
of settling down to work with the days flying by so swiftly and New York and
television rushing towards me. Now the cathartic crisis has occurred and I am
smooth again. It's a lovely feeling.

Sunday 25 March

Well! My sense of relief and release and the feeling that time was at last
stretching before me was very short-lived. Now all is changed round again.
The majestic Ford Motor Company have scrambled down from their high
eminence and I am now to do *This Happy Breed* on 5 May as per the original
contract. There have been angry letters in the Press about me being cancelled
and general publicity. Added to their discomfiture, Ford must have realized
that they have nothing prepared for 5 May and that frankly they are up shit
creek without a paddle. My first instinct was to refuse haughtily, but I

---

1 For trying to censor some of Noël's more *risqué* lyrics and also certain lines in *Blithe Spirit*;
  television audiences in the Mid-West were then considered eminently shockable and likely
  to alleviate their outrage by refusing to buy Ford cars.

telephoned the wretched Bill Paley at Roundhill[1] and he urged me, with pulsating sincerity, to do the damned thing on 5 May, and so that is that and now there will be a great hurrying and scurrying about casting and not 'time stretching before me' but a month of feverish activity. All this being so, I have reorganized my plans and my mind once more and, although regretting the vanished peace, feel quite cheerful and definitely exultant. The script of *Happy Breed* is good and, in order to frame it, I have written an introduction explaining the play and the period, and I shall speak the introduction as myself on film.

South Sea Bubble opened at the Opera House, Manchester, last Monday night and was quite definitely a roaring success. I had a batch of enthusiastic cables from Lorn and Larry and Vivien. She has apparently had a comedy triumph and I am so very, very glad for her as well as for myself. It is maddening to think that I shall not be able to pop over from Paris and see it, but I can't have my cake and lie on it. I shall have to be philosophical and reflect on the lovely television dollars clinking into the Bank of Bermuda and the lovely pounds, shillings and pence *not* clinking into the Inland Revenue.

Sunday 1 April   New York

The week has been full of excessive movement and wear and tear and I am frankly exhausted. We flew, uneventfully enough, to New York on Tuesday, Cole and Graham and me, after lunching with the Paleys at Roundhill. The plane was two hours late and so we didn't get into the city and to bed until after 1 a.m. and had to be hauled from sleep at 7 a.m. to catch the morning plane for Bermuda. It was a pleasant flight, however, and we dozed and read and caught a little rest.

In Bermuda the sun shone fitfully but it was none too warm. We spent the whole afternoon at Spithead Lodge taking measurements and were just about to leave when Jack arrived. He looked absolutely ghastly and quite gaga and could hardly stand. I took him over the house and he mumbled appropriate praise.

On the way back to the hotel the horror of it overwhelmed me and I sat in the front seat of the car weeping silently and remembering the past and how handsome he used to be. I don't see how he can live much longer. He has arteriosclerosis from excessive drinking and the only hope, if any, is to force him into a sanatorium. The next morning I delivered what, I pray, will be my last lecture to Jack. He was looking a bit better, not yet having had a nip, and I gave him the works in the despairing hope that I *might* convince him that he *must* do a cure. I was not harsh but I told him some horrid truths. It seems that I did some good but I have no belief that the effect will last.

On Friday night we went to *My Fair Lady*, the musical version of

1 Where he was on holiday.

Pygmalion, which was really quite enchanting from every point of view. Rex Harrison and Julie Andrews are wonderful, score and lyrics excellent, décor and dresses lovely, and the whole thing beautifully presented.

Tuesday 3 April

Cole and Graham have gone winging their way back to England, and I am left in the middle of casting *This Happy Breed* and rehearsing for the Carnegie Hall next Saturday. I hate people I love whizzing, without me, through the perilous air, and it was a great relief to get a cable saying that they had arrived safely. I shall miss them sorely, but it is good for me to be alone again. Not that I am all that alone for I am surrounded with people from morning till night. Charles and Ham wait on me devotedly and there are rehearsals with Kostelanetz, interviews with the Press, and continual discussion about casting.

Monday 9 April

On Saturday night I made my début on the historic stage of the Carnegie Hall. I cannot, much as I would like to, describe it as a triumph. I spoke the verses clearly and well but the lighting, as in all concert halls, was awful; the atmosphere fusty, and the presentation very bad. Kostelanetz insisted on doing *Carnival of the Animals* second on the programme, which was idiotic, so I came on before the audience were warmed up. It didn't really matter but it was bad showmanship. During the morning rehearsal I asked him to let me come on at the end but he said it was impossible. I couldn't for the life of me imagine why until I realized that, had I done so, it would have interfered with his encores!

Last night, however, was much better. Ed Sullivan[1] was really marvellous to me and I did a cut version of *Carnival* and finished with 'Mad Dogs', all of which brought the place down. Poor Kostelanetz was very firmly put in his place. My lighting and photography were wonderful, which was just as well, as apparently I was viewed by fifty-two million people! The whole show was efficiently and professionally run and I thoroughly enjoyed it.

A great deal has happened. First, and most important, Edna Best is going to play Ethel[2]. She has been dreadfully ill with a mental breakdown for months, but the doctors swear she will be all right for this and that it will be therapeutically the best thing in the world for her. However, she cannot go to Hollywood and so I have finally overridden CBS and Ford and insisted on doing the show from here, which is what I wanted all along. This has caused

1 Ed Sullivan, presenter of the television show.
2 In *This Happy Breed*.

a tremendous sensation in television circles and I am suspected of having sinister powers!

There has been a terrific hoo-ha as to whether or not Kay Kendall should play Queenie. She is coming here anyway to live secretly in sin with Rex, which is madness from her point of view. I managed to get Rex to agree[1] and then the silly bitch refused, so she can stew for all I care and I have engaged Patricia Cutts, who read it very well. We start rehearsals next Monday.

Sunday 15 April   New York

Well, here I am settled into my little apartment and happy as a bee pottering about and cooking little delicacies, which I devour sitting in the minute kitchen. There is little crockery but a great many glasses, so I had a field day in Lewis and Conger's where I bought several fascinating gadgets including a resplendent Waring Mixer in which I frizz up milk shakes, etc. Grace, my coloured daily lady, is very, very grand and rather over made-up. She only appears for a couple of hours on weekdays and so today I am faced with doing my own washing-up, which I should quite enjoy if I didn't get quite so wet. This afternoon I am going to the Lunts to be taught how to make pies!

I had a blissful three days with Kit and Guthrie, and learnt my words thoroughly. The cast is now complete and we start rehearsing tomorrow. I am looking forward to it. This play demands truth but not an excess of vitality, and so I shall not have to tear myself to shreds as I have done at the other two performances. In three weeks' time it will all be over and I shall be free again.

Sunday 29 April   Sneden's Landing

Spring has at last arrived and up here, looking out over the Hudson, it is perfectly lovely. Daffodils are out and the sun is shining. I really cannot imagine why people go traipsing off to Long Island or Connecticut when here, only thirty-five minutes from Times Square, there is absolute quiet and considerable beauty.

Rehearsals of *Happy Breed* are progressing wonderfully well. Everyone is word perfect and we still have another week to go. I am playing it better than I played it originally, probably because I am older and know more, but I seem to feel right as Frank Gibbons the moment I come on in the first scene. Edna is giving an exquisite performance as Ethel; true, uncompromising and infinitely touching. She is a fine actress and no trouble at all. When I look back on the bloody hell that Claudette put me through I can hardly believe my good fortune in having a leading lady who goes about her business calmly and methodically and is only concentrated on getting every ounce of reality out of the character rather than fussing about her angles and her clothes and *not*

1 To her playing it.

troubling to learn the words. The whole cast is eager to be good. Patricia Cutts is excellent and should make a success. They are all playing true and I am very happy with them.

South Sea Bubble opened on Wednesday in London[1], and, in spite of the usual tepid patronage from *The Times* and some other papers, is a smash hit. Vivien has had a triumph and apparently the whole cast is good. The first-night audience were apparently stinkers but the company refused to be got down and finally roused them to enthusiasm.

I detest the London first-night atmosphere and I am glad I wasn't there to suffer and be exasperated. My plays are written for the public and not for that small galaxy of scruffy critics and pretentious *savants* who know little and do less.

On Friday night I did a *Person to Person* impromptu interview with Ed Murrow[2] and got away with it very successfully. I am very proud of the fact that I *really* relaxed and refused to let myself be nervous, although it is unquestionably a nerve-racking business. I did it from Charles and Ham's apartment. Having Ed Murrow's voice firing questions at me from the air was a curious sensation. I concentrated on nonchalance and fortunately didn't say anything dreadful.

Guthrie and Kit are being dear as always, and this is a lovely house to stay in. Last night we went to a cocktail party nearby and there was Osbert Sitwell. He has got Parkinson's disease very badly and shakes continually. I felt suddenly dreadfully sorry for him and also admiring because he is not allowing it to get him down. We had a long talk and he couldn't have been nicer. It seems at long last that the age-old feud will be resolved, with a little effort from me. This effort I shall certainly make. The years go by and old venoms lose their potency and there is no longer any time for such foolishness.

Sunday 6 May   New York

Well, it is all over and, it seems, a much greater triumph than either of the other two. Last night, before the credits were over on the screen, CBS had over a thousand telephone calls. Bill Paley called me immediately and told me it was the greatest thing he had ever seen on television. His voice was still husky with emotion. Marlene called, as always, from Hollywood and I have never heard her in such a state. Clifton and the Bogarts called too, also Kit and Guthrie, and countless others. Apparently I gave a really fine performance, a great deal of which I owe to Edna, who was magnificent. She was calm and sure and infinitely touching and I think has made the success of her life. It is so lovely for her after those dreadful months of mental misery in the clinic to come back like this and she has been so dear all through rehearsals that I am

1 At the Lyric Theatre.
2 On American television.

forever in her debt. The rapport between us was so strong that it gave the play a little personal magic that it has never had before either on the stage or the screen. The whole cast played beautifully. No one grabbed opportunities or fluffed or lost their heads and it was an almost perfect production from every point of view. There have naturally been no notices as yet, but I have a feeling that they will be good. What is much more important than either notices or ratings is that *I* know it was good and I feel really proud of having done it.

If it turns out to be the sensational success that Bill Paley assures me it is, this is certainly a very satisfactory round-off to a triumphant year. My enemies have been vanquished, not by any vitriolic replies from me, but merely by a good performance of a good play.

I am feeling happily exhausted because we had a company party at Edna's plus Gladys [Cooper], Cathleen [Nesbitt], Rex, Kay, and Julie Andrews[1], and it went on until after 5 a.m. I also feel happily liberated. Not that I haven't enjoyed all this hard work, but it is lovely to feel that I have no definite commitment whatever and can really relax and get my brain functioning again on other things. It will be heaven to have time to read and write and paint and not have to gird my loins for a while.

The thing that touched and pleased me most last night was a red carnation and telegram from the technical staff wishing me well and thanking me for my confidence in them.

Sunday 13 May   ss *Liberté*

Eh bien me voici, excessivement épuisé, mais gai comme un pinson, apart from the fact that I have an upset stomach, diverticulitis, wind and a touch of lumbago, all of which is entirely understandable because New York is a rat race at the worst of times and, at the best of times, a three-ring circus. This last week has been full and overflowing. The notices of *This Happy Breed* have been fabulous. The New York ones soberly enthusiastic and most heart-warming but they were nothing compared with the raves from Philadelphia, Chicago, Detroit, Los Angeles, San Francisco, etc. The general consensus of opinion is that *This Happy Breed* is the finest telecast ever done and my performance the best of all! Edna, rightly, shares all honours and the entire cast got good notices and immediate offers of jobs from all over the place. This makes me very happy because they all worked wonderfully and gave an all in all team-work performance which was quite remarkable.

The one discordant note in all this is that the rating was lower than either of my other two. This, curiously enough, almost pleases me. I *know* the rating system is inaccurate and unimportant. It couldn't be anything else considering that it excludes New York and the State of California; also, in fairness, I cannot see why ordinary Middle Western families should be expected to sit

1 Julie Andrews (b. 1935), British musical star.

quietly watching a play about London suburbia when, with the turn of a knob, they could see *The Hit Parade*, Jimmy Durante or George Gobel[1], whom they are used to and understand without concentration. If, last week, there had been a spectacular played by Lynn and Alfred, Kit Cornell, Margot Fonteyn, me, Larry and Vivien, Ina Claire and Toscanini[2], and at the same time an interview with Prince Rainier of Monaco[3], there is no doubt that eighty per cent of the millions would have chosen Prince Rainier. This may be deplorable but it is human enough and I have no complaints. The only thing I do complain about is that the sponsors should value ratings as highly as they do. Particularly sponsors like the Ford Motor Company, who sell expensive luxury products. Twenty million teenagers may prefer to see Eddie Fisher and Debbie Reynolds[4] rather than Edna and me, but it doesn't mean that they would all rush out and buy Ford cars, because they couldn't afford to.

What really pleases me is that my three spectaculars have all won unanimous critical acclaim and have been good performances. I have in no way damaged my reputation or my integrity by embarking on this commercial enterprise; on the contrary, I have enhanced my personal prestige enormously and increased my public by many millions. This is much more than I hoped to achieve and, ratings or no ratings, high ratings or low ratings, I feel completely triumphant.

This has certainly been a fantastic year what with one thing and another. Here I am, *me voici*, aged fifty-six, a resident of Bermuda with over £60,000 in the bank, a smash hit in London, and no less than six successful appearances in America to my credit, all within ten months! It is now time to rest a little and remember with quiet glee how short a while ago it was that Beverley Baxter, the dear fellow, asked me if I considered that I had survived the war! If anyone should ever read this they must pardon my gloating. It is certainly a good moment in my life and, on the whole, I think I have earned it, if only for my grisly determination not to let the dismal 'success-resenters' get me down and, God knows, they tried hard enough. In England I know they will go on trying until the day of my death, but I doubt if they will succeed and even if at long last they do, 'They can't take this away from me'.

Before leaving New York on Friday I saw *The Diary of Anne Frank*[5], which has just been awarded the Pulitzer Prize. It is well directed but not a particularly good play, messy and self-pitying, the sort of semi-significant dreariness that usually wins awards. Susan Strasberg, who plays the lead, is about nineteen and has made a terrific success. She plays it well, very well indeed,

---

1 Jimmy Durante (1893-1980) and George Gobel (b. 1919), American entertainers.
2 Arturo Toscanini (1867-1957), Italian conductor.
3 Prince Rainier (b. 1923) was married this year to Grace Kelly (b. 1929).
4 Eddie Fisher (b. 1928), American night-club singer, married at this time to American actress Debbie Reynolds (b. 1932).
5 Dramatized by Frances Goodrich and Albert Hackett.

but she knows too much. Poor child, in future years it is to be hoped that she learns to know less.

Sunday 20 May   Paris

On Thursday morning last at five I was awakened by Graham and Coley bursting into my cabin. I had fully intended to be up to greet them but Morpheus claimed me. Hot on their heels came three amiable Press gentlemen. I didn't want to see them but thought I had better be polite. They questioned me closely about my 'decision' and I answered honestly. The reports they ultimately wrote were innocuous, badly written and without malice, but the headlines the sub-editors had imposed on them were sickeningly vulgar as usual.

The English Press have really gone to town and I have been insulted and vilified and accused of 'renouncing my native land where I earned all my riches'! John Gordon[1] has had some sorrowful malicious digs, and a gentleman called Bernard Harris has written a long article in the *Express* saying that England can well do without me. This article aroused protest and the next day the *Express* published two letters which said that I was perfectly right and that as a Briton I could live where I chose.

Meanwhile some weekly notices of *South Sea Bubble* have appeared, patronizing and contemptuous for the play, but good for Vivien and the box-office which, incidentally, does not need their help as it is being besieged and the play is sold out for months. I would like to be able to pop over and see it but, from all accounts, I should be fairly irritated if I did. Vivien is apparently enchanting, with dignity, looks and star quality, but *not* technically very expert in comedy. The production[2] sounds to me a lash-up. It is unfortunate to be denied the privilege of seeing it but perhaps, from the point of view of general amicability, just as well. I cannot abide fussy, insecure direction or inadequate comedy acting, and given the opportunity I should most certainly have said so, banished Billy Chappell from the West End, and rehearsed the whole thing inexorably for a week. How lucky they are, to be sure!

Sunday 3 June   Avignon

I drove out to Chantilly to lunch with Diana [Cooper]. It was a sort of a twilight day. Oggie[3] was there having recently had a stroke. Iris Tree[4], whom I haven't seen for over twenty years, was also there. She was dear and looked outwardly the same with the same old Joan of Arc blonde hair and the same clear blue eyes twinkling in a nut-brown, wrinkled face. She looked healthy

---

1 In the *Sunday Express*.
2 By William Chappell (b. 1908), dancer and choreographer who had turned to theatre design and direction.
3 Olga Lynn, opera coach and singing teacher.
4 Iris Tree, bohemian youngest daughter of actor-manager Herbert Beerbohm Tree.

and well *and* her age, which is bloody smart of her. Diana – oh dear – my heart does ache for her. She was enchanting, as to me she always is, but she is beginning, at long, long last, to look old. I wish so very much that she hadn't wasted so much time minding so much and would stop trying. A lot of light went out of her anyhow when Duff died. The past lay over the house heavily, like a curse, instead of something lovely to be remembered. I drove back to Paris rather sadly.

Marlene, with her intense preoccupation with herself and her love affairs, is also showing signs of wear and tear. How foolish to think that one can ever slam the door in the face of age. Much wiser to be polite and gracious and ask him to lunch in advance.

Piaf in her dusty black dress is still singing sad songs about bereft tarts longing for their lovers to come back and still, we must face it, singing them beautifully, but I do so wish she would pop in a couple of cheerful ones just for the hell of it.

Edward [Molyneux] and I dined with Pam Churchill and discussed the Old Man's sudden infatuation with one Wendy Russell which is apparently causing some dismay in the Churchill family.

I now have, in the Bank of Bermuda and owing to me, £111,000 tax-free! Better really than being £19,000 overdrawn. Thank you.

Saturday 9 June   Domaine des Clausonnes, Biot

Tomorrow I have to fly back to Paris because it is the only day that Johnny G. can come over and discuss *Nude with Violin*[1]. This is a bore as I could have done with a couple of days more. This place is enchanting. We are lodged temporarily in a sixteenth-century farmhouse looking out over terraces of carnations to the Mediterranean. Edward is building a truly lovely house nearby which is almost finished. It is too large and too grandiloquent for my personal taste, but it is a masterpiece architecturally and looks already part of the landscape. Edward is, temperamentally, right back where he used to be in the old days. Still capable of tempers and sudden violence but good company. I am so relieved about this because during the last few years I thought our friendship was done for. This time, however, I have enjoyed every minute with him.

We have gambled a little, unsuccessfully, lain in the sun, eaten some delicious meals and enjoyed ourselves. On Thursday, the day he left, Edward and I drove to Rocquebrune to lunch with Emery Reves[2], Wendy Russell, the most fascinating lady, Winston Churchill, Sarah, and Winston's secretary. The lunch was a great success, particularly from my point of view, for it seems, from later reports, that I was charming, witty, brilliant, etc. What I really was

1 Which John Gielgud was about to star in and direct for London.
2 Emery Reves, Churchill's overseas literary agent.

was profoundly interested. There was this great man, historically one of the greatest our country has produced, domestically one of the silliest, absolutely obsessed with a senile passion for Wendy Russell. He followed her about the room with his brimming eyes and wobbled after her across the terrace, staggering like a vast baby of two who is just learning to walk. He was extremely affable to me and, standing back to allow me to go into a room before him, he pointed to a Toulouse-Lautrec painting of a shabby prostitute exposing cruelly and cynically a naked bottom, flaccid and creased, and said in a voice dripping with senile prurience, 'Very appetizing!'

This really startled me. To begin with I doubt if Lautrec had ever for an instant intended it to be alluring, and the idea of the saviour of our country calling it appetizing once more demonstrated his extraordinary flair for choosing the right word. I am convinced that 'appetizing' was what he really thought it. I reflected, on the way home, how dangerous an enemy repressed sex can be. I doubt if, during the whole of his married life, Winston Churchill has ever been physically unfaithful to Lady Churchill, but, oh, what has gone on inside that dynamic mind? This impotent passion for Wendy Russell is, I suppose, the pay-off. Sex heading its ugly rear at the age of eighty-three, waiting so long, so long, too long. It was disturbing, laughable, pitiable and, to me, most definitely shocking. I forgave the old man his resolute enmity of years, then and there. He, the most triumphant man alive, after all has lived much less than I.

Sunday 17 June   ss *Queen Mary*

My last evening in the south was fairly dreary. Edward and I dined with Loel and Gloria Guinness[1] and the Windsors at the Hôtel de Paris. After which I was led to the casino, *not* wishing to gamble, by Gloria, and forced to lose £100! The pleasure of the evening had really not justified so high a price. I comforted myself with inward visions of the dear Bank of Bermuda bulging with my earnings, but the long drive home was bleak and irritable. As usual the Duchess was charming to me. I cannot help rather liking her. He, as usual and as always, was completely idiotic. The difficulties of conversation with him are now enhanced by his deafness. My social sense leapt to the fray and I laid myself out to be pleasant, to which he barked amiably. I reflected wryly on the way home that I had spent two meals in one week sucking up to two men who had been steadfastly against me since I was in my twenties. It seemed a pity that Max Beaverbrook was missing.

Paris was wet and cold. John came over and was very sensible about *Nude with Violin*. It was decided that it should open in Dublin in the autumn so that I can correct whatever is wrong with it. I do not think he is ideal for the

1 Of the Irish brewery family.

part, but he is such a wonderful man of the theatre that I know the production will be done with taste and dignity. The Seidmanns, with whom I stayed, were as sweet as ever and fussed over me like mother birds.

We went to the opening night of the Ballet Soviétique, which was a great social and theatrical event. I sat surrounded by Feuillère, Popesco, Arletty, Marie Bell,[1] etc., in fact all the French *vedettes*. The Russkis chose, wrongly I think, *Lac des Cygnes* in its entirety. The production was reminiscent of *Sinbad the Sailor* in Newcastle *circa* 1908. The *corps de ballet* was excellent. Miss Bout, the leading ballerina, danced brilliantly but without star quality. The orchestra (French) was appalling and the lighting worse. In addition to this the floorboards of the stage of the Châtelet were loose and the din during some of the ensemble dancing was deafening. It was a pity, I think, that the Russians so resolutely refused to allow capitalistic visitors to go to their so beautiful country for such a long time. The result, from the point of view of artistic progress, has been dim.

Monday 18 June

I've just finished Tom Driberg's life of Max Beaverbrook. I can well understand why Max was enraged when he read the proofs; what I *cannot* understand is that Driberg (a) should have shown them to him, and (b) been surprised, as apparently he was, by his reaction. It is a tough book, brilliantly concise and, at moments, devastating. He gives full credit to Max for his performance as Minister of Aircraft Production, which was a truly remarkable achievement, but his assessment of his character and motives throughout his violently misspent life is shattering in its ruthlessness. He, Driberg, seems to have an uncanny gift for picking on the perfect phrase calculated to wound and deflate an ego like Max's. He leaves nothing out and gives little quarter. Max emerges at the end of it as I think he really is, a fascinating, dynamic, repellent, kindly, evil and entirely predictable character. The whole book riveted me from cover to cover and I put it down with an almost panic-stricken sense of relief that England has been able to survive the contemptible machinations of all those gentlemen in power who are purported to have led us through the dark war years to victory. Driberg has tremendous skill in highlighting other people's weaknesses. I wonder what he is like himself.

I am proud that my *Daily Express* episode from *In Which We Serve* is included in the book. It is at least one small but effective protest against the lies and misrepresentations of the Beaverbrook press. I am left with the uneasy conviction, not entirely new to me, that Churchill is a great man with more Achilles heels than are usual in a biped, one of which is a remarkable capacity for self-deception and another a strong vein of cheapness. Anthony Eden, merely adequate and obviously miscast; Lloyd George, a scheming, disloyal

1 Elvire Popesco, Arletty and Marie Bell, three distinguished French actresses.

careerist; the Duke of Windsor, virtually half-witted from first to last (no surprise to me); Brendan Bracken, a sycophantic passenger; Beverley Baxter, an overpaid ass; Dickie Mountbatten, pretty good; Bevin, obtuse but solid; Chamberlain, oh dear!; Simon, a shifter; Roosevelt, good; and Max himself a scarifying mixture of twisted frustrations, social insecurity, spiritual vacuity and defeated lust, both for power and for love. A remarkable book. A truly dreadful exposé of how innocent lives are governed, dominated, and generally buggered about by unscrupulous power hunters. Give me my books, my easel, my piano, anything, anything rather than the opportunity of being engaged in any endeavour whatever with such lost creatures.

The rest of my reading on board has been less explosive. Ian [Fleming]'s *Diamonds Are Forever*, enjoyable schoolboy stuff. *Thin Ice*, Compton Mackenzie's novel about a queer diplomat: well-written but, as usual with books on homosexuality written by heterosexuals, not *quite* right. That dreadful, unconscious superiority.

Wednesday 27 June   Bermuda

Well, chaos is the word: acres of packing cases, armies of overpaid workmen, carpenters, painters, electricians, masons, etc., all hammering, whistling, roaring jokes at each other, all very carefree, as indeed they should be considering that they each get about six bob an hour. The house is going to be lovely and my own little cottage is charming. I am having the rocks below it cemented with a wall at either end to protect me from the tourists, and steps leading down into the water. The bathing is quite perfect, better than almost anywhere I have known. Our neighbours, Joe and Mary Huber, are friendly and hospitable to excess. They pour drinks, very strong drinks, down our throats every evening when our day's toil is o'er, and we drive back, pissed and exhausted, to eat repellent food at the hotel and fall into bed.

My first endeavour on arrival was to pass a driving test and buy a Hillman. The speed limit is twenty miles an hour and very right too, because the roads, designed for more sedate vehicles, are narrow, twisty, and generally enclosed with stone walls which makes it impossible to see anything coming. The most noisy and prevalent means of transport on the island is a contraption called a Mobylette. This is a bicycle with a motor attached and is lethally dangerous, and everyone is warned *never* to ride them at night or when it has been raining. Many people ignore this wise counsel, with the result that it is difficult to walk more than a few yards in the town without meeting someone in a plaster cast. Coley and Graham have, so far, escaped, and as we now have a car they are turning their hired Mobylettes in, thank God. I shall miss seeing them scooting along; Graham, nonchalant and devil-may-care, and Coley, rigid, with set lips and an expression of grim determination.

The island itself is much, much nicer than I thought it would be. In the past, when I have made brief visits, I never cared for it much, but now, in the lovely warmth of summer, I am becoming enchanted. I love the pastel-coloured houses and the little creeks and harbours and islands. It is sad about all the cedar trees having caught a fell disease and died, but their deadness and greyness is offset by the masses and masses of oleanders and the vast flamboyants. The sea, in strong sunlight, is a bright, almost hysterical turquoise, and from where we are, looking out across the harbour towards Hamilton in the far right distance, the water traffic is very gay. Little boats, big boats, yachts, naval craft, ferry boats and Chris-Crafts go scurrying by, and every Monday morning the *Queen* [*of Bermuda*] arrives. She is very large and grey and hoots reassuringly, so unlike our own dear *Queen*. On Wednesday afternoons she steams away again, her rails lined with tourists with peeling skins and curious straw hats and cameras.

Every morning at about noon a crowded ferry boat passes and the gentleman in charge announces places of interest through a loudspeaker. His voice echoes across the still water, and whenever the boat passes Spithead Lodge I hear him explaining that whereas the house was originally the home of Eugene O'Neill, the celebrated American playwright, it is now the new home of none other than Noël Coward. The first time I heard this I was swimming along doing a stately Margate breast-stroke with my head high out of the water. I looked up in dismay, saw about twenty nuns peering at me through binoculars, and sank like a stone. I don't really mind this daily publicity but unfortunately it does encourage the boat's passengers to spring into taxis the moment they land and come belting out to stare at me over the wall and take photographs. The other morning I was caught, practically naked, covered in dust and sweat and carrying a frying-pan in one hand and a slop-pail in the other. I paused graciously while they took their bloody snapshots, and pressed on with my tasks and occupations. Noël Coward is *so* sophisticated.

Wednesday 4 July

Here it is the fourth of July and all over this sun-scorched island Americans are giving jolly little parties to celebrate their spirited escape from British tyranny. Feeling fairly sympathetic to this point of view, I may join some of them.

I have moved into my cottage. There is a drought and very little water, but the sea is handy and I use it for all but the supreme purpose. My concrete dock is being constructed and white cement dust lies thickly over everything. The main house is coming on apace. Our social life has been agreeable and not too strenuous.

I dined, formally, at Admiralty House. The C-in-C and his wife are charming. All the glamour of the Navy was turned on. About a dozen young officers dined; one of them, Captain Jewell, was the submarine commander who delivered the body of *The Man Who Never Was*[1]. His comments on the film were acrid.

Then on Sunday morning more parties on board the three frigates in the harbour; bunting, flags flying, impeccable manners. I find that I have missed all this for many years. Unhappily it will not last long even here because the C-in-C is being moved to Norfolk, Virginia, and there will be no longer an Admiralty House here and no longer a resident C-in-C. This is an edict of the Treasury, who are probably feeling uneasy now that I have left the country.

Wednesday 11 July

On Friday I received a long and affectionate letter from Vivien explaining that she is going to have a baby and will be leaving *South Sea Bubble* on 1 August. This was a considerable shock, particularly as they, she and Larry, have waited so long to let me know. This I consider fairly unforgivable of them, but I rose above my shock commendably and cabled and wrote loving congratulations. Not entirely insincere because, if she does manage to produce a tot and it's an all right tot, it will possibly steady her down and make that uneasy ménage more tranquil. I do really hope this will happen, but I do wish so very much that they had had the moral courage to take me into their confidence before. Larry could quite easily have flown over to see me in Paris but he just didn't. Binkie and I have been exchanging agitated cables ever since. *Nobody* we want is available. There is a dim chance that Katie Hammond might go in for a limited period, but it is a very dim chance. The only other possibility apparently is Elizabeth Sellars[2], whom I know to be an excellent young actress, but whether or not she is an experienced enough comedienne to carry that arduous part remains to be seen.

Judging by all accounts, darling Viv was far from ideal. Charming, distinguished and lovely to look at, but technically insecure. My guess is that the business will inevitably drop when she leaves but will come back again providing the part is well played. The play is strong and so is the rest of the cast. I never thought in any event that Vivien would stick it for long but I *did* think she'd keep on until Christmas. It is dismal to have to juggle with a capacity hit. They aren't all that easy to come by, God knows. However, there is nothing to be done but trust Binkie's sense and judgement, usually pretty infallible, and hope for the best. Obviously there is nothing for me to do but behave well about it, but I shall be hopping mad if, as I unworthily suspect, the whole business comes to nothing.

I also think, from Vivien's point of view, that it is a highly perilous enterprise. If anything goes wrong, it will very possibly send her around the

---

1 Title of the book and film based on a wartime exploit in which an anonymous corpse was landed on a German beach bearing 'secrets' about Allied manoeuvres.
2 Elizabeth Sellars (b. 1923), British actress.

bend again; she is over forty, very, very small, and none too well balanced mentally. I am filled with forebodings and a curious sense of having been let down. Not because of her having the baby, but because they could so easily have let us know before and given us more time to find a suitable replacement. I have had a guarded, business-like letter from Binkie, saying nothing about his personal feelings, but I think I can guess them. Larry irritates him to madness anyway and has been extremely tiresome over the whole production.

Monday 16 July

No definite news about *S.S.B.* yet and no reply from either of the Oliviers. The house is very nearly done but there are still millions of little jobs to do. We have been having great fun cooking and I actually made a sensational Yorkshire pudding. Our kitchen scenes are good sound slapstick comedy and the cursing and swearing and getting in each other's way adds up to some nice clean belly-laughs. It seems to me that I do nothing but buy things. I go into the supermart in Hamilton for one tin of tomato purée and come out wheeling a wire barrow piled to the skies with comestibles for which there is no room at the inn.

But still, while the cooking craze lasts, I had better give it its head. We have electric frying-pans, waffle-irons, egg-beaters, percolators, pressure saucepans, double-boilers, cake tins, moulds and a sea of bowls made of china, plastic and glass. We also have shelves crowded with canned herbs, canned fruit, canned meat, canned everything. I have so far made, unaided, pancakes, a chocolate cake, a coffee mousse, a crab mousse, and the above-mentioned Yorkshire pudding. Aided, I have, or we have, made a dreamy cheese soufflé and an angel cake which looks delicious but which has a curious consistency, like Dunlopillo flavoured with vanilla. Countless sauces, of course, and a number of little snack dishes; some good, some indifferent and some fairly nasty but all, in the last analysis, edible.

Apart from these creative culinary flights, my much-publicized genius has remained dormant. Perhaps one day soon, when the workmen have finally folded their tents and rowdily stolen away, I shall be able to concentrate on my novel and the songs I have to record and an idea for a musical. At the moment there is a dead vacuum and it is rather irking me. We must put our faith in One Above, that's what we must do.

Monday 30 July

Bermuda has taken charge of us. It is a sweet island, much, much nicer to live on than I expected.

The greatest excitement is that I have bought a speed-boat with a thirty horsepower outboard engine. It is a very smart little craft and I am learning by trial and a good deal of error to handle it. To live here and *not* have a boat would be silly because it makes the whole difference. We go off to faraway beaches, deep anchor, clumsily, and have picnics. It is the first boat I have ever owned and I am mad about it. We have learned to moor it, unmoor it, bring it alongside – convulsively, as yet – wash it, fill it with petrol, start the engine, stop the engine, spring out of it clutching tangles of rope, tie up, untie and spring back again. I have rammed it into the dock very hard, I have scraped it over rocks, but so far no serious damage has been done.

I have cooked most of the meals and am really becoming quite good. I have, I think, mastered the simpler forms of pastry-making and have made several exquisite pies, both savoury and sweet. It is enormous fun and I am enjoying myself.

The weather is hot, hot, hot and we have air-conditioning to protect the pianos and the books. It also is a considerable comfort to us.

Monday 6 August

The weather has changed and the blue skies have changed to gun-metal grey and rain pours down; lovely for the garden and the tanks, but depressing for us if it goes on too long. There is a major crisis over the Suez Canal[1] and a war might occur at any moment, but of course it won't. The idiotic Egyptians are making beasts of themselves and Britain, France and the US are *as one* in agreeing that the Canal must be international *or else*. All this could, of course, have been avoided if we had not caved in and been just and fair and decent and foolish. We should never have dreamed of evacuating Egypt in the first place. This is obviously a dangerous moment because Russia is supporting Egypt, but my voices tell me that Russia is no more anxious for a full-scale war than we are so I suppose some compromise will be arrived at. It is the same tedious old story, weak-kneed humanitarianism instead of dignified strength.

Life here continues pleasantly enough. The boat is a great pleasure and we have taken to doing our shopping with it. We scoot across the Sound, man-oeuvre ourselves alongside, fling ropes at each other, tie the boat up and off we go, returning later laden with groceries.

Edith Evans has collapsed and been taken to hospital. Gladys Cooper has flown the Atlantic and opened[2] with only one rehearsal. Poor Binkie[3]. I *was* thinking 'poor Edith' and was all set to write her a letter of sympathy, but I heard from Lorn and Joyce that her real trouble was stoppage, about which she refused to do a thing on account of being a Christian Scientist. That old charlatan Mary Baker Eddy[4] certainly has a lot to answer for.

1 Colonel Nasser had been officially elected President of Egypt in June and had almost immediately nationalized the Suez Canal.
2 In the Edith Evans role in Enid Bagnold's *The Chalk Garden*.
3 It was an H.M. Tennent production.
4 Mary Baker Eddy, American founder of Christian Science.

I have been reading a lot of plays, old plays, and they are curiously stimulating. The dialogue, mostly, is stilted and dated, but my, my! they are well constructed. Clyde Fitch[1] is an excellent case in point. His writing is undoubtedly trivial and his view of life largely circumscribed by the times in which he lived, but they are full of entertainment value, well made and every now and then witty. No wonder they were successful. They were nearly all vehicles for some particular star and they certainly, within their limits, de-livered the goods. Of course he was decried by the critics; anyone so imme-diately successful inevitably would be. There is a certain analogy between him and me, I think, except that my scope is wider and I think and hope that I have a little more depth, even in my comedies. In those days, of course, the theatre was still a place of entertainment and not a platform for propaganda and orgies of racial self-pity. I believe I would far rather, even today, watch a well-constructed Clyde Fitch drawing-room drama than sit through loosely knit, turgid meanderings like *Death of a Salesman* and *The Diary of Anne Frank*, both of which, incidentally, are critics' prize-winners.

I expect I am just a dear, foggy-minded old has-been: oh no, I don't expect any such thing. What I *do* know is that as long as I continue to write plays to be acted in theatres, I shall strain every fibre to see that they are clear, well constructed and strong enough in content, either serious or funny, to keep an average paying audience interested from 8.30 until 11.15. Here endeth the first and last and, for me, only lesson.

Tuesday 14 August

What I, most irritably, expected has now happened. Vivien left the cast of *S.S.B* on Saturday night, had a gay farewell party with the company, drove down to Notley and had a miscarriage on Sunday. She was five months gone and it was a boy. The Press shrieked with headlines on Monday, VIV LOSES HER BABY! etc.; meanwhile the wretched Elizabeth Sellars had to open to a not very large audience in an atmosphere of gloom. Apparently she did all right but of course the business took a nose-dive. Poor Vivien is, of course, miserable and sleepless and everyone is worried about her.

Personally I am naturally very sorry for her, but the hysterical, disorganized silliness of the whole thing infuriates me. In the first place, to try to have a baby at her age is fairly foolish; secondly, it is not very bright, if pregnant, to dance about at the Palladium with Larry and Johnny Mills[2] and go out to parties while playing an arduous part eight times a week. The miscarriage was about as inevitable as anything could be. Meanwhile a smash success is destroyed, she is wretched and on her way round the bend again, Larry is

1 Clyde Fitch, late nineteenth-century playwright.
2 In a charity midnight matinée.

wretched, a large number of people, including me, are inconvenienced, and all for nothing.

I am also pretty angry with them for not replying to my, in the circumstances, very magnanimous cable and letter, which I sent immediately I received their letter with 'the great news'. They should have warned me when I was in Paris anyhow, so that I could have concentrated on getting someone more suitable than E. Sellars, and they should certainly have written to me, even if the letter was bubbling with insincerity it would at least have been a gesture. As far as I am concerned they have most emphatically *not* behaved like the loving friends they are supposed to be. *South Sea Bubble*, if only they had had the sense to see it, was a life-saver for Vivien. It gave her a glamorous success on her own, away from Larry's perpetual shadow, and she should have played it for at least six months and not left it until a really first-rate replacement could be found. Altogether I'm sick to death of them both at the moment. I've been bored and involved with their domestic problems for years and done all I could to help, and as they haven't even troubled to write to me they can bloody well get on with it. I am saddened by this, but not surprised or unduly depressed. Friendship is a rare business and fair exchange is one of its essentials. I have enough true friends anyhow.

Sunday 2 September

Today I fly to New York. The two months here have passed so swiftly and there has been so much to do. The house is settled; my cooking has improved; I became too thin for a little and with the thinness irritation set in – irritation and tetchiness and a feeling of unease and dissatisfaction with everything. Even Coley and Graham, neither of whom could have sweeter dispositions, began to get on my nerves. Fortunately, after a little private seance with myself, I managed to spell out the writing on the wall, which said, in so many words, 'Don't be a cunt!' This is foolish vanity; to be slim and svelte is important only up to a point. At the age of fifty-six youth is no longer essential or even becoming. Fifty-six is fifty-six, rapidly approaching fifty-seven, and health and happiness are more important than lissomness. To be fat is bad and slovenly, unless it is beyond your control, but to have a middle-aged spread when you are a little more than middle-aged is no disgrace and, however slim you get, you will still be the age you are and no one will be fooled, so banish this nonsense once and for all. Be your age and be your weight and conserve your vitality by eating enough and enjoying it.

After this person-to-person reprimand I gained about six pounds and have felt better ever since. My face is not my fortune but it must be watched, if only for professional reasons. It is now all right and the correct shape, but it is no longer a young face and if it were it would be macabre. It is strange to examine it carefully and compare it with early photographs. There it is, the same eyes and nose and mouth, but, oh, the changes! Mostly, I think, for the better. Mutton is so much more acceptable when it is not masquerading as lamb. Physically I have several years ahead of me providing I acquiesce gracefully to the changing years. When people say, 'How young you look! How do you do it?' I must, for my soul's salvation, be able to reply, 'I don't *do* it. I *am* it inside and when I no longer "am it", who cares?' I have no complaints. In the future, when I discover that too much sweets and starch and alcohol are beginning to show, I shall cut them down but not out. I need starch and sweets and alcohol in moderation because I enjoy them, and I am damned if I am going to upset my metabolism and thereby my health and happiness by straining after a youthful line that is gone for ever. If I am happy and at peace and my nerves are cosily enclosed in enough fatty tissue to keep them from twitching, the people near me are also more likely to be happy and at peace. I would really rather be fat than disagreeable, but with a little horse-sense there is no need to be either.

Thursday 27 September   Dublin

Well, I now know the worst and the best and the in-between about *Nude with Violin*[1] and can act accordingly. Actually I have been the centre of such a carry-on during the last few days that I can hardly see straight, but I can at least see straight enough to realize that the play needs stringent cutting, a bit of rewriting, and a hundred per cent redirecting. John, to my infinite relief, is so very much better than I thought he would be that my real apprehensions are gone. He looks fine and, although not yet comedically sure, is neither embarrassing nor mannered, both of which I dreaded he would be. There are a few Terry ringing tones in his voice[2] but these can be eliminated. David Horne is hopelessly miscast and moos and bellows like a mad water-buffalo, thereby completely upsetting the balance of the play. The set, by Paul Anstee, is very good but the lighting far, far too dim. John has directed the play with loving care and reverence and given everyone so much fussy business to do that most of the comedy lines are lost. They get up, sit down, carry trays in and out, change places and move around so incessantly that I nearly went out of my mind.

However, all this can and will be rectified. The play, I think, is genuinely funny and should be successful, but this I cannot be sure of until I cut away all the fussy inessentials and see it clear. It is extraordinary that a fine director like Johnny, who can do *The Cherry Orchard* and *A Day by the Sea* so superbly, should have gone so very far wrong. I can only conclude that it was over-anxiety. I am certainly glad now that I did not see *South Sea Bubble*, for

1 Which had opened at the Olympia, Dublin, on 24 September at the start of a pre-London tour.
2 John Gielgud is a member of the theatrical Terry family.

had I done so there would have been no time to get it right. I wonder why it is that my plays are such traps for directors, as indeed my lyrics are for singers. Nobody seems capable of leaving well enough alone and allowing the words to take care of themselves. Neither my lyrics nor my dialogue require decoration; all they do require are clarity, diction and intention and a minimum of gesture and business.

Since I landed at Cherbourg on Monday evening my life has been made hell by the Press. They have badgered me, photographed me, pursued me, telephoned me, and all of them only interested in my tax avoidance. My night and day in Paris were enlivened by Ginette, Paul-Emile and Marlene, the latter having stayed over especially to see me. All this was great fun and we all stayed in the flat together, Marlene sleeping on the couch in P-E's consulting room so that I could have the spare-room bed. She was in a tremendously *hausfrau* mood and washed everything in sight, including my hairbrush (which was quite clean), and gave me a wonderful new sleeping-pill suppository, which I rammed up my bottom and slept like a top.

All Monday was devoted to eluding the Press. Just before the plane left the pilot came to me and warned me that he might have to land in England as the weather was tricky. This, although agitating, I rose above, and happily all was well and we landed in Dublin if anything a little ahead of time. There I was subjected to a Press carry-on which would have made Marilyn Monroe envious. The whole business was far and away out of proportion to the event, but of course it had nothing to do with my play, only with my financial affairs. They asked me sly, bold, ignorant, insulting and entirely contemptible questions for over half an hour, in the course of which I remained calm, kept my temper, and reiterated that all I had done by giving up my English domicile was to assert my inalienable right as an Englishman to live where I chose and how I chose. I was asked, among other idiocies, whether it was true that the Queen, on hearing of my dreadful delinquency, had firmly scratched my name from the next honours list! I was also asked how much, in cash, I owed the British Government! All the worst questions naturally came from the English Press – the Irish were much politer and more considerate.

Apparently the play had gone very well, although the English papers had, quite unethically[1], given it scathing notices. The whole of Dublin had been in an uproar since the dress rehearsal on Sunday night. I suppose I should be gratified to know that I am still of such headline value. Actually it makes me a little sick when it takes this scurrilous form. Poor John was completely bewildered; he had never had the dubious pleasure of opening a Noël Coward play before.

1 They were not supposed to review until the London opening night.

Saturday 6 October

I am fairly tired, my voice has nearly gone owing to cold and damp, but I am, on the whole, triumphant. I have rewritten two scenes, transposed another and got David Horne to give a quieter performance. He has been very good to work with and has taken direction swiftly and well. But the outstanding behaver has been John. He has never for one instant shown the slightest resentment or even irritation, although I have completely changed his entire production. He has been enthusiastic and helpful and has concentrated on nothing but getting the play and his performance right. He is a great man of the theatre and has true humility and is quite incapable of harbouring a mean or jealous thought. Owing to this almost unique generosity of spirit, it has all been exciting and creative and thoroughly enjoyable. I think now that the play will be a success. Occasionally he starts ranting away in a false 'actor's' voice, but I am round in a flash to his dressing-room and he apparently really knows when he is hitting too hard. Considering that he has never played a modern comedy part before he is remarkably good.

I have had an unexpected *bonne bouche* in the form of a preface written by Terry Rattigan for the *Theatrical Companion to Coward*[1], a preface wittily and charmingly written, in no way effusive yet managing to say the nicest possible things about my work[2]. Real generosity, literately expressed, and I am most deeply grateful to him.

On Thursday Vivien arrived with Binkie. She had telephoned me in Paris and also written me a contrite letter. I met her at the airport with full Press dishonours. After the play and after supper she and Binkie and I retired to my sitting-room and a very great many beans were spilt. All was well until Binkie confessed that he had known about the 'baby' when he saw me in Paris but had sworn to Larry not to tell me! This really made me lose my temper and let them both have it. The scene lasted until 3.30 a.m., but it finished amiably enough. I at least had the satisfaction of saying what has been fomenting in my mind for a long time. Vivien was really very sweet and I think and hope the air is now cleared.

Sunday 21 October   New York

Marlene and I went to the opening of *Around the World in Eighty Days*, which is a great big smash hit. It really is a fascinating picture and none of the multitude of star bit-players attempts any hogging. I have also seen Judy Garland at the Palace; she was superb. And Adrianne Allen playing Celia Johnson's part in *The Reluctant Debutante*, which is a hit; she was excellent,

---

1 Edited by Raymond Mander and Joe Mitchenson, published in 1957.
2 It said, 'He is simply a phenomenon, and one that is unlikely to occur ever again in theatre history.'

but without Celia's curious distinction. *Nude* got raves in Liverpool and played to record business.

Sunday 28 October   Bermuda

Gone is the sunshine and the turquoise water, gone are the tourists and many of the residents, and gone, gone, gone is the warmth and glamour of this enchanted isle. Everyone says that such weather at this time of the year is unprecedented, but we have heard that kind of thing before. The wind is chill, the skies are lowering and gallons of rain fall constantly, penicillin is rife in our shoes and clothes, and both the kittens have gone – vanished – been spirited away. It is hard to believe that tragedy could have come to both of them, so we can only hope that whoever pinched them is looking after them kindly. This is a sadness and I miss them. I am fighting a fresh cold, which is not surprising with this chill dampness on everything. I am longing, longing for the seeping-through-the-bones warmth of Jamaica.

The Admirable Crichton[1] film unit is here with Kenny More, Cecil Parker, Sally Ann Howes, etc.; they all came for drinks yesterday and had a riotous time. Today we bid a sad farewell to the C–in–C, because he leaves on Tuesday and the naval tradition of this island will fade away with his departure. This to my mind is a great, great mistake but I suppose it is more or less in key with the usual idiocies going on in England. Down with pageantry and the past. Up with mediocrity. There is, alas, no new *Cavalcade*[2] to be written. Oh dear, no. A *Cavalcade* of Germany perhaps, or Japan. They are countries of industry and determination. We, alas, were victors and there is little more demoralizing than that, it seems.

Sunday 4 November   New York

On Thursday night I attended the opening of *The Sleeping Prince*[3] and it was completely disastrous. The audience, typical Gilbert Miller-Park Avenue morons, were vile. The play was monumentally miscast. The wit of Larry's performance in London, where nobody really appreciated it, gave the play the lift it needed. This turgid misrepresentation was quite unbearable.

On Friday I finished off my recordings[4], fairly triumphantly. Pete [Matz] had assembled a brilliant rhythm section consisting of piano, double bass, trumpet, guitar and drums, each instrumentalist an expert. The result was, to me, exciting and I sang well. We did 'Time and Again', 'Twentieth Century Blues', 'Sail Away', 'Half Caste Woman' and 'Marvellous Party'. We also did

1 J.M. Barrie's comedy, now being filmed by Lewis Gilbert.
2 Noël's patriotic play of 1931, which had celebrated British history during the first thirty years of the century.
3 Rattigan's comedy which Noël had been offered for London.
4 For the LP, *Noël Coward in New York*.

our experimental remake of the medley, but this didn't come off. Altogether, however, it was a very successful session and the finished record should be good.

On Saturday afternoon I went to Bing's[1] box to hear Callas sing *Norma* at the Met. She was fighting a bad cold and all hell was apparently breaking loose backstage, but she completely captivated me. True, her high notes were a bit scratchy but she is a fine singer, beautifully controlled and in technical command of every phrase. She is also an artist: she did some superb bits of acting which only Mary Garden[2] could have equalled. The mezzo was a fat cow with a good strong voice and a good strong claque which shrieked and roared every time she came on. She tried to pinch the show from Callas but she didn't succeed. At the very end Callas got an ovation the like of which I have seldom heard. She is a perfectionist and a stylist and it was fascinating to see how her quality triumphed with that vast, prejudiced, over-knowledgeable audience. At the Met the rule is that only the voices really count. It is a good rule, of course, for Grand Opera but personally I will always settle for a little less vocal perfection if it is offset by good acting and strong personality. I believe that the public, even the diehards, secretly agree with me.

In the evening I had another treat, *Separate Tables*[3], which was better even than it was in London. Maggie and Eric were superb, so was Beryl Measor and the rest of the cast. It is a smash hit as it fully deserves to be, being a compassionate, beautifully constructed play, expertly and movingly acted.

Monday 12 November

Yesterday I spent eight hours solid recording with Maggie Leighton for a highbrow company called Caedmon, who generally put out records of Edith Sitwell, T.S. Eliot, Dylan Thomas, etc. The eager ladies who officiated were enthusiastic and amiable but amateurish; however, we took charge and whisked through *Brief Encounter*, the breakfast scene from *Blithe Spirit*, the love scene from *Present Laughter*, and the whole second act of *The Apple Cart*. Maggie was quite unequivocally marvellous. She was reading *Blithe Spirit* and *Present Laughter* for the first time and she got every intonation and every emphasis dead right. She is enchanting to work with and she really must play my plays indefinitely because she is one of the very few who really understand the language.

On Wednesday night *Nude* opened in London[4]. I talked to Binkie, etc., at seven o'clock New York time, which was midnight in London. He and everyone seemed delighted. The audience apparently had been very good for

1 Rudolf Bing, director of the Metropolitan Opera House.
2 Mary Garden (1877–1967), Scottish-American soprano.
3 The Rattigan double bill in which Eric Portman and Margaret Leighton were repeating their London success on Broadway.
4 At the Globe Theatre.

once and the play had gone beautifully. The next day I talked to him again. The notices, as usual, are smug and patronizing and full of praise for the acting and blame for the play. The advance, however, is very big and there is a large library deal[1]. It is obviously a big success and there it will sit, next door but one to dear *South Sea Bubble*[2], which is packing them in and shows no signs of weakening. This really is my most effective answer to the critics after all.

I lunched, at long last, with Bill Stephenson on Thursday. We reminisced about the war years and discoursed, gloomily, on the present crisis in the Middle East and Hungary. He is of the opinion that Anthony Eden has gone round the bend and mistimed his gesture completely[3]. This may be so but, unlike the Munich time, I find I cannot work up any interest. The world is so idiotic. There is so much ignorance, superstition, graft, greed and general stupidity that I cannot feel any impulses to do anything about it whatever, even if I could. I shall continue to press on with my own affairs for as long as circumstances allow me to.

General Eisenhower won the election[4] with a landslide and so now *that* febrile, cooked-up hysteria has died down a bit.

A sadness has occurred. Poor Beatrice Eden is seriously ill in the Roosevelt Hospital. She had been taken in to be operated on, but the surgeons merely opened her up, saw that it was hopeless, and sewed her up again. It is apparently cancer of the intestine *and* the liver. If this is true, there is indeed no hope. I went along to see her and found her, considering, comparatively bright. I don't think she knows the full horror yet but I think she suspects. I am so desperately sorry for her, so lonely and alone. She has always had a quality of gallantry about her. I think her life, since she left Anthony[5], has been fairly dreary. She was so eager to break free from pomposities and grandeur, and the last thing she wanted was to be the wife of a Prime Minister, but having achieved her emancipation I have a feeling it went a little sour on her. She has had a few love affairs, of course, but none of them very sparkling, and now, far from home and the Yorkshire moors, she has to face up to dying. I have no doubt that she will do it bravely, but it is sad, sad, sad.

Sunday 25 November   Jamaica

The weather is perfect – 'never did I breathe such pure serene'. Apparent peace broods over the 'paradise of the Caribbean', but alas it is only apparent,

1 An advance guarantee of sales made to the management by ticket agencies (brokers).
2 On Shaftesbury Avenue.
3 Prime Minister Eden had just ordered British and French forces to occupy the Suez Canal Zone ahead of the invading Israeli army, an action condemned by the United Nations and causing bitter controversy in Britain, and which Eden was shortly to countermand.
4 For the US Presidency.
5 Her marriage to Anthony Eden had been dissolved in 1950.

for lurking behind the quiet trees and scampering through the banana plan-
tations are rumours, tensions and wild surmises. Suddenly, two days ago, it
was announced in fierce headlines that the Prime Minister was flying out here
for three weeks' rest and was to stay at Goldeneye! Sylvia Foot immediately
appeared. Policemen formed a cordon round the house, banana birds perched
on the almond trees chirruped, 'Why, why, why should the Prime Minister of
England come so far away from home during a major international crisis?'
whereupon other whimsical wild creatures replied, 'Either because he knows
more than he pretends to know and the crisis is not as serious as it looks', or
'He knows nothing at all and has been advised to beat a tactful and tactical
retreat.' Personally I subscribe to the former theory. Anthony is not a fool and
certainly not a coward. It appears that his recent decision about the Middle
East was a monumental error in timing, but all *we* know about this is what we
have read in the newspapers and I have known the newspapers to be inaccurate,
just once or twice. Anyhow, the poor man is here with Lady E[1]. I delivered a
welcoming note and a box of goodies from Bravo Terrace, our new Fortnum's
in Port Maria, and propose to leave them discreetly alone until they show
some signs of wanting company.

We lunched yesterday with HE and Sylvia Foot, who had just met the Edens
at Montego and dropped them off at Goldeneye. HE said that he looked tired
but that there was definitely nothing wrong with him and no necessity for
medical supervision.

The nastiest aspect of the whole business is that the Press are here, stationed
at Castle Gordon – Don Iddon[2], etc. Don Iddon is quite agreeable and I shall
have to be amiable when he appears on the doorstep, which he most inevitably
will. It seems that wherever I go and however far I travel I shall never get
away from these scruffy, unpleasant scavengers.

I have just received and read the Sunday notices for *Nude with Violin*. They
are all idiotic, all bad, and all, with the exception of the dear little *News of the
World* and some woolly but well-disposed obscurities by Harold Hobson[3],
choked and spitting with personal venom. Kenneth Tynan has really surpassed
himself[4]. He withers my whole career with such subtle brilliance that he might
just as well have written, 'Oh God, oh God, I wish more than anything in the
world to be Noël Coward, if only for one glorious day!' Another of the critics,
whose name eludes me, says that this play places me on the bottom rung of
the ladder (English theatre ladder), which is where I fully deserve to be! Well,
well, well. It is certainly a curious sensation to be the recipient of so much

---

1 Clarissa Eden (b. 1920), daughter of Major John Spencer Churchill, who in 1952 had married
  Anthony Eden, now knighted.
2 Of the *Daily Express*.
3 In the *Sunday Times*.
4 In the *Observer*.

concentrated hatred and abuse. I would love to know, although of course I never shall, how much they believe what they write, or how much their tapping fingers are motivated by grinding subconscious jealousy over which they have no critical control. It must be the latter really, because no sane, balanced critic would give himself away so personally. It would be so much cleverer to damn my work with faint praise than to come roaring out into the market place screaming, 'Yah, yah, yah, I hate you, you're a success and I'm not!'

Sunday 9 December

The Prime Minister slept well. On Friday he took a walk to the end of the property, wearing blue shorts, a 'Tower Isle' shirt and dark glasses. Lady Eden, who accompanied him, wore green shorts, a white shirt and sunglasses. I quote from the *Gleaner*. In England there has been a strained vote of confidence in the Government, and the Prime Minister has hotly denied all rumours that he intends to resign. French and English troops are moving out of Egypt. General Eisenhower is very well. Cole Lesley is much better, although he still coughs like an old gentleman in a workhouse.

My Jamaican company matters are in a state of absolute chaos. I am faced once again with the realization that everyone even remotely concerned with legal and financial business is verbose, boring and dull.

Sunday 16 December

Well, I am fifty-seven today.

Both Gladys and Winnie seem to be genuinely impressed with my verse[1] and so I am pressing on, which I should probably have done in any case. I find it quite fascinating to write at random, sometimes in rhyme, sometimes not. I am trying to discipline myself away from too much discipline, by which I mean that my experience and training in lyric writing has made me inclined to stick too closely to a rigid form. It is strange that technical accuracy should occasionally banish magic, but it does. The carefully rhymed verses, which I find it very difficult *not* to do, are, on the whole, less effective and certainly less moving than the free ones.

Sunday 23 December

Now a new excitement has happened. I have started to model in clay, or rather plasticine. I did a Negro head to begin with and then two full-length statuettes. Really not bad for a very beginner. Coley did an exquisite little woman's head at first go off, and we now spend hours walking round our masterpieces and admiring them, and ourselves, from every angle. The girls are having a lovely

1 Noël had begun to write a series of verses, which he was now trying out on the newly arrived Gladys Calthrop and Winifred Ashton.

time, at least Winnie is – Gladys is a little dim but she is already looking a million times better than when she arrived. Winnie is the supreme dominator. Her vitality is indestructible, her energy fabulous and her untidiness remarkable; she manages to wreak more havoc in a small space of time than an army of delinquent refugees. She talks wisely and informatively up to the point where she gets carried away and begins to show off. Then steps have to be taken. Our evenings are loud with argument. She also, with unmistakable Freudian compulsion, never stops saying hair-raising things such as, 'Stick it right *up* dear, ram it, ram it, and then wiggle-waggle it out again.' This apropos of an armature for modelling. Then, 'You must clean your tool, dear boy!' etc.

She is an extraordinary character and immensely lovable, also immensely irritating when she starts roaring and laying down the law. This holiday is wonderful for her. I am so very glad because, over the years, I have owed her a great deal. She is really enthusiastic about my verses and also most helpful. Her enthusiasm is very good for me and very encouraging, but I suspect it a bit, not because I don't believe it to be sincere, but because she is tremendously ruled by her personal prejudices. She loves me dearly and so everything I do has a glow for her, and if it hasn't an authentic glow of its own, her affection for me proceeds automatically to manufacture one. She is a wonderful, unique mixture of artist, writer, games mistress, poet and egomaniac. She is infinitely kind, stubborn, ruthless in her dislike and certainly capable of cruelty, albeit *un*thinking cruelty. She is acutely sensitive to the coloured world about her and to the sometimes over-coloured world of classic literature, and she is astonishingly *in*sensitive to people. After all these years she is still unsure whether I am mocking or talking seriously. She only really knows little bits of me. These little bits, on the whole, she treasures, but there are other, even bigger bits, which are completely beyond the range of her understanding. It is all fascinating and the visit, so far, is being a triumphant success.

Monday 31 December

Christmas week is over and the giving and receiving, unwrapping and wrapping, determined conviviality, pressure, crushed-down irritations and simulated enthusiasms are over too. Now there is the debris, the letters of thanks to be written, the wondering what to do with and where to put so many of the heart-warming gifts, the physical and mental inertia. It will take a few days yet to be able to get clear of miscellaneous gratitudes.

The Christmas dinner itself was fairly nasty because neither Coley nor I had had time to oversee the preparations. The turkey was passable, but there were no sausages with it, no rolls of bacon and no bread sauce, and the roast potatoes were beige and palely loitering. Croydon obliged by having three kittens under an armchair in my sitting-room during the early hours of the

morning. Judging from their colouring, their conception was far from im-
maculate. She appears to be delighted with them. Boxing Day was rendered
hideous by Alton[1] who, having been sozzling steadily since Christmas Eve,
proceeded to get very drunk indeed, knock a boy off a mule with the car, pass
out and say nothing about it. The boy showed no outward signs of the faintest
injury but groaned a great deal. He was finally taken to the doctor. Alton was
in disgrace, the atmosphere was wretched, all of which went on for two days.
Now these particular clouds have lifted. Charles, who had arrived with Ham
on the twenty-third, got a high fever on Christmas Day, but recovered
afterwards. They were both very sweet and have now gone back to New York.

We had a three-hour session about my financial affairs. Nothing that was
originally promised me has really come true, except that I am a bit better off
than I was. Whether I am enough better off to compensate for the bitter
persecution I have endured from the English Press remains to be seen. I
suppose, on the whole, as the years roll on, it will turn out to have been a good
move, but as things are at the moment I am still paying heavy tax in England,
will have to pay at least company tax here and full tax on anything I earn in
America. The whole business sickens and bores me, and I must admit that I
have been bitterly hurt inside by the English fusillade of abuse. However,
there is nothing to be done but press on and not allow myself to be too
sensitive. I know that I am not good about money matters. These eternal
'expedience' discussions make me feel dirty.

On Saturday I went to Kingston, stayed the night at King's House, and
went with HE and Sylvia to a gala performance of the pantomime, given
ostensibly in my honour. I am, as a rule, the first to encourage theatre
enthusiasm and ambition and sincere effort to do something worthwhile, even
if the efforts are only amateur, but this display of complacent self-indulgence
was hard to bear. The only discernible talent lay in the designing of the dresses
and the sense of colour. The performance from every point of view, even from
amateur standards, was beneath contempt. I had a terrible urge, instead of
smiling and complimenting everyone, to rise up and protest and say that
entertainment was my life's work and to see it prostituted with such breathless
suburban idiocy was a mortal sin and, unlike more conventional mortal sins,
completely unpardonable. I did not obey this urge and retained my sickening
popularity and charm, but inside I was deeply angry.

I have just finished Rebecca [West]'s new novel, *The Fountain Overflows*.
It is a beautiful book, wise and compassionate, and peopled with curious,
believable and most endearing characters. It is also based on a standard of
values, both moral and musical, that is impeccable.

This turbulent year ends with today and I am not sorry. I have enjoyed
some of it but on the whole it has been agitating, distracting and, once or

1 The houseboy at Blue Harbour.

twice, almost defeating. It has brought me three great successes, the television performance of *This Happy Breed*, *South Sea Bubble* and *Nude with Violin*. It has also brought me a torrent of envy and malice from almost every newspaper in England. It has brought me a change of life in the geographical sense and probably a little private menopause as well. It has also brought me, inevitably perhaps, a certain change of heart regarding my own country, which I do not like. I have a core of sadness about England, sadness mixed with a sort of desolate irritation that a country and people so rich in tradition and achievement should betray itself and what it stands for by so whole-heartedly submitting to foolish government, natural laziness, woolly thinking and, above all, the new religion of mediocrity. The age of the common man has taken over a nation which owes its very existence to uncommon men. This is a dismal metamorphosis. Perhaps, however, there is still hope.

1957

A year in which much was started but little actually finished, perhaps because the efforts of emigration and the triumphs in America during 1956 had left Noël uncharacteristically drained of energy; he spent longer than usual wintering in Jamaica, returned to London in the summer, and spent much of it putting a distinctly uneasy Michael Wilding into Nude with Violin *to replace the departing John Gielgud.*

Then he himself began to rehearse the role for Broadway; 'I am staying', he told a Fleet Street enquirer (Alan Brien), 'in the Oliver Messel suite at the Dorchester; all that luxury is not really me, but doubtless I shall be able to rise above it. Thanks to all the vilification poured on my head in recent months I am now as famous as Debbie Reynolds, which is most gratifying.'

Sunday 13 January   Jamaica

Binkie and John Perry arrived last night, Terry [Rattigan] comes tomorrow. I had a sweet letter from Larry which touched me. He has been troubled about my 'great decision'[1] and didn't know how to say so until finally he sat himself down and poured it all out. Knowing him, this was a difficult thing to do. I have written him a long explanatory letter back which I hope will ease his mind on my behalf. I am glad he wrote what he thought. I have felt for sometime that there was an 'uncomfortableness' going on and now the air is clear again. We have been friends for so many years.

I have decided *not* to appear at the Palace[2], *not* to return to Las Vegas and *not* to accept any commitments for any public appearances until I am so bored and so nostalgic for the impact of people and the sound of applause that I can no longer resist. This writing of free verse, which I am enjoying so very much, is wonderful exercise for my mind and for my vocabulary. Most of what I have already done I really feel is good and is opening up, for me, some new windows. My sense of words, a natural gift, is becoming more trained and selective and I suspect, when I next sit down to write a play, things may happen that have never happened before. All this gives me a curious cerebral excitement. I'm feeling happy and creative and non-bothered. I need this peace badly and have needed it for years.

I cannot help what the ill-disposed English journalists write about me. I refuse to be tempted into either bitterness or reprisals. Obviously I am saddened that so many people at home should believe, because they see it in print, that I have abandoned my country and *evaded* paying my dues. On the other hand, a great many people do *not* believe this. When I analyse the situation carefully, which I have been forced to do *ad nauseam*, I see clearly that I would have been insane to keep Goldenhurst and Gerald Road and continue to pay the crippling surtax with nothing to put by for my old age. At this very moment, I at least have more actual money in the bank than I have ever possessed in my whole career. I can afford, if necessary, not to work at all for several years! And although the thought of not working appals me, it is comforting to know that I am free from the strain of having to make money all the time. I have roughly £70,000 in the Bank of Bermuda and the Royal Bank of Canada here. I have the house in Bermuda, a very valuable property and unlikely to deteriorate, and Blue Harbour and Firefly. I suppose if all my assets were realized I am worth about £100,000. Considering that two years ago I was £19,000 overdrawn, this is a marked improvement. All I have to do now is to relax, give myself time, keep healthy and let the creative side of my nature take its course.

1 To emigrate.
2 New York, where he had been offered a season singing in cabaret.

Sunday 20 January

Winnie and Gladys flew away on Thursday, Winnie actually in tears on leaving the house. She cheered up later; we had drinks with Edward and saw his new paintings which are really fine. He has little to worry about when he can paint like that. Then Terry and I saw the girls off and drove back.

Terry is a most curious mixture. His appearance and his ordinary dialogue are deceptive. He is light, sweet, ready to giggle, incredibly silly over his emotional life, weak and stubborn at the same time – they usually go together – and yet capable of writing *The Deep Blue Sea, Separate Tables, The Browning Version*, etc., plays so richly impregnated with human understanding and compassion. He is drinking too much and allowing himself to become podgy; on this I lectured him mildly. I think he must be careful now that he is in the forties: he has so much to contribute and it mustn't be frittered away.

My epic verse is at last within sight of the end[1]. Fifteen pages – it has been a long voyage and I am eager to get the god-damned ship and all who sail in her safely to Tilbury, because I have several other ideas rapping smartly on the door and I cannot let them in until this particular odyssey is completed.

Montego was horrible as usual. They are opening two night-clubs. Round-hill is packed with all the *soi-disant gratin* of New York. How Edward can endure to live in that atmosphere has really puzzled me. I suppose actually it doesn't puzzle me all that much. He has always preferred the company of dull people, which is in itself curious because he is so bright himself, except when he's had a couple. There is no doubt about it, the idle rich are, always have been, and always will be, boring. They have supplied me in my time with some excellent dialogue and situations, but only within a limited scope. I suppose in my early teens I was impressed by them. I don't believe, however, that even then I was as much impressed as I am supposed to have been. Now they not only bore me but depress me. This, I suspect, is age taking its wicked toll. If it is, good luck to it. I would rather live in a shack on a deserted sandbank than be stuck in Roundhill with all those shrill dullards.

Sunday 27 January

Je suis seul. Estoy libre. I am alone! Coley will come up to lunch[2] and we will talk or not as we feel like it and peace will wrap us round like an eiderdown. Not that Binkie, Johnny or Terry were the slightest trouble. They pursued their own course and enjoyed themselves and couldn't have been sweeter, and, of course, the fact of my living up here changed the whole face of the world for me; nevertheless, I am sick of too many people at meals. Last night was bliss. I dined alone up here – steak and onions and sweet potatoes in a purée

---

1 A poem called P & O.
2 From Blue Harbour; Noël was on his own at Firefly Hill.

whipped up by me. I gave myself a gin and tonic and a Spanish lesson, retired to bed at 9.30 and read an extremely good biography of James I and slept like a top.

I have made a secret plan which is that I shall never live here during the season again, i.e. from January to April. In the first place the weather is liable to be tricky, although so far this year it has been wonderful. In the second place I cannot, for tax reasons, live here for more than six months a year, and far and away the nicest time here is September to Christmas and April to July. In March I am going to do some more island hopping and find a really remote and inaccessible place, buy, if possible, a little house, or almost a shack would do providing it is *simpatico*, and nip away there each year from January till the end of March. Then I shall evade all the Jamaican visitors. The locals themselves don't worry me at all – they are sweet and considerate   but since Roundhill opened *everybody* is coming to Jamaica and they all, it seems, *have* to see me! It really would be impossible to write a sustained piece of work here during the season. There are constant interruptions, some of them quite agreeable but all of them distracting. If only I could find somewhere like the little shack I had in Honolulu[1]. No luxury except a frigidaire. No grand furniture, just somewhere that I can lock up behind me when I go. Somewhere, in fact, where there will be literally nothing to do but write, read and paint.

I know this sounds on the surface idiotic as I already have Bermuda and here. But Bermuda and here are quite different. There are too many people, amiable people, kind people, very occasionally interesting people, but too many of them and all encroaching on my time and my vitality. Tomorrow, for instance, Phyllis Calvert and her husband[2] are coming to dinner. I like them both but the dinner has to be planned, etc. On Tuesday Edward is driving over and bringing Natasha to stay. Annie and Ian, whom I love, are just around the corner and would love a canasta evening. There are meetings for 'Designs for Living'. At any moment of any day a telegram is liable to arrive from someone, possibly someone quite nice, saying can we pop in and see you on Thursday on our way back from rafting? One can't say NO, NO, NO, go away from Jamaica, go and live in Palm Beach or the South of France! But, oh dear, I wish they would.

Sunday 3 February

Another lovely week has scurried by. Natasha is here now, perfectly sweet and no trouble at all. She loves peace and being left alone as much as I do. I am reading again through all the dear E. Nesbits and they seem to me to be more charming and evocative than ever. It is strange that after half a century I can

1 In 1926, recovering from a nervous breakdown on Broadway, Noël had been lent an isolated Hawaiian ranch.
2 Phyllis Calvert (b. 1915), British actress, married to bookseller, Peter Murray Hill.

still get such lovely pleasure from them. Her writing is so light and unforced, her humour so sure and her narrative quality so strong that the stories, which I know backwards, rivet me as much now as they did when I was a little boy. Even more so in one way because I can now enjoy her actual talent and her extraordinary power of describing hot summer days in England in the beginning years of the century.

All the pleasant memories of my own childhood jump up at me from the pages. I remember Bay Tree Cottage at Meon, and walking across the path through the cornfields to Tichfield to buy *The Magnet* and *The Gem*; I remember exploring for the first time the 'jungle' round Aunt Laura's lake in Cornwall and the old blue punt and the creek and the wooden swing in the clearing. I can also recapture clearly the early morning, before breakfast bathes at Bognor and the smell of the seaweed and the smell of the bacon frying when we came back to the lodgings. E. Nesbit knew all the things that stay in the mind, all the happy treasures. I suppose she, of all the writers I have ever read, has given me over the years the most complete satisfaction and, incidentally, a great deal of inspiration. I am glad I knew her in the last years of her life. She certainly left me a lot in her will[1].

I have been reading through a series of *Time and Tide* that all arrived in a bunch. It is, to my mind, the only really non-partisan weekly that is intelligent and what I must describe as right-minded, which I suppose really proves how partisan it and I really are. It is so clear, reading through all those weeks of the Suez crisis, that the good old imperialism was a bloody sight wiser and healthier than all this woolly-headed, muddled, 'all men are equal' humanitarianism which has lost us so much pride and dignity and prestige in the modern world. The British Empire was a great and wonderful social, economic and even spiritual experiment, and all the parlour pinks and eager, ill-informed intellectuals cannot convince me to the contrary.

There is much to be deplored in the British character but there is also much, very much, to be admired and respected. We have done a great deal of good to a great many million people, principally by helping them towards common sense.

At the present moment England is in a state of almost complete subservience to America and for the worst possible reason, that America is the richer. I, who genuinely love America and Americans, cannot ignore their only too obvious naivety in world diplomacy. Poor dear Roosevelt, when old and dying, sincerely believed that if we played generously with Stalin he would play generously with us and our Western world. This naive misconception of character (and history) has left Europe in misery and turmoil ever since. Eisenhower, a charming man and an excellent Commander-in-Chief, has not and never had the slightest talent for statesmanship. He has, I fear, seen some

1 i.e. the joy of rereading her books.

dangerous inner light. He is also old and tired and ill. John Foster Dulles[1], a sort of poor man's Neville Chamberlain without that ass's sincerity, has caused irreparable damage to the modern world by the incalculable shadiness of his diplomatic dealings and his immense authority as the representative of the wealthiest country in the world. He, too, is old and ignorant and dying.

In England, poor Anthony has resigned, given up, and is on his way to New Zealand, a tragic figure who had been cast in a star part well above his capacities. All the same I suspect that history will be kinder to him than the contemptible, contemporary English Press. It was obviously dotty of him to embark on the Suez adventure in complete secrecy. The petulant gesture of a weak but stubborn man, but it at least *was* a gesture and more in the tradition of English courage than the milksop compromises of his colleagues. If he had been allowed by world pressure and by English pressure to finish the job, we should at least have knocked Nasser off his perch and controlled the Canal. The, to me, saddest part of this garbled, untidy story is the split that occurred in England itself. All that silly demonstrating and arguing could only have been motivated by fear, as it was during Munich, and the fear was obviously exacerbated, as before, by the misrepresentations of the gutter Press.

I am exceedingly thankful that I wasn't in England at the time. I should have lost many friends as I did at Munich time and made a lot more enemies. I am sorry, desperately sorry, for Anthony personally but I never really thought he had it in him. I have hopes of Harold Macmillan[2]. He is a clever man and I do not think he is weak or liable to be railroaded by phoney American sentimentality into doing what his experience tells him is wrong. This is indeed a sad moment in English history and in the world's history. But England has survived before and so, let's face it, has the world.

Sunday 17 February

I have just read *Look Back in Anger* by John Osborne[3] and it is full of talent and fairly well constructed, but I wish I knew why the hero is so dreadfully cross and what about? I should also like to know how, where and why he and his friend run a sweet-stall and if, considering the hero's unparalleled capacity for invective, they ever manage to sell any sweets? I expect my bewilderment is because I am very old indeed and cannot understand why the younger generation, instead of knocking at the door, should bash the fuck out of it. In this decade there is obviously less and less time for comedy as far as the intelligentsia is concerned. Curiously enough, however, judging by the steady

---

1 John Foster Dulles (1888–1959), US delegate to the United Nations 1946, 1947 and 1950, and Secretary of State under Eisenhower.
2 Harold Macmillan (b. 1894), who succeeded Eden as Conservative Prime Minister 1957–63.
3 John Osborne (b. 1929), British dramatist.

returns for *Nude with Violin*, the public still love it. I wonder how long this trend of dreariness for dreariness's sake will last. Apparently, in the minds of the critics and the aforementioned intelligentsia, significance and importance can only be achieved by concentrating on unhappiness, psychopathic confusion and general dismay. No lightness is permissible. For these misguided souls it is obviously much to be deplored that the great public refuse to be impressed by the Brechts[1] and the Anouilhs and all the rest of the defeatists, and continue unregenerately to enjoy being amused in the theatre. I expect that the public will win in the long run; it usually does.

Sunday 24 February

The novel is progressing doggedly. It is now more than half-way done. I am pleased with it up to a point, it is gay and amusing and at moments there are patches of good descriptive writing, but it is very, very light and trivial and I have a feeling that it would be wiser to serialize it, in England and America, thereby postponing its publication until later on, by which time I might have done something with a bit more weight. I am not decrying my gift for comedy, which is my greatest asset, but I have a hunch that I am right.

Lornie has arrived, funnier and more lovingly sensible than ever. I have just read *Guy Burgess*, a determined journalistic effort by Tom Driberg to whitewash the permanently grey character of Mr Burgess. He tries valiantly, owing to Labour and Communistic sympathies, but he does not succeed. Burgess emerges, admittedly more intelligent than I had imagined, but no less of a fool. This is far from being as paradoxical as it sounds. All those left-wing intellectuals of the Twenties and Thirties were intelligent, well-read and expensively over-educated, but very few of them have yet been proved right and I gravely doubt that they ever will. They joined the Communist Party with adolescent enthusiasm for a cause, plus a certain rebellious superiority; then a number of them saw that they had been fooled and repudiated the Party, etc. All of which seems to me like a most unintelligent waste of time. Burgess did not repudiate his Marxism and now lives, in apparently welcome squalor, in Moscow. I cannot think it is of the least importance whether he lives in Timbuctoo or Alaska. He is obviously a tiresome, wrong-headed, self-indulgent man with faulty emotional balance and little integrity.

It was a splendid gesture on the part of Driberg to write this book about him, but Driberg is a trained journalist, an ex-Labour politician, and on both these counts, to me, suspect. He is readable and the chapters dealing with Munich and all that leads up to the war are exceedingly graphic and lucidly written. It is when he is dealing with his hero that he gets a bit bogged down. I had an uneasy feeling that he didn't care a hoot whether Burgess lived or died, but that the fact of getting his story out of him was a good scoop. Well,

1 Bertolt Brecht (1898-1956), German dramatist.

I suppose it was. I think, however, that I would have preferred Rebecca to have done it[1].

In England it may be, and is, the age of the common man, but in America it is definitely the age of the crazy-mixed-up-kid. With a few notable exceptions, such as Walter Lippman, Joe Alsop[2], Lew Douglas, etc., the whole nation seems to be becoming increasingly juvenile. They are such a kindly, hospitable, vital race, and their traditions are strong, but I wish they weren't so maddeningly volatile and emotionally swayed and so god-damned naive. It is terrifying to think that the future of Western civilization is in the hands of a lot of well-disposed, hysterical, neurotic children. They have all the power and all the resources, and none of the experience necessary to handle either. I, who love America and have received so much from it, am becoming increasingly aware of their pervasive political and general illiteracy. They don't seem to know anything about history, even their own. They live on advertising and getting-rich-quick, and big business and shockingly sentimental reunion lunches. And the clouds they see banking on the horizon and shrink away from are movie clouds on the vast vista-vision screen of the modern world. It's very discouraging and *very* dangerous.

Sunday 3 March

I am getting on steadily with my novel, and reading, in between whiles, a lot of Henry James. This is very good for me and, at moments, very hard going. He really was the king of exquisitely phrased verbosity. It is good for me technically because I am inclined to oversimplify my descriptive passages and reduce them to staccato interludes rather than letting them be part of the general structure. This is the natural result of years of dialogue writing. It is only when I have done a couple of pages of – to my mind – elaborate and drawn-out description that, on reading it over, I discover to my astonishment that it is neither elaborate nor drawn-out. On the contrary, it is usually on the skimpy side. This, I suppose, is the reason that so few playwrights write good novels and vice versa. Particularly vice versa. Most novelists overload their plays with masses of words.

Personally I am quite determined to be good at both. I am not sure yet, judging from my short stories and autobiographies, that I have evolved a personal style. It is not a thing to pursue consciously. I expect that, on the whole, I have, up to a point. But up to date I haven't really written enough fiction and prose to be able to judge clearly. Willie Maugham, of course, is the bonny boyo *par excellence*. On reading his little introductory prefaces to the various sections of his American anthology of modern literature, I am struck, all over again, with the lovely, lucid simplicity of his prose. His critical passages

1 Rebecca West had written a study of treachery, *The Meaning of Treason*, in 1949.
2 Joe Alsop, distinguished American political commentator and columnist.

are so slyly, deceptively gentle and he says exactly what he wants to say with such undecorated clarity. The complete antithesis of poor Mr James who trudges and writhes and wriggles through jungles of verbiage to describe a cucumber sandwich. And yet, with all this undue emphasis on meticulousness, with all his interminable parentheses and attenuated sentences, he manages to convey a true and perfectly moving sense of the facts and also an indefinable gilding of literary elegance.

Sunday 5 May

The only thing that has happened that is nice is *Theatrical Companion to Coward*. Gog and Magog[1] have done a wonderful and, to me, highly flattering job. Thank God for a tiny ray of pleasantness.

Sunday 12 May

I devoted the beginning of the week to some intensive thought. It seems to me that with *Bubble*, *Relative Values* and *Nude*, all good properties and not one of them produced in New York, that the time has come to stir my stumps. I have had seven months, or at least six, of the quiet contemplative life and, being temperamentally restless, I am now sniffing the sawdust again. Something must definitely be done about these plays. I think seriously of playing *Nude* myself for a limited season on Broadway. With me in it it would be practically sure-fire and also make an attractive television and movie proposition.

Then, I think, I must make it my business to reconcentrate on the American theatre. I must do some of the summer circuits and find out the new young and middle-aged actors who are coming up. Casting is always a problem; that it *can* be done successfully was proved by the television *Happy Breed*. But it needs knowledge of who is who and this I must go after. In addition to all this I have a determined urge to do one more good musical before I clamber finally into my luxurious limbo. I have never done an original American musical with expert choreographers, expert orchestrators, expert lighting, etc. I have always had to fight the dear old English *laissez aller* which at the moment seems more indestructible than ever. I have a good idea germinating in my mind and I shall wait until I get to my Steinways in Bermuda to see whether or not I can still hook on to the 'fluence.

On Thursday evening we dined with the Feet at Blue Mountain Inn, which is far and away the nicest place to dine in Jamaica. I had never been there before. Both the Feet were cheerful and charming, and it was only when they had dropped us and driven away that we heard that the governorship of the West Indies had been announced over the radio and it was Lord Hailes and

---

1 Noël's name for Raymond Mander and Joe Mitchenson, the theatrical historians who had assembled this index to all Noël's plays and their first productions.

not Sir Hugh Foot. I am awfully sorry for them both. It must be a bitter disappointment, especially as it was a foregone conclusion on the island that he would land the job. I also think it is a pity. HE, while not being a 'great' man, is most definitely a good man. He has had years of experience in the Caribbean, knows all the problems and genuinely loves the people. The trouble, of course, in Whitehall circles is his political views. The Foot family have taken few pains to conceal their leftist tendencies. In spite of these, however – and obviously they irritate me – HE would be, I should think, a better and more practical choice.

I have just finished the first volume of *The Portrait of a Lady* and have been entirely charmed by it. Mr James's urbanity, taste and sense of behaviour are so consoling in these jagged *Look Back in Anger* years. It is pleasant to feel there is so much of his I have not read. Some, I know, of the later, involved novels and stories I shall find tedious but this one, written in his middle years, is lucid and delightful. I know that all those rigid social codes and snobbishness of the immediate past were frequently frustrating and hypocritical, but compared with the *un*reticence and hurly-burly of today, they have a delicious nostalgia. How agreeable it is to grow older.

Sunday 19 May   Bermuda

A letter arrived from Binkie saying that poor Jack Buchanan is seriously ill and has to have an operation and cannot possibly open in *Nude*[1]. However this morning he, Binkie, telephoned from England in a high state of excitement to say that Michael Wilding has agreed to do it. As he was the one I wanted originally I am delighted.

Sunday 26 May   New York

I like New York in June, how about you? It is, of course, still May but I like New York in May too. In fact I like New York period. It is stimulating and busy and the apartment is charming and I am very happy to be back in it. Charles and Ham are in fine fettle. *Fallen Angels* is a great success in Hollywood at the Huntingdon Hartford Theatre, and the next project is *Relative Values* with Gladys Cooper, John Williams and Millie Natwick. If this too is successful we will bring it to Broadway. I think I have persuaded Maggie Leighton to do *South Sea Bubble* and I shall probably do *Nude* myself before the year is out, so things are popping. Jack has sold Fairfield and is writing a book! He is fairly 'gone' and doesn't make much sense and there is no future for him in the theatre.

1 He was to have replaced John Gielgud.

Sunday 2 June   ss *Queen Elizabeth*

Quite a boatload. Eddie Fisher, Debbie Reynolds, Madeleine Sherwood, Howard Lindsay[1], Dorothy Stickney, Lord Montgomery[2], Alfred, Lynn and me! I won £400 with Eddie in the ship's pool. We bid together for a number which I had a hunch about and it was the right number, 693, and sold for £830. Hurray! The Lunts are sweet as ever.

The British Press are lining up against me. John Gordon led off last Sunday with an insulting piece about me skipping out of England to avoid income tax, etc. I must say I am viewing my homecoming with mixed feelings. It will be sweet to see my loved ones but otherwise I feel fairly dreary about it. Even this ship reflects subtly the insidious influence of the welfare state. It is not nearly so well run as it used to be and the food is just not good enough for this monarch of the ocean. The cabins have been redecorated with a suburban luxuriousness which is awful to behold. The staff are still sweet but seem rather tired. The films are, so far, appalling. The ship's orchestra is still playing 'Samson and Delilah' and 'Bitter Sweet' in the lounge at tea-time, and the passengers, apart from the glamour-pusses above mentioned, are ghastly. Milton, thou really shouldst be living at this hour!

Wednesday 5 June   London

The worst is over, the weather is warm, and here I am home in England again, installed in the somewhat excessive luxe of the Oliver Messel suite[3]. Apart from the highly coloured décor the rooms are full of flowers from loved ones and, outside, London stretches from [Hyde] Park to St Paul's. I can see across the grey roofs, green trees, the thick towers of the Chelsea power-station, the tall red pencil of Westminster Cathedral, the Abbey, Big Ben all 'glittering in the smokeless air'. It is a curious sensation being home again and in an hotel, as though I were here and not here at the same time.

Nine representatives of the gutter Press flew out to Cherbourg on Monday afternoon and crowded into my cabin while I was trying to pack. I dealt with them courteously but with iron in my voice and acid in my words, and they finally slunk away like cringing pariah dogs that have been suddenly shouted at. They asked me silly, vulgar questions but were, on the whole, amiably disposed and there was an air of shoddy contrition about them. Lornie, Coley and Charles met me at Southampton at 7.30 a.m. and we drove up to London in soft rain. After lunch, when we had collected all the cards from the flowers

---

1 Howard Lindsay (1889-1968), American author and director.
2 Lord Montgomery of Alamein (1887-1976); the British Field Marshal was at this time Deputy Supreme Commander, Europe.
3 At the Dorchester Hotel.

and welcome presents, I went to bed. Graham appeared in the evening and we all had drinks and smoked salmon and drove off to the Globe[1] where I had an ovation from the audience, to say nothing of crowds outside the hotel and the theatre.

London has changed, even in eighteen months; the traffic is appalling and all elegance has fled from the West End. Coventry Street, Piccadilly Circus, Leicester Square and Shaftesbury Avenue have acquired a curious 'welfare state' squalor which reminds me of Moscow. Binkie came back to the Dorchester with me and we sat up far too late. He was very sweet but he has changed, too, a little. His 'theatre' energy seems to have diminished. The changing world has affected him too. I don't think he really minds as much as he used to.

Sunday 9 June

The pace has been swift but on the whole I am enjoying myself. I rehearse Mike [Wilding] every morning and see people and plays the rest of the time. So far the theatre-going has been unrewarding.

Last night I drove to Coppins and dined with the dear Duchess and Prince Eddie[2], who, I must say, has improved vastly and was most charming. It was a sweet evening. I drove there and back with Kenneth Rose, an intelligent young man who is the political correspondent of the *Telegraph*.

Today I drove out to Hatfield to lunch with the Salisburys. Betty was friendly and sweet as she always is; Bobbity, however, was rather uppish. The house was fascinating and Betty showed me over it before the public was allowed in. All the Elizabethan relics thrilled me, particularly the Queen's[3] garden hat made of plaited string and her yellow silk stockings, the first to be worn in England. The whole thing, however, depressed me somewhat. His lordship was definitely 'great' and tried, unsuccessfully, to make me feel ill at ease. In any case, I don't mind deeply. I wanted to see Hatfield. I saw it, and that was that. The whole thing reminded me of years ago in 1941 when I returned from Australia and New Zealand and Anthony Eden virtually cut me in the Carlton Grill[4]. A foolish mistake on his part, although perfectly consistent with his whole career. Chilled, more by the weather than anything else, I drove back to London through wet suburbs. Hatfield is no longer in the country. It is a sort of continuation of Golders Green.

1 Where *Nude with Violin* was still playing.
2 Edward, Duke of Kent (b. 1935).
3 Queen Elizabeth I.
4 On that occasion too there had been unfavourable and largely inaccurate Press reports of Noël's decision to go abroad.

Sunday 16 June

The pace, while not actually killing me, is exhausting me. I have set *Nude* in order, though Mike is worrying me. He is so dreadfully nervous, and although he knows the words he stumbles and stammers and gets into an increasing frizz at each rehearsal.

On Monday I visited poor Beatrice Eden. She cannot live more than a few weeks but she was sitting up and seemed cheerful. I think she has the usual cancer immunity and really doesn't know that it is the end. She was paper thin and a tragic sight. I talked to the head sister, who says it will all be over soon. She is not in pain and is being more and more heavily doped every few hours. A calm and not unpleasant way to die really in spite of the nightmare word.

Eddie Fisher's opening at the Palladium was a tremendous success. He sang well and without tricks or affectation. He also made a speech and announced very sweetly, my presence, whereupon there was a terrific hullabaloo, very heart-warming. Wherever I go in London I am hailed as a returning hero. Taxi drivers shout welcoming words to me and pedestrians smile and wave. All of which makes dear John Gordon and the other Press gentlemen look very silly. There is little doubt about my popularity with the English public and this makes me feel very happy indeed.

Sunday 23 June

Apart from my mornings in the theatre, the week has been acutely social. A lunch with Randolph Churchill at White's because he is writing a book about Anthony Eden and wished to pump me for personal reminiscences and anecdotes. This wish was not really gratified because I cannot remember anything very interesting about Anthony except that he was pleasant and had excessively good manners, neither of which attributes makes a strong enough basis for a psychological analysis. There was a noisy lunch party at Pam Berry's. Loelia [Westminster], Annie [Fleming], Virginia Cowles, the ubiquitous Malcolm Muggeridge[1], whom I can't stand, and Patrick Kinross[2]. It was quite funny and everyone shrieked at once. If the dialogue had been transcribed the critics undoubtedly would have stated confidently that such characters did not exist.

On Wednesday I gave a 'free for all' at the Dorchester which was a terrific success. It was also a curious mixture. Hugh and Sylvia Foot, Dorothy Dickson, Deborah Kerr, Mike Todd and Liz Taylor[3], Oliver [Messel],

---

1 Malcolm Muggeridge (b. 1903), British writer and broadcaster.
2 Patrick Balfour, 3rd Baron Kinross (1904–77), writer.
3 Elizabeth Taylor (b. 1932), British film star, had just married Mike Todd.

Freddie Carpenter[1]. Kenny More[2] came late and was very funny and cheerfully disgraceful.

On Thursday I went to have a drink with Dickie and Edwina. Edwina had been rather offish on the telephone and I was quite determined to deal firmly with her. This I did and she relaxed and became more like her old self, but actually not enough. They have both changed beyond recognition. No more humour and an overweening pomposity. It is a shame but there is obviously nothing to be done. '*Tout lasse, tout passe, tout casse*'. Life goes on and little bits of us get lost.

That same evening after I had coaxed the Mountbattens into a semblance of their former selves, I drove to Windsor with Teddie Thompson. John Counsell had sent me two seats for *Four in Hand*, a stupid little comedy[3] redeemed by the performance of my godson, Danny Massey. It was a gala performance because the Queen had taken over the theatre for her Ascot house party. In the entr'acte, when Teddie and I had settled ourselves in the bar with a drink, a grand uniformed gentleman appeared and said to me, 'Her Majesty the Queen wishes to see you', so I was led upstairs to a passage behind the circle, where I talked for about twenty minutes to the Queen, Princess Margaret and the Queen Mother. They were absolutely enchanting to me and the Queen Mother, as usual, surpassed herself in saying the right thing. She said, 'How lovely to see you again. We have been most angry on your behalf. For the Press to attack your integrity after all you have done for England both in the country and out of it is outrageous, but don't let it upset you, and remember that we too have had our troubles with the Press!' I replied gently that if she wished to reduce me to floods of tears she was going the right way about it. Later Prince Philip appeared and the Princess Royal, Princess Alexandra and the Gloucesters[4]. They were all welcoming and friendly and I returned ultimately to Teddie fairly bulging with royal favour. I do think it was very sweet of them to send for me and take so much trouble to prove to me that none of the Press beastliness had had the slightest effect on their opinion of me. Teddie, of course, was in a frenzy of excitement, and afterwards, when we had a nightcap with Norman Hartnell[5] and Winnie Portarlington[6], her eyes were wet with pride. Perhaps mine were too. There is little sense in having a constitutional monarchy and not being a cosy royal snob. I would rather be

---

1 Freddie Carpenter (b. 1908), Australian director and choreographer, based in London.

2 Kenneth More (b. 1914), the British film and stage actor, who had appeared in Noël's *Peace in Our Time* in 1947.

3 By Michael Brett.

4 Henry, Duke of Gloucester (1900–74), uncle of Elizabeth II, and Alice, Duchess of Gloucester (b. 1901).

5 Norman Hartnell (1901–79), couturier and royal dressmaker; knighted 1977.

6 Winnifreda, Countess of Portarlington.

favoured in that particular way by the Royal Family than be knighted to a standstill.

Sunday 30 June   Biot

Here I am with Graham in the glorious South of France sunshine. Edward's[1] new house is really a dream and not too big and grand as I feared it might be. He really has done it beautifully, the most impeccable taste and immensely comfortable. He himself is happier and nicer than he has been for years. He no longer drinks too many martinis and gets fighting drunk. He is no longer petulant. In fact he is enchanting company and we have done nothing but laugh and enjoy ourselves since we arrived.

Mike [Wilding] opened on Monday night. He was fairly all right but mumbled dreadfully and was quivering with inside nerves. He moved well and with assurance but his speech is a serious problem. Nothing can be done until he has played it for a couple of weeks, then I shall come down with my cohorts all gleaming and beat the fuck out of him. Afterwards there was a party at Teddie's. Not a very good party really, owing to a few deadheads. Larry and Viv were there. Larry had been to see me privately in the afternoon and told me ghastly stories about poor Viv[2]. The whole thing is a nightmare. It is awfully difficult to judge the true situation. Vivien, who can be so charming and gay, can also be a terrible little bitch. This I remember from way back when she suddenly attacked me with full viciousness over 'Lie in the Dark and Listen'[3]. They are undoubtedly a curious couple. I am fond of them and desperately sorry for them.

The following evening I took Molly Buccleuch to the opening of *The Prince and the Showgirl*.[4] A great big booming film première. The crowds lining the streets shouted 'Bravo, Nole' as I drove by, which was jolly sweet. The picture is too long. Larry is superb and, as usual, none of the idiotic critics has noted the exquisite comedic subtlety of his performance. Marilyn Monroe looks very pretty and is charming at moments but too much emphasis on tits and bottom. It is, to me, a charming picture, but then I have always liked the delicate irony of the story. It has had bad notices.

I lunched on Monday with the Duchess of Kent at Kensington Palace, which she has done[5] beautifully. So far, so very, very good.

---

1 Edward Molyneux had now moved into Les Clausonnes near Biot.
2 Who was heading for another nervous breakdown.
3 The war poem Noël had written attacking people in 'safe, reserved occupations'; Vivien Leigh had many friends who were.
4 The Olivier-Marilyn Monroe film of Rattigan's *The Sleeping Prince*.
5 Redecorated; it was now her London home.

Sunday 7 July

The holiday has continued to be enchanting, no clouds either in the sky or in the conversation. I have seen multitudes of old buddies – Dickie Gordon, Rosie Dolly[1], Pam Frankau[2], Peggy Webster[3], George Schlee, Somerset Maugham, Garbo, the Gary Coopers, Mike Todd, Liz Taylor, the Van Johnsons, etc. Edward has remained unfailingly sweet and I have a feeling that there will be no more dramas in the future. I am crossing everything as I write this because he has an unpredictable character.

The high spot of the week has been a lovely evening with Garbo. We picked her up at her beautifully situated but hideous villa and dined at a little restaurant on the port at Villefranche. Garbo was bright as a button and, of course, fabulously beautiful; the food was delicious, the evening glorious with lights from ships glittering in the dark sea and the mountains rising up dramatically into the sky. After dinner we were shown, privately, the little chapel which has just been designed by Jean Cocteau. It is beautifully done, lovely draughtsmanship and pale colours, but I had no idea that all the apostles looked so like Jean Marais.

Another high spot was a day I spent alone with Willie Maugham and Alan[4]. Willie was really extraordinary. After all, he is eighty-three and should show some signs of wear and tear but he doesn't. In fact he seemed younger and in better form than he was two years ago. He dived off the diving-board into the pool as usual and, as usual, the lunch was perfect, with a lovely snooze afterwards in a cool room. We gossiped about everything under the sun and I drove home to Biot in the evening sunlight feeling happy and stimulated and deeply impressed by the charm of old age when it is allied to health and intelligence.

Saturday 13 July   Paris

I have had a pleasant week, peaceful and without strain. I dined with Loulou Jourdan[5] at the Tour d'Argent, after which we went to the Alexandre to have a nightcap and decided it would be good for our livers to walk home. Loulou is a dear boy and I am very fond of him. He is also so handsome that it is a pleasure to look at him.

I spent a curious evening at the Véfour where I had gone to dine alone. Barbara Hutton appeared, not very drunk but weaving, and took charge of

1 Rosie Dolly, one of the two actress/singer Dolly sisters.
2 Pamela Frankau (1908–67), novelist and journalist.
3 Margaret Webster (1905–72), actress and stage director, daughter of actor-manager Ben Webster.
4 Alan Searle, Maugham's secretary.
5 Louis Jourdan (b. 1919), French actor.

me, and I finished the evening alone with her in her suite at the Ritz, reading her own poems to her. Actually some of them are simple and moving. She is a tragic epitome of 'Poor Little Rich Girl'. She is capable of great kindnesses but her money is always between her and happiness. It does seem a shame.

I have bought enough scent and toilet water to float the *Queen Mary* and a lot of shirts and handkerchiefs, owing to the fact that on my last evening in Cannes, after Edward and I had dined on the 'port', I went to the casino and won £300 in about forty minutes. Not being a real gambler I grabbed up all the lovely pink biscuits and flew to the *caisse* and out into the car with the crisp notes rustling in my pocket. This has made my Paris visit extra-luxe and most enjoyable.

Sunday 21 July   ss *United States*

Here I am again half-way to America but very definitely on American soil, if one can so describe this chromium floating hotel. It's very comfortable and wicked bellboys, with dreadfully sophisticated expressions, rush in and out at the touch of a button.

I have read Frankie Lonsdale's biography of Freddie[1]: extremely well done but none too kind really. After Daphne's book on Gerald[2] and Marguerite's book on Laurette[3], I am grateful not to have any bright-eyed daughters.

Monday's performance of *Nude* was disaster. Mike had 'one of his heads', his girl-friend Marie McDonald[4] arrived, and he made an absolute shambles of the play and a fucking fool of himself. The house was packed and the wonderful audience died in their seats. My head rested between my knees throughout most of the torture. He mumbled, fluffed, dried up dead, staggered and was completely inaudible. Joyce was nearly in hysterics and small blame to her[5]. The whole company played up marvellously but the last scene went right down the drain and there were only two curtain calls. Afterwards, at Dotty Dickson's party for me to which, astonishingly, Mike came with 'The Body', I let him have the works and told him he was not epileptic but was suffering from hypochondria, hysteria and acute lack of talent. He then burst into tears and it was all charming. The next morning 'The Body' rang me up to ask me to be kind as Mike had 'taken a beating'. I replied that the public had taken a worse beating and so had the play, the company and the author. I rehearsed him for an hour in the morning, but it was obviously no good. Binkie appeared and we tried to talk sense into him.

That night Binkie and John Perry came to dine with me and told me that

1 *Frederick Lonsdale* by his daughter Frances Donaldson.
2 *Gerald* by his daughter Daphne du Maurier.
3 *Laurette Taylor* by her daughter Marguerite Courtney.
4 Marie McDonald, Hollywood actress known as 'The Body'.
5 Joyce Carey was playing opposite Michael Wilding.

the understudy was playing. We spent the evening racking our brains to think of a replacement. The next day Mike played the matinée and I saw the first scene. Quite good. In the evening Joyce arrived at Winnie's farewell party for me and said he had given a good performance for the first time since he had opened! I can only conclude that my flying at him sank in. If he *does* collapse on this job, which is his last chance, he'll never get another. Poor beast, how awful to be so agonizingly silly.

Graham came to say goodnight at the Dorchester [Hotel] and I saw suddenly how deeply unhappy he is. He behaved beautifully as always and went away. A few minutes later I called him up and he was, as I suspected, suffused with tears. This really tore me in two, and I realized how good he has been under all rebuffs and how lonely inside. He couldn't come to the boat to see me off because he had hopes of getting on a television series with Richard Hearne[1]. Yesterday I had a radio from him saying that they considered him to be the wrong type. I radioed back immediately to say that I considered Richard Hearne's programme to be the wrong type for him and I have written him as cheering a letter as I can. I mind about him terribly. I long for him to get a good job and make a success and I believe that eventually he will. But, oh Lord, the waiting about is ghastly. I know how much he misses me and it *can't* be helped but my heart aches for him.

Sunday 4 August   Beverly Hills

The Almighty has withdrawn his hitherto effusive regard for me and struck me down. My flight out here last Sunday was peaceful and uneventful. I read Nevil Shute's new book *On the Beach*, a grisly description of a group of people left alive in Australia when the rest of the world has been annihilated by H-bombs. They are waiting for the spreading radioactivity to spread to them and wipe them out which, eventually, it does. It's written with his usual fluency and is a good idea, but all the characters are so sickeningly decent and 'ordinary' and such good sorts that personally I longed for the slowly approaching 'fall-out' to get a move on. He is suffering from a sort of spiritual diabetes in which *everything* turns to sugar.

Marlene met me at the airport and we drove to Clifton's. He was in bed with a cold. We dined quietly and went to bed early after I had rehearsed Marlene in some cockney speeches for *Witness for the Prosecution*[2]. It is not easy to teach Cockney to a German glamour-puss who can't pronounce her Rs but she did astonishingly well. On Monday I lay in the sun and bathed in the pool, and in the evening, just as I was dressing to go out and dine quietly with Leonard Spiegelgas[3], I bent down to get some socks out of a drawer and was

1 Richard Hearne (1908–79), British comedian, best known in his role as Mr Pastry.
2 Film by Billy Wilder of Agatha Christie's thriller.
3 Leonard Spiegelgas, dramatist and Hollywood screenwriter.

seized with a blazing pain across the small of my back. At first I thought I had slipped something but I suspected, and I was right, that it was my old friend 'lumbago'.

From then on the whole week became a highly coloured nightmare. Clifton sent me to an ass of a chiropractor, who was most sympathetic and kindly and tortured me more thoroughly than the Gestapo ever tortured Odette. After three days of this 'manipulation' I dragged myself to the telephone and told him I was completely cured, then I called up Ed Bigg in Chicago, who at once prescribed meta-cortin, which is a derivative of cortisone, and within twenty-four hours the pain began to go. Meanwhile I hobbled out to dinner parties – George Cukor, Cole[1], etc. I sat in a projection room and saw *Les Girls*, which was an adequate entertainment redeemed by Kay Kendall. I tottered miserably to lunch with Marlene and Ty[2] and Billy Wilder[3] and the Laughtons[4], and saw some of *Witness* which looked good. Then on Friday, more dead than alive, I endured Clifton's party in my honour which lasted from 6 p.m. to 6 a.m. I gave up at 2.30 a.m. I couldn't stand, so I sat in the garden on a chair with a board at my back for the first part of the evening, then I was helped, board and all, into dinner, and later propped up by the piano. By this time I had had several whiskys and was feeling hardly any pain. I was also doped to the eyes with pink pills called 'flexin'. It was a really wonderfully good party and very choicely star-spangled. Ty Power, Fred Astaire, the Joe Cottens, the Gary Coopers, the Robert Mitchums, Cary Grant, Claudette, Hedda[5], Louella [Parsons], Peggy Wood[6], Fritzi Massary, Barbara Stanwyck[7], Frankie Sinatra, Marlene, etc. Roger Edens[8] played the piano. We all performed. I sang duets with Judy [Garland]. The same old routine but a highly enjoyable one.

The next day, yesterday, Clifton and I just lay about. In the evening we watched Billy Graham[9] on television. A curious spectacle preceded by poor Ethel Waters[10], vast and mad, singing with glutinous sweetness but no voice about Jesus being devoted to her and also to every sparrow. Then Mr Graham. Good looking, clear-cut, decisive, expert gestures and voice production, cruel eyes and a cruel jaw. He talks nobly and violently about Christ and the

1 Cole Porter, whose latest film musical was *Les Girls*.
2 Tyrone Power was co-starring in *Witness for the Prosecution*.
3 Billy Wilder (b. 1906), American film-maker.
4 Charles Laughton (1899–1962), also appearing in Wilder's film, and his wife, British actress Elsa Lanchester (b. 1902).
5 Hedda Hopper (1890–1966), American actress turned journalist.
6 Peggy Wood (b. 1892), American actress and singer; she had starred in the London production of *Bitter Sweet* in 1929.
7 Barbara Stanwyck (b. 1907), American film star.
8 Roger Edens (b. 1905), Hollywood producer and lyricist.
9 Billy Graham (b. 1918), American evangelist.
10 Ethel Waters (1900–77), black American actress and singer.

Christian way of life. He raised his voice, he dropped his voice, he wooed, he bullied and worked himself into a beautifully controlled lather. He called for converts, for people who were willing to dedicate themselves to Jesus, and they began to shuffle self-consciously down the aisles of the Madison Square Garden and stood looking up at him. Not very many answered the call and I noted a rather nasty look in his eye and my heart ached for Mrs Billy Graham after the show was over.

It was a remarkable spectacle and I watched him carefully to see if I could detect a spark of true humility, of genuine religious 'flair', and was unrewarded. He is a fine showman, that is all. As much an egocentric as McCarthy[1] or Hitler or almost any other of the great mass movers. He got his audience. Their expressions of moronic ecstasy were horrible to see. If he had asked them to rush out and lynch someone they would have obeyed. As it was they merely shuffled down and stared at him like cringing animals, dominated by his personality, his looks and his masculinity, and believing with all their puny might that they were drawing nearer to Christ. A lamentable spectacle.

Friday 9 August   Wyoming

Here I am in the Rocky Mountain country, looking out of the window of a wooden cabin at a lush green valley surrounded by jagged mountain peaks. A river rushes through the valley and there are no noises at night except the river and an occasional squirrel dropping on to the roof.

My last few days in Hollywood were more cheerful. The pain had almost disappeared and I was able to move without groaning. I dined with Irving Lazar, and Virginia Zanuck[2], and saw a brilliant film, *Twelve Angry Men*, beautifully written, directed and acted[3], and a less good one, *A Face in the Crowd*, which was unpleasant and untidy but redeemed here and there by some good moments of direction. Elia Kazan[4] allowed the job to get out of control. It was primarily a satire on the gullibility of the 'Great American Public' but he mounted the satire, dug his spurs in and allowed it to bolt with him. (This equine simile may be excused as I am staying on a ranch.)

Clifton and I flew to Salt Lake City on Wednesday and stayed the night at the Utah Hotel. We gave some Press interviews, graciously allowed ourselves to be photographed, ate an inedible dinner and saw *Giant*, one of the slowest movies it has ever been my lot to endure. James Dean had some good moments and Rock Hudson and Liz Taylor acted well here and there, but the whole thing was defeated by its own, and the director's[5], lack of tempo.

1 Joseph McCarthy (1908–57), American Senator notorious for his anti-Communist witch hunt.
2 Wife of Darryl Zanuck.
3 By, respectively, Reginald Rose, Sidney Lumet and, among others, Henry Fonda and E.G. Marshall.
4 The director.
5 George Stevens.

The next morning, yesterday, we climbed into an aeroplane filled with girl scouts and did a hedge-hopping journey to Cody. There were no hedges actually, only beige plains and ravines and bare hills like brown corrugated cardboard. We popped down at several small airports filled with Western atmosphere. The girl scouts sang incessantly to their ukuleles and the sun shone down with all its might, making us very hot. After a drink and lunch at the Irma Hotel, plastered with oleographs and engravings of Buffalo Bill, we did a little shopping and drove out here where the peace is profound and the beauty considerable.

Sunday 25 August   New York

A great deal has happened and it has been a full and exhausting week but everything is going swimmingly. The theatre problem was our greatest headache, but we have now settled on the Belasco which the Shuberts have agreed to do up for me, and we open *Nude with Violin* there on 14 November after one week in Wilmington and two in Philadelphia. Most of our days have been devoted to auditions.

Graham is playing *Tonight at 8.30* at the Theatre Royal, Windsor, for two weeks and has made a success of it and is as happy as a clam. Coley arrived on Friday with all the London news and is going to Bermuda on Wednesday. I shall follow him next Friday or Saturday.

I have kept to my diet and have lost eight pounds. My face is lean again and my body so much better that I can hardly believe it. In addition to this the thyroid pills are magic. Usually when I diet I feel crotchety and exhausted. This time I feel really better than I have felt for years. I drink two glasses of skim milk per day (tidged up with vanilla and sweetening), two eggs for my lunch, and steak and sliced tomato for my dinner. For breakfast only fruit juice and coffee. It is monotonous, of course, but the effect is sensational.

I am not looking forward madly to Bermuda but it will be a month to think, learn my part and gird my slimmer loins.

Saturday 14 September   Bermuda

The last two weeks have been a great deal pleasanter than I expected. In the first place the weather, on the whole, has been lovely. We had trouble over the boat because no one had properly looked after it or its engine. However, after much cursing and swearing and trial and error we've got it to work, and both Coley and I are becoming quite expert.

Binkie is behaving badly and greedily over the American production of *Nude*. He is demanding two per cent of the gross and a share of the subsidiary rights. Both of these demands are unheard of. It is sad that, with all his true capacity for friendship, his overdeveloped business acumen should let him down. Friendship and business we know do not marry comfortably, but I am afraid he has taken a good deal more advantage of me over the years than I realized. This is a discouraging thought but it doesn't really matter. Ethical standards in my mind must be upheld. If they are not, measures must be taken to ensure that they are. In future I fully intend to take them.

Sunday 29 September

We've had a busy week. Two farewell cocktail parties and a dinner at Government House, which was ineffably boring except for a conversation I had with HE who is really very funny. We discussed wickedly the Wolfenden Report on Homosexuality[1] with the new American Consul General flapping his ears nearby. The Governor takes a casual and fairly irreverent view of the whole boring subject. He said that at one period of his army career he had to lecture several hundred young cadets. He told them that, as far as he was concerned, they could get pigs in trouble, goats in trouble and themselves in trouble, but that if they got any NCOs or officers in trouble they would be OUT! This, I need hardly say, I enjoyed enormously.

Sunday 13 October   New York

Two very busy weeks have passed. Busy and enjoyable. I am delighted with the cast: the new bits sound good and I am fairly sure I am going to be all right. Everyone made a tremendous effort and was word perfect at the first rehearsal. The result of this is that, in spite of several different members of the company being away with Asian flu, we are now nearly ready to open and have a whole week in hand for polishing.

I have been with Marlene and others to most of the plays in town and have only been genuinely thrilled twice: *West Side Story* and *Look Back in Anger*. The former is brilliantly done and, to me, most moving. The choreography and general direction[2] beyond praise. John Osborne's play was full of vitality and rich language. It irritated me at moments, as it did when I read it, but it was superbly acted and, on the whole, a rewarding evening in the theatre. Peter Ustinov's *Romanoff and Juliet* I thought heavy-handed and 'charade-ish' with a few witty lines and an excellent comedy performance from him.

Nude is still playing to capacity in London and Michael is still woolly, inaudible and idiotic.

The Russians have produced a satellite called 'Sputnik' which circled the globe in an hour and a half and kept on doing it until it wore itself to shreds. This has shaken the Americans to the core and they are, rightly I think, in a high old frizz. The end of the world we know seems to be drawing appreciably nearer.

1 British parliamentary enquiry into the possibility of legalizing homosexuality between consenting adults.
2 Both by Jerome Robbins.

Saturday 26 October   Wilmington

The play opened on Tuesday night and so far it has been a big success.

Just before the dress rehearsal and the first performance I slipped in the shower and crashed down, making a gash across the bridge of my nose and almost breaking it. The whole bathroom was covered in blood and it was a very horrid shock. Fortunately I didn't break a limb or injure my back. As it was, my nose swelled up and I looked like a bruiser for a few days. I could also hardly breathe for coagulated blood at the back of my nose and throat. However, I rose above it and I'm all right now, but I shall step gingerly in and out of baths to the end of my days.

The notices here have been very fine.

My secret news is that I fear that Old Black Magic has reared itself up again. This is stimulating, disturbing, enjoyable, depressing, gay, tormenting, delightful, silly and sensible. Perhaps I was getting a little smug and too sure of my immunity. It may also be that now that I'm slim as a rail again I'm more attractive not only to myself but to others. I can already see all the old hoops being prepared for me to go through. Ah me!

Sunday 17 November   New York

On Monday afternoon I went to a rehearsal of *Conversation Piece* which is being put on at a tiny theatre (the Barbizon Plaza) with tiny, but good sets; a tiny orchestra and a tiny leading lady, Joan Copeland, who is Arthur Miller's sister and is very charming as Melanie. Her French is excellent and her voice true, though light. The whole thing was done with reasonable taste, but it won't really do because *Conversation Piece* needs immense style and a star, if not two, to play it. The hope is that, being an 'off Broadway' production, the critics will be disarmed and see the *true* values of the play. The piece is done pleasantly and gently and is, almost monotonously, charming.

On Monday evening I went to see a sorry spectacle: *Jamaica*[1] with Lena Horne, Ricardo Montalban and an over-vivacious coloured lady called Josephine Premice who carried on like a mad spider. Lena was brilliant and Ricardo Montalban's chest was lovely. Apart from this the evening was a loss.

Our two previews of *Nude* on Tuesday and Wednesday were fairly grim. The audiences, not yet having been told by Brooks Atkinson and Walter Kerr[2] whether to like it or not, preserved a non-committal demeanour which was trying to play to.

On Thursday there was all the hullabaloo of an NC opening night. Flowers and telegrams and gifts and nervous tension. There was also a deluge of rain so violent that we had to hold the curtain for twenty minutes. When it finally rose and I walked on, I received a tremendous ovation, mainly on account of

1 Musical by Harold Arlen.
2 The leading New York drama critics.

my advanced age and past achievements, and from then on the dear first-nighters settled back into a damp apathy from which nothing I or any of us could do would rouse them. The presence of critics nearly always puts a blight on an audience anyhow and this, coupled with the rain and the steamy heat of the Belasco Theatre, was really too much to combat.

After the performance the management gave a party at the Algonquin and everyone was gay and noisy. Later on the morning papers came out and I retired temporarily to my temporary suite to read them. Both Brooks Atkinson and Walter Kerr were contemptuous of the play, although they praised me as a comedian. This I recognized immediately as the kiss of death. Perhaps not quite death in my case, for I am a considerable draw, but lethal enough to take the edge off the play being a smash hit. I returned to the party heavy-hearted but vivacious to the last, but when I went home I felt miserably disappointed. I telephoned to London as promised and talked to Lornie and Graham, and retired bloody but unbowed to bed.

There is obviously a quality in *Nude with Violin* which irritates the critical mind. Perhaps because the whole play is a blistering satire on the critical mind? At all events, in London it didn't receive one even civil notice and has played to capacity for over a year and made me a nice lot of money. I fear, even with me in it, that it will not do that here. In England the audience can identify itself with the family and its dilemmas. Here there is no line of identification with what, to us, is the ordinary, well-behaved middle class. Such a class doesn't really exist in America.

Also, in England the public is more prone to think for itself. In America they have to be told what to enjoy and what to avoid, not only in the theatre but in every phase of life. They are told by television and radio what to eat, drink and smoke, what cars to buy and what laxatives and sanitary towels to use. They are told, in no uncertain terms, what movies to go to and what stars to admire. They are allowed to choose, admittedly from not too glamorous a selection, what gods to worship. The power of individual thought has been atrophied in them by the incessant onslaughts of commercialism. Their reading matter, for the large majority, consists of columnists' gossip, headlines and magazines. Among the so-called intelligentsia there is only one trend at the moment, a sort of defeated psychopathic despair.

Sunday 24 November

We have done a surprisingly good week considering the disdain of Messrs Atkinson and Kerr. We have had a few 'theatre parties' to help us, and the advance, up to Christmas, is good. After that we may be in trouble. The play, of course, goes much better than it did on the opening night, but I am aware of a tremendous change in the quality of the New York audiences since I played here twenty-one years ago. They used to be quick on comedy, quicker often than London audiences. Now, however, this quickness has gone. They are quite appreciative on the whole, but much dimmer. In fact they have lost the capacity for participation.

Possibly this change has been caused by the 'theatre party' habit, which to my mind is a dangerous and intolerable racket. Charity organizers buy out the theatre at the box-office prices. They then proceed to resell the tickets at exorbitant prices to the supporters of some given charities. Thus, most of the members of the audience, particularly the men, arrive at the theatre either consciously or subconsciously aware that they have paid too highly for their seats and that whatever show they see has got to be super-good to justify their expenditure. These 'theatre party' audiences are hell to play to.

The managements, unwisely I think in the long view, encourage this racket. For them it is of course a form of insurance. If they have sold the house out for five or six performances a week for two or three months before the play has even opened they can at least have a chance, in the face of bad notices, of getting some money back. Helen Hayes told me the other night that ever since *Time Remembered*[1] opened (it is a smash success) she has not had *one* happy performance and not *once* played to the real public. Nothing but theatre parties night after night and matinée after matinée. It is another ghastly example of the all-pervasive commercialism which is rapidly reducing this potentially magnificent country to idiocy.

Sunday 1 December   Sneden's Landing

Here I am home again with Kit and Guthrie and the Hudson River rolling by and hearts at peace under an American heaven. The house is lovelier than ever and Kit and Guthrie sweeter and dearer than ever. No fuss, no demands, just good company when you want it and a comfortable bed when you don't.

We have done another good week but slightly less than last. The performances have been good. I have my suite at the Algonquin to retire to in between the shows on matinée days, and everything is jogging along.

My private emotions are going through the usual familiar hoops, hoops that I fondly imagined I had discarded years ago. I am sure it is good for the soul and the spirit and the ultimate creative processes to fall down into the dust again, but it is now and always has been painful for me. My extraordinary gift of concentration, which stands me in such good stead in all other phases of my life, turns on these occasions into a double-edged sword. My imagination works overtime and frequently inaccurately. I scale heights and tumble down lachrymose ravines. My humour retires baffled (but not for long, thank God), and I lie awake arguing with myself, jeering at myself and, worst of all, pitying myself. All the gallant lyrics of all the songs I have ever written rise up and mock me while I lie in the dark and listen. It all has little to do with the person

1 The Anouilh play in which Helen Hayes was then playing on Broadway.

involved, little to do with anyone but myself. To me, passionate love has always been like a tight shoe rubbing blisters on my Achilles heel. That's enough of that. I resent it and love it and wallow and recover and it's all part of 'life's rich pattern' and I wish to God I could handle it, but I never have and I know I never will. Let's hope that it will ultimately rejuvenate my ageing spirits. Let's hope that at least I get something out of it.

Sunday 8 December   New York

Another week gone by. Business all right but steadily declining. I have nothing more to report beyond a charming dinner with Lillian and Dorothy Gish[1] and an evening of snow and sleet driving out to Brooklyn to see Johnnie Ray open at the Town and Country, which is like an outsize aeroplane hangar filled with the most hideous people I have ever seen, few of whom paid the faintest attention to what was going on on the stage, which was less like a stage than a gargantuan boxing ring. Johnnie managed to hold them reasonably quiet but it was agony to watch him fighting.

I have to appear on Ed Sullivan's programme tonight.[2] I am surprisingly nervous. Not perhaps so surprisingly, because I have a new accompanist, Pete Matz being away in Florida with Ginger Rogers[3]; also my voice is tired and not very flexible. However, I am only doing two numbers, the medley and 'Tots'. The medley is what frightens me but I expect I shall get away with it.

I am not enjoying any of this. The weather is vile, rain, sleet, snow and ice. I am inside bitterly disappointed not to be an absolute smash. This is the first time for many, many years that I have had to look for gaps at the sides of the stalls and scrutinize the nightly returns. I expect this, too, will be good for my soul. It had better be, because it certainly isn't very good for my health. I carry on a running campaign against colds. After all, I haven't endured a really bad winter for many years. I intend to press on for my announced twelve weeks whatever happens, but I'm finding it a considerable strain.

Sunday 15 December

I got away with my television appearance by the skin of my teeth. I sang the medley well but I was nervous inside largely because I could neither see nor hear the orchestra distinctly and was worried about my voice. I was told afterwards by my loved ones that I was charming, but this, after all, is what loved ones are for.

I had a pleasant supper with Ty Power, who is going off into the sticks to

---

1 Dorothy Gish (1898–1968); with her sister Lillian, the brightest of D.W. Griffiths' early silent screen stars; Noël had made his first film, *Hearts of the World*, with them in 1918.
2 A popular television show.
3 Ginger Rogers (b. 1911), American musical star and actress.

play a truncated version of *Back to Methuselah*[1]. He, Faye Emerson, Arthur Treacher, and the rest of the cast travel from town to town by bus and play to fabulous business. Ty said he'd much rather play to people in more or less isolated places who really wanted to see him than face the dubious critical acclaim of Broadway. I must say I agreed with him most heartily. I doubt if I shall ever play on Broadway again for longer than a few weeks[2]. It is not stimulating any more, and as long as the New York theatre-goers continue to allow themselves to be ordered about by the critics and marshalled into theatre parties, the New York theatre, which was once so vital, will decline and be of no further interest. A few lauded smash hits do *not* keep the drama alive.

Sunday 22 December

Well, my birthday is over and I am now fifty-eight, two years off sixty and twelve years off seventy and, Lord knows, I should have learnt wisdom by now but I haven't and that's that. Joycie gave me a little lunch and I had some caviare before the show and a party with birthday cake given by the company after the show. It was all very sweet and I loathed it.

On Tuesday Sam Spiegel gave me and the company a private showing of *The Bridge on the River Kwai*[3], a really magnificent picture. Brilliantly directed by David [Lean] and acted superbly by Alec, James Donald, Jack Hawkins, Sessue Hayakawa and Bill Holden. Really satisfying. I rather wish now that I had done it. Incidentally, I forgot to mention that two weeks ago I gave a private showing of *In Which We Serve* to the company after the play one night. It really held up magnificently and I felt very proud of it.

I lunched with Eleanor Roosevelt at the United Nations and she was charming and friendly as indeed she always has been to me.

The business is still gently slipping. We are going all right but it is dispiriting.

Sunday 29 December

A beastly week. All the dreary Christmas fuss and half-empty houses. Then, on Christmas night, on the stage, my voice gave out. I managed to finish the show and came home to bed where I have been ever since, cutting five performances, all of which were sold out! I should have had the sense to stay off before Christ's natal day and not driven myself to collapse at the worst possible moment. I am going back tonight to play a special performance for the Actors' Fund. I am not *really* better but better enough. Christmas was merrie hell.

1 George Bernard Shaw's play cycle.
2 This was in fact to be Noël's last season there as an actor.
3 The Oscar-winning film in which Noël had declined the role of the English officer eventually played by Alec Guinness.

1958

Rather than let Nude with Violin *drift into Broadway failure, Noël decided at the end of its three months there to move the production to California, adding* Present Laughter *(and Eva Gabor) to enliven the company. The result was a resounding San Francisco–Los Angeles success with which to start the New Year. The rest of the year was spent in translating a Feydeau farce,* Occupe-toi d'Amélie, *which became* Look After Lulu; *he also began work on his one and only ballet score,* London Morning, *for the Festival Ballet, and on a play about old actresses in a retirement home,* Waiting in the Wings.

Sunday 5 January   New York

I have decided, with some misgivings and perhaps misguided optimism, to finish here as planned on 8 February and then play four weeks in San Francisco and two in Hollywood. I have also decided to play *Present Laughter* alternately with *Nude* and use the same set with a few slight alterations. Morris Carnovski will not be in *P.L.* but Eva Gabor[1] has agreed to play Joanna. I couldn't bear to fizzle out here drearily with *Nude*. *P.L.* will cheer me up and there are good parts for all the company. Needless to say they are, most of them, raising hell and clamouring for more money and generally making beasts of themselves. The silliness of actors really passeth all understanding and I should like to bash their empty heads together. To appear with me on the West Coast in two different plays will be the most wonderful opportunity for them to be seen by movie and television executives. The silly asses ought to pay for the privilege. However, it will doubtless all settle itself, it always does.

I know it is a good idea to go to the West Coast. It is almost bound to be a success because they are starved for good theatre. The only thing that worries me is my health. I am already fairly exhausted, and my bad throat has pulled me down. However, I hope that the excitement of plunging into *Present Laughter* again may banish my sense of dreariness. Anyhow the die is cast. Roger Stevens[2], although it will probably lose him money owing to the transport expenses, is enthusiastic and encouraging. I shall probably give a few performances of *P.L.* here so as to polish it up for San Francisco. I rather fancy the idea of using New York as a try-out for the road! I shall *not*, repeat *not*, invite the critics.

I am also recording my verses with Maggie Leighton next Sunday. Never a dull moment.

Sunday 19 January

A busy week, rehearsing *P.L.* and playing *Nude* at night. Eva Gabor is going to be excellent as Joanna. In addition to this she is an adorable darling to work with, no trouble and determined to be good. She arrived at her first rehearsal word perfect, which was none too easy for her, being a Hungarian, and she takes direction like a dream. She will, I suspect, make a big success.

Last Sunday Jules Glaenzer[3] gave one of his famous musical parties for me. It was well done, as always, but something was wrong and that something was anticlimax. In the old days in that dingy apartment on 65th Street the parties

---

1 Eva Gabor (b. 1921), sister of Zsa Zsa, of the flamboyant Hungarian family as famous for their marriages as their stage and film appearances.
2 Roger Stevens, theatrical manager, who was presenting this last Coward season on Broadway.
3 Jules Glaenzer, Chairman of Cartier, New York.

were dazzling. It was there I first heard George Gershwin[1] play 'Rhapsody in Blue'. It was there that Richard Rodgers, Larry Hart, Gertie, Beattie, Oscar Levant[2], Arthur Schwartz[3], Vincent Youmans[4], etc., all played and sang and showed off to the delectation of the other guests who, in those days, really knew what they were listening to. Now the magic has evaporated. At this particular party one or two nondescript performers performed with efficient adequacy but *nostalgie du temps perdu* lay on the occasion like a sad blanket. Jules's autocratic manner has hardened with the years and there is a slight rattle discernible. He was sweet and kind and worked away like a Trojan, but although it was quite entertaining it didn't quite come off. I stayed to the end, as the affair had been given for me, and went home feeling sad, as though I had been in a haunted house.

Sunday 26 January

Here I am, stricken down again with violent laryngitis, and utterly miserable. My voice gave out during Thursday's matinée. I got through and then collapsed in my dressing-room. I am completely exhausted physically, nervously and emotionally and at the lowest ebb that I have been for many years. I loathe giving in. I loathe missing performances. I feel perfectly wretched and devoid of energy. After consultations with the doctor and a fumbling old fool of a specialist *and* the poor management, it has been decided that I shall stay off until next Friday and reopen with *Present Laughter*. This actually terrifies me, because it is a long and arduous part. However, I am in constant communication with Ed Bigg in Chicago and he says that if I really rest and take the prescribed drugs I shall be able to get through. I trust him implicitly but at the moment all I want to do is to get away to the peace and sunshine of Jamaica. I know I can't because I'm too deeply committed. And I am afraid I shall survive!

Sunday 2 February

I tottered out of bed to rehearsal on Wednesday. Had a dress rehearsal on Thursday and opened *Present Laughter* on Friday night. It was a triumphant success and the audience cheered the roof off. The performance was excellent on the whole, Eva enchanting and everyone else fine. I gave a good performance and, fortunately, looked about twenty years younger than I should have looked on account of a wonderful front piece[5], some superb dressing-gowns, two very good new suits from Macdonald & Heath, and my own regained slim

1 George Gershwin (1898–1937), American composer and jazz musician.
2 Oscar Levant (1906–72), American actor and composer.
3 Arthur Schwartz (b. 1900), American producer and composer.
4 Vincent Youmans (1898–1946), American film and stage composer.
5 His first toupée.

figure. It is a great part for me and I am obviously good in it. I ought to be by now, having played it so often. But it was fascinating to me to feel so secure, apart from a little inward anxiety about my voice. I know exactly in this play what to do and how to do it from my first entrance to my last exit. It has grown over the years, and little tricks and bits of business have miraculously reappeared without being consciously summoned.

Larry arrived in New York last week on the day when I collapsed. I was supposed to dine with him at the Algonquin between the shows, but of course I couldn't. Now he is in Boston opening *The Entertainer*[1] and I have missed him, which saddens me. However, with *P.L.* safely launched and two performances of it under my belt, Friday and last night, I feel a great deal more cheerful. I am looking forward to San Francisco but not much to Hollywood. However, we shall see. What I am looking forward to most of all is getting out of this town and its winter weather.

Saturday 8 February

Today we give our last two performances in New York, *Nude* in the afternoon and *P.L.* at night. Tomorrow we all pile into a plane and the scenery and props are piled into another plane and we fly to San Francisco, where we open with *Nude* on Tuesday.

Sunday 16 February   San Francisco

The sun is shining with all its might. The city is beautiful. We are a smash success with both plays and got rave notices. I have been praised to the skies and am now ensconced in the presidential suite at the Mark Hopkins, reading, for a change, glowing accounts of myself in the newspapers. The theatre is enormous and I am a little anxious about my bloody voice, but fortunately the acoustics are good and we don't have to force too much. Everyone is charming to us. The weather is divine. The cold and horrors of New York are fading into the past. The audience love us and my dressing-room, after each performance, is invaded by strangers who come to thank me for coming to San Francisco.

The audiences on the two first nights were good but dim. Since the notices came out, however, they have been marvellous. Lou Lurie, who is eighty-three and owns the theatre and a large part of San Francisco besides, is mad about me and deluged me with cuff-links and bad jokes. Eva remains uncomplicated, hard-working and a darling.

Sunday 16 March   Beverly Hills

Well, we opened on Monday to a real Hollywood ballyhoo carry-on. Crowds in the streets; television cameras outside the theatre and, oddly enough after

1 By John Osborne.

all that nonsense, a reasonably good audience. Afterwards there was a really charming party given by Zsa Zsa Gabor at her house in Bel Air. Practically all the audience was there as well as the company. I didn't stay very late for we had to open *Nude* the following night.

The audiences here are infinitely better than they are reputed to be. Fritzi [Massary] came to yesterday's matinée of *P.L.* and this was my real 'accolade'. She had never seen me on the stage before; however, she came round to my dressing-room literally weeping tears of pleasure and excitement. Her praise was articulate and wonderful and she made me know, instead of merely hoping, that I had given a great performance. As a matter of fact, I really do think it was the best I have given to date. I played it, in my mind, for Fritzi for I have always considered her one of the truly great artists of the world. There is also little that she doesn't know about the theatre. My reward was utterly satisfying. I felt a king.

Sunday 23 March

Yesterday we gave our last two performances. *Nude* in the afternoon and *P.L.* in the evening. Last performances, however much one has yearned for them, are always a little sad. These were no exception and the matinée was a nightmare because darling Mike Todd had been killed in a flaming air crash the night before, and in *Nude*, especially the first act, every line is about death. I felt my voice break when I had to say, 'Until death wiped out the twinkle from his eyes, he contrived to enjoy life to the full!' but I recovered myself. After the matinée I had to do a tape recording about him for CBS, then I had my rest and came to play *P.L.*, only to find that the bloody tape machine had gone wrong and I had to do it all over again just before I went on. This was almost unendurable. Almost, but not quite, for I gave a good final performance. After it the company collected in my dressing-room and everybody had drinks and wept a little and kissed everybody else and that was that.

I am deeply sad about Mike's death. He was a human dynamo, insanely generous, a great showman and a wonderful friend.

Earlier in the week Lornie arrived calm and triumphant, having flown over the North Pole! She, who in the past quivered with dread at the thought of travelling to Broadstairs, has now become a confirmed globe-trotter. Coley overheard her say calmly and concisely to the Customs man: 'No, only some old clothes of inferior quality.'

Sunday 30 March   Jamaica

Now it is all over and I can't quite yet believe it. I am sitting here on my verandah looking out at the mountains and sea and the massed bougainvillaeas and the blue sage and the dragon's blood and the tulip trees, and the Belasco Theatre, the New York apartment, Beverly Hills, San Francisco, the Algonquin, the cold, the sleet, the laryngitis and the nightmare are all part of the past, never, never, I trust, to be repeated.

Clifton gave one of his glamorous star-spangled parties for me on the Sunday after we closed. They were all there, all the glitterers, or nearly all. Lornie sat goggle-eyed watching familiar glamour-pusses at close quarters. It really was a well done party, but I was deathly tired and longing to come home.

The next morning we clambered into an almost empty Delta two-engine plane in which we had the worst air journey I've ever experienced. After Havana a storm seized the plane and battered the hell out of it. Poor Lornie was dreadfully ill. Neither Joyce[1] nor Coley nor I were, but it was a horrid and frightening experience. At one moment, after a fifty-foot drop in which everything was broken, I expected the plane to disintegrate in mid-air. However, at long last we landed, shaken and battered, at Montego and I had the not entirely enviable task of driving the Chevrolet ninety miles to Blue Harbour. I managed it successfully although dropping with exhaustion. Since then I have done nothing but sleep and sleep and sleep.

Sunday 13 April

I have some ideas beginning to burgeon. One is a play called *The Wings* about a home for retired actresses. I really do think that this has great possibilities.

I am already nicely sunburnt and in the back of my mind I am nurturing and cherishing a deep nostalgia for France. I always get homesick for France when I am on this side of the Atlantic for any length of time, but this time it is a bit stronger than usual. I need to put some roots down somewhere in Europe. I'm tired of the unbrave New World.

Thursday 1 May

Suddenly, in a wild resurgence of energy, I rushed at *Waiting in the Wings* and wrote away like mad, getting up at 6.30 every morning and fairly flogging myself. Alas, two days ago, when I had nearly finished the second act, I realized with dismay that although the characters are good and the dialogue, of course, excellent, there is no play. I had started too soon and too quickly, without taking enough care to construct properly. I was horribly discouraged by this and felt wretched, but then Coley came up and we talked it over and I *know* I have done the right thing. I love the idea and it should and must be carried out really well. I am no longer twenty-eight but fifty-eight and my processes are inevitably a little slower and my critical standards are higher. I find I can no longer dash off things with quite the *insouciance* I used to have; added to which I am not entirely well yet. Physically I'm all right, I suppose, but I'm still inside-tired. I should have given myself longer grace. Since I

1 Joyce Carey had been appearing with Noël in *Nude with Violin* and *Present Laughter*.

glorious. Best of all, of course, was *The Visit*[1]. It's a good meaty melodrama and Lynn and Alfred are superb in it. It is marvellously directed by Peter Brook and a smash hit in the new Lunt-Fontanne Theatre! They, of course, are over the moon with delight. It really is a triumph for them, particularly because dear Prince Littler refused to have the play in any of his theatres! This prurient idiocy is almost too good to be true.

I spent a lovely weekend with Kit and Guthrie at Sneden's and all was as it has always been. Except that we're all getting a bit older. However, the high spot of my stay was a morning spent at the Actors' Studio[2], which was far more hilarious than I had ever imagined it to be. I was taken by Joan Copeland, who has attended its classes zealously for eleven years. Cathleen Nesbitt was also visiting that day and made the strain of not laughing out loud all the more difficult. Lee Strasberg (God) sits with a henchman on either side of him and a tape-recorder at his feet so that no pearl that drops from his lips should be lost. We saw, first of all, a young man, very grubby, crawling about on the floor making guttural noises and apparently trying to stab a gramophone which was playing one of his mother's records. His mother was apparently Maria Callas. After he had grunted and slithered about for about twenty minutes, he slithered off up some steps, then reappeared and sat opposite Mr Strasberg facing the whole class and explained, completely inaudibly, what he had been trying to do. Then Mr Strasberg went off into a long dissertation on the art of acting, most of which was pretentious balls. He interrupted his discourse with personal reminiscences of Eleonora Duse[3] and explained, nostalgically, that when she smiled she didn't merely smile with her mouth but with every part of her body! Which comes under the heading of the neatest trick of the week.

After this orgy of portentous time-wasting, Geraldine Page[4] and a Mr Gerveh obliged with a scene from *Mourning Becomes Electra*[5]. This was really unbelievable. They were only a few yards away and I only caught about one word in ten. Never have I seen such affected, downright inept acting. When they had finished, they settled down to explain themselves and be talked to by God, and I suddenly got enraged and went out. Cathleen stayed, however, and telephoned me later. Apparently one student had had the temerity to criticize the inaudibility, whereupon Lee Strasberg flew at him and said audibility didn't matter a good god-damn and it was the moment of truth that counted! It is this monumental nonsense which is spreading like a disease over the American theatre. What is so maddening is that out of it have emerged some good actors, but my guess is that talent, true talent can survive anything.

1 By Friedrich Dürrenmatt.
2 Acting school founded by the American Lee Strasberg, for teaching 'The Method'.
3 Eleonora Duse (1858-1924), famous Italian actress.
4 Geraldine Page (b. 1924), American actress.
5 By Eugene O'Neill.

Tuesday 10 June   Biot

I have now been here for a week and very agreeable it is. Edward is fine and well and at his very nicest.

This house is exquisitely '*bijou*' and a bit feminine for me, but the 'couple', Gaston and Henriette, are very good and she is a lovely cook. I have been to the Cannes casino once and to the Juan les Pins casino twice and have made £500 from these three visits, which is jolly gratifying. I don't expect such luck to last but at least I have a nice lot of casino money to play with.

We went over to lunch with Willie [Maugham] and he was enchanting. I am going on Thursday to stay with him for three days and attend the Frank Sinatra Gala at Monte Carlo[1] on Saturday night. It has been announced in the French Press that I am presenting '*Le Spectacle*', which is news to me, but of course if Frankie wants me to introduce him I will do so, remembering his wonderful generosity to me in Las Vegas.

I have just read Beverley Nichols' new book *The Sweet and Twenties* in which, as usual, he says most charming things about me, but alas the book is slipshod and full of minor inaccuracies which are most irritating. At one point the House of Commons listens to a motion with 'pursued' lips! A curious picture. Some of his anecdotes are witty, and his chapter on the Irish excellent, but there is a certain underlying bitchiness about quite a lot of it which I don't remember Beverley being guilty of before. He is incurably sentimental, of course, and always was, but I have a feeling that this wouldn't matter so much if only he wrote a little better. Too many years of journalism and his pervasive passion for barking up the wrong tree have spoiled his style. The whole book, which purports to be a light, gossipy recapitulation of the twenties, is ruined by his not very convincing moralizing and his typically journalistic habit of making comparisons. On finishing the book one is left with the impression that he has observed too much and understood too little.

Sunday 22 June

Coley arrived last Monday, and by slogging away for two or three hours every morning, with him typing in the afternoon, we have managed to inject some wit and tempo into the first act of *Look After Lulu*[2], and it is now much shorter and, I hope, fairly funny. M. Feydeau is a *very* untidy playwright. He leaves characters about all over the place and disposes of them without explanation. Coley's version of the second and third acts is much better. The trouble is that none of it, apart from visual action, is very funny. However, with

---

1 Organized by Sinatra's *High Society* co-star, Grace Kelly, now Princess Grace of Monaco.
2 An adaptation of French farceur Georges Feydeau's *Occupe-toi d'Amélie*.

much tightening, shortening and impacting I think we might make a success of it.

I have gambled a lot more and lost about half of what I had won, but this I do not resent as I am still playing with the dear casino's money and enjoying it.

In any case, I am pressing on and house-hunting in all directions. I am absolutely determined that here is where I intend to settle. I *don't* like Bermuda, and Jamaica is on the turn[1], and both places are climatically ruinous to books and pictures and furniture. The life here appeals to me and the climate is temperate. I would not like to live here all the year round, but then I have never liked living anywhere all the year round. What I do want, however, is a solid house to come back to after frisking about the world. And, curiously enough, I intend to get what I want and that's that.

I spent a lovely four days with Willie. It is an exquisitely comfortable house to stay in. Perfect valeting, delicious food, good conversation and peace. Alan [Searle] and he and I dined at the Réserve with Ruth [Gordon] and Gar [Kanin], who were sizzling with vitality. Ruth, who is sixty, looks about twenty-two. The Frank Sinatra Gala was ghastly but successful. Frankie was good and true as he always is. The '*dîner*' at the Sporting Club was chaos. Far too many people and suffocating. We sat with Leonard and Sylvia Lyons and Ruth and Gar. Willie was getting more and more fractious as the evening wore on and I really couldn't blame him. Finally I went on and introduced Frankie in French and English, then he hopped up on to the stage and sang for an hour, enchantingly. Willie was off home like a shot the moment Frankie's last note had died away. I don't think he enjoyed it much, or that either he or Alan really saw why and how Frankie is such a superb performer. One can't have everything.

I have just finished *The Rainbow Comes and Goes*, Diana Cooper's first volume of memoirs. This absolutely bewitched me. It is quite beautifully written and her letters to Duff and his to her during World War I are infinitely moving. She herself emerges from the book as a darling, capricious and a bit spoiled, perhaps, but intelligent, witty, compassionate and, somehow, touching. I sat straight down and wrote her an effusive fan letter because I couldn't resist it. If the succeeding volumes are a quarter as good I can't wait.

Sunday 27 July

This has been far and away the nicest holiday I've had for years and I'm more enamoured of this coast than ever. Coley and I, by drudging away for three hours a day, managed to finish *Look After Lulu* and, to my surprise, it's very funny indeed and Vivien [Leigh] is mad about it. I have had conversations

---

1 Politically, foreign residents were now less welcome there than before.

with Van Loewen about the contract and I fear Binkie will squeal[1], but it's high time he did a little squealing anyway.

I have just returned from four days in London, where I appeared at the Palladium in *Night of a Hundred Stars*. The show was brilliantly organized with every available star appearing. I came on at the end and received the greatest ovation of my whole career. It was really staggering and most moving. Also, thank God, I was good. I did my old medley, 'Tots' and four new refrains of 'Let's Do It', which really pulled the place down. It was deeply gratifying and I shall never forget the warmth of that audience.

In London I saw Vivien in *Duel of Angels*[2]. She was fine, but the play is a bit tiresome; Maggie Leighton in Terry's play *Variation on a Theme*, which got vile notices but was actually very good. It didn't *quite* achieve what it set out to achieve and Johnny G's direction was restless and irritating, but Maggie was magnificent and young Jeremy Brett excellent. There are lots of bright new young things in London, including two of my godchildren – Daniel Massey, who is wonderful in the Arthur Macrae revue[3], and Juliet Mills[4], who has made an overnight success in *Five Finger Exercise*[5] with Adrianne [Allen], which I haven't yet seen.

I shall be sorry to leave this little corner. I really have enjoyed every minute of it and, what is more, I feel better than I have felt for years. I think maybe I've had too much tropical heat. Here my brain works more clearly. I now have an idea about turning *The Young Idea*[6] into a musical, changing the 'shires' hunting milieu for Long Island. It's a good strong story and might be wonderful for Daniel and Anna Massey[7].

Sunday 17 August   Paris

Here I am with Ginette and Paul-Emile and leaving tonight on the Rome express for Portofino. I enjoyed my two weeks in London, although there was barely a day of sunshine all the time I was there. I saw most of the plays worth seeing and several that were not.

A sadness occurred between me and Edward just before I left Biot. My new French lawyer, Robin Ward, suggested that the best way for me to buy a house there was to borrow half the price, $60,000, from a friend rather than do

---

1 Tennent's were to present the play and royalties had to be paid both to Noël and to the Feydeau estate.
2 By Jean Giraudoux.
3 *Living for Pleasure*.
4 Juliet Mills (b. 1941), actress daughter of John Mills and Mary Hayley Bell.
5 Peter Shaffer's first play.
6 One of Noël's earliest comedies (1922).
7 Anna Massey (b. 1937), actress; she and Daniel Massey were the children of Adrianne Allen by her former husband Raymond Massey.

it on mortgage. I said at once that nothing could be easier because Edward would lend it to me. However, when I asked Edward he refused, explaining that it would mean selling stocks when the market was low (untrue) and that he had to think of Kathleen![1] He also added in rather a flustered voice that it would be horribly embarrassing if I were unable to pay him back. Oh dear. Oh dear. 'A thing called pennies'! Edward's favourite expression. What dreadful havoc 'pennies' can wreak in the human heart! Poor, poor Edward. I felt mortified at having asked him and so terribly ashamed of him. We have been friends for thirty-eight years. I must remember more clearly in future *never* to demand of people more than they are capable of giving. None of it really matters. Once I have 'emigrated' I can either pay the whole amount down or form a Liechtenstein company and take a mortgage.

To return to London, Vivien, alas, is in one of her dangerous moods. I don't think she will be able to play *Lulu* because she has contracted to do *Duel of Angels* in New York as well as two films. Binkie and I have secretly decided to let Dora Bryan do it, who, if carefully watched, will be brilliant. She has not got Vivien's beauty and top-star quality, but she has more warmth and is a much better comedienne.

Maggie Leighton is still havering about *South Sea Bubble*[2]. She is in a highly strung nervous state over her marriage to Larry Harvey, which is pursuing a tempestuous course. Kay Kendall can't do it because of leaving Rex[3] and being fairly scatty anyhow. It is sad to think how many of our glamorous leading ladies are round the bend. I asked Deborah Kerr yesterday if she would like to play it for a three months' season, but *she* refused because she is in a conjugal crisis, living with Peter Viertel[4] at the Trianon Palace in strictest secrecy and in the throes of a divorce from Tony [Bartley], who is demanding custody of the children. I am getting a little tired of badgering leading ladies to play a wonderful part in a jolly good comedy.

One very happy thing about my London visit was going to Windsor to see Graham in *Subway in the Sky*[5]. He played a tough American detective and played it very well indeed. His accent was phoney at one or two moments, but he was relaxed and easy and has apparently conquered that dreadful inner nervousness that used to stand between him and the audience. At Windsor the audience adored him and applauded every exit. He is obviously, at last, on the up and up and really becoming a good straight actor. I am very proud of him for sticking to his guns through all those disappointments and setbacks.

1 His sister.
2 Which Noël had invited her to play on Broadway.
3 Who was tied to the London run of *My Fair Lady*.
4 Peter Viertel, American screenwriter and novelist, whom she married in 1960.
5 Thriller by Ian Main.

Sunday 24 August   St Jean-Cap Ferrat

I am here for a week staying with Rosita and Norman Winston[1]. It is the exact opposite of Biot. Here there is an endless *va et vient*, bridge, canasta, dinners, lunches, etc. The rich riff-raff of the 'international set', Nou-Nou and Nada and Nell and Pina and Boo-Boo and Jonnie and Bi-Bi. It's quite fun for a short time but I couldn't bear it for long. However, Rosita is a darling and there is a speedboat and sunshine and I have rented a car of my own.

My week at Portofino was pleasant enough but the weather was vile. I am very fond of Lilli [Palmer], but she is certainly in a fine emotional and moral jam and there were some high-powered, tear-diffused, heart-to-heart talks. Carlos [Thompson], her new and charming husband, was in Berlin making a picture. She is still carrying a torch for Rex, although she loves Carlos. Rex never stops badgering her with letters and telephone calls. The poor wretched Kay has apparently got leukaemia and cannot live more than a year or so at the outside! This is a truly horrible situation. She, of course, doesn't know, but Rex does and did when he married her! The poor dear may have behaved badly in the first place when she went bald-headed after Rex, but having got her own way she is certainly paying a ghastly price for it.

Sunday 7 September   ss *Queen Elizabeth*

I have agreed to do a ballet for the Festival Ballet. It was Pat Dolin's[2] idea, and after seeing them at it for two performances I became enthusiastic. They are all young and most of them remarkable dancers, particularly John Gilpin[3], who has star quality. So I am now off on a new endeavour. Hurray! My 'stretch' in Bermuda will certainly be musical what with the ballet and *Later than Spring*. I can't wait.

I spent my last evening with Larry and Viv. The latter seemed calmer. Maggie was there and *her* Larry. They all seem to me a bit hysterical.

The first night out on this voyage I won £600 in the ship's pool! Mustn't grumble. My lower plate hurts me and is now in a tumbler in the bathroom. My pen has given out. My eyes are better. I feel comparatively tranquil. We dock at two o'clock on Tuesday.

Tuesday 23 September   Bermuda

I saw Natasha, the Lunts, Marlene, Eva, etc. I went to the Jerome Robbins *Ballet USA* and the opening of the American Ballet at the Met. Neither of them was remarkable. Excellent dancing, great expertise, but a certain lack of

1 Norman Winston, American financier, and his wife.
2 Anton Dolin (b. 1904), dancer and choreographer, who was co-founder of the Festival Ballet in 1950; knighted 1980.
3 John Gilpin, leading dancer with the Festival Ballet, 1950-60.

style. Leonard Bernstein[1] was there. He wants to make a musical of *Brief Encounter* and Hugh Martin[2] wants to make one of *Hay Fever*. I'm all for them having a go if they feel like it.

In the evening, with Guthrie, we saw *Goldilocks*, the much vaunted musical written and directed by Walter Kerr and his wife. I went prepared for it to be pretty bad, but it certainly exceeded everything that the grape-vine had reported. It was frankly one of the most idiotic, formless, amateur productions I have ever seen. The music is entirely dull, the lyrics overburdened with effort and the book non-existent. The production is grandiose and fabulously expensive, it has already cost $500,000; Aggie de Mille's ballets are not really good enough, and the cast, with the exception of Elaine Stritch, is lamentable. I fully intended to try to forget Mr Kerr's unkindness about *Nude with Violin* and view his efforts with a generous mind, but he didn't give me a chance. I was tolerant during the first act but I got angry during the last. It was all such bloody impertinence. How does an eminent critic of his calibre have the impertinence to dish out such inept, amateurish nonsense? I must say I couldn't have believed it if I hadn't seen for myself. It will probably get kindly reviews from his gallant colleagues when it opens on Broadway, but I don't think anything could save it. Serve him and his giggling wife bloody well right.

It is sad to read in the papers that Yvonne Arnaud is dead. She was such a brilliant actress and I have known her for so many, many years. It is better however that she should die, I think, because she had a cerebral haemorrhage and, even if she had recovered, it would have been to half-life.

The international situation is worsening by the minute. Khrushchev has told Eisenhower to get out of Formosa before he's thrown out, which is hardly polite, and Eisenhower has pronounced the letter 'unacceptable'.

I cannot yet quite believe that we are again going to be plunged into war but if we are there really is nothing I can do about it. I shall press on with my own endeavours for so long as I am permitted to. I shall plan cheerfully for the future regardless of the suspicion that perhaps there won't be one. In fact, I intend to remain bloody but unbowed and resolutely captain of my soul.

Sunday 5 October

An immense amount has happened during the last two weeks, and I am feeling understandably exultant. To begin with, music has been flowing out of me in a gratifying spate. I suppose it is because I haven't concentrated on it for so long. Pat Dolin came on Friday the twenty-fifth and left on the Sunday. He was a charming guest and so enthusiastic about the ballet that by the time he went the entire synopsis had been completed. Musically I have already done the main love theme, which I know is good, a duet for sentries based on the

1 Leonard Bernstein (b. 1918), American composer, conductor and pianist.
2 Hugh Martin, American songwriter.

British Grenadiers, a light waltz, a mazurka for the tarts and the businessmen, and several other bits and pieces which can be developed and utilized. In addition to this I have done two new numbers for *Later than Spring*, a waltz, 'Time Will Tell', and a rattling good point number called 'Why Do the Wrong People Travel?' with a complicated but very funny lyric. I have also written the whole of the first scene and got some of my characters established. It is not to be surprised at that I feel rather pleased with myself. It's a tremendous output for only two weeks. Naturally I am enjoying Bermuda more than I ever have before. It's wonderfully peaceful now out of season and I have my pianos, tape-recorder, typewriter, writing blocks, dictionaries and everything to hand.

We had a conference with David Graham[1] last week and he suggested that when I 'emigrate' it should be to Geneva instead of France, because if one is a resident of Geneva one is entirely free of currency restrictions. In fact I can turn my earnings into dollars or francs or roubles whenever I so desire. It will mean renting a small hotel room by the year but apparently no more than that.

Sunday 12 October

I'm beginning to think that my prolonged tropical honeymoon is over for ever. I now pine for cooler airs and drier climates. I dream nostalgically of Switzerland in snow and Vienna in sleet. I don't dream very nostalgically of London because it really is too depressing, but my heart is definitely leaning to the older world.

The Great Reaper has been at it again. His latest acquisitions include Margaret Scudamore[2], Chips Channon and the Pope. As the latter had recently announced that plastic surgery, except for specifically therapeutic reasons, was a sin, I can't feel that the pompous old fool is much loss.

Sunday 19 October

The notices for *Goldilocks*, as I suspected, were kindly to the point of nausea. I can imagine, without difficulty, what they would have said if I had dared to present to the public such an amateur hotchpotch of sprawling inefficiency, but then I am *not* a critic. The show will be a moderate success thanks to advance and theatre parties, but even the kindliest of the notices tacitly admits that it's not very good.

I have just read Agnes de Mille's second book and very good it is. She is really a bloody good writer and, although I suspect she would be fairly tiresome to work with, she certainly knows her onions.

I have decided to spend Christmas in London. I may get a cold, flu,

1 David Graham, his Bermuda financial adviser.
2 Margaret Scudamore, Michael Redgrave's mother.

pneumonia, pleurisy and arthritis, but if I have to go through all the hell of present-giving, I would prefer to give them to people I really love rather than amiable but less intimate friends. Also it is possible that I may have to establish a residence in Geneva and I can pop over there the moment the 'festive' nightmare is over.

I have to be in Barcelona in April for rehearsals of the ballet and, I hope, back in America again in May for the rehearsals of *Later than Spring*, which I would like to open in San Francisco in June. This, of course, depends on whether or not Roz Russell can extricate herself from commitments[1]. I would much rather open out there, play to good audiences, and make any necessary changes at my leisure than open in a flurry in New Haven and Boston and come crashing into New York without everything being spick and span enough. Also, if the show is good, the fact of a West Coast success will build up the advance.

There is no news of the wretched *Lulu* but I presume Binkie will do it the moment Dora Bryan is free. The idea of Vivien, I fear, must definitely be jettisoned. She is in no fit state to embark on a long run even if she wanted to, and I have a clear feeling that all she wants is a month or two, *réclame*, lovely notices and then something else! Great big glamorous stars can be very tiresome.

Sunday 26 October

The book of *Later than Spring* is causing me trouble. Actually I knew it would because books for musicals invariably cause trouble. The very good reason for this is the time factor. In a straight play you have time to develop your characters and lead up to and away from moments of crisis. In a musical you have hardly any time at all. The music and lyrics, on which the show really depends, interrupt all flow and sequence. Then there are the dancing interludes to be considered and the scene-changes. All in all it is horribly difficult to keep a straight story-line[2], amuse the audience and move them when necessary. However, I am pressing on. The dialogue scenes already written are quite good as I cannot help writing good dialogue, but whether or not it is leading anywhere is my principal worry. I am sure the only thing to do is to finish the whole thing roughly and then go back and see what has to be pointed up, filled out, cut or redone. I have no worries about the score and the lyrics. Those already done are excellent, and ideas for numbers come thick and fast.

I see that the German President has had a cool reception in England. So I should bloody well think. I think the Government was idiotic to have invited him and still more idiotic to accept his £5,000 for Coventry Cathedral. God-damned impertinence and *typically* German.

1 Noël had now chosen the American actress Rosalind Russell (1908–76) for the leading role.
2 It was a love story set on a cruise liner.

Sunday 2 November

My emigration papers have gone through and from 1 January onwards I shall be a resident of Geneva as well as of Bermuda. This will mean renting a hotel room or a one-room flat by the year. Apart from that there are only advantages and few disadvantages. I shall be able to spend my own money in whatever quantities I like without asking permission from man or beast. The fact that all this is possible surely proves that there is something very basically silly about international finance and economics but, silly or not, I am most grateful for it.

Friday 14 November   New York

I have been here just over a week and I must say enjoyed every minute of it. The flat is cosy as ever and the telephone can be unplugged and so I can have peaceful days at home without being badgered by anyone. Pete [Matz] came up from Philadelphia on Wednesday and was highly impressed with the ballet music.

There is no chance of contacting Rosalind Russell until after her telecast of *Wonderful Town* on the twenty-ninth. The moment that is over we shall go into a huddle. There is now a faint chance of doing *Lulu* here in February with Shirley MacLaine and Roddy McDowall. This would suit me very well if we could get a really good director.

I have seen lots of plays. *The Pleasure of His Company*[1], a *soi-disant* comedy of manners, quite enjoyable. Cyril Ritchard very good, although unsubtle, Cornelia Otis Skinner excellent. *A Touch of the Poet*, Eugene O'Neill melodrama, good theatre. Helen Hayes, Eric Portman, Kim Stanley all good. *Epitaph for George Dillon*, John Osborne's latest, in collaboration[2]. Mostly very good, but weak last act. Beautifully played by Alison Leggatt, Eileen Herlie and a new young man called Robert Stephens, who is quite wonderful. The play was about to close but Marlene, who came with me, flew at the producers and forced them to keep it on for a little longer. So it is now *not* closing and may transfer to off-Broadway. Actually it deserves to succeed. In addition to the above I saw one act of Menotti's opera[3], which was choppy and rather irritating. It only ran five performances. He doesn't seem capable of writing a true melody line. It's all bits and pieces.

Sunday 23 November

To put first things first. On Wednesday afternoon I read and sang the first act of *Later than Spring* to Roger Stevens and Oliver Smith[4], and I must say the

1 By Samuel Taylor and Cornelia Otis Skinner.
2 With Anthony Creighton.
3 *Maria Golovin.*
4 Oliver Smith (b. 1918), American designer.

response was more than satisfactory. They loved it and Oliver went overboard and said it had more charm, brilliance, style, etc., than anything he had heard for years. He also added that it would be a smash hit whoever played it. I don't quite agree with him but it was very, very encouraging. Now we have to wait to see whether or not Rosalind Russell is equally impressed.

I went to a grand dinner given by Elsa Maxwell for Callas[1] and von Karajan[2] which was quite enjoyable. Callas looked lovely and couldn't have been more charming. On Saturday night I heard von Karajan conduct the Beethoven First and Ninth at the Carnegie Hall. Madame von K. had kindly invited me to her box. It was quite lovely at moments and I enjoyed all of it until the choral part of the Ninth, when I got the giggles. After this musical solemnity I changed the bowling with a crash and went to a party that Leonard and Sylvia Lyons gave for me. It was really great fun, predominantly Jewish, and a glorious *mélange* of people and talent from David Merrick[3] to Abe Burrows[4]. There was music in the air and Arthur Schwartz and Howard Dietz[5] played and sang lovely old songs, and Elaine Stritch[6], sweet but forgot every lyric. Abe Burrows obliged and was extremely funny. I too obliged towards the end and played some of the ballet music, which seemed to impress the assembled company profoundly. Altogether it was a sweet party.

Sunday 30 November

A great excitement has now occurred about doing *Look After Lulu* almost immediately[7] with Cyril Ritchard directing. The first idea was Shirley Mac-Laine but her film commitments are too complicated. Then I approached Carol Channing by telephone in Reno, Nevada, sent her the script, certain that she would jump at it, but she turned it down on account of Lulu being a 'prostitute' and therefore 'unpalatable' and also because it would be too like Lorelei in *Gentlemen Prefer Blondes*. I said fairly acidly that, if so, whatever she played, including Lady Macbeth, would also be exactly like Lorelei. In the meantime Sam Zolotow announced in his column that she was going to play it, whereupon Vivien went up - or further up - in smoke in London and I had to telephone and soothe her.

Now it has been practically decided to do it with Tammy Grimes, a new girl, rich with talent, whom Cyril and Roddy [McDowall] are both mad about. I went to see her appearing in a night-club and she really has star quality, I

---

1 Maria Callas (1923–77), Greek-born opera singer.
2 Herbert von Karajan (b. 1908), Austrian conductor.
3 David Merrick (b. 1912), Broadway impresario.
4 Abe Burrows (b. 1910), American producer and playwright.
5 Howard Dietz (b. 1896), American librettist, Schwartz's partner.
6 Elaine Stritch (b. 1922), American actress and singer.
7 On Broadway; the London production was still awaiting a decision from Vivien Leigh.

think. This is, of course, a frightening risk because it is a terribly expensive production to do without a name. However, if she gets away with it, and I think she will, the critics will 'discover' her, she'll make an overnight success, and we will have a hit. If not, we shall fall flat on our collective faces and close in a few days. Roger [Stevens] has been most awfully good about it all. He, poor dear, has to raise the money, but I have great hopes that all will be well.

I went with Coley to *Cavalleria Rusticana* and *Pagliacci* at the Met. *Cav* disgraceful with Zinka Milanow hilarious. *Pag* brilliant with Mario del Monaco, Robert Merrill and Lucine Amara all wonderful. I also went with Larry to *Tales of Hoffmann*, charmingly done. Larry is miserable. He has firmly left Vivien after terrible dramas – how long for nobody knows. He now has to fly back again because his brother has died. He clings to me rather when he's in trouble, which I find touching. I'm very fond of him. I'm very fond of Vivien too. But, oh dear – what a perpetual carry-on!

Sunday 7 December   ss *Queen Elizabeth*

Far too much has happened during the last week and I feel quite dizzy. The die is cast about *Lulu*; the play is also cast, or very nearly, as we have had some very successful auditions. The play goes into rehearsal on 29 December and opens out of town on 19 January. I shall have to be back for the try-out to take over from Cyril, who can't leave New York because of his show.

I read *Later than Spring* to Roz Russell and Freddie Brisson[1], who received it in stony, non-committal silence. However, we think that this lack of 'give' is a calculated plan to be 'hard to get'. I pressed on gallantly in the face of almost, but not quite, overwhelming odds. She still hasn't said whether or not she'll do it, tiresome bitch; however, if she doesn't, I have some strong plans about Irene Dunne who would, I think, be better.

I had one magical evening with Pete and the tape-recorder during which we played on two pianos and did the 'Changing of the Guard', the 'Rain' sequence and the 'Sailor's Hornpipe', so now the ballet score is virtually complete. It was quite thrilling. The tunes and harmonies came tumbling out and every note was recorded. This was truly exciting and at the end of the evening we were high as kites from sheer creativeness (also from a little Scotch).

I took Marlene to hear Renata Tebaldi tear off the last two acts of Puccini's *Manon Lescaut*, lovely, lovely singing but, oh, I wish it had been Callas.

Larry returned late on Friday night and saw us off yesterday. He has had several more ghastly scenes with Vivien and buried his brother at sea. Apparently, as usual, the Royal Navy did everything impeccably and Larry was deeply moved. I feel desperately sad for him. Not only on account of Vivien and his brother but because everything seems to be downbeat with him

---

1 Frederick Brisson (b. 1915), Rosalind Russell's film producer husband, nicknamed 'The Lizard of Roz'.

at the moment. I think he rather self-indulges this, but I am sure he is genuinely lonely and unhappy.

Sunday 21 December   London

The Almighty, with an unerring aim, has struck me down and here I am lying in bed with pneumonia! I cannot honestly say that I mind very much; the 104° temperature and violent sweating is now over, and I am weak but peaceful. I had a curious feeling, after my arrival last week, that the pace was getting too hot. The telephone never stopped for a minute and invitations and demands came flooding in, and I was beginning to get frantic and panic-stricken. There can be no two opinions about it, I know far too many people and have far too many friends. I love to see them, I am delighted with their attentions, until there suddenly comes a moment when I wish them all at the bottom of the sea. This is not ingratitude, it is merely my physical vitality rebelling. The Almighty, whom I suspect occasionally of being on my side, realizes this with his infinite wisdom, and when he observes me going too far, giving out too much and generally making a cunt of myself, he firmly knocks me out. I am most grateful to him.

Before the débâcle I managed to crowd a lot in. The day after I arrived I went with Lornie, Cole and Gladys to the opening night of *West Side Story*, which hit London like a hydrogen bomb. It was beautifully done, better even than in New York, and its impact was truly terrific. On the following evening, in darkness and fog, Joyce, Cole and I drove down to Cambridge to see Graham in *The Rape of the Belt*[1], and it was a highly enjoyable jaunt and well worth the trouble because he was really excellent and very funny. In addition to this he is happy as a bee at the moment because he is going into *Brouhaha*[2] at the Aldwych to play a good part and at an excellent salary. Things are at last looking up for him and everything he gets he richly deserves.

I have talked to Cecil Beaton and seen his designs for *Lulu*[3] which are brilliant. I lunched with the Duchess of Kent *en famille* and she was sweet as usual. I went to see Kay Kendall in a dreadful little play[4] in which she was enchanting and Gladys Cooper magnificent. Then came my fifty-ninth birthday. I went with Vivien to the opening night of a bad farce. In the car she attacked me violently about doing *Lulu* in America without her and I quickly slapped her back. She is obviously in a bad way, drinking far, far too much and attacking everyone right and left. I know she is unhappy inside, but her predicament has been entirely her own fault from the first and, to me, the whole situation has now become a bore.

1 The touring production of Benn W. Levy's comedy.
2 A comedy starring Peter Sellers by George Tabori.
3 The New York production.
4 *The Bright One*, written by Judy Campbell and directed by Rex Harrison.

Larry has left her, and I for one don't blame him; she is certainly barmy up to a point, but she has been so spoilt and pampered for so many years that the barminess becomes ugly and dull. Everyone is in a state about her, particularly Binkie and those who really love her. I am very fond of her, but I am beginning to lose interest in the drama. For all her beauty and charm and sweetness, she has let Larry down for years and really tormented him. If he can succeed in breaking away, good luck to him. Women of Viv's temperament, looks and exigence can raise too much hell for themselves and everyone near them.

I'm quite aware that the poor thing is frantic and lonely. I am also aware that she is the biggest draw in the business and has been making a conceited ass of herself for years. *Of course* I'm sorry for her, but I'm so bored with the initial premise of her whole behaviour that I would really rather she didn't play *Lulu* in the English production, draw or no draw. I feel in no mood to cope with the carry-on. If she can manage to pull herself out of this ghastly *dégringolade* by taking a six months' cure and really facing up to things, I shall be relieved and delighted. She has a strong character and maybe she will. One thing, however, is quite certain: nobody else can do it for her, so she had better get on with it chop-chop double pronto.

Sunday 28 December

Christmas has come and gone. On Christmas Eve I rose from my bed of sickness and wobbled frailly into the sitting-room for a cosy Christmas dinner with my loved ones. Gladys, Coley, Lornie, Joycie and Graham. We exchanged handsome gifts, drank champagne cocktails, pulled crackers and ate very good turkey and bread sauce and Christmas pudding. It was a dear little party and I enjoyed every minute of it.

Christmas Day itself I spent in bed, feeling much better after my revels. On Boxing Day we went *en masse* to see Sarah Churchill play Peter Pan and she was really quite charming. The production, however, has grown too perfunctory and a lot of the magic has flown. The next day, undaunted, I went to *Where the Rainbow Ends*. The children were rather good and Alicia Markova waved her arms about very prettily as the Spirit of the Lake. These two dainty Christmas productions were for me indeed a *recherche du temps perdu*. I played the *Rainbow* forty-eight years ago and *Peter Pan* forty-six years ago. I find it difficult to believe that I have been at it for so long, but I am now pushing sixty and there's no getting away from it.

1959

Although Look After Lulu *proved a flop in New York, this was for Noël a year of considerable film success as the suave spymaster, Hawthorne, in* Our Man in Havana. *It was also the year in which he settled in Switzerland. On the verge of his sixtieth birthday, he wrote to a friend:*

I am now more of a perfectionist than I used to be; I take pride in being a professional. I don't write plays with the idea of giving some great thought to the world, and that isn't just coy modesty. As one gets older one doesn't feel quite so strongly any more, one discovers that everything is always going to be exactly the same with different hats on.... If I wanted to write a play with a message, God forbid, it would undoubtedly be a comedy. When the public is no longer interested in what I have to write, then it will be brought home to me that I am out of touch: not before. Nowadays, though, I find that I rather enjoy my downfalls; to me it's acridly funny when something flops that has taken me months to write and compose. In private I suppose I am a tremendous celebrity snob, and by celebrity I don't mean Brigitte Bardot but people of achievement like Somerset Maugham or Rebecca West. Looking back through my life I find that my personality only really changed once, and that was when I was twenty-four and I became a star and a privileged person. Yet to my inner mind I'm much the same now as I was before The Vortex; *I'm as anxious to be good as I ever was, only now time's winged chariot seems to be goosing me. It doesn't bother me that I don't write in England any more. I love England but I hate the climate and I have absolutely no regrets about having left.... looking around me I deplore the lack of style and elegance in most modern plays; I long for the glamour of great stars who used to drive up to the stage door in huge limousines. In my younger days I was tremendously keen to be a star and famous and successful; well, I have been successful for most of my life, and if at this late stage I were to have another series of resounding failures, I believe I could regard them with a certain equanimity.*

He also noted, this time for Plays and Players, *that although, unlike Queen Victoria, he would not be celebrating his jubilee by driving through the streets in an open carriage, he would, like her, be holding a service of thanksgiving, in his case 'for all the excitement and happiness the theatre has brought me and for all the love and support the theatre-going public has so generously given me for so many years'.*

Sunday 4 January   Geneva

Well, here we are, Coley and I, in Calvin's hideaway. We arrived on Friday and arrangements are now proceeding for me to be registered as a subsidiary resident of this city, subsidiary, that is, to Bermuda, where I remain domiciled. We have interviewed an amiable lawyer, we have filled in forms. We have interviewed a delightful bank manager at the Crédit Suisse and filled in more forms. Tomorrow I have to register myself at the British Consulate – I hope without the Press finding out – and then it appears all will be well and I can actually use my own money as I like without any exchange control or government to forbid me. This all seems too good to be true except, of course, that I loathe all the carry-on. I hate avoidance and doing things round corners, but obviously in this day and age there is no other way of surviving.

Before leaving London I saw *The Nutcracker Suite* beautifully done by the Festival Ballet. John Gilpin wonderful. *Cinderella* at the Coliseum, the most 'beautiful-to-look-at' pantomime I've ever seen[1], and *Ondine* at Covent Garden in which Margot was superb, Freddie Ashton's choreography brilliant and the music[2] tuneless and hideous.

Carol Reed[3] has asked me to play with Alec Guinness and Ralph Richardson in Graham Greene's *Our Man in Havana*. It's a good script and a very funny though small part. I think I shall do it. It means a few days' location in Havana in April and about three weeks in London in June and July. All of which fits. We shall wait and see whether or not the concessions and money are satisfactory.

I engaged a young and attractive actor called George Baker to play Philippe in *Lulu*. It was all achieved in about ten minutes.

Our flight was uneventful. It's a pleasant town. The weather is bitter cold but I feel all right apart from a slight cough, a sore tongue and my 'understudy' upper plate which, like Gertie Lawrence in *A to Z*, is *better* than the principal but liable to make the gums sore. The 'principal' became looser and looser until it nearly fell into my lap, so this will have to be endured. The sore tongue is, I think, the result of the antibiotics, which kill ruthlessly not only the pneumonia germs but all the other germs in your body, leaving you defenceless against malign newcomers. It's all very interesting in a dull way.

Sunday 11 January   St Moritz

We arrived on Wednesday after a day's journey with two changes, very enjoyable on the whole apart from a beast of a little girl who squeaked and squealed without ceasing.

1 Designed by Loudon Sainthill; this was based on the Rodgers and Hammerstein television musical.
2 By Hans Werner Henze.
3 Carol Reed (1906–76), British film director; knighted 1952.

I duly registered with the British Consul in Geneva and now I am a resident. We had some pleasant junketings, ate delicious food, ran into Pam Churchill and Noel Barber[1] with his Italian wife. Pam C. was in a dreadful dilemma because there wasn't a safe in the Hôtel des Bergues big enough to hold her jewel case!

We were welcomed here in St Moritz with great enthusiasm by dear Loel and Gloria Guinness, and since then it has been nothing but gaiety and luxe. The weather is unfortunately bitterly cold and too far below zero, but we shiver our way up the mountain to the Corviglia Club and eat and drink and are exceedingly merry. I have taken a great shine to Stavros Niarchos[2], who, apart from being a multimillionaire, is a dear. The Guinness children, attractive but delinquent, are causing poor Gloria stepmother's pangs. Old Madame Badrutt – *Die Könige Mutter* of St Moritz – I love and we go to her private apartments – Swiss Baroque – daily for dinner.

I have read Angus Wilson's new novel *The Middle Age of Mrs Eliot*, a quite good idea completely ruined by the ghastliness of the author's mind.

Thursday 15 January   Paris

The last two days at St Moritz were really lovely – wonderful sunshine and much warmer. Gloria, Coley and I slid down from Chanterelle daily on sleds. There was a farewell party on Monday night given by Stavros Niarchos in the Bowling Alley and it was really great fun – about eighteen including Bill Astor. On Tuesday I had a long talk with Loel about my affairs and he advised me very firmly to live in Switzerland rather than France, at any rate to make Geneva my base. Financially this is obviously sensible and Cole and I are flying there on Tuesday to look at an apartment building which is just finished and looks attractive. Loel says that I must have something worthy of my position and must not get a little hole-in-wall, which would be too obvious a trick to avoid taxes. I must say I feel he is right, and as I like Geneva I don't really mind settling there if I can find somewhere really nice. It's very near everywhere else and only one hour's flight from here. It is also attractive in its own right and has much to recommend it.

We had a night train journey from St Moritz – very romantic, whizzing through icy, snowy stations. We are exceedingly *bien installé* here and I tremble when I think of the bill, but I've had my gambling winnings transferred from Nice, so all is well.

We lunched at Maxim's and sat next to Wallis Windsor, who invited us to dine tonight, so we are doing so. Last night we went – in a driving blizzard – to see Georges Guetary in *Pacifico*[3]. He and it were absolutely frightful, so bad

1 Noel Barber, English journalist working for the *Daily Mail* in Paris.
2 Stavros Niarchos (b. 1909), the Greek ship-owner.
3 By Moutet, François and Nivoix.

as to be almost unbearable. He has grown rather thick and wears very high elevators on which he skips about looking like a 1912 French postcard. I'm afraid he's hopeless for *Later than Spring* and it was all deeply embarrassing, although hilariously funny at moments.

Monday 19 January

We have had an orgy of theatre-going and social junketing. The Windsors' party was very gay. She certainly is a most charming hostess and he was extremely amiable. The conversation was mostly general and largely devoted to the question of whether or not the Duchess should have her face lifted. The main consensus was no. Wallis brought this subject up herself with a sort of calculated defiance. I think, however, that she is a curiously honest woman and her sense of humour, particularly about herself, is either profound or brilliantly simulated. The evening finished with a blonde lady (French) pounding the piano and everyone getting a trifle 'high'. Princess Sixte de Bourbon was definitely shocked when the Duke and I danced a sailor's hornpipe and the Charleston, but there was no harm in it, perhaps a little sadness and nostalgia for him and for me a curious feeling of detached amusement, remembering how beastly he had been to me and about me in our earlier years when he was Prince of Wales and I was beginning. Had he danced the Charleston and hornpipe with me then it would have been an accolade to cherish. As it was, it looked only faintly ridiculous to see us skipping about with a will. The Princess needn't have been shocked, it was merely pleasantly ridiculous.

We went to *La Bonne Soupe*[1], Marie Bell marvellous, but a not very good play. *Père*[2] with Yvonne [Printemps] and Pierre [Fresnay]. A very well made play in which Pierre was superb and the whole cast good, but poor Yvonne tragically changed, fat and puffy and overpoweringly 'cute' (always a dangerous tendency with her). There were fleeting moments of her earlier magic but on the whole it was a sadness. We also saw *La Vie Parisienne*, exquisitely produced[3], and had supper with Jean-Louis and Madeleine afterwards in the Little Café, filled with atmosphere and actors, a sort of tiny French Sardi's. In addition to all this we lunched with Nancy Mitford, which was highly enjoyable as usual, and generally enjoyed ourselves very much.

Tomorrow we fly to Geneva to look at a new and very grand apartment building. From the brochure it seems charming, with elaborate modernizing and glorious views and vast terraces.

---

1 By Félicien Marceau.
2 *The Father* by August Strindberg.
3 Offenbach's operetta was staged by the company set up by Jean-Louis Barrault and his actress wife Madeleine Renaud.

Sunday 25 January

We arrived in Geneva in time for lunch on Tuesday – only a fifty-five-minute flight – and on the way from the airport went to see the glorious apartment building but, alas, all we found was a muddy hole in the ground without even any workmen. Dismayed but not cast down by this setback, we sought out a house agent who took us along the lake to Celigny and showed us a house which we immediately loved. The next morning we left at nine o'clock and looked at properties around Lausanne, Vevey, etc., and on the way back returned to Celigny and spent an hour in it, sitting about in the rooms and on the terrace. It was a lovely, cold, sunny afternoon – am loving it more and more. Unfortunately the price is £50,000! This, of course, is ghastly, but maybe – maybe love will find a way. All prices in Switzerland *and* France are astronomical, and France is out of the question because no one knows what will happen to its economics. Switzerland is more stable than anywhere else.

We flew back [to Paris] on Wednesday evening, dined quietly and went to bed. Since then there have been more junketings – including another lunch with Nancy, drinks at the Embassy, Gladwyn and Cynthia[1] very sweet; a divine evening with Princess Olga, Prince Paul, Prince Alexandre and Princess Maria Pia. They took me to the Folies-Bergère which, as regards talent, was ghastly, but as usual the sets and costumes were good and we laughed a lot at all the splendid titties.

Coley and I drove out to Versailles to see the Villa Trianon, which is empty[2]. It was a painful excursion. It had not been entirely dismantled and a great many of Elsie's lovely things have been left to moulder away in the dank cold. A large apartment building has gone up just beyond the garden shutting out the view of the park. We walked shivering through the cold rooms, so full of ghosts for me. We looked at yellowing visitors' books and photograph albums and there I found myself, over and over again, the sophisticated young Noël Coward of the twenties and thirties without a line on his thin, thin face and quite a lot of hair. I blew a gentle and loving kiss to Elsie over the years. She was so very kind to me. How she would have loathed to see her *objets* left to die so slowly and so coldly. Even if I had wanted the house, it is far, far too grand and big and elaborate but I *didn't* – I wanted to get the hell out of it as quickly as possible. We walked back across the sad, muddy garden and life returned to my bloodstream and the ghosts departed.

Sunday 1 February   London

A very crowded and eventful week. I have a charming suite here [the Ritz] and I *much* prefer it to the Dorchester. It is Edwardian in feeling and quiet

1 Lord and Lady Gladwyn; he was British Ambassador to France 1954–60.
2 The house of an old friend of Noël's, Lady (Elsie) Mendl, who had recently died.

and I have a brass 'pineapple' bed which makes me feel rather like the late Mrs George Keppel[1].

I have definitely decided to do the Graham Greene film with Alec Guinness and Ralph Richardson. I have had two lunches with Carol [Reed], who is treating me *en prince*. In fact in London this time I am definitely 'hot'. Every time I go out I am beset by reporters and photographers. The news of me doing the film was heavily headlined. The part is being written up a bit. I am being paid £1,000 a day and expenses with a minimum guarantee of thirteen days. Knowing Carol's reputation for working over schedule I think I ought to get at least £20,000 out of it.

Peter Matz has let me down badly over the ballet. Only *one* tape arrived, and that was muddled, untidy and obviously done in a hurry at the last minute. I shall deal with Pete in New York and get the musical side tidied up, but this will mean a great deal of extra work and concentration. I am *very* angry but will press on.

There has been a huge crisis about *Lulu*, which is well into rehearsal. They sent me an outrageous contract which I have resolutely refused to sign. Obviously they can't jettison the production at this stage so I have actually got them by the short hairs, but I hate all this god–damned American chiselling. I have decided to stay aloof and let the lawyers work it out.

I saw Graham in *Brouhaha* and he was excellent and has made a great success. This is really gratifying because, God knows, he has earned it. This, I am sure, is the turning point. London, except for two days of thick fog, was sunny and wintry and charming. I sail on Tuesday night without Coley, who is flying to Bermuda to put Spithead firmly on the market.

Sunday 8 February   ss *Queen Elizabeth*

It's been a fairly violent crossing, storms and blizzards and pitchings and tossings. I won the pool again the night before last. It was £900, of which I get £690! I just joined in to help the wretched auctioneer and beat up the bidding. I bought the choice of number for £42 and chose 716. That was all I bought and yesterday morning the steward called me to say I had won!

Vivien is in despair about Larry leaving her. I had a long quiet session with her. She was very pathetic and perfectly sane and sweet, and I feel that the shock of Larry packing up and going may have done her a power of good. It is difficult to resist her charm and pathos when she turns them on. I cannot understand why she should be *surprised* at Larry popping off after all the ghastly scenes. Personally I think he will eventually go back to her, although he swears he won't. It is depressing to reflect that two such talented and enchanting people should torture each other so.

1 King Edward VII's mistress.

Wednesday 18 February   New Haven

I am writing this just before the opening night of *Lulu*. Last night we had an invited audience and the play went wonderfully although many, many of the laughs were lost, some from inexperience, some from lack of diction and a great many from over-direction. Cyril has done a brilliant job on the overall production and, what is more, he has achieved it without scenes and dramas and upsetting people. However, his one fault has been over-concentration on business, movement and noise, and not enough concentration on words. The company is excellent and Tammy Grimes will, I am sure, make an enormous success. Cecil [Beaton]'s dresses and sets are magnificent and I have very, very sanguine hopes for the whole thing. I have been rehearsing all day, redirecting the wedding scene, which was badly overdone, and spearing my lines from the debris.

The week in New York was fairly ghastly. It started with a scene with Pete Matz in which he said he couldn't do the ballet in time as he had signed a contract to do three days a week television. This was a bad let-down and I was very angry, also panic-stricken because there is still a great deal to be done. However, I dug my feet in, gritted my teeth and determined to get on with it myself, finish the score, record it on tape and have it transcribed into piano music by a man called Herbert Schutz and orchestrated and arranged later on in London. Actually this, in the long run, will be better as it will be *entirely* my music and not vitiated and changed by anyone else's ideas.

Fortunately, having seen two rehearsals of *Lulu*, I knew it was more or less on the right track so I didn't have to worry about that. What I did have to worry about, however, was an abscess in one of my few remaining capped teeth. This had to be opened twice and cleaned out. I had anaesthetics, naturally, but it pulled me down and made composing light ballet music a bit of a strain. I persevered and did quite a lot including a very good hornpipe for John Gilpin. I went to only one musical in New York, *Redhead*[1], in which Gwen Verdon was superb.

Sunday 1 March   New York

The week in New Haven finished in a blaze of glory. We played to $29,000 in six performances and the audiences rocked and rolled and roared in all the appropriate places. I was invited to a buffet dinner at Yale in the rooms of one of the 'fellows'. It was most enjoyable.

This week has gone by more or less according to plan except that the first preview on Wednesday night was far too chic, from the Windsors downwards or upwards according to your point of view. The company were unsettled, having been halted and nagged at by Cyril all day, who would have been better

1 This year's Tony Award-winner as best musical.

advised to let them play straight through and give them notes after each act instead of pulling them up on every second line, which flustered them. They gave a patchy, uneven performance. The Windsors et al. seemed to enjoy it, but I didn't. The following previews were much better except for Saturday night when the audience was ghastly – a large Jewish benefit who refused with Hebraic fortitude to co-operate in any way. Tomorrow is the last preview before we open and then – ah then we shall see.

I should like to state here and now that I am not too happy about the theatre. It is the wrong side of Broadway, and although it is very nice in itself (I did play *The Vortex* in it) it has run down a bit. If we are a smash hit, none of this will matter but if not, it will be damaging. The other thing that worries me is that I would have liked two more weeks out of town to polish the performance and get the whole thing really slick. However, we must hope for the best. Gilbert Miller[1] has been extremely nice throughout and made only a few minor suggestions, nearly all of which were valid.

I have been working in all my spare moments, which haven't been many, on the ballet music and I have a lot more done. All this is panicking me rather as there isn't much time and it's a long job.

Tonight I appear on *What's My Line* just to give the show a plug.

Wednesday 11 March   Jamaica

Well, the worst has happened and here I am sitting on my verandah at Firefly licking my wounds – wounds physical as well as spiritual and professional. The preview on Monday was fine. The opening night really very good, the company, on the whole, played it well and everyone seemed delighted. Then came the notices. All damning except one, which was a rave. Tammy, while making a success, didn't do what I hoped she would, which was to be 'discovered' and raved about. Roddy, excellent, was barely mentioned. Then, of course, came the recriminatory discussions and the complete lack of interest from movie companies. Then the inevitable jollying up of the company by Cyril and me.

Everyone concerned has behaved impeccably and owing, I think, to word of mouth, the box-office did not entirely die on us. There is still a slim chance that we might survive the notices and drift into being a hit, but I personally think it is a very slim one. Had the same thing happened in London there would be no question. The show is gay and funny and the audiences enjoy it and English audiences like to think for themselves, but in America, where they are resolutely told what to do by the Press, television and radio, the situation is different. Of course I am very disappointed, but much more concerned for the poor company than for myself. However, as I said, there is still a glimmer of hope.

1 Gilbert Miller was presenting *Look After Lulu* on Broadway.

After all this routine theatrical nightmare my tooth decided to flare up violently, and so after a night of agony I had it yanked out on Saturday morning. Rather clumsily, I fear, because my face afterwards looked as if I had been hit with a mallet. On top of this I did three hours' work on the ballet because I *had* to as we were leaving the next day. Then I went to the Saturday night performance with Binkie, who had just flown in. The house was full, but the audience dull, and Binkie thought what I feared he would think, that it was rowdy, noisy and that there was too much business at the expense of the dialogue. Actually the performance he saw was not very good – the whole company were tired and dispirited and, although they tried gallantly not to betray it, they didn't quite succeed.

The two days here, apart from being agitated and wretched about my tooth, have been disturbed by the fact that today I had to do the *Small World* television programme with Ed Murrow. Actually it went off very well and I was too weary to be nervous. I sat, surrounded by curious electrical equipment, in one of the Tower Isle bungalows[1], and talked for an hour and a half with Ed Murrow and James Thurber[2] in New York and Siobhan McKenna[3] in Dublin. We could all hear each other fairly well and some of it was quite amusing. Thurber was the dullest of the three, because he spoke too slowly and mostly about himself. Siobhan was wonderful and I got in a few cheerful contributions. *How* it was done is a mystery to me, but then so many things are. I think it is the first time in my life that I have talked impromptu for so long. After the first few minutes I quite enjoyed it.

Now I have got to settle down and finish the bloody ballet music (fortunately there isn't much more to do), pull myself together, take off four pounds, evade the loving neighbours as much as possible, and relax.

The island is still lovely and it still has magic, but it is losing its charm bit by bit – too many tourists – too many new hotels – too much Americanization. 'The infection of vulgarity that will subdue the world.' Firefly will remain untouchable for quite a while yet but the coast is being ruined. When I consider what has happened to this island in eleven years I shudder for the future of the world. But there is no profit in shuddering and so I shall content myself by praying to Jesus, Mary Baker Eddy, Mahomet, Allah and Buddha that my tooth calms down and does *not* work up another abscess. I can also hope that the Guinnesses[4], when they come, don't stay too long, that the movie is a success, and that I at least finish the god-damned ballet.

1 The Jamaican hotel from which Noël was linked up to Ed Murrow's New York studio; the programme depended on a visual hook-up and split-screen technique, then comparatively untried in television.
2 James Thurber (1894-1961), the American humourist.
3 Siobhan McKenna (b. 1923), Irish actress.
4 Alec Guinness and his wife Merula, who were to stay with Noël before the start of the filming of *Our Man in Havana*.

Sunday 5 April

Poor *Lulu* finally closed last night after staggering along to decreasing business for six weeks. The general consensus of opinion is that Cyril over-directed it, that Tammy didn't quite come up to expectations and that Roddy, although an excellent actor, is not intrinsically a comedian. All of this, I think, is quite true but it doesn't really explain the failure. The reasons for that are deeper. The Broadway theatre for some years has been in the doldrums owing to the racket of theatre parties, which destroy audience participation, and the sheep-like attitude of the public to the two leading critics, Brooks Atkinson and Walter Kerr. These two, maddening as it is, have tremendous power. If they say 'thumbs down', the play is a flop unless it has in it a star of enormous drawing-power, and even then it is chancy. It is not actually the fault of these two men; they are not malign, merely rather dull and, at the moment, entirely hypnotized by 'significance', turgidity and the fascination of doom. Also the American public is not attuned to stylized farce, neither are the American actors. Personally I have few regrets. I saw the play rapturously received in New Haven by audiences who had *not* been told much about it one way or the other. I found it, in spite of the above-mentioned defects, very enjoyable. It was a bit common and lacked coherent style.

When I had slightly recovered my resilience after the 'tooth', etc., I read through what I had written of *Waiting in the Wings* last year. I found it much better than I thought it was and so I set to work and finished it. I think I have done a good job and that it is a moving and valid play. I have worked hard on it and taken great pains. It is too early yet for me to know whether it is really good or not and by the time it has been transmuted by acting and direction it might emerge quite differently, but my hopes are high and I certainly do know that one or two of the scenes in it are among the best I have written.

I have also composed and tape-recorded the last remaining themes of the ballet. So now that is completed too and it's now over to the orchestrator and the choreographer.

For the last week we have had, unlike *Lulu*, a full house. Alec and Merula Guinness and Pat Dolin and John Gilpin arrived last Sunday. Graham and I met them in Montego and it's all been a great success with everybody liking everybody else. Pat and John went off this morning at crack of dawn to catch a plane for New York and, tomorrow, another one for Barcelona, where they open next week. I join them there on 7 May and go with the company to Madrid, by which time the ballet ought to be reasonably well set.

On Friday next Alec, Merula and I fly to Havana where we start shooting the film on Monday the thirteenth. I shall only have about three or four days' work there, after which I fly to New York and sail for England on the *Queen Mary* on the twenty-second. Coley and Graham are staying here to dispatch the Chevrolet and various bits and pieces to Geneva. Then they go to Bermuda for a week and pack up everything and send it across the Atlantic. The house at Celigny, on which I had set my heart, is really too expensive and anyhow the owner doesn't want to sell, so I shall store everything in Geneva and, when I have done with Madrid, meet Coley there and really comb the environs for a reasonably priced property. I would much rather find an old house at a fair price, and spend money on modernizing it, than pay a vast sum down, which at the moment I really can't afford. On 24 June I start the film proper in London which should be, for me, three weeks or so. Then the opening of the ballet, 13 July, and then I shall be free with no commitments at all. I hope by then to have found something in Switzerland so that we can move in. If I haven't I shall go on searching until I do.

I have no 'American' plans for the autumn. I feel that I am no longer in tune with it. This is only temporary, of course, but I do yearn for Europe.

Thursday 16 April   Havana

Alec, Merula and I have been here since last Friday. We flew from Jamaica and arrived in a sort of biblical deluge. Carol [Reed] met us with lots of policemen with long hair, beards and tommy-guns, and Press men with shorter hair and cameras. The hotel is Miami-American with elaborate décor, an ornate gambling casino, freezing air-conditioning, bad service and inedible food. I have done three days' shooting and, on the whole, enjoyed it, although it was fairly exhausting. Carol is a charming, courteous and meticulous director.

On Monday all I did was walk about the streets very fast watched by thousands of bewildered Cubans and surrounded, for protection only, by hirsute armed policemen. In between takes and rehearsals, I sat on a chair in the middle of the road and was ministered to by prop men, make-up men, etc., all of whom are very nice and attentive. I find I have to relearn once more *not* to pitch my voice, *not* to use my lips, *not* to 'put in' expression, and above all to remember that the camera is only a few feet away and registers everything. Carol is adamant about keeping me down and I am grateful to him. I wish to God I had had him on *The Astonished Heart*.

On Tuesday I played a scene with Alec in 'Sloppy Joe's' which I think was all right. In the lunch-break we were all hustled into a car and driven for miles to meet the famous Fidel Castro[1]. However, after waiting an hour, we had to go away again without clapping eyes on him. After each day's work we repair to a gloomy sound-studio and do 'wild tracks' over and over again. This is fairly wearisome but precludes future 'post-sync-ing', which is hell.

The last day I *didn't* enjoy. I had to play a brief scene with Alec out of context in blazing sun, and my eyes were worrying me. It's this damned

---

1 Fidel Castro (b. 1927) had become the Cuban President in February of this year after his forces had finally overthrown Batista.

conjunctivitis that's been hanging about me for months. Last night we dined with Ernest and Mary Hemingway[1] in their house just outside Havana and all got thoroughly pissed, and so today I feel very peculiar and can't wait to get into the plane and go to sleep. I still feel that acting for the silver screen is fairly silly and infinitely difficult, but I expect that this is because I am inexperienced and don't do it very well.

Sunday 26 April   ss *Queen Mary*

New York was pleasant enough but I found it a trifle irritating. On arrival I managed to get two seats for the opening of the Bolshoi Ballet at the Met. It was a very great gala occasion and a very poor ballet. I went with Marlene, who looked lovely. The place was packed to the ceiling and I enjoyed watching them all stand for 'The Red Flag'. Ulanova, who danced Juliet, was absolutely miraculous, a great actress as well as a great dancer. The duelling scenes were good, but the whole thing was heavy and old-fashioned. Everyone went mad at the end and it was all very sincere.

On Saturday I went to Atlantic City to see Kit [Cornell] and Brian [Aherne] play *Dear Liar*, the Shaw-Campbell letters. They were both excellent and had style and charm. Then on to Philadelphia to see Ethel Merman in *Gypsy*[2], which I enjoyed thoroughly. She is a great performer, Jerry Robbins has done a brilliant production, and the whole thing was satisfying.

On Sunday I drove out to Sneden's in the afternoon and read *Waiting in the Wings* to Kit, Guthrie and Nancy Hamilton. They were quite genuinely moved by it and I was highly gratified. Kit is in rather a bad way, poor darling, a sort of inner nerve crisis, fear of acting, etc. I suspect she will get over it.

On Monday I took Marlene to *Sweet Bird of Youth*. Like all Tennessee's plays it has moments of brilliant writing, but Miss Geraldine Page, who is supposed by the critics to give the greatest performance since Rachel, I thought jerky, mannered and competent. It is a great part and needs a great actress. What it gets is technical efficiency and some good and bad tricks. Paul Newman was very good and the production fine. The play is not really good. None of the characters is really valid and the emphasis on squalor – drugs, syphilis, castration, sex, sex, sex – is too heavy and almost old-fashioned.

I have been offered by Warner Bros to play in the movie of *Lolita*[3]. Now I have refused to read *Lolita* for a long time, so at last I have been forced to try. It is well written in a curious way but exceedingly pornographic and quite disgusting. I cannot quite see myself playing a long, lecherous love story with a little girl of twelve. An unsavoury project if ever there was one.

1 Ernest Hemingway (1898–1961), the American novelist, and his fourth wife Mary.
2 The Jule Styne-Arthur Laurents-Stephen Sondheim musical.
3 Vladimir Nabokov's novel; the part was eventually played by James Mason.

I lunched twice with Natasha. The Jack situation is worse than ever. He has, however, *at last* consented to commit himself to a hospital.

So far this voyage has been peaceful. I have conversed – in the Turkish bath – with Louis Rawlings, a rich Jewish wholesale dressmaker who wishes to launch 'Noël Coward' cologne, to be followed by 'after-shave', 'bath oil', 'soap', etc. This sounds quite a good idea providing that the product is very good, and I might make a lot of money out of it. If Larry and Gerald du Maurier can advertise cigarettes[1], I can't see why I shouldn't advertise toilet water. It's certainly less degrading than playing in *Lolita*.

Tuesday 5 May   London

Today I fly to Barcelona after ten London days of *va et vient* and *sturm und drang*. The weather has been, on the whole, surprisingly good, spring in the air, the grass in the park vivid green, and lilacs blowing and a-growing. The *sturm und drang* was caused by me having a quarrel with Binkie about *Wings*. He loved the play when I read it to him the first night I arrived, then when we met the following Monday evening he had been studying the script and was a little too full of suggested alterations. The discussion between us went sour and finally he said he wouldn't do the play. I took this angrily at face value and flounced out with my lovelocks flowing. The next morning an anguished telegram arrived and everyone forgave everyone else and a further, calmer discussion took place and now all is *en train* and the play is to be sent to Frith Banbury[2], whom I still consider the most appropriate director for this particular play. However, perhaps he won't like it. At all events it will be rediscussed in June when I return. Upon mature reflection, I'm rather glad the scene took place; Binkie has changed a bit of late and this row got us down to bedrock, and Binkie at bedrock is entirely to be trusted; on other strata he is apt to be devious and tricky. I love him very much and the friendship will endure.

Vivien I have seen twice. She is calm, sane, incredibly beautiful and heartbroken. She is counting the days until Larry's return and refuses to envisage the possibility that he really intends to leave her for ever. I hope, really for both their sakes, that she is right. Maggie Leighton and *her* Larry are in slight doldrums, but I expect it will straighten itself out. Marriage in the 'theatre' is not an enviable state.

I went to *A Taste of Honey*, a squalid little piece about squalid and unattractive people. It has been written by an angry young lady of nineteen[3] and is a great success. Personally I found it fairly dull.

The high and low spot of my London visit was the opening night of John

1 Both Olivier and du Maurier cigarettes were on the market.
2 Frith Banbury (b. 1912), London stage director.
3 Shelagh Delaney.

Osborne's musical *The World of Paul Slickey*[1] at the Palace. I went with Gladys and the Millses and never in all my theatrical experience have I seen anything so appalling. Appalling from every point of view. Bad lyrics, dull music, idiotic, would-be-daring dialogue – interminable long-winded scenes about nothing, and above all the amateurishness and ineptitude, such bad taste that one wanted to hide one's head. There is a funeral scene of abiding horror which brought forth a storm of boos from orchestra to gallery. The only redeeming feature was Denis Lotis, who was pleasant and sang well.

I fear that Mr John Osborne is not so talented as he has been made out to be. *Look Back in Anger* had vitality and too much invective. *George Dillon*, his first play, written in collaboration with someone else, was his best and even that had a weak last act. *The Entertainer* was verbose, unreal and pretentious, and this is unspeakable. He is cashing in shamelessly on publicity, but this will soon die away and, unless he reduces his head to normal size and gets down to genuine professional playwriting, he will die away too. It is not enough to attract publicity by inveighing against circumstances and governments and traditions. Destructive vituperation is too easy. I cannot believe that this writer, the first of the 'angry young men', was ever really angry at all. Dissatisfied, perhaps, and certainly envious and, to a degree, talented, but no more than that. No leader of thought or ideas, a conceited, calculating young man blowing a little trumpet.

Monday 11 May   Barcelona

I have been here since last Thursday and have spent most of my time in bed and in the theatre. I am learning a lot about 'behind the scenes' ballet life and I find it, like others before me, fascinating. I have, by now, seen most of the ballets in the repertoire and I am genuinely impressed and quite astounded at the vitality of this company and their endless capacity for work. They rehearse and practise all day and every day and then go on and tear themselves to shreds. John Gilpin, I think, is the finest male dancer I have ever seen. Apart from brilliant technique he has taste, acting talent and notably good looks. He stands miles high above the rest, although some of them are very fine. Some of the ballets are sketchily presented, black tabs and tacky lighting. Actually unnecessary because a cyclorama and grey tabs would be no more expensive. The *corps de ballet* are well disciplined and, as a rule, precise. *London Morning*[2] is being rehearsed and I feel sure that it will ultimately be good. At the moment it is in too rough a state to be judged fairly.

The 'time' factor in Spain is *molto curioso*. The evening performances start at ten and the matinées at six. I have been to a couple of parties given for members of the company, the first one lethal, and the second, last night, very

1 About a gossip columnist.
2 Noël's ballet.

gay. A Russian Easter party given in a small flat by a large Russian dance teacher. Coloured eggs, vodka, lots of succulent little Russki dishes and a great deal of toast drinking. A babel of tongues – French, Russian, Spanish, and a little, really very little, English. I spent most of my time with Pat Dolin and John. They are both dears and I'm enjoying myself. The ballet 'entourage' is fascinating – ballet mistresses, wardrobe mistresses, *régisseurs*, etc. – all very concentrated and cheerful. My God, how they all work! It is certainly a dedicated profession and, to me, highly impressive.

Saturday 13 June   Montreux

The day after I arrived in Geneva, 21 May, Coley and I hired a car and set off. We looked at a couple of unsuitable and expensive properties by the lake and then drove to Les Avants to see one there. It is a roomy but fairly hideous chalet in the mountains above Montreux and the views are sensational. Coley had already seen it on his own and was, naturally, dubious about the house. However, when we looked at it together and had a few ideas about what *could* be done, we became enthusiastic. The price is £12,000, whereas all the others I have seen are £20,000, £30,000, etc. I can afford to spend money on it and it has, for me, many advantages. As I said before, scenically it is marvellous. It has four and a half acres of garden filled with wild strawberries, lilacs, gooseberries, blackcurrants and burgeoning English flowers. It looks out over the lake and the mountains, and the air is wonderful. It faces due south and gets the sun all day and it is exactly twenty minutes from Montreux by car or train (a little local one which runs up and down several times a day). The tiny station is two minutes on foot from the house.

The disadvantages are: a) a vast hotel transformed into a girls' finishing school, which is a bit of an eyesore but well below us so it doesn't matter much; b) the ugly 1900 chalet quality of the house. Mr and Mrs Petrie who own it are anxious to sell and retire to Hindhead. Apparently other would-be buyers are after it so I asked for first refusal for one week. Two days later the Petries rang me up in Geneva to say that they had had a firm offer that very morning of £12,000 and would have to accept it unless I would equal it. I hated the feeling of being stampeded and told them I'd call back in half an hour. Coley and I had an agitated discussion and finally I called back and said I'd buy it. Since then we have wavered very little and now we are not wavering at all and have grown to love it. The Petries' furniture doesn't improve the look of the place and there is a great deal to be done, but now that everything is decided I am delighted.

In the middle of all this the Chevrolet arrived from Jamaica and had to be extracted from the Customs in Geneva. This entailed endless interviews and form fillings, and at long last we got the car and had her washed and tanked up. At the same time Binkie rang up from London and said that *Lulu* was to go into rehearsal immediately with Vivien and Tony Richardson[1] directing, and that Tony R. was flying out to discuss it. All the hotels in Geneva were full owing to the bloody 'summit' conference, but we finally managed to get him a room. He missed two planes, which wasted hours of our time, but at last arrived in time to dine and go into the whole matter. He is very intelligent and I think he will do a good job. Vivien is still havering but will eventually agree. The play is to open out of town, 20 July, and at the Royal Court, 29 July, for five weeks, then transfer. All of which is very satisfactory if only darling Viv stays on the rails.

Tony departed for London the next morning and we shot off in the Chevrolet to Pat Dolin's villa in Monaco. It is a sweet little villa but the trains go between one's legs and the church bells ring under one's armpits and there is a great deal of blasting going on because a new tunnel is being made. The house was shuttered and barred so I sat on a suitcase while Coley and Graham went off to find the fairly *bonne à tout faire*. They returned with the keys and we settled in for three days. Very enjoyable days. We lay on the beach in the sun, visited Gloria and Loel Guinness on their yacht, dined luxuriously at the Hôtel de Paris, and I won 600,000 francs at the casino. Pat himself arrived on Sunday evening and we left on Monday, lunched with Edward, stayed the night in Aix-en-Provence (filthy dinner) and the next night in Aix-le-Bains. We arrived here on Wednesday to hear from Lornie that Vivien had stopped havering and that all was under way.

Sunday 21 June   London

The week in Lausanne was more or less uneventful. Pat and John and the ballet company arrived and we went to all three performances, the third rendered acutely embarrassing by Pat dancing *Giselle* with Toumanova, who looked like Peter Glenville in drag. It was a god-awful spectacle and most shaming.

I bought a small new 'Dauphine' which will be waiting for me when I get back, and we've had the Chevrolet tested and insured and suitably plated. We have made ourselves dizzy and quite hysterical trying to choose chintzes, carpets, wallpapers.

Sunday 28 June

On Monday I took Graham to *Medea*[2] at Covent Garden and we were both overwhelmed by Maria Callas, who was completely and absolutely superb. The opera is not really up to much and should have been by Strauss, but she makes up for everything. She is one of the few really great artists that I have

---

1 Tony Richardson (b. 1928), English stage and film director, co-founder of the English Stage Company at the Royal Court Theatre in 1955.
2 By Cherubini.

ever seen in my life. On Wednesday I went to hear Callas again, this time with the Droghedas[1], Vivien and Diana [Cooper] in the royal box. She was more wonderful than ever and it was an enchanting evening.

Graham and I have taken a great shine to the East End and we drive down and go to different pubs, where we find the exquisite manners of true Cockneys, all of whom, men and women, are impeccably dressed and none of whom is in the least 'look back in angerish', merely cheerful and friendly and disinclined to grumble about anything. I am forced to the conclusion that the viewpoint of our younger playwrights is slightly off true. I would like one day to write an intimate, completely Cockney musical without any sordid overtones. The critics won't like it and the left-wing highbrows won't like it, but the public will.

Callas and her husband dined with me at the Caprice and it was a most successful evening. She is a most remarkable creature.

Sunday 12 July

Well, I've done my ten days' filming and enjoyed it more than I ever have before. Carol is a marvellous director and I really think I am good in it largely thanks to him. The whole visit was nice and I loved working with Alec Guinness and Ralph Richardson who, although slightly boring, is a dear. The getting up in the morning was rather tedious but apart from that the whole thing was fun. The weather has been perfect and I felt quite sad when I left the studios on Thursday after an orgy of present-giving and in a blaze of popularity.

I went to John G's opening in his solo Shakespeare show[2]. He was superb in his quiet moments, but not so good when he wept and roared.

On the evening of Wednesday the first, I played the ballet score to Lee Randall of Decca and they are going to make an LP of it. On Friday last I heard the orchestra for the first time and it was a thrilling sensation to hear that big symphony orchestra really letting go! The dress parade was less happy. Some of the costumes are all right but not all by any manner of means, and none of the Guardsmen's uniforms fits anywhere; however, that is to be remedied.

Sunday 19 July   Paris

The ballet has been an enormous success with the public, for whom it was written, but not with the critics, for whom it was not written. One or two rave notices and the rest either patronizing or abusive. It is no use pretending it is not irritating because it is; it's maddening to have a triumphant opening performance with everyone yelling and cheering and then read the next

1 Lord and Lady Drogheda; he was managing director of the *Financial Times* 1945-70 and chairman of the Royal Opera House, Covent Garden 1958-72.
2 *The Ages of Man* at the Queen's Theatre.

morning that the whole thing is terrible. Fortunately by now the English public are so accustomed to me being insulted by the critics that they pay no attention at all. I don't know exactly what makes them so vitriolic; I suppose it's my continued success and something about my personality that infuriates them, in which case I fear that they will have to get on with it.

I flew here on Thursday and dined with the Windsors that night; delicious dinner as usual, and Wallis gay and charming as ever. The Duke very cheerful; however, Elsa [Maxwell] and Dickie [Gordon] not so good. Actually Dickie all right but Elsa thoroughly disagreeable and drunk with imaginary power. It was a sad day when first she began to write that idiotic column and a still sadder one when she was allowed on television. It has given her delusions of grandeur that are quite startling.

On Friday night I went to see Josephine Baker in her revue at the Olympia. She was all right but thickening a bit; her clothes were good and there was some reasonable dancing, but the whole thing went on far, far too long.

Sunday 2 August

Another hectic week is over and here I am where 'burning Sappho loved and sang'[1]. Douglas, Mary Lee and the two girls are flogging their way across an island to see 'temples and theatres open to the sky', and I am sitting on deck amid a cloud of wasps and near the main drain.

Look After Lulu opened on Wednesday night[2] to a ghastly audience. It didn't go very well, although it was excellently played. Vivien was really entrancing and her performance has improved a lot. The notices I read, except for *The Times* and *Telegraph*, were as usual abusive and almost entirely personal attacks on me; however, I am so accustomed to this that it only exasperated me mildly and on Thursday I clambered into a plane and flew to Athens. There I was met by Stavros Niarchos's representative and whisked to the Grande Bretagne [Hotel], where I found the Fairbankses dressed up for *son et lumière* at the Acropolis and an ambassadorial party to follow. I was invited but firmly refused. I sat outside a café for a little and went to bed in a scorching bedroom early, took a large sleeping-pill and slept for nine hours.

The next morning (Friday) we set sail. The *Eros* is the smaller Niarchos yacht, a beautiful boat but accommodation is limited. I sleep (?) in the dining saloon. After four hours chugging along through enchanted waters we arrived at Spetzapoula, Niarchos's new island. We drove round it in clouds of dust, wobbling uneasily in a land-rover. Then we dined on board the *Creole*, very enjoyable. Eugénie Niarchos is a dear and I took a great liking to her. All yesterday we bathed and picnicked and it was really lovely, the sea is

---

1 Noël was a guest on a yacht lent by Stavros Niarchos to the Fairbanks family and now anchored off the Greek port of Nauplia.
2 At the Royal Court Theatre, London.

unbelievable, and although we met far too many people, mostly Greeks, they were all very welcoming and kind. Last night we dined ashore – about thirty of us – fish with two sorts of garlic sauce, roast pig and ice cream – but last night late we sailed away under a crowd of stars. From now on I hope and pray our cruise will be less social.

I have been fairly adamant about too much sightseeing, and Mary Lee and Doug couldn't be sweeter or more understanding. If only we can be by ourselves I shall enjoy the holiday I'm sure, but the trouble with the rich is that they love going about in packs. I cannot say that the yacht, from my point of view, is the acme of comfort, but I do have my own loo which so far works! The crew are attentive and smiling and, at the moment, I have the yacht to myself. Later on, when more rested, I may look at a temple or two, but not yet.

A sweet cable from Viv saying the play is going beautifully.

Sunday 16 August

I transferred from the *Eros* to the *Creole* on Friday and am now ensconced in a super-luxe, air-conditioned cabin with white-coated Italian stewards fluttering round me like moths. The Niarchoses are kind and hospitable, but curiously remote, particularly Stavros. He is the stuff of which dictators are made. Everyone is terrified of him, and the staff cringes and trembles with tears at his frown. To me he is charming, but his Napoleonic quality forbids intimacy and he flies into tantrums easily. Eugénie is attractive and has a fascinating voice. The two little boys are potentially sweet but, of course, spoiled. Oddly enough, amid all this luxe and among all these Renoirs and Manets, the food, except for the caviare, is mediocre. I was told that we were going to be just ourselves but I might have known better than to believe it. Last night we had sixteen people to dinner!

I still hold to my conviction that the very rich lead most unenviable lives. With all the luxury on board this yacht I was happier mucking in with the Fairbanks family on the little *Eros*. They are a devoted family and their affection for each other spreads over whoever is with them. The Niarchoses are also devoted, but there are unscalable barriers of money and power between them and other people. I am enjoying myself fitfully but I shall be glad to fly away home to Les Avants.

On Monday at Corfu the King and Queen [of Greece] came to dine on board accompanied by an immense clutch of minor princes and princesses, all of whom had to be bobbed and bowed to. The Queen has a deceptive laugh based on a strong Teutonic lack of humour. The King has a loud, affable laugh based on nothing at all. The Queen, who is very *bas bleu*, embarked on a long and confused conversation with me about physics, nuclear fission and advanced planes of thought and experience. She then proceeded to bugger up her scientific theses by talking about 'afterlife', etc. I behaved splendidly and agreed with exquisite subservience to everything she said. They didn't leave until 2.30 a.m. so they must have enjoyed themselves.

I remain here in exquisite *durance vile* until Wednesday when, hell or high water, I intend to get myself to Geneva and settle in to the Victoria Hotel at Glion where Coley has booked me a room. The life of the very rich is not for me, and although it is enjoyable to observe at close quarters for a brief spell, it is strangely deadening to the heart.

Monday 24 August   Glion

This hotel is really charming and dead quiet. I have a high sunny room overlooking the lake and the mountains. My new 'Dauphine' was delivered to me the morning after I arrived and it goes beautifully and is very small and nippy on these mountain roads. The house[1] is a complete shambles and there is little hope of moving in under six weeks so I shall settle in here. It's only ten minutes away and I can go to bed early and get up early and revel in being on my own.

I've talked to Binkie and Lorn and Graham, and all is well at home. Coley and I drove in a deluge to Evian and had a fairly disastrous casino evening. However, I am still up 100,000 francs. We dined with the Van Johnsons who have bought a house in Vevey! Saturday night Ferber dined with us. She is at the Montreux Palace.

My painting is improving a great deal and I think I am mastering gouache. I am reading the fourth Madame Sacha Guitry's book about her marriage. It is fairly silly but good for my French. Sacha certainly was a pompous ass.

Sunday 6 September

There is bad news about poor Katie Kendall. She is critically ill in the London Clinic and I have a dreadful feeling that this time it really is the end. I feel so sad because she is a gay, enchanting creature and such wonderful company. Rex is living in the Clinic to be with her and my heart aches for him.

I have reread *Later than Spring* and it really is too good to discard so I am going to press on with it. I can make it fit Judy Holliday[2] with some judicious alterations, and as there is a whole act virtually complete it would be stupid to rack my brains for something entirely different. It was the idea of Roz Russell that put me off in the first place. Judy, although she is not really old enough for Mrs Wentworth-Brewster as I originally planned her, has warmth and heart, neither of which can be said for the metallic Miss Russell, and I think I can make the whole thing very attractive.

1 Which he had now bought at Les Avants.
2 Judy Holliday (1921–65), funny American actress.

Saturday 19 September

Darling Katie Kendall died last Sunday week, the day before I left for London. She died gently without pain and without any idea that she was dying. Poor Coley was deeply unhappy because she's always been so sweet to him and genuinely loved him. Personally I felt absolutely miserable; she was a gay, wonderful companion. Rex really has behaved very, very admirably. I went to the funeral with Vivien, quite small and quiet and nicely done. There were no mobs and shaming demonstrations, only a few scruffy newspaper photographers clambering about on the cemetery railings and snapping the coffin being lowered into the ground.

The opening of *Lulu* at the New[1] was a triumphant success and it's been playing to an average of £500 a performance ever since. I took Margot Fonteyn and Gina Lollobrigida[2] and her husband. He was intelligent and amiable and she, I thought, was a trifle pleased with herself. She was also over half an hour late. There was a pleasant party at Binkie's afterwards.

My other outings in London were *The Aspern Papers*[3], well done but a little dull; *The Hostage*[4], amateur, noisy and unattractive in every way; and a film, *I'm All Right, Jack*[5], which was brilliantly funny. Peter Sellers was superb, so really was everybody in it.

I dined with Binkie on my last evening and he was at his nicest and we heart-to-hearted until 3 a.m., by which time my friend was pissed as a newt. Paris was great fun. I dined on arrival with the Windsors, a party *à quatre* which Elsa [Maxwell] ruined by inviting a strange Brazilian journalist and his wife for coffee. I'm really getting very, very sick of Elsa; she has become a fairly malignant old bag, full of sound and fury and signifying very little.

Monday 28 September

The only important thing that has happened this week is that, after a brisk talk with myself, I decided to be called every morning and work three hours a day on my novel. It was difficult at first plunging back into it, but now the flow is beginning and I am averaging three pages a day. This is a wonderful time to get it finished because there is little to be done about the house and I can just go on working away regularly for the next few weeks, which is the only way to get anything done anyway.

Last Monday I went to Basle for Lennie Bernstein's concert, which was really magnificent. He played a Mozart piano concerto, conducting it from the

1 It had transferred from the Royal Court on 8 September.
2 Gina Lollobrigida (b. 1927), the Italian film star, married to Milko Skofic.
3 Henry James's novel, adapted by Michael Redgrave.
4 By Brendan Behan.
5 Produced and directed by John and Roy Boulting.

piano, and it was lovely. Then the Brahms Number One, which was thrilling. Supper afterwards with the American Ambassador and his wife. The next morning I woke betimes and came back here for lunch. That evening Coley, Van and Evie [Johnson] and Benita and George[1] and I went to Artur Rubinstein's concert in Montreux. Highly enjoyable and he played beautifully.

Since then various projects have reared their heads – one to appear for a month next March with Marlene in Australia, which should be a very chic combination but I doubt if it will come off because we could both of us do it solo and obviously double the dough! The other project is a television series of me interviewing the 'great' of the twentieth century. I have agreed to make one pilot as an experiment, providing I approve of the script. If this goes through and is any good I shall do anything from thirteen interviews to twenty-six for £2,000 each against sixty per cent of the eventual profits. Apparently it can be so arranged that not more than a few weeks of my time need be entailed. There's also been a tentative film offer from Cecil Tennant to play in a picture with Yul Brynner. Unless the part is sensational I shan't do this.

Today I go to lunch in Lausanne with the Queen of Spain. Never a dull moment.

Monday 5 October

The lunch party with the Queen of Spain was a great success. She was absolutely sweet and as merry as a grig, and the food was exquisite. There was also an amiable couple called the Comte and Comtesse Chevreau d'Antraigues. This is a name I must remember as they threatened to ask me to lunch.

The novel is really coming along very well. I am doing a steady three pages a day and am enjoying it. It is really very funny, I think, and it is deeply satisfying to be working steadily again. I have been idle for far too long.

Lulu is still playing to marvellous business, thank God. I don't think the Australian lark will come off because apparently the taxes there are enormous and it wouldn't be worth all the trouble. However, I shall have to earn some big money soon because the house is costing a fortune. It at last shows signs of being habitable and I do think that when it is at long last finished it will be lovely. I'm longing to move in. This hotel continues to be sweet but one by one, singly and in groups, the staff are leaving. All our favourite waiters have gone and we shall soon, I suspect, be hopping downstairs at dawn to stoke up the furnace and get our own breakfasts.

I am reading an over-detailed but fairly interesting biography of Proust. I don't think we should ever have become close buddies.

The English newspapers are churning themselves into a frenzy over the

1 George Sanders (1906–72), British film actor, second husband of Benita Hume.

Election which happens this week. I expect and hope the Conservatives will get in again, but I can't bring myself to be passionately interested either way.

Sunday 11 October

Well. First things first, and I suppose the Election should be regarded as a first thing. Anyhow it is over and the Conservatives won hands down. Labour has taken a terrible beating and serve them right for being so idiotic as to go on pressing their 'nationalization' plans. The British public just don't want it and that's that.

The *bouquet* to celebrate the completion of the new roof[1] was a great success. A trestle table loaded with bottles of wine and cheese tartlets. Adrianne, Bill[2], Evie Johnson and me at one end, playing my ballet record on the lovely tiny portable that Evie and Van gave me. Speeches were made. It was a lovely evening and it all went off a fair treat.

I was right about the Chevreau d'Antraigues. They *did* ask me to lunch and there was the Queen of Spain again. I took a great shine to my host and hostess – she was Mary Latta and was at school with Joyce!

The novel is progressing steadily. The television boys Dennis Vance and Howard Connell are persevering and flew from Paris for the day to discuss my first 'pilot' interview, which is to be with Darryl Zanuck of all people. Not *quite* my idea of the 'great' of the twentieth century, but interesting enough to practise on. So far I am only committed to this one so we shall see how it works.

I took Coley to Evian last night and, apart from buying some nice toilet water and having a 'luxe' dinner, the evening was disastrous and I lost the last of my 'casino' money and came home resolved not to do it again for some time. I have, on the whole, been very, very lucky and so I mustn't grumble. But I am not a *real* gambler, I am thankful to say.

Saturday 31 October

The Paris experiment[3] was gruelling hard work but went off very well. I arrived at Studio Boulogne at eleven o'clock and stayed there until 9.30! Working all the time. Fortunately I had not only rewritten most of Jock Gourlay's script but had learnt it in the train. This stood me in good stead, for I was stuck in front of a camera and just had to talk. It was stifling hot and fairly agitating but I didn't do badly. Most of the afternoon was taken up with photographing Darryl and asking him questions off camera. He was charming and friendly throughout. Then at the bitter end I had to return to the tiny studio where I had been in the morning and do all the questions I had asked

1 At Les Avants, a topping-out ceremony.
2 Major William Dwight Whitney, Adrianne Allen's husband.
3 As a television interviewer.

Darryl in close-up. This was torture because I was exhausted. However, everyone seemed pleased. Be that as it may, I am not going to do a rush job like that again. The next time I must have the script, and a *good one*, at least two weeks before I do it. Dennis Vance is a good and sympathetic director and I think if we really work together and control the situation we *might* get a very interesting series. They will bring the finished product to Geneva in ten days or a fortnight for me to see.

On Wednesday the first truck-load of furniture from Bermuda arrived at the chalet in a blizzard. Coley has moved in and is up there now in one room. It is all chaos but the windows and doors are in, thank God, *and* the water and central heating. I have constructed the novel on paper up to the end and restart tomorrow.

Sunday 22 November   Paris

I am leaving for London today and start shooting the film *Surprise Package* tomorrow. It's a good part and they're paying me £35,000 and all expenses! This really comes in the nick of time because we were running low in the dear Crédit Suisse and beginning to get worried. There was a drama about the script because the Hôtel des Bergues in Geneva completely and utterly lost it! However, fortunately they had sent another to Glion, which I had sent to the Beau Rivage in Lausanne, read it in an hour, and said 'Yes'. I would have said 'Yes' even if it had been in Sanskrit. Actually it's very funny and well written.

My television interview with Darryl Zanuck turned out to be a great deal better than I expected. I am well-lit, look fairly good, and the sound is clear. I have agreed to do the series providing that they, Vance and Connell, agree to my terms, which are steep, I must say.

I spent yesterday shopping wildly. I bought a royal-blue velvet dressing-gown in Sulka's and made them cut it in half to make a smoking-jacket for the film. It cost a hundred quid. Hail Columbia[1].

On Friday there was a little gathering – Lena Horne, Lennie [Hayton] her husband, and Marlene – at Ginette's. Marlene made an entrance looking ravishing and was quite entrancing for about an hour. Then she became boring and over-egocentric. Poor darling. I'm sure she was over-excited but I did suddenly feel a wave of relief that I *hadn't* agreed to do an Australian tour with her. I am quite sure she would have driven me barmy.

I have already learnt quite a lot of the part and I'm really looking forward to it. I'm also looking forward to being able to pay for the house!

Saturday 28 November   London

Well, I've had an exhausting week but very satisfactory. I think I am going to be good in the picture. It's a very good part. Yul is a dear to work with, so

1 Columbia Pictures were financing *Surprise Package*.

is Mitzi Gaynor[1], and Stanley Donen is a really excellent director, gentle, thorough and patient. There is much less tension working with him than with Carol. Actually I am enjoying doing it very much.

Last weekend, while Binkie was in Paris, the Alberys, *père et fils*[2] – horrid *fils* – put up the notice of *Lulu*. True, we had dropped below £2,500 two weeks running and they are *legally* within their rights, but there's the usual general slump before Christmas and it's insanity to close, particularly as all our after Christmas advance will have to be sacrificed. Apparently Donald Albery wants to bring *Make Me an Offer*[3] in. There is nothing to be done. No other theatre is available to transfer to and that's that.

Last night when I went to fetch Vivien and heard the audience (excellent house) roaring and applauding, I felt really good and mad. I'm awfully sorry for Vivien because Larry's off to America, *doesn't* wish her to go with him, and she has now no excuse, from the Press and public point of view, for not going! I have asked her to Les Avants for Christmas. She is desperately unhappy inside although very good and gay outwardly. Larry is still enamoured of his newfound bachelorhood and I think he intends to hold on to it. The fact that all this was tremendously her own fault in no way mitigates the fact that she's jolly miserable and, apparently, mad about the boy! Really, people are *very* peculiar.

Saturday 5 December

It's been a hard-working week but very satisfactory. All my principal scenes are now done, including a musical sequence in which I do a cheerful little number with Mitzi Gaynor. This was given to me on Wednesday morning at eleven o'clock. I learnt it and it was recorded and in the can by twelve o'clock. Everyone was very surprised but it really wasn't very difficult. The next day I mouthed it in the scene. I have never done this synchronization before, but it was all right. I've enjoyed making this picture and have felt relaxed in front of the camera for the first time in my sporadic film experience.

I have made a *great* decision which will, I fear, cause considerable heartbreak and disappointment. I have decided *not* to sign the television series contract. The whole set-up rather alarms me. All concerned are ineradicably common and it will tie me up for a year. True, I should get, personally, £120,000 out of it, but that is not really the point. I *don't* think it will be good enough and interviewing people really isn't my dish. They have been dithering and quibbling about the contract for weeks, which was silly of them because if it had been ready three weeks ago I should have signed it and been properly hooked. The fact that I *said* I'd do it worries me somewhat because I don't

1 Mitzi Gaynor (b. 1931), star of American musicals.
2 Sir Bronson and Donald Albery owned the New Theatre where *Look After Lulu* was playing.
3 The musical based on Wolf Mankowitz's novel.

like going back on my word, but I really have been more or less talked and bullied into it. I would even be willing to pay an indemnity. I've seldom, no, *never* in my life done anything only for money, and certainly to do something I wasn't really enthusiastic about would be idiocy and I should not be good and do myself a great deal of harm.

It appears that I have 'stolen' *Our Man in Havana* and it looks as if I should make a success in *Surprise Package*, all of which means that my cinematic stock will be high and I can just sit cosily in the snow and wait for nice offers to roll in. The film *S.P.* will practically pay for the house and so I have very little to worry about financially.

Poor Madge Titheradge is slowly dying. Rosamond Lehmann has become an over-ardent spiritualist, and the world wags on. Vivien is coming to Les Avants for Christmas. There has been a ghastly dam-burst in Fréjus, five hundred killed. I'm glad I live in Switzerland.

Saturday 12 December   Paris

I finished the film on Tuesday cheerfully and successfully two days before I expected to, and so in order to save myself two of my hoarded days in England I flew here on Wednesday. Ginette and Larry were on the plane and, on arrival, instead of going straight to bed as I had planned, I rapidly changed into *le smoking* and went with them to the opening night of the Lido. It was the great social-theatrical night of the year. Our table consisted of us, Paul-Emile, Jean-Pierre Aumont and, later, Marlene and Raf Vallone[1] who is her new throb! Next to us was Maurice Chevalier and Sophia Loren, etc., and on the other side the Jean-Louis Barraults, Aurics, etc. The show, as usual, was far too long but well done and included a wonderful juggler, a fantastic conjurer, lots of naked titties and the Dagenham Girl Pipers. It was all rather fun really, although it got a bit boring towards the end.

I had a private showing of *Our Man in Havana* and it's very good. Everyone is roaring around saying that I've stolen the picture, but this is not strictly true, although I think I would have if my part had been a bit bigger. As it is I am really very good and there is no overplaying. Ernie Kovacs and Paul Rogers are wonderful, Burl Ives a bore, Jo Morrow barely adequate, Ralphie very good, Maureen O'Hara quite charming, and Alec! well, I'm a bit puzzled. He is a beautiful actor but, to my mind, he plays the whole thing in too minor a key. It is a faultless performance but actually, I'm afraid, a little dull.

Here in Paris the handsome Alain Delon[2] has become engaged to Romy Schneider[3]. I took them both to dine at Maxim's and afterwards to see

1 Raf Vallone (b. 1916), Italian film actor.
2 Alain Delon (b. 1935), French film star.
3 Romy Schneider (1938–82), Austrian film star.

Marlene. They were very lover-like, she is obviously mad about him – after all, who wouldn't be with those looks?

Marlene is a fabulous success[1]. She looks ravishing and tears the place up. Privately I didn't like anything she did except 'One for my Baby'. She has developed a hard, brassy assurance and she belts out every song harshly and without finesse. All her aloof, almost lazy glamour has been overlaid by a noisy, 'take-this-and-like-it' method which, to me, is disastrous. However, the public loved it. All the same, I know that they would have loved her even more if she had been more remote and not worked so blatantly hard.

Larry and the Seidmanns and I lunched with Maurice Chevalier on Friday and he really was very, very charming and looks miraculous. He is seventy-two and as attractive as he ever was.

Larry came here this evening for a heart-to-heart. He is in a bad state. He's madly in love with Joan Plowright and has had to tell Vivien. He obviously hates hurting her but is equally obviously determined not to go back to her. I am desperately sorry for her although it is mostly her own silly fault.

Monday 21 December   Les Avants

It is eight o'clock in the morning and I am sitting up comfortably in bed in my own house at last. Outside it is still blue-dark but the sun is preparing to come up from behind the Rochers de Naye. The mountains are beginning to turn pink and the visible world is white with snow. The house is really beautiful, much more so than I would have believed, but of course it is not nearly as advanced as it should have been by now. However, we have all worked like mad and filled up bookshelves and hung pictures. It has been great fun but exhausting.

The main 'salon' and library are done and look lovely. The French room almost done. The pink room done, Coley's room done, and my suite virtually complete and quite perfect. My work room is a dream and feels really shut away from the rest of the house, and my multiple shower is sensational! I know I am going to be happy here. It is a light house and the sun shines on most days with all its might, so much so that it is dazzling and we're having sun-blinds made for all the windows. Alas, the place is still full of workmen and will be for weeks yet. The dining-room and main kitchen haven't been touched yet and the landings and stairs are still paperless and carpetless. However, there is nothing to do but press on.

Coley has been working like a maniac, too much so really. Fortunately a cook arrived today called Marcel. Coley is at this moment meeting him at the station. I interviewed him in Paris and he *seems* fine, if perhaps a trifle grand. At any rate, he'll save us for the next few weeks at least. I daren't have the

1 In a solo show at the Olympia.

dear dogs home yet because there's still too much paint and plaster about, but I hope to welcome them for the New Year.

I am now sixty years and four and a half days old and it is a curious feeling. There is an implacable ring to the word 'sixty'. Ten years more and I shall be seventy if I am still a-growing and a-blowing, and then there will be old age. I look forward to it with reasonable equanimity. The fact that my story is comparatively nearly over is something that must be faced. I hope indeed that my faculties will remain unimpaired for as long as possible, but if they don't there really isn't anything I can do about it.

The television series is now *on* again and yesterday Howard Connell, Jock Gourlay and, surprisingly, Wee Georgie Wood[1] came to see me. I have agreed, contract being satisfactory, to do thirteen. I am hooked with this so the only thing is to enjoy it as best I can.

The cook I engaged in Paris has just arrived with a *soi-disant* wife! This is a startling development. They seem to be happy enough but I smell trouble.

Sunday 27 December

Christmas is over and has, on the whole, been fairly painless. Up until the last syllable of recorded Christmas Eve the house was thronged with workmen, painters, carpet-layers, electricians, carpenters, paperers, all getting in each other's way. However, the net result is that the house is a great deal more advanced than we hoped it would be.

On Wednesday night we went to the Chevreau d'Antraigues' Christmas party. It was very well done, gay and stately at the same time. We all received handsome and expensive gifts and the dinner was exquisite. The Queen of Spain asked for me to sit on her left, and so there I was again plunged into a torrent of royal reminiscences, which I thoroughly enjoyed. I stayed the night at the Beau Rivage and spent the next morning doing frantic last-minute shopping. Then I drove to Geneva to meet Vivien. We lunched at the Gentilhomme and drove back here. She is desolate and missing Larry every minute, but she is behaving beautifully and her outward manner is gay and charming.

We had a lovely Christmas Day. The sun was shining and the snow glistening and we all four went on luges to the village, had a cinzano in the Buffet de la Gare, and went up, carrying our luges, in the funicular to Souloup, hoping to slide home down the road, but alas the snow was too thick and we had to walk. However, in such sparkling weather it was most enjoyable and we got back in time for vodka, present-giving and lunch. In the evening we dined with Gloria and Loel [Guinness], just the family plus the Bill Holdens[2] and their two sons. Caviare, more vodka and bowls. Yesterday was peaceful. The

1 Georgie Wood (1895-1979), English music-hall comedian.
2 William Holden (1918-81) the Hollywood film star, was living in Switzerland.

Guinnesses arrived for tea and drinks and were mad about the house. Really very impressed, which was gratifying.

Vivien, poor darling, had one breakdown, with Coley not with me, and sobbed her heart out. This was when we got home on Christmas night. Whether or not Larry will ever come back to her there is no knowing, but if only she would face up to the fact that he probably won't, and get on with her life until the great old Healer does his job, it would be *much* better. But her longing for him has become an obsession. It is genuine, sad and almost irritating.

Three Press men arrived yesterday[1] and, after mutual discussion and consultation, I received them politely, gave them a pre-lunch drink, and utterly cowed them with excessive good manners. They were too cowed to ask Vivien a single embarrassing question about the marriage.

1 Chasing the Olivier separation story.

1960

A year highlighted by solid commercial success with a London play (Waiting in the Wings) *and a novel* (Pomp and Circumstance) *which was twenty weeks on American best-seller lists. Both had as usual been greeted by reviews ranging from the appalling to the patronizing, and Noël at last felt the time was right to answer the critics who had made his post-war life if not miserable then at least irritable. Towards the end of the year he fired off a sequence of three* Sunday Times *broadsides at playwrights of the new wave, actors of the 'scratch and mumble' school, and critics who encouraged both. John Osborne replied magnanimously – 'Mr Coward, like Miss Dietrich, is his own invention and contribution to this century; anyone who cannot see that should keep well away from the theatre' – but others were less inclined to forgive Noël his apparent frivolity and interest in the past. 'My novel is so light', he wrote to his American publishers, 'that you will have difficulty capturing it between hard covers.'*

A bout of phlebitis kept him immobile at the Swiss chalet in the earlier part of the year ('My right leg turned bright pink and I had to be carried about like a parcel') but when fully recovered ('I am now scampering about the house like a sixty-year-old waiting eagerly for the first joyous signs of syphilis'), he progressed to Morocco, London, New York and then finally back to a now less enchanting Jamaica for the ritual winter sojourn.

Friday 1 January   Les Avants

The new year has begun. The four of us, Coley, Gladys, Vivien and me, welcomed it in last night cosily and without fuss. We opened the window and heard festive sounds in the village. We kissed and drank each other's healths and settled down again in front of the fire and played 'Twenty Questions'. Vivien, with deep sadness in her heart and, for one fleeting moment, tears in her eyes, behaved gaily and charmingly and never for one instant allowed her private unhappiness to spill over. This quite remarkable exhibition of good manners touched me very much. I have always been fond of her in spite of her former exigence and frequent tiresomeness, but last night my fondness was fortified by profound admiration and respect for her strength of character. There is always hope for people with that amount of courage and consideration for others.

The new year begins for me in a blaze of slightly tawdry triumph. I have had rave notices for my performance in *Our Man in Havana*. The *Daily Mail* carried a screaming headline and stated that I had 'stolen the picture' from Alec Guinness. It then went on to insult Alec and the rest of the cast and abuse Carol Reed. Delighted as I am to have made such a spectacular success in what is after all a minor part, my pleasure is tempered with irritation at being used as a flail against my fellow artists. This is not noble modesty on my part. I *am* very good, the picture *is* slow in parts and Alec *is* dull at moments.

Saturday 16 January

A great deal has happened in the last fortnight. Gladys departed, then Vivien two days later. I fetched the dear dogs and installed them in their new and gracious home, whereupon they both proceeded to shit and pee all over the house, proving that their three months' house-training was not *quite* so thorough as one had hoped it would be. They are very sweet and beguiling, but I wish they would concentrate their attentions on the less valuable furniture and carpets.

The Mountbatten wedding[1] was hilarious and most enjoyable. All the carefully planned organization went wrong owing to a blizzard, in addition to which all the lights fused at Broadlands in the middle of the reception and a greyhound bus in which Biddy Monckton[2] and I were going to the station broke down in the entrance to the drive and all the silk-hatted gentry, including me, had to get out in deep snow and push! We finally budged it, caught the train and arrived in London safely.

The film offers are rolling in. Otto Preminger[3] sent me a script of *Exodus*,

---

1 Of Lady Pamela Mountbatten to designer David Hicks.
2 A friend who was the wife of Walter Monckton.
3 Otto Preminger (b. 1906), American film director.

which I read and turned down. The story is so very pro-Semitic that it becomes almost *anti*-Semitic and is certainly anti-British, in addition to which the part is no good at all. Apparently there are other things sizzling on the hob. I read *all* the notices of *Havana*, which Lornie had saved for me, and they are unanimous raves for me. I am, of course, delighted. I am also absolutely free to relax, get on with my novel, and pick and choose what lucrative film offers come along. It is a wonderful feeling.

Wednesday 27 January

I am ill again. This time with phlebitis of all things! I have been in bed for five days with my leg up and shall have to stay in it for another week at least. Coley has been wonderful and Piero[1] has carried me about like a baby and placed me on and off the loo. Lornie has gone back to London. It was lovely having her here; she never changes and never fails. Before my phlebitis débâcle I made a great spurt at *Pomp and Circumstance*, and so now, when I am a little stronger, I shall get it finished which will be a great relief.

I have plunged firmly through *Our Mutual Friend*. What a great writer Dickens can be at moments, and how completely he fails when he becomes sentimental. Some of the characterization in *O.M.F.* is masterly and some, particularly Lizzie and Jenny Wren, abysmally bad. I suspect that he suffered from a fundamental lack of taste. The descriptions of the river and London and the general atmosphere of the period are all superb, but why, oh why, those treacly, tear-sodden, pious, noble, completely unreal scenes which I cannot believe that he believed himself.

From the almost sublime to the quite ridiculous we come to Pat Dolin's autobiography which he has been firmly reading aloud, not, thank God, to me, but to Lorn and Coley. I have read extracts. It is quite ghastly, well-intentioned, kindly, but so dreadfully badly written that one can hardly believe one's great big violet eyes. It is continually astonishing to me that so many people write books without the faintest suspicion of talent. There was one lovely phrase that I will always treasure. He went to visit the grave of the late Argentina[2] in Madrid, and after laying six red roses on it he came away 'with her tomb embedded in his heart'!

Bill Holden suddenly arrived yesterday from Hong Kong and brought me some lovely coolie coats and Chinese silk dressing-gowns. Very sweet of him.

Friday 19 February

The Queen has had a royal son[3] and my bloody leg is at last better. I have had a fairly dismal time feeling depressed and rather scared because a blood clot

1 An Italian butler engaged for Les Avants.
2 Famous Spanish dancer.
2 Prince Andrew.

is a tricky business. However, the sombre clouds are beginning to roll away and tonight I walked down and up stairs without aid.

Fred Sadoff[1] and Mike Redgrave are keen to produce *Waiting in the Wings*, and Peggy Webster (my idea) is available and eager to direct it. This, I think, is a very, very good idea and I am most sanguine about it.

Ginette and Nancy Spain[2] came for the weekend and were wildly exuberant and very sweet. Unfortunately Nancy let down the side rather badly by writing a eulogistic but acutely embarrassing article in the *Daily Express*. Neither she nor Ginette knows that this was bad taste, but dear God! I do! Nancy is gay, intelligent, affectionate and well read, and yet she is so trapped in her journalistic training that she cannot see or feel how vulgar it is to betray to the world the intimate jokes and fun of a private weekend among friends. There is *no hope*!

I have just finished Arthur Bryant's *Triumph in the West*, which is the second volume of the Alanbrooke[3] diaries. I found it enthralling from beginning to end and most beautifully written. Winston Churchill emerges, in spite of his intrinsic greatness, as a spoiled, petulant, gaga old sod, which is no surprise to me. Eisenhower comes out of it as a well-meaning, regular-good-guy sort with no military knowledge whatever. In fact most of the Americans, except MacArthur[4], show up in a ghastly light. It is a remarkable book, but it somehow leaves one with an impression of hopelessness. How *could* so many people be so bloody petty and silly? Alanbrooke himself appears to be clear and tolerant and highly civilized.

Sunday 28 February

A black week. On Sunday last the news came through that Edwina [Mountbatten] had died, in Borneo, suddenly in her sleep. This upset me much more than I could have believed possible. During the last few years she *hasn't* been all that close or nice to me. But there were the early years and there was a few weeks ago at the wedding when she was so gay and welcoming and charming. I am desperately sorry for Dickie and Prince Philip. Then poor old Drino Carisbrooke[5] died. I've been doing nothing but write royal letters of condolence. I said to Benita [Hume] on the telephone that all I expected from my friends nowadays was that they should live through dinner.

My leg improved beautifully and I did a lot of work on the novel until suddenly last Friday I found I was running a temperature. The lower part of my leg had swollen again and was bright pink and I sent for the doctor

1 Fred Sadoff, American actor and producer.
2 Nancy Spain (1917–64), English journalist and television panellist.
3 Lord Alanbrooke (1883–1963), British Field Marshal.
4 Douglas MacArthur (1880–1964), American General.
5 Alexander, Marquess of Carisbrooke (1886–1960), a grandson of Queen Victoria.

immediately. He, obviously worried, said he must have another opinion, and so a specialist was sent for and came yesterday. Meanwhile I had been attacked by violent wind in the night and had only slept three hours. This insane agony swiftly transformed itself into congestion of the left lung and so now, after forty-eight hours of hardly being able to breathe, I am lying here, still over a hundred, but feeling a *little* better. If I don't sleep tonight I think I shall die. The trouble is that I have to sit bolt upright; the moment I lie down the pain is intolerable.

Princess Margaret has announced her engagement to Tony Armstrong-Jones[1], Oliver [Messel]'s nephew. He looks quite pretty, but whether or not the marriage is entirely suitable remains to be seen.

Monday 7 March

One more week passed in bed. Injections, pills, thermometers, lemonade, more pills, more injections. The pain at the bottom of my lung has all but vanished and I can now breathe deeply and do so whenever I can remember to. I have now been ill for a long time. I think, taken by and large, the longest time in my life. It gives me a curiously detached feeling. I find the idea of going about again, travelling to different places, going to theatres, seeing people, etc., quite extraordinary, as though it were something I didn't know anything about. I feel, however, very much better in myself.

I had a very sweet letter from Prince Philip, in reply to mine. Not a scurried 'thank you' note, a really old-chum letter, which touched me. From Dickie, however, a not very well-phrased, typewritten form-letter, which touched me less.

The novel is nearly finished, only a few more pages. I shall save doing them and polish them off at leisure during the next two weeks. I read it right through from the beginning, cutting out adjectives, adverbs and redundancies, and I must say I think it's very amusing. It will probably get contemptuous reviews, but I am well used to that. Actually I think I have achieved very successfully what I set out to do, which was to write a light comedy in the form of a novel. It is entertaining, the dialogue and characterization excellent, and it is pretty well constructed. I am a little too near it now to see it quite dispassionately, but when it returns from London, retyped, I shall be able to judge it better.

After a splash of spring and snowdrops and primroses, the snow has returned and, with it, the Nivens, who are coming to lunch.

I am engrossed in *The Forsyte Saga*. A magnificent novel. *What* a comfort!

Sunday 20 March

I finished the novel at 7.30 on Thursday evening so *that's* out of the way. On Tuesday last I drove to Vevey and had my lungs x-rayed. There remains a

1 Anthony Armstrong-Jones (b. 1930), at this time a well-known London photographer.

tiny spot which is rapidly diminishing. I am feeling practically normal and I am leaving for London on Tuesday. I shall stay there for ten days, then Paris for three days, then back here for two or three days, and then I shall fly away by myself either to Tangier or Tunis or Beirut and get some sunshine and have a real holiday. The novel being done is a tremendous relief. I shall now, in my own good time, turn my attention to verse and perhaps short stories.

Larry came on Thursday and stayed two nights. He was absolutely sweet and at his most beguiling best. I really am becoming more and more convinced that he won't go back to Vivien. He's happier than I have seen him for years. I *hope* he won't get a divorce yet and marry Joan Plowright, but I have grave fears that he will. Vivien has gone to America, miserably, to play *Duel of Angels*. If only she has a great success in it, which she probably will, it will be a step in the right direction. She will have to face up to the truth sooner or later and the sooner the better. She will inevitably suffer less as time goes by, but she's still at the stage when she doesn't wish to believe this.

Sunday 27 March   London

I flew here on Tuesday, feeling all right but a little wobbly. On arrival I went to bed for a couple of hours and then went to the opening night of *Look on Tempests*[1] with Gladys [Calthrop]. An excellent play impeccably acted, particularly by Gladys Cooper and Vanessa Redgrave. Theme – homosexuality – well and intelligently treated. Needless to say, the notices the next day were idiotic, principally, I suppose, because the ambience was educated middle class and not forbiddingly squalid.

On Wednesday I went out to Harrow to see a sneak preview of *Surprise Package*. It is a funny picture, injured considerably by Yul's inaudibility and helped very much by me. Mitzi Gaynor charming. It will probably be a success but I am not dead sure. I think I'm fairly certain to be because my part is very funnily written and I do it very well.

On Thursday I went with Binkie to see *The Dumb Waiter* and *The Room* at the [Royal] Court, two *soi-disant* plays by Mr Harold Pinter. They were completely incomprehensible and insultingly boring, although fairly well acted. It is the surrealist school of non-playwriting. Apparently they received some fine notices. Nobody was there. I have also seen *The Angry Silence*[2], absolutely wonderful, superb direction, acting, script and photography. It will *not* be a commercial success because it is too true for the 'big' audiences. It is a bitter indictment of 'wildcat' strikes and the idiocy of the working man.

Lunched with the Duchess and Princess Alexandra. They are *not* pleased over Princess Margaret's engagement. There was a distinct *froideur* when I mentioned it.

1 By Joan Henry.
2 British film scripted by Bryan Forbes and directed by Guy Green.

Talked to Sybil Thorndike about *Wings*. She loves it and there is a strong hope she will do it. Lovely evening with Peggy [Webster] and Pamela Frankau. Peggy gave me some really constructive criticism of the play which I shall follow. It means a little rewriting and transposing and one short extra scene, but I *know* it will improve the play enormously.

Thursday 31 March

The Royal Command Film Performance was fairly funny. The Royal party – Prince Philip, the Duchess of Kent and Princess Alexandra – arrived half an hour late having got stuck in the lift at Buckingham Palace. We all nodded and becked and bowed and curtsied. When I went on to introduce the three French girls, Marina Vlady, Mylene Demongeot and Leslie Caron, I got a really tremendous ovation. Very heart-warming.

Lunch with Frere and Pat, who are really delighted with *Pomp and Circumstance*. It will be published in October, before which I hope to get some lolly for the serialization rights. A very agreeable lunch on Tuesday with Sybil Cholmondeley, in the course of which I sat next to the Duchess of Devonshire[1] and hadn't a clue who she was. However, we got on a treat and I thought she was a dear grey duck and somebody's companion. Liza and John Hope[2] were there, also Betsey Whitney[3] and Harold Nicolson[4], who has shrunk a bit but still looks like a summer pudding.

London is rather oppressive, I find, on these short visits. There are so very many friends and so many telephone calls and so many things one *must* do. The trouble is, of course, that I know far too many people.

Monday 4 April   Paris

I flew here on Friday. The last part of London was quite fun really but exhausting. A gay lunch with Ian, Annie and Loelia. The première of *Once More with Feeling*[5], which was frankly bad. Kay [Kendall] was marvellous and it was heart-breaking to see her being so funny and alluring and realize that she was in that gloomy little grave in Hampstead. Yul looked very attractive. There were some funny lines in the picture, as indeed there were in the play, but it is a common business.

Yesterday I drove out to Chantilly to lunch with Diana [Cooper], who looked lovelier than ever and was welcoming and sweet. There were too many people, but Annie [Fleming] was there and so I had a good time.

1 Deborah (Debo), Duchess of Devonshire, one of the Mitford sisters.
2 Liza and John Hope, daughter and son-in-law of Somerset Maugham.
3 Betsey Whitney, wife of American financier, John (Jock) Whitney, later Ambassador to London.
4 Sir Harold George Nicolson (1886-1968), English diplomat, author and critic.
5 Film directed by Stanley Donen.

I came back to Paris and went to two films on my own. The first, *Suddenly Last Summer*, beautifully acted by Kate Hepburn, Liz Taylor and Monty Clift, was poor Tennessee Williams at his worst. It was full of horrors, so many really that it was idiotic. Madness, brain operations, queerness, cannibalism and a few high-flown observations on life, no particular shape and badly directed by Joe Mankiewicz. Fresh from this fragrant affair, I went to see *En Plein Soleil* with Alain Delon in it. He looked handsome, as usual, and acted much better. He played a wicked, murderous little villain with charm. As he was in bathing trunks throughout most of the picture the charm was adequately displayed.

Friday 15 April   El Jadida, Morocco

The remainder of my Paris visit was enlivened by Coley, with whom I went to *The Nun's Story*[1], very good. On Thursday evening Marlene appeared from New York and I took her to dinner at the Berkeley. She was in a dim mood because she has mismanaged the arrangements for her German tour and it is all in a state of chaos, in addition to which the German Press has come out against her. She looked tired and staggeringly beautiful and I felt sorry for her, not too sorry, however, to tell her a few home truths which have been necessary for some time. I must say she took the 'finger-wagging' very sweetly. Let's hope it does a bit of good.

Sybil [Thorndike] and Lewis [Casson] have definitely signed for *Waiting in the Wings*, which is wonderful.

Tangier is *not* for me. There are too many cliques and feuds and, of course, too many people. I dined with Rupert Croft-Cooke[2] and his black Indian secretary. He was extremely nice, inclined to be aggressive, and somehow pathetic. He never stops writing books, thrillers, novels and autobiographies, and I came away with a small library. He writes well, I think, but obviously neither well nor badly enough because he apparently doesn't make much money. I felt almost ashamed the next morning when Lornie cabled that we had been offered £15,000 for the serialization of *Pomp and Circumstance*. This is three times more than I had hoped and there's the American serialization to come. Hurray!

I left Tangier without regret at eight o'clock yesterday morning in a nasty little 'Consul' with an amiable but unattractive Spanish driver who speaks no English and hardly any French. A hell of a long journey over mostly bumpy roads and bad springs. Here I shall rest for a week, read a lot and get some sun. There is sea on one side and a swimming-pool on the other. The sun is certainly blazing hot but when it goes in it's bloody cold.

1 Film based on Kathryn Hulme's novel, directed by Fred Zinnemann.
2 Rupert Croft-Cooke (b. 1904), British novelist and biographer.

Friday 22 April   Marrakesh

I tired of El Jadida very quickly. The hotel was built for great heat and *not* the icy wind which blew steadily through it. I endured it for two nights and a day and then came here. There was no room at the super-duper Mamounia but this hotel is quite nice. I have a large, comfortable room and a private balcony looking over gardens to the snow-capped Atlas Mountains. The food is unspeakable, but I have found a place in the town called La Taverne which is much better. Marrakesh is very lovely and full of beautiful gardens, particularly the Jardins de Majorelle which are fabulous, like a Dulac illustration for the *Arabian Nights*, all on different levels with blue and yellow jars and trellises and a riot of flowers and flowering shrubs.

I spent two bad nights gambling at the casino, no luck at all but of course enjoyable. I have wandered about the Medina and mingled with the Moors. The colours are fantastic and it is reeking with atmosphere but, like all Eastern bazaars, a little goes a long way.

I had a cable from Lornie saying that she has to have her left breast taken off as soon as possible. This is a dreadful shock and I feel miserable. I *know* that nowadays it's ninety-nine to a hundred per cent certain to be successful, but I also know that the poor darling will have to endure hideous discomfort and a certain amount of pain. I love her so and I can't bear to think of it. I am well aware that we are all nearing the end of our lives but I don't want Lornie to go away yet. However, she is brave and sane and practical and will probably come through it all right. Thank God money is no object and she can have a lovely long convalescence at Les Avants. All the same, *I hate it*!

I am very proud of myself because I have reconstructed *Waiting in the Wings* really satisfactorily. It has entailed a tremendous amount of cutting and snipping and transposing, but I have actually enjoyed doing it. I have a feeling now that the play has a very good chance of success because, in spite of the modern contempt for craftsmanship, it generally wins in the long run. At all events, it is now a strong, well-constructed play and if the critics don't like it they can stuff it. I have a feeling that the public will, if it is directed and played as I hope it will be. Sybil is a draw and, combined with me[1] and Marie Lohr[2], etc., we should get over the first hurdles.

I have just read a book called *The Alleys of Marrakesh* by Peter Mayne. It is extremely well written but I have to admit I found it faintly irritating. He describes his voluntary life for a year in the heart of the Medina. I know it is admirable to be able to endure poverty, stinks and acute discomfort in order to learn Arabic and learn really to *know* the people. It is all gently whimsical and something about it doesn't quite ring true. Perhaps this is more my fault

1 As author.
2 Marie Lohr (1890–1975), distinguished Australian-born actress.

than his. In all my travels I have endured discomfort fairly cheerfully when I have had to, but I never have sought it out. There is a certain smugness, a sort of inverted snobbery in someone highly intelligent who deliberately wallows in foreign gutters. He writes with gently humorous understanding about the Moors and their quaint carryings-on, and I suddenly wanted him to burst into tears, bang his head against one of those colourful mud walls and scream nostalgically for the Ritz. Again I must apologize to him. I have a Ritz mind and always have had. It is a genuine hangover from when I was really poor and had to endure bedbugs and cheap digs and squalor. I am unregenerate about this. To hell with local colour. I'd go mad if I spent one night in the ever so fascinating native quarter and that's that!

Tuesday 26 April   Paris

I flew here from Morocco yesterday having left Casablanca at 8 a.m. The last days in Marrakesh were really charming and included a fabulous Arab meal in an ornate Moorish courtyard hidden away in the slums of the Medina. We sat on cushions, washed our hands in rose-water, and ate, with our fingers, a dish called pastillia. This was a sort of flat, covered pancake made of chiffon-thin pastry with sugar on top and partridges, bacon, herbs, etc., inside. Then a delicious dish was brought in under an enormous straw hat, which was baby chickens done with lemon and spices. Then, I think, sweet coffee. No wine or spirits. We all got in rather a mess but it was worth it. One of the most entirely satisfactory meals I have had anywhere.

Ginette and Paul-Emile were sweet and welcoming as usual. Coley called up an hour after my arrival and said Lornie's operation was entirely satisfactory and far less deep than had been anticipated. This was a wonderful relief and I went out and dined with a light heart. Tomorrow I fly to London.

Monday 2 May   Dorchester Hotel, London

I arrived on Wednesday evening and was met by Coley and Graham, and went straight to Westminster Hospital to see Lornie, who was bright as a button and overwhelmed with relief. Her room was crammed with flowers from everyone. I warned her, wisely, that she would have a let-down later. She was, if anything, too cheerful and I know that a serious operation is likely to take its toll when the immediate fears and discomforts have worn off.

Peggy Webster came to dine and we discussed the play and casting *ad nauseam*. It all looks very healthy. We go into rehearsal 11 July and open in Dublin 8 August for two weeks.

I have got a lovely suite and, apart from the caravanserai atmosphere of the lobby, this hotel is really a good deal more efficient than the Ritz. I *love* the Ritz but it is running to seed a bit.

On Thursday – fighting a cold which has been plaguing me ever since Paris

- I went with Gladys to *Rhinoceros*[1]. A tedious play, directed into the ground by Orson Welles. The beginning was brilliant and Larry, as usual, superb, but then it began to drag, principally because after half way through the first act you know exactly what is going to happen and there is no more interest. I am sick of these amateur, pseudo-intellectual scribblings – Ionesco, in my opinion, is *not* a playwright and not a particularly original thinker. He merely tries to be, which is fatal.

The Caretaker at the Arts by Pinter, which I went to with fear and dread, was *quite* another cup of tea. I loathed *Dumb Waiter* and *The Room*, but after seeing this I'd like to see them again because I think I'm on to Pinter's wavelength. He is at least a genuine original. I don't think he could write in any other way if he tried. *The Caretaker*, on the face of it, is everything I hate most in the theatre – squalor, repetition, lack of action, etc. – but somehow it seizes hold of you. It was magnificently acted by Peter Woodthorpe and Alan Bates and effectively by Donald Pleasance. *Nothing* happens except that somehow it does. The writing is at moments brilliant and quite unlike anyone else's.

Last evening Coley and I went to *Fings Ain't Wot They Used T'Be*[2] at the Garrick, which is a smash hit saved by a true performance by Miriam Karlin. It is maddening as a show because, without the indelible stain of Joan Littlewood's effective but restless direction, it might have been very good. As it is, there are some very amusing lines but as, with the exception of Karlin, almost the entire company is inaudible, the thing is ruined. Apparently Miss Littlewood encourages the not very experienced young actors to improvise and say whatever pops into their minds. The result of this 'freedom from convention' results in chaos. They all talk at once and the timing is lost for ever.

On Sunday evening I gave a little party for six in my suite to look at the television of *The Vortex*. Coley, Graham, Fred Sadoff, Joycie, Maggie [Leighton] and me. Ann Todd played Florence; David McCallum, Nicky; and Ann Castle, Helen. Patience Collier was quite brilliant as Clara, which is hardly a part at all. Ann was nearly good but not quite good enough and looked far too young. McCallum looked fine but seemed muffled. Ann Castle excellent and the whole production fairly good. Unfortunately neither the actors nor the director seemed to have realized that the last act *must* be an explosion of emotion and not a muttered argument. Both mother and son appeared to me to be speaking through veils. There was no violence or cruelty or deep feeling. Not unnaturally, we were all a trifle irritated, but it was apparently a great success.

Incidentally, at Larry's first night Gladys Cooper asked me why I had written a play about retired actresses and not offered her a part in it! I

1 By Eugene Ionesco at the Royal Court Theatre.
2 By Frank Norman and Lionel Bart.

explained that I had written it *for* her but that Binkie had told me she had turned it down without comment. This is rather shocking, I'm afraid. I originally planned it with her as Lotta and Sybil as May. Now Sybil is playing Lotta and Marie Lohr, May. It will probably be as well in the long run because Gladys's trouble with learning lines has certainly not improved, but the point is that Binkie just told a black lie. I am making no issue of this, but I am wondering whether or not Edith Evans, whom Binkie told me *loathed* the play, ever had it sent to her? It's not very nice, is it?

Sunday 8 May

This has been the big week, the glamorous week, the Hurrah for England week! And, in spite of a hacking cough, I have enjoyed every split second of it. Less important things first. A delightful lunch here with Mollie Buccleuch, in course of which we gossiped about everything and had a lovely time. A fairly disastrous supper party at Maggie [Leighton]'s with Larry [Harvey] in a Rodin *penseur* mood and the Henry Fondas, who lay on the evening like a damp mackintosh.

And now for the high festivities. On Wednesday night the court ball at Buckingham Palace[1]. Everybody looking their tiptop best and the entire Royal Family charming. From the pictorial point of view the whole affair was dazzling. The lovely rooms and pictures, the preponderance of red brocade and glittering chandeliers; the fabulous jewels and the *excellent* lighting and the whole atmosphere of supreme grandeur without pomposity.

I had enjoyable conversations with Prince Philip, the Queen Mother, the Queen – brief but amiable – the dear Duchess of Kent, of course, and family, and the radiant engaged couple. He is a charmer and I took a great shine to him, easy and unflurried and a sweet smile. A rather sad little conversation with Lady Churchill about Sarah[2]. It is wretched for her and for poor Sarah too. A jolly reunion with Bob Menzies. Even Bobbity Salisbury was affable to me. I think Sybil Cholmondeley must have had a go at him.

Maggie arrived late after her play and we wandered about and bobbed and bowed and had a lovely time. Her dress split and an Adonis of a footman produced a pin and we screened her while she fixed it up more or less satisfactorily. Finally, after she had borrowed half-a-crown for the loo from the bridegroom's father, whom she didn't know, we were swept out into the small hours with the garbage. A really lovely rout and something to be remembered.

Then, on Friday, the wedding. God in his heaven really smiling like mad and *everything* in the garden being genuinely lovely. I escorted (not took, escorted) Maggie and we drove down Constitution Hill, along the Mall,

1 To celebrate the wedding of Princess Margaret and Anthony Armstrong-Jones.
2 Her daughter, then in marital difficulties.

through the Horse Guards Parade and along Whitehall to the Abbey. The morning was brilliant and the crowds lining the streets looked like endless, vivid herbaceous borders. The police were smiling, the Guards beaming, and the air tingling with excitement and the magic of spring. One old girl in electric blue pranced in front of our car and sang 'Mad Dogs and Englishmen' waving a flag!

The wedding itself was moving and irreproachably organized. We had good seats but couldn't see much, but it was thrilling all the same. The Queen alone looked disagreeable; whether or not this was concealed sadness or bad temper because Tony Armstrong-Jones had refused an earldom[1], nobody seems to know, but she *did* scowl a good deal. Princess Margaret looked like the ideal of what any fairy-tale princess *should* look like. Tony Armstrong-Jones pale, a bit tremulous and completely charming. Prince Philip jocular and really very sweet and reassuring as he led the bride to the altar. The music was divine and the fanfare immensely moving. Nowhere in the world but England could such pomp and circumstance and pageantry be handled with such exquisite dignity. There wasn't one note of vulgarity or anything approaching it in the whole thing. In America such a balance between grandeur and jollity would be impossible; in France or Italy hysterical, in Germany heavy-handed, and in Russia ominous. But in dear London it was lusty, charming, romantic, splendid and conducted without a false note. It is *still* a pretty exciting thing to be English[2].

After the ceremony a wild but beautifully organized lunch party for fifty people at Annie's. A glorious mix-up – the Duchess of Devonshire, Nancy Spain, James Pope-Hennessy[3], Jock and Betsey Whitney, Lucian Freud[4], Bob Boothby, Hugh Gaitskell[5], Judy Montagu, etc. Great fun and highly enjoyable. I forgot to mention that during the week I met, at long last, John Betjeman[6] and, of course, loved him immediately.

After the wedding I watched the whole thing, including the embarkation on the *Britannia*, on the television. It was moving and romantic and the weather still held, and when the Tower Bridge opened and the yacht passed through with those two tiny figures waving from just below the bridge I discovered, unashamedly and without surprise, that my eyes were full of tears.

---

1 He did not become Lord Snowdon until 1961.
2 As he had first announced from the stage of Drury Lane on the opening night of *Cavalcade* in 1931.
3 James Pope-Hennessy (1916–74), English writer and a friend of Noël's; he had begun work on the authorized biography of Noël Coward when he was murdered in 1974.
4 Lucian Freud (b. 1922), English painter.
5 Hugh Gaitskell (1906–63), leader of the Labour opposition 1955–63.
6 John Betjeman (b. 1906), poet, knighted 1969; Poet Laureate from 1972.

Sunday 15 May   Les Avants

Home again. Spring has not failed us. The lilies are out and the hillsides white with narcissi, and the sun is warm and tender.

The week following the wedding festivities included an excruciatingly dull lunch with Duncan Sandys. Some fruitful auditions; we have now completed the cast and it looks hopeful. We engaged Mary Clare who was tremulous and, I fear, barmy, and a first-rate Canadian actor called William Hutt, who read Alan beautifully.

On Thursday I lunched with Pam and David [Hicks] in their minute but charming flat. Dickie was there, aged a good deal since Edwina's death, but genuinely sweet and his own dear self again. Pam has blossomed and looked charming. They both seem very happy. In the evening, went with Gladys to the opening of Terry's play *Ross*[1]. It is beautifully constructed and movingly written and, on the whole, superbly acted. There was a lot of scenic trouble which should *not* have occurred after four days of preparation. I think with Binkie's subtly decreasing interest in the theatre, the H.M. Tennent personnel are losing efficiency. Alec [Guinness] looked very like Lawrence of Arabia and played it well enough, but there was something lacking. He has a certain dullness about him and his 'big' moment seemed contrived. He also wore a blond 'piece' which was too bright and remained blandly intact even after he had been beaten up and buggered by twelve Turks.

Saturday 21 May

Annie and Ian's visit was a great success and they were both gay as be damned and very funny. I took them to dinner with Charlie and Oona and a good time was had by all except, secretly, by me. George and Benita were present and Benita and Annie took one of those heart-felt female dislikes to one another. Under cover, of course, but clear to me. Charlie went into his act a thought too thoroughly and was a trifle embarrassing, but maybe I am hypercritical.

For the first few days here I felt not very well, exhausted after the London junketings and with my cold, like the melody, lingering on and filling my head with catarrh. However, that has all practically vanished and I feel fine.

Poor Aly Khan was killed in a car crash last week, which saddened me because he was always so generous and affectionate to me. It really is infuriating that a man like that, comparatively young, full of *joie de vivre* and vitality, should be snuffed out by a foolish accident while so many monsters of dullness and boredom live on to plague us.

Yesterday was turbulent with the air humming and twanging with staff dramas. Piero suddenly exploded and packed his bags and said he was leaving

1 Rattigan's life of Lawrence of Arabia.
2 Prince Aly Khan (1911–60), leader of Ismaili Muslims.

forthwith because Françoise[1] had been consistently beastly to him for months. I was angry with him for not warning me and let him go. I thought the time had come to take a firm stand, so I sent for Marcel and delivered an ultimatum, which was that she must be out of the house for ever today. If he wanted to stay, I said, he could, but if he wished to leave with her I should quite understand. To my relief and surprise he agreed enthusiastically, so off she goes. This is truly wonderful because she's no good at the job and we never wanted her in the first place. He is, I think, getting sick of her. Hurrah! Then I popped down to Glion, talked to dear Monsieur Ernest and asked if he would release the peerless Enzio[2]. He couldn't have been nicer and said yes providing Enzio gave him fifteen days' notice. I then talked to Enzio, who was a little reluctant owing to having *une petite amie* at the Victoria Hotel. However, he is coming up to see me this afternoon. If we get him it will be ideal. He is a marvellous worker and with him, Marcel and Marie we shall be *en velours*.

Thursday 2 June

Everything is calm on the domestic front. Enzio, alas, couldn't come because he didn't want to leave his little Italian mouse called Caterina. Gennaro, the substitute he suggested, refused because he said the salary wasn't enough, so now we have Gino, who is short-arsed, quick, eager, efficient, and with hardly any legs at all. Socially we have been fairly active. The Brian Ahernes, the Sanders, Van Johnson, etc. The house is becoming dangerously popular.

In London the television performance of *Hay Fever* with Edith [Evans] was a triumphant success and got rave notices in all the papers. There is just a chance, I think, that she might agree to do a revival of it. Graham arrived last week and is struggling, but so far not very successfully, to lose weight. This he *must* persevere with before he starts rehearsals[3]. Colcy and he and I have taken savagely to painting again and the atelier is sonorous with muttered oaths. I have done two jackets for *Pomp and Circumstance* so Heinemann's can take their choice. They're highly coloured and quite good, I think.

The Larry and Vivien situation has now bust wide open and they are going to divorce and he is going to marry Joan Plowright. Poor Vivien is, I am afraid, on her way round the bend again. I am deeply sorry for her. *Duel of Angels*, in spite of her enormous personal success, failed to run even for its specified three months. She is apparently staying on in America for the time being. Meanwhile Joan Plowright has left the cast of *Rhinoceros* (which is transferring, unwisely I think, to the Strand Theatre). Joan's father owns the Scunthorpe Daily something or other and she has delivered a muted message to its avid

1 The '*soi-disant* wife' of Marcel, the chef.
2 From the kitchen of the Victoria Hotel.
3 For *Waiting in the Wings*.

readers. She is a good actress and seems a nice enough girl, but I do wish Larry wouldn't marry her. However, that's his look-out. He has never been remarkable for organizing his life efficiently.

The American magazines have refused *Pomp and C.* on moral grounds! The American magazines are very, very silly.

Sunday 19 June

A great deal has happened. I flew to London last Sunday, at the request of Stanley Donen, to do the music for the film of *The Grass is Greener*[1]. I dined with him on Sunday night, saw the film, which so far is only fairly good because it is too slow and the colour is hideous; however, these defects, I hope, can be remedied. I spent Monday and Tuesday at Shepperton closeted with Muir Mathieson going through the picture reel by reel and deciding where and when the music should be used. They want to have all my famous songs such as 'Stately Homes', 'Secret Heart', 'Mad about the Boy', etc., as background music, also a new theme for Bob Mitchum and Deborah Kerr, which I have already done and recorded. Now the technical assembling and scoring of the material is Muir's responsibility. For this little jaunt I get $15,000. Not to be sneezed at.

Vivien has appeared in London and is busily employed in making a cracking ass of herself. She is right round the bend again, as I suspected, and looks ghastly. What has driven her round the bend again is the demon alcohol; this is what it has always been. I suspect there is far less genuine mental instability about it than most people seem to think. I went to see her 'alone' and found the flat full of people. She arrived from Notley, where she had been insulting the new owners. She was almost inarticulate with drink and spitting vitriol about everyone and everything. The next morning she called me at 8.30 and said she wanted to see me alone, and I refused flatly and said I didn't want to speak to her so long as she continued behaving like that, whereupon she said 'Oh God!' and hung up, and that's the end of that. I have a dreadful suspicion that all this disgraceful carry-on is really a *vino veritas* condition! She has always been spoilt and when she fails to get her own way she takes to the bottle and goes berserk. *Of course* I am fond of her and *of course* I am sorry for her, but however upset she may be about Larry she should control herself and behave better. It's all her own fault anyhow and I am now abysmally bored with the whole situation. It has been going on for far *too long* and I'll have no more of it.

I dined with Lynnie and Alfred, who were dear and enchanting. Lynnie looked so incredibly young and beautiful that I could hardly believe it.

On Wednesday evening Peggy [Webster] came to the flat and we discovered that we were expected to open in Dublin on the Monday night, having arrived,

1 Based on the play by Hugh and Margaret Williams.

company and all, on the Sunday and *without* having had a previous set-up of the scenery in London. Later we adjourned to the Brompton Grill, where Mike [Redgrave] joined us, slow, pompous and obstructive, and there was a real blazing row in the course of which Peggy and I roared at him, banged the table and generally frightened the fuck out of him. Eventually, of course, we got our own way, but the whole thing was tiresome and unnecessary. Mike is a curious character. So much niceness and intelligence, and so little humour.

However, all was forgiven, but I *hope* not forgotten, by the next day, and we *are* going to have the set put up in London for several days, and we are travelling to Dublin on the Saturday, so the prospects of a fairly smooth opening performance are improving. But oh, oh, oh, I wish Binkie had done the play. I am so used to a really efficient organization and this cheerful, optimistic, shoe-string stuff terrifies me. Both Peggy and I are old pros and we *know* how important it is, particularly with a new play of mine, to start off on the right foot. God knows, Mike should have realized this too, but he really wasn't making much sense. I see breakers ahead, but fortunately he will have opened in the new Bolt play[1] and will *not* be with us.

Thursday 30 June

Hester Chapman has been staying for ten days and it has all been a great success. We talked our heads off about this, that and the other thing, particularly the other thing. We took her to a grand buffet soirée given by the Chevreau d'Antraigues in order to see the annual firework display, but it rained and there were no fireworks. We also took Hester to the Chaplins. Charlie was really sweet and immensely entertaining. Evie Johnson had reappeared with Kay Thompson and we played the piano and roared far into the night. We went to Evian to see some French amateurs do *Hay Fever*, which wasn't as ghastly as it might have been, after which I won a bit at the green baize, so the evening was satisfactory.

I have finished 'Wild Weather', 'Over the Hill', 'Mr Kaiser', 'Miss Mouse', etc., for the play. Tomorrow Coley, Graham and I leave like a flock of starlings. They go to London by different planes and I fly to Nice to join Gloria and Loel [Guinness] on the yacht.

Sunday 10 July   Monte Carlo

I have had ten days of enchantment, marred only by a recurrence of lumbago, which although not very bad has prevented me from bathing and put a slight brake on my enjoyment. On arrival at Nice on the first I was met by Loel, driven to the yacht in Antibes harbour, and we sailed within the hour. There are only Gloria, Loel and me on board and it has been highly luxurious. We sailed up the Spanish coast to Cadaques, where we had a cocktail 'do' with

1 *The Tiger and the Horse* by Robert Bolt.

Dali[1], who couldn't have been nicer. We visited Palamos, where Truman Capote is working on his new book. It was all great fun. Then we turned in our tracks and came back to Porquerolle, which was lovely. Saint Tropez was the next stop, apart from a few hours at Le Lavendou, and now we are back in Monte Carlo.

The whole of the Côte d'Azur has become one vast honky-tonk. Millions of cars, millions of people, thousands of 'motels' and camping sites. The coast, viewed from the sea, is still romantic and beautiful, but once ashore it is hell.

Loel and Gloria are charming to be with. There is none of that strain of being confined together in a small space. She is gay and funny, he is a dear, and we've really had a lovely time. Now that we are back in civilization the atmosphere has subtly changed a little. People, of course, are the trouble. Gloria no longer sits bashing away at the play she is writing. I no longer paint bad watercolours in peace on the quarterdeck. There is no peace on the quarterdeck because we are stern to quay and crowds of tourists stand and stare at us all day long.

Elsa Maxwell is staying at Cap Ferrat and I don't really feel I can bear all *that* sort of thing so I shall remain *caché*. Tomorrow we return to Antibes.

Thursday 21 July   Les Avants

I flew back here on the fifteenth and was met by Coley and Joycie at Geneva, and it was lovely to be home again. The last part of my holiday was less enjoyable than the first part. Loel and Gloria left on the twelfth and thirteenth respectively and said I could stay on in the yacht for as long as I liked. This was very sweet of them, but after two days I had had enough of it. The whole place was filled with ghastly tourists augmented by hordes of gormless American sailors with vast Adam's apples and rimless glasses. Except for Felix au Port at Antibes, the South of France, as far as I am concerned, has had it.

Waiting in the Wings is coming along well and we are definitely going to the Duke of York's, which delights me. It is an intimate, cosy little theatre and dead right for the play.

I have had an injection of Irgapyrine and my lumbago is rapidly disappearing. Lillian Gish is at the Victoria in Glion writing a book on D.W. Griffith. The Niven family have moved into a chalet at Château d'Œx. We had lunch with them yesterday and thoroughly enjoyed ourselves. David junior, my godson, is now seventeen and handsome and full of charm. David *père* is as sweet as ever. Hjordis very gay and charming, but fairly silly as usual. Jaimie, the youngest, a nice boy but in danger of becoming Americanized.

---

1 Salvador Dali (b. 1904), the Spanish artist.

Sunday 31 July Fyefield Manor[1]

This is a beautiful house and the garden is divine, but like most old English houses it is *not quite warm* enough. Anthony is very sweet and Clarissa a dear. I think she has been wonderful for him. He was fascinating about the Suez crisis and I am fairly certain that history will vindicate him completely. The Americans really behaved vilely and stabbed us well and truly in the back. This is neither prejudice nor hearsay but the unhappy truth. Dulles, of course, was the real villain, but Eisenhower was weak and silly. It is so horrible about appeasers. I should have thought the world would have learned its lesson by now, but it hasn't and I suppose it never will.

I am delighted with the progress of the play. Sybil gives a really great performance and so, to my joy and relief, does Graham. I've never seen him so relaxed and charming. Marie Lohr is a bit slow and singsong but began to show marked improvement after some gentle words from me. Poor Mary Clare looks wonderful but can't remember a word. The rest are excellent and Peggy has done a fine and tactful job. I have a strong feeling that the play will be a success. I want it to be particularly, for all the usual reasons and one or two extra ones, such as H.M. Tennent, for instance! It will, of course, get some maddening notices, but it is pretty strong in itself and with Sybil and a really fine cast it really should do, I think.

I saw *Oliver*[2], the new musical of *Oliver Twist*, and found it really remarkable. The best English musical I've seen for years. The boys are wonderful and Miss Georgia Brown a whacking new star. Production and lighting beyond praise, lyrics a bit weak, but music charming and cheerfully devoid of imitated Americanisms. It was a thoroughly rewarding evening and a *great* relief.

Saturday 6 August Paris

I've enjoyed my week. Ginette, Marlene, Josh Logan, Emlyn and Molly [Williams], Margalo [Gillmore], Lulu [Louis] and Kiki Jourdan, the Paleys, etc. I've seen *La Dolce Vita*[3], which has brilliant moments and is far, far too long.

I have just read, very carefully, *Waiting for Godot*[4], and in my considered opinion it is pretentious gibberish, without any claim to importance whatsoever. I *know* that it received great critical acclaim and I also know that it's silly to go on saying how stupid the critics are, but this really enrages me. It is nothing but phoney surrealism with occasional references to Christ and mankind. It has no form, no basic philosophy and absolutely no lucidity. It's too conscious

---

1 Noël was back in England and spending a country weekend with the Edens.
2 Directed by Peter Coe, with music and lyrics by Lionel Bart.
3 Federico Fellini's film.
4 Samuel Beckett's play (1953).

to be written off as mad. It's just a waste of everybody's time and it made me ashamed to think that such balls could be taken seriously for a moment.

To continue in this carping vein, I have also read *The Charioteer* by Miss Mary Renault. Oh dear, I do, do wish well-intentioned ladies would *not* write books about homosexuality. This one is turgid, unreal and so ghastly earnest. It takes the hero – *soi-disant* – three hundred pages to reconcile himself to being queer as a coot, and his soul-searching and deep, deep introspection is truly awful. There are 'queer' parties in which everyone calls everyone 'my dear' a good deal, and over the whole book is a shimmering lack of understanding of the subject. I'm sure the poor woman meant well but I wish she'd stick to recreating the glory that was Greece and not fuck about with dear old modern homos.

Monday 15 August   Dublin

My arrival here last Saturday week was in the full film star, Jayne Mansfield[1] tradition. Batteries of cameras, special privileges, Press reception, etc. The dress rehearsal on Sunday was not so bad as I feared, although the technical staff of the dear Olympia leave a great deal to be desired. The opening performance on Monday, apart from erratic lighting and too long waits in the scene changes, was an unqualified triumph. It was an over-sweet 'gala' audience but they settled down and quite obviously loved the play and everything to do with it. The performance[2] was excellent and the ovation at the end tremendous. I clambered up on to the stage and made a 'thank you' speech and it was all highly gratifying.

The next day the local papers, all except one, came out with rave notices and everybody, not unnaturally, is very happy. On Tuesday and Wednesday we – Peggy and me – did a little snipping and tightening here and there. Marie Lohr has come up like a dream. She is still a little slow but has discarded 'booming' and is playing it much more simply and movingly. Sybil is quite wonderful. Nora Nicholson, impeccable; Margot Boyd wonderful as Miss Archie. Maidie, Una and the old guard strong as rocks, and Graham relaxed and easy until he gets to the song, which is still a bit strained, but this, I hope, will adjust itself in time.

The news that the play is a hit has been flashed all over the world and offers from America are already coming in. I am sure some of the London critics, if not all, will be patronizing and beastly, but having seen the reaction of ordinary audiences to the play, I am sure that it won't matter what they say. The play

1 Jayne Mansfield (1933-67), glamorous Hollywood star.
2 Among those in *Waiting in the Wings* were some distinguished elderly actresses; the complete cast was Marie Lohr, Una Venning, Maidie Andrews, Norah Blaney, Maureen Delaney, Mary Clare, Edith Day, Margot Boyd, Sybil Thorndyke, Betty Hare, Jean Conroy, Nora Nicholson, Jessica Dunning, and Molly Lumley, together with Graham Payn, Lewis Casson, Eric Hillyard and William Hutt.

is well-constructed and entertaining and it is superbly acted, and the public will respond accordingly.

Coley and I have just returned from a three-day motor trip to Galway. Unbelievably beautiful, purple hills, blue sea, lovely light, fuchsia hedges, gentle rain and rich Irish charm oozing out of the treacherous peat! We've thoroughly enjoyed ourselves. This is a truly beautiful country, full of melancholy and not to be trusted, but the charm is authentic and the people, outwardly at least, well-mannered and friendly.

Sunday 21 August

Another triumphant week of packed houses and wonderful audiences, culminating in a 'company' party given by me in the hotel on Friday night, very sweet and touching and successful with all the old girls having a whale of a time. I sang, Norah Blaney sang, Edith Day got up and did 'Alice Blue Gown'[1] with little voice left but infinite professionalism – not a dry eye anywhere. Coley left this morning to go back to Les Avants. The company leave for Liverpool this afternoon. I am staying on until next Tuesday week when I fly to Manchester[2].

I am enjoying Ireland. The pubs are peculiar and very, very full of stage characters. In fact the Irish behave *exactly* as they have been portrayed as behaving for years. Charming, soft-voiced, quarrelsome, priest-ridden, feckless and happily devoid of the slightest integrity, in our stodgy English sense of the word. I had supper with Micky Mac Liammoir and Hilton Edwards[3] in their dingy but gentle house. We reminisced about *The Goldfish* and *Peter Pan*. Micky, who is two months and ten days older than I, has a jet-black toupée and a full Max Factor make-up, but is full of charm and dubious sentiment. There is an atmosphere of amiable retrogressiveness over everything and everyone which, for a little while, is curiously attractive. The countryside is bathed in rain and magic light and feels like England, particularly Cornwall, felt fifty years ago when I was a little boy. One can drive for miles along excellent roads without meeting a car. There are occasionally little governess-carts and herds of cattle, and the sight of a penny-farthing bicycle would not surprise me in the least. There is little or no television as yet, hardly any hoardings along the roads and the minimum of Coca-Cola. The Church has set its face against 'progress' and I for one am very grateful to it. Elizabeth Bowen[4] came to the play and was appropriately moved by it. In fact the floor of the box was ankle-deep in Kleenex by the end of the performance.

1 Which she had first sung more than half a century before.
2 To rejoin the *Waiting in the Wings* company.
3 Hilton Edwards (b. 1903), Mac Liammoir's lifelong friend and partner in the running of the Dublin Gate Theatre.
4 Elizabeth Bowen (1899-1973), Anglo-Irish novelist.

Sunday 28 August

The play opened in Liverpool last Monday and got rave notices. This is a *great* relief. Meanwhile I've been jogging about socially. On Friday night I went with Marjorie and Mac[1] to *The Quare Fellow* at the Abbey [Theatre]. Afterwards the company were lined up to meet me and I felt rather like the Queen inspecting her guard of honour. The play was really pretty good and, on the whole, well acted. Brendan Behan[2] appeared, strictly sober, very grubby and really very beguiling. We all adjourned to a pub and then to his house, where we sat and roared at each other. I think he was surprised that I could say cunt and fuck as easily and naturally as he could. At any rate, we got on like a house on fire and he appeared here the next morning bearing signed copies of *Quare Fellow* and *The Hostage*. I was touched by this.

Sunday 11 September   London

I flew here on Tuesday in the morning. Was feeling seedy with slight temperature. The dress rehearsal that evening went smoothly and the play looks lovely in the Duke of York's. It's a real 'theatery' theatre and dead right for it.

The opening performance on Wednesday was an unqualified triumph from the moment the curtain rose until its final fall. The audience, unlike average first-night audiences, was marvellous, swift in all the laughs and quiet as mice when required. At the end there was a really tremendous ovation, and when I finally emerged from the theatre an hour later there were cheering crowds on both sides of St Martin's Lane. The next morning the notices! With the exception of *The Times* (guarded), *Telegraph* (kindly), *Chronicle* (good) and *Herald* (fair), I have never read such abuse in my life. The *Mail* (Muller), *Express* (Levin) and *Standard* (Shulman) were vile, but the *Evening News* was violently vituperative. I was accused of tastelessness, vulgarity, sentimentality, etc. To read them was like being repeatedly slashed in the face. I don't remember such concentrated venom for many a long day. Even *Nude with Violin* at least won some praise for the actors. In this play poor Sybil's *great* performance, to say nothing of Marie's and the others, was barely mentioned. I did a thing I very rarely do. I gave two interviews, one to Bill Boorne of the *Evening News* and one to Cecil Wilson of the *Mail*. They were dignified and to the point, and I think did some good.

Meanwhile the business looks healthy and the advance is good, but this blast of spleen has of course altered the atmosphere. We are not a 'smash' hit, which we should be judging by the audience reaction, and, I fear, we may have to fight a bit to survive. I am terribly sad for the company's sake. This ghastly cold douche after that heart-warming triumph cannot but have laid

1 Anew McMaster, Irish actor-manager; his wife Marjorie was Micheal Mac Liammoir's sister.
2 Brendan Behan (1923–64), Irish dramatist.

them low inside. I know it made me frankly miserable. To be the target of so much virulence is painful, however much one pretends it doesn't matter. It breeds hatred in the heart and that is unedifying and uncomfortable. I suppose it is foolish to wonder why they hate me so. I have been too successful too long.

Monday 26 September   Les Avants

·*Surprise Package* opencd in London and I have had rave notices and several headlines saying I 'steal' the picture from Yul. This, of course, is true but it is petty larceny. Yul and Doris [Brynner] came to dine last night and took Coley and me to hear Isaac Stern[1] in Montreux. He was brilliant, but looked dreadfully funny. Yul was sweet, as indeed he always is. It is true that he is not a very accomplished comedian, but he is attractive and charming, and there was no need to be so beastly to him, but beastly they are in praise or blame and it's useless to expect them to be anything else. Meanwhile *Waiting in the Wings* is playing to virtual capacity business and is obviously an enormous success. This, of course, pleases me more than anything.

The 'new movement in the theatre' has really been taking a beating lately. The dear Royal Court produced a little number called *The Happy Haven*[2] about an old people's home. This is performed in masks and is apparently disastrous. Miss Shelagh Delaney (*Taste of Honey*) has produced a turkey, and that staunch upholder of the revolution, Ken Tynan, has slithered backwards off the barricades and is now enquiring rather dismally *where* all the 'destructiveness' is leading us and *what* is to be put in place of what has been destroyed! What indeed? They really are almost intolerably silly. *Nothing* has been destroyed except the enjoyment of the public and the reputations of the critics, and the former can be and is being remedied. The latter is of no consequence.

Sunday 9 October

I have written a 2,500-word article on 'The New Movement in the Theatre' which really is rather good, I think. When I've done one or two more I shall send them to the *Sunday Times* and later use them as the nucleus of a book on theatre. I think, by now, my age and experience entitle me to write one. I have been plodding through the works of Beckett, Wesker[3], etc., all filled with either pretentious symbolism or violent left-wing propaganda, and none with any real merit. I have also been gallantly persevering with Stanislavski's *Life in Art* and *An Actor Prepares*. Both intolerably turgid and dull and completely devoid of humour. Quite a lot of *An Actor Prepares* I find almost incomprehensible. Of course he manages from time to time to say – in a very complicated way – some hoary old truisms which any reputable actor has known all his life. It

---

1 Isaac Stern, distinguished Russian violinist.
2 By John Arden.
3 Arnold Wesker (b. 1932), British playwright.

really is staggering to think of all those earnest young American would-be Thespians poring over this soggy, pseudo-intellectual poppycock and taking it for gospel. However, I shall touch lightly on all this in my next little essay.

Meanwhile *W. in the W.* is really triumphant. The advance is rising higher and higher and people are fighting for seats. Last week John [Gielgud] and Ralph [Richardson] opened in Enid Bagnold's play[1] and the whole thing got the most terrible notices I have ever read, much, much worse than I got, and unanimous. As it is a very expensive production *and* at the Phoenix, which is a big theatre to fill, this looks like disaster for Binkie and, as far as I am concerned, serve him bloody well right. He has really behaved badly to me of late and his treatment of *Waiting in the Wings* was bad and hurtful. Also very, very foolish. In the old days he used to love the theatre and allow himself to be gently advised by John G, me, Joycie, etc. - now his advisers are John Perry, Prince Littler and Irene Selznick and the change is *not* for the better. I am sad about this change in him because I thought he was really a friend. Perhaps he still is deep down, but I'm not very sanguine. Too much power and too much concentration on money grubbing.

Larry and Joan Plowright have opened in New York and both made smash hits apparently.[2] This is lovely for them but, of course, horrid for Vivien. The mills of God!

Maggie Leighton is divorcing Larry Harvey and is in a sort of frenzy of doubt, disillusion, sadness and downright rage. I telephoned her immediately and she flew here on Friday. She is very sweet and very funny and I'm very fond of her, but, oh, it saddens me to see how these silly ladies muck up their lives. The moment they get their hooks into the gentleman of their choice they proceed assiduously to bash the whole thing to pulp with their tantrums and exigence. The ladies of earlier years were far smarter, no pants, drinking, swearing and competing with the boys; they just stayed put and, as a general rule, got their own way and held their gentlemen much longer. It really isn't surprising that homosexuality is becoming as normal as blueberry pie.

We had a good evening at Evian last night and made about £160 (Maggie) and £260 (me) – not bad.

Friday 21 October

Maybelle Webb died a couple of days ago. I had a cable from Clifton. Poor dear, I'm afraid he will feel dreadfully lonely without her. The late sixties is rather late to be orphaned. I hope he will rise above it and not collapse into aimless melancholia.

Maggie left yesterday. I am deeply fond of her and very sorry for her, but she did carry on a bit. I do wish these ladies who drive their gentlemen away

1 *The Last Joke*; it survived less than a month.
2 In Anouilh's *Becket* and Shelagh Delaney's *A Taste of Honey*.

with a mixture of over-love and neurotic possessiveness would cultivate a little more repose and a good deal more reticence.

Hugh French[1] came for the night on Tuesday and tried to persuade me to do a movie script of Winston's *My Early Life*. The old boy himself is apparently very keen that I should, but I am not so sure. However, I will read through the book and see.

The arrival of Hugh, very forceful and full of American 'salesmanship' overdrive, overdrove Maggie into a hysterical outburst, augmented by several vodkas. He had come from Hollywood, seen Terry [Rattigan] and apparently discussed her break-up with Larry H. Whether they had discussed it too much or too little I was unable to discover, but the evening ended in tears.

Lionel Bart[2] arrived today for the weekend. He is a curious creature, not actually very prepossessing looking but rich with talent and a certain Jewish-looking charm. In looks he reminds me of Jed Harris when younger, but with more sympathy.

I am going to London next Thursday for a slight theatrical whirl around.

Sunday 30 October   Dorchester Hotel, London

So far the London visit has been enjoyable. I arrived on Thursday afternoon after a perfect flight, was met by Lornie, and moved in here – after buying two suits off the peg at Aquascutum. I fought my way into a dinner-jacket and took Joycie to *The Tiger and the Horse*. Beautifully played by Michael and Vanessa [Redgrave] and indeed the whole cast. An interesting play but a trifle arid. After this a party at Jamie Hamilton's[3]. Nancy Mitford, Debo Devonshire, Diana Cooper, Harold Nicolson, etc.: very civilized and charming and an irrefutable proof that, in spite of the 'modern trend', genuinely witty and educated conversation can *still* take place.

On Friday I lunched in and attended the Fairbanks wedding, which was pleasantly done in the Guards' Chapel and free of royalty. The reception was a bit of a shambles owing to Press cameras and lights, but I didn't stay very long. In the evening I took Maggie to *W. in the W.* – a packed house and a too glib performance, but fairly good. Maggie obviously *very* much better and in excellent control.

On Saturday I had a drink with Willie Maugham. He looked well and was quite remarkable, also a bit acid. Jolly good for eighty-six. A theatrical orgy in the evening with Joycie. *Billy Liar*[4] at 5.30. *The Last Joke* at 8.30, with some oysters in between. The former horrible and violently overplayed by Albert Finney. The second elegant, unreal, impeccably acted and, on the whole,

---

1 Hugh French, actors' agent.
2 Lionel Bart (b. 1930), British composer and lyricist.
3 Hamish (Jamie) Hamilton (b. 1900), publisher.
4 Comedy based on Keith Waterhouse's novel.

enjoyable. A wonderful antidote anyhow to *Billy Liar*. First act excellent, but no play really. Some lovely stylized language, lovely set, and good acting, but it won't really do.

Graham is going through hell with Sybil[1] in the flat getting iller and iller and refusing to move. Soon, poor dear, she will get so bad that she will have to.

Sunday 6 November

A very busy week. Plays seen: *A Man for all Seasons*[2], beautiful performance by Paul Scofield, but play a bit dull although well written. Micheal Mac Liammoir's one-man version of Oscar Wilde, highly successful, particularly the prose bits. At the Redgrave party afterwards discovered from John Foster[3] that (a) he had money in *W. in the W.*, which I didn't know, and (b) that Binkie had urged him *not* to invest in it, which I didn't know either. No comment.

Revisited *Oliver* with Lionel and Maggie. As good as ever. *The Most Happy Fella*[4] – well sung but overdone. *Platonov*[5] at the Royal Court, ghastly. Rex good as always, but the play and production beneath contempt.

An excellent rehearsal on Tuesday. I delivered a 'method' pep talk and told them I would rather they lost laughs than lost character. Took the Duchess of Kent on Friday and saw the best performance of the play to date. Really wonderful. Lovely evening all round. Ovations in each entr'acte. Jolly supper at the Caprice.

Lord Reith[6] gave luncheon for me at the Athenaeum. Was received by staff like prodigal son. Dingo [Bateson] at lunch, also Sir Gilbert Rennie, High Commissioner for Central Africa. Amiable but desiccated. All very agreeable and John Reith a dear.

Saturday Night and Sunday Morning[7] good. Albert Finney excellent. He is obviously a good actor but mustn't play comedy. Two luncheons: one with Hester [Chapman], very sweet; the other with Rosamond [Lehmann], also very sweet but sadder. She is truly immersed in spiritualism and there is nothing to do but acquiesce and let it ride. *Pomp and Circumstance* out and selling well. Snooty notices, but one or two good ones.

Sybil getting steadily worse. Graham behaving beautifully but miserable inside. The Lunts can't after all come to Les Avants as Alfred is ill and must get back. I do not think it is really serious; he's a terrible old hypochondriac.

1 His mother.
2 Robert Bolt's play about Sir Thomas More.
3 John Foster (1904–82), lawyer and Conservative MP 1945–74; knighted in 1964.
4 By Frank Loesser.
5 By Chekhov.
6 Lord Reith (1889–1971), director-general of the BBC 1927–38.
7 Film of Alan Sillitoe's novel.

Friday 11 November   Les Avants

Flew back last Monday. Met by Vivien, Jack Merivale[1] and Coley. Vivien in splendid form, outwardly at least; inwardly she is still hankering after Larry. However, she is putting up a gallant performance and seems very fond of Jack, who is constantly fulfilling a long-felt want. They were gay and sweet guests and left on Wednesday. Adrianne and Bill are ecstatic about their chalet[2] and all is well with them, apart from Jeremy Brett[3] having left Anna. She was obviously too bossy and possessive. Ah me! The ladies. God bless them. What silly cunts they make of themselves. It's quite all right to say cunt now because the *Lady Chatterley* case has been won, and already fuck, balls, arse and shit have been printed on the second page of the *Observer* and the *Spectator*. Hurrah for free speech and the death of literature.

I have just finished Diana Cooper's third volume of memoirs. It is quite exquisite and so very beautifully written. It is also deeply moving. I must write to her immediately.

We lunched yesterday with the Nivens at Château d'Œx. They were sweet but, oh dear, I fear Hjordis will *never* make a good housekeeper. The lunch was fairly dreadful and the house *could* be made charming but I doubt if it will be.

Sybil [Payn] has at last gone back to the Westminster Hospital at her own request. I am desperately sorry for her, her gallantry and fighting spirit are admirable, but I fear that this really is the end. Poor, poor Graham. It is so ghastly for him. Thank God he is playing a good part in a success.

Hedda Hopper came to lunch on Wednesday. She has had the Niehans[4] injection treatment. She looked fine but seems to be a bit deaf. In spite of her ignoble profession I am fond of the old girl. She has wonderful vitality and would, I am sure, continue to have, Niehans or no Niehans.

Sunday 20 November

I am flying to New York this afternoon with a certain amount of pleasurable anticipation mixed with dread. Too many parties – too many people – ah me!

Graham is enduring a living hell with Sybil slowly, slowly dying. He knows there is no hope and, of course, he is behaving beautifully. He particularly wants us *not* to be with him because sympathy will break him. However, Coley is going over this week. God knows how long she will last but it *can't* be long.

I had another lunch with the dear Nivens and the Rainiers[5], who couldn't have been sweeter. They have painted me two funny, ghastly little pictures.

1 John Merivale, English actor.
2 Adrianne Allen and William Whitney, her husband, had moved nearby.
3 Jeremy Brett (b. 1935), English actor, who had married Anna Massey in 1958.
4 Professor Paul Niehans, a specialist in rejuvenation treatment.
5 Prince Rainier and Princess Grace of Monaco.

The Great Reaper has been at it again. Gilbert Harding[1] and Clark Gable[2] both gathered on the same day. An orgy of nauseating journalistic sentimentality in the Press.

My blood count is exquisite and *Pomp and Circumstance* got a full rave in the *New York Herald Tribune*. *Waiting in the Wings*, although suffering slightly from the pre-Christmas slump, is still doing marvellously.

It feels strange to be uprooting and setting off again. I expect I shall enjoy it, and anyhow a few weeks of Jamaican warmth and sun will do me a power of good. Actually I feel very well indeed. I am mulling over a musical in my mind but have no intention of rushing it. There is so much I want to write and time's winged chariot is fairly whizzing along. I can't believe I shall be sixty-one in a month's time.

Monday 28 November   New York

The jet flight from Geneva was wonderful, smooth as velvet. Binkie called me up half an hour after I got in. He sounded rather drunk and was with Irene Selznick and the Leland Haywards[3]. At any rate, I got to bed early and faced the week bright on Monday morning. It seems to me that I have already since then seen *millions* of people and there are still millions to come. However, I am taking good care, *not* drinking, and insisting that I get a nap every afternoon. I lunched with Maggie Case, Jack and Natasha. Jack ghastly, grey and insecure and pathetic; Natasha puffed out and looking fairly dreadful.

I have seen Tammy Grimes, who is wonderful in a not good show, *The Unsinkable Molly Brown*[4]. *Fiorello*[5] excellent. *Toys in the Attic*[6] pretentious but well acted. *Bye Bye Birdie*[7] very bad and bought by Binkie for London. *Period of Adjustment*, Tennessee's new play, which I found tasteless, dull and disgusting. Binkie took Lynn and me to *Birdie* and came back here for a heart-to-heart. He never mentioned *Wings* and so I didn't either, and whatever was possible to put right between us was ignored. He was amiable and gossipy and I didn't really care for him any more. This is sad, but I suddenly saw all the pallid little wheels whizzing round: the fear of me, the lack of moral courage, the preoccupation with money, etc., and there it was, clearly and unmistakably the end of a long friendship. We shall always have an agreeable relationship, I am sure, but no more reality. Perhaps there never was any.

1 Gilbert Harding (1907-60), irascible English broadcaster.
2 Clark Gable (1901-60), American film star.
3 Leland Hayward, American agent and producer, and his wife Pamela, married 1960-71; she had previously been married to Randolph Churchill.
4 Musical by Meredith Willson.
5 By Jerry Bock and Sheldon Harnick.
6 By Lillian Hellman.
7 By Michael Stewart, Charles Strouse and Lee Adams.

A brief weekend with Kit and Guthrie. Peaceful and unchanged. Thanksgiving lunch with the Paleys – enchanting. Roger Stevens and Oliver Smith are very enthusiastic about *Later than Spring* (new version), so is Bill Paley, so I have decided to go blazing ahead with it and go into rehearsal in July! If I can really pull it off, it will mean financial security for life. If it flops, I shall still survive. But it would and *will* be fun to do a nice big fat musical.

Friday 16 December   Jamaica

My sixty-first birthday. I am now definitely beyond middle age and well on the way to the sere and yellow, and I find it very difficult to believe. I feel very little different from twenty years ago, or even thirty! Here I am again, anyhow, sitting on my verandah at Firefly and looking out over the sea and the mountains. It is as beautiful as ever and I am happy to be back.

The last two weeks in New York were even more hectic than the first. It would be tedious to list every show I saw and everyone I lunched and dined with: enough to say that I did the lot. Outstanding among the former were Elaine May and Mike Nichols[1]. They are brilliant. *Becket*[2] was a common translation and production, beautifully played by Larry and very well, really, by Anthony Quinn, although he is entirely miscast. The rest shameful and abominable. Joan Plowright excellent in *Taste of Honey*. It remains, however, a sordid little play by a squalid little girl of nineteen. The opening of *Camelot*[3] was *the* event of the season. I took Marlene, who looked lovely and was fairly tiresome throughout the evening. The show itself was beautiful to look at but otherwise disappointing. Music and lyrics uninspired and story uninteresting. Richard Burton, however, gave a superb performance and made the whole expensive evening worthwhile. Afterwards a vast party at Luchow's. Enjoyable if you like vast parties.

The next evening, Sunday, I flew to Milwaukee where Lynnie met me. Late that night I went by train – ghastly – into Chicago and spent the whole of the next day with Ed Bigg having blood tests, liver tests, etc. He was sensible and down to earth as usual and finished up by saying, almost wistfully, that there was nothing wrong with me at all. My liver is not the least bit enlarged, my blood count normal, my blood pressure that of a boy of sixteen (his words, not mine), my heart vigorous and youthful, in fact all my organs functioning away like anything with apparently nothing to discourage them. After this fabulously good news I expected to drop down dead, but I survived and flew back to New York comfortably and was in bed by midnight.

Kay Thompson gave an eccentric party for me which was highly enjoyable, although it started with near disaster as she had forgotten to order any food at

1 In a two-character collection of revue sketches.
2 By Jean Anouilh.
3 Lerner and Loewe musical.

all! The Burtons[1], Joan [Plowright], Larry (I find it so difficult not to say Larry and Vivien), Tammy Grimes, Rex [Harrison], etc., were all famished so we sent out to Steuben's and ultimately all was more than well and it went on until nearly five. We played double pianos, everyone sang and performed, uninhibitedly and repeatedly. Ginette was in seventh heaven. There were only a few civilians[2] present.

I went to *The Sound of Music*[3] with Ginette. It was embarrassing at moments, mainly owing to some of the late Oscar [Hammerstein]'s lyrics being sawney and arch, but the music was lovely, the sets superb, the story straightforward and the performance fine. Mary Martin, although much too old to play a roguish young postulant, was wonderful and, at moments, genuinely moving. There were too many nuns careering about and crossing themselves and singing jaunty little songs, and there *was*, I must admit, a heavy pall of Jewish-Catholic schmaltz enveloping the whole thing, but it was far more professional, melodic and entertaining than any of the other musicals I've seen.

Sybil Payn died on Friday 2 December. I happened to ring up at six o'clock (11 p.m. London) and got Graham. He was wonderful and has behaved superbly throughout all the dreadful weeks of strain. Fortunately Coley was with him. He had been that night as usual to see her before his performance and found her unconscious. The doctor said she couldn't last through the evening and would definitely not regain consciousness, so Graham said he didn't wish to be disturbed with messages at the theatre and went off and gave a good performance. After it Coley and he went back to the hospital and were told that she had died. His behaviour over the whole tragic business has been sane and brave and has touched me deeply and made me love him more than ever. Coley flew over the day after the funeral and told me all the details. Thank God he was there. Sybil Thorndike was angelic throughout and Lornie, of course, a rock of strength as always. This is Graham's first major sorrow and I have no fears for him ever. He has courage, balance and humour and is much loved.

Poor Clifton, on the other hand, is still, after two months, wailing and sobbing over Maybelle's death. As she was well over ninety, gaga, and had driven him mad for years, this seems excessive and over-indulgent. He arrives here on Monday and I'm dreaming of a wet Christmas. Poor, poor Clifton. I am, of course, deeply sorry for him but he must snap out of it.

On Lynn's and Alfred's advice I have taken shares in a Texas oil field! Lynn and Alfred have already made nearly a million dollars out of it. It's a good gamble. Meanwhile I am itching to get down to *Later than Spring*. It is

1 Richard Burton (b. 1925), the Welsh-born stage and film star, and his wife Sybil.
2 i.e. non-professionals.
3 Rodgers and Hammerstein musical.

bubbling in my mind. And so I enter my sixty-second year, with a well-ordered liver and high hopes.

Christmas Day morning

This is a day of goodwill to all men and the giving and receiving of presents which nobody particularly wants, a time for planned gaiety, determined sentiment and irrelevant expense; a religious festival without religion; a commercialized orgy of love without heart. Ah me! I fear I am becoming cynical, but how lovely it would be if it were an ordinary day on which I could get on with my work and read and play patience and perhaps paint a picture; if there were not so many ecstatic 'thank yous' looming ahead and *not* an accumulating pile of thank you letters waiting to be written. But heigh-ho, away we go, and in a couple of hours from now I shall rattle down the abominable road and give myself up to the present-giving which is timed to go off at noon.

Dear Blanche's[1] party (birthday) for me, although beautifully done, so very nearly ended in tragedy. Morris Cargill[2] organized fireworks, very good fireworks, and some Jamaican cretin placed a clump of rockets on the terrace wall facing the home. These were touched off by sparks and shot at the assembled guests. A flaming rocket-head missed *my* head by inches and embedded itself in the roof. If it had hit me I should have been killed or blinded for life. As it happened no one, miraculously, was hurt. Blanche's new terrace was scarred by flame and will probably have to be resurfaced. The incident put a decided damper on the party. Everyone behaved very well, particularly poor Blanche, but voices were strained and there was fear underlying them.

The once peaceful island is full of noises – noises of tourists and noises of underlying discontent. All wages and prices have risen astronomically. The roads are, mostly, in a dreadful state and the whole atmosphere has changed. I owe Jamaica much happiness and peace and enjoyment, and I know now beyond a shadow of doubt that all that is over. I shall strain every nerve to sell Blue Harbour and, perhaps a little later, Firefly too. I love it and shall always love it, but my trust in this place has gone. I have always been fairly good at saying goodbye and now I know I must do it again. I have Les Avants as a permanent home and in future, when I want rest and a holiday, I shall do what I always did before I came here: get myself on to ships and sail away and back. I am tired of the responsibility of this place and to pay out thousands a year regularly just for a couple of months here is no longer worth it.

On Monday last I drove to Montego, lunched with Carmen [Pringle], Jack and Natasha, met Charles [Russell] at 2.30 and Clifton at 5.30 (two hours late).

---

1 Blanche Blackwell, Jamaican resident and good friend and neighbour to Noël.
2 Morris Cargill, a friend and Jamaican resident.

Clifton was fairly all right during the long drive, but since then he has devoted a lot of time to weeping and telling very, very long stories about the various deaths of his various beloved friends. He retails these gruesome memories with a wealth of maudlin detail. Neysa [McMein], Dorothy di Frasso, Adrian[1], Valentino[2], Jeanne Eagels[3]. How he first heard the dreadful news of their demises, how he reacted, how they were laid out, how the memorial services were conducted, etc. These slow, slow ramblings inevitably end up with Maybelle, her last rites and the ear-rings which he remembered at the last minute to fix into her dead lobes, and then he breaks down and sobs and we all gaze at each other in wild surmise.

He admitted to me under a pledge of deep secrecy the other morning that he was seventy-one. I expressed token amazement because the poor dear looks and behaves like ninety. There is much that is sweet about him but he is, and always has been, almost intolerably silly, and all this self-indulgent wallowing in grief and the dear dead past is dreadfully exasperating. Coley and Charles are behaving wonderfully and so am I really, but it is tough going. He is leaving on 3 January to stay with Edward for ten days in a rented bungalow at Half Moon. That should be a morose little holiday if ever there was one.

In the meantime I'm rumbling away in my mind about the book of the musical. It is really beginning to take shape. I have decided to change the title from *Later than Spring* to *Sail Away*, which is a gayer title and more appropriate. I wrote yesterday a wonderful opening number for Kay Thompson. It really is exactly right and my talent for lyrics obviously hasn't abandoned me. I had begun the tune before but now three refrains are complete and the verse will be easy. Verses always are.

Marti Stevens[4] arrives tomorrow and stays until the third, when everyone goes.

1 Adrian (1903-59), American costume designer.
2 Rudolf Valentino (1895-26), Italian-born Hollywood star.
3 Jeanne Eagels (1894-1929), flamboyant Broadway star.
4 Marti Stevens (b. 1933), actress and singer whom Noël affectionately called the Blonde Beast.

1961

Sail Away *was the last Broadway musical for which Noël was to bear almost total responsibility as author, composer, lyricist and director; he even designed its posters, and finished the year by issuing a solo album of its songs. Though it received the usual mixed critical reaction, this romantic cruise comedy made an international star of Elaine Stritch and contained many of the best of Noël's post-war songs; it had lain long on the typewriter (originally entitled* Later than Spring), *had been tailored at various stages for Kay Thompson and Rosalind Russell, and even when it finally opened on tour with Stritch was to undergo drastic major surgery. More than any other of Noël's later shows,* Sail Away *reflected his passion for travel, his loathing of tourists, his horror of old age and his love of the sun. It was a show about escaping the cold and, as such, perhaps more fundamentally autobiographical than was realized at the time even by its more enthusiastic critics.*

Sunday 1 January   Jamaica

Seven a.m. The first morning of the first day of the New Year is auspicious at least. The sun has just climbed out of the sea into a cloudless sky, the birds are garrulous and everything is shining and bright. Brightest of all is the thought that my house party breaks up tomorrow.

Poor Clifton has been and is, frankly, a ghastly bore. He embarks on endless, slow, pointless stories, very often the same ones he has told the day before; he has just one drink too many every evening before dinner and then his speech becomes blurred and he either gets maudlin or launches forth into a vicious attack on someone or other. His present hates are Marlene and Elsa Maxwell, presumably because they didn't write him letters of sympathy. Frank Sinatra has had a bit of a bashing too, but I intervened. I fear the *vino veritas* is true. He really does display a very bitchy, unpleasant character when fried. Oh, poor Clifton, I shouldn't be so unkind as to belabour him. He is so basically idiotic and the whole thing couldn't matter less beyond putting a damper on what might have been a very cheerful little house party. Still, he is looking much better and I think *is* much better than when he arrived. Anyhow, on Tuesday Coley, Charles [Russell] and I will be left on our own and I can stay up here working without a feeling of guilt.

I had a touching letter from Graham. Sybil left him £20,000! A really remarkable woman to have managed to save that much. Naturally he is delighted and at the same time dreadfully touched. Anyhow, it will enable him to pay the £5,000 required for the new house without having to worry about a mortgage or me selling out securities to help him.

Waiting in the Wings took a bad, a very bad drop before Christmas, so bad indeed that I am worried. It would be too awful if it had to close after only four months. I should be humiliated on account of Binkie and the bloody critics. However, it played to £750 on Boxing Day in two performances, which is hopeful. *Pomp and Circumstance* is creeping up and up on the best-seller list in New York and in London. The American reviews were much, much better than the English. I really do seem to be without honour in my own country so far as the critics are concerned. I believe that if I turned out a real masterpiece it would still be patronized and damned with faint praise. Fortunately the public seem to be on my side.

Now 1961 begins. I have made no particular resolutions except to see to it that *Sail Away* is a nice big fat sweet hit, and to face whatever the year holds for me with as much equanimity as possible. But after the sixty mark – excuse me, the sixty-*one* mark – the months become dangerous. Not only for myself but for those I love. I must remember to count every happy day as a dividend. I've had a wonderful life. I've still got rhythm, I've got music, who could ask for anything more?

Saturday 7 January

The party's over now. Coley drove with Clifton, drenched in tears, to deposit him at Edward's bungalow at Half Moon. I somehow feel that it *might* not be an entirely cloudless visit. Edward is not exactly tolerant or kind when he gets a few drinks inside him. Poor Clifton! I gave him a loving but firm pep talk the night before he left and I think it helped a bit.

I have been working very hard indeed and have finished the first act, book, lyrics and music[1]. It is, I think, well constructed and good so far. I shirked doing the book but I am finding it easier than I anticipated because the characters have come to life. Mimi Paragon is certainly a marvellous part for Kay Thompson. I hope to God she plays it and doesn't make a fathead of herself which, I fear, she is quite capable of doing. However, all that is in the dear dim future, and in the meantime I must concentrate on getting the second act done. Then I really can relax for a little because there will be a lot of time between February and July to polish up the rough edges.

Poor *Waiting in the Wings* has not properly recovered from its pre-Christmas plunge and is going to close on 18 February. I am deeply angry about this. Perhaps, after all, those bastards of critics did some damage. Patronizing, dismissive reviews of *Pomp and Circumstance* continue to arrive from England. But it *is* on the best-seller list in both countries. I am sad, sad, sad about *Wings*. So many people have loved it. However, we shall have got six months out of it, which is a good deal better than nothing. But, oh Lordy, Lordy, there is quite an accumulation of bitterness in my heart for those mean, ungenerous, envious, ignorant little critics.

Wednesday 18 January

I was right about Edward and Clifton. Apparently there have been some very nasty scenes. Edward is rapidly becoming loathed wherever he goes. Carmen [Pringle] says he is a bitter, disagreeable old queen and she won't have anything more to do with him. It is that violent temper that breaks out whenever he's had a few drinks. I know it only too well. He always had it, of course, but in the old days there was considerably more charm to compensate for it.

I spent two days at Sunset Lodge. Carmen was sweet as always and I drove over to Roundhill for lunch and enjoyed it very much. The greatest surprise of all is Jack. He is practically back to normal. He has two or three drinks a day without them affecting him in the least. His eyes look clear and he is once more very good company. Natasha looks a million times better than when she arrived. I think her idiotic doctor is giving her curious pills of some sort because she is extremely wobbly on her pins, which she really shouldn't be, being in her early fifties. I spent most of the time with both of them and it was

1 Of *Sail Away*.

quite like the old days. It really would be wonderful if Jack could snap out of it for good. I have horrible doubts, because with alcoholics you can never be sure. However, he is obviously making a tremendous effort and we must hope for the best.

Loelia Westminster arrived on Sunday and I met her and drove her here in time for tea. She has been great fun so far and no trouble at all.

Sunday 29 January

Sail Away is nearly finished except for the final pulling together of all the strings. I am going to leave this until later and until I have had some auditions and have some idea of the personalities who are going to play the parts. It is wonderful having so flexible a formula, because I can add or subtract scenes and numbers without interfering with the basic structure. The music and lyrics have been and are still in full spate. I've done a calypso duet and a new number, 'Something Very Strange', which I really love. So far it all looks more than hopeful.

Loelia left on Tuesday. Her visit was an unblemished success, except for the weather which wasn't too encouraging. She was very good company and we had a gay time. Annie and Ian arrived last Sunday, Ian with a temperature of 103°. I went over with Annie, who had dined with us looking exhausted and strained, and found him scarlet and sweating in a sopping bed and in a hellish temper. I dealt with him firmly and made him rub himself down and get into the other bed, while Annie and I turned the damp mattress and put on clean sheets and pillow cases. All this was achieved to a running accompaniment of violent cursing from the patient. It was all too exactly like the scene in *Pomp and Circumstance*[1] that I fully expected him to burst out in a rash of spots. In fact I almost wished he would; it would have been so tidy and satisfactory. Their connubial situation is rocky. Annie hates Jamaica and wants him to sell Goldeneye. He loves Jamaica and doesn't want to. My personal opinion is that although he is still fond of Annie, the physical side of it, in him, has worn away. It is extraordinary how many of my friends delight in torturing one another.

My articles[2] have appeared in the *Sunday Times* and caused an uproar. There have been so many letters for and against that they have been forced to publish only brief extracts. These have been, on the whole, idiotic. Most of them woolly-minded and malicious. It is of course unfortunate that *Waiting in the Wings* is closing. This has given some of the enraged correspondents a handle. One lady called Pamela Platt wrote that I should realize that my career was over and that it was unkind of the *S.T.* to allow 'the silly old man to make

---

1 Where the hero develops chicken-pox.
2 About the declining standards of British theatre and the inadequacy of the 'angry young men' as dramatists.

such a spectacle of himself'. This I considered to be on the rude side. I am happy to announce, however, in my quavering, senile voice that *Pomp and Circumstance* has already sold over 28,000 copies in America and is climbing higher and higher on the best-seller list. It saddens me to think that my career is over and done for, but there *are* compensations.

Sunday 5 February

The Press in London are still squealing like stuck pigs over my articles. Mr Levin in the *Express* outdid himself in insulting abuse. I really must write some more when I have time.

Our life has been intermittently social. Annie and Ian and the Donaldsons (Freddie Lonsdale's daughter and son-in-law), Maureen Dufferin[1] and John Maude[2], very sweet. Carmen drove over especially to hear my new tunes and was suitably enthusiastic. This evening we give a 'free for all' farewell cocktail 'do' down at Blue Harbour. I'm desperately sorry to be leaving, much more sorry than I could ever have dreamed I would be when we arrived. This place has magic for me and I suspect that it always will have. The peace of working up here; the lovely long mornings and the fabulous moonlight nights ablaze with fireflies are really too enchanting to consider saying goodbye to for ever. Not yet at any rate. I shall try to come back in June to fortify myself before rehearsals begin.

Monday 20 February   New York

We arrived after a perfect jet flight, so smooth that we were able to play Scrabble.

The week passed in a whirl of music rehearsals with Pete Matz and Fred Werner, a young pianist whom Pete recommended and who couldn't be nicer or more efficient. On Thursday I read the rough draft to Roger [Stevens], Oliver [Smith], Carol Haney[3], Goddard [Lieberson] and Levy Lyder[4] (representing Bill Paley). I explained carefully that the book was deliberately unfinished and that the moment I knew who was going to play the principal parts I would retire to Switzerland and rewrite it. Everybody raved about the score but Oliver and Goddard were dubious about the book. This was tiresome but not important because I know perfectly well what I am going to do with it and they don't. I think actually it was a mistake to have read it to them in an unfinished state. Their imaginations are limited.

Kay [Thompson] came to dine on Monday and *raved* about everything, but doesn't want to play Mimi because she has a complex about appearing on

1 Maureen, Marchioness of Dufferin and Ava.
2 John Maude, QC; son of comedian Cyril Maude.
3 Carol Haney (1928-64), Broadway dancer and choreographer.
4 Levy Lyder, of CBS records.

Broadway. Two or three days later she said definitely she wouldn't do it! This, of course, is irritating but we are now after Elaine Stritch, who is an excellent comedienne and will probably be fine.

Patrice Munsel[1] has also refused, to my great relief, as she is too soubrette for Verity and, although her voice is marvellous, has not got the right quality. Also she wants to be *the* star of any show she does. It was all quite amicable.

Tuesday 28 February

Last Monday I appeared at the Author and Book Club at the Waldorf Astoria and talked to two thousand ladies from Westchester. My fellow speakers were Morris West (*Devil's Advocate*) and Mary Ellen Chase (*Lovely Ambition*). Both their speeches were excellent and I came last and it all went beautifully. In the evening I went with Maggie Case to hear Leontyne Price sing *Aïda* which was exquisite. One of the loveliest voices I have ever heard. I have seen *Wildcat*[2], bad except for Lucille Ball who was brilliant, and *Turandot* at the Met, beautifully sung and an entirely new production designed by Cecil [Beaton]. Quite lovely. I have visited Cole Porter in hospital and he is much better. I have dined with Marlene, who was at her very best, and last night Coley, Charles and I went to *Leave it to Jane*, an off-Broadway musical (Kern, 1917). Not at all bad.

On Thursday I appeared on the Jack Paar show and was a tremendous success. He was amiable and sweet and so horribly nervous that I had to calm him. Anyhow, the whole thing went splendidly and was apparently a triumph.

Sunday 5 March

I have been photographed rapidly and efficiently by Dick Avedon[3] and taken to hear Joan Sutherland[4] at the Carnegie Hall. She sang an early Bellini opera, *Beatrice di Tenda*, in concert and was magnificent, although she looked rather peculiar on account of having a Widow Twankey hair-do and being very tall indeed. It is a glorious voice, however, and she sings with perfect control.

Auditions are continuing but we haven't found anyone startling yet. On Friday Coley and I went to hear Price sing *Butterfly* and it was glorious. On Saturday, yesterday, we journeyed to Philadelphia, where we saw *The Happiest Girl in the World*, which was boring, tasteless and ghastly beyond belief. The sets were rather good and very elaborate. Poor Cyril Ritchard was quite, quite dreadful. He camped about like an old-fashioned queen at a drag party. All his innate vulgarity came bubbling unpleasantly to the surface. The book is

1 Patrice Munsel (b. 1925), American operatic soprano.
2 Musical by N. Richard Nash, Cy Coleman and Carolyn Leigh.
3 Richard Avedon (b. 1923), American photographer.
4 Joan Sutherland (b. 1926), Australian opera singer; created Dame in 1979.

the old *Lysistrata* play set to an Offenbach score, which is ruined by bad orchestration, common lyrics and indifferent singing. The whole thing was arch and lascivious. I do wish that years ago Cyril had faced up to the fact that he was as queer as a coot, renounced the Catholic faith, and given way horribly to his sexual urges rather than bottle them up. The performance and the production was an orgy of frustrated sex. Naked young men lying about; no jokes above the navel; an appalling scene in a Turkish bath, and Cyril bouncing on and off the stage in ladies' wigs and ladies' hats. It was all so embarrassing that at moments I was unable to look at the stage. I fear the poor beast will be massacred in New York.

Sunday 12 March

I took Elaine Stritch to dine at the Chambord. She is wildly enthusiastic and very funny. She will, I am sure, be wonderful as Mimi, but I foresee leetle clouds in the azure sky. She is an ardent Catholic, and has been 'in analysis' for five years! Oh dear. A girl with problems. However, I think I shall be able to manage her. If I can, all will be fine and dandy, if not, ze scenes zay will be terribile. I must engage an expert understudy.

At Roger's request I gave an 'audition' of the score to eight ladies who organize theatre parties. As I despise and abominate theatre parties this went against the grain, but I persevered in the cause of true art and a healthy advance, and charmed the shit out of them. The most important of them asked for thirty dates right off the bat. This, in a large theatre, amounts to about a quarter of a million dollars. Fortunately Jack Small, the Shuberts' representative, was present. He was tremendously impressed and offered me an absolute guarantee of the Shubert Theatre and the promise of the Winter Garden if it is free, which I think it will be. He also went all over New York trumpeting the news that it was a *great* score and rang up Roger offering to put up, on behalf of the Shuberts, half the money! So taken by and large it was a successful afternoon. However, I would rather not have Shubert participation if I can help it. We shall see.

I saw Jean Kerr's play *Mary, Mary*; very funny lines and I enjoyed it, but some of it is laboured. I have also seen *Advise and Consent*[1] and *The Best Man*[2]. Both about homosexuality and politics. On Monday I took Coley to *Trovatore*, Price again, more marvellous than ever, also Franco Corelli. Beautiful voice, very handsome and *very* delighted with himself.

Friday 17 March   Jamaica

My whole month in New York finished at concert pitch and I am now back here again looking out over the mountains in the evening light and

1 By Allen Drury.
2 By Gore Vidal.

feeling cheerful if a trifle exhausted. I made a sudden decision *not* to return to London and Switzerland but to come here and get the book completed. Oliver Smith is at Silver Seas and we are going to spend the next month really concentrating.

On Monday morning I interviewed Joe Layton, who is the most sought after and up and coming young choreographer on the scene at the moment. He was intelligent and I took a great liking to him. He is also available in May after he has finished with *Sound of Music* in London. I had a television spectacular called *The Gershwin Years* run through for me which he had choreographed and his work is brilliant. It now only depends on the terms being satisfactory, and I shall bloody well see to it that they are.

While all this excitement has been going on, Roger has been getting gloomier and gloomier. He has had so many recent disasters that I know he is finding it difficult to raise the money. He asked me to go to Chappell's and see if they would be willing to contribute. This I did, and Charles and I had an interview with Max and Louis Dreyfus and Irving Brown, who is bright and more or less runs the business now. The old boys, as always, were sweet to me and said they would do anything I wanted. I got them to promise, more or less, to put up a third, i.e. $120,000. Then we heard from Don Seawell[1] that Helen Bonfils would finance the show entirely and put up $400,000 without batting an eyelid! She is apparently the third richest woman in America. Within an hour he telephoned to say that he had talked to her in Denver (which she practically owns) and that she had said that as the show was mine he could have committed her without troubling to telephone! This, I must say, was one of the most gratifying compliments I have had for a long time.

Personally I am immensely relieved and happy. Roger was nice to me over *Nude with Violin*, etc., and I wanted him to do the musical for sentimental reasons. Sentimental reasons, however, are *not* the thing in business, as I have learned to my bitter cost over the years. Cochran, Charlot[2], John C. Wilson. I have been taken advantage of by all of them and downright cheated by some of them. I am now sixty-one and at long last the penny has dropped. I intend that my declining years shall be at least thoroughly secure.

Coley and I flew away exhausted at ten o'clock and arrived at Montego at 1.30 on the dot. A perfect flight. We broke down – morally – and graciously accepted three champagne cocktails before lunch. After lunch we went off into our individual comas; I awoke feeling fine but poor Coley, on the other hand, woke feeling ghastly and looking bright green. He tottered off to the loo and came back a few minutes later minus his plate, which he had dropped down the 'thing' while he was being sick! This is too famous an old joke to be enlarged upon. Eventually, when we had landed and were going through

1 Don Seawell, New York lawyer.
2 André Charlot (1882–1956), London revue impresario of the 1920s.

immigration, an angelic steward sidled up to him, pressed the retrieved teeth into his hand, and murmured, 'Safe and sound and *thoroughly* disinfected!' We set off giggling weakly in a Hertz drive-yourself Consul, and here we are with a month of peace before us and a lot of hard work.

Monday 3 April

I finished the job yesterday and the relief was considerable. I think the second act is better than the first, which is all to the good. I read it aloud to Oliver last night. Coley did a rough timing and it isn't as over-long as I feared. In fact, I think it's about right. I don't remember ever having worked with such dogged determination. It had to be dogged because I have not enjoyed it – the actual working, I mean. I've loved doing the music and lyrics, but not having to sit down every morning at seven before a blank page and know that it had to be filled with apparently inconsequential dialogue, every word of which has to count as there is no time for irrelevancies.

Meanwhile Oliver is concentrating equally hard, and from the drawings he has already done it looks to me as though the production is going to be absolutely beautiful. He always manages to bring a fresh and unexpected angle to every set. In addition to which, his scale-planning and meticulous blocking-out of the scene changes are efficient to the last degree. Oh dear, if only I had had that for *Pacific 1860, Operette, Ace of Clubs,* etc.

Vivien and Jack [Merivale] came on Friday and stayed only until Saturday afternoon. She was perfectly sweet and normal, and I think that Larry's marriage really has made her face up to the inevitability of not getting him back. Jack is good with her and a gentle, nice creature. I wouldn't care to change places with him. Anyhow, the visit was a great success and it was lovely to see her cheerful and happy again. I'm very fond of her, although there are certainly moments when I could throttle her.

Yesterday John Wyndham, Harold Macmillan's secretary, came to lunch with rather a nice ADC. Dorothy Macmillan[1] popped in for a moment before lunch and knocked back two rum punches. She was cheerful and nice as always, and I was delighted to see her. John Wyndham not very prepossessing to look at but highly intelligent and very funny indeed. He regaled us at lunch with hilarious stories about his Great Uncle Charles, a sort of Mitford character. Oliver was entranced. His bawdy vocabulary, together with a typical British upper-class voice and throw-away technique, appeared like every parodied stage Englishman ever imagined. I do see that this particular product of our rain-sodden little island is a great puzzlement to Americans. It was all extremely funny. The chaos at King's House is apparently considerable, what with the Macmillans and entourage and Winston Churchill suddenly arriving on the Onassis yacht for twenty-four hours. They are all flying to Washington

1 Lady Dorothy Macmillan (d. 1966), wife of Harold Macmillan, who was now Prime Minister.

tomorrow and everyone will be left munching aspirin and gasping for breath.

Sunday 9 April

The Happiest Girl in the World, the Cyril Ritchard horror that we saw in Philadelphia, has opened in New York and got not exactly rave notices but very nearly! No critics have apparently noticed the hideous vulgarity and snide lasciviousness of the whole thing. Nobody has commented upon Cyril's dreadful, unfanny camping! In fact they have been very, very kind. How unpredictable and inexplicable they are! If that show had appeared on Broadway under my name it would have been blasted off the face of the world – or would it? I am really at a loss, and also discouraged. It is dampening, after spending endless hours working with the utmost conceivable care to write a show with taste and genuine humour, to see in print enthusiastic reports of something which, spiritually and psychologically, is beneath contempt and profoundly dirty. Ah well. It has happened before and will undoubtedly happen again.

We leave for New York on Wednesday, and England presumably about ten days later. This has been a wonderful time here. Peaceful and productive and, except for some black moments over the script, I have thoroughly enjoyed myself. The mornings, as always, are wonderful, and I've seldom had breakfast on my verandah later than 6.30.

Friday 5 May   Les Avants

Coley and I flew away from New York on 22 April. London settled down on us like a comfortable old army blanket. It is extraordinary the difference in tempo. One feels it in the air.

The fever pitch of New York was upheld virtually until the moment we left. No definite news of whether we are going to get the Broadhurst or the Martin Beck. Complicated auditions, complicated dress conferences, etc., in addition to which I recorded the entire score on to tape at six o'clock on Friday evening when I and my voice were exhausted. However, it came out quite well.

Everything is proceeding fairly well. Our only serious worry is Charles [Russell], who has taken to having hysterical scenes, going white to the lips, hurling insults at me, then, when his ardour has spent itself, saying he feels *much* better and is *glad* to have got everything off his chest. I think he has developed a sort of *folie de grandeur* and sees himself as a great impresario. His values are all wrong, poor dear, and he *has* been alone and rather frustrated for a longish time, but these violent outbursts augur ill for the future, and I certainly do not intend to tolerate them when I am in rehearsal. They are a waste of time and energy. At the moment all is apparently well and, in addition to co-producing, he is to be billed as 'assistant director'. The emphasis on 'billing' in the American theatre has reached the pitch of lunacy.

London, as usual when visited for a short time, was hectic and somehow dreary. I saw Anna Massey give a wonderful performance in *The Miracle Worker*[1]. Maggie Leighton was, in an almost unplayable part, fine in *Lady from the Sea*[2]. Apart from these I saw two limp revues and the Crazy Gang[3], which was robust and cheerful. I visited Ian Fleming, who has had a coronary thrombosis and is in the London Clinic. It is awful for him to have to give up golf and all forms of exercise for a year or more. He was very good about it, but I am sincerely sorry for him. Other friends encountered were Dickie [Mountbatten], Walter and Biddy [Monckton], Molly Buccleuch, Fairbanks, Princess Margaret, Tony A-J, Duchess of Kent, Irene Browne, Lionel Bart, Tony Richardson, Vivien, Jacko [Merivale], Bobbie Helpmann, etc. I gave two interviews to Milton Shulman, who is writing four vast articles about me for the *Sunday Express*. There is no way of stopping him so I thought it best to co-operate. Actually he was very agreeable, but God knows what will emerge. I lunched with Pam and Michael Berry, Willie Maugham, Annie and Loelia.

Our theatre for *Sail Away* is still undecided but it looks like being the Broadhurst. The advance is mounting towards one million dollars!

Graham and I flew here the day before yesterday. The house is enchanting.

Saturday 27 May   Les Avants

My month here is over and tonight I take the train for Paris. It has been a lovely time. Just Coley, Graham and me. We have played croquet, we have played Scrabble and have enjoyed daily sessions of painting. Apart from these agreeable relaxations, I have managed to do quite a lot of work: a foreword for Loelia's book; a foreword to my sixth volume of plays; a rousing march, 'You're a Long, Long Way from America' for the *Sail Away* first act finale; the music for the first act opening, and a very pretty melody for Verity and Johnny in the Naples scene, no lyric as yet.

Joe Layton and his wife Evelyn came for a weekend and couldn't have been nicer. She is going to play Mrs Lush. Joe is bright, sensible and constructive, and we went through the whole script placing each musical number. He is full of ideas and I am sure will contribute a great deal to the show. Helene Pons arrived from Rome with efficient and comprehensive dress charts for every dress, every character and every scene. Within five minutes of her arrival the library looked like a jumble sale. She really is a wonderful old girl, professional and thorough and, what is most important, she really understands the characters and her designs have humour. Meanwhile the Broadhurst Theatre has

1 By William Gibson.
2 Ibsen's play.
3 Popular English comedy team, in a show entitled *Young in Heart*.

been settled, although it may be arranged to move to the Shubert or the Winter Garden. In fact everything is well prepared in advance so that whatever emergencies arrive they can be dealt with without involving too much chaos.

I have had one social outing: a luncheon with the Niehans at the Montreux Palace. Prince and Princess Nicholas of Romania, Ram Gopal[1] and the Kokoschkas[2]. I have completely fallen in love with Kokoschka. He is full of charm and humour and authentically a 'great man'. They both came yesterday for a drink and were enchanting. We went with Adrianne and Bill to see the Belgrade Opera do *La Pique Dame*[3], which was quite appalling but at moments hilarious. That old iron curtain really shouldn't be lifted. Adrianne's chalet is very, very much more than twopence-coloured. She has run riot with patterned wallpapers and rainbow hues in every direction. Personally I think she has gone much too far, but it is what she wants and is, of course, excessively feminine and comfortable.

Tonight I have to make a public appearance in Montreux and present the prizes for the Concours de Télévision[4], after which the Swiss express is being stopped for me at 1.55! It will be a long, long evening, but I feel it is a good idea to make a gesture to Switzerland in general and Montreux in particular.

That, frankly, is the end of the news.

Sunday 4 June   London

Paris was pleasant. On the night of the day I arrived, last Sunday, I went with Ginette, Paul-Emile and Nancy Spain to *West Side Story*. Grover Dale, who was the main object of the exercise, was extremely good. I knew beforehand that he was a sensational dancer but I was not sure of him as a personality. However, he has considerable charm, and although not the type I had envisaged for Barnaby I think he will do. Joe Layton is very keen to have him and he does seem a nice creature. Anyhow, I took him out to supper, told him he was 'in', and flung him into a frenzy of delight. I also flung him, the following day, into the 70 Avenue Marceau[5] circus, from which he emerged, all things considered, with flying colours. It must have been startling for the poor boy to be faced suddenly with Ginette, Lena Horne, Sue Fonda[6], Nancy Spain, etc., all shrieking at the tops of their voices in different languages.

My other Paris outings included a lunch with Nancy Mitford, an evening with Ned Rorem (avant-garde American composer, amiable but a trifle too 'advanced' for me), a funny dinner with Ruth [Gordon], Gar [Kanin], Kate

1 Ram Gopal, Indian dancer.
2 Oskar Kokoschka, Austrian-born British painter, and his wife.
3 Tchaikovsky's *The Queen of Spades*.
4 First of the now annual Montreux television festivals.
5 Home of Ginette Spanier and Paul-Emile Seidmann.
6 Sue Fonda, third wife of actor Henry Fonda.

[Hepburn] and Spence [Tracy][1] at the Escargot, and a visit to *Tis Pity She's a Whore*[2] in French with Alain Delon and Romy Schneider, both of whom, considering they had never been on the stage before, were remarkable. The Visconti production was wonderful.

I arrived here on Thursday and went to the opening of *Dazzling Prospect* by John Perry and Molly Keane. It was quite disastrous. Disgracefully directed by Johnny Gielgud. Booed whole-heartedly by the audience. Margaret Rutherford was funny at moments. Poor Joyce [Carey] struggled through a non-existent part. The whole thing was really shameful and, naturally enough, got the most appalling reviews. I also saw the incoming H.M. Tennent revue *On the Avenue* at Streatham. Beryl Reid fine, the rest simpering, esoteric and old-fashioned. Binkie is obviously losing his mind. Yesterday Coley and I saw *The Devils*[3] in the afternoon, not very good; and *Beyond the Fringe* in the evening, absolutely marvellous – those four unprofessional, professional young men[4] are brilliant and *not* circumscribed by old formulas and little gossipy campy jokes.

Oliver appeared with some coloured sketches of the *Sail Away* sets. They are excellent but need a little colour control.

Sunday 11 June

A full week. Last Sunday a charming party given by Dirk Bogarde for Judy Garland[5] at Beaconsfield. Joyce and I drove down and enjoyed ourselves thoroughly.

On Monday night Maggie [Leighton] and I dined with Princess Margaret and Tony at Kensington Palace, just the four of us and, after dinner, drove secretly to Tony's place or 'studio' in Rotherhithe, where we banged the piano and threw empty cointreau bottles into the river. Not an intellectual occupation but enjoyable. They were both very sweet and obviously happy.

On Tuesday I went to the Royal Tournament with Dickie and some decrowned heads in the royal box. Really very enjoyable. Dickie kept on bobbing up and down and taking the salute, and the RAF PT display was truly miraculous.

The next morning I went by train to Kettering, where Mollie Buccleuch met me and took me at a high speed all through Boughton[6], which is perfectly beautiful and filled with incredible treasures, including fabulous presents from Louis XIV to Charles II, van Dyck sketches, two van Ruysdaels from the Vatican, several ghosts and an almost overwhelming sense of England's past.

1 Spencer Tracy (1900-67), famous American film star.
2 John Ford's Jacobean tragedy.
3 Play by John Whiting, based on Aldous Huxley's book *The Devils of Loudon*.
4 Alan Bennett, Peter Cook, Jonathan Miller and Dudley Moore.
5 Who was making her last film, *I Could Go On Singing*, with Bogarde.
6 The Northamptonshire family seat of the Dukes of Buccleuch and Queensberry.

After lunch we drove to Sledmere in Yorkshire where I was lovingly greeted by Virginia Sykes (née Gilliat) whom I haven't seen since she was a deb. Sledmere is a beautiful Adam house and the party was very gay. Liza Hope, Fairbanks, etc. The next day we all drove to York Minster for the royal wedding[1].

Everything perfectly organized and the ceremony, for me, very moving. Prince Eddie looked so exactly like his father. The Duchess's looks, poise and glorious dignity were infinitely touching. Prince Eddie had given me a wonderful seat in the choir where I could see everything perfectly. The reception was beautifully done. The Queen and Prince Philip were charming to me, although at one point I nearly knocked Her Gracious Majesty for a burton and some moth-balls bounced from my trouser pocket.

After another dinner at Sledmere I came up to London on the Friday morning. All very gay and cheerful. That night I went to hear Joan Sutherland in *Lucia*, which was marvellous and a brilliant production. Yesterday we did a sort of theatre marathon. Act One of *Music Man*[2] in the afternoon – dreadful. *Bird of Time*[3] at 5.30. Very bad play but, at moments, unintentionally hilarious. Then *Sound of Music*, really very good except for its embarrassments. Today we have lunched with Vivien in her new Sussex mill where Maggie [Leighton] fell down and bruised her bum, and tonight we have sat through *Gone with the Wind*[4] and found it quite remarkable and Vivien's performance superb. Tomorrow we – Coley and I – fly to New York.

Wednesday 21 June   New York

Coley and I arrived last Monday week after a perfect flight. Charles met us and there was a slight showdown when we got back to the apartment. He was still wrapped in his grandiose dreams. He has succeeded with uncanny skill in antagonizing everybody and is still, I regret to say, blandly unaware of it. However, he has had to face hard facts and is, at the moment, subdued and unhappy. I am, of course, sorry for him and have done my best to stand up for him, but his general tactlessness and folly have manacled me. He is still co-producing the show, but only nominally, and is also being billed as my personal assistant and being paid, by me, $300 a week against his ultimate $12\frac{1}{2}$ per cent of the profits. Through his having talked himself out of actually co-producing, the management have now complete control. I don't really mind this as they are financing the whole thing and I have in my contract complete artistic control over everything to do with the production. They have been unfailingly courteous to me and I have no complaints. They obviously consider me a

1 Of Edward, Duke of Kent, and Katharine Worsley.
2 By Meredith Willson.
3 By Peter Mayne.
4 The 1939 film.

proper Charlie to have Charles anywhere near me, and I'm not dead sure that they're not right. Meanwhile, apart from the Charles situation, everything is going wonderfully. The dances are all under way and I am seeing the sets tomorrow. The demand for theatre parties is sensational and we are already sold out through next April! This, considering we haven't gone into rehearsal yet, is really fantastic. Everyone concerned seems to be bubbling with enthusiasm and I have really high hopes.

Coley and I are flying to Bermuda on Saturday for a week to get a little sun; then back we come and plunge into rehearsals. It was blazingly hot when we first arrived but now it has cooled down. I have done a very effective poster for the show in gouache and ink, and everyone is delighted with it.

Sunday 9 July

Everything is going so well that it is almost frightening. I have seen a couple of dance rehearsals and there is no doubt at all that Joe is a brilliant choreographer. The dancing boys and girls themselves are excellent and enthusiastic. Grover Dale and Pat Harty are charming together. Meanwhile – behind the back of Equity[1] and *strictly* against the rules, I have had Margalo [Gillmore], Bill Hutt and Jean Fenn here two or three times, just to read through. Now they are all word perfect in all their scenes.[2] The day before yesterday Jean Fenn arrived for the first time. I have taken a really immense liking to her. She is direct, simple, completely *un*tiresome and has taken the trouble to learn the part accurately. To my relief and surprise she is neither over-sweet, over-vocal nor in any way false. She has obviously studied the words carefully and sings them with truth. Last night she came for a two-hour music 'go-over' with Pete and, at moments, I was hard put to it not to cry. Her voice is really perfectly glorious. Kay [Thompson] arrived in the middle of everything with roses and champagne and her particular vitality. It was a brief period of enchantment.

Elaine Stritch is now my only problem. She buggered off to Nantucket and hasn't been near me. Perhaps – I repeat, perhaps – she has really been *studying* her part. But if only she had been here for just the last three days to get the benefit of the quiet reading it would have helped her and me considerably. Something tells me she may be going to be tiresome. She certainly has a reputation for it. I don't think bitchy and vile like some, but complicated and difficult. However, I may be misjudging her. In any case, everything else is going so well and everyone else is so good that I can't expect to have absolute perfection. The sets, incidentally, are going to be fine.

The world news is fairly ominous. There are growing rumours that America

1 Because he was not yet paying rehearsal salaries.
2 Grover Dale, Patricia Harty, Margalo Gillmore, William Hutt, Jean Fenn and James Hurst were all in the *Sail Away* cast.

will go to war with Russia in December! This I do not quite believe yet, although it may well happen. If so the whole world will be involved, of course, and it will probably be thanks very much! Ernest Hemingway shot himself through the head. It was quite obviously deliberate, although there has been a lot of the usual talk about cleaning the gun. I believe he had the beginnings of cancer and knew it. In which case I think he was very sensible to do it.

Sunday 16 July

The first week of rehearsals is over and really triumphantly over. I don't remember, since *Bitter Sweet*, being so completely happy with a company. There is not one of them that I don't like. Stritch, as I suspected, began by being tiresome, over-full of suggestions and not knowing a word, but after a couple of days she saw the light. She was never, I hasten to add, beastly in any way, just fluffy and nervous inside. If, like the others, she had done what I asked her and arrived at the first rehearsal without the book, she would have saved herself and me a lot of time and trouble. Actors are incredibly silly, and leading ladies idiotic. I except Jean Fenn from this generalization and Jimmy Hurst. I have never known people work with such concentration.

Stritch is going to be wonderful. Sure, authoritative and a real deliverer. Joe continues to do prodigies. The Taormina ballet is hilarious. In fact the whole thing is quite obviously headed for enormous success. There will probably be a few minor dramas and miseries but I do not envisage serious ones.

Sunday 13 August   Boston

Well, the show has opened and is a sell-out for the entire time we are here. It is, so far, a smash hit, but there is a lot to be done and Joe and I are doing it. The Saturday and Monday previews were dreary, the Tuesday one much better, and the opening night a wonderful audience and, of course, the whole show came to life. Afterwards there was a vast and ghastly party given in my honour by the Statler Hilton Hotel. It was a real publicity brawl and the heat was appalling. However, we lived through it. The whole opening night was a full-blooded jamboree. Crowded sidewalks. Flash bulbs - celebrities - tension and hysteria. Boston has apparently not seen its like for years. The performance was fairly slick and, considering it was, after all, an out of town opening, miraculous.

Lynn and Alfred have been here since Saturday and have attended gleefully every performance. Judy [Garland], Kay [Thompson], Loelia, the Richard Rodgers, Dorothy Hammerstein, etc., all came and were highly enthusiastic. The notices, from the box-office point of view, were excellent. Stritch was marvellous and deservedly got raves. Grover and Pat, to my joy, made a tremendous success. Jean and Jimmy came off less well. They sang beautifully but were far from convincing as actors, also the love story is not right and I have been busy revising and reconstructing it. They were, after all, engaged for their voices and I fear I have asked too much of them. It is madness to expect two singers to play subtle 'Noël Coward' love scenes with the right values *and* sing at the same time. However, all this will be worked on.

The orchestrations are beautiful and Pete Matz has been truly remarkable throughout. The sets are only fairly good. Dear Oliver Smith, although the winner of countless awards, is not really all he is made out to be. The show curtain and some of the painting is frankly very bad indeed and these are going to be changed. The dresses are pretty bad. Jean Fenn, who has a lovely face and a beautiful figure, has chosen for herself a series of pastel iron lungs and instead of looking chic manages to look sedate and suburban. However, I am pleading with Mainbocher[1] to dress her entirely for the New York opening.

The whole production, owing to foresight and careful planning, is $100,000 under budget, which is really remarkable. It also means that we can afford to spend a bit more now to get everything right. We have eight weeks before we open in New York, so all should be well, providing we work hard. Joe Layton has remained throughout shrewd, wise, unflagging and constructive. I have never worked with anyone that I have loved and respected so much. He has no stubbornness and no false 'values'. We shall have a hit eventually when all the loose ends are tidied up.

Sunday 20 August   Martha's Vineyard

A week of high tumult and excitement. On Tuesday night Mrs Roosevelt came. I dined with her and took her to the theatre. She was absolutely charming as always and I presented the company to her afterwards. On Thursday night Jackie Kennedy[2] came with the Paul Mellons[3]. This was arranged secretly between Adèle [Astaire] and me on the telephone. However, the secret got out and the theatre was a howling inferno of Press photographers and reporters. I felt extremely embarrassed about all this. The editor of one of the local papers apparently saw the party dining at the Ritz at 6.30 and sprang to the nearest telephone. However, the whole business hit the headlines in both the Boston and the New York papers; in fact, the Press of the world has been plastered with photographs of Mrs Kennedy and me, all of which, despite the fact that I had nothing to do with it, is marvellous publicity for the show. I should have been much angrier if it had been the Queen or Princess Margaret, but here in America where publicity is the breath of life I cannot feel that it matters very much. Anyhow, Mrs K. couldn't have been nicer and was sweet to the company and the whole evening was a triumph.

1 New York fashion designer.
2 Jacqueline Kennedy (b. 1929); her husband John F. Kennedy had been elected President the previous year.
3 Paul Mellon and his wife, American millionaire art collectors.

In spite of forebodings that it was dangerous to open in Boston in August we are a complete sell-out. Last week we played to $61,000! The show is now the right length and the right shape, and as there is really not a dull moment in it, I don't see how it can fail with the public even if we get poor notices in New York. Poor Jean Fenn has been tiresome about her dresses and idiotic about her hair; however, faced with the fact that she has had much less success than anyone else in the cast, she is now amenable to anything I suggest.

When I eventually write my book on the theatre there will be a whole chapter devoted to leading ladies' dresses and hair. They are invariably the main stumbling-blocks. Leading ladies' husbands may also come in for some acrid comment.

I came up here yesterday to stay with Kit and Nancy [Hamilton]. Guthrie is coming up on Wednesday. He has been very ill with a tumour in the bladder but is apparently much better. Secretly I have grave suspicions because they have been treating him with radium and this to me means only one thing. However, I hope I'm wrong.

It is divinely peaceful – as indeed it always is staying with Kit. It is not *quite* as warm as I should like but I can at least put myself down and relax completely for a few days. I am not by any means as exhausted as I should be, because everything is going so well, but I do feel the need to get away from the show for a little and return to it with a fresh eye.

The international outlook is getting gloomier and gloomier. I do not yet feel the imminent inevitability of war that I felt in 1938, but the threat of it is growing. The same 'Hitler' pattern is repeating itself. The Americans are now on the spot and I can sense hysteria rising.

John Osborne has written a violent, hysterical tirade against England[1]. I think he must really be a little bit unbalanced. Whatever is going on in the world at the moment is not directly the fault of England and the Royal Family and the 'establishment'. It is sad that an intelligent young man should be so basically silly. Perhaps, however, he is only doing it for publicity reasons.

Tuesday 29 August   Boston

Coley and I had a lovely day on Sunday. The Mellons sent their private jet plane for us and we were whisked to Osterville on Cape Cod, an exquisite house, where we had lunch with the President and Mrs Kennedy, both of whom were charming. I was impressed with him. Although the burden of the Western world is on his shoulders, he resolutely insists on relaxing completely every weekend. They arrived on the *Merlin*, the presidential motor cruiser. Secret Service gentlemen were festooned from every tree. She was pretty, cheerful and full of star quality. In fact they both are. She is also, to her everlasting credit, an ardent Coward fan. Adèle was there, and full of vitality

1 In a letter to the *New Statesman*.

and gaiety as always. Mrs Mellon is a dear woman with perfect taste and perfect manners. The Kennedys left at about four o'clock and we waved them away from the jetty. It was curiously moving to see that attractive young couple wearing gay colours, shooting off across the grey-green 'Boudin' sea followed and preceded by armoured coastguard cutters. At 4.30 Coley and I took off in the 'luxury' plane and we were back in the hotel at 5.15. Altogether a day to remember.

Monday 4 September   Philadelphia

We arrived here last night after a typical 'theatrical' train call. Coley and I had a drawing-room but we mingled most of the time with the cast, who were merry as grigs and behaving as actors always behave on train calls – drinks out of paper cups, singsongs, card games, jokes, gossipy get-togethers. It was all great fun and the long journey – six and a half hours – passed in a flash.

This last week has been remarkable for several things. The Russians resumed their nuclear tests in spite of having promised not to, which has shocked the world and, it is said, has brought the dreaded nuclear war so much nearer. President Kennedy seems to be keeping his head. The Berlin crisis has lessened slightly. Jean Fenn has had her hair cut. It is much better but not quite right. The whole show is now set and moves swiftly. It won't tomorrow night because the stage crew is apparently terrible and so there will probably be hitches, but all the essentials are now right.

Sunday 10 September

We opened on Tuesday night to a ghastly 'subscription' audience. The performance was smoother than I had hoped and the notices were all good except for the love story. There is no question about it, Verity and Johnny are a bore and the show sags whenever they come on. I was feeling fairly despairing about this when Joe walked in on Wednesday morning while I was having breakfast and said we should cut Jean's part of Verity entirely and let Johnny play the love story with Stritch.

I realized at once that, though this idea was revolutionary and entailed a major reconstruction job, it was also a life-saver. It means cutting 'Changing World' and 'I Am No Good at Love'. Apart from this the sacrifices were negligible. Everything began to fall into place. Stritch can really speak my dialogue, which Fenn never could – in fact there was nothing against the idea and everything in favour of it. We've still got three weeks before we open in New York.

Meanwhile Jean was in bed with laryngitis and not playing anyhow. There were terrific dramas and comings and goings. The next night Jean appeared at the theatre. She really behaved very well, poor thing. The whole company were in a state of suspended frenzy. According to Equity rules she will have to be paid eight weeks' salary, which will come to exactly the same as her new dresses would have cost. Friday and yesterday I rose at 7.30 and worked all day. The reconstruction of the whole thing is now done and is a vast improvement. We rehearse all day today and tomorrow and put all the new scenes in tomorrow night, hell or high water. Personally I think it will make all the difference between a moderate 'season' success and a smash. There have, of course, been headlines in the papers saying that we're in trouble, which is much healthier publicity for our New York opening than saying we're a smash hit and Mrs Kennedy thought it marvellous. We are much more likely to get good notices if the critics are not told in advance that the whole thing is a *fait accompli*. Anyhow, away we go. The next days are going to be exciting.

Sunday 17 September   New York

The new, reconstructed show went in last Monday and it was a complete triumph. Fortunately it was a good audience and the company were 'up'. Stritch's performance was nothing short of miraculous and she did 'Something Very Strange' so movingly that I almost cried. There is no doubt about it, I made the right decision. There are now no dull patches.

Maddening news from England. Poor darling Lornie fell down, for no apparent reason, and cracked her kneecap in addition to hurting her wrist and bruising her face. She is now in St George's Hospital in a plaster cast and of course won't be able to come next week and very probably will have to miss the New York opening too. This is dreadfully hard luck and I am miserably sorry for her. I know how bitterly disappointed she will be, as indeed I am.

Sunday 1 October

Here we are three days from the opening. The previews have been progressively better as the tiresome week wore on. The first one on Wednesday was ghastly. The company was down and nervous, the audience was moronic, and the scenery looked as though everyone had slept in it for a week. I called a brisk managerial conference on Thursday morning at which it was decided to have a full lighting rehearsal on Friday. This we did, and from that moment on things have looked up considerably. I stayed in bed yesterday in order to fight a cold, which I think I have succeeded in doing, so I missed two performances, both of which were apparently very good. Judging by the way the show has gone even with those ghastly preview audiences, I am fairly certain that it will be a success. If we get rave notices we shall have a smash hit; if not, we, like Mother Godamn, will survive.

Guthrie is desperately ill and I fear that it is the end. He looked ghastly when I saw him in Boston several weeks ago. Since then he has apparently lost twenty-five pounds and is now having transfusions. All this slow death is saddening.

I dined at the Maison Basque with Lynn and Alfred and Natasha. Joe and I recorded 'Dear Old Couple' and a hill-billy version of 'This is a Night for Lovers' as a first night present for the company. I must say they both sound very funny. The excitement about the opening night and the present-giving and the party afterwards is now rising to fever pitch. Coley has been really marvellous and everything has been organized perfectly with the minimum of fuss. I am so sad that darling Lornie isn't here but it can't be helped and she must come in November.

Tuesday 5 October

The opening night is now two days behind us and all is well. *The Times* notice was a rave. The *Tribune* was disagreeable but praised Stritch extravagantly and took its hatred out on me. The rest of the notices were carping but on the whole favourable. There has been an enormous line at the box-office since we opened and there isn't a seat to be had for months. The first-night performance was magnificent, the audience chic to the point of nausea but, for them, enthusiastic. The party afterwards at Sardi's given by the management was beautifully organized hell. Everyone in New York was there, invited or uninvited, from Adlai Stevenson to Jean Fenn. My little lot consisted of Marlene, who behaved fairly well, Dotty Dickson who behaved divinely, Myrna Loy[1] ditto, and Stritchie. Also Coley, Graham and Charles, later Maggie Leighton. Everyone concerned had gone out of their way to make it a tribute to me. My music was played incessantly and the walls were covered with blown-up reproductions of my posters and my drawing of Joe, and one room was entirely devoted to caricatures of me. I had, of course, millions of telegrams, masses of flowers and several expensive presents. In fact it was a real Noël Coward night. When I pause to reflect on the number of people who seem genuinely to wish me well from all corners of the world, I am really very proud and pleased.

Last night I took Maggie Leighton, who arrived too late for the opening, rather dreading second night flatness, but I needn't have worried. The performance was even better than ever and the house jammed to the last standee with a wildly enthusiastic audience who cheered the roof off at the end. Everyone on the business side seems to think it will run for two years at least and I think very possibly it may but, owing to the carping of the critics, it is not quite the immediate smash I hoped it would be. However, as even a moderate musical can make a fortune in this country and *Sail Away* is far above moderate, I really have no cause to complain. We shall play to capacity for months and I am on 13 per cent of the gross. We record the LP on Sunday, which ought to sell marvellously because everyone is mad about the music. *The Caretaker* opened last night and got rave reviews in *The Times* and

1 Myrna Loy (b. 1905), American film actress.

Tribune but, alas, no line at the box-office today. I really don't think, good as it is, that Broadway audiences will look on it as entertainment.

Sunday 15 October   Jamaica

Back where it all began. This time the beginning of the rainy season and everything luminous.

We flew down on Thursday and I am beginning to unwind. The sensation of having nothing particular to do is extraordinary. We drove into Kingston yesterday and exchanged the Consul we'd got at Montego for a Triumph Convertible which opens and closes in a flash and is a little dear. We lunched with Charles and Mildred[1] and they were pleased to see us again after a fairly long while. I was pleased to see them, too, as a matter of fact. They are, after all, my earliest Jamaican friends, and so long as one doesn't see too much of them they are very kind and sweet.

I love this place more and more. Changes are still happening now, a little for the better, I think. In the first place all the ghastly new hotels have failed and gone bankrupt and the tourist invasion is dropping off owing to the ridiculous prices. All this, from my point of view, is definitely good news. The island feels more peaceful than it did a year ago. It has withdrawn from Federation and is now in a state of suspension.

I have some letters to write and, within the next five weeks, I must make some lyric changes for my own recording of *Sail Away*. I can't very well sing 'If only I was younger I'd put ribbons in my hair'!

I have just finished Emlyn [Williams]'s autobiography, *George*. It is perfectly enchanting. Beautifully written, honest, witty, compassionate and, at moments, profoundly moving. The Cinderella story of all time. His more than humble beginnings are never overstated and his early sex burgeonings in both directions described with exquisite taste. It is truly a marvellous exhibition of objective self-analysis as well as being a gripping story. I don't see how it can fail to have an enormous success. I suppose it won't be long before I start writing myself. I can already hear the internal rumblings, but for the moment I am going to relax and paint and lie in the sun and play patience. It's a lovely prospect.

I can hardly believe those hectic, over-strained months are over. *Sail Away* is already slipping into the past and my mind is stretching itself. There is no more news except that for the first time for ages I am at peace.

Monday 23 October

How to Succeed in Business Without Really Trying has opened in New York and received the ecstatic raves that I should have liked to have had. This

1 Charles and Mildred D'Costa, Jamaican residents who had befriended Noël from his first visit to the island.

surprises me a little. I saw it in Philadelphia on its opening night and thought it would be a hit all right; it has a very funny, funny book and Robert Morse, who is wonderful, but I don't care much for the rest of the cast or the production, and the music, although it is by Frank Loesser, I found disappointing. However, it has now emerged as the greatest smash since *My Fair Lady*. It is a fast-moving, common, enjoyable musical farce and is about as comparable to *My Fair Lady* as *The Caretaker*. However, although I feel a little sad that they didn't blow their trumpets and sound their timbrels for *Sail Away*, I am all in favour of rival musicals being successes. It is good for box-office. The more people have a good time in the theatre, the more they want to come.

Meanwhile *Sail Away* continues to play to standees at every performance. How long that will last there is no knowing. The difference, for example, between Boston or San Francisco audience reaction and New York is quite extraordinary. *Sail Away* in Boston went marvellously at every performance for four solid weeks in the full blazing heat of summer and with the dreary Jean Fenn love story still in. In New York it still goes wonderfully and they cheer at the end but, on the average, they are not nearly so quick on the comedy lines and lyrics and, of course, the theatre parties are ghastly. They arrive late and talk and leave early, still talking. I have actually seen gangs of chattering, overdressed people get up and leave ostentatiously while Stritch is singing the 'Later than Spring' reprise. This abysmal lack of theatre manners was never apparent in the old days. However, theatre parties are the rule of the day and they have brought us in $1,400,000 advance, so I suppose one should be grateful. I am *not* grateful nevertheless. I deplore the damage they are doing to the theatre.

Sunday 29 October

Charles won a jeep in a raffle at the 'April in Paris' Ball and is shipping it to me here as a birthday present. This is very generous and sweet of him and it will be, to date, the largest birthday present I have ever received. It will be wonderfully useful here because the road is getting worse and worse.

At the moment there is a hurricane threatening and we have had an unceasing deluge for two days and nights, and although it has now let up a bit, the clouds are banking on the horizon and we shall get it again. In the middle of all this Don Seawell flew dramatically from New York to discuss *Sail Away* urgently. He arrived last night and the facts are these. (1) The carping notices did us damage. (2) We are not the smash hit we hoped to be. (3) The company is giving a slack performance. (4) Joe Layton is in Europe. (5) The Shuberts are *not* pushing the ticket sales at the box-office for some reason. (6) Our $1,500,000 advance is diminishing and the daily box-office sales are not compensating as they should. (7) A certain section of New York theatre-cum-café society is spreading the word that the boys in the show are all pansies and the girls not attractive enough. (8) The ushers report to the Shuberts that a number of people are leaving after the first act and a further number leaving before the end of the show. (9) The consensus of opinion (apparently) is that Grover Dale and Pat Harty are not good enough. (10) The love story is not strong enough and Jimmy Hurst is big, handsome and dull. There are several more quoted opinions that it would be waste of time to go on about.

Now then: this is a moment when I must strain every nerve to assess the situation clearly and keep my head. At present the general impression is that we are a smash hit. There are standees at every performance and we have never failed to play to capacity. The long-playing record is apparently selling very satisfactorily and is being played over the air a great deal. I receive a large number of fan letters from strangers thanking me extravagantly for providing a light, cheerful entertainment without emphasis on squalor and devoid of message or social significance. The management, Haila[1] and Don [Seawell] – Helen Bonfils doesn't count – are comparatively inexperienced. They love the show and are determined to do everything in their power to keep it on for a year at least, although, according to present box-office portents, it looks as though it wouldn't last beyond May or June. They are willing to spend lavishly on advertising; in fact, they are behaving very well, as they have all along. I have really no complaint against them. They have given me everything I wanted and backed me up over every issue since the word go. I think perhaps at the moment they are paying a little too much attention to little niggling comments and criticisms. I cannot blame them for this because the comments and criticisms are there.

Now the thing is to decide what, if anything, is to be done. The answer is to advertise judiciously and well, leave the show intact without further cutting and fiddling, and hope that the big public will eventually find its way to it and enjoy it. There is still a more than reasonable chance that this will happen. We played in Boston for four weeks in the blazing heat without one empty seat and without any star name on the bills except mine. The vast audience applauded and cheered at every performance. In Philadelphia we played three weeks, mostly to ghastly guild subscription audiences, and broke the theatre record. Why? If the men are too campy and the girls not attractive enough and the love story is thin, and Grover Dale and Pat Harty without charm and Jimmy Hurst dull, why did the audiences crowd into the theatre and enjoy the performance when they got there?

The gloominess of the present situation can be accounted for up to a point by the tone of the notices. They weren't all bad by any means, but there was much emphasis on it being 'old-fashioned' and 'thin'. Then Dorothy Kilgallen slammed it on the radio (she has recently done the same for Puccini and

1 Haila Stoddard, the show's co-producer with Don Seawell.

Leontyne Price). Then *Variety* came out with an idiotic and almost entirely abusive notice. On the other hand the *Times, Cue* and certain other columnists and critics have praised us to the skies.

Don says that the word-of-mouth which was good to begin with has now changed round to bad. This can only be accounted for by the theatre party audiences who pay too much for their seats, pay little or no attention to the show they are seeing, arrive late, leave early, and consider it more smart and sophisticated to disenjoy a show than to enjoy it. In addition to this, there is a certain quality in my work that does not and indeed never has appealed to this particular mentality. In the old days, when there were no organized audiences, the situation didn't exist. The public paid box-office prices, and if they liked a show it was a success and if they didn't it was a failure. In those happier days a certain number of theatre devotees read the notices but the large majority judged for themselves, nor were their opinions prejudiced in advance by radio and television comments.

Another fact that I must face is that I am rising sixty-two, whether I like it or not, and it is perfectly possible that I *am* out of touch with the times. I don't care for the present trends either in literature or the theatre. Pornography bores me. Squalor disgusts me. Garishness, vulgarity and commonness of mind offend me, and problems of social significance on the stage, unless superbly well presented, to me are the negation of entertainment. Subtlety, discretion, restraint, finesse, charm, intelligence, good manners, talent and glamour still enchant me. Is it because I am so much older that I am unable to distinguish these qualities in the majority of present-day books I read and shows I see? Am I falling into the famous trap of *nostalgie du temps perdu*? Have I really, or at least nearly, reached the crucial moment when I should retire from the fray and spend my remaining years sorting out my memories and sentimentalizing the past at the expense of the present?

I would be prepared to admit this if I were convinced that it was true, but I am *not* convinced. It is no use, of course, appealing to Coley or Lornie or any of my contemporaries for an unbiased opinion because they are all in the same boat. This is something that I must decide for myself. I know, with my deep instinct, that there is something about *Sail Away* that doesn't satisfy me. I am proud of the music and the lyrics, I am not especially proud of the 'book', but it is adroitly constructed, does not drag, and fulfils its purpose, which is to carry the show through to its conclusion. The 'books' of musicals, with one or two notable exceptions, are always unsatisfactory. There is never enough time to develop characters, and the music and the dancing, which after all is what the public come for, take up the major portion of the time allotted. In this instance I have deliberately kept the 'book' down to the minimum, in the belief that the public would be relieved at not having to sit through acres of dialogue between numbers. In fact I have used a revue formula with a mere thread of story running through it. Presumably I was wrong. Most of the critics seemed to mourn the lack of 'strong' story without realizing that a 'strong' story was never intended in the first place. I planned a light, musical entertainment with neither overtones nor undertones of solemnity, and this, so help me, is exactly what I have achieved. It will have to succeed or fail on its own merits, there is nothing more to be done with it. It is, of course, disappointing that it didn't get raves and become an immediate smash, but I have had disappointments before and a great deal worse than this.

When I get back to New York I shall do everything I can to help as far as intelligent publicity goes but, beyond this, no more. I have had enough of *Sail Away* and must now gather my wits together and decide what to embark on next. A novel? A book of short stories? A movie? Another musical? A book of essays on the theatre? At the moment I have no particular bias in any direction. I am, I suspect, creatively tired, but that won't last long. However, I shall encourage it to last as long as possible because I want to relax, really to relax, and give myself time to think and read and paint for pleasure and set my mind in order. I do not think this will be achieved just yet. At any rate not on this side of the wide Atlantic. There is no business like show business, but there are certain other businesses which are not quite so demanding and exhausting. One of them is to sit or lie quietly and meditate and eventually to put whatever one has meditated about neatly on paper, so effectively that it gets on to the best-seller list. With this commercially tainted but comforting thought I shall bring this overlong entry in my journal to a close. The wind is rising and before many hours have passed I may no longer have a roof over my head.

Thursday 2 November

Jack and Guthrie have both died this week. Apparently Natasha found Jack dead on the floor of his bedroom. Guthrie's death I knew was inevitable. I don't think he had any pain. He was a sweet friend and I shall always miss him. Jack, of course, is quite another matter. He was a part of my life for so very many years. I cannot feel sad that he is dead. He has been less than half alive for the last ten years, a trouble and a bore to himself and to everyone else. Naturally, now that he is dead, my mind is inclined to skip the disintegration and fly back to when he was handsome, witty, charming, good company. What a hideous, foolish waste of life! His character was never good. Perhaps he knew that, perhaps he knew something unpleasant about himself which served as an excuse for drinking. I am almost sure he was aware of inadequacy. I believe, in his heart, he knew he couldn't direct well and that all he did know about it was second-hand. Of course I am sad. Of course I feel horrid inside. But not nearly so much as I might have. To me he died years ago. Poor Natasha, she will feel wretched for a bit and then, I should imagine, immensely relieved. However, she will probably go through some strong Russian gloom before she emerges. I have asked her to come here immediately and to come to Les Avants for Christmas.

Ah me! This growing old! This losing of friends and breaking of links with the past. One by one they go – a bit chipped off here, a bit chipped off there. It is an inevitability that one must prepare the heart and mind for. I wonder how long it will be before I make my last exit. Probably quite a while, both Mum and Father[1] had long lives. I shall probably live to see many other, more poignant deaths. Unlike Edna St Vincent Millay[2], I *am* resigned. There is no sense in rebellion. I suppose I should envy the afterlife believers, the genu-flectors, the happy-ever-after ones who know beyond a shadow of doubt that we shall all meet again in some celestial vacuum, but I don't. I'd rather face up to finality and get on with life, lonely or not, for as long as it lasts. Those I have really loved are still with me in moments of memory – whole and intact and unchanged. I cannot envisage them in another sphere. I do not even wish to. If I were to see darling Mum again, which phase of her should I choose? The last sad months when she was deaf and nearly blind? The earlier years when she was vital and energetic and frequently maddening? Or the earlier still years when I was tiny and she was my whole world? It's all too compli-cated. I'll settle, without apprehension, for oblivion. I cannot really feel that oblivion will be disappointing. Life and love and fame and fortune can all be disappointing, but not dear old oblivion. Hurrah for eternity!

Sunday 12 November

We went to Goldeneye and snorkeled with Blanche [Blackwell]. My principal joy is to get out into the deep water beyond the reef where the big fish are. Blanche, overweighted with responsibility for my safety, discourages this. However, we did get out a little way but saw nothing but exquisite coral, vast sea eggs and a few parrot-fish. It was on the way back that drama set in. We were almost within our depth when Blanchie gave a sort of underwater shriek and pointed with her spear. I heard the word barracuda and looked and saw one, but only a baby of about a foot long. Then I looked beyond it and there, I must admit, was the largest barracuda I have ever seen; it must have been five feet at least. It was cruising along minding its business, thank God, and obviously was not in an irritable mood.

I have written an introduction to a Dolphin paperback edition of seven of my short stories; fortunately they have chosen the seven best ones. I reread them and was pleasantly surprised. They are very sure and lucid and well constructed, more so than I had remembered. Encouraged by this glimpse at my past endeavours I am now, with immense enjoyment, rereading *Present Indicative*. An excellent autobiography.

1 Arthur Sabin Coward (1856–1937).
2 Edna St Vincent Millay (1892–1950), American poet.

The hurricane 'Hattie' that threatened us and caused us three days of deluge hit Belize in British Honduras full on and laid it flat, killing over a thousand and injuring thousands more. It is the worst hurricane disaster ever, I believe. Shortly after this a vast and violent fire broke out in Beverly Hills and frizzled up a great many houses both gracious and ungracious, including those of poor Zsa Zsa Gabor, Burt Lancaster[1], Walter Wanger[2], etc., all of which goes to prove that God's in his heaven and not just sitting there either. He's *doing* something.

Sunday 19 November

The Great Reaper has been at it again. This time he has carried off poor little Madge Titheradge. Of course, it is a mercy that she should at last be free of all these years of pain, but I hate to think of her dead. What an enchanting actress she was and how sweet to me always, even when I was a small boy.

Cole and I had a long and cosy talk about death the other evening, sitting up here watching the dark come and waiting for the fireflies to appear. He is so sensible. We discussed what would happen if I died and what would happen if he died, and came to the sensible conclusion that there was nothing to be done. We should have to get on with life until our turn came. I said, 'After all, the day had to go on and breakfast had to be eaten', and he replied that if I died he might find it a little difficult to eat breakfast but would probably be peckish by lunch-time.

Well, enough of that. The Queen is in Ghana. Princess Margaret is presumably nursing her baby[3] and as happy as a bee. I had an enthusiastic letter from her thanking me for the record. *Sail Away* is still playing to standees. The jeep arrived and I am mad about it. It is wildly powerful and *loves* the bad roads. It comes flying up here in a second without a backward look. I have left instructions for a new verandah to be built with a studio over it, for the whole house to be rendered and plastered, and for a bit of extra terrace to be built by the pool at Blue Harbour. When I return in March all this should be done.

Monday 27 November   New York

We arrived on Wednesday at 5.30 in good time to go to the show in the evening. The audience was deadly and the performance desperately energetic. It was the night before Thanksgiving and a pall of anticipatory turkey and pumpkin pie lay over the city. Everyone was overacting like mad and so I called a rehearsal on Friday. The rehearsal started with me giving a three-quarters of an hour homily on the art of acting truly, disregarding dull audiences, *not* coming out and begging for laughs, and *not* interpolating lines

1 Burt Lancaster (b. 1913), American film star.
2 Walter Wanger (1894–1968), Hollywood producer.
3 David, Viscount Linley, born on 3 November.

and business without the permission of the author–director. This obviously had an effect because since then the performance has improved one hundred per cent. The business is still causing concern, but as this is happening all over town I am not as anxious as the management is. What I am anxious and determined about is that the *performance* shall be held up to standard.

On Saturday evening, after a long and valuable heart-to-heart with Stritch in the course of which I persuaded her to pay more attention to the love story and *not* persistently run away from it, I dined with Alfred and Lynn – just the three of us. We started at a quarter to eight and finished at a quarter past one, during which time we never drew breath. We wandered back and forth happily over the forty-one years we have known and loved one another and it was altogether enchanting and, above all, comforting. Lynn looks marvellous and Alfred much better than he has looked for years. They are a fabulous couple.

We went to see Natasha – Coley and I – she was set for tears but we forestalled them. She is in a curious state of widowed remorse exacerbated by vodka and really not making much sense. Apparently the financial situation is all right. I hope to God it is. I talked to Kit about Guthrie. She was awfully good but obviously very unhappy. Poor Ruth Chatterton died – one more to join the throng.

Monday 4 December

My first day of recording[1] was disastrous. Pete was exhausted and the orchestra was cumbersome and slow. Fortunately my voice was in good condition. The next day was a bit better because we used only a rhythm section; also I had delivered a few sharp words. The third day was good, and when we had done the numbers we were scheduled to do I insisted on re-recording all the ones we had done on Monday. The result, after much exhaustive work, is one of the best records I have ever made. It really is good and will, I am sure, help the show enormously.

Friday 8 December   ss *Queen Mary*

Lornie and I set sail yesterday. On board are the Richardsons[2], Kate [Hepburn], Spencer [Tracy], Beverley Nichols and Victor Mature[3], but so far all is peace. A much-needed peace because the last few days have been fraught with horror. Lornie, Coley and I had a two-hour conference with Jay Kramer[4] about Charles who, having announced that he wished to terminate our contract in April, suddenly changed his mind and said he wished to continue as my American representative and have the *first refusal* of all my future products

1 An album of songs from *Sail Away*.
2 Sir Ralph Richardson and his wife, actress Meriel Forbes.
3 Victor Mature (b. 1915), American film star.
4 Jay Kramer, Noël's New York lawyer.

and the right to raise money for them! I put my foot down and said 'No!' And that was that. It is all sad and horrid really but I am too old for such goings on.

Tuesday 19 December   London

There has been quite a lot accomplished in my week here. It is all settled with Harold Fielding[1] (whom I rather like) that *Sail Away* opens at the Savoy on 21 June after a two-and-a-half-week try-out at Bristol. I have a feeling that the show will be better appreciated in London than in New York. We had a sensational drop to $37,000 last week which is sinister but, all alibis apart, everything in New York has dropped. We are hoping for a resurgence of business after Christmas. I don't know what the world is coming to and that's a fact, except that it obviously is *not* coming to *Sail Away*.

Poor Arthur Macrae is in the University College Hospital dying of cancer of the lungs. He hasn't the slightest idea that he is dying, and although he looks ghastly with that unmistakable grey-yellow look, he has no pain and has never been happier. Everyone goes to visit him and he is surfeited with caviare and champagne and all conceivable goodies. Joyce goes twice a day and is behaving wonderfully. I am deeply sorry for her. Art is her nearest and dearest next to me. She refused to come to Les Avants for Christmas because she felt she should stand by. Binkie has been a wonderful friend which, under all his devious business aspects, he always is. He is paying for everything and seeing to it that poor Art has nothing financial to worry about. It is a sad, sad business. Apparently it will all be over in a few weeks. No pain has been guaranteed.

I heard Lionel Bart's score for *Blitz* and it is very good. I saw, or half saw, the new Michel St-Denis production of *The Cherry Orchard*.[2] It was dimly lit and, to my mind, untidily played. I much preferred John Gielgud's Lyric Hammersmith production seven years ago.

Tuesday 26 December   Les Avants

Well, we have had our Christmas and I must admit it was entirely enjoyable. Everyone had champagne cocktails and kissed one another ardently and it was all great fun.

On Saturday we went to a highly *recherché* party at the Chevreau d'Antraigues. It was grand and exquisitely dull. I, as usual, sat next to the Queen of Spain who, as usual, was merry as a grig. She really is a gallant old girl and I am fond of her. She is at least a 'giver' rather than a 'taker'.

We dined on Thursday with Adrianne, Bill and Anna [Massey]. I had a long heart-to-heart with Anna, who couldn't have been nicer or more sensible. We went into the whole Jeremy [Brett] business and she evinced no malice or

1 Harold Fielding, London theatrical impresario specializing in musicals.
2 At the Aldwych by the Royal Shakespeare Company.

spite, merely a dignified and resigned acceptance of the situation. I really was deeply impressed with her wisdom, maturity and plain horse-sense. Adrianne, on the other hand, who got herself firmly on to the wrong track at the outset, is plainly miserable. However, there's no sense in going on about it. The young must cope with their own problems.

The Great Reaper had a final fling just before Christmas and whisked away Moss Hart. He died swiftly of a heart attack in his car at Palm Springs. I don't know whether or not Kitty was with him. Poor darling, it is ghastly for her.

I have just finished Evelyn Waugh's latest book, *Unconditional Surrender*, sadly disappointing. There are intermittent gleams of the old magic but long tracts of well-written boredom. The whole book is shadowed by a dark cloud of Catholicism which suffocates humour and interferes with the story. Oh dear, I do wish highly intelligent writers would not unconditionally surrender themselves to specific religious dogmas, it really does bugger up the output.

I have risen above a brief but sharp bout of lumbago and am now busily fighting – with cortisone ointment – a recurrence of my bloody paint allergy. Never a dull moment.

1962

Apart from one brief, profitable film appearance in Paris When It Sizzles, *the year was largely taken up with moving* Sail Away *from Broadway to the Savoy Theatre in London, where it opened to a generally grudging Press but managed to survive a healthy nine months. Noël was also beginning now to work on what would be his last score, the words and music for Harry Kurnitz's musical adaptation of Rattigan's* The Sleeping Prince. *Called* The Girl Who Came to Supper, *and concerned with an American chorus girl working in London at the time of the 1911 Coronation who falls in love with a Carpathian Prince Regent, it allowed Noël to write lilting, lyrical numbers about most of his favourite themes in one of his favourite periods.* Sail Away *had, after all, only allowed him to write about travel, whereas* The Girl Who Came to Supper *allowed him American showbusiness, London, royalty and the Edwardian music-hall. Sadly, that score has, in his own country, only ever been heard on disc and on radio.*

One of the best things about Sail Away's *London reception was the review of the author it elicited in the* London Magazine *from Noël's fellow-playwright John Whiting: 'We have had him with us now for sixty glorious years; we had better accept him. That extraordinary piece of landscaping which he uses for a face, and the dying dove which he pretends is a voice, are always hinting nowadays that he is forgotten, old-fashioned and un-loved. That he is forgotten is demonstrably untrue ... that he is old-fashioned is another matter. But is he unloved? Speaking as one twenty years his junior, all I can ask is: who doesn't love his youth? For that is what Coward is to men of my age:* Private Lives, Conversation Piece, Operette, Tonight at 8.30, *'The Scoundrel' and all those songs we sang to our girls driving back in the red* MG *from the Thames pub on a summer night in 1936.'*

Monday 1 January   Les Avants

The New Year starts today unburdened for me with too many good resolutions, merely a decision to smoke a tiny bit less, to write more, to keep as
healthy as possible by watching my diet and my weight, and to keep my mind
alert and prepared to grapple with whatever the year may bring.

Adrianne and Bill and Anna came to dine last night and we all sang 'Auld
Lang Syne' and wished each other Happy New Year and played games and
enjoyed ourselves. Adrianne is rising above her domestic troubles with great
panache and was at her gay best.

Poor Spencer Tracy was taken ill during the Berlin première of the [*Judgment
at*] *Nuremberg* movie and was flown back to America. Apparently it is cancer.
Also apparently he knows, because he gave a Press interview implying clearly
that he thought his life was over. Kate will be dreadfully unhappy[1]. I wrote to
her yesterday to ask if there was anything I could do, but of course there isn't.
I talked to Joycie, who is seeing Arthur every day. He is beginning to slip a bit
and has complained of slight pain, so they have put him back on drugs again.
It's a macabre and desolate situation. I hope they will have the sense not to try
too hard to keep him alive.

The snow is lying all about but it is neither smooth, crisp nor even on
account of a thaw having set in. There is nothing to be seen outside but the
shapes of trees looming through thick clouds. Guido[2] has his *soi-disant* uncle
to stay with him for a few days. This is apparently not going down very well
with Enzio and Ugo[3]. The general consensus of opinion is that it is not his
uncle at all. His auntie possibly but *certainly* not his uncle. It is nice for Guido
to have a friend but I think Coley and I will have to suggest tactfully that he
leave soon. I do *not* want dissension among the staff.

Coley bought two copies of *Pomp and Circumstance* in French. He got them
in a shop in Lausanne. It is a beautiful edition and appears to be very well
translated. The title is *Amour, Délices et Protocole*. All this is very gratifying
but a complete surprise to me and to Lornie. I had no idea it had even been
translated, let alone published. Nobody ever tells me anything.

My new Triumph has arrived. Coley and Graham fetched it from Lausanne.
It is bright scarlet and, although a convertible, warm and snug as can be. It is,
of course, useless at the moment because of the snow but it will be lovely to
have in the spring.

Monday 8 January

It has been a lovely holiday and we've painted and luged – the snow was only

1 Katharine Hepburn's successful on-screen partnership and close off-screen friendship with
  Spencer Tracy had begun in the early 1940s.
2 The cook.
3 The butler and gardener.

really good on one day – and done crossword puzzles and made some very good jokes. Altogether one of the nicest Christmases I have known for years. Yesterday Kit and Nancy [Hamilton] drove over to lunch with Brian and Eleanor [Aherne]. Tarquin [Olivier], my godson, was here so we were quite a crowd. Kit was really wonderfully good, sad underneath but gay on top. She misses Guthrie every minute, poor love, and I fear will go on doing so for quite a while.

Tarquin is really a bright and sweet boy. Jill [Esmond], rather surprisingly I think, has been a wonderful mother to him and he quite genuinely adores her. Larry, as a father figure, has not come off quite so well. Tarquin is small, pale, vulnerable and, I think, fairly tough. He recently spent twenty-one months in Indonesia living, in acute discomfort, with the natives and working out theories about how the West can ultimately understand the East. Personally I think this unlikely, but in any case he seems to be very dedicated and has written a book on the subject, which he is now rewriting, as well as working nine hours a day doing a news broadcast service in Berne. I do *hope* he has genuine talent for writing and that his book is good. My other godson, David Niven [junior], nearly but not quite broke his leg skiing last week and is now in a cast and unable to return to his studies in Grenoble, which delights him.

Tuesday 16 January

Kit and Nancy are here. I had a feeling that Kit needed a haven and so did she, so they arrived on Friday and are staying on after we leave next Saturday. It is lovely to be able to repay even a bit of her loving hospitality over so many years. I drove to Geneva, then met Loudon Sainthill[1], whom I drove back. His designs for *Sail Away* are wonderful, much, much better than poor Oliver [Smith]'s. They will give me a new angle on the show which will be a great help. He has lovely taste and a beautiful colour sense.

Last week Arnold Wesker, much to my astonishment, telephoned from London and said he wanted to come and see me! I invited him immediately, devoured by curiosity. He arrived looking grubby and peculiar in drab colours and his wife's sweater, which was definitely a mistake either for her or for him. It turned out that he wants me either to donate money or to give a preview of *Sail Away* in order to raise funds for 'Centre 42', a Labour-promoted scheme for bringing culture to the masses. They propose to organize festivals all over green England which will include plays (unspecified) in the round, little exhibitions of modern painting and sculpture, merry folk-singing and dancing, etc. This is all designed to wean the workers away from football pools, doggies and bingo and such wickedness, and teach them really to appreciate Henry Moore and Benjamin Britten and, at a pinch, me. This whole project, of

1 Loudon Sainthill (1919–69), Australian-born designer.

course, sent me off into dreadful giggles, from which I later recovered and gave him a sharp talking-to about wasting his talent and energy on an already gained cause and an old-fashioned one at that. I refused absolutely to contribute a penny or even a thought to such a lamentable waste of time.

He left the next day rather desolate and, seized by pangs of guilt, I read the *Trilogy*[1] right through. He has undoubtedly got great talent but everything, or nearly everything, is spoiled by old-fashioned, 'up the workers', left-wing propaganda. The critics have hailed him as a 'great writer', which automatically puts him alongside Tolstoi, Dickens, Shakespeare, Shaw, etc., whereas he really happens to be an over-earnest little creature obsessed by the wicked capitalists and the wrongs of the world. He complained that he, and his avant-garde colleagues, have been victimized by the Press and is suddenly dismayed to discover that his plays aren't box-office. He explained all this to me honestly and naively. I reminded him that that was exactly what I had prophesied in my articles in the *Sunday Times* last year. Since he left he has written me a very sweet, sentimental, 'serious' letter, and *The Kitchen*, which really is very dramatic and better, I think, than his other works. I really do like him.

Tarquin has given me the first chapter of his book to read. Oh dear. It *isn't* very promising. Dear Ernie Kovacs[2] has been killed in a car crash. *Sail Away* is doing drearily bad business. Heigh-ho!

Sunday 28 January   London

We have had a successful ten days of activities. I've taken a great liking to the Harold Fielding set-up, particularly Joan Preston, the stage manageress. We have seen many good actresses and actors.

There have been miseries about poor Arthur. He insisted on going home to his Mum in Hove, which he has now done. Poor Joyce went down with him. I *know* that somewhere inside him he knows he is dying. I went to see him before he left and he looked ghastly of course. How long he will be able to stay at home no one knows, but there are nurses and doctors laid on in readiness for the least emergency. It is horribly sad and poor Joyce is fairly distraught.

Apart from auditions I have seen various entertainments both actual and celluloid. The outstanding of the latter was *Judgment at Nuremberg*[3], superbly directed, written, acted and photographed. Last night Coley and I went to see *Luther*, and in a way I'm glad we did if only to prove something that I have long suspected, which is that John Osborne is a talented, shrewd, calculating fake. There is *no* play there. Just a series of disjointed monologues and duologues. Albert Finney (the Great) talented but inaudible, the production

---

1 Wesker's *Roots, Chicken Soup with Barley* and *I'm Talking about Jerusalem*.
2 Ernie Kovacs (1919-62), American film actor who had been with Noël in *Our Man in Havana*.
3 Produced and directed by Stanley Kramer.

fairly good but pretentious, John Moffatt excellent. I left the theatre knowing as much about Luther as when I went in. Fortunately there are some programme notes, which I read when I got home. John Osborne's obsession about shocking the susceptibilities has not abated, he has merely rechannelled it. There are constant references to anus, farting, excreta, wet dreams and copulation, many of which may conceivably have been actually said by Martin Luther in the course of his unattractive life, but when crammed into two and a half hours of playing time become monotonous, facile and profoundly vulgar. What is even more vulgar is Osborne's misuse of the English language. To write of the early sixteenth century colloquially is not only understandable but necessary, but to employ cheap American idioms such as 'way out', 'snarled up', etc., is not. It has been a great success for a long time, but to date I have found no one who liked it except Tony Richardson, who directed it. A baffling and fairly boring evening in the theatre.

Sunday 4 February   New York

Poor *Sail Away* is stumbling along here. We took Loudon to the Wednesday matinée, which was a dull audience, contrary to expectations as matinées are usually good, and only half full. Loudon loved it, however, and is full of inventive ideas. Since then we have had unsatisfactory auditions almost devoid of talent, and I am getting seriously worried about who will play Nancy.

We have seen *New Faces*[1], absolute disaster. A movie, *The Children's Hour*[2]. Not good enough in spite of Audrey Hepburn and Shirley MacLaine. And *The Night of the Iguana*. For this Oliver [Smith] has done a really brilliant set. The play is interesting and I think the best Tennessee has written for some time. There are some moments of fine writing and some moments of sordid sex imagery, which he seems unable to avoid. However, it is an absorbing evening in the theatre. Bette Davis is effective, if a little obvious. Alan Webb gives a marvellous 'old man' performance. Maggie [Leighton] is quite beyond praise, subtle, quiet and infinitely moving. She really is a magnificent actress. The play is a smash hit and she has made the triumph of her life, which is just as it should be.

Monday 19 February   Jamaica

The principal event of the last week is that I have constructed a new comedy. The title, at the moment, is *Three for the Money* and it is about a ramshackle Irish castle and a ramshackle Irish lord who has three beautiful but undisciplined daughters, upon whose charms he relies to save the family fortunes. An ex-mistress of his takes them off to France, educates them in the suitable graces and, in one way or another, they all manage to find rich gentlemen. At

1 Revue conceived and directed by Leonard Sillman.
2 Film version of Lillian Hellman's play (retitled *The Loudest Whisper* in the UK).

the end of the play they are all three, for various reasons, free of their encumbrances and ready to set forth on further adventures. Meanwhile the house is restored and the family estate secured. This is a very bald outline but it offers opportunities, I think, for good comedy situations. I intend, if I can, to write it on a plane just above reality, as I did *Blithe Spirit*. If it comes down to solid ground for a moment it will disintegrate. I am looking forward to having a bash at it.

For the last fourteen months I have thought and talked of nothing but *Sail Away* and I have got to talk and think of it all over again in the spring. In the meantime I am revelling in a sort of 'intellectual prison break'. I am reading voraciously and my mind, freed from the exigencies of American musical comedy, is beginning to get a little colour in its cheeks again. I am rereading the Trollope 'Palliser' novels, which are soothing.

Sail Away, owing to an almost sensational lack of enthusiasm from the New York public, is closing next Saturday, thereby putting an end to my optimistic dreams of a two-year run, a national company[1] and a nice old-age pension. However, I have not done so badly out of it financially, having made, from royalties alone, at least £30,000. If it should be a success in London, much will be retrieved; if not, to hell with it. My mind, which is feeling very healthy and creative, will occupy itself with other projects, perhaps remunerative, perhaps not, but in any case exciting. I am sick to death of poor *Sail Away*.

I have just reread Trollope's autobiography and can well understand why the publication of it depressed the sales of his books. He emerges from it as incredibly industrious, pompous, self-righteous and lacking in humour. In it there is little or none of the wit of his own dialogue. However, I am finding *Phineas Finn* and *Phineas Redux* as enchanting as ever.

Thursday 22 February   San Francisco

Coley saw me off in Kingston on Tuesday, and I sped off through the bright skies at approximately the same moment that John Glenn Junior sped off in his capsule into outer space. He had been round the world three times before I landed at Miami airport. I did a little shopping and had my hair cut, and while this was going on I heard over the radio that Glenn had landed safely. It was a tremendously exciting moment, ruined for me by a blonde manicurist with a voice like a corncrake who made it almost impossible to hear what had happened.

Arrived here 2 p.m. (San Francisco time) after a seven-and-a-half-hour flight. Very pleasant really. Finished *Phineas Finn* and Ernest Gann's *Island in the Sky* as a chaser. Dined last night with Ina [Claire] and Bill [Wallace]. Rather foolishly, I think, they had arranged a dinner party - I should

1 Which would play other American cities on tour.

have been much happier alone with them – however, it was quite all right. Ina looks wonderful and is as full of gay vitality as ever. Bill also in cracking form.

Talked to Ed [Bigg] on the telephone about my leg and he told me unequivocally and firmly that I must *give up smoking entirely*. I *know* he is right, so I made my great decision. I dread the next few weeks but I must really persevere this time. It's no use cutting down, one must really stop and suffer whatever is necessary. I must watch that I don't put on weight, so I suppose I shall have to starve myself as well. It's going to be a lovely holiday, but I suppose I shall profit spiritually as well as physically by being captain of my soul. At least I hope I shall be able to walk a hundred yards without having to sit down.

Sunday 25 February

Well, here I am in the middle of the night bumbling about at 35,000 feet over the Pacific Ocean. The plane is luxurious and practically empty so I propose to stretch out and sleep – a seven-hour flight during which we lose Sunday entirely owing to the international date-line. I presume I shall recover it on the way home.

What has happened to Honolulu is indescribable. It is a cross between Miami Beach and Coney Island. The loveliness and peace have gone for ever. It is now crammed with shrill-voiced tourists who make the air hideous with their loud-mouthed arrogance. Every effort is concentrated on catering for them. Nothing is real any more. The leis, the hula dancers, the gently spoken 'alohas' are all shrill and synthetic. It is sad and hateful to reflect on what progress in general and American progress in particular is doing to the world. It is not only that they have loud, ugly voices and too much money, it is that their basic sense of values is dead wrong. Nothing is any good unless it is big and expensive.

Wednesday 28 February   Suva, Fiji

I arrived Monday morning five o'clock Fiji time. I'd slept not too badly on the plane, so I decided to get a car and drive straight on here. When the sun rose at about 6.15 I was bowling along on a vile road by the side of a young Hindoo. The country looked lovely though the day was overcast – very like Jamaica, only more lush – all my old friends – breadfruit, flamboyant, tulip tree, wild banana, etc., plus lots of different varieties of palm.

I arrived here at about eleven o'clock. Typical going-to-seed British colonial hotel – on the same lines as the Queen's Park in Trinidad but smaller and much nicer really. The Fijians are very attractive and they all wear skirts regardless of gender. As they also go in for 'Jackie' hair-dos[1] this is apt to

1 Mrs Kennedy's bouffant style.

cause confusion. The skirts are called sulus. The policemen's are flared slightly and pointed at the bottom like the elves in *Where the Rainbow Ends*.

Today I'm starting off in an eighty-foot ketch for two days' island visiting. The owner is an ex-RNVR, Stan Brown. I took an immediate liking to him. If it's a success I shall go for a longer trip with him next week.

Cable from Joyce saying that poor Arthur had died peacefully on Sunday. I'm very, very sad for her. For myself, too, because I was so fond of him and he was a real wit.

Sunday 4 March   Nandi

The three days on the *Maroso* were very enjoyable but impaired somewhat by the weather. The first day was all right and I got a lovely tan; from then on wind and rain and, on the way back, a very rough sea. We anchored on the second day between two uninhabited islands with a sort of sand-bar running between them. Wonderful shells and a real South Sea magic quality. The *Maroso*, which is the pride of Stan Brown's life, is far from luxurious and, I fear, on the dirty side. It was not too bad, but when the weather played up there was nowhere to sit except down in the saloon, which smelt of copra and kerosene. Stan I liked very much. Ex-Merchant Marine, then RNVR. A wonderful seaman. The crew was a mixture of Fijians, Gilbertese, Chinese, etc. My cabin was on deck and not bad. There *was* a loo, with a pink plastic seat, and altogether I enjoyed myself, but I think for long it might get me down. However, there are many more islands I should like to see.

Wednesday 7 March   Tahiti

Well here I am in Tahiti at last. It's beautiful and exotic and fascinating and all the things it is supposed to be, or nearly all. What is wrong is 'progress'. In a very short while it will be spoiled utterly. This hotel – on the American plan of course – is self-consciously Polynesian, with thatched roofs and pretty little Tahitian girls wearing flowers behind their ears and throwing sex at you with every dry martini. Music is played through loudspeakers from 7 a.m. throughout the day and night. When they run out of commercialized Tahitian music they fall back on 'Roll out the Barrel'. It is also, in the evening, pitch dark so that you cannot see to read the menu, which doesn't matter really because you seldom get what you order. Cutting through this incessant, soul-annihilating din rises and falls the eternal nasal twang of the Middle West. The port is attractive, with a café called Vaimar's, where you sit on picturesque but uncomfortable painted chairs and watch the Gauguin types whizzing backwards and forwards on Vespas.

I chartered a boat and set off with a wiry little Frog called Alain Brun to see Moorea. He was an excellent seaman, had built his boat himself and was passionately proud of it. We encircled Moorea inside the reef, which was absolutely beautiful. The whole island is fantastic. Sharp volcanic mountains rising sheer out of the sea. Dazzling white beaches and millions of coco-palms. The lagoon crammed with rainbow fish. We landed at a small, newly built hotel. There was a pert Tahitian waitress, an Italian proprietor and an old, queer Chinese cook who was very pissed and had been on the *rosé* since 9 a.m. The whole day was enjoyable and coming back through the sunset was exquisite.

MGM and the *Mutiny on the Bounty*[1] set-up have added their modest quota to the undoing of one of the world's beauty spots. Marlon Brando and Trevor Howard between them apparently did incalculable damage. Trevor nearly got killed by driving down the runway at the airport when a plane was trying to land. Altogether a highly unedifying carry-on all round. I got most of this from a nice, civilized French Pressman who interviewed me. Today I met at lunch a really charming young Englishman called John Everett, who used to row at Oxford with Tony Armstrong-Jones. We are dining together tonight. Tomorrow I fly to Bora Bora.

Sunday 18 March   Bora Bora

I am flying back to Tahiti today, after ten days here. It ranks high among the few really lovely places I have been to. The hotel is very pleasant and run by an American who has had one American wife and two Tahitian ones. His present one, Mari, is an ex-dancer, singer and guitar player. She has a strong personality and an individual voice and, when worked up, can wriggle her bottom with incredible speed. Alex Bourgerie, her husband, regards these exercises with complacent pride. I've picked up two really charming new friends, Pat and Joe Costello from San Francisco. They are the nicest sort of Americans, youngish, attractive and well-mannered.

John Everett came from Saturday to Thursday and couldn't have been nicer. We paddled about the unbelievable lagoon in a pirogue and snorkeled among the fabulous reefs. I have never in my life seen anything so beautiful as that particular reef and this particular lagoon. The myriads of coloured fish, the coral formations, are all beyond description. Alex took me to the outer reef in his speedboat. Out there, just inside the reef, it is more marvellous than ever. I was paddling along happily on the surface in my mask when I came face to face with a six-foot shark. I did *not* panic, but it was a frightening moment. I slapped the water hard with my fist and it gave me a look of infinite disdain and swam away. A short while later John, who had just speared a fish, met it suddenly coming at him from behind a rock, gave a yell and hopped on to the reef. However, it went its way without attacking. We have also seen a number of big sting-rays and a sinister-looking sea-snake which I nearly decapitated with a paddle.

1 The 1961 remake was shot largely in Tahiti.

John left on Thursday and missed the loveliest adventure of all. Joe and Pat and I set off with Mari, Alex, two musicians and two crew in the big sailing pirogue and, in full moonlight, sailed to a little atoll at the other end of the lagoon. When we arrived a fire was made and we had a feast of fish, breadfruit, yams, bananas, etc., on the sand. We also had several dry martinis and a lot of *vin rosé*. The view from the atoll of Bora Bora itself was exquisite. The bright white sand and the silver sea and the unbelievable stars. Mari and the musicians strummed away at their guitars and sang old island songs. Altogether an evening of complete enchantment. We sailed and paddled gently home at two in the morning.

We have seen the 'satellite' several times. It encircles the world every ninety minutes. It looks like an extra star and then you realize that it is moving. Apparently it will stay in orbit indefinitely. Science has certainly progressed since whoever it was discovered the wheel.

I shall leave here with regret. It will, of course, become spoiled within a very short time. Happily, however, there are lots of other islands in these magic seas.

Saturday 24 March   Beverly Hills

Well, the contrast is considerable. My last few days in Tahiti were hectic but, on the whole, enjoyable. I went on a whole day's outing with Joe Costello and visited an island, or rather a collection of islands, called Tetiaroa. We went in a motor fishing boat but, as there was no entrance through the reef, we had to wait until a Tahitian fisherman fetched us in a boat. This was all very exciting and fairly risky because we had to time the waves to the split second. There was nearly disaster when the fisherman was swept overboard. I sat in the bottom of the boat holding on like a vice and deciding, when flung into the water, to swim out to sea rather than attempt the reef. However, the fisherman managed to clamber back and we slid and bumped finally into the lagoon. The main island is inhabited by an American lady of eighty-six who is stone blind. She was very bright, however, and I listened to Joe bargaining with her. He is trying to form a syndicate to buy the whole atoll and make it into a San Franciscan sporting club! Then I got tired of this demonstration of the march of progress and went out and snorkeled in the lagoon. Our ultimate return over the reef was less spectacular, but on the way back to Tahiti – three and a half hours – we ran into bad weather and got fairly wet.

Tahiti itself was living up to its sex reputation with splendid enthusiasm. A friend had rented a sort of beach shack in which he was lording it with two Tahitian tarts, one a striking-looking lesbian. Really, I *don't* know what the world is coming to. However, he seemed to be having himself a ball, if perhaps a rather complicated one.

On arrival here I got a violent welcome from the hotel. Flowers, fruit, etc.

I went round and surprised Clifton, who nearly had a fit. The next day I lunched with 'Swifty' Lazar and suggested he take over the disposal of my properties for movies or television. I think this is a wise move.

Saturday 31 March   New York

I flew to Chicago on Tuesday from Hollywood. Ed Bigg and I dined in the Pump Room, and on Wednesday morning I reported at the ghastly Passevant Hospital at 7.30. Everything had gone wrong with Ed's organization of my day, so I lay in bed for two hours without even a cup of coffee, waiting for my first blood test. The silly girl who finally arrived jabbed me over and over again in the wrong places until finally I flew at her and showed her the right vein. Strange women and dwarfs walk in and out of the room without knocking and there is *always* a pneumatic drill going on outside. Fortunately, however, all my tests were accomplished satisfactorily and I am in perfect condition except for an artery in my right leg which is closing up! This has got to be watched. There was a long discussion about non-smoking. I asked if I could smoke an average of five a day and they advised me not to, without much conviction. I *don't* want to stop entirely so I think I shall winsomely disregard their advice, but I shall certainly watch that the maximum stays constant.

Sunday 8 April   Les Avants

Back home again after a not very pleasant week. It began badly with me arriving at Idlewild last Sunday at 8.45 a.m. to catch the plane and *still* being there at 8 p.m. after a day of misery and frustration. There was fog and the BOAC plane which was *en route* from San Francisco couldn't land. If I had been travelling Pan-Am I could have taken off on time. As it was the whole day was hell. I eventually arrived in London on Monday morning at 9.30 (my stomach time 3.30 a.m.). I naturally didn't feel too well what with my cold and lack of sleep. However, I did my best to rise above it.

I saw three plays: *The Keep*[1], which I couldn't bear; *Look Homeward Angel*[2], not as well done as in New York; and *The School for Scandal*[3] opening night at the Haymarket. Beautifully done, everybody good, particularly Ralph [Richardson] and Anna [Massey], lovely décor and dresses, charm and style, bad notices. Not for the play, of course, which was dull, but for the production and acting which were not. The London critics are even sillier and more ignorant than the New York ones. My feelings about the theatre in both countries are not happy. None of it seems any longer to be worth the trouble.

I lunched with Dickie Mountbatten, Biddy Monckton and Doreen Brabourne and we discussed the Royal Gala Performance of *Sail Away* and,

1 Comedy by Gwyn Thomas.
2 Pulitzer prize-winning play based on Thomas Wolfe's novel.
3 Sheridan's play produced by John Gielgud.

God help me, the suggested cabaret afterwards! I think I'm hooked. However, it's all in two good causes: Edwina's charity fund and publicity for the show.

On Friday Coley and I flew here, gaily clad for spring, and expecting primroses, violets and wild narcissi. What we got was ten feet of snow. So deep was it that we couldn't get the car into the gate. I, feeling like death anyway, retired to bed immediately, where I have been ever since. I have slept and slept and read and slept again and *at last* I am beginning to feel rested.

I've read Ian's latest thriller[1], which starts brilliantly and goes too far as usual, *The Prime Minister*, Trollope, entirely satisfying, and Chris Isherwood's new autobiographical novel[2]. Really very curious. Well-written, intelligent, silly, naive, sophisticated, untidy. Oh dear, what a scrambled mind. Not without charm but certainly without balance.

Sunday 15 April

Joe and Evelyn [Layton] arrived on Wednesday, gay and full of niceness. I love them both very much. It is extraordinary that Joe, having achieved one of his ambitions very early, which was to be a director as well as a choreographer, and having achieved it triumphantly with *No Strings*[3], should show not a sign of being spoiled or grand. He is as full of enthusiasm for *Sail Away* as ever he was. I am thankful to God he is doing it with me. He will be a life-saver as he was before.

Herman Levin[4] has called me up from New York and asked me to do the score and lyrics for *The Sleeping Prince* which is being turned into a musical by Harry Kurnitz[5]. I feel rather torn about this. At the moment I naturally feel that I don't want to have anything to do with an American musical ever in my life again, but this, of course, will pass and I have always loved *The Sleeping Prince*. Also it is period and a perfect period, what's more, for my music and lyrics. I have given an evasive answer.

My photographs of Tahiti and Bora Bora have all been developed and printed and they are absolutely marvellous. The colour is clear and accurate and out of all the rolls I took there were only two or three bad shots. When I think of the time I've wasted with expensive, complicated cameras when all the time I might have had this little $4.50 job, which takes brilliant photographs without having to frig about with focussing or light meters or anything!

Sunday 29 April

Two weeks have gone by and at long last 'frosts are slain and flowers begotten

1 *The Spy Who Loved Me.*
2 *Down There on a Visit.*
3 Richard Rodgers' musical currently on Broadway.
4 Herman Levin (b. 1907), Broadway producer whose productions included *My Fair Lady.*
5 Harry Kurnitz (1907–68), Hollywood screenwriter.

and in green underwood and cover, blossom by blossom the spring begins'. The spring here is really fabulous. Adrianne and Bill are back and their garden is a dream, blazing with hyacinths and daffodils and crocuses. We, being much higher, are not so advanced, but the sun is suddenly hot enough to lie out in and there are only diminishing vestiges of snow on the mountain peaks.

Coley and I went to stay two nights with Lilli [Palmer] and Carlos [Thompson]. They have bought a vast property about forty-five minutes from Zurich and are building a dream house on the top of it. At the moment they are living in what will ultimately be the guest-house. We had a lovely time and they were both enchanting to us.

Willie Maugham and Alan [Searle] came over for lunch. They are staying at the Beau Rivage. Willie looks wonderful, bright as a button. His stammer is a bit heavier and he is a trifle deaf but shows no other signs of being eighty-eight.

We have also had Stritch for five days. She was really very good and I am awfully fond of her but, oh dear, she *is* a problem girl. Coley was wonderful with her and has given her a list of five words which must never again cross her lips – guilt, problem, scared, frightened, insecurity! It is really surprising how many American adults are virtually illiterate, and how very many of them have plunged into psychiatry so that their egos have grown inwards, like toenails. Poor darling Stritch, with all her talents, is almost completely confused about everything. She is an ardent Catholic and never stops saying fuck and Jesus Christ. She is also kind, touching and loyal and, fortunately, devoted to me. She is also, like most Americans, dreadfully noisy. We took her to Evian to gamble and she had a wonderful time, but the sound was depressing.

We packed her into the plane for London yesterday. Apart from her suitcases she had lots of little bags and some dresses wrapped in cellophane on hangers! The hullabaloo was considerable.

I have read a thriller by my godson Alan Williams[1] called *Long Road South* and it is really very good indeed. He is an authentic writer. There is, as with all his generation, too much emphasis on sex, squalor and torture and horror, but it's graphically and imaginatively written.

Saturday 5 May   Hôtel Lotti, Paris

Here I am comfortably installed in a small room with douche under the eaves. I leave for London this afternoon. I left Montreux on the night train on Wednesday after a very 'old times' reminiscent dinner at Les Avants, with Adrianne, Bill, Bobby Andrews and Phyl Monkman. It was great fun and I regretted having to bowl down the hill to catch my train. Phyl looks marvellous considering she must be seventy or more. So many memories came flooding back. Bobby was cheerful, his older self became almost his old self. We

1   Alan Williams, novelist son of Emlyn.

plunged back into long-ago gaieties and I finally settled myself in my wagon-lit in a welter of nostalgia.

On Thursday night, Ginette and I dined at Le Bistroquet and then went to the Olympia to see Marlene, who really was marvellous. I have never seen her so good. She has learned a lot during those racketings from capital to capital, and now puts her numbers over with far more authority and technique. Afterwards we supped at the Club d'Elysée and it was 'gay and sweet and terribly exciting'[1], and we were joined by Burt Bacharach[2] and got into a discussion about crabs. Marlene sorrowfully announced that she had once had them for Christmas.

The next morning – last night, to be exact – there was a cocktail rout at 70 Avenue Marceau: Marlene, Marti [Stevens], Maurice Chevalier, Paul-Emile, etc.

Sunday 13 May   Paris

Me voici back again. The first week of rehearsals is behind me and I must say I am more than delighted. Joe has achieved prodigies with the dancers who are, under his choreography, actually better than our New York lot. Stritch is really trying her utmost and is at last beginning to get the sentimental values right. We – Coley, Graham and I – took her, Joe and Grover [Dale] to The Cricketers on Sunday night and it was a triumphant success. Everyone sang and enjoyed themselves and the good old 'English pub' atmosphere entranced our transatlantic visitors.

On Tuesday Stritch, Gladys, Coley and I went to the opening of *Blitz*[3]. From the production point of view it was marvellous, but alas the book and the direction were bad. The music and lyrics are fairly good but the whole thing is overwhelmed by Mr Sean Kenny's moving sets which never stay still for a minute. It got pretty bad notices on the whole but I think it will be a hit. I am sorry for Lionel Bart, he has rich talents, but in this he aimed too high. It probably won't do him any harm to fail a little. God knows we all have to go through it from time to time.

Arnold Wesker, on the other hand, has written a bitter, exciting and moving play called *Chips with Everything*. It is full of good theatre and brilliantly directed by John Dexter. The acting is superb and Frank Finlay and John Kelland are remarkable. Only every now and then does class hatred rear its ugly head; in fact I do really believe that Arnold has taken a little heed of my sharp *Sunday Times* articles and realized that too much obvious propaganda spoils the broth. Anyhow, it was a wonderful evening in the theatre.

I visited Diana Cooper in her new house in Warwick Avenue. She looked

1 From a 1932 song of Noël's, 'Let's Say Goodbye'.
2 Burt Bacharach (b. 1929), American composer, then Dietrich's conductor-arranger.
3 Lionel Bart's epic World War Two musical at the Adelphi.

fabulously lovely and pathetic. She will never get over Duff's death and never be really happy again, but she puts on a magnificent front and talking to her was light and magic like it always has been.

On Friday I flew here with Binkie. We gossiped incessantly all the way over and he was at his best. I discovered a lot. Unfortunately his hand has lost its cunning as far as dealing with people is concerned. He came over to persuade Marlene to appear at Her Majesty's in June and to persuade Louis Jourdan to play Lancelot in *Camelot*. He handled neither of these missions very successfully.

Sunday 27 May   Paris

Two more weeks have passed during which a great deal has happened. First of all there has been the threatened strike of musicians, which has been a terrible worry. For a while it really looked as though *Sail Away* would not be able to open. This would have been real disaster not only for Harold Fielding, who has already invested over £40,000 in it, but for me and everyone concerned. However, Harold, who is nothing if not smart, suddenly resigned from the West End Managers' Association and came to a private agreement with the Musicians' Union. So we now have an orchestra guaranteed for two years whether the others strike or not! I am immensely relieved and, although I cannot entirely take off my hat to him morally, I can certainly drop a grateful curtsey to his guts and determination. I cannot feel that the other managers will be altogether pleased. If the strike *does* start we shall be the only musical playing!

Rehearsals have continued to go well and I am really pleased with the whole company. Last Saturday I went with Stritch and the Laytons to the farewell of the Crazy Gang, a very moving occasion. On the Sunday night I endured a 'tribute' to me from the Gallery First Nighters Club. It took the form of a dinner and cabaret in the banqueting hall of the Criterion. Poor wretched Leslie Bloom, the President, who had been waiting for the great moment for years, was stricken with gastro-enteritis and couldn't be present.

I saw Peter Shaffer's two one-acters at the Globe[1], exquisite both of them and wonderfully played. I also saw *Castle in Sweden*[2], which was pretentious and boring although well acted.

I flew here on Thursday night with Gloria in Loel's private jet! It is fetching me on Tuesday night to take me in style to Bristol! On arrival here I received a perfectly sweet small Corot oil painting from Rosita Winston! All these exclamation marks are to prove the highness of my life at the moment. I have agreed to do the score and lyrics for *The Sleeping Prince* for Herman Levin.

1   *The Private Ear* and *The Public Eye*.
2   By Françoise Sagan.

Harry Kurnitz is doing the book and Cecil [Beaton], I hope, the décor and dresses.

Princess Marina came to a rehearsal and was as dear as ever. I dined with Marlene the night before last and she was at her best. Life, on the whole, is not entirely without interest.

Tuesday 5 June   Bristol

I arrived in style last Tuesday in Loel's private jet. Three pilots, two steward-esses, one steward and me. The Press and Coley greeted me and it all caused a minor sensation. We had a couple of gruelling dress rehearsals. The show opened on Thursday night and was a triumphant success. Stritch tore the place up and I made a tactful speech at the end and led various actors forward. The notices were good. The production is lovely, Loudon has done a wonder-ful job. The Parthenon set is the only failure on account of being, surprisingly, raspberry pink. However, this is being redone. David Holliday is quite re-markable. His voice is lovely and he can really act with truth and sincerity. He is a dear boy and I'm very proud of him. Grover was not good on the first night but has improved since. Cary Grant[1] came to the second performance and couldn't have been nicer, sweeter and more enthusiastic.

Monday 2 July   Les Avants

There has been a considerable gap since my last entry. The opening night and the Royal Gala and all their excitements are now behind me and I can now relax for a little and then start work on the score and music for *The Sleeping Prince*.

Sail Away is a smash hit and the advance is tremendous. The opening night was triumphant from beginning to end. The audience was warm and friendly from the moment the curtain went up, and at the end Stritchie got a tumul-tuous ovation. My party consisted of Joycie, Gladys, Graham, Coley and Jack Merivale. Vivien crept in for the last scene. Later there was a gathering in my suite and she and Kenny More got fried and flung four-letter words about like confetti, but it was all nice dirty fun and nobody seemed to mind except me, who wished they would go home. The little American group consisting of Stritchie, David [Holliday] and Grover [Dale] behaved impeccably, and so it was all the more irritating that big glamorous English stars should make such asses of themselves.

The next morning the notices, with the exception of *The Times*, were just as mean and grudging and unkind as I had expected them to be. The *Telegraph* wasn't bad, if a trifle patronizing, and Milton Shulman in the *Evening Standard* was quite civil for once. The rest, and also the Sunday papers, were degrading.

1 Cary Grant (b. 1904), the British-born film star long resident in Hollywood was visiting his
   family in Bristol.

They hate me very much, these little men. Fortunately they were all enthusiastic about Stritch and the show was quite obviously a hit from the word go, so it really doesn't matter. There is no doubt, however, that these continual streams of abuse I get whenever I put anything on the stage *are* a bit discouraging. It would be so nice, just for once, to receive a little generosity or at least a little justice, but I fear that there is small likelihood of that happening so long as I continue to entertain the public.

We recorded the cast album on Sunday, Monday and Tuesday, which was exhausting, but I think it will be good.

The Royal Gala was highly successful on Thursday night. It was all beautifully organized and the Queen looked dazzlingly beautiful, so, for that matter, did Prince Philip. I presented Stritch and Joe in the entr'acte, Joe resplendent in a Moss Bros tail suit. After it was all over and the Queen had departed amid cheering crowds, Vivien, Jack, Joyce, Coley and I drove to Charing Cross pier and embarked on the Harold Fielding boat for a perishing trip down the river. It was a very well done party and quite enjoyable. Stritch, however, overcome by the strain of curtseying twice to the Queen, proceeded to get exuberant, made a great deal of noise and threw a lot of champagne glasses into the river. The next day she was filled with remorse, guilt and basic insecurity, all of which was enhanced by me ticking her off. I do really love her very much, but I wish she wasn't a dear little delinquent of thirty-six!

On Friday I took an understudy rehearsal, which was very satisfactory, and went with Graham to Covent Garden to see Nureyev and Margot Fonteyn in *Giselle*. She was marvellous and he, of course, remarkable, but a thought too pleased with himself. I had already made a vow never to see *Giselle* again. It is a ghastly ballet and I loathe it, and so help me God that was the last time.

I lunched with Liza and John Hope and had a heart-to-heart with Liza, who is miserable over the 'picture' feud[1]. There may be faults on both sides, but I cannot feel that dear W. Somerset Maugham has behaved very nicely. He is devoured by retrospective hate of poor Syrie and it has become an obsession.

I have read the Oscar Wilde letters and have come to the reluctant conclusion that he was one of the silliest, most conceited and unattractive characters that ever existed. His love letters to Lord Alfred Douglas are humourless, affected and embarrassing, and his crawling letter from prison to the Home Secretary beneath contempt. *De Profundis* is one long wail of self-pity. It is extraordinary indeed that such a posing, artificial old queen should have written one of the greatest comedies in the English language. In my opinion it was the only thing of the least *importance* that he did write.

I flew to Paris on Saturday morning, lunched with Harry [Kurnitz] and

---

1 Which centred on Somerset Maugham's decision to adopt his secretary Alan Searle as his son, thus making Searle, and not Maugham's only child Liza, heir to most of the estate.

Herman Levin and Swifty [Lazar], and conferred about *The Sleeping Prince* all the afternoon. Harry has done half the first act and I am absolutely delighted with it. If he keeps it up we shall have a hit, provided that I can do a good score and good lyrics, which I think and hope I can. On Sunday night, after dinner with Swifty, Herman, Harry, Howard Hughes[1], etc., I boarded the night train and arrived here this morning. The house looks sweet, the staff are smiling. Toto is lyrical and God, I presume, is in his heaven.

Monday 9 July

There has been a tremendous drama over Godfrey Winn[2] and his first-night seats. He was infuriated at being offered row O and wrote an abusive letter to poor Lornie saying it was an affront to his reputation as a writer! She wrote back tartly and firmly, and then another blazing effusion arrived, really quite unbelievable. He is obviously off his rocker. Which brings me with a jolt to the wretched Charles [Russell], who is making a hysterical, cracking fool of himself and consulting lawyers to bring suits against me. This is another case of ego blown up so big that it bursts and causes a sort of mental peritonitis. It's all hideously unpleasant and has made me ashamed of ever having been fond of him. He has certainly sent the scales whizzing down from my eyes. I could never have believed he could be so deeply horrible. Oh dear. It is a discouraging world at times.

On the credit side, however, *Sail Away* is a smash. Pat Wallace came out in the *Tatler* with a rave review, a rave in the right way. I am very grateful to her for saying quite a lot that should be said, particularly about the general attitude of the critics to me and my work.

I have already roughed out three numbers for *The Sleeping Prince* and I find that the talent is still there waiting to drip off my fingers. It *is* a comfort.

Monday 16 July

Harry Kurnitz has been here for a week. He is a dear character and I love him very much. He has nearly finished the first draft of act one and it is perfectly enchanting. I am really excited about it and I have a strong feeling that if my music and lyrics are good enough we should have a smash hit. Still, there's many a slip. However, I am thoroughly enthusiastic and have already done a good point number, 'Put Not Your Trust in Princes', and a lovely ballad with no lyrics as yet.

Coley and I had a session about my business affairs and it has been decided to give up my domicile in Bermuda, which I have never approved of, and become resident here [Switzerland]. The tax situation is more than reasonable

1 Howard Hughes (1905–76), the eccentric American millionaire.
2 Godfrey Winn (1908–72), British journalist and author; as a young man he had appeared in Noël's *The Marquise* (1927).

and now apparently I can spend six months a year in England if I want to. This is a great comfort.

There has been another six-page letter of gibbering paranoia from Godfrey Winn to Adrianne, which she has answered with dignified restraint. The poor little creature is really making a screaming ass of himself.

I am rereading Dakin's *Life of Mary Baker Eddy*. It is a brilliantly satisfactory biography. I had forgotten how good it was. Her curious life is a monument to the incredible gullibility of the human race. It is also an astounding proof of what can be achieved by utterly humourless egomania. The poor woman was obviously mentally adrift from the age of five, querulous, hysterical, unscrupulous, snobbish and almost unbelievably stupid, and yet by sheer determination she achieved everything she thought she wanted. I say 'thought she wanted' advisedly because her life was fairly wretched. I think hers must be the greatest case of self-deception in history. To be a moral thief, an unblushing liar, a supreme dictator, and a cruel, self-satisfied monster, and attain, in the minds of millions, the status of a deity, is not only remarkable but a dismal reflection on the human race. She had much in common with Hitler, only no moustache.

Sunday 29 July

I flew to London last Friday and went to *Sail Away* with Lornie the night I arrived. The house was packed with a wonderful audience and the whole company gave a fine performance.

Princess Marina came with Princess Chichibu [of Japan] and there was a great hoo-ha. In the entr'acte poor Princess Marina fainted dead away on the stairs. I flew about with glasses of iced water, which she upset over herself until she was lying in a sort of marsh. Poor dear, I was dreadfully sorry for her because she was really distressed. However, I finally packed her off home in a car and returned to cope with Princess Chichibu, who turned out to be a living Japanese doll.

I saw *The Collection* by Harold Pinter and was immensely impressed. He is the only one of the *soi-disant* avant-garde who has genuine originality. I saw Graham in a thriller at Windsor and he was really excellent. I also drove to Chichester with Joyce to see Larry's production of *Uncle Vanya*[1], which was sheer magic. The entire cast was wonderful, especially Mike Redgrave, Joan Plowright and Larry. A really glorious experience.

Charles is still huffing and puffing and threatening dire law suits. Godfrey Winn is still writing incredible letters. Kay Thompson is staying here. I suddenly bought a new Steinway yesterday and it's bliss. I've written a lovely song, 'I'll Remember Her'. Kay is going to Niehans for treatment. Rebecca West and Mary Borden lunched with me in London on different days. Both

1 Chekhov's play.

enraged about Willie Maugham publishing his disgusting autobiography in an American magazine. It really is beneath contempt and crucifies the wretched Syrie. I don't think I want to see him again.

Monday 6 August

It has been a successful week. Kay and I have played double pianos almost incessantly with the result that several new tunes have emerged. She is really a tremendous help; she goes off into a rhythmic accompaniment and I compose a melodic line against it. Tomorrow Coley and I join Gloria [Guinness] and Harry [Kurnitz] at Geneva Airport and fly to Sardinia for a visit in a private Viscount. Loel's plane is temporarily occupied in flying some Eastern potentate across far-away deserts. The yacht will be waiting for us in Sardinia and then hurrah for the hols, except that a good deal of work will have to be done with Harry over the book, which is still far too long.

Marilyn Monroe committed suicide yesterday. The usual overdose. Poor silly creature. I am convinced that what brought her to that final foolish gesture was a steady diet of intellectual pretentiousness pumped into her over the years by Arthur Miller, and 'The Method'. She was, to begin with, a fairly normal little sexpot with exploitable curves and a certain natural talent. I am sure that all the idiocies of her last few years, always being late on the set, etc., plus over-publicity and too many theoretical discussions about acting, were the result of all this constant analysis of every line in every part she had to play, and a desperate longing to be 'intellectual' without the brain to achieve it. It is a sad comment on contemporary values that a beautiful, famous and wealthy young woman of thirty-six should capriciously kill herself for want of a little self-discipline and horse-sense. Judy [Garland] and Vivien in their different ways are in the same plight. Too much too soon and too little often.

I have read Willie Maugham's final spate of venom in *Show Magazine*. It is well written and entirely contemptible.

Sunday 19 August   Rome

Well, the yachting holiday is over and here I am in solitary splendour in the Eternal City out of season, which is very relaxing and just what I want. The holiday, taken by and large, was a great success. Gloria and Loel were sweet and kind and the food was glorious, so glorious indeed that I am now living on salads and cold ham. We flew from Geneva to Sardinia in a private Viscount which took an hour and a half. We then drove to the coast and embarked on the yacht, which sailed immediately to a remote corner of the island where we remained for three days, lashed by a mistral. The weather was blazing hot and sunny but the mistral was, as it usually is, maddening. However, after the third day it blew itself out and we bathed and lay in the sun and visited the property Loel has bought. It looked a bit arid to me, but that is his affair.

When we finally left Sardinia we spent one night at Porto Vecchio in Corsica and the next two at Elba, Portoferraio and Porto Azzurro, both of which were enchanting. From there we set sail for Portofino, which was lovely. Here Rex and Rachel[1] were with us for most of the two days we were there. We aroused Rex's interest in *Sleeping Prince* and I sang him 'I'll Remember Her', which obviously impressed him. We sailed from Portofino to Monte Carlo, where we spent one hectic night, and then Antibes the next morning. Gloria and Loel are possibly the only rich people I know with whom it is possible to have a good time, but even they are a bit tricky just because they *are* rich. Stone walls do not a prison make nor iron bars a cage, but millions of pounds can make, very subtly, both.

Tuesday 28 August   Les Avants

Home again. Glorious weather – house looking lovely – Graham and Coley looking lovely – staff looking lovely. My week in Rome was a complete success. I have a little fallen in love with the Eternal City. Kay [Thompson] came back the last day I was there and we dined peacefully, and sat afterwards on the Via Veneto and had ice creams while we watched the gay throng of hustlers, pimps, queens, faggots, priests and tourists ambling past. I left Rome with regret.

I've just reread *Cakes and Ale*. A brilliant novel but, oh, how poor Willie's unfortunate character shines through it. There is neither kindness nor compassion in it, wit, narrative quality, diamond-sharp observation, one or two streaks of profound vulgarity, much malice and no heart. Considering that he wrote it in 1930 it is not surprising that now, in 1962, he should be writing with even more venom. I think this particular spiritual malaise, allied to certain annoying literary mannerisms, may dim his posterity.

I am waiting in a state of suspended frustration for Harry's completed script of *The Sleeping Prince*. Apparently, owing to Joe Layton having to do another show first, this will not be done until next autumn. I don't much mind, but it is a danger to enthusiasm. In the meanwhile, however, I must really get back to my pens and paper and typewriter. I have an idea of doing a series of short plays, two a night, under the collective title of *Neutral Territory*; each play, separate in itself, will take place in a hotel suite in Switzerland. I intend to write them for myself as a sort of acting orgy swan-song. It is a fascinating project if I can get enough variety into it.

Sunday 9 September

We – Coley, Graham and I – spent an enchanting and curious evening with Marlene and Marti [Stevens] and the youngest grandchild[2], eighteen months,

1 Rachel Roberts (1927–80), British actress whom Rex Harrison had married after Kay Kendall's death.
2 Of Marlene's, by her only child, Maria.

who I must say was beguiling. Marlene – incognito in a black wig at dinner in the inn next door – still contriving to look lovely. Before this, *without* the black wig, we watched her under the summer trees, changing, expertly, the baby's napkin and feeding it and, later, bathing it. All done with indestructible glamour and, for Marlene, considerable humour.

Above and below and aside and apart from all this, I finished my long-short story, *Me and the Girls*, and I think it is good. The balance between comedy and tragedy was difficult to achieve but I think I've achieved it. I have also written two complicated refrains for 'Long Live the King'. *I* can sing them but whether or not Rex will be able to remains to be seen. Tonight we are taking Adrianne to dine at the Montreux Palace and then to Verdi's *Requiem*. The Montreux Festival Musicale is still flourishing.

Tuesday 18 September

Last Monday night's performance of *Sail Away* was excellent, and the business was up £1,000 on the week before. Harold Fielding has done a new library deal, which will take us comfortably into December, by which time I shall have taken myself comfortably to Jamaica.

Hester Chapman came to lunch looking handsome and distinguished. Coley, Graham and I, all looking handsome and distinguished, drove down to lunch with Vivien at Tickeridge[1]. She was at her tiptop best, calm and wise and pretty and *off* the bottle. Then we drove back and took George Cukor to dinner and on to The Cricketers, which was a howling success. Everybody sang and I think our transatlantic visitors were truly impressed by the uninhibited enjoyment of Londoners.

Tuesday 25 September

Today I am going to Paris and returning on Friday night. George Axelrod[2] rang me up and asked me to play a small but effective part in the movie[3] he is doing with Audrey Hepburn and Bill Holden. He hurried the script to me and the scene *is* effective although tiny, but I am being paid $10,000 and all luxe expenses, and so I said yes. I think it will be rather fun. The part is that of a Hungarian movie producer (Alex Korda?) dressed in a Roman toga at a fancy dress party. I shall enjoy doing the accent.

I went into Lausanne and had all the tests done on my leg, and it looks as though I shall have to have the operation, probably next week. They will put in a plastic artery! I shall have to be in hospital for fifteen days! But still, if it has to be done I had better get on with it.

I have made up my lifelong feud with Edith Sitwell. I wrote her a fan letter

1 The house she had bought in Sussex.
2 George Axelrod (b. 1922), American comedy writer and dramatist.
3 *Paris When It Sizzles*.

about her book[1] which, in spite of what Hester and other lady writers may say, is wonderfully readable and, at moments, brilliant. Anyhow, she sent me a sweet and friendly telegram back and I shall go and see her when I'm in London at the beginning of November. Coley and I have decided to sail with Vivien on 16 November on the *Q.E.* or the *France.*

Meanwhile, I've written another article for the *Sunday Times* about the nonsense that is talked and written about the theatre in these so glorious days. I think it is quite funny. At least it is sensible. The amount of balls talked by the modern young directors and printed in the *Sunday Times* supplement is not to be believed.

Coley and I went to two concerts running. Cziffra – a Hungarian pianist – on Thursday, very enjoyable if not quite first rate; and dear Artur Rubinstein on Friday, this time with Adrianne. He played the Schumann Concerto with exquisite taste but he is, poor darling, looking a bit old.

George Cukor is staying. He arrived on Sunday and is leaving with me today. He is a dear and I love him very much.

Monday 1 October

My four days' sojourn in Paris was really an unqualified success. George and I left on the new crack train which leaves Lausanne at 6.10 and arrives in Paris at 10.50. It was smooth and comfortable. We were met by George and Joan Axelrod and I was conducted in state to the suite at the Bristol which they had engaged for me. A duplex suite with five bedrooms, library, dining-room, salon, private lift, etc. It took me quite a while to find my way about it.

George A. said that they did *not* want me to play the part with an accent but to be super Noël Coward. This rather threw me; however, I decided to use irrepressible laughter as the basis of my performance and just wing it on that one technical trick. It worked like a charm and I have never had such a fuss made. Dick Quine, the director, and a sweet man, carried on alarming. Audrey H, unquestionably the nicest and most talented girl in the business, deluged me with praise and roses. Bill Holden, *off* the bottle and looking fifteen years younger, absolutely charming to work with. We exchanged confidences and bottles of eau de cologne in the interminable waits. The set, the Eiffel Tower Restaurant, was marvellous, but the heat of the lights appalling. I worked for three days dressed in a white and gold satin tunic, laced up gold boots, a magnificent scarlet, gold-fringed cloak, and a wreath of gilt leaves on my head! George showed me about half of the picture – rough-cut; it really is very funny and Audrey and Bill are enchanting. So is Tony Curtis and so, apparently, am I. So that is a neat little job done. I did my big speech in two takes without fluffing once, and I must say I thoroughly enjoyed myself. I like the shooting hours in Paris – twelve o'clock to 7.30 straight through.

1 *The Queens and The Hive* (1962).

I dined one night with Ginette and George Axelrod. The next night with Dick Quine, Kim Novak[1], Bill [Holden], George [Axelrod], and Capucine[2], who is a dear. The third night by myself. Heaven. And the last night with George Cukor.

I don't think I want to play a very, very long movie, but I do like nipping in and playing a good scene or two. I am much more relaxed in front of the camera than I used to be.

Tuesday 16 October

Two uncomfortable weeks have gone by. Uncomfortable for me because I finally got a room in the Central Hospital, where I subjected myself to an examinatory treatment under anaesthetic and came to feeling dreadful. I was told the next morning by Dr Mosimann, who showed me x-rays, that I should have to have a major operation, or rather three operations in one.

In the meantime, Rebecca West arrived to stay and wanted to see Niehans. Coley called him and he said he was dreadfully worried about me being operated on as he did not consider it necessary. I went to see him with Rebecca and he explained that surgeons, however brilliant, only think surgically, and that surgery isn't inevitably the sure answer. He outlined his own idea of injecting me with placenta, and says that in a few months it is more than probable that new cells will form fresh arteries. I have agreed to go into his Clinique and have the lot – rejuvenation shots and all. I don't see how they can do me any harm and they *might* do me a lot of good. At any rate it will enforce my not smoking and not drinking, which *must* do me good. I have a profound respect for the old boy. He has, I believe, a streak of genius. Everyone I know who has been treated by him swears that he is marvellous. Hedda [Hopper], Gloria Swanson, Ram Gopal, Willie Maugham, etc. They can't *all* be idiotic! Anyhow, I really don't relish a major operation at my age and if it can possibly be avoided I intend to avoid it.

Rebecca, on her first night here, had a dreadful *crise* of her gall-bladder, and Dr Spuhler was sent for and stuffed her full of morphine. She is now fine after three days in bed. She is also a sweet house guest, gay and considerate and, oh, how gloriously intelligent. Rebecca and I are going into the Clinique together on Wednesday evening. Coley has thought of our theme song, 'I've Got EWE under my Skin'.

The Lunts arrive shortly. I have given up smoking and sleeping pills and look forward to a drugless future.

1 Kim Novak (b. 1933), the American film star.
2 Capucine (b. 1933), French model and film actress.

Wednesday 24 October

Well, it's all over and done with and my system is now overrun by jostling crowds of fresh cells which, I presume, are joining up and dividing and multiplying and subtracting and generally doing what comes naturally. The actual operation was painful but not intolerably so. What I hadn't anticipated was that it would be funny. This it was, owing to the time element. It was all done at the double. The door of my room burst open and in flew Professor Niehans robed in white like an archangel, accompanied by two firm, blonde German nurses and wheeling a sort of aluminium cocktail cabinet filled with vast syringes all containing different liquids in pastel shades. In a twinkling they hurled me on to my face, the doctor cried 'prick' in a hoarse voice and plunged the first syringe into my bottom – I gritted my teeth and gasped. This happened five times on my right buttock and twice on my left. They then flew out and left me spread-eagled on my face. Half an hour later they returned and Niehans plunged one last and enormous syringe into me and that was that. My bottom was stiff for a bit but not really bad. Apart from this I have suffered no inconvenience. The Clinique is beautifully run, the nurses wonderful and the food excellent. I have had five days of complete rest and feel fine. It now remains to be seen whether or not the fresh cells dilate my veins and arteries and thereby avoid the necessity of the major operation next spring. I have a curious, hopeful feeling that this may happen. As far as the rejuvenation lark goes, for that also we must await results for three months, and then! *Quien sabe?*

The Lunts arrived yesterday, bright as buttons and looking splendid. Herman Levin, Joe and Harry arrive on Sunday week. Then on 7 November we have the momentous meeting with Rex in Paris[1], after that a week in London, and Cole and I sail on 20 November on the dear old *Queen Mary*.

The Lunts are terribly anxious for me to write a farewell play for them[2] and, of course, last night an idea came – whether it will develop or not remains to be seen. It's to be called *Rehearsal Period* or perhaps *Swan Song*, and concerns two elderly stars, separated thirty years before, coming together again in the course of rehearsing a new play. The whole thing should be done on a bare stage during the three weeks' rehearsal period. It feels hopeful to me. I want it to be pure comedy with just a couple of sentimental moments. I wonder, oh, I wonder!

President Kennedy has delivered an ultimatum forbidding *any* ships to take arms to Cuba. We presume that if a ship disobliges it will be summarily sunk. This, my darling, means war! Isn't that fun?

---

1 To decide whether or not he would play the Prince Regent in *The Girl Who Came to Supper*.
2 Both Lunts were by now over seventy.

Sunday 11 November

Since I last addressed myself to these pages a great deal has happened. The world crisis is now over and Kennedy's determination won the day. So far, at least. Khrushchev has dismantled the missile bases in Cuba and international hysteria has subsided. Dear Mrs Roosevelt is dead, which saddens me because I was very fond of her.

The Lunts' visit was a terrific success and they were as sweet and dear as ever.

The last few days have been a little bit of a strain. Herman, Harry and Joe in the house and endless *Sleeping Prince* discussions. Actually it is all coming along very well. Joe has had some brilliant reconstruction ideas with which he mowed down the wretched Harry on the first evening. I lectured him the next morning on lack of tact and he was suitably contrite. Darling Joe. He really is an enchanting character, and I am so thankful he is directing the show. Incidentally, I think I have found a title in the lyric of the first big ballad, 'Come Be My True Love'. Joe is very keen for Florence Henderson to play Mary. So am I, if all he says of her is true. I only saw her once, in Joe's *Gershwin Years* on television, and loved her. Since then she has been a triumphant success in the first road company of *Sound of Music*. Joe says her voice is wonderful. So let's cross everything.

I've just ploughed through Cecil Woodham Smith's new book, *The Great Hunger*. It is tremendously well done but depressing. Not that I expected a book concerned exclusively with the Irish potato famine to be one long crescendo of belly-laughs, but it is a bit too gruesome, I think, also too repetitious. I am now in the middle of Allen Drury's *A Shade of Difference*. It's really excellent, very entertaining, almost better than *Advise and Consent*. Too many split infinitives, but you can't have everything.

I may have to pop over to London next Wednesday to endure a few auditions with Herman. Coley has retired to bed with a sore throat. I hope it's not going to turn into anything.

Wednesday 21 November

I *did* go to London last Wednesday and endured two days of auditions with happy results, because we found an excellent boy and girl for the King and Louisa respectively, and also Richard Wattis, I think, will sign. Martita Hunt has made an ass of herself and says she *cannot* appear in a vulgarized edition of dear Terry's play. If she's going to carry on like that we're better off without her. I think Brownie [Irene Browne] is the next best bet. George Sanders *won't* do it, so now Herman is in New York concentrating on Chris Plummer.

I had a blazing scene with Ian Bevan[1] on the telephone. Harold Fielding has embarked on a 'new' advertising campaign which consists of dropping Stritch's

1 A member of Harold Fielding's production team.

name and my name from the bills entirely! This, apart from being breach of contract, is imbecile. I think the poor little creature is barmy. Stritch, naturally enough, is upset. The show is jogging along all right. A long way off capacity but quite satisfactory.

I went to *Rattle of a Simple Man*[1] and enjoyed it. Edward Woodward marvellous, Sheila Hancock excellent, not *quite* as good as he is, but very nearly. Altogether a rewarding evening in the theatre.

On Sunday I went to tea with Edith Sitwell in her flat in Hampstead. I must say I found her completely charming, very amusing and rather touching. How strange that a forty-year feud should finish so gracefully and so suddenly. I am awfully glad. She gave me her new slim volume of poems. I am fairly unrepentant about her poetry. I really think that three-quarters of it is gibberish. However, I must crush down these thoughts otherwise the dove of peace will shit on me.

Saw *Dr No* all by myself. Thoroughly enjoyable but, of course, idiotic. I'm glad I didn't play it.[2] Arrived back the day before yesterday with streaming eyes, a lacerated gum and an incipient cold. Coley still choking. Deep snow. Oh dear!

Tuesday 4 December

I have been, as usual, a martyr to minor ailments. I have conjunctivitis, which means that my eyes are bloodshot and I look ghastly. I have a 'chapped' face on account of the extreme cold which is, today, twelve below zero. However, in spite of these manifestations of wrong thought, I am very well. I have taken to walking! Every day I stride off and do three or four kilometres. The basic idea of this is to force blood through the failing artery in my right leg, which I *think* it is beginning to do. What is so curious is that I am beginning to enjoy it. It is painful every now and then, but then I stop and look at the view until the pain stops and I am able to press on again. I usually make Enzio drive me up to above Souloup and leave me there to walk down. *Up* hill I really cannot manage.

The Christmas miseries are upon us. I have signed millions of Christmas cards. Coley is working like a slave.

My volume of collected short stories is out and seems to be quite a success. I am waiting daily for the 'Niehans' metamorphosis to take place, but nothing spectacular has happened so far. I long to smoke sometimes, but the misery is lessening.

---

1 By Charles Dyer at the Garrick.
2 The first of the Fleming novels to be filmed; Ian had asked Noël to play Dr No, to which Noël had replied, 'No, no, no, a thousand times no!'

Tuesday 11 December   London

Coley and I left Les Avants in fine style on Wednesday morning, and then spent until 6.30 in Geneva airport because the fog in England prevented planes from coming in. The next morning we took off, arrived at Gatwick and drove to London. In the evening *and* the fog I went by myself to see Larry in *Semi-Detached*[1]. It had had vile notices and I prayed it would be good. But it wasn't. It's a dreary, untidy little play with Larry good in spots. Oh, what a bad judge he is. To do this play was a major mistake.

On Friday I lunched with Liza and John Hope and drove to Fairlawne where the Cazalets[2] received us cosily. Altogether a lovely weekend. The Queen Mother absolutely enchanting and particularly sweet to me. I really do love her very much. We discussed all sorts of forbidden topics such as the abdication, my long-ago refused knighthood, Tony Armstrong-Jones, etc. The other guests, apart from the Hopes and me, were Virginia [Cowles] and Aidan Crawley, and Martin Gilliat[3], all very nice. I had to leave on Sunday evening and drive up to the Savoy to dine with Herman [Levin], Harry [Kurnitz] and Christopher Plummer and wife[4]. After dinner I played him the score and he seemed impressed. I hope he'll do it, he has great charm. I'm not *absolutely* sure that he's right for it, but we shall see.

On Monday I lunched with Joyce and did some shopping, and in the evening took Rebecca to the première of *Lawrence of Arabia*. It was a grand gala with the Queen, Prince Philip and all. A truly magnificent picture, brilliantly directed[5] and acted and superbly photographed. Peter O'Toole[6] very fine and far, far more attractive than Lawrence could ever hope to be. I said to him afterwards that if Lawrence had looked like him there would have been many more than twelve Turks queueing up for the buggering session. The picture is, I suppose, a bit too long – four hours! But it held me riveted all the time. The party afterwards at Grosvenor House was vast and ghastly and, of course, *very* late because we didn't get out of the Odeon until twenty to one.

Lily Elsie[7] is dead. So is Pops d'Erlanger. Very sad.

Christopher Plummer has turned down *The Sleeping Prince*. So now what?

---

1 By David Turner.
2 Peter Cazalet, the Queen Mother's racehorse trainer, and his wife Zara.
3 Martin Gilliat (b. 1913), Private Secretary to Queen Elizabeth the Queen Mother since 1956.
4 Christopher Plummer (b. 1929), Canadian stage and film actor, and his second wife, journalist Patricia Lewis.
5 By David Lean.
6 Peter O'Toole (b. 1932), Irish-born actor.
7 Lily Elsie, musical comedy star of the 1920s.

Thursday 20 December   Les Avants

The rest of the London visit passed in a whirl. I became sixty-three on Sunday and Gladys gave a party – quite fun, but no party is one hundred per cent enjoyable if you neither drink nor smoke. However, I rose above it. It was a cheerfully mixed bag.

I saw *The Tulip Tree*, a charming play by N. C. Hunter with Celia [Johnson] and John Clements giving lovely performances. Needless to say it got bad notices, but then Norman Hunter never gets good ones, neither does he ever write bad plays. I suppose they resent his quality and class. On the same evening I went to the opening of *King Lear*. It was very fine and Paul Scofield was superb. It was *too long*, however, and as usual I found a great deal of the first part of the play incomprehensible.

A lovely photograph arrived, frame and all, from the Queen Mother with a sweet letter. I had two social lunch parties, one with the Lunts at Sybil Cholmondeley's, and the other, without the Lunts, at Annie [Fleming]'s. Diana Cooper, Debo [Devonshire], Paddy Leigh Fermor, etc. Very enjoyable. I had tea with Princess Marina and Princess Olga and the young enchanted: Angus Ogilvy seems extremely nice and Princess Alexandra obviously radiant[1].

I went to a cocktail 'do' at the Freres to meet John Steinbeck[2].

On Sunday, my natal day, I did a taped broadcast to the Commonwealth and, in the afternoon, saw with Joyce, Coley and Graham a private showing of Terry Rattigan's television play, *Heart to Heart*. Goodish only and much too slow. Tea with Joyce Grenfell and then a snooze and my packing. Quite a day.

Lunched with Binkie on Monday before flying here. Marlene is here, having been through the Niehans mill. She is being very sweet and tranquil.

Monday 31 December

Tomorrow 1963 begins and today 1962 is expiring in a splutter of gossip. The Duke of Windsor has been attacked in the Press for having hob-nobbed with Hitler in the late thirties. Secret papers have disclosed his pro-Nazi perfidy which, of course, I was perfectly aware of at the time. Poor dear, what a monumental ass he has always been! William Somerset Maugham has adopted Alan Searle as his son and is suing Liza under French law for, apparently, everything he has given her. It really is very silly indeed and he is making a

---

1 The Princess had recently become engaged to businessman Angus Ogilvy, son of the Earl of Airlie.

2 John Steinbeck (1902-68), the American novelist, whose books were published in England by Heinemann.

cracking fool of himself. The newspapers are sending him up sky-high, of course. Perhaps it is not a good idea to live quite so long.

The Chevreau d'Antraigues' party was fairly disastrous but mercifully brief. Marlene was in a bad temper at having to go and wasn't very gracious. As a matter of fact, the whole thing was a bore. Marti [Stevens] and Kay [Thompson] arrived from Rome, Graham from London. We have descended the mountain several times on luges and bob-sleighs, not really at breakneck speed because the snow is too soft. We fly to London tomorrow.

Sail Away is not doing well and Harold Fielding is threatening to put the notice up. I don't somehow think he will just yet. It's very disappointing. It has the aura of success about it but actually has never played to smash business. Perhaps I really am getting too old and out of touch. I can't really believe this but I suppose there are several pointers. The score and lyrics of *Sleeping Prince* so far show no signs of hardening arteries. I intend to have a careful period of introspection in Jamaica. In these cold airs three-quarters of my energy is occupied in fighting the temperature.

Queen Marie-Jose, Princess Marie Gabriella and Prince Peter of Greece came to lunch on Thursday. It was all very amiable and *comme il faut*. I've been seeing a lot of place-cards lately. I am reading an American novel, *Another Country* by James Baldwin. It is filled with every imaginable four-letter word and pages of pornography. I look with dismay at the jangling world around me, at the close of this clamorous year. How much longer can all this lack of control, non-discipline, self-indulgence and wild futility last? The books I like to read, the music I like to hear, the paintings I like to see all belong to the past. This is really old age, I suppose. And yet there is a margin for doubt. I never liked formlessness, bad manners, obscurantism and vulgarity even when I was young! Hail 1963!

= 1963 =

A year of great activity on three major musicals: first Sail Away *had to be safely launched in Australia, then Noël had to take over the Broadway production of* The Girl Who Came to Supper *(for which he was also composer and lyricist) from an ailing Joe Layton, and within days of that he had to start casting* High Spirits, *the musical that Hugh Martin and Timothy Gray had made of Noël's* Blithe Spirit, *which he was also then to direct, though with a little last-minute help from Gower Champion.*

This was also the year when London, or at any rate the Hampstead Theatre Club, rediscovered Private Lives *and when it began to occur to at least a few theatre-goers and critics that, with three major musicals in production and a hit revival, he perhaps might not be the old dodo several journalists had been writing about. Asked in Australia for his idea of a perfect life, Noël replied simply, 'Mine'; asked by his agent to wire instructions about a seven-thousand-dollar offer for the magazine rights in a new short story, he wired simply, 'No instructions, just grab'.*

Elsewhere, critics were still reeling from the shock of the Coward renaissance: 'Can it be', asked one, 'that we have underrated Coward all these years, and that Private Lives, *far from being a badly dated relic, is in fact the funniest play to have adorned the English theatre in this century?' Audiences rapidly answered that question by forming box-office queues; Noël was back in business.*

Saturday 12 January   ss *Queen Mary*

Coley and I went aboard at noon, having endured two hours of purgatory in an unheated train on which was served the most disgusting breakfast. 'Milton thou shouldst be living at this hour: England hath need of thee.' I am aware that this quotation seems irrelevant and that perhaps it should be Shakespeare and not Milton, but I am sure that either Milton or Shakespeare could run British Railways more efficiently than this bloody Welfare State. I am becoming almighty sick of the Welfare State; sick of general 'commonness', sick of ugly voices, sick of bad manners and teenagers and debased values.

I am also fairly cross because Ian Bevan telephoned me just before the ship sailed to announce that Harold Fielding was putting up the notice at the Savoy tonight. Poor old *Sail Away*, it has done pretty well but it has never been a real smash. However, a seven months' run is not to be sneezed at. I think with a little more nursing it might have teetered on for a few more weeks, but this is doubtful. Although I didn't care much for Harold Fielding, I cannot really blame him for refusing to play to a loss. It is a fast-moving show and most people who have seen it seem to have enjoyed it, but there is obviously something about it that fails to appeal to the large public. Perhaps the book is not strong enough, perhaps Stritch, with all her talent and vitality, hasn't enough star sex appeal, perhaps some of the lyrics are just a bit too clever. At any rate, that's that and, apart from an Australian production, I have seen the last of it. I have already risen up and twitched my mantle blue.

I have enjoyed my two weeks in London on the whole, but it has been bitterly, bitterly cold. I have seen *The Physicists*, the new Dürrenmatt play, well played but not as good as it ought to have been. I spent a day at Brighton and saw Robin [Maugham], Kate [Hammond] and John [Clements], Joan and Larry, etc., and made a conquest of Cuthbert Worsley[1], sincerely amiable but fairly idiotic. I also, after the Palladium pantomime, had a *rapprochement* in the White Elephant with Kenneth Tynan, who was also amiable. All his views on life and the theatre are diametrically opposed to mine, and I discovered that he is deeply scared of the atomic bomb. I mean genuinely, gibberingly scared! This I find surprising. It seems to me far too vast a nightmare to be frightened of.

Sunday 20 January   New York

We arrived in due course on Thursday morning after five days of bliss. Made a new friend, Joan Sutherland[2], who is a dear, jolly girl, and tried to cheer up an old friend, Harold Nicolson, who was being rather tryingly morose.

1 T.C. Worsley was at this time drama critic of the *Financial Times*.
2 Joan Sutherland (b. 1926), Australian soprano, created a Dame 1979.

We saw some ghastly films including *Jumbo*[1] and *Five Finger Exercise*[2], both horrid.

On landing I was met by Geoff Johnson[3], Jay Kramer and a strange gentleman who pressed a writ into my hand in such a furtive cloak and dagger manner that I giggled and handed it immediately to Jay. Charles and Ham were apparently watching this thrilling spectacle from a distance but I didn't see them. The whole thing is so incredibly silly. The case they are attempting to bring is apparently for a percentage of my royalties from *Sail Away*. As, I believe, according to contract Charles is entitled to this anyway in America and had it, and now there is no more coming in and the contract is terminated, I cannot see much point in the suggested legal proceedings. He is obviously round the bend and it is all a great pity and to hell with it. I was an idiot to have been fond of him. This betrayal of his true character is very startling. I presume he will go on trying to be a nuisance for some time and then give up and sink into the obscurity he deserves.

At our first audition[4] we heard Florence Henderson who was enchanting, a really lovely voice, sweet looks, and read well and with authority. No question in anyone's mind, she is it. Unfortunately Florence is pregnant! Her wretched baby is due at the end of July or the beginning of August, so we have decided to postpone rehearsals until 27 August. I don't really mind. It gives me more time and there is a lot to be done.

On the night we arrived, Coley and I went to *A Funny Thing Happened on the Way to the Forum*[5]. I thought at first I was going to loathe it but it turned out to be very funny.

Last night Herman [Levin] gave a very sweet dinner party at the Colony. Ruth [Gordon] and Gar [Kanin], Kitty Hart, Betty Bacall, Coley and me. Really a great success. We met for drinks at Herman's apartment and I played some of the score to the assembled company and it was received with violent professional enthusiasm.

Sunday 27 January

On Monday Coley and I went to Philadelphia to see Vivien open in *Tovarich*[6]. She was quite remarkable. She looked ravishing, had wonderful star authority, and when she did attempt to sing, in a deep bass-baritone, she got away with it brilliantly. The same cannot be said for the wretched Jean-Pierre Aumont,

1 Billie Rose's *Jumbo*, directed by Charles Walters with songs by Rodgers and Hart.
2 The film of Peter Shaffer's play, directed by Daniel Mann.
3 Geoffrey Johnson, New York casting agent who became Noël's American representative during the last decade of his life.
4 For *The Girl Who Came to Supper*.
5 Musical by Stephen Sondheim, starring Zero Mostel.
6 A new musical version of the Jacques Deval-Robert Sherwood comedy.

who can't even attempt to sing and has in addition – or perhaps I should say in subtraction – a built-in, Gallic cuteness which is quite dreadful. He is not quite so bad as he was in *Anatol*, but good, bad or indifferent, whoever plays that part opposite Vivien *must* be able to sing. To have two leading characters in a big musical with no voices at all is idiotic. We sat up with Vivien until 4 a.m. She knows it's not good enough and that she should never have done it. She also knows that it's entirely her own conceited fault. I warned her against it nine months ago in Hollywood and she flew at me. Poor darling. She is a bad judge. They will sell out on the road on her name, the show will be torn to pieces in New York, she will probably make a personal success, but it will not be worth it.

On Saturday Jose Ferrer appeared from Hollywood, where he is making a movie. I played him some of the songs and he couldn't have been more appreciative. In the afternoon he gave us an audition at the Winter Garden. He was beguilingly nervous and sang perfectly charmingly. Perfect diction and perfect stage authority. He *is* ugly but he is also curiously attractive. He is the right age for the part and a good name. There was no doubt in any of our minds, except still a small weeny one in mine. Anyhow, he was engaged then and there and a wire was sent to poor Keith Michell[1] putting him off. We are now set with our two leading parts.

Monday 4 February   Jamaica

I can't believe it. The soft, warm air, the glorious sunshine, the peace! We arrived yesterday afternoon and got here just before dusk.

Our last New York week increased in tempo until it became frenzied. Plays seen include: *Who's Afraid of Virginia Woolf?*[2], fine, scathing, sublimely acted. *Adrienne Lecouvreur*[3] at the Met: Renata Tebaldi, very slim and glamorous, and Franco Corelli. I thoroughly enjoyed it. It is not an 'important' opera, but it is melodic and pretty to look at. On Friday we took Lynn and Alfred to *Oliver*, a great success. They were thrilled. They go to the theatre so seldom, it was like taking the kiddies to the panto. On Saturday matinée Coley, Hugh [Martin] and I went to *Milk Train*, Tennessee's new opus. I found it so intolerable and Hermione Baddeley's acting so vulgar that I left after about twenty minutes and went home. Cheap, exterior acting infuriates me as much as fine, interior acting elates me. Both, alas, are equally well received by indiscriminate audiences. But to see poor Baddeley in a monstrous star part, after Uta Hagen, was too much.

A great surprise happened. Hugh Martin and Timothy Gray[4] came on

1 Keith Michell (b. 1928), Australian-born actor.
2 By Edward Albee, starring Uta Hagen and Arthur Hill.
3 Opera by Cilèa.
4 Timothy Gray, British lyricist.

Thursday morning to play the score of *Blithe Spirit*[1]. I was all set to turn it down because it really has been going on far too long and I was sick of all the frigging about. Coley and I sat with our mouths open. It is quite brilliant. The music is melodic and delightful, the lyrics really witty, and they have done a complete book outline keeping to my original play and yet making it effective as a musical. I really am not only relieved but delighted. I've told them to go ahead, discussed the contract, and everything is on the way. I would like it to be played by Gwen Verdon, Celeste Holm, Keith Michell and Kay Thompson, and directed and choreographed by Robert Fosse. However, ideal castings seldom come true. The business set-up for this is fairly simple – a three-way cut throughout.

I am at least eight pounds overweight and cannot get into any of my last year's shorts and trousers. This enrages me and I am off on a rigid diet.

Sunday 10 February

On looking back over the last few pages of this journal I am horrified to observe that I have made not a single mention of the Common Market drama[2]. This, I presume, must be basically because the subject doesn't interest me. I know it *should* but, compared with really vital issues such as Florence Henderson being pregnant or whether or not Jose Ferrer can sing, it doesn't seem to matter. Anyhow, De Gaulle has made a pig of himself[3], which should occasion no surprise to anyone who has glanced at any photograph of him. I know none of the ins and outs of the case. I merely hoped we *would* go into the Common Market for the simple but valid reason that Beaverbrook was so dead against it. This I have always found a fairly safe hoe to furrow, or is it furrow to hoe? Anyway, now we're out and the newspapers are trying to make the best of a bad – or good? – job.

Then, to occupy our errant minds there has been the Vassall case[4]. Clearly one of the most absorbing trials of the century. The Press, who are really on trial, have been getting a good trouncing and I couldn't be more delighted. Three of the reporters have been given suspended prison sentences for contempt of court. They refused to divulge their sources of misinformation. If they don't give in in five days they'll go to jail for six months and serve them bloody well right. It's high time the impertinence and maliciousness of those squalid little men was shown up. Nobody at the trial has hitherto pointed out the vital fact, that if the idiotic penal law against homosexuality did not exist, Vassall would never have been blackmailed and probably led a blameless life.

Coley and I spent a happy day in Kingston and managed to spend just over

---

1 Which they were adapting as a musical.
2 Should Britain be allowed to enter and if so, on what terms?
3 By refusing to let Britain join.
4 In which William Vassall, an Admiralty clerk, was charged with spying for the USSR.

a thousand pounds. A new Morris station-wagon, a new frigidaire, a sofa, two chairs for my verandah, and nine lampshades!

There has been a drama of magnitude over Mr Hopper and whether or not he should be 'put away'. He barks wildly and attacks cyclists and has to be shut up permanently in the pen where he cries all day. Having finally decided that 'easeful death' was the kindest solution, and wept copiously, Mae intervened and categorically forbade such an evil deed. She whisked Mr Hopper away to a *good* home before you could say 'chloroform', and so everyone is very relieved.

Annie and Ian have been dined with and were very sweet. A great deal of painting has taken place and I've started a short story.

Sunday 10 March

I have completed four numbers[1], all good ones. I did all four complete, words and music, in one morning, and I am very proud of them. They really are like old London pub songs and are funny without trying to be. So altogether I am doing very well. Added to which I am painting much better. My daily programme is: called at 7 a.m. – write a few letters – work until one o'clock – Coley arrives with mail – lunch – perhaps brief snooze – paint until 6.30 or seven, then a couple of drinks, looking at the view. Coley retires to Blue Harbour, I dine alone and listen to Miss Price, Miss Sutherland, Miss Callas or Miss Tebaldi. Then at about ten o'clock I go to bed and read a bit. It's a lovely existence and I adore it more and more.

I have decided to take Coley to Australia with me. I should have stipulated this in the first place, but it is now too late to ask them. However, I may stay a few days in Sydney and perhaps do a television or broadcast and make a little to pay for it. All my expenses and fares there and back are being paid. It will be an entirely different *Sail Away*, played by Maggie Fitzgibbon and Kevin Colson, both of whom are apparently big draws in Australia. I am taking Coley because I know what it will be like. Considering how they carried on in 1940[2], I tremble to think what will happen now when I am twenty-three years more famous! I *couldn't* cope with it entirely alone. It will be lovely for Coley. We will fly out together, maybe stopping off for a day or two here and there *en route*, then Coley will fly back and I shall try to sail back and get on with some writing. It should be quite fun although certainly exhausting. I'm actually looking forward to it.

I am feeling remarkably well. Perhaps, after all, the dear Herr Professor Niehans *has* got something in this 'fresh cell' idea. I've had a letter from Rebecca [West]. She also says she's never felt so well in her life!

1 For the score of *The Girl Who Came to Supper*.
2 When he first went there on a concert tour.

Sunday 17 March

The record of *Faster than Sound*[1] arrived. Hugh and Timothy have done it brilliantly. A thoroughly professional job. There really isn't a moderate number in it – they are all first-rate and about three obvious hits. Now all that remains to be done is to see to it that it is perfectly cast and directed and choreographed. Not so easy. The boys have done an admirable job on the script. They've kept to my dialogue throughout and yet contrived to open it up into 'musical' shape. The few lines they have had to interpolate are completely in key. In fact, taken all round it is one of the best potential musicals I have ever seen. Let's pray that nothing goes wrong between now and production. So much depends on playing and direction. I intend to keep a firm eye on it from the word go. It is planned, on my suggestion, to play it for three months in Los Angeles and San Francisco first.

What I predicted about the New York theatre parties killing audience participation has come true. *Oliver*, which is a smash hit, hasn't had one good audience since it opened, with the result that the performance is deteriorating fast. When I think of how wonderful New York audiences used to be, my heart is very sad.

Sunday 31 March

Joycie, Coley and I went on a lovely expedition. We drove to Buff Bay and then up into the mountains along by the foaming Buff Bay River. The scenery was sensational. The road got worse and worse and, owing to violent rains, because we'd had a bad gale for three days, at moments almost impassable. However, the gallant little Triumph managed to battle through. We drove through Hardware Gap and down through Newcastle to the Strawberry Hill Inn, which has the most fabulous views on each side of it and is really attractive. Quite small, good food and a glorious garden with everything imaginable growing. It was suddenly bitterly cold when the sun went, but the night was clear, there was a fragile new moon and the lights of Kingston glittered like rhinestones.

Then we all went to the factory[2] where I sat with Professor Baker discussing my designs. Baker, who is the boss, was entirely enthusiastic, and they're going to put two or three NC dinner and dessert services on the market! We then drove home, stopping off for tea at the Shaw Park Beach Club where we encountered Walter Wanger with Joan Bennett[3] lurking round the corner.

---

1 Working title for the *Blithe Spirit* musical.
2 Of the local Royal Worcester china business, for which Noël had been asked to do some designs.
3 Joan Bennett (b. 1910), American actress married at this time to Walter Wanger; he had recently shot her agent in the groin.

Quite a change! I am at the moment concentrating on an epic poem about the English upper middle class[1].

Monday 15 April   New York

Coley and I flew here on Sunday, since when a great deal has happened. Herman Levin is really wildly enthusiastic about the score. Yesterday I recorded the whole thing. It took four hours but is now down on tape and disc. Then I have had conferences about the *Blithe Spirit* musical and have agreed to direct it, starting rehearsals on 2 January. This will give me a month in Jamaica after *The Girl Who Came to Supper* opens.

Today we heard Edward Woodward (*Rattle of a Simple Man*) sing, and he was fine. It's a lovely voice and we *know* he is a good actor. Bea Lillie is mad about playing Arcati. She will bring to it star quality, moments of genius and little or no acting talent, but I'll settle. There's a strong possibility of Eileen Herlie for Ruth, and Gwen Verdon has been so idiotic over Elvira that, although she'd be a big draw, I've decided to let her stay at home. No coaxing. It's a waste of time. The next choice is Zizi Jeanmaire, who might be wonderful.

Tonight George Axelrod called me and asked me to do an extra day on the Paris film[2]. I said I would but he would have to pay me the same as I got before. This shook him, but he called back in ten minutes and agreed, so on 29 April I fly to Eden Roc for two days, play the scene, and return with 10,000 bucks. Not bad really. Since I've been here I've seen *Otello*[3] at the Met, abominable except for Macracken who was good, but poor old Milanow should be put down. *Tovarich*, disaster except for Vivien. Peter Glenville[4] has *not* improved it, if anything he has made it worse. On Friday Coley and I went to *La Sonnambula*[5]. Joan Sutherland was perfectly glorious, never have I heard such beautiful singing or so great an ovation. Afterwards she came to supper with us at the Plaza. She is a dear and I like her absolute unpretentiousness. On Saturday we went to Philadelphia to see Danny Massey in *She Loves Me*[6], a charming, untidy, over-gentle musical in which he is excellent.

Maggie Leighton is, at the moment, churning steadily round the bend. She's violently involved with Tony Quinn and having a masochistic beano. Vivien, on the other hand, is calm as a cucumber, deeply unhappy inside, but outwardly captain of her soul and looking wonderful. Stritch is very busy with rehearsals for *Virginia Woolf* (matinées only) in which she should be

1 *Not Yet the Dodo*, published in 1967.
2 *Paris When it Sizzles*.
3 Verdi's opera.
4 The director.
5 Bellini's opera.
6 By Sheldon Harnick and Jerry Bock.

very good. I met Edward Albee, very intelligent but badly tainted with avant-garde, Beckett, etc. He talked quite a lot of cock.

Friday 26 April   London

Arrived here on the sixteenth, since which happy day a lot has happened. Gladys is recovering rapidly from her nerve crack-up but is sofa-bound with a slipped disc. Lornie is fine; Graham is fine but still virtually out of work.

Long conference with Joe [Layton] and Harry Kurnitz re the book of *The Girl Who Came to Supper*. Everyone agrees that this is a good title; everyone also agrees that the book is not yet right and far, far too long. However, after the conference with Joe and me I think Harry will really get the book right. We have engaged Tessie O'Shea[1] to sing the 'London' song, and Irene Browne has finally got the Queen Mother, so *that's* all right.

The royal week was fine, beginning with the ball at Windsor Castle, a truly beautiful sight and wonderfully done. All the Royal Family particularly sweet to me. Then, two days later, the wedding[2]. Marvellously timed and performed. I was in the nave with the Norfolks, the Cholmondeleys, the Buccleuchs, the Fairbanks and Mrs Danny Kaye! In the evening I dined with Princess Margaret and the Queen Mother and we watched the whole thing on television and proceeded to have a very gay evening which went on until 2 a.m. Poor Tony and Princess M. are really upset about their bad Press. I tried to comfort them as well as I could. The next day I had tea with Princess Marina, who was happy but tearful over everything. In the evening, as an antidote to so much grace and favour, I went out to Stratford East with Joyce, Coley and Graham to see *Oh What a Lovely War*, a highly imaginative, brilliantly directed production by Joan Littlewood. The class bias strong and not accurate, and a definite debt to *Cavalcade*. The whole thing is a savage satire and really pretty remarkable.

Sunday 5 May   Les Avants

This time next week I shall be at the other side of the world, in Bangkok, having already had two days in London and two days in Beirut. It hardly seems possible.

My two days' filming at Eden Roc was successful and, on the whole, enjoyable. Dick Quine is a dear man and a good director; the weather was sublime and I spent most of each day in trunks sitting in the sun. I only put on my bath-robe for takes. I took Dick up to Biot to see Edward. He was perfectly amiable but, I thought, sillier than ever. The house, of course, looked beautiful as usual, and as usual there was an air of melancholy enveloping it. Kathleen [Molyneux] came up for a minute and made *far* too much fuss of

1 Tessie O'Shea (b. 1917), British music-hall singer.
2 Of Princess Alexandra and Angus Ogilvy.

me. I could feel Edward quivering. The next day they all came down for a minute to watch us filming, but Edward whisked them reluctantly away. I dined alone with Dick the first two nights and heard of his sad heart over Kim Novak! However, I think he is gradually recovering. Time, as I have so often wittily said, is a great healer.

David and Hjordis [Niven] came over to lunch and were very dear as usual. There has been a revival of *Private Lives* in a tiny theatre in Hampstead and it has had rave notices! Some critics even praised the play!

Sunday 12 May   Bangkok

A violently crowded week. First of all, London. We dined and went to *Whatever Happened to Baby Jane?*, a macabre movie with Bette Davis and Joan Crawford, both of whom were good, obvious and effective. On Tuesday afternoon a special performance in my honour of *Private Lives* by the Hampstead Theatre Club. Very well done on the whole but not, I fear, *quite* elegant enough. In the evening a party in the River Room at the Savoy. I sat next to the Queen Mother at dinner and she was gayer and more enchanting than ever. Actually it was a very delightful party.

The next morning Coley and I took off for Beirut where we spent two enjoyable days. Lunched with old Linda Sursock[1] in her Lebanese town house, a sort of early Oscar Asche production with lots of stained-glass, tinkling fountains and attar of roses. The next morning we were driven up into the mountains by Sir Moore Crosthwaite, the British ambassador, a dyed-in-the-wool beauty lover but quite nice. He is one of those rather sad, art-loving bachelors who are so often to be found in the Diplomatic Corps.

In the evening we took off for Bangkok. A troubled night, coming down at Karachi, Calcutta and Rangoon. We arrived here about midday. Blazing hot and hideously disappointing. All the beauty of the place has been banished for ever by progress and American tourism. The klongs (canals) have mostly been filled in. The crowded bazaars have disappeared. There are wide, dusty boulevards decorated with ghastly slang signs advertising Esso, 7-Up, etc. There are still flowering trees and temples but the whole place has so miserably progressed that one feels that they have only been put up for the Americans. *Everything* is for the Americans. Presumably there are still a few Siamese nooks and crannies into which they have not penetrated, but I have neither the time nor the inclination to search for them. We are leaving for Hong Kong tomorrow instead of Wednesday. This hotel is German-run so the décor is predominantly dark and gloomy. There is, fortunately, air-conditioning. The pool is quite nice but surrounded by Middle-Western ladies with tortured hair. The orchestra plays – atavistically – *Tales from the Vienna Woods*, *Intermezzo* and *William Tell*. Coley has gone off on his own to see the

1 Linda Sursock, celebrated hostess.

Emerald Buddha. I suspect that by now it has a Kotex advertisement in its navel.

Sunday 19 May Kowloon

We leave tonight for Australia. Our week here has been really lovely. Hong Kong is still one of the most fascinating places in the world. I have a lovely, over-air-conditioned suite overlooking the harbour, and at night, with all the lights glittering on the Peak opposite and the ferries darting back and forth and the warships and freight boats and liners and sampans and junks all lit up, it is perfectly beautiful. True, there are numbers of skyscrapers, but because of the height of the island they are not so oppressive as they might be.

I had a meagre but agreeable lunch with Sir Robert and Lady Black at Government House. A less meagre but equally agreeable lunch with Admiral Scatchard in *Hermes*, and a really enchanting evening with Prince Eddie and Kathy[1], who live in an ordinary officers' issue flatlet in the New Territories and are merry as grigs and having a lovely time untrammelled by royal pomposity. They really are a sweet couple and it is a pleasure to see two people so entirely happy with each other. I also saw George[2], who is thirteen months and blond and pink and smiling.

Various other characters have swum across our vision, including some of the resident Hong Kong homos, who behave and talk exactly like all other parochial homos and serve canapés and have *My Fair Lady* discreetly playing in the background. We had made, between us, four tropical suits, eight pairs of trousers and two raw silk dinner-jackets, all exquisitely made and completed in three days with two fittings! The bill for the lot came to just under £90. We have been jabbed for cholera on account of there being quite a lot of it about, and tomorrow we shall have left this lovely tropical heat behind and be plunged into the chills of an Australian winter.

Saturday 1 June Sydney

All is now over bar the shouting, but the shouting is happily continuing with great vigour. A great deal has been crammed into the last thirteen days. We arrived at Sydney as ordained at 9.15 and I had given myself time to get shaved and spruced up before facing the Press. It was quite a hullabaloo. I was broadcast and televised and interviewed *ad nauseam*, but they were all very pleasant. Two hours later I went through the whole thing again at Melbourne, where I was met by John McCallum[3], Lady Tait[4] (Frank had

1 The Duke and Duchess of Kent; he was at this time stationed in Hong Kong with the army.
2 George, Earl of St Andrews, their first child.
3 John McCallum, director of productions at J.C. Williamson who were producing *Sail Away*.
4 Lady Tait, doyenne of the Williamson business run by her husband Sir Frank Tait and his two younger brothers, irreverently known as hesitate, agitate and cogitate.

met me in Sydney), and had lunch at the airport with Maggie Fitzgibbon and Kevin Colson, a very attractive young man who is playing Johnny. In the afternoon I rested, then had a large Press reception, then met the company in a rehearsal room.

The next morning I went to work and the opening night was a howling success, the notices enthusiastic and the advance wonderful, so there it is. Maggie really is excellent and warm and lovable, but of course the brilliance of Stritchie is lacking. It's all been a great success and I must say I am really touched by the way Australians welcome me. They are wonderful people.

Sunday 9 June   Singapore

Back in the blessed, glorious, tropical heat again. I have a luxurious suite opening on to the pool and a personal Chinese servant to wait on me. He has a bright red nose and is called Coco. I have done little but write letters and postcards and read. I went one evening to Bugis Street, which is more wonderful than ever. Pimps and pedlars and whores and sailors, like a very sophisticated Oscar Asche production. One sits at tables in the street and it is fascinating. I was swiftly surrounded by British sailors, who were sweet-mannered, as always, and invited me on board the following morning, so the following morning I hired a car and drove out to the naval base at Aeleta.

I was received on board by the officer of the day, who looked rather startled, and before he could say, 'Have a gin, sir', I was whisked down to the lower deck by one of my friends in a pair of shorts and there I sat, in the steaming heat, while they 'spliced the main brace' and poured gallons of rum and water down my throat. They were all fat, thin, short, tall, impeccably mannered and happy as bees because they were sailing for home that afternoon. They presented me with a wooden shield with the ship's crest on it and signed by the entire mess. I was charmed and touched as I always am with the slightest contact with the Royal Navy. I was whisked from there to several other messes and finally to the wardroom where, as usual, I was enthusiastically received.

After all this, just as I was about to leave and was bidding goodbye to my lower deck chums, I was seized by a rubicund PO from the sister ship HMS *Brighton* (mine was HMS *Llandaff*), which was lying alongside, and forced on board to the PO's mess, where I was given more rum and a lighter with the ship's crest. They, too, were as nice as they could be, and I finally drove back to Singapore in an agreeable haze of sentimental euphoria, convinced more than ever that my rapport with the Navy is as strong and loving as ever.

Curiously enough, I woke up after my afternoon snooze feeling slightly light-headed but none the worse. A little of what you fancy does you good. How glad I am that I did *In Which We Serve* and how proud I am that it was as good as it was. There are restless stirrings within me about writing a play

– the one I mapped out in Switzerland. Maybe I shall. Anyhow, this period of being on my own is doing me – as usual – a power of good.

What is also doing me a power of good is a book called *African Genesis* which is a superbly written essay on the beginnings of man. It is written by Robert Ardrey who wrote, many years ago, *Thunder Rock*. I think it is possibly one of the most stimulating, brilliant, witty, well-informed and thrilling books I have ever read in my life. The thesis he proves is that instead of us being descended from those amiable Darwinian apes in Asia, we are actually descended from killer apes in South Africa. The book disposes of Freud, Marx and organized or, indeed, any religion. It says so many things that in my deep mind I have thought but not formulated. When I have finished it I shall go straight back and start again at the beginning. I have also read *Kim Novak, Goddess of Love*, which is hilarious. Written by a journalist with a ghastly mind and not even a nodding acquaintance with the English language. The amount of clichés and split infinitives is glorious.

Poor Jack Profumo – idiotic Jack Profumo – has resigned from the Government and there is a full-blooded scandal flooding the newspapers[1]. Poor Valerie[2]. I am so very sorry for her.

Bill Holden and Capucine are here, just having finished making a movie in Kuala Lumpur. Bill entirely teetotal and very sweet.

Sunday 16 June   ss *Chitral*

Here I am at sea again in a luxe cabin in a P & O. This sounds like a contradiction in terms but many things have changed and both P & O have pulled up their socks.

My stay in Singapore was very restful. Bill Holden and Capucine stayed only two nights and flew off to Bangkok. She is a keen talker and they are both, I fear, cracking bores. Adam Faith[3] appeared with a Jewish manager and four young rhythm boys called 'The Roulettes'. I went to see his second performance in the Happy World Stadium. It was all so deafening that I wished to God I had brought my ear-plugs. Adam is very attractive and has considerable charm. He wore a midnight-blue Italian silk suit and rocked and rolled with the utmost authority to the ear-shattering accompaniment of the Roulettes, who played electric guitars, drums and a double bass, all violently over-amplified. The din was quite incredible and punctuated by piercing shrieks from the teenagers. It was all most curious and I failed to hear one word. Apparently this is not important. It is only the 'beat' that is important and it is this that 'sends' the teenagers. The acts that preceded him were fairly

1 John Profumo (b. 1915), Secretary of State for War, had admitted that he had lied to the House of Commons about his affair with prostitute Christine Keeler.
2 Valerie Hobson, English actress, who had married John Profumo in 1954.
3 Adam Faith (b. 1940), British pop star turned actor.

horrible and equally noisy. I talked to him by the pool the following day. Simple, unaffected, a very nice boy. Like an island, he is always entirely surrounded by teenagers, photographers, and the lint-white Roulettes, who are uniformly hideous. What a peculiar life. By now he is back in London recording and rehearsing for a summer show at Bridlington.

I had one more farewell evening in Bugis Street and was rewarded by meeting a heavily tattooed, bearded sailor with a parrot on a bit of bamboo. He was charming and very funny. His friend was called 'Biscuits' because his name was Crawford. They finally disappeared, parrot and all, into the seething world, having completely made my evening.

Monday 8 July   San Francisco

The ship became more and more boring and so I decided to get off at Honolulu. The flight here, Pan-Am, was perfect. I spent a pleasant evening wandering about. Talked to Herman and Coley on the telephone. The news is that *Private Lives* has had absolute rave notices at the Duke of York's![1] It has suddenly been discovered, after thirty-three years, that it is a good play!

Willie Maugham has lost his case against Liza and the French courts have decreed that, everyone concerned being English, she *is* legitimate and the adoption of Alan [Searle] as Willie's son has been annulled! Serve the disagreeable old sod right. The Profumo scandal is getting worse and worse and more and more people are being involved. Bill Astor, Douglas Fairbanks, etc. The Press are having a field day. The high moral tone continues to be nauseating.

Sunday 21 July   New York

I have had ten days of auditions, conferences and arguments. Joe is getting irritated with Herman. We're all getting irritated with Harry, who has *not yet* finished the book. It is the jittery pre-rehearsal period. I have discussed orchestra and orchestrations with Russell Bennett and Jay Blackton. I have rewritten – at Joe's earnest request – 'Lonely Man' and made it a more schmaltzy tune. I have also done the Carpathian National Anthem and a page of Cockney dialogue for Harry.

There have also been great carryings-on about *Blithe Spirit*. I took Beattie to lunch. She looked wonderful and was very funny and sweet, but also she couldn't even remember the beginnings of the sentences she'd started. As she was *never* good on words, this augurs ill for the future. I intend to give her a good talking to when I get back from Jamaica, where I go on Tuesday for three weeks. There is still more music to be done and there's really no point in hanging about in the hot city. I gave up the idea of going to England and Switzerland because it would be too exhausting. The present cast for *Blithe Spirit* (*High Spirits*) is Beatrice Lillie, Edward Woodward (fixed), and Celeste

1 In a transfer from Hampstead Theatre Club.

Holm and Tammy Grimes being negotiated. I want Tammy because she is a strong personality and will be good competition for Beattie. She wants to do it. We have definitely got the Alvin Theatre and will open there on 31 March after a week in Newhaven, three weeks in Boston and three weeks in Philadelphia.

Coley and Geoff [Johnson] are nosing around for an apartment but no luck so far. Nothing much is left in the theatres but *Tovarich* is still on, entirely owing to Vivien. She, incidentally, is gayer and sweeter and calmer than she has been for years. I think, at long last, she really is getting over Larry. I do love her very much and it is a great relief. She told me – via Binkie – that poor Terry [Rattigan] *has* got cancer, of the liver presumably. Apparently he knows. This is desperately sad. I wrote a long letter to him all about the show, without of course even hinting that I knew everything. I wonder if he really knows. Perhaps just at moments, like Arthur [Macrae], who, I was always convinced, had sudden flashes of desolate realization.

I've talked to Lornie and Graham. *Private Lives* is a big hit at the Duke of York's. Graham has bought a house in Kensington which he intends to furnish and let. A very good idea. It's a pity he didn't think of it sooner. I had a very nice letter from Robert Ardrey in reply to my fan letter about *African Genesis*. He and his wife live in Rome and urge me to come and stay. This, of course, I cannot do. Nor would I. I'm a big hotel boy. However, I do long to meet them.

I had a truly touching letter from Valerie Profumo. She certainly is a gallant behaver. Meanwhile the squalid Ward case[1] is spread thickly over every newspaper. Those miserable little tarts Christine Keeler and Mandy Rice-Davies are having a ball and implicating everyone they can think of. They have both, apparently, been given vast sums for their sordid life stories. I *do* know what the world's coming to and that's a fact. It's coming to complete moral and mental disintegration. We all know that sex orgies, flagellation, homosexuality, adultery and procuring have gone on since the beginning of recorded time, but never before has it been so widely and vulgarly and lasciviously publicized.

Most of the vulgarity can, as usual, be blamed on the Press. The policy of most leading newspapers has been for years based on a cynical appeal to the lowest in human nature. I think, in a troubled world, when the yellow and black tides are rising, the Western white people are displaying singularly little foresight or imagination. To take a gloomy view of life is not part of my philosophy; to laugh at the idiocies of my fellow creatures is. However, at this particular moment I cannot find so much to laugh at as I would like. It is a dismaying spectacle, this almost universal decay of values. Money, publicity, sex, political corruption, bad manners and incomprehensible silliness. No

1 Stephen Ward, a society osteopath associated with the Profumo scandal, had been charged with living on immoral earnings.

standards left but the *Evening Standard*! As Queen Mary said on being informed that the King[1] intended to abdicate, 'Here's a pretty kettle of fish!'

I dined the other evening with the two Kennedy sisters, Pat Lawford and Jean Smith. They were very gay and it was quite enjoyable. Today I drove out with Harry to lunch with Leland and Pam Hayward. A lovely house, everything beautifully done. Pam, I have always thought, is a very remarkable girl. Leland is much nicer and cosier than he used to be.

I saw an off-Broadway revival of *The Boys from Syracuse*[2]. What a brilliant score and what witty lyrics. Here indeed are the stimulating snows of yester-year. I also saw two films, *This Sporting Life*[3], unreal but effective, and *Sparrows Can't Sing*[4], moments of brilliance ruined by Joan Littlewood's calculated lack of discipline. A formless muddle with a lot of silly actors improvising, but perfect Cockney atmosphere. I'd like to throttle that tiresome talented woman for not taking more trouble.

Sunday 28 July   Jamaica

Coley and I flew here last Tuesday. We flew low over this house [Firefly] and saw everything a-growing and a-blowing. Once more, once more ye laurels. The magic of this island has taken charge. It's slightly different in high summer. Fewer flowers but more flowering trees. The temperature is a bit hotter but not too much so. There are gigantic biblical thunderstorms. What remains constant is the peace.

I had a letter from Terry. He admits that he is ill but says he has put on weight. I think, reading between the lines, that this optimism is false. But it just may not be. I am determined to pop back to London in October when the show is in Toronto. I shall know when I see him.

Sail Away has opened in Sydney and is apparently a big success. Incidentally, I went to see Stritch play *Who's Afraid of Virginia Woolf?* in New York. She was absolutely magnificent. A truly great performance. If only she could play it in London. She really is an astonishingly fine actress.

The man is coming on Monday to discuss the swimming-pool! It is an extravagance but, oh, how I long for it. I think it can be done by Christmas. Taken by and large, the world is quite full of a number of things!

Monday 5 August

The odious Ward case is over. Those disgusting girls[5] showed off and made pigs of themselves. The jury returned a verdict of guilty; meanwhile the

1 Edward VIII, her son.
2 By Richard Rodgers and Lorenz Hart.
3 Based on David Storey's novel.
4 Film version of Stephen Lewis's comedy, *Sparrers Can't Sing*.
5 Christine Keeler and Mandy Rice-Davies.

wretched Ward, who was on bail and staying in a friend's flat, took an overdose of sleeping pills the night before he was due to be sentenced and was taken to hospital in a coma. He died yesterday. As he was likely to get fourteen years, I think this was very sensible of him. The whole business has been sordid, exacerbated by the Press, and a very dangerous slur on the English. Somebody said the other day that the scandals in England were nearly always about sex, whereas the scandals in America were nearly always about money. Quite a shrewd observation, I think.

I have read Walter Wanger's paperback account of the making of *Cleopatra* from the beginning. It is a saga of such paralysing silliness that one can hardly credit it. The behaviour of everyone concerned is appalling, the waste of time and money insane, and the ultimate result dull. It is playing to enormous grosses and I suppose will eventually make a profit. But what an expense of spirit in a waste of shame!

I have ordered the swimming-pool for up here! One is only old once.

Sunday 11 August

I have had another letter from Terry raving about the music. I told Graham to send him the record. The letter was brave all right, but I'm sure he knows he is dying. Perhaps he only knows at moments. It is too horrible. Evil, cruel men live on and the nice ones go.

I've just finished rereading [T.E.] Lawrence's *The Mint*. I don't think I have actually read it since he sent it to me in manuscript years and years ago. It is really glorious writing. All the four-letter words are singularly unshocking because of his taste. It is obviously a profoundly true picture of the Air Force at that time. What is extraordinary is that he *wished* to endure all that abusive bullying by sergeants and corporals and all that hideous discomfort. Obviously he had a strong streak of masochism, despised his own body, and subconsciously, or perhaps consciously, loved the better bodies of other younger men close to him and in his vision. I rather doubt whether or not in his whole life he ever did anything actively homosexual. Perhaps early on in his salad days. I wish now that I had probed a bit deeper when I knew him. Whatever they may say of him, however, he was unquestionably a great writer of the English language.

The repercussions of the Ward trial are still going on. Apparently he left several letters of considerable interest. His last girl-friend is spitting fury and vowing to avenge him by spilling a number of highly-placed beans, and a group of twenty artists and writers sent a vast wreath of white roses to his funeral with a card on which was written, 'For Stephen Ward, victim of British hypocrisy'! The inquest was last Friday, but there is to be an inquiry. Meanwhile those ghastly girls are not enjoying themselves quite so much.

The world spins on. Florence Henderson has had a bouncing boy and is doing fine, thank God. Jacqueline Kennedy has had a tiny premature boy, who is not so good and has been rushed to hospital. My investments, looked after by Tom Roe in Switzerland, are doing fine.

Sunday 18 August

These four weeks have been tremendously valuable. 'Time and to spare, my love.' I've really got through a lot of work. I've finished a story. It is about 40,000 words. I have also typed and revised it. It's really very good, and although at one point I got a bit panicky and stuck, I surmounted the hurdle and the end is now charming. I have also got on quite a lot with *Not Yet the Dodo*. I do love writing verse. I have also been right through the book of *High Spirits*, making notes, cuts, revision, etc., as well as having done the trio and the soliloquies for *The Girl Who Came to Supper* when I first arrived, so there is no doubt about it, this place is a gold-mine for me as far as creating is concerned. I've always worked better here than anywhere else. If the musicals are both successes and a reasonable amount of lolly comes rolling in, Coley and I are planning for the future. First of all, about £5,000 will have to be spent on Blue Harbour to make it a saleable property.

From tomorrow onwards I am going to have a busy three months. *The Girl Who Came to Supper* rehearsals and try-out and stresses and strains. Auditions and conferences and technical planning for *High Spirits*, plus a brief but necessary visit to London and a charity gala in Washington on 9 November. It is fortunate, I think, that I was born with a lot of vitality.

Graham arrived in New York on Tuesday to help Coley, take Irene Browne to lunch, help me with the *High Spirits* preparations, etc. It cannot be said that I lead a monotonous life exactly. So again I must rise and twitch my mantle blue.

Sunday 25 August   New York

First week over. The dancers are good. The singers are good and Joe is more inventive and dear than ever. The principals start rehearsing next Monday and the whole atmosphere is fairly quivering. Everybody is delighted with the 'Soliloquies' and the 'Trio', so I really think that now I have done all that was required. Herman is in a bubbling state of excitement. In addition to all this, *High Spirits* plans are progressing. Celeste Holm has dillied and dallied and finally refused Ruth, so we shall have to think again. Hugh and Tim have written a new opening number and an extra one for Ruth and Charles.

Claudette Colbert has opened, with Cyril Ritchard, in *The Irregular Verb to Love*[1], in which she is completely miscast and has begun to make a beast of herself. Maggie Leighton has put on a little weight and is a trifle less scatty and very sweet. Vivien is, I fear, embarking on one of her zizzing periods. She has

1 Comedy by Hugh and Margaret Williams.

forsaken the play[1] for a week and gone to Martha's Vineyard to stay with Kit. Maggie, Coley and I went to *Cleopatra*, which is a monument to vulgarity. Very, very long and completely tasteless from beginning to end. We also saw Garbo in *Camille*[2] which, even after thirty years, is exquisite.

Brownie has arrived, looking fine and not, so far, grumbling too much. Tessie O'Shea also has arrived exuding synthetic good humour from every pore, but she is going to do the 'London' song marvellously and will probably tear the place up.

Jessica Mitford has written a brilliant book called *The American Way of Death*, which is a savage and very funny satire on funeral parlours, like *The Loved One*[3] but basically much more serious.

Monday 2 September

Last week was fairly fraught. First reading by the principals on Monday. Everyone very excited and, I am delighted to say, very, very good. It is a beautifully balanced cast. Jo Ferrer is charming to work with and is going to be fine. Florence Henderson is enchanting and will, I think, become a great star. Joe is excelling himself and the whole thing is coming to life.

I saw Gingold in *Poor Dad*, etc.[4] She was excellent and the idiotic, occasionally effective, amateur romp was brilliantly camped up by Jerry Robbins. We have dined with Oliver [Smith] and seen his *Girl Who Came to Supper* sets in colour, and they're very good. I had supper with Vivien, who really is getting near the edge. She was rude-ish and fairly tiresome. Oh dear, I wish she could keep level. She is such a darling when she is all right and such a conceited little bitch when she isn't all right. She is missing performances on and off and grumbling about how tired she is.

I came back last night having spent Saturday and yesterday on Fire Island. I don't really think I shall ever go again. It is lovely from the point of view of beach and sun and wearing no clothes, but the atmosphere is sick-sick-sick. Never in my life have I seen such concentrated, abandoned homosexuality. It is fantastic and difficult to believe. I wished really that I hadn't gone. Thousands of queer young men of all shapes and sizes camping about blatantly and carrying on – in my opinion – appallingly. Then there were all the lesbians glowering at each other. Among this welter of brazen perversion wander a few 'straights', with children and dogs. I have always been of the opinion that a large group of queer men was unattractive. On Fire Island

1 *Tovarich*.
2 The 1936 film directed by George Cukor.
3 Evelyn Waugh's novel, published in 1948.
4 *Oh Dad, Poor Dad, Mamma's Hung You in the Closet and I'm Feelin' So Sad*, play by Arthur Kopit.

it is more than unattractive, it's macabre, sinister, irritating and somehow tragic.

For the benefit of future historians who might avidly read this journal, there has been a large 'Civil Rights' march on Washington during which both Negroes and whites behaved in an exemplary manner and nobody got hurt. 'The world is too much with us; late and soon.'

Sunday 8 September

Rehearsals are still going wonderfully. There was a run-through of the first act on Friday night, and I must say it was very exciting. There are a few things wrong, but I am being like Dad and keeping Mum until we get into the theatre.

We still haven't got a Ruth for *High Spirits*. Hugh and Tim are fussing a bit about finishing off the extra numbers, but I have been firm and made angry noises and they are now concentrating like crazy. Peggy Wood and Max Gordon have both written books[1], both of which I have had to read and comment upon. Peggy's is arch and only passably interesting. Max's is really very good and simple and honest.

I have had my last remaining tooth out. It was so wobbly that it was becoming a menace. My new plate is remarkable. I haven't *quite* got used to it yet, but it is much firmer and more solid than I anticipated and, thank God, it has made no difference whatever to my speech. I am a little agitated about it holding still when I sing, but I am sure that in a week or two I shall have it completely under control.

It is a curious feeling being concerned with a big endeavour like *The Girl Who Came to Supper* and yet *not* being concerned with it. I find it a trifle frustrating. Actually I would prefer to be rehearsing from ten to ten. However, I *know* I'm wise to stay, for the moment, in the background.

Saturday 14 September

This will be a melancholy entry in this journal. I have just come back from the 'Battle of Britain' dinner given in remembrance of those young men who saved, temporarily, the world. It was simple, dignified, sparsely attended and, to me, almost intolerably sad[2]. Air Vice-Marshal Esplin made an excellent, British throw-away speech, marred by rather roguish allusions to the Profumo scandal. The atmosphere, for me, was thick with dreadful nostalgia. The Battle of Britain was twenty-three years ago and the world has forgotten it. Those young men, so many of whom I knew, flew up into the air and died for us and all we believed in, and all we believed in has so changed that

---

1 About their lives in the American theatre.
2 An event Noël later wrote of in his poem 'Battle of Britain Dinner', published in *Not Yet the Dodo*.

they really needn't have died at all. It was ail a nonsense. So incredibly brave, so beautiful and true, and now, twenty-three years later, it is remembered for one night in the year, by a handful of people assembled in a New York hotel. There they were, a few of the survivors, middle-aged, swinging round in the air above our heads, being remembered for a brief moment in a world which is not worth their dying. Their enemy, the German nation, is now flourishing. The tears shed for their deaths àre dried and forgotten. Nobody knows or cares really if they ever existed, except this little group of Britishers gallantly making a salute over the years to a courage and valiance far beyond praise.

The Air Vice-Marshal in his speech reminded, lightly, the Americans present that they had not even been aware of what was going on so long ago, before Pearl Harbor had dragged them kicking and screaming into a war which was being fought for them as well as for us, and the so-called civilized world. He talked of the future and asked us not to dwell too much on the ageing past. He had been a pilot in those agonizing years, and I heard in his voice an almost flippant despair. It's all over and done with and forgotten except for a few brief moments on this one night each year. Sitting there, signing autographs and listening to him, I listened further back to the planes flying over to the hated Germany, now hailed as a friend, as indeed is Japan, and my stomach turned and my heart sank. What did they die for? I suppose for themselves and what they believed was England. It *was* England then – just for a few brave months – so perhaps they were right, except that they are dead and would have been alive today but for the dissolute foolishness of war. Now there is peace and their sacrifice seems so idiotic, such aimless waste. The peace we are enduring is not worth their deaths. England has become a third-rate power, economically and morally. We are vulgarized by American values. America, which didn't even know war on its own ground, is now dictating our policies and patronizing our values.

I came away from that gentle, touching, tatty little party with a heavy and sad heart. The England those boys died for has disappeared. Our history, except for stupid, squalid, social scandals, is over. I was here twenty-three years ago during the Battle of Britain and I was profoundly unhappy. Tonight I am profoundly unhappy all over again, but for different reasons. Now my unhappiness is impersonal, then it was personal. Then I worried about being away when great things were happening. Now I know that it didn't matter. This is a more desolate unhappiness.

To hell with it. Life is for living and I must concentrate on *The Girl Who Came to Supper* and *High Spirits* and trying to keep Joe Layton from *over-directing* and seeing that the people round me are all right and that all relationships are well balanced. But oh, oh, oh! What was it that I so minded about twenty-three years ago? An ideal? An abstract patriotism? What? I wouldn't have missed that undistinguished little evening for anything. There were such poignant moments of memory and a churning-up of the heart. All quite unintentional. It was a sedate, tired little occasion. An *effort* – quite well organized – to revive a few memories, and it was almost intolerably sad. I wanted suddenly to stand up and shout, 'Shut up! Stop it. What's the use of this calculated nostalgia? Let's face the truth. The England we knew and loved was betrayed at Munich, revived for one short year in 1940 and was supreme in adversity, and now no longer exists.' That last great year was our valediction. It will never happen again.

We are now beset by the 'clever ones', all the cheap, frightened people. The young men who are angry and mediocre, the playwrights who can see nothing but defeat and who have no pride, no knowledge of the past, no reverence for our lovely heritage, nothing but a sick kowtowing to fear of death. Perhaps – just perhaps – someone will rise up and say, 'This isn't good enough.' There is still the basic English character to hold on to. But *is* there? I am old now. Sixty-three is old all right. I despise the young, who see no quality in our great past and who spit, with phoney, left-wing disdain, on all that we, as a race, have contributed to the living world.

I have been to the Battle of Britain dinner on 14 September 1963 and tomorrow I shall start re-concentrating on whether the show has enough style or not and who shall play Ruth in *High Spirits* and how my financial situation can be satisfactorily arranged and how I can get enough put by for my really old age which will soon overwhelm me. In the meantime, I say a grateful goodbye to those foolish, gallant young men who made it possible for me to be alive today to write these sentimental words.

Sunday 22 September   Boston

The week has been fairly fraught one way and another. I spent three hours of Monday being interviewed on television for a two-hour 'salute' to Noël Coward. Skitch Henderson played some of my tunes very well. Sally-Ann Howes sang. Bea Lillie sang. And two very dull men asked me a series of very dull questions about my life to which I replied, I fear, dully.

The first run-through of *The Girl Who Came to Supper* was disastrous. Vastly over-directed. Too much movement, too many props and everybody overacting like mad and trying to be funny. So much of it is brilliantly directed and the brilliance was obscured by Joe's choreographic passion for incorrect movement. *Why* have choreographers no respect for words or lyrics? Anyway, I let fly, lost my temper and flounced out, and the next day refused to go near the theatre. Herman Levin, I may say, was entirely on my side. I threatened, not idly, to go to Jamaica as I did not wish to be associated with vulgar acting, etc. This caused a dreadful sensation and late the next night Joe called me up and all was well. I can't bear disapproving of what he does because I really love him. He is cursed by a sort of personal insecurity and is afraid of credit being taken away from him. As he is really richly inventive and talented, this is plain silly. At all events, now all is rosy and he has achieved miracles of subtraction. Nearly all the unnecessary violence has been taken away and the last two run-throughs have been wonderful. Florence is superb. So is Jo Ferrer. Irene is a frizz. Tessie O'Shea fine, when reduced. The book has emerged really well and I think there is little doubt that it will be a smash hit.

High Spirits is now cast completely. We had an interesting audition and finally engaged Louise Troy for Ruth. She read it very well, twice, and sings adequately. Her looks are splendid.

On Friday night I dined with all, or rather most, of the Kennedys. It was an enormous party. I have never seen so many really attractive women. Bob Kennedy, Ted Kennedy, Pat, Ethel, etc., were abundantly cheerful and very noisy indeed. I finished the evening with Sharman Douglas[1] and we had a slightly bibulous heart-to-heart talk about Stritch, the Royal Family in general, and Princess Margaret and Tony in particular. She is a nice girl, Sharman. The whole evening was quite enjoyable, but I *do not like* big parties and that's that.

My new lower plate is behaving *much* better than I expected. It only occasionally tries to escape me.

I've just arrived here. First orchestra rehearsal tomorrow morning.

Saturday 5 October   Martha's Vineyard

Well, *The Girl Who Came to Supper* opened last Monday in Boston to a rapturous reception. The next morning rave notices and it is so far quite palpably a smash hit. The orchestra is excellent. The lighting – by now – improving. The whole show, by now, much better and will be better still on Monday after Joe has rehearsed and redone 'London' over the weekend. Tessie O'Shea stopped the show cold on the opening night and has done so ever since, but the number is still too long and complicated. Florence is miraculous and I love her every minute. Jose Ferrer a bit inaudible and an ugly voice and appearance, but great charm, a fine comedian and will be vocally improved after I've been after him. The orchestrations are fine and my music has received paeans of praise. There was not any undue chaos. The preview last Saturday night was successful but fairly dreary. The lighting was catastrophic. I took over for five hours on Sunday and made a few improvements.

Marlene appeared while I was rehearsing the orchestra last week and was really very sweet and at her best. Poor Vivien, on the other hand, went barmy again on Saturday, slapped Jean-Pierre Aumont and walked off the stage and later attacked him in his dressing-room. The next day, after untold horrors,

1 Sharman Douglas, daughter of former US Ambassador to London, Lewis Douglas.

she was put in an ambulance and flown to London. She called me up three days ago and sounded odd but calm.

Bea Lillie has announced through her agent that she will *not* appear in *High Spirits* unless she has two more numbers and this and that. I have talked to her firmly. Personally I wish to God she wouldn't do it. She's bound to be a bloody nuisance apart from not being able to act and not knowing a word. Really, these female stars!

Chips with Everything and *Luther* are both big hits in New York. Both my television appearances – interview with Elliot Norton and *Salute to N.C.* – have been triumphant. The Noël Coward renaissance is in full swing.

Tuesday 22 October   London

There is quite a lot to write about really. Here I am, flower bestrewn, in my dear old Savoy suite. But, as in *Bitter Sweet*, I must flash back.

After my gentle few days with Kit at Martha's Vineyard, we drove back to Boston and saw the show, which went very well. There was still, obviously, a great deal to be done. The week whizzed by. I had a jolly visit to Harvard and the 'Lampoon' Club. On Thursday the tenth, flew back to New York. Had *High Spirits* meeting. Lunched with Bea, who wasn't tiresome at all, but very sweet. Drinks with Terry [Rattigan], also very sweet. Everyone concerned so far most enthusiastic. Coley and I had a film 'orgy' – *Tom Jones*[1] wonderful, *Wuthering Heights*[2] dated, and *In the French Style*[3] quite charming. On Sunday night we went to Martha Graham's opening night. Company brilliantly disciplined but, oh dear! I *know* she is a great genius and the foremost innovator of modern ballet, etc., but I wish, I wish, she didn't make me laugh! She really is a bit long in the tooth now to go running about the stage on her knees, and even when she was young it wasn't a very sensible thing to do. There was a vast party afterwards at which I paid my respects and buggered off fairly rapidly.

Flew to Toronto on Monday. Opened Tuesday. *Not* a good performance – even Florence forcing and overplaying. Notices very bad. One headline, 'Boston loved it. Toronto deplores it!' Harry Kurnitz, who had been taking several bows in New York, went into deep shock. Personally I was delighted. Everyone concerned was far too complacent.

Coley and I flew to New York. Saw *Jennie*[4] with Mary Martin – ghastly. *The Ballad of the Sad Café*[5] pretentious balls. Two heavy days of auditions. We have collected a fine cast for *H.S.* Am getting sick of *The G. Who Came*

1 Produced and directed by Tony Richardson.
2 William Wyler's 1939 classic.
3 Produced and directed by Robert Parrish.
4 Musical by Howard Dietz and Arthur Schwartz.
5 Carson McCullers' story adapted for the stage by Edward Albee.

to S. and the frustration of not being able to put things right myself. However, I suppose it's good for my soul.

Tuesday 5 November   New York

Here I am back again after four tiresome days in Toronto. The show is much improved but Jose Ferrer is ghastly and it's no good wishful thinking any longer. However, we must see what happens in Philadelphia.

The London visit was a great success. A satisfactory 'summit' conference about finance. I am now definitely to be a Swiss resident and Tom Roe is working to get a satisfactory tax arrangement with the Swiss government. If he succeeds it will mean that my financial life will be far less complicated. All my loved ones were well. I saw Peter O'Toole's Hamlet[1] and thought it wonderful and enjoyed the whole production. Terry's play[2] I also saw and I'm afraid it won't really do, although Charles Boyer is very good. I lunched with Princess Marina and dined with Princess Margaret and Tony *and* Marlene! A curious evening. I didn't feel exactly a warm glow between the two ladies. I gave a farewell drinkery at the Savoy – mixed bag – Marlene, Lionel Bart, Adam Faith, Dick Rodgers, Maggie Fitzgibbon, loved ones, etc. I visited Larry and Joan in Brighton, also Robin [Maugham], John [Clements] and Katie [Hammond], Terry and, on the way home, visited Vivien at Tickeridge. She is much better. I dined with Binkie, who was back on form and very sweet. In fact the whole visit passed in an enjoyable flash.

Last night Coley and I saw *Barefoot in the Park*[3], a truly funny comedy well constructed, beautifully acted and directed *and* a smash hit!

A great sadness. Poor old Elsa [Maxwell] died. Another old friend gone. How glad I am that I went to see her a couple of weeks ago and made her laugh. I had a feeling that she was on her way, poor old duck.

Sunday 17 November   Jamaica

Bad weather but blissful peace. The new swimming-pool is beautifully done. It will make a tremendous difference to my life here. They start to fill it tomorrow by the truck-load, which will take about a week. I know it was a wild extravagance but it will be worth it.

The Girl Who Came to Supper opened in Philadelphia to a madly enthusiastic audience and unanimous rave notices in the Press. Even Jo Ferrer came off fairly well and his performance *is* improving. He has all the signs of being a good comedian, but those evil fairies at his Puerto Rican christening bestowed on him short legs, a too large nose, small eyes, a toneless singing voice and a defective sense of timing. It is extraordinary to me that an actor with his years

1 The opening production of Olivier's National Theatre Company at the Old Vic.
2 *Man and Boy* at the Queen's Theatre.
3 By Neil Simon.

of experience should still, after six weeks' playing, misjudge his effects and talk through laughs. However, he sings my lyrics clearly and has, at moments, a certain curious charm. Tessie O'Shea tears the place up at every performance with monotonous regularity. Florence is wonderful. Irene too slow and over-acting, but effective. The show is now very good and there is little more to be done except let the company play it in.

I went to Washington on Thursday the seventh and stayed with Grace Phillips[1]. A cosy, sweet house and *everything* done, but I would still rather have been at an hotel. Grace gave a dinner party the night I arrived. Bunny and Paul Mellon, Mrs Kennedy's mother, etc. Very agreeable but time-wasting. Peter [Matz] arrived and we rehearsed with the band on Friday – not a very good band but Peter got the best out of it. Lunched at the British Embassy. The Ormsby-Gores[2] were charming and friendly. In the afternoon I went to the immense, ghastly ballroom in which I am to appear to test the sound which, thank God, was all right.

A full rehearsal on Saturday and a long, boring evening alone because I naturally refused to go to the dinner, as I was appearing. Peter came to the house at 10.30 and I rehearsed for an hour. The forty-five minutes I spent in my beastly little dressing-room were hell. Not because I was nervous but because I was cold and tired. I finally went on at 12.30. The audience, considering they were *crème de la crème*, were surprisingly attentive, and on I went, hoping that my lower plate wouldn't jump up and down, rattle or fly into the senators' laps. It actually behaved as well as the audience. I had a triumphant success but I didn't really enjoy it much. The only thing I did enjoy was the consciousness that I still had the knack and had not forgotten how to do it. Everybody cheered and roared. I got to bed about 4.30!

Poor darling Joe had been ill for four days and it was finally diagnosed as infectious hepatitis, so he went back to New York and into hospital. The whole company, including Coley, Graham and me, were inoculated. The performance on Monday night was excellent and the new middle bit in 'Middle Age' went beautifully. On Tuesday night I took Herman to hear Joan Sutherland sing *Traviata*. She was glorious.

The next day Coley, Graham and I drove back to New York. Took Maggie Leighton to dinner. She was well but fairly raving. In the middle of the night I was just about to go to sleep when I heard a curious noise in the sitting-room. I jumped out of bed, opened the door, and was beaten back by smoke and flames. I managed to crawl out through the kitchen into the hall in my pyjama top. Fortunately the bathroom door didn't stick as it usually does. I

1 Noël was in Washington for a charity gala performance and was the guest of Washington society hostess Grace Phillips.
2 Sylvia and William Ormsby-Gore; he was British Ambassador to Washington 1961–65, created Baron Harlech 1964.

yelled blue murder and rushed down in the elevator. The fire department arrived in five minutes – ten vast men in big boots and two cops. Meanwhile, a dear man who lives on my floor called Chris George had been rushing valiantly in and out of my apartment with plastic jars of water. Graham and Coley arrived, pale and agitated. Poor Mrs Hambly next door had hysterics. A whole shelf of books was destroyed, including all my reference books and some unfinished manuscripts. All one side of the fireplace was burnt and the whole room reduced to a charred and stinking shambles. If I had been asleep with my ear-plugs in I should probably have been trapped, and suffocated and burnt to death. There is a sheer drop from the window and no way out except through the kitchen which, in a few more minutes, would have been on fire. It was a horrid experience and I had a slight delayed reaction.

Sunday 24 November   Philadelphia

The most horrible and incredible catastrophe. On Friday President Kennedy was shot dead in Dallas, Texas, by a young man of twenty-four called Oswald apparently. Oswald himself was shot this morning while he was being transferred from one prison to another. The whole country is in a state of deep shock. Mrs Kennedy, who was with the President in the car when he died, has behaved throughout with dignity, grace and magnificent self-control. I watched her today on television accompanying the President's body from the White House to the Capitol and was moved to tears. The shooting of the suspected murderer by an exhibitionistic night-club proprietor is too idiotic to be believed. That the Dallas police should have allowed it to happen is so stupid that the brain reels. Now it will never be satisfactorily proved whether Oswald shot the President or not, and there will be a jungle of rumours.

I came back yesterday from Jamaica. Having had an urgent cable from Herman on Friday (before I knew of the assassination), I decided to come on Sunday because Joe is still in hospital and there is no one to command the ship. The moment I heard of the President's death – Friday afternoon – I decided to come yesterday. Coley and I made all arrangements and left Boscobel airstrip at ten o'clock – then Miami – then Newark – then New York. My apartment is still a shambles so I changed clothes, visited Joe, who is better, dined at the Drake Room and drove directly here.

I am now faced with the task of writing a new number – comedy – for Jo Ferrer because 'Long Live the King' had, of course, to be cut immediately as it deals exclusively with assassination. This is a dreadful job. I am genuinely upset over the President's death and the whole atmosphere is quivering. Hardly conducive to writing frivolous lyrics and music. However, I must go on trying. We are giving a performance tonight as there is to be a day of mourning tomorrow and nothing will be open. It is impossible to evade the general feeling of shock. It seems so desolately wasteful that a virile man in the prime of his life, to whom the whole world was looking for leadership and who, incidentally, was doing a gallant job of it, should be wiped out of life by the action of a zany delinquent with Communist tendencies. I feel that I am living through too much history and that my own life is becoming more and more hectic. However, I feel all right so far. Now I have to take charge, write the bloody song, rehearse the company and get on with the job. Still, I had a week in Jamaica and shall get some more over Christmas.

Monday 2 December   New York

The beginning of the week was horrible owing to the President's funeral, etc. Coley and I glued our eyes to the television for hours. In the meantime business has been really fabulous and the performances fine. Joe Layton is better but still in bed in the Park East Hospital. He may be let out for a preview. Anyhow, I have taken charge and cheered up the company and everything is set fair for New York. Now, of course, we are plunged into the usual chaos of first-night seats. However, we are crashing through somehow or other.

Ginette came to the Saturday matinée in Philadelphia and went articulately barmy with enthusiasm. She even told Jo Ferrer that he moved beautifully, which is entirely inaccurate. Coley is keeping his head. The telephone never stops ringing. I had quite fun in Philadelphia. I am bound to admit that to be complete boss again was soothing. The company are marvellous and work like fiends. Coley and I drove back yesterday through the late afternoon sunlight, which even made the New Jersey marshes and factories look beautiful. I must now get on with my brush work.

Wednesday 11 December   Jamaica

I can hardly believe it but I am back again on my beloved verandah. The pool up here is full and glorious, the most glorious present I have ever given myself. The weather has been vile and Port Maria was flooded over the weekend, but now the late sun is shining and I wish to God I had three months here instead of only three weeks. However, three weeks is a good deal better than nothing, and I feel very well.

The last ten days have been tricky. Joe got out of bed to come to the first preview on Thursday. He made a sweet speech to the company and fled back to the hospital, where he has been ever since. He really has been horribly ill but he is definitely on the mend. Florence, who had been working herself into a state of self-indulgent 'nerve' panic, suddenly refused to play the Saturday matinée preview an hour or two before curtain time. This might have demoralized the whole company; however, I made a brief speech before the overture and cowed the audience into submission. No one walked out!

The opening night on Sunday was the most fabulous evening I can ever remember in the theatre. The glittering, star-spangled audience was wonderful from the very beginning. The company gave a brilliant performance (if any one of them hadn't with *that* audience they should have been shot). Jo Ferrer was better than he has ever been hitherto, and although that is not good enough for me he made a great success and nearly stopped the show with 'Middle Age'. Florence was excellent, not a fault, an efficient, perfectly timed performance which only lacked the essential – heart. She was too sure, too competent and had lost the charm she had in Boston. Irene was really brilliant, and the star of the evening was Tessie O'Shea, whose ovation during and after 'London' held up proceedings for almost five minutes. I have never heard such cheering. She fully earned it because she was warm, friendly and gave a perfect performance. Not unnaturally, she got all the notices. It was truly thrilling to see that rumbustious, bouncing old-timer, after some years of limbo, come back and tear the place up. The whole evening was quite extraordinary.

A lovely party given by Herman at the Plaza and a company party in a mock Hawaiian joint on Broadway. I will write down a few of the 'names' present just for the record. My party alone consisted of Lynn and Alfred, Kit Cornell, Tammy Grimes, Lena Horne and Joan Sutherland. Then there were Mary Martin and Richard [Halliday], Claudette [Colbert] and Cyril [Ritchard], the Paleys, the Richard Rodgers, [Edna] Ferber, Sam Spiegel, Otto Preminger, Walter Wanger, the Josh Logans, Alec and Merula Guinness, Edward [Molyneux], the Loel Guinnesses, Norman and Rosita Winston, etc. I felt an extraordinary personal warmth from that audience and was properly gratified by it. Among others, I left out Valentina and Ruth [Gordon] and Gar [Kanin], who were the most enthusiastic of the lot. I was as deluged with praise as the city was deluged with rain at the end of the performance. We all hung about in the empty auditorium for ages until cars appeared to bear us to the Plaza.

The notices next day were all raves except for Taubman in the *Tribune*, which was bad, and Kerr in the *Times* which, surprisingly, was good for me and my music and lyrics, wonderful for Tessie, and very good for Jo Ferrer and Florence, but *bad* for the book. None of them has been really very good for the book. Poor Harry. He is such a dear, but he is a writer of lines and jokes rather than a writer of plays. The *Times* and *Tribune* took the edge off us being a smash hit. But there is little doubt that we are. It has all been rather a gruelling and frustrating experience for me and I shall never again put myself into such a tricky position.

I have had tremendous conferences over *High Spirits* and it is all shaping up beautifully. I wish it could be postponed for a month to give me more time to rest, but it can't be so that's that. It feels to me that it will be a hit. The book, we know, is solid. The score is excellent and the lyrics funny. We also have two authentic stars. I shall make the most of these three weeks and march with stately dignity into my sixty-fifth year!

Monday 16 December

Well, I have now stepped tentatively into my sixty-fifth year. I cannot quite bring myself to believe it but statistics, like the camera, cannot lie. Yesterday the sun blazed all day and it got me tanned to the colour of a Bechstein grand. Coley arrived from New York on Saturday looking paper-white and thoroughly exhausted from having dealt with all the first night telegrams, etc.

According to Coley, *The Girl Who Came to Supper* is apparently a real hit. There was bad business on Wednesday on account of a small flurry of snow, but all the other performances were packed and the show went wonderfully. Herman made one of his speeches to the company assuring them, rather belligerently, that all was well. I do wish he wouldn't. It's bad psychology. Personally I still entertain some doubts that all is well. We've just missed being a real smash hit. We may build into one. The two factors in my opinion which mitigate against it are not enough heart in the book (and particularly at the end of the play), and Jo Ferrer not being physically attractive enough. He gives an excellent performance but I feel in my bones that the great public wants that extra star quality which actually neither he nor Florence possess. On the credit side, however, the show looks marvellous, it is brilliantly staged and performed, my music and lyrics are very good, and the audience appears to love it. A musical 'smash' on Broadway is a successful getting together of imponderables. It is only rarely, as in the case of *Oklahoma!* and *West Side Story*, that a big show can succeed without a star name. Fortunately, in *High Spirits* I shall have two, Beattie and Tammy. Also the book is solid.

Sunday 29 December

Well, Christmas is over once more. We had a great present-giving tree party on Christmas morning. Then in the evening we dined at Blanche [Blackwell]'s and played games. After that the skies opened and have been open ever since until this morning when the sun is out again. I have never known such a continuous deluge. It was almost frightening. There have been landslides and ghastliness all over the island and roads washed away. I haven't seen the road between here and Blue Harbour, but according to the boys it hardly exists.

The Girl Who Came to Supper played $92,000 the *week before* Christmas. The *Time*, *Newsweek* and *New Yorker* notices are bad. *Time* very bad, in fact insulting. Dick Watts has come out in the *Post* and *re*affirmed his opening night notice, which was a rave, and announced that it is far and away the best musical in town and enchanting anyway. The *New Yorker* dismissed my score as being mainly recitative! What *could* he have meant? *Time* said – wittily – it was marshmelody! There is unquestionably a certain type of scribbling gentleman who is basically antipathetic to me. It *cannot* be anything but personal. No one in their sane senses could say the lyrics and music of *The Girl Who Came to Supper* were not good. They *are* good. Very good indeed. As a matter of fact, this is the first time I have had – on the whole – enthusiastic notices for my music for years, if ever. Very few dramatic critics can distinguish a good tune from a bad one.

In any case, *T.G.W.C.T.S.* is fairly obviously a smash hit so far. How long it continues to be remains to be seen. It will be all right, I think. It is excellent entertainment value and audiences like it, but oh, alack and alas, with just a little more it could have been a real block-buster. If Harry had written it with more 'heart'. If Joe had directed it with more 'heart', and if Jo Ferrer and Florence could have emanated more '*heart*'. This specific warmth is what it lacks and because of this basic sentimental lack it will never quite sweep the board. Perhaps *High Spirits* will suffer from the same defect, except that it sets out to be high-powered satire from first to last and the least suspicion of genuine sentiment would destroy it. Also we have Miss Lillie and Miss Grimes, both of whom have star personalities. We shall see. Oh, indeed, we shall see, and alarmingly soon.

1964

With The Girl Who Came to Supper *and* High Spirits *launched on Broadway, in his own country Noël was agreeably surprised to find himself, at the age of almost three score years and five, at last regarded as indeed a 'national treasure'. Laurence Olivier, who had last played with him in* Private Lives *in 1930, suggested that* Hay Fever *should be the first play by a living dramatist to be staged at the Old Vic under the new National Theatre management, and that Noël himself should be the one to direct it. 'When I tapped out this little comedy so exuberantly on to my typewriter, I would have indeed been astonished if anyone had told me that it was destined to re-emerge fresh and blooming forty years later.' But it did, and as Ronald Bryden in the* New Statesman *then noted: 'Who would have thought the landmarks of the Sixties would include the emergence of Noël Coward as the grand old man of British drama? There he was one morning flipping verbal tiddly-winks with reporters about "Dad's Renaissance"; the next, he was there again . . . slightly older than the century on which he sits, his eyelids wearier than ever, hanging beside Forster, Eliot and the OMs, demonstrably the greatest living English playwright.'*

Monday 13 January   New York

A great deal has happened. There is at the moment a raging blizzard. Jose Ferrer, without permission, flew to Puerto Rico for Rosie Clooney's[1] opening night and is stranded there. David Brooks, his understudy, left his gracious New Jersey home at two o'clock this afternoon and has not been heard of since. The audience, what there was of it, has had to be turned away and there has been no performance. *T.G.W.C.T.S.* is far from being the smash hit we hoped for. We are still doing the best business in town and we have a certain amount of theatre parties booked, but our get-out figure is $55,000 a week. Last week we climbed laboriously from $68,000 to $75,000 but the situation is not healthy.

High Spirits is progressing very well indeed. Tammy Grimes is going to be brilliant, Teddy Woodward excellent, Louise Troy ditto and Bea Lillie - well - it is impossible to decide. She has worked really hard for months, cannot retain more than a few sentences at a time, cannot act *at all*, has no idea of moving from one side of the stage to the other and yet contributes a curious quality of genius. She is driving me shrieking mad at every rehearsal and yet I know she is aching to please me. Today, after a week of indescribable hell, she got through the first act comparatively fluently. One can only hope, grit one's teeth and pray for patience. Graham is being really invaluable as my assistant director. He is shrewd and authoritative and has got the company on his side. If Beattie really delivers, which I believe she will, we shall probably have a real smash hit.

Panama is in revolt against America, Zanzibar is in revolt against England, India is in revolt against itself, and I am in revolt against Jose Ferrer, *The Girl Who Came to Supper* and everyone connected with it.

Friday 24 January

This is a day off for the whole company including the wretched director, so I am springing to these pages to put on record that I am patient, kind, forbearing, sensible, gentle, decisive and brilliant. If I were not all of these things I should now be nestling cosily in a strait-jacket in some loony-bin. I have been rehearsing intensively and day after day I have sat quietly with my nails dug into the palms of my hands while Miss Lillie stumbles, flounders, forgets, remembers, drives the company mad and is as much like Madame Arcati as I am like Queen Victoria.

I went with Claudette to the opening preview of Arthur Miller's play *After the Fall* at the Lincoln Center Repertory Theater on Washington Square, which turns out on closer inspection to be a gloomy hangar painted black with a jutting out stage made of steps and levels and no curtain. The play is a

---

[1] Rosemary Clooney, American singer, married to Jose Ferrer.

three-and-a-half-hour wail about how cruel life has been to Arthur Miller. What it does *not* mention is that the cruellest blow life has dealt him is that he hasn't a grain of humour. He is capable of writing one or two fairly effective 'theatre' scenes. His philosophy is adolescent and sodden with self-pity. His taste is non-existent. The Marilyn Monroe part of the play[1] is really vulgar beyond belief. Out of all this pretentious, turgid verbosity emerges the character of a silly, dull man with a mediocre mind. It has, needless to say, been hailed as a masterpiece and treated with the greatest possible reverence. There is more human truth in the first ten minutes of *Barefoot in the Park* than in the whole three and a half hours of *After the Fall*.

Carol Channing has returned in *Hello Dolly*, a musical version of *The Matchmaker*[2], which is patchy with two or three effective moments. This has received unanimous praise and is described as the greatest musical since *My Fair Lady*. It *isn't*. Meanwhile Joe [Layton] is back and slogging away at *T.G.W.C.T.S*. We will play to $68,000 this week, which is not bad, but not good.

Sunday 9 February   Boston

Coley and I have just arrived here after spending a night with Lester Osterman[3] and his wife and granddaughter in their gracious home in Darien, Connecticut. The food was delicious, the house hideous, and the peace of the occasion was shattered by the grandchild, Sheila – a pretty little girl of two and a half, who resolutely refused to allow any conversation to last longer than four minutes without shrieking or calling attention to herself. Nobody admonished her, nobody told her to shut up, she was gently advised once or twice to stop stuffing herself with whatever food happened to be handy; she completely ignored the advice.

The day before the company was due to leave for New Haven, Graham was suddenly seized with agonizing pain in his left buttock and thigh, and couldn't move. We had to leave him behind, since when he has been in a 'traction' hospital and is unlikely to get out of it for some time yet. This was not only miserable for him but highly inconvenient for me to be deprived of my assistant director during the time I needed him most. However, there was nothing to do but to press on. We managed to get the show on the stage for the Saturday night preview – 1 February. It went fairly well and was only twenty minutes over time.

On Monday night we opened. Beattie fucked up the whole business in so far as the book was concerned, but managed to make a great success at the expense of the play, the cast and my nerves. However, the whole thing got

1 A thinly-veiled account of Miller's marriage to Marilyn Monroe, 1956-61.
2 Thornton Wilder's play.
3 Lester Osterman, one of the producers of *High Spirits*.

rave notices and on Tuesday night she was more relaxed and actually got through the first scene without drying up more than twice. She went off into Turkish later on, but we mustn't ask too much. Her name and her personality and charm are enormous assets to the show. Her complete lack of concentration and inability to remember lines is catastrophic, but to replace her with anyone else would be more damaging than allowing her to play it. Her pet swain, John Philip, is being a crashing bore and a bloody nuisance but he has been squelched for the time being. At one moment Beattie turned on me and was perfectly idiotic; however, she apologized within the hour and so I rose above it. Tammy is brilliant, Louise good. The show patchy and in need of a couple of new numbers. We are, however, completely sold out for the road tour – three weeks here and three weeks in Philadelphia. I have remained calmly at the helm although there have been one or two moments when I would have liked to let fly.

Tuesday 10 March   Philadelphia

It is possible that a note of gloom will be sounded in this particular entry. First of all, *The Girl Who Came to Supper* is closing next Saturday night. This is fairly shocking and I cannot feel that Herman Levin has put up a very valiant fight to save it. Three factors have contributed to this disaster. Jose Ferrer, the book and the Broadway Theater, all three of which I have shrieked about from the beginning. Florence [Henderson] didn't really come off either. I think, however, she would have had a better chance with a physically attractive leading man. I tried to wishful-think myself into believing that Jose would be good, but I knew in my heart from the very beginning that he was miscast. Another factor – which I hate to have to admit – is that dear Joe Layton really directed it wrong from the very first. He *staged* it brilliantly but the actual direction was common and farcical, whereas it should have been witty and romantic. However, that is that and it is definitely spilt milk department. There is, I believe, a distinct possibility that Binkie and Prince [Littler] might do it at Drury Lane. It won't cost them much because the entire production could be shipped. God alone knows who will play it.

In addition to this disappointment I have developed a stomach ulcer and I have had great pain from it. Ed Bigg – via telephone – has put me on a pap diet and I am beginning to feel better although terribly weak. I think it has been caused by the ceaseless irritation of Beattie not knowing a word culminating in a hideous scene with John Philip[1]. I have managed to remain calm but at a considerable cost to my nervous system. Happily, however, the show is much better. Beattie has improved beyond belief and we are a sell-out here.

In under a month's time I shall be lying in the sun by my pool at Firefly. I

1 Who accused Noël of 'not appreciating' Miss Lillie.

expect the usual Jamaican miracle will occur if only I can hold out until then. I am now, incidentally, a firmly established Swiss resident.

Monday 23 March   New York

Now a ghastly tragedy has happened. Poor dear Nancy Spain was killed on Saturday in a chartered plane on her way to the Grand National; Joan Werner Laurie[1] was killed with her. I have just talked to Ginette in Paris. She is distraught, naturally, but behaving beautifully. It is cruel that all that gaiety, intelligence and vitality should be snuffed out when so many bores and horrors are left living.

The news from the *High Spirits* front is curious. Tammy spent the last Philadelphia week in hospital suffering from self-induced hysteria and Beattie's notices. Lester [Osterman] and Dick[2] came to me and asked if I minded them calling in Gower Champion[3] to pull the show together. I said I would be only too delighted. In due course he arrived and, at the first conference, listed everything that I have been saying for eight weeks. In addition to this he has some constructive ideas. I immediately, spurred on by his enthusiasm, wrote a new ending to the play as the present finale is hopeless. This went in on Friday night and was fine. Meanwhile, we have postponed the opening until 7 April. This has put Jamaica one more week away from me. However, I am flying out to Chicago on Wednesday to be thoroughly checked, x-rayed, etc. The ulcer is better but I'm still on a diet and feel exhausted.

Binkie has completely cooled off *The Girl Who Came to Supper* for London because Herman closed it so arbitrarily in New York. Herman is still moaning and screaming. Personally I cannot care very much any more. After plodding through these two musicals I am really very tired indeed. I took on far too much. I am sick to death of *High Spirits* and everyone connected with it. I think, galvanized by Gower, it may be a success. At any rate, I have done all I can do. My next assignment is *Hay Fever* for the new National Theatre in London[4], and I intend to worm my way out of it. In the meantime I must search for or write a play for myself to do in London next year as a sort of swan-song. I would like to act once more before I fold my bedraggled wings.

Monday 30 March   New York

Well, after a two-day check-up in the Passevant Hospital in Chicago it has been proved that I haven't got an ulcer after all. What I have been suffering from is acute gastritis caused by continual irritation. The Passevant has improved. A strange woman with orange hair bounced into my room and asked if I was Miss Davis and if I would like a shampoo! I replied to both questions in the negative.

1 Joan Werner Laurie (1920–64), English magazine executive.
2 Richard Horner, the second of the three producers involved.
3 Gower Champion (1920–80), American director and choreographer.
4 Olivier had suggested that Noël himself should direct this revival of his comedy.

I flew back here on Friday, and on Saturday night went with Binkie, Graham and Johnny Gielgud to *High Spirits*. To date the worst performance I have seen of it.

Last night we went to the Hasty Pudding Show at the Lamb's Club. It was very funny and the Harvard *jeunesse dorée* were beguiling. I heard *Falstaff* last Saturday at the Met. A lovely opera[1] but too long. Wonderful Zeffirelli production. Tonight I go to *High Spirits* again, God help me, and afterwards to a party given in my honour.

Friday 10 April   Jamaica

At last – at last – it is all over and I'm here again in the most perfect weather and utter peace. It is almost unbelievable. I have been longing for it for so many weeks. The last three months have been a nightmare. Never, never again will I take on so much, too much.

High Spirits opened on Tuesday night and was an immediate success. Beattie came on with a star mixture of assurance and humility, took the audience by the scruff of its neck and shook it into a state of adoring frenzy. Tammy was brilliant and gave a fine performance but, owing to Gower Champion's over-direction, was considerably less good than she had been in Boston and Philadelphia. Teddy Woodward was very good, which is all he ever can be in this part. He sang well and acted well, but he is essentially a character actor and he will never really dominate in a straight part. Incidentally, he is one of the nicest, most co-operative actors I have ever worked with. In all the hurly-burly, indecisiveness and inefficient chaos of this production he is the only one who has given me no trouble at all. Louise Troy came up a fair treat and made a great success. In fact, the performance was very good. The sets and dresses remain muddled, uninspired and tatty.

The calling in of Gower Champion in Philadelphia turned out on the whole to be a very good thing indeed. He has achieved some minor miracles and the whole show moves with more smoothness, speed and ease than it did before. He is a remarkable man of the theatre, and as at the moment of his intrusion I was ill and exhausted and really incapable of fighting any more minor battles, I am extremely grateful to him. I think he has contributed a great deal to the show's success. His own error, and it was an important one, was that he fiddled about too much with my direction of the dialogue scenes, which were always good anyhow. Like all choreographers, he hasn't enough faith in words and repose. His worst error has been to try to 'bring Tammy up'. What he has succeeded in doing is making her restless and fidgety.

Beattie, with all her fluffy-mindedness and lack of any *acting* technique whatever, is unquestionably a great star and has that indestructible capacity for making the audience love her. Her beguiling smile and her, at moments,

1 By Verdi.

incredible funniness are magical and, so far as the public is concerned, it doesn't matter how many lines she forgets and how many mistakes she makes. She is adored. The public are amused by Tammy and they admire her, but she is not *loved*. At any rate, the show is a hit and I can only hope and pray that it doesn't droop and die in a few months.

For the present I am going to rest, read, paint and contemplate my remaining years. Coley, who has been wonderful through all this ghastliness, needs a good rest too. We are both worried about Graham who seems, dear and lovable as he is, quite incapable of doing anything at all. He is, I fear, a born drifter. He just wanders through his life with no impetus and no genuine ambition. I know his theatrical career has been a failure, but there *are* other ploys to go after. He sleeps and sleeps and the days go by. I love him dearly and for ever, but this lack of drive, in any direction, is a bad augury for the future. I am willing and happy to look after him for the rest of my life, but he must do *something*. If only he would take up some occupation and stick to it. If only – if only! He is extremely popular and everyone loves him, but he is almost pathologically idle. It was dreadfully unfortunate that he should have got ill just as he was starting out as my assistant director. I know that he is unhappy inside, but alas, with his natural resilience, these moments of self-revelation dissipate and on go the years and soon he will be an elderly man who has achieved nothing at all. It is indeed a sad worry. However, hope springs eternal and there may be – just may be – a solution. But I, with my advancing years, am less capable of driving people than I used to be. The whip no longer cracks so sharply as it once did, which is not entirely surprising as I shall be sixty-five next December! I, of course, am the lucky one. For me no day is long enough. There is so much I want to do.

Sunday 19 April

I am by now back to being well again. My diet has disappeared. Last night – all by myself – I indulged in a whisky and soda. It was lovely. The first alcoholic drink for six weeks. I do not intend to get back to the nonsense of 'drinking normally'. It doesn't agree with me and never did. But I do like a couple at the end of the day before my dinner. I waited anxiously to see whether or not the unaccustomed fire-water would wreck my tender stomach, but it didn't. Happily nothing much has happened. I have read and slept and read and slept again. I have not budged out of this house for ten days. Now that I have the glorious pool there is no need to go down to Blue Harbour. It's paradise up here anyhow and the peace is quite indescribable.

High Spirits continues to flourish, apparently. My stocks have now been sold at the right moment, making me £1,000! Not bad. I have started a new short story called *The Captain's Table* which promises well. I have read *The Prime of Miss Jean Brodie* by Muriel Spark, which is witty and touching. She is an excellent writer. Maggie Leighton is going to do a play adapted from the book which ought to be charming[1]. *The Night of the Generals*[2] is a 'sex-murder' story translated from the German and tied up with the Generals' conspiracy to assassinate Hitler in 1944. Very good indeed. *Verandah* by James Pope-Hennessey is certainly unusual and entirely satisfactory. It is based on the life of his erratic Irish grandfather, who was one of Britain's more spectacular colonial governors. It is wittily and exquisitely written and I hoarded every page. It is comforting after so much slipshod American writing to read first-rate English devoid of slang, vulgarisms and tortured syntax.

Although I have so many loving American friends, the American 'way of life' and the American values have been depressing me for a long time. True, I have had a considerable dose of them lately, but it is not only that. There is an underlying 'commonness' in the general American viewpoint. The pioneer valiance with which they started out has degenerated sadly into a nationwide decadence, an accepted emphasis on all the wrong creeds. Too much publicity and commercial advertising – too much reverence for money – too much Press-engendered hysteria over the threat of Communism, the Negro problem, etc., etc. Too many sleeping pills – too many pills of all sorts – too much 'know-how' and too little knowledge. And far, far too much television. The current President[3] seems affable and reasonably sound, but the assassination of Kennedy was a lethal blow to the future. Catholic and self-willed he may have been, but he had courage, comparative youth and style.

Sunday *10 May*

Only one more week here. In a way I am sorry and in a way I am glad. I have a longing to get back to Europe. Graham flew away yesterday. I think we have found a way of solving his problem. Geoffrey Russell[4] is going to present *High Spirits* in London. Dick Horner suggested that Timmy [Gray], Hugh [Martin] and Dany[5] should go over and direct it as it is done in NY. As the three of them together are the worst time-wasters extant, my heart sank at the thought. However, if Graham co-directed with Tim (although he missed New Haven and Boston he attended every rehearsal), I would have someone concerned who could watch my interests. Tim is quite bright and has a lot of drive. Graham has much more taste and is *infinitely* more tactful. I really think this might work.

In the meantime negotiations are still limping along regarding *The Girl Who Came to Supper*. Donald Albery keeps on grinding away at everyone's

1 In the event Vanessa Redgrave did it.
2 By H.H. Kirst.
3 Lyndon Johnson.
4 Geoffrey Russell (b. 1921), 4th Baron Ampthill; theatre producer.
5 Dany Daniels, the third of the *High Spirits* producers.

royalties. I wrote a new last scene and sent it to Herman. He seems to like it. At least it's brief and not repetitious. *High Spirits* continues to stay in the smash hit class. It's one of the three sell-out musicals in New York. I tremble to think what will happen when Beattie finds out that Cis Courtneidge is going to do it in London. John Philip will blow up. After all, she has made the greatest success of her life in it! Personally I am certain that she wouldn't get such notices in London. To begin with they would resent her treatment of Madame Arcati. In the second place she has never been as successful in London as in America. The New York critics have, as they so often do, gone far too far. She is very, very funny and very, very beguiling and the audiences *do* adore her, but quite a lot of what she does is at the expense of the play and the rest of the cast. She certainly has a streak of comic genius but so, modestly, has the play. And although she is blissfully unaware of it, it is the play and the part that carry her. Unlike all the revues she has done, she is not on too much and when she *is*, she has a structure under her.

My short story, *The Captain's Table*, has reached fifty-four pages and shows no sign of ending. It is, I think, very good and I don't want to rush it, but I did *hope* to finish it before I left. However, if I don't, I don't and I shall just have to finish it at Les Avants. My stomach is at long, long last really getting better. It's not quite right yet and it plays up immediately if I work too hard or do too much. I've had some bad depressions but very firmly snapped myself out of them.

Larry has made the success of his life as Othello[1]. I can't wait to see it.

Saturday 16 May

Tomorrow we fly to New York. The weather has given up being blissful and taken to raining and blowing quite a lot. Of course, it's still warm and lovely, but what with one thing and another I've had enough for the time being.

Poor Diana Wynyard[2] died the other day of a kidney ailment. She was only fifty-eight. I feel sad. Although I didn't want her to play *Hay Fever*, I didn't want her to die in order not to. Celia [Johnson] has taken over her part in *The Master Builder*. Perhaps she will be suggested for Judith. I don't really think that she's right for it, although she's a beautiful actress.

High Spirits is still playing to capacity. Let's hope it doesn't do that famous 'Noël Coward musical nose-dive' after three months. I have been slogging away at my Italian grammar and I am making progress. My stomach has cleared itself up. I am looking forward to the rest of the year with *no* commitments other than those made to myself. I shall miss the lovely timeless mornings here, but it will be spring in Europe and then summer, and when the damp

1 At Chichester, in a production by John Dexter.
2 Diana Wynyard (1906–64), distinguished English actress; she had starred in the film of Noël's *Cavalcade* (1932).

winds of autumn come and I see the slightest sign of either *High Spirits* or *The Girl Who Came to Supper* being done in London, I shall fly to Mauritius, the Seychelles, the Canaries or Hong Kong.

Saturday 6 June   Les Avants

The ten days in London were full to overflowing. I saw some of the best acting I have ever seen in my life. Peggy [Ashcroft] and Vanessa [Redgrave] in *The Seagull*. Mike [Redgrave], Larry, Rosemary Harris and Joan [Plowright] in *Uncle Vanya*, better than ever. Joan and Frank Finlay in *Hobson's Choice*[1]; and, towering above all, Larry as Othello. A truly great performance. His whole conception was extraordinary. I know certain 'clever' carpers disagree with it, but to me it is beyond doubt greatness on the stage.

I discussed – *ad nauseam* – *High Spirits* with Geoffrey Russell. A very talented and pretty girl called Jan Waters auditioned for Ruth and was engaged immediately. It is now arranged that Graham and Timmy will co-direct it, with me taking the first three days' rehearsal and reappearing with cohorts all gleaming with purple and gold at the end of the first week in Oxford. We have no Charles as yet but hope for Denis Quilley.

I discussed *Hay Fever* with Larry and took Edith Evans to lunch. She is rather morally bound to do *The Chinese Prime Minister*[2] but I *think* she wants to do *Hay Fever* more. I certainly hope so. We shall know within a week or so. Meanwhile everything must be crossed. I discussed *The Girl Who Came to Supper* with Binkie, who is still dead against doing it owing to Herman having closed it too soon in New York. At all events, I think it is wise to leave it lie for a year or so. I lunched with Vivien at Tickeridge. She was fine and gay. I went to Brighton to see Larry and Joan, and dined with Terry [Rattigan] and Robin [Maugham] and finished up at Alma Cogan's[3] in London at 12.30, where I met two Beatles[4].

I lunched with the dear Queen Mother at Clarence House. She was more enchanting than ever. I took tea with Princess Marina and Princess Olga and, the night before I left, dined *à trois* with Princess Margaret and Tony. Very cosy and enjoyable. I gave a mixed cocktail party in my suite at the Savoy. Tommy Steele[5], Joan Sutherland and Ricky[6], Gladys, Joyce, Daniel [Massey] and Adrianne [Allen], and Patrick Woodcock[7]. Lunched with Hester [Chapman]. In fact a very, very gay week. Then two rather more peaceful days in

1 Comedy by Harold Brighouse.
2 By Enid Bagnold.
3 Alma Cogan, British singer.
4 John Lennon and Paul McCartney.
5 Tommy Steele (b. 1936), Cockney singer and actor.
6 Richard Bonynge (b. 1930), Australian conductor, married to Joan Sutherland.
7 Patrick Woodcock, Noël's London doctor.

Paris, mostly with Ginette and Paul-Emile. Another mixed cocktail rout. They sent me off on the 11.53 train on Thursday night and here I am!

Tuesday 16 June

Coley and I spent three days in Milano with Joan and Ricky. On the way there our train stuck for two hours in the Simplon Tunnel and we had to sit with the windows shut, sweating, in the company of a vociferous Greek and a handsome Lebanese. The next night we went to *La Bohème* at La Scala, an absolutely magnificent production by Franco Zeffirelli – really staggering – well sung, although the Mimi was a bit sharp here and there. We wandered about Milano in the lovely heat and I bought a lot of new trousers which I hardly need owing to my wasp-waist having jumped from thirty-four to thirty-six! It's no use worrying about it. I feel healthy and well, and intend to stay so.

Before our Milano trip we went to the exhibition in Lausanne, known as 'L'Expo', with Adrianne and Bill and dined with Brian and Eleanor Aherne. It was great fun. The fun-fair, although small, was darling. A really excellent little roller-coaster on to which I forced Brian twice running. The whole thing looks really charming at night and is well lit, but in daylight it's a bit arid. Joan and Ricky and I discussed the projected record[1]. I think it might be marvellous. They really are dears, and Joan is certainly the most glorious singer I have ever heard. It is a great, great voice. I feel, however, that she is doing too much. I may give Ricky a little finger-wag.

Max Beaverbrook died on Friday. This long – too long – delayed occurrence requires no comment. God is still presumably in his heaven unless he has been forced to move over.

Thursday 25 June

The die has been recast and I am going to direct *Hay Fever* after all. Larry rang me up today in a frizz because he has to take over *The Master Builder* from Michael [Redgrave], who is leaving, and therefore can't direct it himself. He was very dear and persuasive and said how important it would be to the company, and so I said yes. Edith Evans is now fixed and it will be a glorious cast including Maggie Smith, Bob Stephens, etc. John Dexter[2] has promised to take over if I get maddened or exhausted. In fact, I must admit I'm very excited about it. It will all fit in beautifully with *High Spirits*. Both *Hay Fever* and *High Spirits* will be in Manchester the same week and open in London the same week. It will be quite an autumn. Four plays on television[3]. A new

1 Joan Sutherland was to sing some of Noël's more operatic numbers.
2 John Dexter (b. 1935), British stage and film director.
3 Granada were televising 'A Choice of Coward' (*Present Laughter*, *Blithe Spirit*, *The Vortex* and *Design for Living*).

book published[1]. *Hay Fever* and *High Spirits*. I wonder if the late Beverley Baxter is at last convinced that I've survived the war. Incidentally, it appears that dear Granada Television expected me to perform four introductions – one for each play – for a token fee of ten guineas each! Bloody sauce. I told them, via Kenneth[2], that my absolute minimum was £250 apiece. This they have agreed to. I am going to make each one an excerpt from the *Play Parade* prefaces. They are very good, but quite a chore to learn by Tuesday next.

Feeling an urge for a slightly heavier and grander car than the dear Triumph Herald, I've bought myself a perfectly beautiful Mercedes Benz – only 38,000 francs (£3,000) second-hand and in perfect condition. The price of a new one is £5,300. I'm collecting this treasure tomorrow and driving over to Goldingen to stay a couple of nights with Lilli and Carlos.

Now that I am a bona-fide Swiss resident, all moneys earned by me will be paid to me here into Crédit Suisse on which I shall pay 7.4 per cent tax. At the moment I am paying 50 per cent company tax in England. The difference between 7 per cent and 50 per cent is considerable.

I am reading Rupert Croft-Cooke's life of Lord Alfred Douglas called *Bosie*. It is really quite well done but miserably vulgar at moments.

Thursday 9 July

I accomplished my trip to Lilli and Carlos in my new Mercedes with great élan and fortitude. It goes like a dream but the weather was infuriating – a series of violent thunderstorms interspersed with blazing sun. Fortunately the hood goes up and down easily. I spent one night with them – they were very sweet – unhappily, Carlos has written a long, over-sexed novel which I brought with me and have since, aided by Coley, read and corrected here and there. It's a bugger.

I spent a night of peaceful but paralysing boredom at the Hotel Schweizerhof in Berne, and returned here on Sunday afternoon to find I was not allowed up the hill to the house because the road was closed for Karti racing. Kartis are small, low scooters-cum-cars and very fast. Coley came down and we sat and gossiped outside the Buffet de la Gare until the god-damned festivities were over. The next day the television unit[3] arrived including the director, Joan Kemp-Welch. There were fourteen of them, and all that evening and all Tuesday I worked away, changing my clothes and speaking my introductions. They were all extremely nice and the whole business finished with a buffet luncheon. It was all a great success.

Graham arrived on Wednesday. We've had a lovely few days, me bashing away at Italian, which is really coming on a treat. We went to the Impressionist

---

1 *Pretty Polly Barlow*, a short story collection.
2 Kenneth Carten, now Noël's London agent.
3 From Granada Television.

exhibition at Lausanne. Some of the loveliest pictures I have ever seen until the last few rooms, which were full of hideous and meaningless Abstracts. On Monday Geoff Johnson arrived from New York quivering with excitement, and Geoffrey Russell, a little later, bearing the set designs for *High Spirits* and some new croquet balls which I had asked for. The set designs are charming (so are the croquet balls). He too was charming. All so far is going well except that Larry rang up in a panic to say that he wanted *Hay Fever* to open on 3 November, which happens to be the opening date of *High Spirits*.

The Japanese wish to do an 'all girl' production of *High Spirits* in Tokyo. I can't wait to see a large-hipped geisha as Dr Bradman.

Last night the Ahernes came, bringing Garbo who was really enchanting. After drinks here we all went to Adrianne's and had a buffet dinner and played games. Phyl Monkman and Bobby Andrews were there. Phyl is truly marvellous, seventy-three, racked with arthritis, and merry as a grig. I am very, very fond of her. Tonight I go to the Chevreau d'Antraigues to dine with the Queen of Spain, who has been having trouble with her lower plate. Tomorrow I take off for Rome for my holiday.

Tuesday 14 July   Rome

Independence Day in America[1]. Most of the inhabitants of that vast, unwieldy continent seem to be proving their independence by coming to Rome. The next afternoon I took off from Geneva. Brian, Eleanor and Garbo (quivering with neurosis) were on the plane. They travelled tourist, presumably because La Divina feared recognition in the more sophisticated atmosphere of the first class. She needn't have worried because no one recognized her at all. The officials, however, did recognize me so I was whisked through the Customs and Immigration at record speed. I left poor Brian valiantly identifying luggage. Garbo and Eleanor disappeared into the loo. They are all embarking on a little yacht. As it was blowing a gale when we arrived, I cannot feel that they will be very comfortable.

The magic of this city has once more taken charge of me. I wander through the incredible streets and sit outside cafés and allow the past to seep into my old bones. The Via Veneto is more 'Via Veneto' than ever. I got dragged to a ghastly cocktail party by John Barrymore Jr[2] (bearded and eccentric) and had to endure a clutch of randy elderly film and television tycoons with attendant Roman starlets with vast bosoms. I escaped at ten o'clock and dined alone on the Via Veneto.

Last night was the best night of all. I dined (first meeting) with Bob

---

1 Not in fact, although it was of course France's national holiday.
2 John Barrymore Jr (b. 1932), American actor; son of the famous matinée idol and film star John Barrymore and silent film heroine Dolores Costello.

Ardrey[1], his wife, her married daughter (*very* pretty), and his sixteen-year-old son (also very pretty and highly intelligent). They have an apartment in the Piazza di Mercanti with a terrace looking over the Piazza and next door to the house in which Michelangelo used to have his statues cast. The whole setting was exquisite and the dinner perfectly delicious. Having loved his book so much, I was a bit leery of meeting him, but my leeriness was unfounded. He is a dear man – rather loud-voiced, of course, brilliantly informed and immensely friendly. Birdine, his second wife, is South African and, although plump, extremely pretty. Her voice is occasionally rather a worry because she has superimposed over an Afrikaans accent a cautiously modulated voice which deteriorates into piss-elegance rather like Greer Garson's. However, she herself is not in the least piss-elegant, and I took a great shine to her. I arrived at 7.15 and left at 3 a.m. Bob is writing a new book (beginning it in a few weeks after eighteen months of research). It is to be called *The Territorial Imperative* and is a follow-on to *African Genesis*. He talked about it without a trace of egomania, but with scientific detachment. I was riveted.

After dinner, when I had played their lovely Steinway and we had all returned to the terrace, the conversation really started hopping. It was so very, very much what I needed. I felt my brain stretching its muscles. He has an extraordinary mind and, having been a playwright, his explanations of even abstruse anthropomorphic and biological theories are economical and clear. Down below in the Piazza there is a famous restaurant and the noises of people talking, crockery being banged about, and a sour little brass band wafted up over the terrace wall. There were coloured lanterns strung round the Piazza and along the beautiful, curved street, which has remained unchanged for hundreds of years. An almost new moon sat in the sky above us and the city was palpably breathing all round us. Altogether an evening of enchantment. I came back through the empty streets, bumping along in a minute taxi driven by a Roman maniac, feeling thoroughly rejuvenated. I did *not* drink too much. The latter part of the evening I drank nothing but water. Bob got a bit pissed and the more pissed he got the better he talked, which is a rare accomplishment. Compared with the conversation of some of the other dinner parties I have attended (and given) lately, it really was a breath of new air.

Monday 20 July   Rome

Well, I have returned from two hectic days in Spoleto. An orgy of 'culture' mainly musical. It was the end of the Festival and all the feuds and discontentments were sizzling near the surface. I saw *Raymonda* with Nureyev and Doreen Wells. He was fine. She perfectly efficient and the ballet well danced but not enthralling. Yesterday Margot [Fonteyn] returned so I stayed over and saw it all again. The most magical, moving experience. She was exquisite

1 Whose book *African Genesis* Noël had so much admired.

and her presence lighted up the whole thing. It was radiant and the two of them together will go down in my memory as one of the *great* moments of my life in the theatre. After the matinée I took them both (and several others) to dinner and I drove back to Rome with Margot. Rudi Nureyev at the last moment decided to hop into a Ferrari with some friends. Margot slept on my shoulder all the way home. I love her very much.

Apart from this truly glorious performance, the Festival was very much as I imagined it would be. Chamber music from twelve to one every day in a sweet little theatre, well done but not my diet. On Saturday night a Beethoven cantata and Rossini's *Stabat Mater*, both well sung and played and both too long. Afterwards a grand party at Gian Carlo's[1], followed by fireworks. Gian Carlo was sweet but *affolé*. There is a slight but perceptible smear of amateurishness over the whole affair; earnest, humourless and very, very American sincere. I stayed in a Victorian *ottocento palazzo* and slept in a brass fourposter draped with lace. There are, of course, a thousand short stories waiting to be written about the Festival – *Dei due Mondi*. All the little disagreements and umbrages and hurt feelings. I would rather have a truck run over my head than have any part of it. However, the whole hysterical carry-on was made worthwhile by Margot and Nureyev. He is a curious wild animal, very beguiling and fairly unpredictable. He is given to sudden outbursts of rage and is liable to bite people. He actually bit me during dinner but it was only on the finger and didn't draw blood.

Tuesday 28 July   Istanbul[2]

I flew here last Saturday and I am firmly leaving tomorrow. I have seen the Blue Mosque, the Seraglio, the Crown Jewels and the covered market. I have also seen a great many very ugly people and very little glamour. I made a mistake in not going to the Hilton. The Hilton is ultra-modern and filled with American tourists, but it is luxurious and the food is edible. In this dump, however, the food is uneatable, the waiters are filthy, the furniture bad art nouveau, and although the view over the Bosphorus is lovely it is not worth it. On the whole it is one of the scruffiest, dirtiest cities I have ever been to. I doubt if I shall come again.

My last week in Rome was quite interesting. Desmond O'Donovan[3] arrived from London with the 'set' for *Hay Fever*. Very good and some excellent dress sketches. He is a soft but pleasant young man who is to be my assistant director. He spent six years in a monastery and then jumped over the wall into the National Theatre. I think he has given up God, which is just as well really.

1 Gian Carlo Menotti (b. 1911), Italian composer who was the founding father of the Spoleto 'Festival of Two Worlds'.
2 Where Noël was, he said, known as 'English Delight'.
3 Desmond O'Donovan, National Theatre Company.

Kay Thompson reappeared. Sweet as ever and barmy as ever. I took her to visit the Ardreys, which was a great success.

On Friday night I dined with Tommy S.[1] and Leontyne Price. It should have been a lovely evening, but it wasn't. Leontyne doesn't really like Tommy and he knows it. This she confessed in the car going home. She is a bright cookie and sees through him. I don't really like him either. He talked a lot of idealistic balls and Leontyne remained earthy and unimpressed. She is at the moment recording *Forza del Destino* with him and yearning for von Karajan. I think he is a silly character underneath his great talent and good looks, also a fairly bitchy one. However, this does not astonish me.

Sunday 9 August   Les Avants

I flew here from Rome yesterday and, although I have enjoyed my holiday on the whole, I am delighted to be home. Indeed, during the last month there have been several moments when I have reproached myself sharply for ever having left it. However, it's all been grist to the mill, I suppose.

Capri swirled around us and we swirled around Capri. Nobody ever sat down to dinner before 11.30. Everyone bought shirts and trousers and pullovers. We visited the Blue Grotto in a rubber boat. The island is still wickedly enchanting and enchanted. A vivacious American lady, who looks twenty-eight and is actually sixty-eight, very sweetly offered me her little house in the old part of the town whenever I wanted it. She only uses it for two months a year. Her name is Joan Baruch-Bové, and I must say I took to her. The little house is exquisite and stares across the bay to Vesuvius. I also saw Graham Greene, Gracie Fields and several others. The bells clanged on the Piazza and the tourists wandered up and down. I really would like to know what it all is like out of season. I suspect enchanting. I might pop down for a couple of weeks at the end of November.

Here all is merry and the news from the various battle fronts is good. 'Hero' the Alsatian was killed by the train – actually, I am rather relieved. I didn't trust him. However, that's the fourth dog killed since I've been here, so no more. Perhaps a Siamese cat would be a good idea.

Sunday 16 August

Now Ian [Fleming] has died and it is a horrid but expected sadness. He went on smoking and drinking in spite of all warnings. Annie has been distraught for months watching the inevitable approaching, and now it has happened. I am horribly distressed for her and miserable for myself. He has been a good and charming friend to me ever since I have known him.

Joyce, Hester and Ginette are here. The weather has cheered up, and there

1 Thomas Schippers (1930–77), American conductor who was the artistic director of the Spoleto Festival from 1958.

is much laughter learnt of friends and gentleness in hearts at peace under a Swiss heaven. Coley and Joyce and I went with Adrianne, Bill and Margalo [Gillmore] to hear Yehudi Menuhin's concert in a church near Gstaad. It was very enjoyable, but there has never yet been composed a piece of classical music that was not too long.

Hester's book, *Charles II*, dedicated to me, is wonderfully good and I feel very proud. Winnie's new book about Covent Garden is enchanting[1].

I have been asked by the BBC to present on television a tribute to Winston on his ninetieth birthday. Apparently he is very keen on my doing so. Doubtless he has forgotten how disagreeable he frequently was to me during the war. However, he is a very great old man so I shall forget it too. I have agreed to do it. We must only hope that he stays with us until 29 November!

Present Laughter on television has received rave notices in all the papers and I have been 'God blessed' and hailed (in the *Daily Mail*) as a proper ray of sunshine! Which only goes to show that tides ebb and flow and that the stars in their courses are far from static.

There is no more particular news. Wars continue to rage in various quarters of the harassed globe. Little girls continue to be interfered with on Wandsworth Common. Maggie Leighton has married Michael Wilding.

I really *must* settle down and finish *Bon Voyage* (new title for *The Captain's Table*). It's weighing on my conscience. I wish I could have finished the bloody thing in Jamaica and not been forced to leave it three-quarters done.

Sunday 23 August

I have pulled up my socks, girded my loins and, at long last, finished *Bon Voyage* and, what is more, made a very good job of it.

There is little to report. The television of *Blithe Spirit* was apparently not so hot, and *Camelot* has opened at Drury Lane with the most ghastly notices I have ever read. Larry Harvey, however, has apparently got away with it. I'm glad really because, although he is far from universally popular, he has always been charming to me.

The Royal Court Theatre has announced with winsome candour a change of policy. And a very drastic change indeed it is, including *A Cuckoo in the Nest*![2] It is now two or three years since my articles in the *Sunday Times*. It has taken all that time for the penny to drop. It seems that *at last* our quasi-avant-gardists have realized that success in the theatre is more attractive than continued failure and that the dear public *must* be entertained.

---

1 *London Has a Garden*, under Winifred Ashton's pseudonym Clemence Dane.
2 By Ben Travers, now well into his seventies; hardly an angry young man.

Sunday 30 August

The Vortex television play received wonderfully good notices for me and reasonably good for the production. This 'Coward Renaissance' is bewildering me. It can't last!

Irene [Browne] has been here for a week, a perfect house guest, enjoying every moment. She is going back to illness, and possible death. She has to have another operation for a malignancy. It might be all right but I am worried. She is an old friend and, with me, always a dear one.

John Dexter came for three nights. Very sweet, consciously and rather touchingly 'rough diamond'. I have read carefully Christopher Hassall's *Life of Rupert Brooke*. He – the soldiers' poet – emerges as a rather tiresome young man, *too* preoccupied with being 'open-air' and tramping through England's green and lovely land. Unmistakably a bloody good poet. The book is too long and his letters are also too long. A fascinating but curiously irritating character.

I have been correcting the proofs of *Pretty Polly Barlow*. Comparatively few errors on the publisher's side, but far, far too many adverbs and qualifying adjectives on my side. I have been fairly, greatly, firmly, winsomely, rather, almost, very, briskly ruthless! I have now got to start on the proofs of *Me and the Girls* and *Mrs Clapper*[1]. I have also got to read *Hay Fever* as Edith arrives tomorrow.

The *High Spirits* preliminary rehearsals have started and all seems to be going well. This time next week I shall be in London, buckling on my armour to start them off on the right foot. There is a tremendous argle-bargle in the papers about 'dirty plays' being done at the Aldwych. Emile Littler has emerged in a haze of moral rectitude. It is all pretty silly.

John Dexter is very keen on me playing the Shaw *King Charles*[2] in the spring. I am quite keen too, but apparently Larry isn't. However, we shall see. It would, I think, be fascinating to do, particularly at the National Theatre with a bang-up cast.

Saturday 5 September

A really very enjoyable week. Edith has been absolutely sweet and obviously has enjoyed every minute. We took her to Evian – to dine with Adrianne, etc. We read through *Hay Fever* and she is, of course, perfectly brilliant. I can't wait to get into rehearsal. Apart from having a fine cast, to have a really great actress to work with will be thrilling. She *may* be tiresome (particularly with the other actors) but I don't care because she will deliver the goods, and what goods! Wonderful speaking voice, perfect timing and every comedy implication in its place. She also, I must say, looks wonderful. The fact that she is –

1 The other two short stories making up the collection.
2 *In Good King Charles's Golden Days*, for the National Theatre Company at the Old Vic.

in years – too old for the part couldn't matter less. Personally I believe she could play Juliet.

Joan Sutherland arrived on Thursday. She has definitely decided to buy the house next door. It will be lovely to have her installed there. She is a dear and I am very genuinely fond of her. We had a cocktail party yesterday; it was a great success and Charlie [Chaplin] was dear and at his best.

The last of the Coward quartette has been done, *Design for Living*. Opinions are varied. I have a sinister suspicion that Joan Kemp-Welch isn't quite such a good director as I hoped she was. However, I shall be able to judge for myself when I see the kinescopes, which I fear I shall have to do. I had a very insulting notice in the *Daily Mail* by a gentleman who admitted that my personality brought out the devil in him. Actually it wasn't really a devil it brought out, merely a small, envious, journalistic dreariness.

Sunday 13 September

Well now I've got a thorough-going, snuffling, choking, dripping, rasping, fucking cold and I am resenting it very much indeed. I am not used to having colds. My head is full of moist cotton-wool and I am in a rage.

The London visit was successful. On Sunday Coley, Graham and I went to a common, vulgar movie[1] in which David Niven and Marlon Brando tried to be untrue in the South of France. Brando was good at moments. David dull throughout.

A reading of *High Spirits* on Monday morning and rehearsal Monday afternoon. To rehearse Cis Courtneidge after Beattie Lillie is such paradise that I can hardly believe my ears and eyes. In the first place she is a thorough professional and can act. In the second place she can sing and dance. In the third place she is quick-witted, intelligent and hilariously funny, even with the book in her hand. I cannot believe what I endured with Beattie. I *know* she has genius and I *know* she tried, and I also know – thank God – that she got rave notices and saved the day. But never, never, never again. Life is too short for such incessant torment. This cast is excellent. Jan Waters is a 'find', acts well and has comedy inflections. Denis Quilley is a dear man with a really lovely voice. He is a good actor, but there is a shade of dullness which I think may evaporate. Fenella Fielding is a problem. She has evolved a veneer of personal style, somewhere between Gingold and Joan Greenwood. It is all a set-piece and none of it real. She may, I believe, turn out to be very effective, but she is a bloody nuisance, brimming with theories and suggestions. She requires knocking on the head fairly regularly. The set and scene designs are charming and all seems to be going well. I am going back on Friday to give them *all* Saturday with their books out of their hands.

I had a charming evening with Binkie, Joyce and John Perry. Binkie is

1 *Bedtime Story* directed by Ralph Levy.

planning a slap-up revival of *Present Laughter* probably with Nigel Patrick[1] or Johnny Gielgud. Of the two, Nigel will play it better and Johnny is the greater star. We shall see.

Sunday 27 September   London

First of all I am sublimely happy with *Hay Fever*. The cast is fine, disciplined and quick and wonderful to work with. Edith is being very good – a *great* actress. Bob Stephens, Lynn Redgrave, Maggie Smith, Derek Jacobi, all first rate. In fact there was only one sore thumb, which was Sarah Miles who, fortunately, after the first day's rehearsal, swallowed a fish bone, got flu, and hasn't been seen since. Meanwhile her understudy, Louise Purnell, is so pretty and such a good actress that I told Larry I *must* keep her. So after, apparently, some tears she – Sarah Miles – is shedding her inaudibility and lack of technique on *The Crucible* and *The Recruiting Officer*[2]. It has so far given me such deep pleasure directing these lovely actors that I feel quite reborn.

High Spirits, on the other hand, is, as usual, a pain in the crutch. Cis, Denis and Jan Waters good but it has now been decided that the wretched, synthetic Fenella must go. We are trying out Marti Stevens this afternoon. She is no Ina Claire but at least she looks nice and can sing. Oh, this god-damned *High Spirits*. It has caused me nothing but trouble from the outset. Neither Coley nor I can bear to look at it any more. However, we must press on.

I went with Larry to the John Osborne play[3] which, apart from fine acting and production and one or two moments of good invective, is intolerable. Undisciplined, self-indulgent, vulgar and psychologically inaccurate. I went to the opening of *Maggie May*[4] which is a smash hit and, on the whole, deserves to be. Personally I wouldn't care to see it again on account of being allergic to strikers and squalor, but it is very well done. *Wait a Minim* is a cheerful South African revue – charmingly done but a bit attenuated. I spent last Sunday afternoon being photographed by Tony Snowdon all over London – Trafalgar Square, fun-fair, Covent Garden, zoo, etc., very enjoyable. In the evening I dined with him and Princess Margaret. An agreeable evening. With the exception of fucking *High Spirits*, a profitable ten days. I also saw the first act of Zeffirelli's *Amletto* – wonderful production beautifully played.

Sunday 4 October

A good week on the whole. Edith floundering over her words and getting crotchety, but not seriously so and she *is* making a supreme effort. If only the

---

1 Nigel Patrick (1913–81), British actor.
2 These two plays, by Arthur Miller and George Farquhar, were also in the National Theatre repertoire at the time.
3 *Inadmissible Evidence*, produced by Anthony Page and starring Nicol Williamson.
4 Lionel Bart's musical.

stubborn old mule had taken my original advice and studied the words meticulously *before* we went into rehearsal, she would have saved herself a lot of nervousness, frustration and panic and me many hours of irritation. However, that is all part of the gay, mad world of powder and paint. I seem to be doomed to sit patient and still, watching elderly actresses forgetting their lines.

High Spirits is going well. Marti is excellent, sings well, moves beautifully and looks lovely.

Socially I have had a varied week. A large dinner party for Charlie[1] rendered embarrassing at moments by J.B. Priestley making a cracking fool of himself. A lovely evening with the Dowager Duchess of Devonshire and John Betjeman. Another enjoyable evening with Vivien in honour of Tarquin [Olivier] and his fiancée, who is a nice, intelligent girl and very pretty. Diana [Cooper] was there – enchanting as ever – Vivien a bit strained but looking wonderful.

I have seen two movies: *Goldfinger*[2], well done balls, and *The Night of the Iguana*[3], beautifully made with Deborah [Kerr] giving a perfectly glorious performance. Ava Gardner also wonderful. Richard [Burton] a bit scruffy.

I am reading Tom Driberg's book on Dr Buchman and the Moral Rearmament lot[4]. What a lot of nonsense people believe in. And, oh dear me, *all* the thousands of ardent followers! As I think I have mentioned before once or twice, the human race is *very* silly.

Sunday 11 October

I've just driven back from Oxford with Coley. We drove down on Saturday – lunching with Rebecca [West] on the way, which was very enjoyable. We got to Oxford in time for the five o'clock matinée[5] which was quite ghastly. The audience was bad and the performance slow, slipshod and utterly without vitality. The second show (eight o'clock) was entirely different; a packed and enthusiastic audience and a very much better performance.

Meanwhile *Hay Fever* is coming along. Edith still floundering but improving. We had one hour in the set, about which I am reserving my judgement. We rehearse in it all this week at the Phoenix. I saw Larry's *Othello* again on Monday and thought him more wonderful than ever. I also saw *The Recruiting Officer* which I adored. All the cast good, particularly Maggie [Smith] and Bob [Stephens], who were superb.

---

1 Charlie Chaplin, who was publishing his autobiography *My Life*.
2 Based on Ian Fleming's novel and directed by Guy Hamilton.
3 John Huston's film of Tennessee Williams's play.
4 *The Mystery of Moral Rearmament*; Noël was particularly interested because the movement had a large establishment near Les Avants.
5 Of *High Spirits*.

Sunday 18 October   Manchester

Well we now have a Labour Government[1], with a majority of four which isn't, fortunately, enough to permit them to nationalize *too* much. Pam Berry's election party at the Savoy was quite fun really; all sorts and kinds from Diana and Vivien to Bernard Levin[2] and Anthony Powell[3], whom I took quite a fancy to.

Rehearsals have gone very well during the week. The dresses are wonderful and the cast also. The set a bit tatty but can and will be improved. The news from the *High Spirits* front is less secure.

During the week I have managed to see several varied entertainments. *The Dutch Courtesan*[4] at the Old Vic, which I left so eagerly at the end of the first act that I knocked a man down. It's dirty, dull, badly directed, indifferently acted and largely – thank God – inaudible. I have seen *Camelot*, which remains a great big glamorous cracking bore. The production – particularly the first act – is superb; Larry Harvey looks fine, has great authority and, unfortunately, does such an accurate vocal imitation of Richard Burton that if you close your eyes you might just as well be at *Becket*. The dialogue of *Camelot* is so interminable, flat and vulgar, and the music, except for three good tunes, so uninspired that the success it has been both in America and here is incomprehensible.

Poor Cole Porter has died. Another figure from the merry early years. I think it is as well really. He has had so much pain and misery for so long. There is no more particular news to record. The Midland Hotel stands where it always stood and there are still electric drills in the street outside. Dickie Attenborough gives a magnificent performance in *The Guns of Batasi*[5]. I am very well. Whether or not I shall be the next time I write remains to be seen.

Sunday 25 October   London

Well, here I am back again after a week of hell in merry Manchester. The fun really started at 4.30 p.m. on Sunday when Coley woke me from my snooze to announce that Edith was in a state of collapse and couldn't play the dress rehearsal, to which an audience had been invited. I flew upstairs and found her moaning on the bed saying she had a dry mouth and a dropped stomach. Gwen ffrangçon-Davies, whom she had brought along as a comforter, was hovering about looking distraught. I dealt with the scene gently, although

---

1 The first Harold Wilson victory at the polls.
2 Bernard Levin (b. 1928), British journalist and drama critic of the *Daily Mail*.
3 Anthony Powell (b. 1905), British author, best known for his novel sequence 'A Dance to the Music of Time'.
4 Early seventeenth-century comedy by John Marston.
5 Film directed by John Guillermin.

inwardly seething, then whisked Gwen down to my suite for a conference with John Dexter. Gwen was almost as angry as I was and we decided that the only thing to do was to give the Dame hell. So back we went upstairs again and I let fly and told Edith that she was a disgrace to herself, the theatre *and* Christian Science[1], and that unless she got down to the theatre immediately she would never appear again. Gwen interposed a few Mary Baker Eddy platitudes and the net result was that she finally *did* get herself to the theatre. The audience had to be sent away and the dress rehearsal was funereal. After it was over I went through the whole play again with Maggie Smith, who is word perfect[2] and incredibly funny. *Her* understudy, Pauline Taylor, was also word perfect and so I knew that in a supreme emergency we were safe.

On the opening night (Monday) Edith tottered insecurely through the play, drying up, mistiming and cutting lots of important lines. However, the play and the brilliance of the cast got us through. The notices were marvellous. Larry came down, was delighted with everything and everybody but Edith, who appalled him. When he asked her why she had not put on her false eyelashes she replied that it was because she didn't want to feel she was giving a performance! As she had been bellowing for weeks about old-timers setting an example to the young ones, this didn't sound *quite* right. She dried up and fluffed through all the performances, played slowly and down, and took her curtain calls as though she had just been un-nailed from the cross. I have a stop-and-start dress rehearsal tonight, an invited dress rehearsal, and we open on Tuesday, so we shall see.

Meanwhile the wretched *High Spirits* opened at the Palace on Tuesday to a handful of people who seemed to be as bored with it as I was. Marti looked nice, Cis tried with only occasional success to be funny. Jan Waters and Denis Quilley were good, and the orchestra appalling. Since then there have been scenes and dramas with Dany Daniels screaming and decamping for London. The notices were dreadful and the business virtually non-existent.

During the week poor Joan [Plowright] had a miscarriage, so poor Larry had to open *The Master Builder* on Friday night with the understudy, Jeanne Hepple, who incidentally was quite brilliant. Celia [Johnson] marvellous, Larry superb, and the play beautifully done. Larry has been very, very sweet to me all through and, Edith or no Edith, I am very proud to be with the National Theatre.

Sunday 1 November

Well. *Hay Fever* opened on Tuesday night and was a triumph. The notices, with the usual exception of the *Daily Express*, were raves. Edith gave an

1 In which Dame Edith had deep faith.
2 In the role of Judith, which she was understudying while playing Myra.

adequate performance, too slow and insecure, but the rest of the company were brilliant. I have had tremendous praise both for the play and my direction, so for the moment I have nothing to complain about. Edith, on the *second* night, was merry and gay and gave a quite sparkling performance. The box-office is besieged and it is obviously the biggest hit the National Theatre has had since *Othello*. Larry, as usual, has been wonderful to me and so far as that little enterprise goes I am very happy.

On Friday evening I dined with the Quentin Crewes[1], Rosamond [Lehmann], Edna O'Brien[2] and Bernard Levin. He was very amiable and is obviously intelligent. My personal party for the *Hay Fever* opening consisted of Diana Cooper, Judy Garland, Mark[3], Margot Fonteyn, Nureyev, Lena Horne, Vivien and Jack [Merivale], over and above Joyce, Gladys, Graham and Coley. Poor Lornie was ill in bed with flu. She *is* unfortunate. Coley, as usual, has coped serenely with everything – first-night seats, telegrams, fuss and fume. Tuesday, of course, we are dreading. We are both so utterly sick to death of *High Spirits*, which isn't altogether surprising. However, after the first night I shall never, I hope, have to sit through it again. My party this time will be the Fairbanks, Leontyne Price, Lilli and Carlos, Lena, Judy, etc. Pray God we shall be a frolicsome party.

Sunday 8 November   Les Avants

That *was* a week that was, and I arrived here on Friday evening with Coley absolutely exhausted, almost in a trance. With the exception of last night, when we dined with Adrianne and the Chaplins, I have been in bed and am at last beginning to unwind.

High Spirits opened on Tuesday night to a wildly enthusiastic audience, much more so than ever hoped for. The show went wonderfully and the next morning, as I anticipated, disaster. All the notices horrible with the exception of the *Financial Times*, whose critic[4] must be mad because he said, among other things, that Marti and Denis play the comedy scenes beautifully. As they neither of them get one laugh throughout the evening with all those wonderful lines, I cannot quite agree. The main burden of the notices is that the beautiful play has been mucked about with. Timmy [Gray] and Hugh [Martin] have properly bought it[5]. Considering their insensate obstinacy from the very beginning, I cannot feel altogether sorry. Cis also got some well-deserved cracks for vulgarizing Madame Arcati, and serve her bloody well right. I told her in Oxford to redress it entirely, play it in character and

1 Quentin Crewe (b. 1926), writer and journalist, and his wife, novelist Angela Huth.
2 Edna O'Brien (b. 1936), Irish novelist resident in London.
3 Mark Herron, Judy Garland's current husband.
4 B.A. Young, who had just replaced T.C. Worsley.
5 From the critics.

take out the cheap interpolated gags. She has *not* done so. The one I am really sorry for is Geoffrey [Russell]. He has behaved so very well all the way along and I am afraid, unless a miracle happens, that he will lose a packet. The miracle just *might* happen, but I fear it is unlikely. The only hope is that the audiences love it and the only problem is – with these notices – that we may not get them into the theatre. The Sunday notices are equally damning except – surprise, surprise – a spirited defence from the *Sunday Express*.

On Wednesday I taped the Winston tribute. It was a long job but, I think, successful. On Thursday I dined with Liza and John [Hope] and Princess Marina, who was particularly sweet. On Monday Coley and I went to the Variety Command Performance at the Palladium. Some of it good, notably Lena Horne and Tommy Cooper; Gracie Fields a tiny bit worrying but still a bit left. The young singing ladies headed by Cilla Black ghastly beyond belief. The Queen, as usual, looked enchanting.

Since getting here I have read a not-so-good thriller by Eric Ambler[1], and young Winston's book about his flight across Africa[2] – informative, lucid and occasionally rather naively pompous, but he emerges as a dear young man with a lot of his grandfather's courage. I can hardly believe that these last two frantic months are over but they *are* and, like a poltergeist, I intend to lie doggo for days.

Wednesday 18 November

The days have passed peacefully enough and in course of them a rip-snorting scandal has blown up and looks like going on blowing until it achieves hurricane velocity. It concerns George Sanders and his wife Benita Hume. George, who has always been one for having grandiose ideas and splendid pipe-dreams about making vast amounts of money for nothing, dreamed up a scheme for making sausages in Scotland! A company was formed named, roguishly but unfortunately, 'Cadco'. A week or so ago the whole thing went sky high. George and Benita have lost so far £150,000. There is to be a question asked tomorrow in the House of Commons and there is a full enquiry pending. I am sorry for Benita. I am not all that sorry for George because he has behaved like a perfect ass. At all events, we now wait and see what develops.

High Spirits is hobbling along convulsively. *Hay Fever* more and more triumphant. *Pretty Polly Barlow* has so far received one abusive notice from a ghastly young squirt called Julian Jebb in the *Sunday Times* and two other rather patronizing ones.

---

1 *A Kind of Anger.*
2 *First Journey* by Winston Churchill, Randolph's son.

Sunday 22 November

Nothing very much has happened but the scandal is a-growing and a-blowing. We dined the other evening with the Norman Krasnas[1] in the house they have contrived to imbue with an atmosphere of Beverly Hills. Norman gave me one of his new plays to read. I ploughed through the script, fished out some minor criticisms, telephoned to him and he was delighted. Alas and alack, the more I read and see concerning American values the more my crusty old heart sinks. There is so much kindness and friendliness and, frequently, authentic humour, but the basic vulgarity of viewpoint pushes its way up and permeates everything they say or do. There are, of course, notable exceptions and much to love and admire but, oh, how glad I am to be on this side of that turbulent Atlantic.

On the other side of the medal, David Cecil's biography of Max Beerbohm[2] is a joy. Exquisitely written, compassionate and evocative. Following on that, I have read Max's letters to Reggie Turner and his theatre criticism, most of which was brilliant. Our own dear Levins and Shulmans should study them carefully and perhaps learn to decry with grace and style rather than with abusive invective. I have read the first volume of one of Anthony Powell's sagas[3]. Very well written, at moments witty, but on the whole a trifle arid, a mixture of Proust and bromide. The critics who have compared him to Evelyn Waugh are far from accurate. Evelyn, in his earlier books at least, had zest and brevity and was irresistibly comic. Powell is meticulous and, by comparison, stodgy. The difference between the Yorkshire pudding you get in restaurants and the Yorkshire puddings I used to make in Bermuda.

There has been a rumour floating about, secretly, that I *may* be asked to direct *Love for Love* for the National Theatre. I have read it and would rather die. It's no good, I simply cannot abide Restoration comedy. I am sure it was good in its time, but now its obvious, bawdy roguishness bores the hell out of me. *Love for Love* seems to me to be appallingly overwritten. It is, I suppose, kind of critics to compare me with Congreve, but I do wish they hadn't. We return to London tomorrow.

Sunday 6 December

It has been snowing steadily for four days and it is now over a metre deep. Very beautiful to look at but a trifle inconvenient. The London visit was exhausting but, on the whole, enjoyable. We went to see Rudi and Margot dance *Le Corsair* and *Daphnis and Chloë* (Margot without Rudi) and had supper with them afterwards. Their dancing was exquisite. We all went to Marlene's

1 Norman Krasna (b. 1909), Hollywood playwright and his wife.
2 Entitled simply *Max*.
3 *A Question of Upbringing*.

opening night[1] and to a party at Binkie's afterwards. She was really stagger-ingly good and had a triumph. She has learnt so much, so much. I dined with Princess Marina and Princess Olga, sweet but a tiny bit dull. My weekend with Zara and Peter Cazalet was far from dull. In the first place the Queen Mother was sweeter to me than ever, and in the second place Peter, Zara and the Shawcrosses[2] couldn't have been nicer. We raced on Saturday at Lingfield and on Sunday morning went to church! A pleasant enough little service with a mercifully brief sermon. My mind, however, is not really attuned to the Church of England or any other church for that matter. I loathe all that insistence on being a miserable sinner and asking for forgiveness. The tradi-tional part of it is all right with the squeaky hymns and the choir (mixed) and the best bibs and tuckers and all the age-old carry-on, but the fundamental faith underlying it is missing in me. I never have felt and I don't feel now the call of the Holy Spirit, and I suspect I never shall.

The house party was fun all the time. We played croquet, we giggled, I played the piano a lot, everyone was gay and sweet. Mary and Christopher Soames came over for dinner on Saturday night and she and I had a long Churchill heart-to-heart. She is a dear and I have always liked her the best of the lot. Her opinion of Duncan[3] coincides with mine – i.e. that he is a shit. She is writing a biography of Lady Churchill and I have a feeling she will do it well. She is honest, unbiased and nobody's fool. On Sunday evening we all watched *Ninety Years On*[4]. Thank God it was good and I was good. Everyone present was very impressed and I have since been flooded with letters of praise. I sat next to the darling QM who was palpably moved. The next morning I drove up to London with her through sun and frost and fog. I have a feeling I might become a bore about the Queen Mother. I have always liked her since we first met in the twenties, and of late years I have come to adore her. She has irrepressible humour, divine manners and a kind heart. My affection for her has gone far beyond royal *snobisme*. She is also, I am proud and happy to say, genuinely fond of me.

On Monday I went to a lunch (fork and nasty) given for me by Heine-mann's[5]. It was really very agreeable and I was made much of. In the evening Coley and I went to a dress rehearsal of *The Royal Hunt of the Sun* which I most thoroughly enjoyed. Bob Stephens and Colin Blakely were fine, the direction[6] superb, and it is a beautifully written play. The difference between Peter Shaffer and all the Osbornes and Weskers is that he has no hatred in his

---

1 In solo concert at the Queen's Theatre.
2 Sir Hartley William Shawcross, lawyer and politician, and Lady Shawcross.
3 Duncan Sandys, her ex-brother-in-law.
4 The Churchill birthday tribute written by Rattigan and narrated by Noël.
5 To celebrate the publication of his short story collection, *Pretty Polly Barlow*.
6 By John Dexter.

heart and no partisan axe to grind. He writes compassionately about human beings. He also has more than a touch of poetry. I only wish he would write more.

Since coming back here I have had some very snooty, patronizing notices of *Pretty Polly* and some raves for the Winston tribute mixed with some snarling attacks. I know that this is the age of 'the common man' but I do wish there were not quite so many of them writing for the newspapers. Several have commented on my 'hat-in-hand' subservience, presumably because I addressed him [Churchill] throughout as 'Sir'. To the common mind, 'sir' appears to be a symbol of slavery, whereas of course the omission of it in the proper circumstances would be a huge symbol of social insecurity. The dreadful silliness of the human race continues to amaze me. The embittered fighting for territory all over the world. The balls written in newspapers, both common and intellectual, about all essential problems. I am too old to allow it to infuriate me but not too old for it still to surprise me. Personally I intend to continue my life as cheerfully as I can until I arrive at the end of it. 'As cheerfully as I can' is, of course, the operative phrase, but come weal, come woe, I believe I stand a better chance than most owing to a basic irreverence for the whole silly business.

Wednesday 16 December   Capri

Well, I am now half-way through the sixties and can honestly be said to be pushing seventy. At the moment I feel as if I were pushing ninety. This little jaunt has been a dreary failure, and oh, what high hopes we started out with![1] We drove to Naples, had a nasty-ish lunch, caught the Aliscarfi and arrived here at four o'clock. Lovely weather but nippy. The divine villa was freezing. Nobody had warned anyone that I was coming. The night was hell and I steadily perished. The next morning I discovered that in the winter the villa gets no sun at all even in the late afternoon. In the evening, when seven beastly maids with seven beastly mops had been at it, the house was only tepid and the lavatory refused to work. This decided me and I moved there and then to a hotel, which is second class but warm and the proprietor is a dear. Coley and Graham organized my luggage the next morning. We had quite a pleasant day on Monday and lunched in the sun at the Piccola Marina. Yesterday, however, the weather changed violently and has remained completely *cattivo*.

Capri out of season is not only quiet but moribund. There is nowhere to go, no one to see, nowhere to eat except two crummy restaurants, added to which the necessity of having to walk up and down narrow cobbled streets is exhausting and hurting my legs badly. In fact the whole thing is a bugger

1 Coley, Graham and Noël had decided to see what Capri might be like in midwinter, staying in Jean Baruch-Bové's villa.

and I have decided that my head should be very thoroughly examined. I have in Switzerland a divine house, wonderful servants, exquisite food, lovely country, everything my heart can desire, and here I am sitting on a deserted rock in the pouring rain getting more decrepit and cross with every breath I take. This is not – repeat *not* – going to continue. I have decided to leave for Switzerland, home and beauty on Saturday and put myself down in peace and comfort.

Poor old enemy-friend Edith Sitwell died. I am sad, and glad that I talked to her before I left London.

Sunday 27 December   Les Avants

Christmas is now over and done with and, contrary to all expectations, I enjoyed every minute of it. Just Coley, Graham, me and the staff. Everybody kissed everybody else and exchanged many, many presents. We all drank too much and ate too much and it was lovely.

Yesterday we went to the dear Nivens where everybody kissed everybody else, exchanged presents, drank too much and ate too much and it was also lovely. We played games and giggled and David was dearer than ever. The snow lay all about, deep and uncrisp and uneven. Hjordis, the two boys and the two little adopted girls were enchanting and we staggered off the train at Les Avants giggling like idiots and feeling fine.

I have decided, after quite a lot of reflection, that the most important thing for me to do next is a not too long autobiography of those unrecorded years from 1931 to 1939. God knows, enough occurred during them to justify their being rescued from oblivion. I can embark on the latter years of my life – since 1945 – later on. But those eight years *must* be remembered and put down. I wish, I wish I had kept a diary in those days, but I think I can rely fairly well on memory.

Pretty Polly has received not one really good notice. A few quite good, a lot very bad, and all brief and patronizing. It is foolish for a writer constantly to decry the critics; it is also foolish, I think, for the critics so constantly to decry anyone who writes as well as I do. They have been proved wrong before often enough and, who knows, they may be proved wrong again. I *know Me and the Girls* is good, also *Mrs Capper. Pretty Polly* is less interesting, being more conventional in theme, but it is at moments very funny and eminently readable. The battle, of course, will never end until the grave closes over me, and then! oh dear, the balls that will be written about me.

I have just reread the last two volumes of Diana [Cooper]'s autobiography. Exquisitely written and a mind incapable of the smallest vulgarity. I have also read a book about the last years of President Wilson called *When the Cheering Stopped*. Execrably written and a mind incapable of anything but vulgarity. Enjoyable in a way in spite of continual wincing at the false values and clumsily expressed sentiments. I cannot feel that Mrs Wilson emerges as a very attractive character. She is the epitome of the dominant American female at her worst. The President appears as a pretentious, conceited, pathetic ass. A fascinating document.

1965

A varied year, highlighted by the visit of the Queen Mother to Jamaica in general and to Noël's Firefly and Blue Harbour in particular. This was the year in which he wrote his last major play, A Song at Twilight, *in whose central character, Sir Hugo Latymer, is to be found a remarkable amalgam of Max Beerbohm and Somerset Maugham. It was also the year in which he worked with Laurence Olivier for the first time since* Private Lives *(in an Otto Preminger thriller called* Bunny Lake is Missing*), the year in which he lost his beloved Winifred (Clemence Dane), and the year in which he set out on his last major holiday alone, to the Seychelles, a holiday which left him with an illness from which it could be argued that he never totally recovered. It left his wanderlust curiously undimmed: 'My passion for journeys is unchanged by the passing years. I am, however, always either too late or too early; I arrive in Japan just when the cherry blossom has fallen. I get to China too early for the next revolution. I reach Canada when the maple leaves have gone, and the snow hasn't arrived. People are always telling me about something I have just missed; I find it very restful.'*

Tuesday 5 January   Les Avants

The New Year festivities were very funny and most enjoyable. Johan Cast-berg[1] came and brought his violin! I only asked him because his wife and children are away and he was all alone. No good deed goes unpunished. He had also ordered a car for 1 a.m., whereas we were all ready for bed at twelve o'clock sharp. Altogether, however, it was a hilarious evening. Kit [Cornell], Nancy [Hamilton], Binkie, Coley, Graham and me. They are very sweet, but Nancy talks far too much. Binkie was sweet and right back again to the old Binkie of past days.

I am worried about Graham. He is so dear and loving and all his essential values are right, but his future career seems to me fairly hopeless. If only *High Spirits* had been a success.[2] If only he could find a steady job. If only he wasn't so young at heart and so immature in brain. He has had so many chances and failed. He knows this, of course, and I am sure that he has many miserable moments, but he *won't* work unless he has to, then he is at it like a tiger, but he lacks the self-discipline to force himself. He also, I fear, lacks physical vitality. He sleeps and 'rests' far too much. He *hasn't* pressed on with learning to type. He only reads trash and that very seldom. It's a despairing situation because unless he does *something* soon he will decline into a pathetic, elderly failure. I can't bear to think of it. Something must be done.

I'm busy making notes for *Past Conditional*[3], and, my God, there is much to remember.

Sunday 17 January

The time has passed quickly. Winston Churchill, I fear, is dying at this very moment. I suppose it's just as well really. Ninety years is a long, long time. Personally I would rather not wait until the faculties begin to go. However, that must be left in the hands of 'The One Above' and I hope he'll do something about it and not just sit there.

This begins my last week here. I have written two 'theatre' pieces and am now embarking on a third. These will, I hope, be serialized and eventually help to make up a book. I have read a detailed biography of Alfred and Lynn[4] on which I have had to write a guarded comment for *Life* magazine. *High Spirits* is closing next Saturday. Celia Johnson is taking over *Hay Fever* when Edith leaves in March. I shall rehearse her the week of the twenty-fifth. We dined with the Sanders and met Lex Barker[5]! Sophia Loren and Peter

1 Johan Castberg, a Swiss neighbour.
2 For Graham as co-director.
3 The volume of 1930s memoirs he was never to write.
4 *The Lunts* by George Freedley.
5 Lex Barker (1919–73), American actor famous for playing Tarzan; he had just finished filming *Kali-Yug, Goddess of Vengeance*.

Ustinov[1] are dining tonight. I have reread all three volumes of Diana [Cooper]'s, autobiography – exquisite. Also Lady Longford's immense biography of Queen Victoria, one of the best I have ever read. Also I have read Barrilet and Gredy's *Fleur de Cactus*, a really very funny, thoroughly commercial play[2]. Coley and I slide down the mountain daily on luges by which we inhale enough fresh air to fortify ourselves for *The Times* crossword.

Sunday 24 January   Paris

Arrived here on Friday evening by the Cisalpine de luxe train from Lausanne. So de luxe was it that I had to fight my way into it and out of it with no porters. Yesterday I lunched with Edward [Molyneux], who is starting up as a couturier again and is merry as a grig. Ginette gave a fairly violent 'cocktail' for me with most of the *crème* of the French theatre: Maurice Chevalier, Sophie Desmarets, Jean Poiret, Nicole Courcelle, Gaby Sylva, François Perrier, etc., after which we dined – Ginette, Paul-Emile and I – at the Berkeley and very expensive it was too.

On Sunday afternoon I went to see *Fleur de Cactus*, grossly overplayed by everyone but Jean Poiret, and vilely directed. The play somehow survived. After this, a pleasant tête-à-tête with Maria Callas, who looked wonderful and couldn't have been sweeter.

My last week in Switzerland was occupied to the full. I went on racking my brains to remember my lost years of the thirties and finally managed to get them and their events into some sort of order. I wrote another theatre article, so now there are three done towards my ultimate book. Sophia Loren and Peter Ustinov came to dine, and two days later Coley and I stood about for hours in the withering cold watching them shoot some scenes on the lakeside at Montreux. She is a dear, I think, and a hundred per cent professional. Peter seemed to be a bit woolly and indecisive, but he is a brilliant creature and I am very fond of him. I don't think, however, that I would like to be directed by him. He is very slow.

Now my travels start again. I've got a hell of a week ahead of me but I suppose I shall survive.

Winston Churchill died this morning.

Thursday 4 February   New York

Coley and I arrived here last night. The flight was uneventful, but the ten days preceding it were very eventful indeed. In course of them I rehearsed Celia Johnson in *Hay Fever*, in which she is going to be marvellous. Cast *Present Laughter* with Binkie and Nigel Patrick; an extremely good cast – Nigel Patrick, Phyllis Calvert, Maxine Audley, Richard Briers, Graham Payn,

1 They were in Switzerland filming *Lady L.*
2 Which went on to a long London and New York stage and screen success as *Cactus Flower*.

Avice Landon, etc. On Sunday my whole day was spent in the Queen's Theatre rehearsing for the *Golden Hour of Drama*[1] which I had to introduce with a succinct two-and-a-half-minute speech, after which I popped along to Kensington Palace and watched the programme through with Princess Margaret, Tony, and Sharman Douglas, and very enjoyable it was too, although much too long, and I stayed far too late after it.

I saw *The Crucible*, brilliantly directed by Larry – a thrilling evening in the theatre. I went to *Marat/Sade*[2] at the Aldwych with Joycie, which I thought pretentious balls. Joyce rechristened it *Brookery Nook*[3]. I will always despise talented directors who choose a stinkingly bad play just because it offers directorial opportunities. It was over-directed anyhow. On Monday night *Divorce Me Darling*, Sandy Wilson's follow-up of *The Boy Friend*, some good tunes but pretty dismal on the whole.

I lunched with the Queen Mother the day after I arrived in London. She is coming to Firefly on the twenty-fourth to lunch, so it's out with the curry powder. I do love her.

I was taken to see the lying-in-state of Winston Churchill, infinitely impressive – those endless crowds moving slowly and silently by after waiting in the bitter weather for many hours. On Saturday morning Vivien, Jack, Bumble[4], Billy Chappell, Graham, Coley and I watched the funeral on television from 9.20 until 1.30 – in floods of proud tears most of the time. No other race could have done so great a tribute with so little pomposity and so much dignity. The arrival of the barge we could see from the window of my sitting-room[5], directly opposite us. A great and truly noble experience. Other personal social carry-ons were a lunch with darling Diana and the Snowdons and Judy [Garland], and a farewell cocktail party given by me on Tuesday. A mixed bag ranging from dear Bob Menzies to Nureyev, Margot, Phyllis Monkman and Lionel Bart.

Sunday 14 February   Jamaica

Coley and I arrived here on Thursday more dead than alive, utterly exhausted. New York was as hectic as it always is. We went to *Tiny Alice* and were as bewildered as everyone else including the cast. Edward Albee has a strong sense of theatre and he writes good parts. The first act was hopeful, after that a chaotic mess of sex and symbolism. Beautifully directed and acted except for poor Johnny G. who was strained and unconvincing. Altogether a maddening evening in the theatre, so nearly good and yet so bloody pretentious. I told

1 An ATV spectacular from the West End.
2 Drama by Peter Weiss.
3 Peter Brook was its director.
4 Beatrice Dawson, costume designer.
5 On the Savoy Hotel's embankment side.

Edward what I felt and he was very amiable about it. He and his firm, Clinton Wilder and Richard Barr, want to do a Noël Coward repertory next autumn: *Hay Fever, Private Lives, Present Laughter* and *Design for Living*. They want to do a slap-up production on Broadway and at the same time do a Samuel Beckett repertory with a slap-down production *off* Broadway. I wonder which will be the bigger success.

I saw the second act of *High Spirits*, Beattie outrageous but terribly funny. Tammy gabbling. Alfred and Lynn arranged for us – Kit, Nancy [Hamilton], Carol Channing, Coley and me – to see *The Magnificent Yankee*, the television play they did about Oliver Wendell Holmes. Absolutely superb. The best acting possible. They are both incredible. Lots of argle-bargle about *The Girl Who Came to Supper* in London and a possible national tour of *High Spirits*. Long and idiotic conversation with David Selznick about electronic theatre! All too much, too much, too much.

Sunday 21 February

Things are looking up. My stomach, which was bad for several days, has now decided to behave. The magic of this island plus a lot of rest has done the trick. Coley and I had one of our shopping sprees in Kingston on Monday, in the course of which we bought an electric typewriter (not yet arrived), two new beds for Alfred and Lynn, an armchair, a Sony television set and six pairs of jockey shorts.

The hubbub about the Queen Mother coming to lunch with me, far from being a secret, is the talk of the island. The whole place has been hopping with security police for weeks. I drove to Kingston on Friday to lunch at King's House. A very pompous lunch, but the Campbells (Governor-General and wife) were welcoming and sweet. The Queen Mother, as always, enchanting, and her entourage dear as can be. Instead of her coming across the Junction Road, which would have taken her an hour and a half, it has been arranged for her to pay a state visit to Spanish Town and drive here via Bog Walk, Fern Gully and Ocho Rios, which puts fifty miles on to her journey. Poor dear, I *did* so want her to relax; however, she plans to get here about 1.15 (I doubt this). After lunch she has a three-hour drive to Tryall. However, there is nothing to be done except pray the weather is good. I sensed bewilderment among the officials that she should wish to come to my tiny, ungrand house when there are so many more apparently suitable ones. They just don't know the Queen Mother. I am having her whole party, and am looking forward to it, but shall be relieved when it is over.

Lynn and Alfred arrived on Thursday, gay and well and as dear as ever. I have read about eight books since I arrived, including *The Happy Foreigner* and *The Squire* by Enid Bagnold. Both exquisitely written. She really is an extraordinary writer and her use of English is magical. Also Ludovic Kennedy's account of the Stephen Ward trial, a scathing and, I fear, justified attack on English justice and London police methods. Today Maureen Dufferin and party are coming to lunch. We shall give them a dress rehearsal of what we are giving the Queen Mother, i.e. curry in coconuts, fish mousse and rum cream pie. Soon I shall start to work. There is much to be done.

Sunday 28 February

On Wednesday the weather was crystal clear and sunny but a bit windy. The Queen Mother arrived at 1.20 and was gayer and more enchanting than ever. The place was littered with security agents, policemen and ebony chiefs of police, all very large, but I managed to keep them at bay. Lunch was a great success. I had to make an iced soup twenty minutes before the QM arrived because the fish mousse collapsed into a grey heap and had the consistency of an ordinary Slazenger tennis ball. The curry was delicious served in steaming coconuts, then there was a vast bowl of strawberries and a rum cream pie. We sat on the verandah before lunch and introduced the Queen Mother to bullshots. She had two and was delighted. The view was dazzlingly beautiful and absolutely at its best. She was supposed to leave at three o'clock for her long drive to Tryall, but she insisted on visiting Blue Harbour as well, so I drove down with her through the cheering citizens of Grant's Town and she didn't actually leave until ten to four.

Coley, Blanche [Blackwell] and Lynn and Alfred inevitably fell in love with her. As for me, I am at her feet. She has infinite grace of mind, charm, humour and deep-down kindness, in addition to which she looks enchanting. She puts everyone at ease immediately without condescension or apparent effort. She did me great honour by driving nearly eighty miles off her course to come to see me and I do really believe she enjoyed it. Everyone waited on everyone else at lunch. The houseboy – by his special request – wore white gloves and a white coat. It was all tremendous fun, without a moment of strain, and she left behind her five gibbering worshippers.

I have sold *Bon Voyage*, or rather Curtis Brown[1] have, to *McCall's* magazine for $12,500! I have virtually given up smoking. Five a day maximum. The weather has changed and become stormy and freezing; however, I don't suppose it will last. That was another week that was!

Sunday 14 March

Quite a good week. I have written the first act of a new play called *A Song at Twilight*. So far it is good, I know, and I've got the fireworks yet to come in the last act. The original idea has been in my mind for some time. It was suggested by a scene in David Cecil's biography of Max Beerbohm when Constance Collier, after years of non-contact, suddenly descends on him when

1 His literary agents.

he is an old man and flattens him with her vitality. My play is more sinister, and there is Maugham in it as well as Max. All this is very exciting, but what is most exciting of all is my extraordinary facility for writing dialogue. Too great a facility really. I have to force myself to go slowly. And oh, how much easier it is to write than prose! Anyhow, at the moment I'm functioning happily.

The rehearsals of *Present Laughter* are apparently going very well. Graham has lost eleven pounds and is as happy as a bee. The Noël Coward Repertory Company in New York is coming along. They have agreed with me to cut *Present Laughter* and only do three – *Private Lives*, *Hay Fever* and *Design for Living*. They have suggested Alfred to direct *D. for L.* which is a fine idea, and Eileen Herlie to play *Hay Fever*. She should be quite good, she is an excellent comedienne. But oh, casting the rest after my darling National Theatre Company will be a desolate endeavour. Team-work is not a strong attribute of the current American theatre. However, I am sure this particular management will do its best. The days here pass by with the speed of light. Because, I suppose, I am working and happy. The tediums of the outside world seem remote.

I have been offered five days' work in a film[1] by Otto Preminger at the end of May which I will accept if the part is good enough. Joan Sutherland and family arrive tomorrow week. Until then, quiet flows the Don. Which reminds me, Donald Albery is still frigging about over the London production of *The Girl Who Came to Supper*.

Sunday 21 March

A Song at Twilight is nearly finished. I am purposely not hurrying because if I type for more than three hours a day I get tensed up and feel exhausted. It is a good play, I really believe, and has some important things said. I am going to do a little rewriting at the beginning before I go on further because the characters have taken over and the present beginning is no longer quite valid. This is in no way a bore. I am enjoying writing dialogue again so very much. The script that Otto Preminger wants me for is bloody good and so I've said I'll do it. Thirty thousand dollars for one week's work plus suite at the Savoy and car. The part is a drunken old queerish masochist. Could be effective, I think. Bill Marchant[2] has done a fine job on the television script of *Pretty Polly*, so good is it that I would like him to do the movie script as well.

We – Coley and I – have come to a great decision. We have been discussing it for over a year. Coley is now fifty-six, Lornie over seventy, and I am sixty-five. Sooner or later we've got to have extra help. Coley now does all business letters, etc., runs the houses here and in Switzerland, deals with the guests, books all reservations and organizes all journeys. There are also lots of other

1 *Bunny Lake is Missing.*
2 William Marchant, British writer.

things, such as the sorting of my private letters and journals, which he hasn't time to attempt. We have therefore been searching in our minds for a sort of secretary-cum-dogsbody for him, whom he could train to take more and more of the burden off his shoulders.

Two days ago I offered the job to Nicky Malabre. He is office-trained, having been with Pan-Am for years. He is thirty-five, nice looking, presentable, excellent manners and great charm. He is also quite bright, can type, drive a car, etc. Above all he has humour and a nice character. He also has a strong Jamaican accent! Personally I think he's a very good bet. He has flown to Miami until tomorrow when he will give us his decision. I think it will be yes. It is, of course, an added expense, but it must be realized that if anything should happen to Coley I should have *no one* who knew the ropes and was *au courant* with all the complications of my very complicated life. I don't want one day to be faced suddenly with an emergency. Much better have someone waiting in the wings.

Sunday 28 March

I am wagging my tail hard. Yesterday I finished the play and I really think it's a rouser. Of course, it may turn out not to be and everyone will hate it, but I doubt this. In the first place I intend to play it myself with, if possible, Maggie Leighton and Irene Worth. There are only four characters and three of them are fine parts. I am now preparing two long one-acters to play as contrast in the same set. One, *Concert Pitch*, about a great conductor, and the other, *Shadows of the Evening*, about a north-country business tycoon. We shall see.

In the meantime *Present Laughter* has opened in Brighton and received a screaming rave notice from the usually rather acid critic there. Graham is apparently very good, which is of course a tremendous relief to me. They all seem to be good; only Maxine Audley hasn't quite made it, but she will probably improve before they get to town. *Hay Fever* opened in Glasgow and got *two* rave notices! Celia is apparently enchanting in it. It is small wonder that I am purring.

Nicky has accepted the job with immense enthusiasm. He has been so really good during the discussions. We are all getting steamed up about the Sutherland-Coward record which is to be made in November. It will be very thrilling to hear that glorious voice singing my music. Coley and I flew to Montego on Tuesday to have lunch with Lady Churchill, extremely nice and obviously pleased to see me. I haven't seen her for a long while and I found her a little frail, not surprisingly as she is eighty, and a tiny bit deaf, but her charm was undiminished. She had been delighted by my tribute to Winston and apparently he did sit through the whole thing and asked for more! I am reading Violet Bonham-Carter's book on Winston[1] which is very good indeed,

1 *Winston Churchill as I Knew Him.*

and rereading Evelyn's *Vile Bodies*, which is masterly and as fresh and wildly funny as it ever was. Maria Callas has had a supreme triumph in *Tosca* at the Met. I never stop plunging into the pool to rescue grasshoppers, bees, beetles and other insects. I cannot bear to think of those intricate, sensitive mechanisms perishing in chlorine. I also salvage an occasional frog. Not one as yet has had the gratitude to turn into a Prince Charming.

Sunday 4 April

This week started with tragic sadness. Two cables, one from Lornie and one from Dick [Addinsell], saying that darling Winnie had died. Although at the back of my mind I had been expecting it, it was a miserable shock. She'd been in pain for months. Later I had a letter saying that on the evening before, she rallied suddenly, tied a purple nylon scarf round her head, slapped on some lipstick, and sent for Dick and Victor[1] and had a little farewell party with them for an hour. She was certainly a gallant old girl. I find it hard to bear the thought that I shall never see her again. When I think of all the war years and the fun we had in her little Tavistock Street house and all the arguments and jokes and violent enthusiasms, I realize how much I am in her debt. What is particularly horrid for me is that I wrote to her on Friday – the day she died – a loving letter. If only I had done so a few days before. I would so have liked her to hear from me and know that I was thinking of her. Well, that's one more old friend gone – the cupboard is getting barer. There is no sense in grieving; at my age these partings must be expected and accepted. I wrote a brief tribute to her for *The Times*. Irene [Browne], on the other hand, has had her operation very successfully and looks forward to several more years of life. Patrick [Woodcock] gives her about a year.

I have temporarily abandoned the short plays and started on *Past Conditional* which so far is going well, but it will be a long job. However, I find now that I am writing prose much more easily than I used to and I am still besotted about my electric typewriter. The Great Reaper swooped down again and carried off the poor Princess Royal, suddenly and swiftly with a coronary thrombosis. In fact he has had quite a busy time lately.

Joan and Ricky are here. They are no trouble at all and I am really fond of them. Joan is a dear character. I've been bullying her about her Australian accent. James Pope-Hennessy arrived last night, and today, after a week of blissful sunshine, the heavens are greyly disgorging a steady deluge. It's all the moon's fault. I've finished Violet Bonham-Carter's book on Winston which is beautifully done. What an extraordinary character. Deeply as I revere and admire him, I could never have loved him. I've now taken to reading some

1 Victor Stiebel, designer.

of the longer poems of Wordsworth and very rewarding they are. Only just over three more weeks and we shall be winging away again.

Sunday 11 April

Joan and Ricky left today. James is still here. The mixture has been a tremendous success. James is a dear and so very comfortingly intelligent. Joan I really am deeply fond of. She is honest, uncomplicated, nobody's fool and so absolutely and genuinely herself. I painted a portrait of Ricky with which he seems delighted. I think it is ghastly. We gave a grand cocktail party for Joan last night. It was a perfect, pluperfect, evening; absolutely clear and not a breath of wind, so we gave the party round the pool – all the locals plus a few strangers they brought with them. It did look enchanting, I must say. When the light had nearly gone, the moon appeared. Coloured lights were placed round the pool. I turned on the pool light and the verandah lights, which are red. The effect was magical. I also put on two Rachmaninov concertos as background music. A sweet Airedale-ish dog gatecrashed early on and we took such a mutual fancy to one another that he is still here. The whole thing was a fine success.

Now I have had an idea for one of the long-short plays and I've started it today. It's called *Come into the Garden, Maud*. I have therefore temporarily abandoned *Past Conditional*, but I've done twenty-five pages and it's looking good.

Only ten more days in my Jamaican paradise. I do believe that I love this place better than anywhere but, as usual, I shall be ready to plunge once more into the hurly-burly. I've had cheerful letters from Graham and Binkie about *Present Laughter*. I *know* there will be certain things I *don't* approve of but I suspect that, on the whole, it's all right. *Hay Fever* has reopened with a flourish at the Old Vic. Peter Sellers and his wife[1] came over to lunch the other day and were sweet. No more particular news. Life grinds on.

Tuesday 20 April

Only one clear day more. On Thursday we fly to New York, Coley, Nicky and me. There have been a series of farewell parties for Nicky who is very popular indeed.

I have today finished *Come into the Garden, Maud* and I think it's really very good. I've been rather foolishly working against time and overtiring myself which is not very sensible when I have so much before me, but I *love* working here and I must say I have done a hell of a lot since we arrived in February.

Gladys Cooper arrived yesterday looking wonderful and talking without

1 Britt Ekland, Swedish film star, married to Peter Sellers 1964–69.

drawing breath. We took her to the 'Nicky's Farewell' dinner. It was all a great success but slightly exhausting. Gladys left for Montego today where she is planning to build three houses!

Saturday 1 May   London

Coley and Nicky and I arrived last night. A rapturous welcome from Lornie, the Lunts and Graham. The time in New York was, as usual, pretty hectic. We saw some plays including *The Odd Couple*[1], which was wonderful. There were lengthy discussions about the Noël Coward Repertory Company. The boys seem very bright and it all looks hopeful.

I flew to Chicago on Sunday, had a complete check-up on Monday, and flew back that night. Ed [Bigg] was wonderful. I had to have the bloody barium enema *and* be blown up with air, which was hell. However, nothing sinister has been discovered anywhere and all my organs are in splendid condition. There was, as I suspected, a tiny bug in my bowels which is being dealt with by various pills.

We saw Margot and Rudi dance *Marguerite et Armand* at the Met. Absolutely magical. Maggie Leighton has enthusiastically agreed to do the plays with me next spring, which is very good news. *Pretty Polly* is going to be made into a movie and shot on location in Singapore. *Hay Fever* is still packing them in and so is *Present Laughter*, which I am going to tonight. I lunched today with Otto Preminger, Larry, Anna Massey, etc., in a garage in Swiss Cottage. They are shooting 'on location' with a vengeance. I start on Wednesday in a mews just off Trafalgar Square. Otto very amiable but *vedremo* as the Italians say. Nicky is doing very well and being a great success with everyone. He really is a dear boy. We saw *Ship of Fools* in New York. A badly-directed[2], dull picture except for Vivien [Leigh], Simone Signoret and Oskar Werner. I also saw Natasha, who is off the booze and looked sweet, almost back to normal except that her legs are wobbly. I really am beginning to hate New York. It is getting commoner and commoner.

Joe Layton did an hour-long television spectacular on Barbra Streisand and over-directed it badly. It really is very sad. Ever since *The Girl Who Came to Supper* there has been a change in our relationship. I'm still fond of him although Evvie[3] gets me down a bit, but I have lost faith in his talent. I thought he was going to be a fine director but he is too visual and fussy. I'm afraid now, unless he is willing to learn a few sharp lessons, that he may never make the transition from choreographer to director. As a matter of fact, they seldom do, with the possible exception of Jerry Robbins.

1 By Neil Simon.
2 By Stanley Kramer.
3 Joe Layton's wife.

Sunday 16 May   Les Avants

I finished the film last Monday night. I found Otto P. an excellent director
and I think I am good in it. I saw *Present Laughter*. All *apparently* very good
but badly gabbled. Nigel Patrick plays so fast that you miss words *and*
meaning. So I had two rehearsals and improved things considerably. I didn't
have a chance to see Celia in *Hay Fever*, for the only night they did it I was
working; however, I go to London on Tuesday to record *The Critic*[1] and shall
see *Hay Fever* on Thursday. There have been great complications over the
Pretty Polly film deal but we hope that everything will be straightened out. I
read *A Song at Twilight* and *Come into the Garden, Maud* to Binkie and he was
truly enthusiastic and most intelligently critical. So I am going to sit down
and do some rewriting when I get back from London. I must also write the
extra play or two.

I have just been to the Cannes Film Festival as a guest of Otto's. *Never*
have I seen such an 'expense of spirit in a waste of shame' – the milling
crowds, the hordes of photographers, the insensate vulgarity of the whole
thing. I really was fairly nauseated, but in a ghastly way I enjoyed it. There is,
of course, a short story in a film festival. Otto's film *In Harm's Way* was
well-acted but interminable. The dinner (gala) afterwards was also interminable, the crowds suffocating and Diahann Carroll[2], who performed, was
deafening, too slow and inaudible. I had lunch with Edward at Biot. All very
sweet and ineffably silly. I stayed an extra night at the Carlton. Had a brief
encounter with Rex and Rachel [Roberts], Rachel noisier than ever, took
Kevin Colson[3] to dine and gambled a bit. I returned here on Friday.

This morning Lornie told me that she had a recurrence of cancer under her
left arm. They apparently do not consider it bad enough to operate, but are
going to give her six weeks' cobalt treatment. My heart sinks at the thought.
It will probably be all right but it is a dreadful sign and portent. A few more
years? Who knows! This is the deep sadness of getting old. However, I must
be prepared for whatever is to come. Phyl Monkman has had both her hips
operated on. All very cheerful. Meanwhile another spring has come and this
country is radiant.

Wednesday 26 May

Coley and I flew back yesterday after a week in London. I did my recording
of Mr Puff in *The Critic*. I think it will be all right but the other acting, except
for George Baker and John Moffatt, was not of the highest order. I went to
Hay Fever. The cast was as good as ever with the exception of Maggie [Smith]

1 Noël was making an LP of Sheridan's comedy.
2 Diahann Carroll, black American entertainer.
3 Kevin Colson, Australian singer.

who was overplaying. Celia was quite enchanting and very, very funny. The audience was rapturous. I also saw an hour and a half of *Mother Courage*[1], which was intolerable; all of *Much Ado*, which was inventive, noisy, nice to look at and nothing *whatever* to do with Shakespeare[2]. We saw Dorothy Tutin play Queen Victoria very, very well[3], but the rest was tatty; also *A Heritage and its History* taken from Ivy Compton-Burnett's book[4], which was witty but done without style and with hideous dresses, hideous scenery, bad direction and only adequate acting.

Incidentally, the Actors' Studio production of *The Three Sisters*[5] and *Blues for Mr Charlie*[6] were torn to pieces by the Press and booed off the stage. They were apparently absolutely despicable! Personally I am rather glad because all this 'method' balls has done considerable harm to the theatre. John Osborne has directed a comedy at the Royal Court which is apparently unfunny and disgusting[7]. Edith got away with the opening performance of *The Chinese Prime Minister*, having given everyone concerned hell for weeks. *Present Laughter* still doing very well and playing to four thousand a week. We have had endless legal meetings regarding the *Pretty Polly* movie. Too exhausting to go into in detail.

Lornie is fine, her daily treatment tires her but the cancer is shrinking. Phyl Monkman's operation was a success and she is going to be able to walk without pain. I believe from now on it will be possible for me to spend six months in England if I want to.

There has been a reading of the Homosexual Bill in the House of Lords with a large majority in favour of it. Montgomery made an ass of himself and so did Lord Goddard (eighty-eight) and Lord Kilmuir, Rex's idiotic brother-in-law. Lady Gaitskell, Lord Arran and the bishops were sensible and tolerant. The ignorance of Lord Montgomery really does astound me. He so brilliantly commanded so many men and obviously knows nothing about them. Such desperate prejudice is quite terrifying.

Monday 14 June

I am in the process of rewriting *A Song at Twilight*. I have finished the first act which was the most difficult and it is much improved. I have been reading an excellent biography of the Empress Elizabeth of Austria. Clearly one of the most beautiful women in the world and beyond a shadow of doubt the silliest. Conceited, selfish, neurotic, humourless and, so far as I can judge, nutty as a

1 Bertolt Brecht's play at the Old Vic.
2 It was a Zeffirelli production, in the Old Vic repertoire with *Hay Fever* and *Mother Courage*.
3 In *Portrait of a Queen* at the Vaudeville.
4 Adapted by Julian Mitchell.
5 Chekhov's play.
6 By James Baldwin.
7 *Meals on Wheels* by Charles Wood.

fruit cake for most of her life. It is sad to reflect how many beautiful women are idiotic. It's bad enough in the theatre when they bash about and make asses of themselves, but when, like Mary Stuart, Marie Antoinette and 'Sissi', they are in a position to affect history it is more serious. I am reading at the moment a fairly intelligent analysis of the modern playwrights[1]. It is, of course, irritating me because a great deal of it is pretentious balls, but at least it tries to give a little explanation of what has been going on in the theatre for the last few years. I'm afraid that ghastly Brecht has a lot to answer for. Poor Judy Holliday died the other day aged forty-eight of cancer. This, I think, is a real sadness, she was such a good comedienne.

I think I have an idea for the third play of my series, but as yet it is only an idea and hasn't begun to be constructed. I want to write about a celebrated actor and entourage who settles in Switzerland to avoid the English tax situation. Based on my own experiences, I cannot see that I can fail to make it fairly funny. However, the shape of it has to be worked out. Once that is set the dialogue will take care of itself.

Guido has been caught by the police for speeding and his licence has been (temporarily, I hope) taken away from him. There is a pall of gloom on this particular Alp.

Wednesday 23 June

I have finished the rewriting of *A Song at Twilight*, and I really do think I have improved it enormously. The weather has slightly improved. The Swiss social world continues to revolve sluggishly but quite agreeably. I dined with the Chevreau d'Antraigues and visited the Queen of Spain after dinner. The poor old girl is not well and shows signs of breaking up.

I have had to deliver a lecture to Nicky. He must concentrate on learning about me and my life and works, even if it means the dreaded necessity of reading the printed word occasionally. He is a dear boy and everyone likes him, but he *is* thirty-five and not twenty-two.

There has been another high-flown debate in the House of Lords about suggested (idiotic) amendments to the Homosexual Bill, in the course of which Lord Montgomery announced that homosexuality between men was the most abominable and bestial act that any human being could commit! It, in his mind, apparently compares unfavourably with disembowelling, torturing, gas chambers and brutal murder. It is inconceivable that a man of his eminence and achievements could make such a statement. The poor old sod must be gaga.

The Beatles have all four been awarded MBEs, which has caused a considerable outcry. Furious war heroes are sending back their bravely-won medals by the bushel. It is, of course, a tactless and major blunder on the part of the

1 *Anger and After* by John Russell Taylor.

Prime Minister, and also I don't think the Queen should have agreed. Some other decoration should have been selected to reward them for their talentless but considerable contributions to the Exchequer.

Sunday 4 July

Today Audrey and Mel[1] came to lunch. She enchanting as ever and he really extremely nice. I got back on Thursday after an interlude in Rome in time to dine with Adrianne and Dorothy Hammerstein[2], whom I love. Rome was fascinating and fraught with drama. The temperature all the time hovered between 88° and 98°. Princess Torlonia's wedding was beautiful to look at but too many '*paperazzi*' flashing cameras all through even the most serious parts of the ceremony. I went with Kay Thompson and Merle Oberon. I then changed into a dinner jacket and went to the '*Grand Recepsione*' which was *inferno* owing to there being no air-conditioning. It looked beautiful, however, and was crowded with Maria Pias and Maria Gabriellas.

On the Sunday night, I went to see the Beatles. I had never seen them in the flesh before. The noise was deafening throughout and I couldn't hear a word they sang or a note they played, just one long, ear-splitting din. Apparently they were not a success. The notices were bad the next day. I went backstage to see them and was met by Brian Epstein[3], who told me they had gone back to the hotel and would I go there. So off I went and, after being received by Brian Epstein and Wendy Hanson[4] and given a drink, I was told that the Beatles refused to see me because that ass David Lewin[5] had quoted me saying unflattering things about them months ago. I thought this graceless in the extreme, but decided to play it with firmness and dignity. I asked Wendy to go and fetch one of them and she finally reappeared with Paul McCartney and I explained gently but firmly that one did *not* pay much attention to the statements of newspaper reporters. The poor boy was quite amiable and I sent messages of congratulation to his colleagues, although the message I would have liked to send them was that they were bad-mannered little shits. In any case, it is still impossible to judge from their public performance whether they have talent or not. They were professional, had a certain guileless charm, and stayed on mercifully for not too long.

I was truly horrified and shocked by the audience. It was like a mass masturbation orgy, although apparently mild compared with what it usually is. The whole thing is to me an unpleasant phenomenon. Mob hysteria when commercially promoted, or in whatever way promoted, always sickens me. To

1 Audrey Hepburn and her then husband, American actor Mel Ferrer.
2 Dorothy Hammerstein, Oscar's widow.
3 Brian Epstein, the Beatles' manager.
4 Wendy Hanson, the group's publicist.
5 David Lewin, columnist on the *Daily Mail*.

realize that the majority of the modern adolescent world goes ritualistically mad over those four innocuous, rather silly-looking young men is a disturbing thought. Perhaps we are whirling more swiftly into extinction than we know. Personally I should have liked to take some of those squealing young maniacs and cracked their heads together. I am all for audiences going mad with enthusiasm after a performance, but *not* incessantly *during* the performance so that there ceases to be a performance.

I had a pleasant morning with Diana Cooper, Liz and Raimund von Hofmansthal[1], and Princess Olga and Prince Paul. I took Sarah Churchill to dine. She was somehow heart-breaking. She looked beaten up and papery. I have always liked her. We had a nice reminiscent evening and she remained sober. Two days later I went to have a drink in her apartment, where she lives with a coloured abstract painter with a very abstract talent. He is three-quarters Negro and one quarter Arab. The apartment was ghastly, squalid, incense burning, tatty. Sarah was sweet and obviously desperately eager that I should like her dark cardboard lover which, alas, I was not able to do. There she is, that pretty, aristocratically born woman, now aged fifty and quite obviously done for. She had talked, wistfully and defiantly, at dinner about living her own life, etc., and I longed to wag my finger and say that self-indulgence and lack of discipline seldom add up to happiness, but it is too late. I could only stare at her and wonder *why*. She adored Winston. I cannot believe that Lady Churchill could have been all that bad a mother. Mary, after all, is wise and good. What a silly tragedy.

Bob Ardrey came here for the night and talked brilliantly and wonderfully. He is, to my mind, probably the most extraordinary brain I have ever encountered. I am longing for *Territorial Imperative*. He left me with a lot to think about and with a refreshed mind.

Saturday 17 July

Joyce has been here for ten days which has been lovely. We wrestle with *The Times* crossword. On Tuesday Bill Fairchild came to dine with his colleague David Stone to discuss *The Gertrude Lawrence Story*, a project of which I heartily disapprove[2]. Bill was nice as always. David Stone was also, *au fond*, nice. They stayed for ever. We argued back and forth. Julie Andrews is to play Gertie, about as suitable as casting the late Princess Royal as Dubarry. However, she's a clever girl and will at least be charming and sing well. *Why* they are doing the film I shall never know. There isn't any real story beyond the fact that she started young in the theatre, became an understudy, then

1 Lady Elizabeth and Raimund von Hofmansthal, Diana Cooper's niece and her husband.
2 British screenwriter William Fairchild, and David Stone from Twentieth Century-Fox's studio, were beginning work on a Hollywood musical version of Gertrude Lawrence's life, eventually entitled *Star!*.

a star, lived with Philip Astley, Bert Taylor, etc., married Richard Aldrich, and died. I really do think that the Hollywood film mentality is worse than ever.

I have had a sweet letter from the Queen Mother asking me to stay Tuesday night at Sandringham. John Osborne's homosexual play about Colonel Redl has opened and is apparently years too long and a bore[1]. As Redl was a brilliant man and a fascinating character, it *must* be Osborne's fault that he is a bore. I intend to go and see for myself, however. I have read Cecil [Beaton]'s diaries (wartime) which are brilliant and beautifully written. I am now embarked upon the vivid but inconclusive short stories of Elizabeth Bowen and Elizabeth Taylor. Fine writing but irritatingly over-sensitive. Of the two I prefer Taylor to Bowen. She is less barmy. Adlai Stevenson dropped dead in Grosvenor Square. The weather has blown cold again. I am arranging my freight boat, Congo trip in October. I have not yet written the third play but an idea is churning. I read *A Song at Twilight* to Robin [Maugham] who nearly fainted. He was deeply impressed but agitated because people might think it was based on Willie! Actually it isn't, although there are many similarities.

Tuesday 3 August

Home again after two violent weeks in London – absolutely exhausting; will I never learn? No. Went on arrival Sunday to *Von Ryan's Express*[2], a lovely thriller with Sinatra, etc. On the Monday lunched with Vivien and she was calm, sweet and at her best. I saw *The Killing of Sister George*[3], not perfect but highly enjoyable and the right length, beautifully played. Drove down to Sandringham on Tuesday through biblical storms – nearly four hours' drive – the Queen Mother as dear as ever. Nice house party. We all had high tea then whizzed off to the church in King's Lynn to hear Rostropovitch, the Russian cellist. I drove with the Queen Mother and we sat together in the first row. Rostropovitch really was marvellous, thank God, otherwise there would have been grave danger of giggles. Afterwards dinner at Sandringham and piano playing, etc. I shall always cherish the memory of the Queen Mother and me singing as a duet 'My Old Man Said Follow the Van'.

At twelve o'clock the next day, after a cheerful, gossipy morning, we were all rushed off to picnic on the beach thirty-five minutes away. As I had to leave Sandringham at two o'clock to get back to London, this was unfortunate. There was a plague of thick black flies and we disenjoyed our picnic lunch in a wooden hut with all the windows shut. I could only stay about twenty minutes (happily). The QM adored it. She's a great outdoor girl. I drove the four hours back to London reflecting cheerfully on my good fortune. She is,

1 *A Patriot For Me* at the Royal Court.
2 Directed by Mark Robson.
3 Frank Marcus's play.

I think, the most genuinely charming woman, and I am so deeply pleased that she is as fond of me as she obviously is.

I dined with Binkie and we made elaborate plans about the plays, including deciding on Glen Byam Shaw[1] as director. The next day, Thursday, was hectic. I did the Michael MacOwan television interview from 10.30 until five[2]. I think it was good; at any rate, I never hesitated and did enough for two! The set-up was excellent. After this Coley, Gladys and I went to the John Osborne play *A Patriot for Me*. Three hours and three-quarters of muddled, undisciplined writing, adequate acting, vile lighting, good performances by Maximilian Schell and George Devine and Jill Bennett, and good, largely unnecessary sets. Interminable scenes and acres of appalling bad taste. He really *won't* do. Colonel Redl is a fascinating character and the story is strong. Osborne has missed all the main points. The 'drag' scene is so embarrassing that we could hardly look at the stage. After this curious experience we dined well at the Empress (thank God) and went on to Danny La Rue's[3]. He also was in 'drag', in fact it was a big 'drag' evening, but he was also witty and utterly charming and the whole show completely enjoyable. It finished with a long musical and vocal tribute to me, beautifully done.

The next day was peaceful. A brief drink with Lionel Bart and Joan Littlewood, dinner with Peter Arne[4], and bed early. On Saturday Coley and I drove to Chichester to see *Trelawny*[5], which was enchanting. Marvellously played – Bob [Stephens] wonderful and Louise Purnell really very good indeed. Sunday, Graham, Coley and I lunched with Vivien at Tickeridge. Monday, Phyl Monkman and Bobby Andrews came to lunch. Phyl on crutches but without pain at last. Gave an interview for the Norwegian Broadcasting Company on tape. My interviewer looked about nine and a half. In the evening went with Gladys [Cooper], Joyce and Coley to *The Homecoming*[6]. An extraordinary play, fairly obscure, superbly done and utterly professional. Ian Holm and Paul Rogers sensational. Pinter is a strange playwright. A sort of Cockney Ivy Compton-Burnett. The end of the play went off a bit, but I was never bored for an instant.

On Tuesday Willis Hall and Keith Waterhouse came to discuss the film of *Pretty Polly Barlow*[7]. It all seems to be going well. Lunched *à trois* with Princess Margaret and Tony, which was great fun. I even found myself playing ring o' roses backwards with the children. Chichester again with

1 Glen Byam Shaw (b. 1904), British stage director.
2 For a BBC series entitled *Great Acting*.
3 Danny La Rue, British female impersonator.
4 Peter Arne (b. 1922), Anglo-American actor.
5 Pinero's comedy, *Trelawny of the 'Wells'*.
6 By Harold Pinter.
7 Which they were to adapt for the screen.

Coley, this time, opening night of *Miss Julie*[1] and *Black Comedy* by Peter Shaffer. *Miss Julie* too turgid and long, but magnificently played by Albert Finney and Maggie [Smith]. *Black Comedy* immensely funny, slightly overdone but entirely successful.

Wednesday, Irene Worth lunched and we yakked away until four o'clock. Cocktail party – Anna Neagle, Danny La Rue, Nigel [Patrick], Avice [Landon], Maxine [Audley], Phyl Calvert, etc. Dined with Viv. Thursday morning operated on by Matt Banks. Three hours on the table and had claustrophobic panic afterwards when I had half come round; apart from that, lots of heroin and everything fine. Under-chin jowls now completely gone. Must remain bandaged until Monday when I return to London to have stitches out.

Darling old Irene Browne died (without pain). I have just written a tribute to her which Johnny G. is going to read at the memorial service. Another dear old friend gone. She has behaved so superbly during this last year, knowing all the time that she was under sentence of death. With all her grumbling and faults, she was a wonderful friend and I shall never forget her.

Friday 20 August

This is a good day because I have this morning finished *Shadows of the Evening* and I think it is one of the best plays I have ever written. I may have to eat these words later on and consider myself a proper Charlie for having written them, but that is how I feel at the immediate moment. It is a sad theme but not entirely a sad play. It also has wonderful parts for all three of us[2], particularly me. I really do think that to have written one full-length and two one-act plays all in the same set[3] with three characters and a waiter is a remarkable theatrical feat and I am mighty proud of myself.

I went to London to have my stitches out, which was successfully accomplished. Apart from a couple of scabs behind my ears which are fast disappearing, my face looks fine. Poor Matt Banks who did the operation so brilliantly was hauled off to hospital almost immediately after doing it with a coronary thrombosis, and is now dying, if not already dead. This is a sadness because, apart from being a great plastic surgeon, he was a dear man. I stayed with Graham for the three nights I was there and it was great fun.

I came back here on the Wednesday and went on with *Shadows of the Evening*. I had already done four pages. Glen [Byam Shaw] came on Monday and I am so very, very glad that he is going to direct the plays. He is sensible, extremely experienced and has a loving character. I *know* he will be of the utmost help to me. We have been having silly telephone calls from Maggie Leighton, who is making a dithering fool of herself. She is too besotted about

1 By Strindberg.
2 i.e. Noël, Irene Worth and Margaret Leighton.
3 A Lausanne hotel suite.

Michael Wilding and *cannot* come to England without him, and permission
has to be granted by Hugh French, who is his employer, to let him come.
Neither Glen nor Binkie nor I want him to come. He'll only be an amiable
nuisance and justify his idiotic existence by making suggestions and getting in
our hair. Also Maggie seems to have changed and become more scatty than
ever, and the Hollywood values have obviously corrupted what there was of
her mind. In the meantime, I am popping off to Cap Ferrat tomorrow for four
days' sunshine with the darling Nivens. I am sad about Maggie, but I am not
going to tolerate any more leading-lady airs and graces and tantrums for
anyone. I have too much to do in creating my own performances.

Tuesday 7 September

A lot has happened. First of all Binkie and I decided to ask Lilli [Palmer] to
do the plays. We did and she accepted enthusiastically, so we cabled Maggie
that the deal was off. She's been frigging about for four months and kept us
waiting too long. Also, I really don't want Michael Wilding lolling about
during rehearsals. I have had enough of stars' husbands and lovers. I took
Shadows of the Evening to Lilli at Goldingen. She was mad about it, so is
Binkie. All of which makes me very happy. Now – today – suddenly out of the
blue comes a letter from Glen saying that he doesn't like it at all and refuses
to direct! He also cheerfully suggests that I should write another play in its
place – a thriller or something! This has not unnaturally infuriated me. I
haven't talked to Binkie yet, but I intend to this evening. Obviously we shall
have to find another director. I will *not* be dictated to over anything so
important as this. If I really feel it is good and Binkie, Lilli, Coley, Graham,
Adrianne, Carlos, etc., all agree, I can't see why Glen's contrary opinion
should affect me in any way. It's all very tiresome, but I do know that I've got
to press on with what *I* believe to be right, even if I am ultimately proved to
be wrong.

I spent a divine four days with the Nivens on Cap Ferrat. I called on Willie
Maugham and I am glad I did because he was wretchedly, pathetically
grateful. He is living out his last days in a desperate nightmare, poor beast. He
barely makes sense and, of course, he *knows* his mind has gone. I managed to
cheer him a bit and certainly helped poor Alan [Searle] who is going through
hell.

Tomorrow I am going to the South of France again, this time to Sam
Spiegel's yacht. The weather here has been so bestial that I can't stand any
more. I shall stay in the yacht for a week, then Rome for a few days to find a
Felix[1], then London for four nights before coming back here for a full week
before I start off on my grand safari. I cannot say that my life, on the whole,
is dull exactly, but I do wish Glen hadn't suddenly turned silly on me. I had

1 An actor to play the Italian waiter in *Suite in Three Keys*.

so hoped that all was set and that we were going to enjoy working together. However, all may be well yet. Lilli I am enchanted with from every point of view. She is shrewd, sensible, untiresome and also glamorous, in addition to being a really fine actress.

Sunday 19 September   Rome

An enjoyable week on Sam's yacht which is the acme of luxury. Burt Lancaster appeared with his girl-friend and was amiable and fun. We cruised up and down the Riviera. The weather was only fairly good. I went, not entirely willingly, to the casino in Cannes and won £1,000! I did *not* go back. On Tuesday Sam flew to London. I couldn't fly here because they hadn't a reservation until Thursday. Therefore I stayed on the yacht in Monaco harbour. The first night I dined with Evelyn Baring[1] and met the Graham Sutherlands[2], with whom I immediately fell in love. He has promised to paint me next July in Venice. On the second night I took several of the crew out to dine at Villefranche, after which they took me on a proper piss-up. I have seldom enjoyed an evening more. Why is it that all English seamen have such unfailingly good manners? I felt dreadful next morning and lapped up oceans of Fernet Branca. I managed to get myself on the plane and managed to get myself here in reasonably good order. So far I have dined with Bob [Ardrey]. This was, as usual, a perfect evening. We talked our heads off and Bob gave me the first four chapters (typescript) of *Territorial Imperative*. It's going to be a brilliant book, although I found quite a lot to criticize. He is an extraordinary man and I love and admire him very much.

I have interviewed various agents and also several spectacularly handsome young men, but so far none of them has seemed quite right. They either can't speak English well enough or have had no stage experience. Also nearly all of them, although beautiful as the day, looked shaggy and scruffy. I *know* it is the fashion to have long unwashed hair and rough sweaters and no ties, but I do wish they wouldn't. However, I have already collected a wad of photographs and have still a few more to see. The agents, I must say, are being very helpful.

Monday 27 September   Les Avants

Oh dear, oh dear, a very great deal has happened. Nobody could describe my life as dull. Before I left Rome I found a perfect Felix, a handsome young actor called Carlo Palmucci who, having already been suggested to me by the agents, appeared with a letter of introduction from Franco Zeffirelli. His English is all right, his looks marvellous, and he has had considerable stage experience. I dined once more with Bob Ardrey and gave him *Shadows of the*

1 General Evelyn Baring, retired British administrator, ex-Governor of Southern Rhodesia and of Kenya, knighted 1960.
2 Graham Sutherland (1903–80), British artist, and his wife.

Evening. He was brilliantly articulate and critical and said I had nearly pulled it off but not quite. He said, in fact, what Lilli had said, that there was not enough conflict between the two women and that the whole thing was too fucking noble. I listened to him with the closest attention and much gratitude. Later on I supped with Zeffirelli, Bob Stephens and Maggie Smith. A perfectly enchanting Anglo-Italian theatrical carry-on.

The next day I took off – two hours late – for London. The journey went like a flash, and at seven o'clock I arrived at Binkie's as arranged. Glen was due to come at eight. Unfortunately, however, Binkie's chauffeur had made a balls-up and he was there when I arrived. There then ensued a scene of such horrendous idiocy that it is almost beyond description. In the first place he'd had a couple, which is *not* a good business method of dealing with me. At all events I did my best – without real conviction – to cajole and coax him but he moaned and argued and kept on saying how brilliant *I* was and how slow *he* was and that we should never be able to work together because I *frightened* him and would undermine him with Lilli and Irene. At this Binkie lost his temper and flew at him. In fact Binkie was strong as a rock throughout the whole imbecilic episode.

Finally, at long last, after dinner was over and the silliness was reaching fever pitch, I said that I must have another director. Glen retired to the other room because the car wasn't ordered until eleven o'clock and it was then only ten. Binkie and I sat on the floor hissing like schoolgirls in the dorm after lights out, and trying to get Vivian Matalon[1] (whom I have always wanted) on the telephone. Glen then came back, said he hated and loved me, and cried and said he *would* do the plays if I really wanted him to. This was a ghastly moment. I said firmly that whereas I *had* wanted him to, I didn't any more because he himself had talked me out of it and that I was convinced he was right and that we could *never* work together. Still he lingered and went maundering on until I told Binkie firmly to take him away, put him in the car and send him home. It really was a most extraordinary performance. Thank God it happened when it did. I couldn't have put up with that sort of high-charged juvenile emotionalism when I'm in rehearsal. Finally we located Vivian Matalon who came round immediately. I took a great liking to him. He read the plays the next evening. Had the same criticisms as Lilli, Ardrey and Irene, but said *Shadows of the Evening* could be the greatest of the three. Anyhow, all is well and I am starting rewriting today.

I had a private showing of *Bunny Lake*. It is a thrilling picture and I am very good. After this I took Irene to lunch and we had a lovely time. She produced sheaves of highly critical notes, ninety per cent of which were intelligent and constructive. We parted in a haze of mutual admiration.

We are all worried about darling Lornie. The thing under her arm has

1 Vivian Matalon (b. 1929), English-born actor turned director.

started kicking up again. She is obviously worried too but behaving so beauti-fully as always. I do hope to Christ it isn't serious. She's going to be examined on Wednesday and will telephone here on Thursday morning. I'm dreading it. It is indeed tough to envisage life without Lornie's love and loyalty and indestructible humour. I suppose I shall have to some day, but I do pray it isn't just yet.

Sunday 3 October

Things are looking up. First of all Lornie telephoned on Thursday morning and the thing under her arm isn't serious at all. It has merely collected some fluid as a result of the previous treatment which will disperse. She doesn't even have to see the doctor again for four months. This is a glorious relief not only for Coley and me but for her. Secondly, I have rewritten *Shadows of the Evening* from beginning to end. I have kept all the good bits but ruthlessly cut out all pretension and nobility. It is now, I really do think, a very true and moving play. Curiously enough I enjoyed rewriting it. I respond most effec-tively to constructive criticism and I know my critics were right over this. The play is now tougher and consequently more touching.

My whole holiday itinerary has been buggered up by an Italian freighter becoming suddenly capricious and being eighteen days late leaving! Therefore I have changed everything round and now fly to Bombay next Saturday – three hours to Cairo, five hours on – there I wait for a week and catch the boat for the Seychelles on the seventeenth. I shall now have a month there and then take the boat to Mombasa and cut out Lourenço Marques and Johannes-burg. I can fly direct to Cairo from Nairobi and then home after I have wandered about a bit among the wild animals. All this, of course, makes my holiday much simpler. I shall be in cable communication most of the time; also a month in the Seychelles is obviously better than twelve days. There are many small islands to be explored and I shall be able to charter a little boat and whisk off on my own (with a captain and crew, of course). I am looking forward to it all very much. Something tells me there is gold in them thar hills. Also I shall have the two voyages of five days each, which I love.

I am at the moment reading an extraordinarily original novel by – of all people – Irene Handl[1]. It is at moments quite brilliantly written. She really has an authentic touch of genius. While I was in London poor darling old Juliet Duff died. It was apparently a sweet and easy death. She had her breakfast in bed and it was a lovely day and she was merry as a grig. When the maid came to fetch the tray she was unconscious and died at 7.30 in the evening without coming round. She was eighty-five and had had an interesting and gay life. I shall miss her.

1 *The Sioux.*

Sunday 10 October   Bombay

I arrived here in blazing heat at 8.30 this morning, after a very long but luxurious flight. Air India is really a very fancy line indeed and the pilots seem able to fly quite nicely. We've had a fairly emotional week in Switzerland. Patrick Guinness[1] was killed driving his Alfa Romeo at 170 kilometres an hour on Tuesday morning. This is a deep and dreadful blow for poor Loel, who worshipped him. Coley and Hjordis and I went to the funeral service in Lausanne and it was all very miserable. Loel, who was completely shattered and had been crying for two days, behaved so wonderfully that it was profoundly moving. Instead of driving off with Gloria he stayed behind to thank us all for coming. Later on in the evening I called him up and he was heartbreaking. Patrick was the white hope of his life and was only thirty-four. Oh, how foolish people are to drive so dreadfully fast. We ran into most of the family again at Geneva airport yesterday. They were all flying off, with the remains of Patrick, to Billancourt, where he is to be buried.

To change to brighter subjects, Binkie and Irene are mad about my new version of *Shadows of the Evening* and I suspect Lilli will be too. All this is very satisfactory.

It is strange finding myself in India again. It seems at first sight to have decayed considerably since the hateful British were banished. The dirt is unbelievable. I have been treated with the greatest possible VIP courtesy. They are nothing if not polite, but there is a sense of *dégringolade* in the air. Nothing *quite* works. I am having grave trouble with my bath taps, which refuse to work without the hand-spray running too, and therefore the whole bathroom is sopping wet. Several green bowing gentlemen have come and gone but so far with no effect.

I find this ingrained wanderlust of mine very curious. I am *not* very comfortable but extremely happy. Even the teeming squalor doesn't depress me unduly. I love the feeling of being entirely on my own for a while, with no pressing jobs to be done and time to think. On Saturday I sail for the Seychelles; I suspect that they are going to be a bit seedy too, but it won't matter because of the sea and the lagoons and the islands to visit.

Among other things this is a *dry* state so I have had to procure a permit to buy a bottle of Scotch and *that* I can't get until tomorrow because today is Sunday! Well, well!

Sunday 24 October   Seychelles

I arrived here on Thursday morning; Gerry Le Grand, the proprietor of the hotel, met me on board and conducted me ashore in a launch. He is bright-eyed, dapper, a little over-affable, and has a languid wife who puts Alice-blue

1 The son of Loel Guinness by his previous marriage.

on her eyelids and seems to be swimming eternally in her own private aquarium. I have a private aquarium of my own but it is called a bungalow. It is, shall we say, on the primitive side, but comfortable enough. There is a shower with cold water only and a wonderful beach is only a few yards away across a not very main road. The service is erratic and conducted at a slow tempo by a bevy of dusky Seychelloises in green dresses who chatter to each other in a high-pitched Creole patois. Whenever I sit down on my verandah to have a cup of tea and a biscuit, I am immediately surrounded by a lot of small grey doves. They are appallingly tame and stamp about all over the table snatching crumbs from my hand. The food – served in an open dining-room – is indescribable. I don't think in all my journeyings I have ever encountered worse. The butter is always rancid and what they do to the meat and fish is macabre. Everything seems to taste of something else and the something else it tastes of isn't very nice. All the mothers and fathers and children that accompanied me on the *Karanja* are milling about. The children shriek continuously like engine whistles. Happily they are most of them sailing back to India today on the *Kampala*.

On Thursday evening, after I had unpacked and had a snooze, I was taken on board *Albion*, an aircraft carrier. It was an enormous naval 'showing-the-flag' cocktail party. The Navy, as always, was impeccable. I was presented to the Governor, Lord Oxford and Asquith, who looks a soppy date if ever I saw one. He was dreamily amiable and turns out to be Lady Horner's grandson. I have written my name dutifully in the book, so I presume I shall be invited to something or other. In the meantime I have met a great number of the locals and a very curious lot they are. Everybody drinks from morning till night and nobody seems to like each other very much.

It *is* undoubtedly a beautiful island but any vague ideas I had about buying some land are rapidly fading. However, I am pressing on and going to have a dekko at some of the other islands. The sea is wonderful and the beaches superb. There is much charm in the air, largely, I think, because of the population being so multicoloured. Some of the girls and boys are very beautiful, cross-breeds of Indian, Chinese, Polynesian and Negro. Today it is pouring again so I am going to have a quiet time and get on with learning Sir Hugo[1]. I have already mastered twenty pages. The vegetation has a lot in common with Jamaica – lots of old friends like breadfruit, poui and allamandar, etc., with some new lusher varieties thrown in. The shopping facilities in Victoria, the main town, are about half as good as Port Maria was in 1948. But still it too has charm – Victoria, I mean. There is a tiny, tiny clock tower like a baby Big Ben stuck in the middle of it.

The rain is now coming down in torrents and there is nothing to do but read *Martin Chuzzlewit*, learn some more lines or look at some naked Ameri-

[1] His character in *A Song at Twilight*.

cans playing handball on the beach. I think I shall enjoy my time here well enough, providing the weather clears and I can head off too much hospitality from the locals.

Wednesday 3 November

Last Wednesday I was taken to dine in the bosom of the Man-Chan family. It was very enjoyable. Madame Man-Chan is an ebullient Creole lady with rolling chocolate eyes and a high-pitched laugh. She is given to bursting into song without sufficient warning in a high-pitched soprano. The Creole dinner was highly spiced and excellent. She has two vast sons, one married to a *soi-disant* Persian princess and the other to a pretty Cockney lady from Richmond. The house is crammed from floors to ceilings with every conceivable sort of ornament, good, bad and indifferent. It was a very funny evening. The next night I dined at Government House and took an immediate shine to Lady Oxford, who is charming looking and has a lovely sense of humour. He is extremely affable and, I suppose, painfully shy. They have invited me to stay for as long as I like so I am going on Friday week for a long weekend. The rest of the dinner party was a mixed bag – the Pomeroys (do-good ladies from South Carolina but very nice), the Minister of Justice, an exuberant Frenchman who sighed for Yvonne Printemps and *le temps perdu*. In fact a very charming evening.

The next morning at crack of dawn I embarked on the *Lady Esmé*, the Government ferry boat which goes three times a week to Praslins and back. Gerry Le Grand took me to lunch with an old doctor called Elgood and his amiable but complaining wife, who had an Irene Handl voice with that ineffable veneer of refinement superimposed on basic Cockney. Dr Elgood *has* false teeth but refuses to use them. He hasn't been to a theatre since 1914 so we discussed Gertie Millar, Lily Elsie, etc. At 2.30 I was fetched by the proprietor of the hotel I was staying in on the other side of the island. He is a Welshman called Alec Lewis. I took a fairly instant dislike to him. We drove in a Land Rover over an appalling road which makes Firefly Hill look like an autoroute. He and his wife have built a hotel which consists of a main building and three grey bungalows. His wife Peggy looks exactly like Moo [Meriel] Richardson if she had been laid out in the sun for three years to dry off.

That first evening was the nadir of my holiday to date. After a jolly communal dinner we sat on the verandah eaten alive by mosquitoes and sandflies and tormented by flies while Alec expounded his views on life in general and the Seychelles Government in particular. I retired to bed exhausted and was allowed to read a little of *Martin Chuzzlewit* before the lights were switched off. This was Friday night and I knew I was trapped until Tuesday because the *Lady Esmé* was going to be a day late.

Sunday was a bit better. We went (accompanied by a mechanic) to La

Digue, which is a dear little island, and while my hosts went off on their own business I sat on the steps of the police station and had a fascinating conversation with the Seychellois superintendent in Italian because he had served in Italy during the war and wished to brush up his lingua. That evening an attractive young couple from Kenya, whom I had noticed on the boat, appeared. On the following evening I went to their house for a drink. An old thatched job with wooden balconies, *no* amenities but considerable charm. He is a good-looking boy, rather like a young Michael Redgrave. He is an elephant hunter! She is ravishingly pretty and very bright and they are both, believe it or not, educated, intelligent and speak the Queen's English. Their name is Forgan, Neil and Storm Forgan. They have settled on Praslins to plant tea and sell the seeds. This was a pleasant interlude and on the Tuesday morning before I left they took me sailing and it was lovely. During this interminable weekend I ploughed right through *Martin Chuzzlewit*, nine hundred pages. Apart from Sairey Gamp, Betsy Prigg and the Pecksniffs, *not* really a very good novel, too sprawly and self-indulgent.

Friday 12 November

I am back here [Hôtel des Seychelles] after a crowded and unpleasant week. The day after my return from Praslins I was taken by Gerry in his boat to Silhouette. Very rough sea, two hours each way, but lovely sunshine. There we were entertained by a splendid 'Peter Sellers' Indian called Narriman and the implacably friendly Pomeroys. We had an enormous Seychelloise lunch, all of which tasted distinctly of paraffin.

On Friday I went to Government House. Both the Oxfords were sweet to me and we played croquet and dined quietly. On Saturday morning we went in state to the opening of the newly-built Barclays Bank building. It was stiflingly hot and I had a terrible suspicion that I was going to be ill. After lunch I snoozed and woke feeling dreadful. That evening there was a dull dinner party. When it was over I went to bed and found my temperature was over a hundred. The next morning the 'trots' began. A Scottish doctor was sent for and I was whisked into the hospital, where I languished in acute discomfort for three days and nights. The dear Oxfords brought me a chaise-longue, toilet paper, books, rolls and honey, and visited me twice a day. It was finally discovered that I had 'round' worm which one gets from water – particularly, rumour has it, from Government House! At all events, I was inspected and drugged and let out on Wednesday. I still feel very weak and I've lost pounds, but the 'trots' are subsiding.

Through all these dire experiences it has rained ceaselessly. However, I *still* have the Government House chaise-longue and am beginning to feel a little better. Today there is a steady deluge. All my clothes are patched with mildew and penicillin is growing in every shoe. Rhodesia has declared its independence. Harold Wilson's 'mission' has failed and England has had one more kick in the puss. The Welfare State may be all right for improving the living conditions of the mediocre, but it isn't dazzlingly successful in dealing with foreign affairs and colonial administration. I don't see why it should be really, as few of its leaders have been further than Blackpool.

Sunday 21 November

The blow has fallen again and I have been horribly ill for the last week – diarrhoea and vomiting. I am having injections but I refused to go back to the hospital. I have a dreadful suspicion that it *may* be hepatitis but I am praying that it's not. Only a few more days and I shall be away from this curiously ghastly place. There is an undercurrent of evil here which I am very much aware of. The islands are beautiful enough, but to be beautiful enough is not enough. Everything is scruffy and tatty and running to seed. The weather has been vile up until the last week when it has been lovely but, alas, too late to be of any good to me. All I do is lie on my chaise-longue all day and stare at the sea.

I am nearly word perfect in *A Song at Twilight* and am about to begin on *Shadows of the Evening*. I have read an enchanting book by Alan Moorehead called *No Room in the Ark*, and I have at last got round to Errol Flynn's autobiography, which I found painfully irritating. *What* a silly man. It is indeed as outspoken as it is reputed to be but with the sort of outspokenness which curdles the blood. Such a wealth of unnecessary vulgarity. I have also read about two hundred pages of Gibbon[1], which is rewarding in some ways but a bit monotonous. It is certainly a horrifying comment on the human animal.

Monday 6 December   Les Avants

Home at last. I can hardly believe it. The weather is vile but I couldn't care less. I have my own comfortable bed and delicious food and peace. Coley is wonderful apart from a racking cold. I arrived on Friday morning more dead than alive. I am feeling fifty times better already and Dr Spuhler is looking after me. No more nausea and no more 'trots'.

My few days in Mombasa could have been enjoyable if only I had felt better and if only the hotel food had been eatable, which it wasn't. However, I managed to have a few good moments. A nice sailing jaunt and a lovely picnic. We flew in a private plane to Voi in the Tsavo Reserve. Here we were met by two elephants and a young, tame rhino called Rufus. Also by a good-looking man called David Shelbrick, who is the boss of the whole thing and who drove us for a couple of hours about the countryside where we saw baboons, zebra, impala, tek-tek, oryx, etc., etc. Then we flew low over the

1 *History of the Decline and Fall of the Roman Empire.*

vast plateau and looked down at giraffes, elephants, rhinos and all sorts of deer and buffalo. We picnicked by a river and got back to Mombasa about 4 p.m. This was my last day and although it exhausted me I enjoyed it. I flew to Nairobi on Thursday morning where I had a marvellous suite at the hotel for the day and – at last – an excellently cooked steak for lunch. This I brought up a few hours later. Nairobi looked fascinating – masses and masses of flowering trees – whole avenues of jacaranda, and a beautifully laid-out city. That was the end of the most disastrous holiday I ever had. It will take me a good long time to get over it. I'm still on a careful diet, of course, and still not drinking a drop, but oh, the bliss of being home again!

Thursday 16 December

Sixty-six years ago today I was propelled from the womb. There were no electric trains, and motor cars were exciting curiosities. There was not even the thought of an aeroplane in the winter skies, and horse-buses clopped through the London streets. There were no buses at all in Teddington. I can hardly believe that so much has happened in sixty-six years, but it has, and now men are whizzing about in outer space and taking photographs of the remote stars. Which only goes to show that man is a very remarkable animal. So remarkable that his main instinct – over and above his incredible cleverness – is still to kill and be killed, to maim and torture and massacre other animals for sport. Capital punishment having been abolished by the woolly-minded humanitarians in England, there has now been disclosed a hideous and revolting series of murders on the Yorkshire Moors by a girl of twenty-three and a man of twenty-seven. They have so far betrayed neither feeling nor interest in the progress of their preliminary trial. They have killed several children, apparently for 'kicks', and lastly battered a boy of seventeen to death with a hatchet. While the man was doing this, the girl sat with her feet on the mantelpiece, smoking. They will get a life sentence, which means fifteen years. So they will be out again and ready for more outrages. I have never thought the abolition of capital punishment a good idea, and I think so less than ever now.

My health has returned to normal and I am still glowing with the relief of being home. I am having a happy birthday. I have a fabulous little pocket tape recorder, which no one thought to give me on my sixth birthday so I have had to wait for it for sixty years. None of that threading on of the tape – you just pop in a little cassette and it works like a dream. I have learnt all the three plays and, with the exception of a few non-sequitur cues, I am word perfect in them. Willie Maugham died this morning. Poor miserable old man. Not very sadly mourned, I fear. Coley and I have written to Nicky giving him the definite sack. Now we are about to try out Calvin Darnell, who has worked for Vivien for years and is apparently a treasure. He arrives on Sunday to help us over the Christmas ghastliness. It will be *such* a relief to me if he really is good and can take some of the burden off Coley's shoulders. I have been completely happy since I've been back and feeling myself getting stronger and stronger. This at least is a pleasant way to start my sixty-seventh year. I wonder what it holds for me?

— 1966 —

The year of Noël's last London stage appearance, in the three plays he had written to make up Suite in Three Keys, *was also a year of crippling ill-health which he overcame only just in time to make sure that what he very well knew to be his farewell appearance (the last words of the last play are 'Goodnight, Sweetheart') would also be one of his most successful. As a critic in the* Daily Mail *wrote: 'At curtain fall one felt oddly elated, as if recapturing the flavour of an elusive drink once tasted when young but which has never been mixed quite right since. I now know the name of it: not mannerism, not bravura, not histrionics but style.'*

But Noël himself now knew that it was almost all over: 'It's terrifying', he told a friend in this year, 'how little time there is left. Every day now is a dividend and there is still so much I want to do. But my life until now has left me with no persistent regrets of any kind. I don't look back in anger, nor indeed in anything approaching even mild rage; I rather look back in pleasure and amusement. As for death, it holds no fear for me, provided it is not going to be a painfully lingering affair.'

Sunday 2 January   Les Avants

1966 has begun amiably enough. Binkie is here, Gladys [Cooper] and Vivian Matalon. Christmas has come and gone and so has Joan Sutherland. It was all very sweet, although not perhaps terribly exciting.

We have an elaborate film projector which Coley has mastered up to a point. We have shown *King Rat*[1] but will have to show it again because, owing to Coley omitting the second reel due to inadequate packing, we got *very* confused over the plot. However, it looked very good once we got the sound right.

The world is wagging away. My wigs – brought by Vivian – are wonderful. I have made no specific New Year resolutions, except perhaps to smoke a little less and keep my stomach from rumbling. I have read Truman Capote's *In Cold Blood*, which is magnificent. *Charlie Girl* with Anna Neagle and *Twang*[2] without Anna Neagle have both opened in London to appalling notices. There has been a heavy snowfall which is now thawing, so I have not yet been able to try the luge that Lilli gave me. Mary Chevreau d'Antraigues' Christmas party was very grand indeed. I sat next to the Queen of Spain as usual. There were lots of Spanish and mixed royalties present, and everybody was bobbing up and down like corks. Actually it was quite fun.

Calvin Darnell is doing quite well. He is willing and industrious and almost obtrusively unobtrusive. He also has a few minor mannerisms that drive me mad, such as a nervous wink and a compulsion to say, 'Do you know what I mean?' in every sentence. Apart from these small defects he is quite nice. I cannot *quite* envisage him as being my life's companion, but that perhaps would be asking too much. But he *is* well disposed and nice mannered.

Vivian is very bright and I like him more and more. All seems to be set fair for the plays.

Tuesday 18 January

Lilli arrived – Irene already here – both of them going to be marvellous. Yesterday I collapsed at rehearsal and I am now waiting for a stomach specialist who is coming at 7.30. I feel very ill. The griping has stopped but the gas pains are cruel and incessant. What is haunting me, naturally, is the fear that I won't be able to open. The set-up is perfect. I am delighted with every aspect, but I am so ill and exhausted that I can barely lift my hand let alone play three long parts. It is all utterly discouraging and I have little hope.

Sunday 23 January   La Source, Lausanne

The nightmare continues and the days go slowly by. I moved into this most excellent clinique on Friday afternoon after a morning of general hell with

---

1 Based on James Clavell's novel and directed by Bryan Forbes.
2 Musical by Lionel Bart which closed within days.

Lilli hysterical and insisting that I go immediately in an ambulance to Basle to be diagnosed by Professor Nissen who is 'great'. He is also a surgeon and I am liable to distrust surgical diagnosis *before* I know what is wrong with me. She flew at Coley who, poor darling, having been harassed all the week, broke down – privately, with me. Lilli meant it all for the best, I'm sure, but it was no moment for hysteria. Anyway she and Irene went away after an early lunch. Irene was superb and very dear.

Meanwhile I telephoned to Binkie to cancel Dublin[1]. A dreadful thing to have to do. Now we are all hanging on to the hope that I shall be able to rehearse in three weeks' time and open at the Queen's on 7 March as arranged. Personally my hope is diminishing rapidly. They have discovered that I have a urinary infection, which indicates something wrong with my kidneys. A kidney specialist is seeing me tomorrow, and on Tuesday I shall have to endure the test, which is horribly disagreeable and painful. On Wednesday I am to endure the barium enema just to check on my diverticulum. In the meantime I am being plugged full of penicillin, streptomycin, etc. I am losing weight alarmingly and now weigh only sixty-one kilos. I am, of course, hideously depressed and unhappy. I know, in my heart, that even if they find nothing devastatingly wrong with my kidneys, I still shan't be ready to open in London in six weeks from tomorrow. The whole project will have to be postponed until I'm well enough to do it and that's that.

The disappointment is hard to bear because I know the plays are good and the whole set-up was fine. I am also *very* interested about what is the matter with me. It may be our old friend cancer. If so, this is definitely the decline of my life. This I will face when I come to it. I don't relish prolonged illness and operations and attenuated death. But I suppose I shall have to cope with it as well as I can. On the other hand, it may be a swiftly curable disorder and I shall soon be well again. However, my voices tell me *not* soon enough. It would be neatly 'macabre' if *Shadows of the Evening* turned out to be the last play I wrote. A lesson in life construction for all promising playwrights. Watch these columns closely for any fresh bulletins from La Source.

Sunday 30 January

The nightmare is practically over. I have *not* got a growth anywhere, my kidneys are fine, my bladder is radiant. What I *have* got is an inflamed sigmoid and diverticulum. It is this which has been causing the blood and albumen in my urine *and* my temperature. It is perforated in one place – the sigmoid – and there is a remote chance that an operation may be necessary, but getting more and more remote as I am so far responding to treatment. I am at last beginning to feel better – weak as a kitten, obviously, but that is not to be surprised at.

1 Where *Suite in Three Keys* was due to open pre-London.

Binkie flew over yesterday and we have made plans. I shall not have the *definite* go-ahead until the end of this week but I really do think all will be well. The plans are for me to rest here in Switzerland for the next three weeks – then go away – probably to Monte Carlo to the Hôtel de Paris, where the food is *certain*. Then start rehearsing in London 21 March and open the week of 11 April. I really do think I shall be strong and well enough by then. Lilli is in a panic about learning the words, but I shall give her a week at Les Avants before we go to London. I am so relieved. I loathed the idea of putting the whole thing off until much later. At least now I shall be playing in England in any *good* weather there is.

Sunday 6 February

Still here [La Source] and likely to remain so for another ten days or two weeks. This was a bit of a blow when the doctor told me, but I am now resigned. Coley brings me dainties. I am sent orchids and eau de cologne by the Shereks[1], and life is far from unbearable. I read incessantly and do crosswords. Since being here I have read three books by Elspeth Huxley – African and enjoyable; two novels by Elizabeth Jane Howard – excellent; *The House of Arden* and *Harding's Luck* by darling E. Nesbit; *Madame Bovary* and *Flaubert and Madame Bovary*; *The Comedians*, Graham Greene's latest – well written as usual and, as usual, unpleasant. Also Arnold Bennett's *The Old Wives' Tale*, to me one of the few great novels in the English language. It is my third reading of it and it held me entranced as though I had never seen it before. Now I'm on dear *Pride and Prejudice*. *Madame Bovary* is another great novel. Francis Steegmuller, who has done this particular translation, has done it well but there really are too many Americanisms. American idiom really does *not* mix with the classics. It is not all that offensive in this instance but it is startling and curiously vulgarizes the text. Graham Greene, good writer though he is, has such an unsavoury mind that it is difficult not to cringe at moments. *The Comedians* is the mixture as before – sex, Catholicism, sadism and back to sex. The modern Hall Caine.

Lilli has been making a beast of herself and Binkie is not unnaturally furious. Considering how really wonderful he was to Lilli over her Rex troubles, I don't blame him. I am fond of Lilli, up to a point, but the mixture of female film star and Kraut is not entirely felicitous. Buster Keaton has died and so has poor Hedda Hopper. Audrey H. and David N. have been to see me; apart from them, no visitors. I am not entirely disenjoying my rest cure. I am *determined* to crush these bloody amoebas.

Sunday 13 February

This is the day when I should have been flying to Dublin. However, I am *not* flying to Dublin but still languishing here in my hospital bed, which I am

1 The impresario Henry Sherek and his wife Pamela were at this time living in Geneva.

beginning to think I shall never leave. The Emetine is making me feel fairly awful, ghastly attacks of nausea particularly in the mornings as though I were going to have a dear little baby.

Meanwhile in the great world outside, life goes on and death too. Irene Ravensdale[1] has gone, so have Sophie Tucker and Billy Rose[2]. The Great Reaper is certainly having a ball. The Homosexual Bill has passed through the House of Commons with a majority of fifty-five votes. I read the debate in the *Telegraph*. Really some of the opposition speeches were so bigoted, ignorant and silly that one can hardly believe that adult minds, particularly those adult minds concerned with our Government, should be so basically idiotic. However, now all will be well apparently and the law will be changed at the next session. Nothing will convince the bigots, but the blackmailers will be discouraged and fewer haunted, terrified young men will commit suicide.

I have toiled through two long volumes of *Can You Forgive Her?* It really isn't one of Trollope's happier efforts owing to the heroine, Alice Vavasour, being a humourless prig and a cracking bore. Lady Glencora, however, saved the book and there is fortunately a good deal of her. I am now embarked on *He Knew He Was Right* which I've never read before. Trollope is fortunately inexhaustible.

The dear Queen of Spain came to visit me, which was very sweet of her. She is a gallant woman if ever I saw one. Irene has apparently come to heel and Lilli is all sweetness and light, so for the moment we've got the girls under control. I've just been reading the French edition of *Pretty Polly Barlow*. It's really very well done and nicely presented. The Russians have landed on the moon, which looks from the televised photographs very, very unattractive. I have started a short story which so far is going slowly but well. It is called *Penny Dreadful* and concerns a male sob-sister journalist not unlike Godfrey Winn who is continually the housewives' choice and finally dies of a heart attack because he has been given inferior seats for a fashionable first night. It might be good.

Tuesday 22 February

Let nobody be surprised. I am still here. Just as I am beginning to feel better I am flung down again by some fresh drug. It is sadly discouraging. I have had some very black moments. Apparently I really have been in some danger, if not of death, at least of a dreadful operation. The operation still hovers if all else fails. It's a horrible possibility on account of being a particularly nasty operation.

I'm still hoping against hope that I shall be able to do the plays. I shall really be heart-broken if I can't. Binkie is being wonderful: calm, cheerful and

1 Mary Irene Curzon, 2nd Baroness Ravensdale.
2 Billy Rose, Broadway showman and circus proprietor.

encouraging. I've still got just under a month but the time is going by and I am very apprehensive. Coley, of course, is saving my life. He comes every day with edible dainties and little surprises. He is unfailing in love and tact and goodness. I have sheafs of 'get well' cards from all over the world. The Press are being successfully kept at bay. I am fairly unhappy for a lot of the time but not all of the time. The food is ghastly. And the times of serving it barbaric. To have to face a badly cooked steak swimming in unutterable gravy at 11.30 a.m. is a lot to expect. I'm constantly sending things back and stuffing myself with sugar and cream and eggs, but it's all pretty difficult with incessant gut pains and no appetite.

Monday 28 February

The nightmare is at last coming to an end. I woke up four days ago and decided to take a very firm grip both on myself and on my circumstances. I have had too much despair and gloomy forebodings and I don't intend to have any more. I have no temperature and haven't had for four weeks. My bowels are working normally and I feel astonishingly well considering that I have been bed-ridden for seven weeks. The only thing that is perplexing is the fact that my blood sedimentation and white cell count remain obstinately high. However, on looking back on my check-up here in the Nestlé Hospital in 1960 – Coley unearthed all the data – there it is stated that my white cell count and sedimentation rate were high then. So it seems that I am a natural white cell and sedimentation boy and had better get on with it. I *know* I am no longer ill and I *know* that the sooner I get out of this hospital and eat proper food and begin to live normally again the white cells will diminish, the sedimentation decrease, and Bob will be my uncle.

I have given up the idea of Monte Carlo. I intend to go to London next week, settle into Johnny Gielgud's house and get myself acclimatized to the brisk airs of London before starting rehearsals on 2 March. I also know that I shall have to be on a careful, although not appallingly strict, diet for several months, and that I must keep quiet, not see too many people and conserve my vitality for the theatre. All this I am willing and prepared to do. What I am *not* willing and prepared to do is to have any more rectal examinations, aortographs, barium enemas, etc., until it is considered by *really* expert opinions to be necessary. My diverticulum and sigmoid are obviously on the high road to recovery, if not completely cured. I now intend to give my own body a chance to reassert itself and do its own carefully organized magics. It has had a tough time with all these antibiotics and drugs. I am convinced that if left alone it won't fail me, provided that I take reasonable care, eat with discretion, and try not to do too much too soon. Today the final blood and urine tests are coming through. Whatever they say I am leaving this hospital and starting to live again. These have been the most miserable weeks of my life and I don't intend to risk enduring them again. Anyway, I'm sick of being ill in French.

Sunday 13 March   London

It is quite incredible the difference that has happened in my life during the last fortnight. Two weeks ago I was in that bloody clinique and here I am back at the Savoy leading a normal life again. I had a consultation on Friday with Dr Avery Jones, who is apparently the top gastro-enterologist in the world today. He was uneffusive, authoritative and gloriously sensible. He listened to my garbled medical history attentively – glanced expertly at the x-rays, gave me a swift and unexpected sigmoidoscopy which his expertise made entirely painless, and then talked to me sanely and in English. I have obviously been very seriously ill. Dr Jones told me to eat what I like, in reason, drink what I like, in reason, smoke for pleasure rather than habit, and get on with my life and the plays. I am not *quite* well yet and my two weaknesses are my colon and my feet! I must be very careful not to wear tight shoes or get anything wrong with them at all. It's that old arterial circulatory trouble. I am, however, *thankful* to myself for snapping out of that dreadful slough of despond. I am being careful and not doing too much and I rest a great deal. It is lovely spring weather.

I have been to *Charlie Girl*[1], *The Match Girls*[2] and *Hello Dolly*[3]. The first had a certain common entertainment quality and contained quite a lot of talent. The second had also talent, excellent choreography and a depressing, miserable book and appalling score. The last had Mary Martin who was, I thought, brilliant. Gower [Champion]'s production is wonderful, and although I didn't really like the show I enjoyed it thoroughly. On Thursday I saw myself on the television screen talking for fifty minutes about acting. Really very good. I endured a Press reception at Binkie's. I am *not*, repeat *not*, going to accept Johnny's sweet offer of his house. It has *no* central heating and the bath and loo are on the top floor *above* the main bedroom. It is also terribly *bijou* and I should go mad in it in two days. We are all apartment-hunting like crazy. Meanwhile the Savoy enfolds me in its expensive arms and my heart is at peace under an English heaven. I am taking *no more pills*.

Sunday 20 March

Coley ill! With bronchitis and near pneumonia – absolute hell. Oh dear.

I have had a busy week, overdone things a bit and had slight relapses, but all is well really. I gave a large cocktail party on Tuesday – a necessity to get everyone off. This was a great success but a strain. A wonderful mix-up.

1 The musical with Anna Neagle at the Adelphi Theatre.
2 Musical by Bill Owen and Tony Russell.
3 The London production of the Broadway hit by Jerry Herman and Michael Stewart.

Margot and Tito[1], Zena [Dare], the Redgrave girls[2], Phyl [Monkman], Maidie [Andrews], etc. The next day I had my first rehearsal and went on too long because I was enjoying myself. On Monday night I had a little supper with the Queen Mother here on the floor below. On Thursday I rehearsed again and went to *A Flea in her Ear* at the Old Vic[3]. Perfection of acting and direction. Friday, a *very* good rehearsal in the afternoon. Irene coming along fine. Last night I took Lilli to the five o'clock matinée of *You Never Can Tell*[4]. Oh, what a brilliant comedy, very well done by all concerned, Ralphie [Richardson] in particular. I have found a perfect apartment - 37 Chesham Place, plumb in the middle of all my loved ones - most luxurious with a glorious big room and a terrace garden and dead quiet. I move in on 6 April. It's a real find, although terribly expensive.

My stomach has its ups and downs - sometimes I feel awful and it hurts and I get worried, but Patrick [Woodcock] has been a real comfort and has warned me that I must prepare to face this 'feeling ill' for a long time to come. There is no more inflammation and, providing I don't get constipated - which I won't - all will be well. I shall *not* feel ill on the stage, but before and after I probably shall from time to time. I can face this all right so long as I know it is inevitable.

On Wednesday I lunched with Princess Marina and Prince Paul - very quiet and enjoyable. Tomorrow rehearsals *really* start. Coley returns from Valley of Shadow.

Sunday 27 March

A most successful week - the whole of *A Song at Twilight* blocked without books[5] but with a certain amount of spluttering from Lilli. However, she is a fine actress and is going to be wonderful. So is Irene and so, I devoutly hope, am I. Vivian is a sensitive and highly intelligent director, and although I get a bit tired after each day's work, I am thoroughly enjoying myself and getting stronger every day. At the moment, unfortunately, I have the inevitable cold, but thank God it has come now instead of two weeks hence.

I went with Coley and Lilli to *Love for Love*[6] on Wednesday - perfect production and Larry glorious. On Tuesday I dined with Princess Margaret and Tony. An entirely enjoyable evening. Apart from these outings I have come home dutifully every evening. Albert Mason suddenly called up, said he had to see me as he had something urgent to tell me so he came round for a

1 Margot Fonteyn and her Panamanian husband Roberto Arias.
2 Lynn and Vanessa Redgrave.
3 Feydeau's play, produced by the National Theatre Company under Jacques Charon.
4 Shaw's play at the Haymarket Theatre.
5 i.e. all moves arranged, and spoken from memory.
6 Congreve's play at the Old Vic.

drink. What he had to tell me was that when I was having my chin operation by poor Matt Banks I died under the anaesthetic! In fact my heart stopped beating for forty-five seconds! Indeed a startling bit of information. They had to hit me very hard with their fists, which of course accounts for the chest pain and panic I suffered when I came round. I have often wondered if people who die in their sleep feel anything. Now I know. They don't. I am terribly sorry for poor Banks. He must have been in a dreadful state. The headlines would have been charming: 'N.C. dies having chin lifted'! Albert was most troubled as to whether to tell me or not but felt that I should certainly be warned in case of future operations! Well, well. Actually I'm delighted to know because it has proved something. However, it was a very narrow escape.

Sunday 3 April

A successful week on the whole but a lot of irritations caused entirely by Miss Lilli Palmer who does *not* know her words well enough of *Song at Twilight* and obviously hasn't attempted to learn either of the other plays. I have been adamant and so has Binkie. Vivian less adamant and frightened. Today we had a really marvellous rehearsal of *Twilight*, then a tea break and then *Maud*. Lilli read from her script sulkily at first and then, because I started playing rings round her, began to perk up. She will obviously be charming when she knows it but *when* will she know it? I am, inside, bitterly angry and disgusted with them both, although they are brilliant actresses and wonderful to act with. *I* could open in all three plays by the end of this week, if only they had really co-operated and learnt their words. If I could have opened the plays on consecutive nights, which was what I originally planned, it would have been sensational. As it is there is to be almost a fortnight between the two openings. I have kept calm but do not intend to repress too much. If I am provoked into a scene they will both buy it.

I went with Gladys to see a film called *Alfie*[1] with Michael Caine. Absolutely brilliant. Everyone in it first rate, Vivien Merchant brilliant, and Michael Caine superb. A big new star. Hurray! Let's hope he doesn't get swollen-headed and take to the bottle. The gay, mad world of powder and paint is dangerous.

Gerry and Jackie Durrell[2] came to dine on Wednesday. Both charming and the evening a great success. My cold continues but is slowly fading.

Sunday 10 April

Here I am installed in my new flat which is quite perfect. Beautifully furnished, comfortable and dead quiet. Apart from this the week has been hell, made so entirely by Lilli who has contrived to make a bitch of herself with untiring energy. Carlos [Thompson], on Tuesday, sent me a peremptory note saying

1 Based on the play by Bill Naughton.
2 Gerald Durrell (b. 1925), writer and zoologist, and his first wife Jacqueline.

he was waiting for me in my dressing-room and I must come at once. I went and he affectionately suggested that, as Vivian was no good as a director, he should direct the play himself as neither Vivian nor I knew its real possibilities! He said that *he* could bring 'music' to it and inspire me to give a better performance! This appalling impertinence so staggered me that I was speechless. The next day Vivian lost his temper and really went for Lilli who – privately directed by Carlos – had given a performance of incredible melodramatic vulgarity. I myself had let fly at both the girls two days previously because I felt if I didn't get the fury out of my system I should get ill again. There have been continual dramas involving Binkie, Vivian, Lilli, Irene, etc. A ghastly waste of time. Lilli threatening to go back to Switzerland, etc. All absolutely horrible. I really do wonder how I have survived it. However, I *have*. Two public performances have been given. The play rapturously received. Rehearsals continue. I have made a truce with Lilli because I have to play with her. But I have never – with the possible exception of Claudette Colbert – worked with such a stupid bitch. On this cosy, affectionate note, dear diary, I will close.

Tuesday 19 April

Well, the most incredible thing has happened. Not only has *A Song at Twilight* opened triumphantly but the Press notices have on the whole been extremely good. Most particularly the *Express* and the *Evening Standard*! Fortunately the *Sun* struck a sour note and said 'Coward's Return Very Tedious', which convinced me that I hadn't entirely slipped. The Sunday notices were less good but excellent box-office, and the play is such a sell-out smash that we have had to engage extra people to cope with the ticket demand. On the opening night I gave an excellent, un-nervous, controlled performance, thank God. My letters of praise have been fabulous. Irene was brilliant. Lilli still shrill and insecure but much better. Her notices were tepid. London really feels as though it were *en fête* with my success, and it is a warming and lovely feeling. All, however, is not as jam and treacle as it should be, owing – I need hardly say – to the behaviour of dear Miss Palmer. There were grand reconciliations with Carlos at Binkie's party, and so far as she and I are concerned, outwardly all is roses. Inwardly the thorns are a bit prickly. She does *not* – repeat *not* – know the other two plays, which is maddening.

I feel physically like death, and this is a hell of a week with dress rehearsals of the second bill every day and playing *Twilight*. I played tonight under considerable stress but did all right. Nothing would induce me to disappoint these wonderful audiences. I feel a warmth and a genuine 'love' emanating from the front of the house at every performance. I have been away too long, but it is truly moving to come back to my age-old job again, more triumphant and more loved than ever. My heart is very cosy and warm and gratified. The dreadful hospital days are over; I'm back again, like Dolly, where I belong and have always belonged. My stomach is better. The virus makes me feel awful, but who cares! To have one of the most radiant successes of my life forty-two years after *The Vortex*, *and* to have won over those bloody doctors in Switzerland, makes everything – even Lilli – worthwhile.

Wednesday 27 April

After an exhausting week of two performances a day, a Sunday night *and* a Monday matinée, we opened *Shadows* and *Maud* on Monday night to a fantastic audience. *Shadows* I played well apparently, and the customers were attentive and controllable. *Maud* was an absolute riot from beginning to end and the ovation at the final curtain was quite, quite wonderful. I haven't experienced anything like it for many a long day and it made everything worthwhile. People came pouring on to the stage afterwards and it was altogether a heart-warming triumph.

We all went on to a party at Binkie's which was charming and not too big. Binkie was tremendously moved by the whole thing and we had a few moments alone in my dressing-room which I shall never forget. He has behaved so wonderfully all along and I am so very, very glad for him. Lilli has calmed down and is amiable to everyone – not, of course, to the extent of sending a goodwill flower or note or telegram, but at least not screaming. Irene is fine but going through a rather unpredictable phase. She wrote me a very loving letter, however, and has made a terrific success. Lilli is very good in both the short plays, not sensational but good. The notices mostly excellent and the *Express* and *Mail* rapturous. It really is, I suppose, one of the greatest successes I have ever had and I really feel so immensely relieved and happy.

Sunday 22 May

I have not devoted myself to these fascinating pages for nearly a month which is disgraceful, but there has been nothing much to report beyond continued success which is apt to become repetitious. I am feeling much, much better in health. The plays are, all three, triumphant successes and I am enjoying every minute of them. I am also improving my performances. We are playing to a steady £10,000 a week, which is fabulous. My dressing-room each night is a three-ring circus.

Coley and I went to Binkie's last weekend and it was enchanting. Absolutely perfect weather – hot sun – croquet and much laughter. I have decided to do the plays in New York but not until January. We are hoping to get Maggie [Leighton]. I do hope she doesn't fuck it up again because they *were* written for her and she should be marvellous. Lilli is behaving perfectly, no more troubles and scenes. She is very effective *and* improving, but her English is a bit dodgy and her acting a little too gesticulative. However, all is peaceful and to play to these wonderful audiences every performance is really lovely.

Beverley Nichols has written a ghastly book purporting to defend Syrie's memory[1]. He has been, rightly, crucified for it. It is vulgar, tactless and inaccurate. I have retitled it *I've Just Come Up from Somerset*! Lord Moran's book on Churchill is brilliant[2]. There is a great hoo-ha as to whether or not he should have written it on account of contravening medical ethics. Personally I am glad he did because it's a very important historical document.

I have just come back from appearing in the *Eamonn Andrews Show*[3] with Dudley Moore, Lucille Ball and Cassius Clay. It was great fun. I have seen many, many old friends during the last few weeks ranging from the Queen Mother to Florence Desmond[4]. This flat is really exquisitely comfortable and I am enjoying my life very much. I keep on getting wonderful letters and praise from everyone. I shall be losing my head next, I *don't* suppose! However, I really am acting very well and I know it, which is a great comfort. That is the end of the news.

Monday 30 May

By leaving England when I did ten years ago and incurring all that high-powered journalistic wrath, I have managed to get enough money put away to give me a cushion for my old age. It isn't very much considering, but it is enough. I still detest the English climate and London's face has sadly changed, but I know and I have always known that this is where I belong. Now that old age is zooming towards me I have to take sensible stock of the future. If anything happened to Coley and Lornie and my dear ones, it is absurd to imagine myself sitting alone in Les Avants where, lovely as the house is, I have never been really well. This is possibly because of the altitude and the air being too bloody pure. Jamaica I shall always hang on to, although it wouldn't be a bad idea to sell Blue Harbour, if possible, and stick to Firefly.

I shall go into all this in the autumn. In the meantime I intend to look into the financial situation very thoroughly. Other people (Binkie, for instance) manage to be very rich and live in England. When I upped and left, it was necessary because I couldn't afford to work and hadn't a big enough nest-egg. In the future, obviously, as I grow more and more decrepit and need to travel less, I shall need to be near friends, good doctors and the Odeon! Perhaps this decision has been hastened by having read Lord Moran's book on Churchill and Garson Kanin's book on Willie Maugham[5]. The latter very readable and

1 *A Case of Human Bondage*, which was a hatchet job on Somerset Maugham.
2 *Winston Churchill: the Struggle for Survival*; Moran had been Churchill's physician during the war.
3 On television.
4 Florence Desmond, celebrated impersonator and revue artist of the 1930s.
5 *Remembering Mr Maugham*.

compassionate. All his idolatry cannot erase the fact that Willie was a very unpleasant character, but Garson has been kind, which is what Willie's talent, if not his character, deserves.

The thought of old age is, not unnaturally, in my mind a great deal nowadays. The weeks and months and years pass with disconcerting swiftness. In only thirteen years' time I shall be eighty! I cannot say that this realization doesn't depress me a little because it does, but not to an excessive degree for the simple reason that there is *nothing* I can do about it. I don't mind whether the final curtain falls in Jamaica, Japan or Fiji, but I am determined that the last act shall be set mainly in 'This realm, this dear, dear land', in which the people are sillier than ever and the succeeding governments also are idiotic, but my roots are sunk deep in it[1].

I attended, at Dickie's bidding, a *Kelly* reunion on board a ship on the Thames[2]. The forty-eight survivors were there with their wives and cousins and aunts. I was officially presented with a *Kelly* tie as an honorary member of the ship's company. It was so unimportant and so very, very important.

Monday 6 June

Another week has whizzed by. A rather royal one really. On Tuesday I had supper with Princess Margaret and Tony and the Queen Mother, which was very enjoyable. Yesterday was mainly a highly royal orgy. I called for Princess Marina at 11.45, left my car there and drove with her to Richmond Park to see Princess Alexandra – *very* pregnant – and Angus. Then we drove off to Coppins to have tea with Prince Eddie and Kate. It was quite a day. In the evening I went with Coley and Graham to the dress rehearsal of the new John Osborne–Lope de Vega play at the Old Vic[3]. Beautifully directed and played, at moments well written but, alas, pretentious and annoyingly obscure. *Black Comedy* which followed was disgracefully overacted and has deteriorated dreadfully since I saw it in Chichester. After that we went for a little while to Danny La Rue's party, which was violently noisy but redeemed by the niceness of Danny himself.

I am still enjoying playing the plays and the audiences continue to be fantastic. It is a most effulgent renaissance, I must say. Millions of people crowd into my dressing-room every night and the stink of success is quite overpowering.

---

1 The sentimental notion of a final homecoming was abandoned. Noël's last will and testament (November 1971) states: 'I intend to live and die in Switzerland, I regard Switzerland as my permanent home and I have no intention of ever permanently residing again in England.'

2 The *Kelly*, Mountbatten's wartime command, was the ship around which Noël had constructed *In Which We Serve*.

3 *A Bond Honoured*, which Osborne had adapted from the Spanish.

Monday 13 June

Only seven more weeks to go. I am far from bored with playing the plays, but I am beginning to feel very tired. I am not gallivanting too much but a certain amount is unavoidable. Yesterday I spent – unnecessarily – four hours at the Old Vic in wig, eyebrows and moustache, waiting to say my five lines in Wesker's *The Kitchen*. It's a memorial performance to George Devine[1]. Oh dear. Having seen so many excerpts from so many of those verbose, irresolute plays, I am very thankful that I stayed away. Everybody acts well, but the lack of technical knowledge on the part of most of the playwrights is most irritating. I do detest pretentiousness and there really is far too much of it about.

Wednesday 6 July

I have finished the preface to Gar Kanin's book about Maugham. It really was difficult to do. Poor Willie was such an unadmirable character. Liza and John came to lunch yesterday and I read it to them and they seemed to be pleased. John, who loathed Willie, was afraid I was going to whitewash him, and Liza was dreading another essay in bitchiness like Beverley's. Last Friday Alan Searle came to lunch and retailed the whole saga of the last difficult years, so altogether I have had a Maughamish time. Alan, of course, is lost and lonely and says so frequently, which is not exactly enlivening. I urged him to cheer up and look about him at the merry busy world, but he seemed disinclined to try.

On Sunday evening I went for a pub-crawl in the East End with Julian Pettifer[2] and two young men whose names elude me. It was for me a completely enchanting outing. I was recognized wherever we went, but never once intruded upon or asked for autographs. The instinctive good manners of the true Cockney never ceases to impress me. It seems to me to be a simpler and much happier world. Nobody got roaring drunk, a great many of both sexes were extremely attractive, and nearby was the river and the docks and freight boats lit up and the feel of the sea. A lovely time was had by all.

On Tuesday I recorded in the morning with Joan [Sutherland]. I had very little to do. I merely spoke bits of the verses of 'Secret Heart' and 'Dearest Love'. Her voice really is incredible and to hear her singing my music with a big orchestra was a rare treat.

After much discussion Coley and I have decided to ask Peter Arne to come and be Coley's deputy-understudy-aide. Peter is a dear and has known us all for years. He is also efficient and a very good character. He starts as a permanence next Monday, but is here today being briefed. This is a great relief to us. I am terribly dependent on Coley and if he got ill or anything

1 George Devine (1910–66), director of the Royal Court 1956–65.
2 Julian Pettifer, BBC television reporter.

happened to him I should be in a bad way. Peter, among his other nice qualities, has the capacity for devotion which, as the years close in on me, I shall certainly need.

Saturday 16 July

It has been a fairly heavy week. I did a television interview about Dickie Mountbatten on Tuesday. Had a Press reception and lunch for *Pretty Polly*[1] on Wednesday. David Merrick lunched with me on Thursday before my matinée. I may live to eat my words, but I really do like him. His reputation for being a theatrical fiend in human form I think is rather exaggerated. However, we shall see. On Friday I went to the Sidcup drama students' matinée of *Cavalcade*, presented with an immense cast at the Scala. It really wasn't very good. They all tried hard but acting isn't so easy as it looks. There was no real potential talent in the cast. The girl who played Ellen was the best. The rest were fairly frightful. People continue to flock to the theatre and flock round to my dressing-room afterwards. It is all very triumphant and flattering and I am grateful for it, but I do want now to relax a little. Peter Arne is mingling well. He is a dear and tremendously anxious to help in any and every way.

Last Sunday Coley, Graham and I drove down to Kent. We lunched with Gladys and Patience [Erskine] and had tea with Elizabeth [Taylor]. It was a *nostalgie du temps perdu* and I wasn't somehow all that sorry that the *temps* were *perdu*. Gladys was snarling at Patience and vice versa. Elizabeth, on the other hand, was very gay and amusing and her house is far the nicest of the lot. We drove back through pissing rain, but it was all a duty done.

Tuesday 26 July

I've just come back from having supper with the Queen and Prince Philip and Princess Anne. They all came to the plays – double bill – and the supper was at the Brabournes' flat. Just them, Dickie, the Royals and me. It was really very relaxed and cosy and the Queen was enchanting. She also looked lovely. Apart from admiring her a great deal, I really do like her very much; she is easy and gay and ready to giggle. In the interval between the plays the Duchess of Kent fainted in the ladies' loo, so I told Eddie to bring her to my dressing-room where she remained all through *Come into the Garden, Maud*, so she didn't see it but only heard it through the tannoy. Prince Eddie came round and fetched her at the end, poor dear.

I drove Dickie home after the supper party and he went on about me having an OM. He is determined that I should have an honour of some sort. He's a dear friend, I must say. He seems to mind about me being decorated much more than I do. It will probably come to pass eventually.

---

1 The film was about to start shooting, with Hayley Mills and Trevor Howard directed by Guy Green.

The audience tonight was marvellous and *Maud* went very well. I am in the process of being elected to the Garrick Club. I have lunched there twice, once with Jamie Hamilton and once with Robin Maugham. I am not really club-minded, but it has a great deal of solid theatrical atmosphere and some wonderful pictures. Perhaps when I am really old I can sit in it with my OM.

Maggie [Leighton] has arrived and is coming to Paris with me on Sunday to deal with her clothes at Molyneux. She is in fine form, very funny and very enthusiastic about the plays. I am so glad that she is at last going to play them.

I am counting the minutes until the end of the week. I am longing to be free of routine and really put myself down.

Monday 8 August   Les Avants

I arrived here last Thursday morning after three days in Paris, fairly peaceful days on the whole with no staying up late, but it is still taking me time to unwind. I dined with the Windsors at Neuilly. She, as usual, was charming to me, he very amiable. It was not a violently stimulating evening but agreeable. I saw a lot of Ginette and Marlene. They all saw me off on the night train.

The last two performances of the plays were tumultuous with the audiences cheering their heads off. I gave a small party at Chesham Place. Just Lilli, Carlos, Irene, Binkie, Maggie, Gladys, Joyce, Peter, Coley, Graham and me. A gentle occasion only very slightly tinged with 'last night' nostalgia. The house here is in perfect condition. The weather, however, is *not* in perfect condition. It is grey and chilly and wet, which is all right with me as it offers no temptations to rush out into the dangerous mountain air. We have had drinks with Joan and Ricky and they have had drinks with us. The waltz-song I long ago promised Joan is beginning in my mind, and at the piano. I am *not* forcing it but it feels as though it might be all right.

Monday 12 September

I am working hard on my unfinished epic *Not Yet the Dodo*. I intend now to finish it once and for all and then my book of verse will be complete and ready for publication. I truly love writing both rhymed and unrhymed verse. It's complicated and exasperating but rewarding when it comes off.

Peter O'Toole came for the weekend to discuss *Present Laughter*, which he is going to do on television. He was bright and full of charm. And Dulcie and Michael[1] came to lunch a few days ago and were gay and amusing. One curiously forgets how really nice and intelligent they are.

Coley and Graham are now back from the South of France and very cheerful and brown. Zena [Dare] arrives today, and John Osborne for the weekend. Then Sheridan Morley, who wants to write my biography[2]. I personally think

1 Dulcie Gray and her husband Michael Denison, frequent English stage partners.
2 Sheridan Morley wrote the first Coward biography, *A Talent to Amuse*.

he might do it very well. He writes good English and regards me with, I hope, suitable reverence. I shall make him do a few preliminary chapters before I give my full support, however. The Sutherland-Coward record is finished. She sings gloriously and my music sounds wonderful. I, on the other hand, sound a trifle constipated, which I am most determinedly *not*. However, there is mercifully very little of me on the disc, just the verses of 'Secret Heart' and 'Dearest Love'.

We all paint violently every afternoon. I have inaugurated a new 'period'. Masses of figures scampering about all over the canvasses. In two weeks' time we shall uproot and set off for London, New York and Jamaica. My life really cannot be described as dull. My stomach is still occasionally a nuisance, but I am sure this prolonged rest will finally do the trick.

Thursday 6 October   Jamaica

Coley and Peter and I arrived last night or, rather, yesterday afternoon. We sat on the verandah [at Firefly] watching the sunset. The night fell and the stars came out. Coley and Peter left me and I had dinner by myself and went to bed at 8.30. Never have I felt so overwhelmingly but happily tired.

Having spent a brief few days in New York, I know beyond doubt that I could never stand playing a season there. We saw two shows: Gwen Verdon in *Sweet Charity*[1], and Betty Bacall in *Cactus Flower*, the former a brash musical with a negligible score, the latter a vulgar translation by Abe Burrows which was exuberantly overacted. We dined with Alfred and Lynn who were dearer than ever. Natasha has cured herself and is off the bottle and on the beam again. I am naturally disappointed that they will not see me in *Suite in Three Keys*; so are they, but that can't be helped. If I had not made my great decision I am convinced I should have cracked up after the first three weeks. Even in London, where the response was so marvellous, I felt dreadfully tired and strained. Now I am free to do what I like, go where I like and stay as long as I like. I can write and paint and read with no pressure and no time limit. I suspect that a great deal more good will come out of it than trudging for three months on the Broadway treadmill.

Sunday 16 October

The weather has been sublime ever since we arrived last Wednesday week and it still is. I am feeling much better but I really *am* worried about my damned diverticulum. I am far from being free of it and sometimes, for several hours of the day, I feel downright ill. I dread further experiments and tests. My body would *much* rather be left alone, but still I don't intend to spend the last few years of my life feeling *sous le temps* all the time. Apropos of which, poor

1 Cy Coleman and Neil Simon's adaptation of Fellini's film *Notti di Cabiria*, directed by Bob Fosse.

Clifton died two days ago. Another old friend gone. For his sake I'm glad. He's been miserably ill for a long time now. He was dreadfully preoccupied with his own bad health, poor dear. If Maybelle had died ten years earlier he might have survived better, but she left it too late and he wrapped himself in grief and dread every morning when he woke. He used to be such good company in the past. Age defeated him. I wonder if it will defeat me? I *feel* it won't, but you never know. Invalidism is a subtle pleasure.

I have just read the Harold Nicolson diaries. So beautifully written, witty and wise; his son Nigel has edited them brilliantly. Charming as they are, however, a certain intrinsic softness of character emerges. He was given to making wrong decisions, impelled by a sort of basic silliness and sentimental-ity. I know it's a dreadful thing to say, but there was a Beverley Nichols streak in him, the difference being, of course, that Nicolson had a first-rate mind. But a certain similarity is there. They were both pink and summer puddingish and liable to be swayed by sawney sentimental values; kind, gentle, witty and, when driven into a corner, inclined to be bitchy. Vita[1] emerges as much the stronger character. I wish I had known her better.

Tuesday 25 October

'Across the wires the electric message came: "He is no better, he is much the same".' I *am* much the same. My stomach still worries me but I do believe it is getting a little less. We shall see. The weather remains unbelievable. Every morning at 6.15 I open my shutters and there is the day waiting, perfect and without a cloud. I don't ever remember anything like it. At the moment – 7 a.m. – I am sitting on my verandah wearing only a sarong. The mountains are blue and clear, there isn't a breath of wind, and it is warm, warm, warm!

I have finally finished *Not Yet the Dodo*. It's on the long side. I know it has some good things in it but whether or not it is all pure gold remains to be seen. Anyhow, now the whole verse book is complete and all that is required is to write an interesting preface. I am struggling valiantly with Rebecca [West]'s *The Birds Fall Down*. It is everything that I *should* enjoy, but her writing is maddening. A novelist's job is to write her characters and situations lucidly and, by so doing, hold the reader's attention. Rebecca, in this book, is self-indulgent and verbose. I have read three-quarters of the book and I am still in the middle of finding out who is who and what is what. I resent having to go back and reread a whole page to find out not only who is talking but what they are talking about. In addition to which all the characters are called Alexander Alexandrovitch or Nicholai Nicholaievitch which makes confusion doubly confused. To weave intricate patterns with words may be fascinating for the writer, but however fascinating the patterns are, they become a pain in the arse for the simple reader. Henry James, of course, was one of the double-

1 Vita Sackville-West, writer, married to Harold Nicolson.

dyed, double-Dutch deans of this particular school and, now I come to think of it, Rebecca was a great James girl; in fact, her first book was a monograph on him. I do wish she hadn't been. Here am I thrashing around in a jungle of spies and Orient Expresses and lovely 'turn of the century' intrigues, all the ingredients I like best, and instead of being thrilled and riveted I am merely frustrated. It is very disappointing and extremely irritating.

News of the outer world comes to us convulsively through the smudgily printed pages of the *Daily Gleaner*. As far as I can gather, all is normal. People are still killing each other gleefully in Vietnam; brides are continually being led to the altar swathed in illusion, tulle and 'drama' overskirts; there is the usual trouble about the Jamaican water supply and a drought is imminent. The gardener has scythed the grass next to the swimming-pool, covering it with a scum of grass and leaves, etc., so that it now has the consistency of bouillabaisse. This is particularly infuriating because we can't possibly refill it or even have it topped up owing to the water shortage. However, I must count my blessings, one of which is a heart at peace under a Jamaican heaven.

Monday 7 November   Passevant Hospital, Chicago

10.30 a.m.: The merry Calvary has started. An enema last night and another this morning. Later the dreaded barium. The nurse who gave me last night's was gentle, efficient and immensely considerate. It was hell, as it always is, but it was bearable. The nurse who gave me this morning's was kindly, large, clumsy and stupid. She rammed the nozzle up so violently that I screamed. 'It's better that way,' she assured me. Then she let it slip and so the bed got soaked and finally left me a quivering wreck.

Ed Bigg has just been to see me. Apparently so far nothing sinister has appeared in the tests. My diverticulum is pretty bad, covered with ghastly little nodules. Personally I long to have them all cut away but Ed is still obdurate. We shall have to make the 'operation' decision in a few days' time when *all* the beastly tests are through. Tomorrow I have the kidney caper to look forward to. This, as I know only too well, is a bugger, although not as literally so as the barium. I shall have to lie on my back while they squeeze down on my stomach, at the same time injecting dye into a vein in my arm with an implement the size of a knitting needle. I am pretty miserable, of course, but doing my best to rise above it.

Coley, of course, is being a rock of comfort and sweetness. This is a bad period I'm going through and if I had to face it entirely alone it would be so much, much worse. However, there is nothing to do but read and relax as much as I can in the circumstances. I've certainly had a bad year from the health point of view. I am determined that from now on I am going to be well – if it kills me.

Tuesday 8 November

I have now a television in my room which Coley procured for me. I watched, hypnotized, a lot of rubbish and a great number of commercials. Among other things was a fairly terrifying sort of documentary about commercial aviation! It showed the techniques and hazards involved in a routine flight from Paris to New York. It really is very alarming to reflect how *very* many people are involved in one's safety. And so very many instruments! Just a couple of mistakes – and thank you!

4 p.m.: My daily torment is over. It was fairly beastly but not so hideous as yesterday. The important injection into my vein hardly hurt at all, but before this a vivacious young nurse injected some sort of 'allergy test' serum into my right arm which hurt like hell and what is more went on hurting for quite a while. It was rather like being stung by a giant hornet.

Ed appeared and discussed the tests. So far the looked-for cancer has not evinced itself. My kidneys are apparently normal. However, we are not giving up hope. Further tests will be made tomorrow. Including – perhaps – a sososcopy, which means a wire with a light on the end of it being rammed into my penis up as far as the bladder. It's not definite that I shall have to have this. I have had it before, and although they give an anaesthetic with it, the after-effects are dreadful. A violently burning sensation and a fruitless longing to pee. Or perhaps I should say urinate. Even 'making water' is considered vulgar in this vast land of opportunity and oppressive refinement. On the plane, just before landing, it was announced over the loudspeaker that we – the passengers – would notice a 'marked increase in the sound level'! *Not* that we should notice a louder noise. The English language sure takes a beating, brother, in these United States.

I certainly notice a marked increase in the sound level in this hospital whenever I compose myself for an hour's sleep. Things don't only go bump in the night, they go crash-bang-wallop all day long. Added to which the peculiarly penetrating whine of Middle-Western voices cuts through the ears like a buzz-saw. There is an elderly lady – rather distinguished looking, with white hair – just across the passage from me, who indulges in endless telephone conversations with her family and friends. The noise she makes is quite extraordinary. I, together with everyone else on the floor, know by now all her symptoms by heart. She is – I trust – soon going under the knife, which may take the corncrake quality of her voice down a bit, but I have little hope of this.

Wednesday 9 November

9.30 a.m.: The day has started in the usual wild flurry. At 6.30 I was wakened from a deep sleep by a very black lady who crashed into the room, placed a notice on my bed-table and crashed out again, leaving the door wide open.

The notice said 'Breakfast Deferred'. Shortly after this, when I had managed to doze off again, a handsome young doctor appeared and tried – for a long time unsuccessfully – to inject me with a dye. After experimenting with several different veins, he finally managed to get the needle in. This process was fairly painful. When he had gone away in triumph, a blonde lady appeared and said she was my second team captain. I asked what game we were playing and whether we were winning, but she ignored this and said her name was Mrs Berrington. We conversed politely for a moment or two and she went away. Then, according to instructions, I drank three glasses of water and peed into a bottle. A few moments ago there was a sudden humming noise and a very loud female voice shrieked out of the radio 'Can I help you?' This startled and confused me. I replied that I strongly doubted that she could help me in any way whatever, but that she was welcome to try. Then the crackling and humming stopped and there was silence. Two large trays of breakfast have already been brought to me, but I have dutifully sent them away. It seems odd to me that nobody has been *told* that I am *not* to have any breakfast until after the dye tests are completed.

9 p.m.: I've just been through a pretty bad time. Without Coley I couldn't have endured it without breaking down. My morning tests have disclosed unmistakably that I have a stone the size of a walnut in my kidney. This, it is surmised, may be the cause of all the pain I have been having and not the diverticulum at all. On looking back, all the doctors I've seen during the last ghastly year have been perplexed and worried about red cells in my urine. The kidney stone, of course, would account for this. Obviously the stone must be cut out, but I don't think they can do this until Monday. In the meantime several surgeons are going to consult.

It's been a horrid day of waiting and apprehension, three-quarters of which was unnecessary, and it is no good pretending I am happy because I am bloody miserable. However, there is nothing to be done but grit the dentures and take what comes with as much dignity as possible. Tomorrow there will be further blood tests but not painful ones – if they manage to find the right veins, but I am well inured to all that. From the operation onwards I shall have private nurses.

I shall now burrow my way into *Barchester Towers* and wait for the sleeping pills to begin to work. There is a biblical thunderstorm going on outside. The lightning is searing the heavens, the thunder is crashing and roaring, and the rain is pissing down with concentrated venom.

Thursday 17 November

9 p.m.: Well – the worst is over. The operation on Monday was clear-cut and with no sinister undertones. It certainly is a ghastly-looking stone and I am not in the least surprised that I have been in pain for so long. It was indeed

lucky that Dr Lewis spotted it on the x-ray. It was almost completely hidden. It would have been horrible if they had operated on my diverticulum and *not* on my kidney. A narrow squeak. The pain I have endured for the last four days has been really grim, the worst I can ever remember suffering. However, I managed to get myself out of bed three times on the day of the operation to go to the loo, which was bloody torture but Ed says that by doing so I have shortened my convalescence by many days. The nurses, I must say, have been wonderful and at last, this very evening, I am virtually out of pain.

Saturday 19 November

7.30 p.m.: No pain! A whole day with no pain at all! I find it difficult to believe. These last two weeks have been dreadful. In all my life I cannot remember so much actual suffering going on for so long. However, now perhaps I shall be allowed to relax.

Lynn and Alfred are working away at Genessee plotting menus for me. I am to have 'toad in the hole', chocolate pudding, buttered carrots, steaks, broiled hams – Ah me! I shall come away blown up like a balloon.

The great big world outside rolls on. There has been a tremendous controversy about eating meat on Fridays. The Pope has suddenly said it's okay by him, but there are rebellious spirits abroad and it is all very alarming. Some people just *will not* eat meat on Fridays because it would be against the word of God, who is obviously touchy about such vital matters.

Thursday 24 November (*Thanksgiving!*)

9 p.m.: This is my last night in this bed and in this room and, oh God, am I glad. My wound has healed remarkably quickly and there have been no complications. Coley, of course, has been an angel throughout. Graham is flying to New York next Tuesday to come with Coley and me to Jamaica. I have decided once and for all that he must do the job as Coley's 'understudy'. It doesn't matter that he can't type. He has a loving and loyal heart and no future anywhere but with me. He will do all he can to help and now, having made this decision, I feel happier than I have felt for a long time. I am sick to death of being let down by inadequate characters. Graham's stage career is non-existent. It has worried me for ages thinking of him struggling to get work and failing. He will be forty-nine next birthday and the jig is up. By joining Coley and me he can help over a number of things. He can even learn to type. If by any chance things ever happened to Coley, I shall not be left lonely and stranded. In the natural course of events I haven't got so very many years left to live and I am determined to live those I have with the minimum of irritation and the maximum of happiness.

Tomorrow I leave this dreary pest-house and go to Alfred and Lynn who are, at this minute, in the kitchen dreaming up gastronomic treats! My stone has gone. I have no commitments, and a good deal of enjoyment in store. I really mustn't grumble.

Wednesday 7 December   New York

The week with Lynn and Alfred at Genessee was, as expected, perfect. I was cossetted, tended and fussed over. I am feeling daily better and better, but I know from experience that it will be a long while before I am really well. However, I am even now well enough to enjoy myself and, in spite of the theatrical excitements of New York, I am yearning for Blue Harbour and Firefly.

I have seen Mary Martin and Robert Preston in a musical version of *The Four Poster*[1]. Both of them superb. I have seen *Cabaret*, a very, very good musical[2], and I have also seen a revival of *Dinner at Eight* directed abominably by Tyrone Guthrie and with the worst cast of actors I have seen for many a year. I think he must have gone mad! Ferber, of course, is livid and fulminates down the telephone[3]. I also saw the film of *Is Paris Burning?*[4] which, contrary to reports and reviews, I thought extremely good.

Friday 16 December   Jamaica

Today I am sixty-seven. Three years off seventy! I find it difficult to believe but it is true. The day seems more depressed about it than I am, for the sky is heavy with cloud and there is a chill wind blowing.

I have no particular news to report beyond the fact that I intend to start a new play today – just as a sort of private celebration. It is to be a light comedy based on *Star Quality*[5], so I shall have a good deal of the dialogue already done. It should, I think, be fun to do.

Lornie is apparently better but will be kept in bed over Christmas[6]. I am far from happy about her but there is no urgent problem.

Christmas is coming with all its ghastliness. Coley and Graham are saving me from the worst of it by shopping for me and wrapping for me. It is as well they are, because if they didn't I shouldn't do either.

---

1 A two–character comedy by Jan de Hartog retitled *I Do! I Do!*.
2 By John Kander and Fred Ebb based on Christopher Isherwood's Berlin stories and the play *I am a Camera* by John Van Druten.
3 She had written the play with George Kaufman.
4 Based on Dominic Lapierre and Larry Collins' best-selling novel.
5 Noël's short story about an actress.
6 She had gone into hospital with a recurrence of her arm trouble.

1967

Having decided that he lacked not only the energy but also the desire to take Suite in Three Keys *to Broadway, Noël opted instead in this year for two less demanding acting assignments. For American television he played the Emperor in a musical adaptation of* Androcles and the Lion, *though the notion of Coward appearing in a Shaw classic scored by Richard Rodgers seems to have been received with a certain casual disregard by viewers. From that he went on to play the Witch of Capri in* Boom, *and here again the idea of Coward working with Richard Burton and Elizabeth Taylor in a script by Tennessee Williams was more impressive on paper than celluloid.*

Towards the end of November, a few days after he had returned to Switzerland, Lorn Loraine died in London at the age of seventy-three. For forty-seven years she had been Noël's closest friend, confidante and adviser; she had run his professional life with a mixture of efficiency and brisk critical devotion which he found both invaluable and irreplaceable. Now, with Lornie dead, he had lost one of the few deep friendships which had survived throughout his adult life. However, he did have Graham and Coley with him at Les Avants, and the three of them commuted between Switzerland and Jamaica, finding it hard to think of anything that they really missed by not living in London.

Tuesday 10 January   Jamaica

The days slide by. I've started the second act of *Star Quality* but I'm not hurrying. The urge to get something done in as short a time as possible, which I used to have, has diminished a bit. A sign of age, no doubt. I find it pleasant to have something on the hob simmering away and requiring from me only an occasional progressive stir.

Darling old Mary Garden has died, aged eighty-nine, in Aberdeen. One of the greatest musical artists I have ever known and a generous and enchanting friend. What a strange, flamboyant career.

I have read a lot and rested a lot. I still lack a certain essential energy and suspect that I will continue to do so for quite a while yet. A major abdominal operation at my age is a shock to the system that takes a long time to fade. I feel perfectly cheerful and well, but my urgency has dimmed, temporarily I hope, but permanently perhaps. After all, I am three years off seventy! I spend relaxed hours painting in the studio. Perhaps relaxed is not the word. Concentrated, oblivious hours is a better description. The results are unimportant but the peace highly enjoyable. I wonder if one day I may write a 'Resistance' play. It is a subject that fascinates me. I have read several excellent books on it lately, notably *Pin-Stripe Saboteur* and *Death Be Not Proud*. What incredible courage and swiftness of resource those brave people had! It is hard to believe now that all those horrors were endured less than a quarter of a century ago.

Sunday 22 January

I have finished the second act of *Star Quality*. I am pleased with it but only up to a point. The dialogue is good but it lacks something; perhaps the something it lacks is better construction. I will press on and finish it and then leave it lie for a bit and have another look at it. My voices tell me that a certain amount of rewriting will have to be done.

I have just finished a book on the French Revolution called *Paris Under the Terror*. A very good book indeed. The ghastly atrocities and horrors committed during that blood-stained period have by now retreated into history, but when I reflect on the unspeakable carnage which has occurred during my own lifetime it is fairly obvious to me that human nature, every time that it is temporarily freed by special circumstances from conventional and social restrictions, is as cruel and contemptible as it ever was. Apart from the inherent sadism, callousness and illogicality of my fellow beings, I become more and more appalled by their insensate silliness. Another point that has struck me is that women in power are a menace; the unstable, bossy, emotional idiocy of women like Madame Roland, Charlotte Corday, and that royal ass Marie Antoinette still, if given the chance, have their counterparts today. Imagine the chaos that would ensue if our destinies were ruled, even temporarily, by

Nancy Astor or Clare Booth Luce! Beatrice Lillie would be infinitely less perilous. Some day I must really settle down to writing a biography of that arch-idiot Joan of Arc.

Wednesday 1 February

The weather has changed violently. Not only the outward weather, which has become grey, wet, windy and gloomy, but the inward weather of my hitherto relaxed and lovely holiday. Yesterday was a sad and dreadful day. First of all a cable saying that Dingo Bateson had been killed in a shooting accident. Then a letter from Joan[1] telling me that Lornie is badly ill, a sort of physical and mental decline. Her arm still gives her a lot of pain and her spirit has collapsed. Dingo, apart from being a brilliant lawyer, was a wise, shrewd, infinitely kind friend to whom I could comfortingly turn in any sort of crisis, personal or general. Lornie, of course, has been one of the principal mainstays of my life for forty-six years. Loving, devoted, passionately loyal and one of the most truly important characters of my life. There will be no more of it now. Even if she lives on for a few more months she will become increasingly ill and probably suffer more pain. For her sake it would be kinder if she could die. This is an intolerable sentence to have to write but I know, miserably, that it is the truth. Coley is telephoning to Joan this morning. He and Graham have already made reservations for us all to fly to New York on Friday. From there we will fly to London and face the sad music. Of course, I shall ultimately get over it and go on living my life as cheerfully as possible, but I shall have lost something absolutely irreplaceable. The immediate future, however, is dark with unhappiness. It is said that old age has its compensations. I wonder what they are.

Sunday 19 March   Les Avants

For various reasons I find that there has been no entry in this journal since 1 February, so I must now try as best I can to recapture those forgotten weeks. Here goes.

On Friday 3 February Coley, Graham and I flew to New York. On arrival there we telephoned to Joan and talked briefly to Lorn herself. She seemed cheerful but sounded weak, though apparently was improving. Maddeningly we were cut off and couldn't get back. However, we were leaving anyway on the following Tuesday and there was no violent urgency.

On the Monday I was guest of honour at a vast Doubleday cocktail party given to hundreds of buyers and booksellers from all over the States. I signed Christ knows how many autographs and was so charming that I felt quite sick in the car afterwards. We had a sweet lunch with Kit [Cornell] and Nancy

1 Joan Hirst, who had been helping Lorn to run Noël's London office and was now beginning to take charge of it with the same loving care.

[Hamilton] on the Sunday. We also went to see darling Benita [Hume] who was gay and brave as usual. I don't believe that now she can live more than a few more months. How much she is aware of this I don't know, but her performance is magnificent. I suppose I do admire courage and humour more than any other human qualities and she has both.

We arrived in London on Tuesday night and I was enthusiastically welcomed as usual by the dear Savoy. On Wednesday morning I saw Lornie. She looked fairly ghastly and was a bit tearful at first, but cheered up a lot after a while. I saw her every day while I was in London and, according to Joan, who has been and is an angel, I really have done a lot of good, and at least I am now available here and can fly over at once if needed. When that will be there is no knowing, but that it will be fairly soon there is little doubt. I have steeled myself to endure it as much as I can but there is an ache in my heart all the time. I had a talk to the doctor and the matron and made it fairly clear that pain must be reduced to the minimum *at all costs*. Both of them understood and I am sure will see to it.

I dined with Binkie who, as I suspected, was not enthusiastic about *Star Quality*. He was highly amused by it personally but thought it too esoteric for the great public. He was rather flummoxed when I entirely agreed with him. So that's that. It wasn't a waste of time because I enjoyed writing it. I shall now write something quite different.

Larry was fine in *The Dance of Death* but, oh dear, what a humourless ass Strindberg was. I enjoyed *Staircase*[1] in which Paul Scofield was beyond praise, and also fairly enjoyed *The Sacred Flame*. Gladys [Cooper] was superb and it certainly is a professional, well-constructed play. Willie Maugham certainly knew how to do it. It *is* a comfort in these days of self-indulgent verbosity to see a play that is technically fine and written with proper respect for the medium. There is, however, a certain unsatisfactoriness in the play, as in so much of Willie's writing. I think it is an inherent vulgarity, not vulgarity of words but vulgarity of emotion. Be that as it may, I was duly grateful for it.

I also saw *The Promise*[2], a nearly good play perfectly acted by Judi Dench, Ian McShane and Ian McKellen. It really is fascinating to see the young do it as well as that. I came away from the theatre bubbling with pleasure.

I had a lovely lunch with Diana [Cooper] at the Mirabelle. Her beauty and her intelligence both seem to be indestructible. There is no subject on earth that I wouldn't freely discuss with her except perhaps commonness of mind, which would be a waste of time because she wouldn't know what I was talking about. A rare friend.

I gave a minor cocktail party at the Savoy, very enjoyable, only about twenty in all, if that. Apart from my usual loved ones, my two handsome godsons

1 Play by Charles Dyer.
2 By Alexei Arbuzov.

came – Danny Massey and David Niven Jr – and very beguiling they were, too.

I dined quietly with Patrick [Woodcock] on Sunday. He was sensible and wise as usual. I have been increasingly worried lately about my memory. Not my far-away memory. I can still remember accurately plays and events of 1909. But my immediate memory, which has been behaving in a disconcerting manner. A sort of curtain descends in my mind veiling what happened last week! If I concentrate for a minute all is well, but it is rather alarming suddenly to be pulled up by a blank. Patrick thinks it is not so much anno domini as I do. He says it might easily be linked to my circulatory troubles, which have haunted me ever since that damned phlebitis. I know, ever since Chicago, that my right side is arterially less good than my left. So there is obviously much sense in what Ed [Bigg] has bullied me about. Walking! I've just got to walk so much a day from now onwards, even if it's only as far as the village. Certainly not back because it's uphill! Those sweet little peripheral veins have *got* to be encouraged. Ah me! All I have to console me now is bad weather when it is either raining too heavily or snowing too heavily for me to go out. I greet each radiant new day with a sinking heart!

It has been snowing violently today so I am happy as can be. But tomorrow will come and I shall have to go stumping down the bloody hill. I must *learn* to like it.

Thursday 20 April

Another shameful lapse, over a month. I really must try to be more conscientious. However, nothing very much has happened within the confines of my little private shelter. A great deal continues to happen *outside* it, but there's nothing I can do about it so they'd all better get on with it. Hester [Chapman] is staying here for the moment and is being, as usual, the perfect house guest, perfectly happy to be left alone with a book and not demanding to be entertained.

I have done act one, scene one, of a new comedy called *Age Cannot Wither*. So far it is good and funny, but whether I can keep it up or not remains to be seen. Gone are the days when I could cheerfully polish off a complete play in a few days. Perhaps my standards are higher. At any rate, my impetus has lessened. Not entirely to be wondered at in the late sixties.

Lornie is lingering on. Apparently she is suffering a little less pain. They have put her on heroin (a sinister sign). I don't believe she can live very much longer. I try to keep this out of my mind as much as I can. There is no sense in moaning and groaning. Joan continues to be rock firm and telephones us every day or two if we don't telephone her. I am no longer as unhappy about it as I was. The unhappiness sits there like a shadow in the back of my mind, but I have become accustomed to its face. We've none of us got all that much longer to live anyhow. This reflection doesn't depress me unduly. It is, of course, possible that with my constitution I might stagger on into the nineties, which would mean nearly another quarter of a century! I cannot say that I find this prospect very alluring. I would prefer Fate to allow me to go to sleep when it's my proper bedtime. I never have been one for staying up too late.

It must not be imagined, however, that I am mellowing away into a tranquil decay. Oh dear me no. I am already beginning to feel the travel itch again. In a couple of weeks' time I shall probably fly to Rome for a little jaunt to change the ambience. It will be nice to sit on the Via Veneto and watch all those Americans stamping by. I think, however, that I shall try to finish the play before I go. My ingrained sense of tidiness will not be stilled.

Sunday 14 May

Another long lapse but I have been trivially occupied with one thing and another. Darling Lornie is still alive and still in pain, although the heroin mitigates it to a certain extent. I don't see how she can last much longer. She's good and brave about it, but I can tell from her voice on the telephone that she is unbearably weary of it all. The whole business is a long-drawn-out, lingering nightmare.

I have done an act and a half of *Age Cannot Wither* and I am now letting it simmer for a little. I shall probably finish it within the next few weeks. So far it seems all right, but we shall see. Here everything is peace and plenty and the weather is lovely. Coley and Graham and I go to the piscine every afternoon and watch the *jeunesse dorée* romping about in their abbreviated trunks.

The news from America is that the Theatre Guild wished to do *Suite in Three Keys* in the autumn, an idea which was immediately jumped on and squashed by Binkie who wants to present the plays with David Merrick. I am all for them doing so, but the difficult question is who is to play my parts. Maggie and Irene are available, but no talented gentleman has yet appeared on the horizon. I wanted Freddie March but apparently he isn't well enough, and Henry Fonda has been suggested. He is a beautiful actor but lacks the versatility. He would obviously play *Come into the Garden, Maud* perfectly and *Shadows of the Evening*, but I cannot envisage him in *A Song at Twilight*. He is too stubbornly Middle-West to play Hugo. The whole play would be flung out of balance. Also I am convinced that an English actor should play all three. Half the comedy in *Maud* lay in the fact that I was playing an American. If a genuine American did it, it wouldn't be nearly so effective. Oh, how I wish darling Larry wasn't so grand and important and executive. He, of course, would be perfect.

Sunday 21 May

I entirely forgot in my last entry to report on my week in London. It was a crowded week and on the whole rewarding. I saw an enjoyable play by Alan Ayckbourn called *Relatively Speaking* in which everyone was good and Celia [Johnson] superb. I had a lovely evening with Binkie, a gay lunch with Vivien, and an enchanting lunch with Diana [Cooper] and Iris [Tree]. I visited Lornie every day and, I hope, cheered her up. She is still in pain most of the time. I interviewed her principal nurse and her doctor and inveighed, as strongly as I could, against the necessity of her suffering so much. I know that too much heroin can't be given because of setting up immunity, but there must be some way of alleviating her misery. I do wish so deeply that her darling old heart would give out one night when she is asleep. She hasn't a vestige of hope. She knows this as well as I do in her inside mind; in fact she has more or less admitted it to me. I suppose some day someone will discover a cure for this bloody disease. I only know that if I had it, or indeed if I do have it, all I shall want is to be put out of my misery and, if it is humanly possible, I shall see to it that I am.

I am reading the letters of Franz Joseph to Catherine Schratt. Really very touching. The Empress Elizabeth, of course, appears a great deal. Another monumental historical ass, meriting a niche along with Marie Antoinette, Mary Stuart *et al.* I can't think of one beautiful historical lady in a position of power who wasn't a dithering idiot. I suppose it's the beauty that does it. Oh for the humour and horse-sense of Queen Elizabeth I. I have a feeling that Boadicea might have been fairly bright, but they were neither of them Gladys Coopers.

Thursday 8 June

I have finished act one of *Age Cannot Wither* (two scenes). As far as dialogue is concerned it is very good, but I had a terrible time trying to get the curtain down. Finally, with a scream of relief I managed it and shall now wait until I return from London next week before starting on the second act. I have it fairly clearly constructed in my mind so it shouldn't be too difficult. I have been suffering rather from my recalcitrant diverticulum. It is becoming a chronic worry, not unbearable but uncomfortable. My spastic colon sends me clattering to the loo three or four times a day instead of once and it is a great bore.

Tomorrow we all go to London. All being Coley, Graham and Joyce and me. On Tuesday next I have to traipse to Bury St Edmunds to see George Baker's production of *Private Lives*. I have promised to do this but I wish to God I hadn't. I hope that my virtue will be rewarded, but doubt it. No good deed goes unpunished.

Darling Lornie continues to linger on. She has been brighter and more cheerful during the last few days and has had less pain, but I fear that the decline is pretty steady.

Thursday 22 June

Darling Larry-boy has cancer of the prostate. It is at a very early stage so there is hope of a successful operation, but this has to be postponed for a week or so because he developed pneumonia as well. I've just talked to Joan [Plowright] on the telephone and he is much, much better. Loel Guinness is being operated on tomorrow for stones in the kidney. He has *all* my profound sympathy. I have refrained from warning him what hell it is going to be afterwards. Darling Lornie is still lingering – ups and downs – I saw her every day while I was in London.

I made the noble gesture of driving all the way to Bury St Edmunds to see George Baker do *Private Lives*. Ninety miles there and ninety miles back, but my virtue was rewarded because he was very good indeed; in fact the whole production was excellent.

In addition to all this I had an enjoyable evening with Patrick [Woodcock], a not very enjoyable memorial service for Pamela Frankau at Farm Street, a jolly 'five o'clock' with Binkie, a tape-recording of a tribute to Dick Rodgers on his sixty-fifth birthday (nobody paid any particular tribute to me on my sixty-fifth birthday – *very* remiss), a visit to Vivien, who is in bed with a recurrence of TB! Oh dear! However, it's apparently very mild and curable. I also watched, with mounting irritation, the film of *Pretty Polly* which, as I deduced from the first script, was common, unsubtle and vulgar. Nobody was good in it and Trevor Howard was horrid. When I think of his charm and subtlety in *Brief Encounter*. Hayley [Mills], poor child, did her best, but there was no hope with that script and that director. Guy Green should have remained a cameraman.

I still haven't embarked on the second act of *Age Cannot Wither*. I've been too agitated by everything. I shall get after it when I'm good and ready. Spencer Tracy has died, so also has Dotty Parker. Life is so full of comical surprises that one daren't open the newspaper. My diverticulum is still making a pig of itself but not so enthusiastically as it was. Ed's pills are doing the trick. No more news for the moment.

Sunday 2 July   London

Coley, Graham and I arrived back here on Monday. On Tuesday I went off on my district visiting. First of all Lornie, who looks ghastly but was quite lucid and cheerful. Then Vivien, who was sitting up in bed looking pale but lovely, and smoking, which she shouldn't have been doing. She was gay and enchanting as she always is. Then Larry, writhing about on a bed in St

Thomas's Hospital. I was relieved to find that although they *have* diagnosed cancer of the prostate, it is apparently very slight and is responding to treatment satisfactorily. I hope to God this is true, but at least he showed no sinister physical signs. The colour of his skin was good and none of that grey-yellowish look. He was also cheerful.

During my week in London I visited Lornie every day. I have now become accustomed to the idea that she is dying. It is extraordinary how efficiently the mind adjusts itself. I know that when she does it will be ghastly, but in the meantime I seem to have been granted a sort of amnesty. It is impossible to go on being miserable and I try hard not to indulge in self-pity and *nostalgie du temps perdu*. It's a waste of time and there isn't too much of that left anyway.

Sunday 16 July

A journal by rights should be full of observations, psychological reflections and witty comments on the passing days, not merely a flat report of engagements fulfilled. I stare at my engagement book blankly, however, and it provides me with sparse inspiration. 'Theatre with Joyce' – 'Lunch with Gladys' – 'Movie with Cole and Graham'. I note, among other things, Tuesday 4 July, National Theatre, seven o'clock. This was *The Three Sisters*, magnificently played, particularly by Joan [Plowright] but, to me, always rather a tiresome play. Then Friday 7 July, Zena [Dare] to lunch – Donizetti's *Fille du Régiment*, Covent Garden. Zena was a darling as always and Joan sang *Fille du Régiment* divinely, but the whole thing was too arch. I had a pleasant interlude with Peggy Ashcroft in her Hampstead garden. I like her as much as I admire her, which gives her star billing all right. We gossiped away under the trees and I left with reluctance. Then on Monday the tenth, lunch with Sybil Cholmondeley and *Getting Married*[1] in the evening. Too long and verbose but quite well done. The opening night of *Mrs Cheyney* to which I went with Gladys was fairly dreary. Freddie Lonsdale's dialogue sounds curiously laboured and dated.

I can't even remember the date of the morning that Coley came into my suite at the Savoy, suffused with tears, and told me that Vivien had died[2]. The shock was too violent. I mind too deeply about this to go on about it very much. She was a lovely, generous and darling friend, and I shall miss her always. Apparently Jacko [Merivale] came back from his theatre, saw her sleeping peacefully and went to warm up some soup for himself in the kitchen. When he came back a few minutes later she was lying on the floor in a welter of blood, having had a haemorrhage. Jacko, with almost incredible courage and tact, cleaned up all the hideous mess because he knew that she would hate anybody, even the doctor, to see her like that. Then he telephoned for the

1 Shaw's play at the Strand Theatre.
2 It was 8 July.

doctor. Jacko is a good and kind man. A day or two later he rang me up and asked me to read the address at her memorial service which is, I believe, to be on the twenty-fourth. I lovingly but very firmly refused. I truly do not believe I could have done it without breaking down and making a shambles of it. I know this was cowardly, but I can't regret it. The emotional strain would be ghastly, and as I am not feeling any too well at the moment it would possibly cause me great damage. All my own loved ones agree and I can only hope that they're right. If it could have helped Vivien in any way I would have done anything, but it couldn't because she's gone for ever. I loathe and despise the miserable Christian trappings of death.

Sunday 30 July   Paris

I arrived here yesterday after the miseries of London and dined quietly with Ginette. And a great relief it was. These last two weeks have been ghastly. The happier moments were the Royal Tournament, a quiet evening with Binkie, a pleasant party at Peter Daubeny's, and a gay lunch with Loelia [Westminster]. The unhappier moments outweighed the happier ones. My daily visits to darling Lornie which tear me to pieces. The Cecil Tennant memorial service, which was beautifully done and Larry's reading of the lesson was deeply moving. Actually waking up each morning with a load on the heart was the worst. Since I have come away the load is still there every day but the weight has curiously lightened. One cannot go on being miserable. Life must be got on with and I hate self-indulgent moroseness. My visit to Paris has already been made for me by Marlene last night. I said to her, with an effort at grey comedy, 'All I demand from my friends nowadays is that they live through lunch.' To which she replied, puzzled, 'Why lunch, sweetheart?'

Sunday 13 August   Les Avants

My week in Paris was quite agreeable. Actually it was just under a week. There were no particular highlights, but I mooched about and sat outside cafés and enjoyed the lovely city as I always do. I flew back to London on Thursday evening. On Friday I went to *The Flip Side*, Hugh Williams's reminiscent but quite enjoyable comedy about two married couples who pair off with each other! Fancy[1]! It was well played, particularly by Anna Massey who was really brilliant. Stanley[2] came to fit my wigs for the Tennessee Williams film[3].

I lunched with Tony and Princess Margaret and was photographed all over

1 Echoes of *Private Lives* were strong.
2 Stanley Hall of Wig Creations.
3 Noël had signed to play the Witch of Capri with Richard Burton and Elizabeth Taylor in *Boom* for Joseph Losey; the film was adapted from Tennessee Williams's play *The Milk Train Doesn't Stop Here Any More*.

the garden. She was really very sweet and even took the trouble to ring Coley up in advance to find out what I could or could not eat for lunch.

I flew back here on Tuesday and arrived home in time for dinner and bed. On Thursday we went to the Chatelard[1] to see and, alas, hear the 'Jodellclub'. It was hilarious and quite, quite dreadful. A group of earnest Swiss young men with one fierce lady in the middle, all in national costume and all yodelling like mad. We went with Joan and Ricky and only just managed not to make beasts of ourselves. Then on Friday we went to hear dear Josephine Baker doing a one-night stand at the casino in Montreux. She really was remarkable. Immensely chic and accomplished and sang really charmingly. Personally I thought the audience was deadly. They just sat and goggled at her, but she managed with firm professional skill to get them. I expect they preferred the dismal yodelling.

Last night we dined with Adrianne and Bill and played the hiding game. The evening was ruined for us by dear little David[2] who gave an exhibition of infant megalomania which was nauseating and went on relentlessly all through dinner. Bill was enraptured throughout, but Adrianne after a while got the message and tried to shut the little beast up, but with no success. He is a flagrant example of the 'children should be seen and not heard' theory. It isn't entirely the poor little bugger's fault, of course. Bill and Adrianne spoil him outrageously. Personally I should have liked to cleave his winsome little blond head in two with a meat axe. Unfortunately there wasn't one handy. I owe the fact that I have been virtually clamped to the loo all day entirely to him. He overstimulated my spastic colon into a state of gibbering hysteria.

Thursday 7 September

A big jump since my last entry but a great deal has happened, including a brisk trip to New York to play Caesar in Dick Rodgers's *Androcles and the Lion*[3] for a television spectacular. Joe Layton directed it very well, everyone was extremely nice, but I didn't enjoy any of it. I hate television anyway. It has all the nervous pressures of a first night with none of the response. However, I was apparently very good. Friday was spent recording the bloody thing, and on Saturday Coley and I flew to London. Lornie still lingering. Fortunately she has been moved into the South London Hospital where she gets better attention than at home. How long Lornie can stay there is uncertain, she may have to be moved to a nursing home. This, I am afraid, she will hate.

Graham, Coley and I flew here on Monday. Coley has been in bed ever since with one of his ghastly colds. I feel exhausted and have to gird up my loins to travel to Sardinia next week to do the movie with Richard and

1 Girls' school near Noël's chalet at Les Avants.
2 Adrianne's grandson.
3 A musical version of Shaw's comedy.

Elizabeth. I am quite looking forward to this but I should like to feel a bit better. Perhaps I shall after a few days' rest. Saying 'goodbye' to Lornie was awful. I don't suppose I shall ever see her again.

Warren Beatty[1] popped into my life in London and dined with me at the Savoy. He is an attractive creature with a comforting sense of humour.

Sunday 17 September

Ina Claire is at the Beau Rivage and came over and we had a very gay evening. She is quite remarkably and quite genuinely as vital as ever. She talks away without drawing breath and her eyes twinkle and she looks at most in her forties. As I was taken by Mum to see her in *The Girl from Utah* on my thirteenth birthday, when she was admittedly only eighteen, this makes her seventy-three! A truly comforting phenomenon.

Sunday 15 October

Well, Sardinia is now behind us and very enjoyable it was. In the first place, most beautiful and bathed in lovely sunshine all the time. In the second place, everyone concerned with the picture was charming and friendly. I love Liz Taylor and found her a million per cent professional and wonderful to work with. Richard, of course, was sweet and the director, Joe Losey, a dear man. I had a bit of trouble with Tennessee's curiously phrased dialogue, but apart from that everything was halcyon. Acting for the movies in such very pleasant circumstances is really great fun. Our hotel – the Cappo Caccia – was perched up high looking over a picture postcard sea. There were very few people in it, being the end of the season. When I had time off, we went off in a boat and explored little caves and beaches and swam. The water was bloody cold but the sun was bloody hot, so all was well. We spent a peaceful evening in Milano on the way back and got home last Thursday. All is the same in London. Darling Lornie is still hanging on. Joan is being wonderful as ever and goes to see her daily.

Last night we went to the Knie Circus in Vevey and it was perfectly wonderful. The best I think I've ever seen. Every act was good and none too long. The animals were enchanting, particularly an over-amorous baby bear which kept on giving everybody French kisses regardless of gender. Afterwards we were invited by Madame Knie to have drinks in her elaborate, fifty-year-old caravan. I sat next to the lion-tamer on one side and Charlie Chaplin on the other. It was all very gay. Obviously circus people are just as fascinating as they are cracked up to be. There was quite a moving moment during the show when the principal clown presented Charles with a large bouquet of roses. Charles accepted it charmingly, and then unfortunately they presented

---

1 Warren Beatty (b. 1937), the American film actor, who had just produced and starred in *Bonnie and Clyde*.

James Mason with another bouquet which was a bit of an anticlimax. Later Madame Knie's son apologized profusely for not having given me a bouquet but they had no idea I was there. It really was a most 'enchanted evening'.

I have just finished a remarkable biography of the Tsar and Tsarina called *Nicholas and Alexandra*, very well written by a youngish American[1]. It really is such an appalling story. The Tsar amiable, kindly and stupid, and the Tsarina, a hysterical ass. The most fascinating character to emerge is, as usual, Rasputin. What an extraordinary phenomenon! His murder is brilliantly described and coincides in every detail with what Dmitri told me years ago. The only thing I query is that Youssoupoff lured Rasputin to his house to meet his wife Irina, who was in the Crimea. Rasputin would have known this perfectly well. The truth, I think, is that Rasputin had a tiny little lech on Youssoupoff himself.

Friday 3 November

Robin Maugham has been here for three days and left yesterday for Australia via Marseilles. He is good company and we laughed a lot.

I have just finished an autobiography by Herbert Wilcox called *Twenty-five Thousand Sunsets*. It is curiously endearing. His unquestioning adoration of Anna[2] shines through every page. You would think, from reading it, that dear Anna is the greatest actress, singer and dancer and glamorous star who ever graced the stage and screen. The fact that this is not strictly accurate never for a split second occurs to him. It is one long paean of reverent, ecstatic praise. Of course, what does emerge from the ardent treacle is the unimpaired 'niceness' of both of them, added to which comes the faintly bewildered reflection that Anna is and has been for years one of the greatest box-office draws in the English theatre. She has now been playing *Charlie Girl* at the Adelphi to capacity for over a year. She has a vast and idolatrous public. It is a very, very strange phenomenon.

Sunday 3 December

I was in London a week. Nothing worthy of mention happened before I left except a very agreeable visit from Joe and Patricia Losey. They really are dears, both of them. We took them to drinks with Adrianne, and she and Bill came to dinner. All very successful. On the seventeenth Ginette came for the weekend and was gay and vital as ever. On the nineteenth Coley, Graham and I flew to London. We saw a rough-cut of *Go-Forth*[3]. I'm not sure whether or not it will storm the world, but I'm quite good and look all right. While in London I recorded some poems, me on one side and John Betjeman on the other.

1 Robert Massie.
2 Anna Neagle, his wife.
3 The working title for *Boom*.

I went with Joycie to a jolly Sunday evening with the Jack Hawkinses[1]. On Monday saw *Mrs Capper*[2]. Rather disappointing, but well enough directed. I had lunch with the Queen Mother on Tuesday and sat next to her again the following night.

We all went in Joan's box for the opening of *Norma*[3]. She sang it divinely and there was a party afterwards. I gave a free-for-all cocktail party on Friday which was a great success.

On Thursday we endured with difficulty Lornie's memorial service[4]. It was well and simply done and quite intolerable. I staggered blindly away from it and went to lunch at Diana's, which was an excellent thing to do. She, of course, knew I was in misery, and why, and was utterly sweet. Coley, Graham and I flew home to Les Avants on Saturday, thankful to be back.

Thursday 21 December

Two weeks have sailed by with nothing eventful happening. I've had a few come-overs of misery about Lornie, but that was only to be expected. I snap myself out of them as swiftly as I can because there is no sense in grief, it wastes emotional energy.

Tomorrow the Christmas lot arrive. Binkie, John Perry and Gladys. The weather so far is fine and Yuleish with quite a lot of snow. I dread a thaw and a slushy Christmas but perhaps the Almighty will be amiable; after all, it is a celebration of his own boy's birthday.

Joyce has opened in a revival of *Dear Octopus*[5], which is a smash success. This is encouraging because it is a well-written and well-constructed play. I really do believe the avant-garde Royal Court gurglings are beginning to fade.

I'm in the middle of reading an excellent biography of Lytton Strachey by Michael Holroyd. It's a fascinating picture of the Bloomsbury lot. Oh, how fortunate I was to have been born poor. If Mother had been able to afford to send me to private school, Eton and Oxford or Cambridge, it would have probably set me back years. I have always distrusted too much education and intellectualism; it seems to me that they are always dead wrong about things that really matter, however right they may be in their literary and artistic assessments. There is something to me both arid and damp about dwelling too much among the literary shades of the past. My good fortune was to have a bright, acquisitive, but not, *not* an intellectual mind, and to have been impelled by circumstances to get out and earn my living and help with the instalments on the house. I believe that had my early formative years been passed in more

1 Jack Hawkins (1910–73), British actor, and his wife Doreen.
2 A television adaptation by William Marchant of one of Noël's short stories.
3 Bellini's opera at Covent Garden.
4 She had died on 21 November.
5 By Dodie Smith, at the Haymarket.

assured circumstances I might quite easily have slipped into preciousness; as it was I merely had to slip *out* of precociousness and bring home the bacon. The world of the theatre is a strong forcing-house, and I believe I knew more about the basic facts of life by the age of fourteen than the more carefully untutored knew at twenty-five. In any event, my own peculiar circumstances suited me and on the whole the results haven't been too bad. After which encouraging self-slap on the back, I will bring this entry to a close.

1968

The year of Noël's last film (The Italian Job) *was also the year of his last round-the-world journey, one which took him to Hong Kong and the ritual firing of the noonday gun, immortalized in his 'Mad Dogs and Englishmen'; it was also a year when he began to make more frequent television appearances, notably as a guest of David Frost and as one of the subjects in a study of old age by Lord Snowdon called* Don't Count The Candles. *Four of his short stories also turned up on television in dramatizations by William Marchant, while* Brief Encounter *became a stage success in Paris.*

In London, Paris and New York Noël's work came up increasingly frequently for rediscovery and revival, and he no longer felt the need or the urgency to do a great deal; he had his painting, his friends, his Jamaican winters and his Swiss summers. Above all he had the certainty that at long, long last he had come back into his own, and that others could now be left to get on with his work on stage and screen.

Wednesday 3 January   Les Avants

Well, Christmas is over and, what is more, very successfully over. Binkie and John and Gladys arrived as planned on the twenty-third, and we all had a lovely time with lots of present-giving and receiving and seasonable merriment. They went back to London yesterday, so Graham, Coley and I are left until next Monday when we too go to London for a week. Then heigh-ho for New York, California and Tahiti. A pleasant prospect.

The weather has been entirely satisfactory – a lot of snow and sleds and jingle-bells. I feel a little curious about being only two years off seventy! My health is all right and my heart is pure, which I put down to excessive smoking. However, a reckoning will probably come. It usually does. I read in one of my journals of a few years ago a triumphant account of giving up smoking for ever; after a few weeks I decided I could bear it no longer so back I went to the darling weed and have felt splendid ever since. It may, of course, shorten my life by a year or two, but I haven't got all that longer to go anyhow and I couldn't care less. It's been a nice and profitable buggy ride and I've enjoyed most of it very much. The loss of a few years of gnarled old age does not oppress me. I hope the South Sea Bubble won't burst. I am longing to show Coley and Graham all those lovely places.

Peter Bridge[1] is about to do a revival of *Hay Fever* with Celia [Johnson]. She is charming in it so it ought to have a reasonable success. Good old *Hay Fever* certainly has been a loyal friend. Written and conceived in exactly three days at that little cottage in Dockenfield in 1922! What a profitable weekend *that* was.

Sunday 14 January   Tahiti

Well, it's been a crowded week but on the whole very enjoyable. On Monday we flew to London on the afternoon plane. On Tuesday there was a run-through of *Hay Fever* which was excellent, Celia, of course, enchanting. On Thursday evening we all trailed off to Golders Green to see Danny La Rue in *Sleeping Beauty* in which he played the Queen Mother with his usual style and elegance. He is a remarkable performer, incapable of bad taste, the only female impersonator I've ever seen who is not embarrassing. After that we went to Binkie's party for me which was lovely, just the right number and just the right casting. Ted Seago[2] lunched with me on Friday, and in the evening I gave a select little cocktail party, most enjoyable, after which a quiet dinner in the Grill and early to bed. On Saturday evening we went to see *Rosencrantz*

---

1 Peter Bridge (b. 1925), London impresario.
2 Edward Seago, artist, who painted three portraits of Noël, one of which was commissioned by the Garrick Club and now hangs there.

and Guildenstern are Dead[1] at the National. Very well played, of course, and a fascinating idea. Sunday was peaceful. Joyce and I lunched and went to a movie and Jeremy Thorpe dined with me. He is a nice new find, attractive and very bright and the head of the Liberal Party.

On Monday Coley, Graham and I flew to New York on the afternoon plane. Our four days in New York were a bit hectic. On Sunday we flew to San Francisco and had dinner with Ina and Bill. On Thursday we took off across the Pacific. We dropped down at Honolulu for an hour or so, and then the long hop to Tahiti where we arrived at 11 p.m. By this time our insides were in a muddle. I *think* we lost a whole day, or gained one. I'm not sure which.

Tuesday 5 March   Fiji

We have had a lovely three weeks on Bora Bora and are now about to take off for the *extreme* Orient. We fly to Singapore tomorrow via Australia. We are all three richly suntanned, having spent most of our time here cruising about in a motor launch. Fiji has changed very little since I was here before. It is still as hot as hell and the policemen still wear their pointed white skirts. Being a British island there are comparatively few American tourists. It is strange that a people so charming and hospitable at home should be so ghastly abroad!

My passion for the tropics remains unimpaired. I am sitting at the moment stark naked in my sitting-room (to coin a phrase) and sweating profusely on to a leatherette chair. I wonder who thought of introducing leatherette into the tropics? Whoever did should have his balls snipped off and fastened to his nose with a safety-pin. This should also happen to whoever thought of leatherette in the first place.

Sunday 17 March   Kowloon

I have got into quite a muddle with dates and departures and arrivals, but we are definitely here, looking out across the harbour at the lovely Peak of Hong Kong. Singapore was as fascinating as ever. It is flat and quite hideous, of course, but the 'atmosphere' remains unimpaired. We did all the things we should do such as sit in Bugis Street for hour after hour watching the strange Oscar Asche world go by. It is a curious place and will always have allure for me. On our flight to Singapore we stopped for an hour in Sydney where I had the usual amiable mobbing by the Press. Actually this place is the best of all for me. I never get tired of watching the shipping in the harbour and the ferries darting back and forth. We drove across the Peak and down the other side to Aberdeen the other evening, just for old times' sake, but we were wise enough not to eat there and came back here. The drive was sensational and Graham, who had never seen the island before, was suitably thrilled and impressed.

1 Play by Tom Stoppard which views *Hamlet* through the eyes of the two courtiers of the title.

There is nothing to report but pleasure, which of course is liable to become a bit monotonous. Dreadful things are happening all over the great big glorious world according to the newspapers, but so far we have remained untouched. Such selfish callousness is indeed shameful and I couldn't care less. It is 'hurrah for the hols' and there is no urgency to be anywhere at any special time. That, if I may smugly say so, is the *right* way to travel.

Wednesday 3 April   Bangkok

We are leaving tonight at midnight to fly to Beirut – a hell of a long flight. Coley and Graham went to Angkor, leaving me for three days on my own. I got up to a few highish jinks, including being taken to a lovely restaurant run by two Danish queens called the Two Vikings, exquisite food and very luxe atmosphere. Afterwards to an open-air theatrical production which was very colourful, as our transatlantic cousins would say, and, as is usual with Oriental entertainment, absolutely deafening.

The remainder of our stay in Hong Kong was enjoyable but uneventful. Robert, my pet Kowloon tailor, took me out for an 'evening' which was enchanting. First of all, his 'gracious home' with wife, two children and mother-in-law, all perfectly sweet and with cosy, exquisite manners. Then out to a dinner *à deux* and a cabaret! He is a dear man. I wasn't even allowed to pay for one cocktail. On Wednesday last I was invited up to the Peak to fire off the noonday gun, which made the hell of a noise and scared the liver and lights out of me. However, it all went off very well (with a bang, in fact) and I was photographed all ends up.

This hotel has a terrace overlooking the swift river where we have drinks every evening watching the liver-coloured water swirling by and tiny steam tugs hauling rows of barges up river against the tide. It's a lovely place and I am fonder of it than ever.

Thursday 11 April   Beirut

We leave here in a few hours to fly home to Les Avants. It's been great fun. Larry Harvey appeared and was merry as a grig and took us to dine at an Italian restaurant with some of his film crew[1]. We lunched with dear old Linda Sursock, which was lovely. She really is a marvellous old girl, sitting there glittering with jewels and made up to the eyes directly under a portrait of her when young and staggeringly beautiful. She had lovely gifts for us and made us very welcome.

A deputation from Beirut College appeared, as they are rehearsing a production of *Blithe Spirit*. They presented me with a really lovely coffee tray and sat round in a circle while I obliged with a few 'production' hints. They were very eager and beguiling and, to me, very touching.

1 He was producing and starring in a little-known film, *He and She*.

I've always loved this place since I first came to stay here years ago with Edward and Mary Spears. He was High Commissioner or something and they had a slightly sinister house up in the mountains at Alex which he said was like living in a hollow tooth! Actually it was, rather. This time we are at the St George's Hotel, very modern and luxe, with a beautiful swimming-pool and excellent food and service. So our holiday has ended in a blaze of enjoyment. Actually it has all been enjoyable – very little 'rough' to be taken and a maximum of 'smooth'. I don't suppose I shall ever get over my wanderlust and I don't particularly want to. One of the pleasant aspects of a 'wanderlust' is the anticipation of going home. I'm longing to see my polite green Swiss mountains and be greeted hysterically by Guido. I also hope that the *avion* stays up in the air and carries us safely back. As it usually does, I will waste no time in foolish apprehension.

Wednesday 1 May   Les Avants

Consulting my day-to-day engagements I am horrified to discover that nothing whatever has happened to me for weeks! This is very disconcerting because it means brain-racking. Nothing of grave import occurred, obviously, otherwise it would have been noted. My mind is a blank. I see by my 'Day-to-Day' on Friday 26 April Ginette arrives and on Sunday 28 April Ginette leaves! Surely a sadly brief little visit. Still, even only two days of Ginette are better than no Ginette at all. It is agreeable to reflect upon Ginette. Over these last few years she has so definitely established herself among the very old friends. It would now seem absurd to go to Paris without going direct to 70 Avenue Marceau. They are both, she and Paul-Émile, so immediately welcoming. I don't *stay* at Marceau; I much prefer a hotel to staying with people, even loved ones. I like the feeling of being able to ring the bell and ask for a cup of cocoa and a steak at 3.30 in the afternoon.

Sunday 9 June   London

We flew here last Monday and dined with Billie More[1] and Betty Bacall, highly enjoyable. They are both darling, noisy broads.

On Wednesday we went to an afternoon theatre party at David Pelham's[2]. He is full of schemes for staging a vast tribute to me at the Albert Hall! This I have most firmly discouraged, but he has that old 'promoter' gleam in his eye and I fear I have not heard the last of it.

Dottie Dickson gave a very grand lunch party at Simpson's to which we all went, Graham, Coley, Joyce, Gladys, etc., and very pleasant it was.

In the evening we went to see George Baker in *The Sleeping Prince*. He was very charming and looked very handsome, but the play is no good and never

1 Billie More, Kenneth More's second wife.
2 David Pelham, London entrepreneur and occasional theatre producer.

will be, as I know to my cost. When I think of all the lovely music and lyrics I wasted on *The Girl Who Came to Supper* I grind my plates with frustrated rage.

Dear Stanley Hall gave a lovely party for me. Not enormous but with everyone I wanted to see. He is a most enchanting host and I thoroughly enjoyed myself. Now I come to think of it, I have never *not* had a good time at Stanley's. He is a sweet friend.

On Friday I went to a jolly supper party given by Carol Channing[1] at Grosvenor House, noisy and theatrical and very enjoyable. On Saturday John and Ross Taylor came to play the score of *Mr and Mrs*[2]. We all went down to the ballroom. Some of the tunes are very good, I think. John sang them very loudly indeed. Whether the mixture of *Fumed Oak* and *Still Life* will really work or not remains to be seen. John Neville apparently is mad to play both plays and it will be on us in December. If enthusiasm is anything to go by – and it *sometimes* is – it ought to run to capacity for eleven years.

I had a nice long evening with Binkie, one of our recurrent gossipy heart-to-hearters. We got amiably pissed and discussed everything under the sun. It was the mixture as before and a very agreeable mixture too. I always enjoy our evenings and go home far, far too late. Dear Binkie.

Sunday 16 June

On Wednesday we drove out to see Sheridan Morley whose small boy[3] took a flattering shine to me and sat on my lap throughout without moving. He was very, very sweet. Dined with George Cukor at eight o'clock and had a thoroughly satisfactory gossip about everybody and everything. He was as funny and cheerful as ever. On Thursday John Dexter came to lunch here. In the evening Graham, Coley and I went to *Elektra* at Covent Garden and to Danny La Rue's, a varied programme but very enjoyable. I love dear Herr Doktor Strauss but he does go on a bit, I fear. If only – if only someone could have persuaded him to do some brisk cutting. Danny La Rue, on the other hand, always goes off leaving you wishing for more. He is brilliantly professional and better than ever.

I gave one of my 'drinks parties', very successful, and when it was all over, including the shouting, I dined quietly in the Grill with Michael Caine and Tony Beckley[4]. They were both charming and we had a lovely time. I love Michael, he is so utterly and completely himself. No amount of stardom could undermine or overwhelm his native Cockney simplicity. Considering how

---

1 Carol Channing (b. 1921), American musical star.
2 A musical they had written based on two of Noël's one-act plays from *Tonight at 8.30*.
3 Hugo, Noël's sixteenth and last godson.
4 With both of whom Noël was soon to film *The Italian Job*.

immensely successful he is, this is remarkable, but on the other hand perhaps it isn't. He has a basically sweet character and much humour. I don't feel somehow that he could ever go far wrong. He came up the hard way and if he was going to become inflated it would have shown by now. I'm very, very fond of him.

Sunday 23 June   Les Avants

I forgot in my last entry to mention the Cazalet wedding[1], which was glamorous to a high degree. The reception, of course, was at Fairlawne and was most beautifully done. Zara and Peter had organized it a fair treat. I sat next to the Queen Mother at lunch. She was as dear as ever. The weather behaved with royal consideration and it was all enchantment. Sheran and her groom looked lovely, in fact everyone looked pretty lovely. I was resplendent in my morning coat and grey topper.

On Monday the seventeenth we flew back here and, exhausted by my London junketings, I retired to bed for a couple of days, not with illness but with relief. The week has been peaceful with nothing to report beyond the fact that Adrianne and Bill dined on Thursday and Cathleen Nesbitt arrived on Friday. There was a grand balls-up at Geneva because for some obscure reason she didn't know she was being met and headed for the train before we could get at her. We winkled her out of it just as it was about to glide out of the station.

Sunday 30 June

A pleasant, uneventful week. Cathleen, as always, a perfect house guest. Merle and Bruno[2] came to lunch on Monday. They urged us lovingly to stay with them in Acapulco in January, so that is what we are going to do. It may be a bit social but we can hop off to Jamaica if and when we become overwhelmed. They are both so nice and understanding that we shall probably outstay our welcome.

Yesterday we dined with Adrianne and Bill to meet Field Marshal Sir Claud Auchinleck. I was delighted to see him again. He is a real charmer. I told him that I had bought one of his pictures some years ago and treasured it, and he blushed like a schoolgirl. As he was already fairly pink this put him into the magenta class. A dear man.

Monday 15 July

Nothing eventful has happened. Cathleen's visit was a great success and she was succeeded by Hester [Chapman] who was in fine form, talked beautifully

---

1 Zara and Peter Cazalet's daughter, Sheran, was marrying Simon Hornby, a director of W. H. Smith.
2 Merle Oberon and her third husband, Bruno Pagliai.

as always, and dropped cigarette ash over herself and the furniture with the greatest nonchalance. Yesterday – rather surprisingly, I think – George Balanchine came to tea. He turned out to be a cuddly character and was highly entertaining about early days with Cochran at the Pavillon[1]. He did ballets assisted by Elsie April and Cissie Sewell[2], and we went hopping down memory lane with the greatest exuberance. As someone once wittily remarked, 'It's a small world.' Tomorrow we go to London.

Friday 26 July   London

Quite a lot has happened during the last two weeks, but nothing of world-shattering importance. Unless you can call the movie of *Star!* world-shattering. Julie Andrews was talented, charming, efficient and very pretty but *not* very like Gertie. Danny Massey was excellent as me and had the sense to give an impression of me rather than try to imitate me. He was tactless enough to sing better than I do, but of *course* without my special matchless charm!

On Sunday we all – Coley, Graham and I – went to Danny La Rue's party which was very enjoyable indeed. He is a dear creature and a marvellous host. On Friday I went and had tea with Princess Marina. She was in bed and looked very papery. I am worried about her. She was very cheerful, however, and we gossiped and giggled. Ali Forbes came to lunch with me on Tuesday. He is lovely company and makes me laugh a great deal. We sat in the Grill and put the world to rights, with the greatest *insouciance*. Lunched with Cathleen Nesbitt on Thursday. She really is a miracle. Full of vitality and great fun as always. It is unbelievable that she is on the eighty mark!

Sunday 4 August   Les Avants

Last weekend I went to stay with the Queen Mother at Royal Lodge and very gay and charming it was. I even went to church with her on Sunday morning because I thought she'd like me to. The service was mercifully brief.

Sunday 18 August

Still nothing epoch-making to report. I gave a recherché little dinner here for Adrianne, Bill and Dorothy Hammerstein. We went the day before yesterday, or rather night before yesterday, to hear Mireille Matthieu[3] at the casino in Montreux. She seemed a nice enough girl and sang agreeably, but I did not feel myself to be seared and scorched with her blazing talent. The others were most enthusiastic, however, and I was a disgruntled minority.

Life passes gently on, but the smooth pattern will soon be shot to hell as I go to dear old Dublin the day after tomorrow to start work on *The Italian Job*.

1 The Russian choreographer's sole venture into the commercial world of West End revue.
2 Cissie Sewell, ballet mistress for many of Noël's early musicals.
3 Mireille Matthieu, French singing star.

It's a good part and a good script so I expect I shall enjoy it. It is also to be directed by Peter Collinson, who has offered to have his Rolls Royce specially sprayed white for me! This is heart-warming when one reflects that he was the little Actors' Orphanage boy whom I saved from expulsion by giving him a brisk heart-to-heart talk on a garden seat! He is now married and has two children – I think – and a heart – I *know*!

Sunday 1 September   London

Well, the Dublin filming is over and great fun it was. There are still a few interiors to be done here, at Isleworth. Michael Caine is a darling to work with, swift, efficient and with a comforting sense of humour. It's incredible to think, listening to his light, charming speaking voice, that he started life as a Cockney barrow-boy in Whitechapel. We had a lovely time working together and I enjoyed every scene I played with him. Peter reigned benevolently over us with his heart glinting in the sunlight. It will be, I think, a good picture. Altogether a very satisfying experience.

We came back yesterday on a chartered plane which always frightens the shit out of me. However, we landed gracefully and no wings fell off.

Sunday 8 September

On Friday I dined with Binkie. Jill Bennett and John Osborne[1] came in later especially to discuss *Design for Living*, which she is to play and he is to direct. To our horror Binkie got pissed as a newt and proceeded to insult John Osborne violently! The subject of *Design for Living* never came up. After the barrage had lasted about an hour, Jill and John – not unnaturally – left, followed hotly by me. It really was extremely entertaining and quite idiotic. I saw that there was no use staying to tick Binkie off. Apparently they lunched amicably at Scott's a week later and all was forgotten and forgiven. Personally I thought the whole carry-on a waste of valuable time.

Tuesday 17 September   Les Avants

We got back here yesterday after a merry few days in Paris. The week started with me doing an interview with David Frost on the box – not live, taped. I actually rather dreaded it, but he turned out to be bright, co-operative and thoroughly charming. No snide remarks, no nonsense, extreme professionalism.

On Tuesday, after drinks with dear Stanley Hall, we went to the opening of *Gone with the Wind*[2] at the Empire. It really is a marvellous picture, but it upset me dreadfully seeing Vivien in all her loveliness, radiant and alive. I wished I hadn't gone in one way, and in another I was glad because she was so very, very good.

1 Then married.
2 The first major reissue of the film in fifteen years.

In Paris dined with Marlene and Claudette. Took Diana to lunch at Fouquet's – lovelier and dearer than ever. Went on Saturday night to the Folies-Bergère, gloriously ghastly. Saw Ginette, of course, every day and on the last night we dined – should auld acquaintance be *oublié* – at the Méditerranée.

Sunday 13 October

Peace, peace, perfect peace. A pleasant evening with Brian and Eleanor Aherne. A dreadful séance with a mad masseur – recommended by Adrianne – who plonked me into an electric bath and nearly killed me. I think he really was a bit mad. He suddenly turned a very strong hose douche straight into my eyes. I was out of the bath in a flash. My eyes were scarlet for days. A very unpleasant experience.

Sunday 3 November

The two weeks in London went off satisfactorily. I got through the dubbing[1] all right, in fact with flying colours, considering how much it irritates and bores me.

I saw *The Secretary Bird*[2], which was not bad and much enhanced by Kenny More, who is a lovely, deft comedian in the proper Hawtrey, Du Maurier, Coward tradition! In fact he doesn't apparently make any effort to get his effects and manages to get every one. No asking for laughs or begging for attention. Very satisfactory.

I went to dear Princess Marina's memorial service at the Abbey[3] which was fairly miserable, and lunched afterwards with Mollie Buccleuch, which was a cheerer-upper. She is a bright and darling friend and I am very fond of her. Incidentally, it was Peter Coates who gave the lunch in his flat in Albany. He is still as nice as ever he was when I first encountered him as Wavell's Comptroller of the Household (how grand that sounds!) in Viceregal Lodge in Delhi[4].

Monday 4 November

Ali Forbes is here for the weekend, which is nice because he is very funny and no trouble at all.

The rest of the London visit was very enjoyable, including, rather surprisingly, a lunch with Michael and Dulcie Denison at their house in Regent's Park. They were so very nice and I so seldom see them. Went to see my Seago portrait at the Garrick Club. Most impressive.

1 For *The Italian Job*.
2 By William Douglas Home at the Savoy Theatre.
3 She had died on 27 August.
4 During Noël's wartime concert tour.

Sunday 24 November

Life has been very serene in the Chalet Covarr[1] and the sun has shone – for most of the time – with nearly all its might. Joan Hirst has been staying. She is such a dear, and what wonderful chance that she spent all those years with Lornie watching the wheels go round. Joe Layton also appeared for two days, sweet as ever.

Monday 16 December

Oh, how I used to look forward to this magic day[2]! Now that I have had sixty-nine of them my enthusiasm has faded. Coley and Graham loaded me with gifts, and I sat up in bed submerged in wrappings and looking like an ancient Buddhist priest with a minor attack of jaundice. One year off seventy now! Just fancy. The snows of yester-year are a bloody long way off.

We flew to London on Tuesday. Saw *Forty Years On* for the second time and enjoyed it more than ever. Alan Bennett[3] came to supper with us afterwards at the Grill and was gently funny and entirely beguiling. He's a clever cookie all right. On Wednesday night the opening of *Mr and Mrs*. Oh dear! John Neville sang very well and was charming. Honor Blackman was equally charming but did not – alas – sing very well. It was all, I fear, a bit of a botch up[4].

Hal Burton came to see me to discuss the Noël Coward Festival week next year to celebrate my seventieth birthday[5]! It is not a subject that appeals to me greatly. However, it is inevitable and I must rise above it unless the *angelo di morte* whisks me off in the nick of time.

We all went to the movie of *Oliver*. Absolutely brilliant, beautifully played and gloriously directed by Carol Reed. I had a nice gossipy lunch with Bobby Andrews. Old times not only reared their heads but tossed their curls. I gave a select little cocktail party in my suite and then dined with Maggie [Leighton] and Mike Wilding, in the course of which we laughed so much that we were nearly sick. It was a right lovely evening.

Sunday 29 December

Well, Christmas is over, the pall of good will has evaporated, and we're back to normal. Binkie and John [Perry] and Gladys were sweet and cheerful and we all had a lovely time, including the hectic last-minute shopping in

---

1 The Swiss pronunciation of the Chalet Coward.
2 His birthday.
3 Alan Bennett (b. 1934), English playwright whose first West End play, *Forty Years On*, had opened at the Apollo in October of this year.
4 And closed rapidly.
5 BBC television were planning a week of Noël's plays, films and music.

Montreux and the routine drink at Seychaud's before flogging home up the hill.

We had a jolly Boxing Day with the Nivens at Château d'Œx. Alas, no Burtons because Liz is ill in Paris. Adrianne, Bill, Anna and young David came to lunch on Christmas Day, and we returned the civility by dining with them in their new apartment in La Tour de Peilz. Very enjoyable. Adrianne has done the whole thing beautifully – lots of blue and pink, of course. Her bedroom is vast and very luxurious, Bill's tiny and less so – there's just room for a bed and board which looked synonymous.

It has been a full and variegated year and I've enjoyed it very much. Now I must turn my questing violet eyes to 1969. My seventieth year! There is really no comment to make about that except perhaps 'Well, well', 'Fancy', or 'Oh fuck'. Still, I suppose it is comforting to be able to remember the first aeroplane and almost the first motor car! I am very well except for a violent itching inside my right nostril which is driving me mad. But, like everything else in this mutable life, that too will go. Meanwhile I wish to hell it would get on with it.

We take off for New York tomorrow.

1969

The last year for which Noël kept a diary was an uneventful prelude to 'Holy Week', his own irreverent nickname for the December celebration of his seventieth birthday, one which the BBC took only fractionally less seriously than a coronation; for seven nights his plays, songs and films were poured out over both radio and television airwaves, as though suddenly Britain was trying to take back to her heart a son who had been allowed too long to roam. Not to be outdone, the National Film Theatre also came up with an entire season of his films, the Phoenix Theatre (which he and Gertie had opened with Private Lives just forty years earlier) staged A Talent to Amuse, a midnight gala celebration of his words and music featuring at least as many stars as were in the heavens, and the University of Sussex offered a doctorate. Across the Atlantic Private Lives was back on Broadway, and in Vancouver a late-night cabaret called And Now Noël Coward paved the way for a large number of shows (most notably Cowardy Custard and Oh Coward!) which were to reopen the treasury of Noël's songs and bring them to an entirely new audience.

All these celebrations, marking as they did the culmination of the Coward renaissance which had started six years earlier with that little Hampstead Theatre Club run of Private Lives, were for Noël ample proof (if he required any) that he had returned to public grace and favour both as an artist and as a man.

Most important of all, at the end of 1969 came the news that a Labour government had recommended to the Queen a knighthood which many thought remarkable only for the length of time it had been overdue. With that, Noël saw a fitting end to his public and professional life and to these diaries, simply because there was no way of following it without anticlimax. His timing was, to the last, faultless.

Sunday 26 January   Acapulco

Well, here we are in Acapulco, in Merle and Bruno's exquisite house, sucking up the lovely sunshine and being waited on hand and foot.

The two weeks in New York were enjoyable but, as usual, hectic. We saw all loved ones such as Lynn and Alfred, Natasha, etc. We went to all the plays and musicals, notably *Boys in the Band*[1], *George M*[2] (Joel Grey brilliant), *Dear World*[3] (Angela Lansbury brilliant), *The Great White Hope*[4] (beastly), *Forty Carats*[5], *Dames at Sea*[6], *Promises, Promises*[7]. A lovely Sunday lunch with Kit and Nancy [Hamilton]. In fact we had a lovely time and are now putting ourselves down very gingerly to recover from it. New York, champagne air and all, is always exhausting for a short visit. There are too many friends to see and too many plays to enjoy, or not as the case may be.

Sunday 9 February   Jamaica

Our visit to Merle's was a terrific success. She is a dream hostess. She leaves you alone when you want to be left alone and entertains you when you want to be entertained. At all times she is gay, considerate and kind. Nor has she the faintest inclination to show you off as a visiting lion. We had a truly lovely time with them both.

Now here we are back in our earthly paradise; everything is a-growing and a-blowing, including, at the moment, a norther, but not a bad one. I sit on my verandah and look out over the sea and the lights of Port Maria twinkling and the dark blue mountains silhouetted against the stars and I am completely at peace. I still can't believe that I bought this magic mountain top for £150! It has been a life-saver. There is nothing much to report except peace and quiet, and peace and quiet make dull reading.

Adrianne and Bill arrive on the twenty-first which will be lovely. Apart from them no distractions except pleasant ones. (That looks wrong somehow, so I must add that they will be the pleasantest distraction of all!)

Sunday 9 March

Another peaceful month has whisked by. Adrianne and Bill left yesterday. They had a wonderful hol. Today Lionel Bart came over from Port Antonio where he is composing in the rain. He was very sweet as usual. Tomorrow Joycie arrives.

1 Play by Mart Crowley.
2 Musical based on the life of George M. Cohan.
3 Musical version of Giraudoux's *The Mad Woman of Chaillot*.
4 Play by Howard Sackler.
5 Adaptation of a French comedy by Barillet and Grédy.
6 1930s pastiche musical.
7 Burt Bacharach's and Neil Simon's musical version of Billy Wilder's film *The Apartment*.

Sunday 23 March   London

Well, we've been through a bad time. On Thursday the thirteenth, Graham had a sort of seizure while driving down from Firefly. He suddenly collapsed over the wheel. Fortunately Joyce grabbed the wheel while Fabia[1] switched off the ignition, and also, by a miracle, a police car suddenly appeared and drove him home to Blue Harbour. I knew nothing of this until the next morning when Coley appeared. We at once decided to get him back to London as soon as possible. Dr Harry was awfully good and advised keeping him quiet for a week and agreed to send his son, Philip Harry, home with us in the plane. Graham has no memory of any of this. It really was horribly frightening. Fabia and Joycie stayed behind and we flew here on Friday. Philip Harry kept Graham comfortably sedated throughout the journey. Now he is safely installed in his own bed and dear Patrick [Woodcock] is on the job. There have been no recurrences. Patrick thinks, and I agree with him, that it was a tiny cerebral haemorrhage which stopped for a moment the blood flowing to the brain. The saddest part is that he really mustn't be allowed to drive any more. At the moment he sees the sense of this, but it's a dreary outlook for him in the future. He drives so well and loves it so much. However, we will cross all those bloody bridges when we come to them. It's all been ghastly and I've been utterly miserable. Coley, of course, a rock as always. Graham is very well and cheerful and the nightmare is receding, but alas the memory lingers on.

Sunday 6 April

I lunched on 28 March with dear Sybil Cholmondeley who suddenly broke down over Rock[2]. I was dreadfully sad for her. She is such a loving old friend. She soon recovered herself and I felt somehow glad that I had been there and touched that she should have trusted me enough to give way in front of me.

I went with Joyce to the film *Isadora*[3] with Vanessa Redgrave clumping about very like the original. Isadora Duncan was really a fairly silly lady, I fear, and by the time I got round to see her at the Prince of Wales Theatre with Walter Kummell at the pianoforte she was a fairly *old* silly lady, at any rate far too old to leap about in a chiffon tunic.

I also went with Joycie to *Plaza Suite*. Such a good idea having different plays all played in a hotel suite! I wonder where Neil Simon got it from?[4]

1 Fabia Drake (b. 1904), British actress then staying in Jamaica with Noël.
2 Her husband had died the previous year.
3 Directed by Karel Reisz.
4 A barbed reference to *Suite in Three Keys*.

Sunday 13 April

Just back from seeing *Oh, What a Lovely War!*, a brilliant film brilliantly directed by Dickie Attenborough. Larry as Sir John French is beyond praise and hilariously funny. What a miraculous actor he is. Every detail perfect.

Sunday 27 April   Les Avants

A sadness has happened. The dear Queen of Spain died. She was a sweet neighbour and I shall miss her very much. She was always gay and good company and I was very, very fond of her.

Sunday 11 May

Today we fly to Antibes, Coley and Graham and I, to join Loel and Gloria on the *Sarina*. The weather is set fair, so it ought to be lovely. The programme is to bounce about the Mediterranean for a bit and visit Corsica, Sardinia, etc. Knowing Loel's scale of living, we shall suffer few deprivations. Our Riviera wardrobes have been scrupulously selected and we are all set for the dangerous sea.

Sunday 18 May

Well, that little excursion is over and we enjoyed every minute of it. The sea behaved with the utmost discretion and the skies were clear. Nothing dramatic happened. Everyone was sweet to everyone else. The food was exquisite and we lay in the sun and relaxed. It was a lovely and effortless holiday – Loel is one of the very few really rich people I know who knows how to enjoy it. This is a fairly rare gift. We were not hustled or bustled about and forced to do anything we didn't want to do. Sardinia aroused a few pleasantly poignant memories of Joe Losey[1], and Corsica aroused less agreeable memories of long ago when I chartered that bestial little yacht and set off with Louis Hayward, emphatically not one of the happier episodes of my life[2]. This time, however, there was complete serenity and a lovely time was had by all, and here we are back again on our Alp, all three of us elegantly tanned and merry as grigs.

Sunday 22 June

Valentina arrived yesterday and then there was the Chaplin wedding (Josephine), very charming and well done. I still maintain, however, that weddings are depressants. Valentina in fine form and spent a lot of time lying flat on the carpet showing us health-inducing exercises. I should die immediately if I tried one of them. Coley rather stole her thunder by sticking his leg straight up into the air which he is inclined to do on the least encouragement. Actually

1 During the filming of *Boom*.
2 A 1930s adventure with actor Louis Hayward which ended abruptly in a storm at sea.

it proves very little beyond the fact that he is double-jointed. She was impressed and suitably discouraged. Apart from these excitements there is nothing to report.

Sunday 27 July   London

I've just got back from my royal weekend with the Queen Mother. She was charming, gay and entirely enchanting, as she always is. The Queen came over to lunch on Sunday looking like a young girl. It was all very merry and agreeable but there is always, for me, a tiny pall of 'best behaviour' overlaying the proceedings. I am not complaining about this, I think it is right and proper, but I am constantly aware of it. It isn't that I have a basic urge to tell disgusting jokes and say 'fuck' every five minutes, but I'm conscious of a faint resentment that I couldn't if I wanted to. I told the Queen how moved I had been by Prince Charles's Investiture[1], and she gaily shattered my sentimental illusions by saying that they were both struggling not to giggle because at the dress rehearsal the crown was too big and extinguished him like a candle-snuffer!

On Wednesday the sixteenth we sat in a row on the sofa at Les Avants and watched the moon 'take-off' while we casually sipped our after-lunch coffee. I seem to remember that someone once remarked that we live in a marvellous age. Whoever it was, they were dead right. There have been no other comparable excitements.

Sunday 24 August   Les Avants

Dottie Dickson has been staying, also Boo Laye[2], both sweet and appreciative and no trouble at all. Radie Harris[3] came to tea, I can't think where from. She was very gossipy and entertaining. Edward came for one night, at long last, and was suitably enthusiastic and at his benign best. It is being, on the whole, a fairly peaceful summer and I have no complaints.

Sunday 7 September

A pleasant *va et vient* of amiable cronies. John Gilpin, Pat Dolin, etc. Autumn is on us and all too soon Christmas will be at our throats. The leaves are brown – season of mists and mellow fruitfulness. 'And the "something" bells chime to the sentinel Angel of the Watch who smiles to heaven and answers back, "All's well, sweet bells, all's well." ' (*Charley's Aunt*, act three).[4] Thank God for my classical education.

---

1 As Prince of Wales earlier that month.
2 Evelyn Laye (b. 1900), British comedy actress, who had starred in Noël's *Bitter Sweet* in 1930.
3 Radie Harris, Hollywood gossip columnist.
4 Noël had toured as Charley in Brandon Thomas's farce in 1916.

Wednesday 31 December

I perceive, now, 31 December, that there has been no entry since 7 September. With my usual watchful eye on posterity, I can only suggest to any wretched future biographer that he gets my daily engagement book and from that fills in anything he can find and good luck to him, poor bugger. Personally I have neither the will nor the strength to attempt the task.

So here we go firmly with 31 December. A great deal has happened during the recent unrecorded months. I opened the National Film Theatre season of my films[1] with *In Which We Serve*, which I am the first to admit is a rattling good movie. I wept steadily throughout, right from the very beginning when they were building the ship in the shipyard. The BBC gave a terrific birthday party[2] for me in the Lancaster Room at the Savoy which was a terrific success. My birthday lunch was given by the darling Queen Mother at Clarence House, where I received a crown-encrusted cigarette-box from her, an equally crown-encrusted cigarette-case from the Queen herself, and some exquisite cuff-links from Princess Margaret and Tony. During lunch the Queen asked me whether I would accept Mr Wilson's offer of a knighthood. I kissed her hand and said, in a rather strangulated voice, 'Yes, Ma'am.' Apart from all this, my seventieth birthday was uneventful.

The knighthood ceremony takes place on 4 February. Then we go to New York for about ten days and, at long last, my beloved Jamaica.

1 To mark the opening of 'Holy Week', a celebration of Noël Coward's seventieth birthday on London stage, screen and television.
2 Televised, with after-dinner tributes by Lord Mountbatten and Sir Laurence Olivier.

Noël Coward's diaries end here; three tranquil years later, at the age of seventy-three, he died of a heart attack at Firefly on his beloved Jamaica.

Chronology

1899   Born on 16 December in Teddington, Middlesex.

1911   Made first stage appearance in *The Goldfish*, London.

1914   Began writing songs, sketches and short stories (with Esmé Wynne).

1917   His play *Ida Collaborates* (written with Esmé Wynne) produced on a British tour.

1918   Wrote first play as sole author, *The Rat Trap*, produced in Britain in 1926.

1919   Wrote *I'll Leave It To You*, produced in Britain in 1920 and in USA in 1923.

1921   Wrote *The Young Idea*, produced in Britain in 1922 and in USA in 1932, and *Sirocco*, produced in Britain in 1927.

1922   Wrote songs and sketches for the revue *London Calling!*, produced in 1923, and *The Queen Was in the Parlour*, produced in Britain in 1926 and in USA in 1929.

1923   Appeared in London in *London Calling!* Wrote *The Vortex*, produced in Britain in 1924 and in USA in 1925, and *Fallen Angels*, produced in Britain in 1925 and in USA in 1927.

1924   Directed and appeared in *The Vortex* in London. Wrote *Hay Fever*, produced in Britain and USA in 1925, and *Easy Virtue*, produced in USA in 1925 and in Britain in 1926.

1925   Continued appearing in *The Vortex* in London and also in USA. Wrote book, music and lyrics for *On with the Dance*, produced that year in Britain.

1926   Wrote *This Was A Man*, produced that year in USA, *The Marquise*, produced in Britain and USA in 1927, and *Semi-Monde*, produced in Britain in 1977.

1927   *Easy Virtue*, *The Vortex* and *The Queen Was in the Parlour* filmed. Wrote *Home Chat*, produced in Britain that year and in USA in 1932.

1928   Wrote book, music and lyrics for *This Year of Grace!*, produced in Britain and USA that year – also acted in American production.

1929   Completed operetta *Bitter Sweet*, produced in Britain and USA that year. Wrote *Private Lives*, produced in Britain and USA in 1930.

1930   Appeared in *Private Lives* in Britain. Wrote *Post-Mortem*, first professional production on British television in 1968, and started *Cavalcade*.

1931   Appeared in *Private Lives* in USA. *Cavalcade* produced in Britain. *Private Lives* filmed.

1932   Wrote book, music and lyrics for *Words and Music*, produced in Britain that year. Also wrote *Design for Living*, produced in USA in 1933 and in Britain in 1939. *The Queen Was in the Parlour* filmed again under the title *Tonight is Ours*. *Cavalcade* filmed.

1933   Appeared in USA in *Design for Living*. Wrote *Conversation Piece*, produced in Britain and USA in 1934. *Design for Living* and *Bitter Sweet* both filmed.

1934   Appeared in *Conversation Piece* in Britain. Wrote *Point Valaine*, produced in USA that year and in Britain in 1944.

1935   Wrote *Tonight at 8.30*, produced in Britain that ycar and in USA in 1936. He appeared in both productions.

1937   Wrote *Operette*, produced in Britain in 1938. First volume of autobiography, *Present Indicative*, published in Britain añd USA.

1938   Adapted *Words and Music* for its American production, entitled *Set to Music*.

1939   Wrote *Present Laughter* and *This Happy Breed*. Rehearsals for both interrupted by the war and not produced in Britain until 1942. *Present Laughter* produced in USA in 1946 and *This Happy Breed* in 1949. *To Step Aside* (short stories) published in Britain and USA.

1940   Toured Australia and also wrote *Time Remembered* (*Salute to the Brave*), unproduced to date.

1941   Wrote and directed *Blithe Spirit*, produced in Britain and USA that year. Wrote screenplay for *In Which We Serve*.

1942   Appeared in and co-directed (with David Lean) *In Which We Serve*. Toured Britain in *Blithe Spirit*, *Present Laughter* and *This Happy Breed*. *We Were Dancing* (from *Tonight at 8.30*) filmed.

1943   Appeared in London in *Present Laughter* and *This Happy Breed*, and co-produced film version of the latter.

1944   Toured extensively in South Africa, Far East and Europe. Co-produced film of *Blithe Spirit*. Wrote screenplay for *Brief Encounter* (based on *Still Life* from *Tonight at 8.30*). *Middle East Diary* published in Britain and USA.

1945   Wrote *Sigh No More*, produced in Britain that year, and started writing *Pacific 1860*, produced in Britain in 1946.

1946   Started writing *Peace in Our Time*, produced in Britain in 1947.

1947   Appeared in *Present Laughter* in Britain. Wrote *Long Island Sound*, unproduced to date.

1948   Appeared in French production of *Present Laughter* (*Joyeux Chagrins*). Wrote screenplay for *The Astonished Heart* (from *Tonight at 8.30*).

1949   Appeared in *The Astonished Heart*. Wrote *Ace of Clubs*, produced in Britain in 1950, and *Home and Colonial*: as *Island Fling* it was produced in USA in 1951 and revised as *South Sea Bubble* in Britain in 1956.

1951   Wrote *Relative Values*, produced in Britain that year, and *Quadrille*, produced in Britain in 1952 and in USA in 1954. Made first cabaret appearance at Café de Paris, London. *Star Quality* (short stories) published in Britain and USA.

1952   Three plays from *Tonight at 8.30* filmed as *Meet Me Tonight*.

1953   Wrote *After the Ball*, produced in Britain in 1954 and in USA in 1955.

1954   Wrote *Nude with Violin*, produced in Britain in 1956 and in USA in 1957. *Future Indefinite* published in Britain and USA.

1955   Cabaret season in Las Vegas, USA. Wrote and appeared in *Together with Music* for US television.

1956   Appeared in *Blithe Spirit* and *This Happy Breed* on US television. Wrote *Volcano*, unproduced to date.

1957   Appeared in USA in *Nude with Violin*.

1958   Appeared in USA in *Present Laughter* and *Nude with Violin*. Adapted Feydeau's *Occupe-toi d'Amélie* as *Look After Lulu*, produced in USA and Britain in 1959. Composed score for the ballet *London Morning*, produced in Britain in 1959.

1959   Wrote *Waiting in the Wings*, produced in Britain in 1960.

1960   His novel *Pomp and Circumstance* published in Britain and USA.

1961   Completed *Sail Away*, produced in USA that year and in Britain in 1962.

1962   Wrote music and lyrics for *The Girl Who Came to Supper*, produced in USA in 1963.

1964   Directed *High Spirits* (musical of *Blithe Spirit*) in USA and *Hay Fever* in Britain. *Pretty Polly Barlow* (short stories) published in Britain.

1965   Wrote *Suite in Three Keys*, produced in Britain in 1966 and (as *Noël Coward in Two Keys*) in USA in 1974.

1966   Appeared in Britain in *Suite in Three Keys*. Started writing stage version of *Star Quality*, unproduced to date.

1967   *Bon Voyage* (short stories) and *Not Yet The Dodo* (verses) published in Britain and USA.

1970   Received knighthood in the British New Year Honours List.

1972   *Cowardy Custard* produced in Britain and *Oh! Coward* in USA.

1973   Died on 26 March in Jamaica.

Index

The numbers set in italic indicate a footnote on that page. People's names appear as they do in the Diaries, with or without a title. The plays and films that Noël Coward saw and the books he read are given in his entry.